AF342217

EXTREME
LIKE
A GIRL

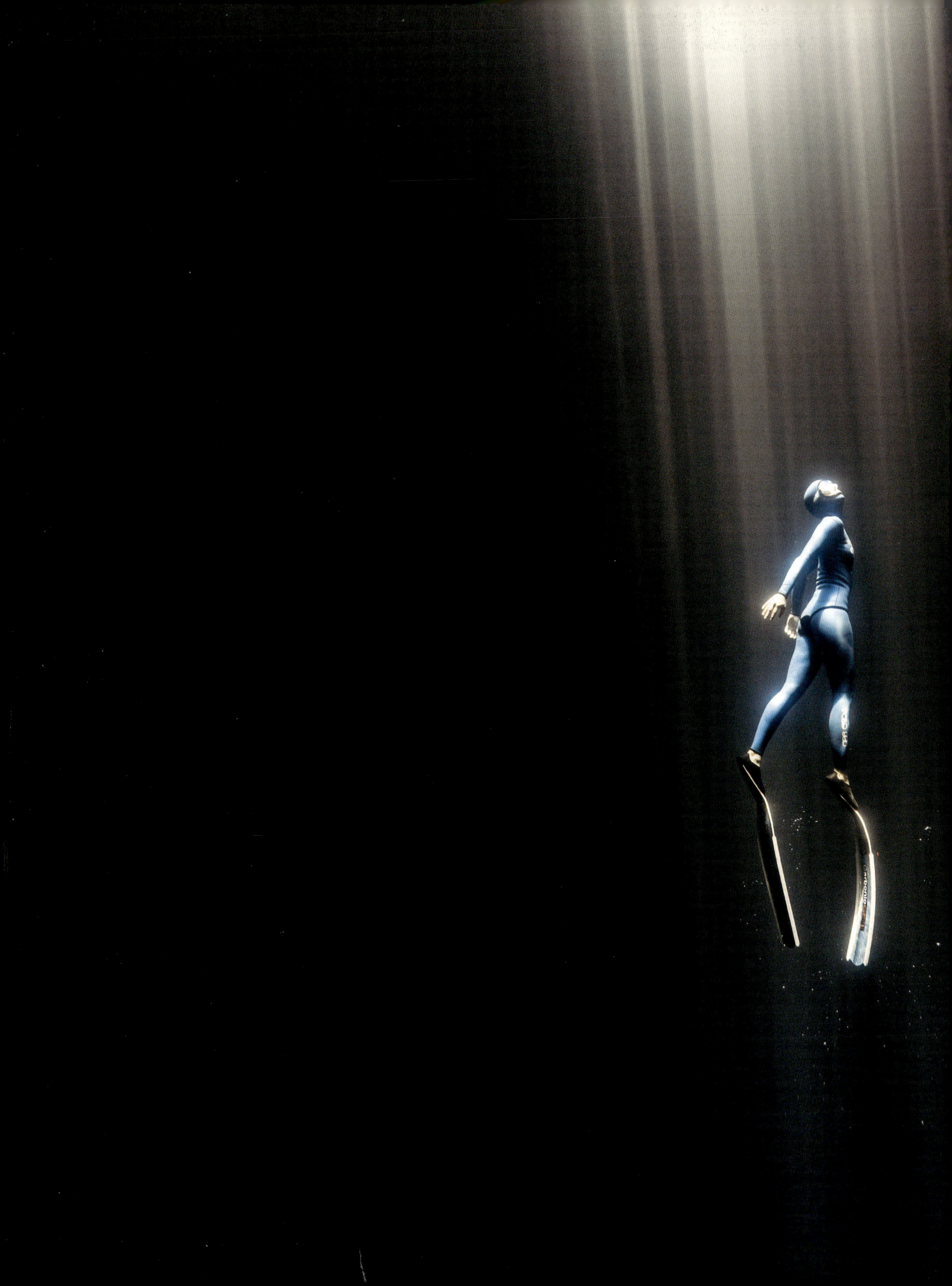

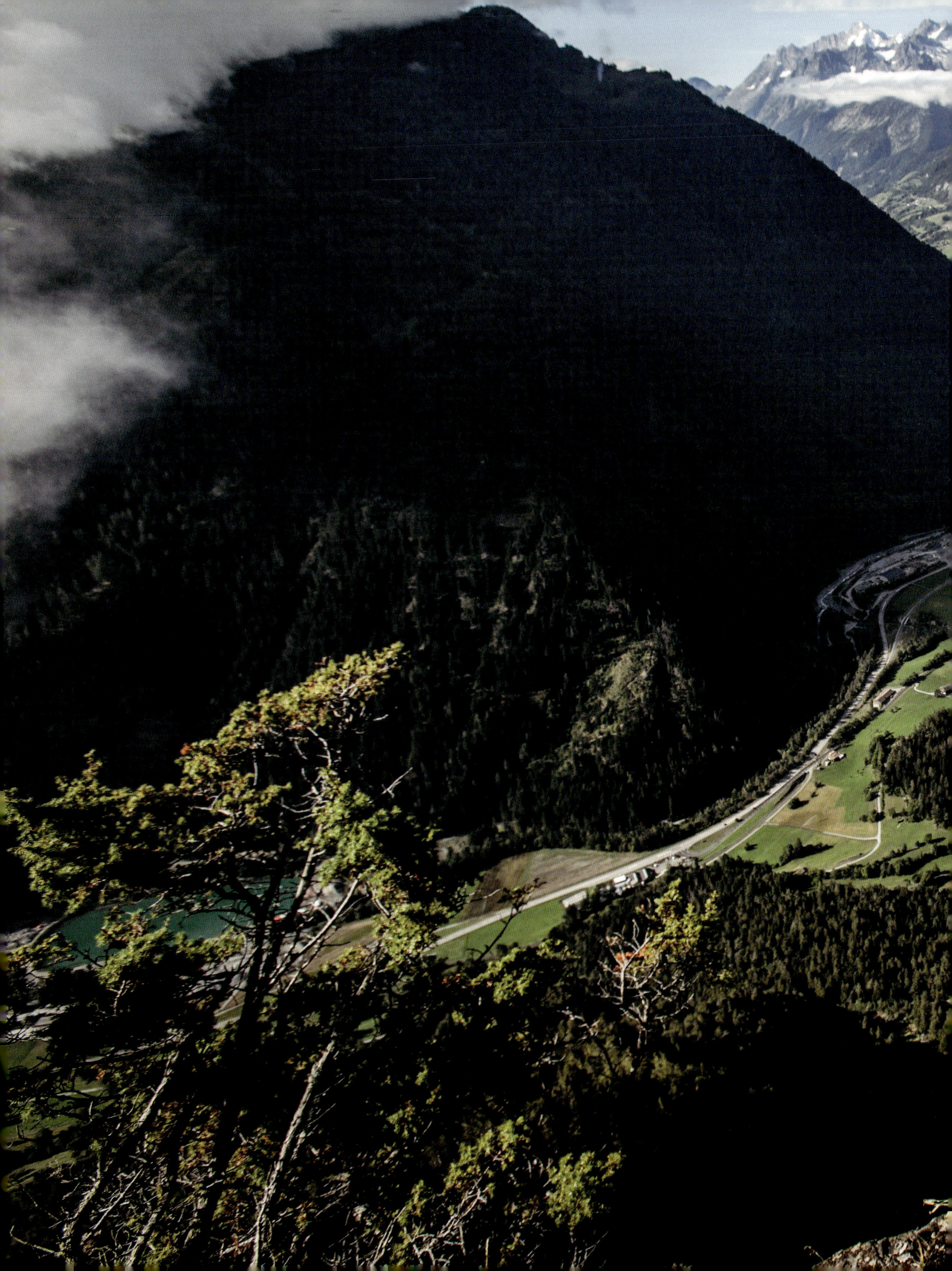

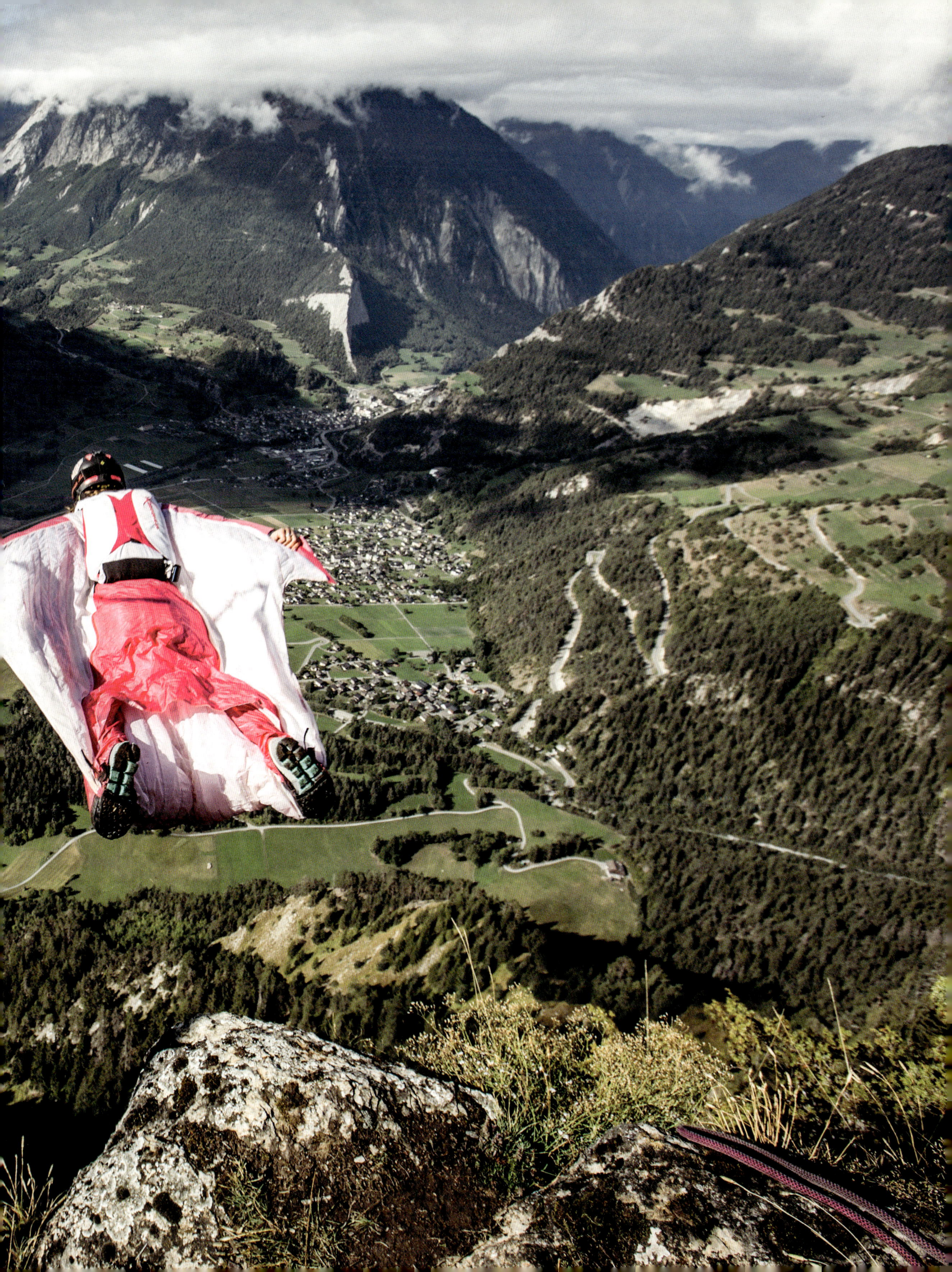

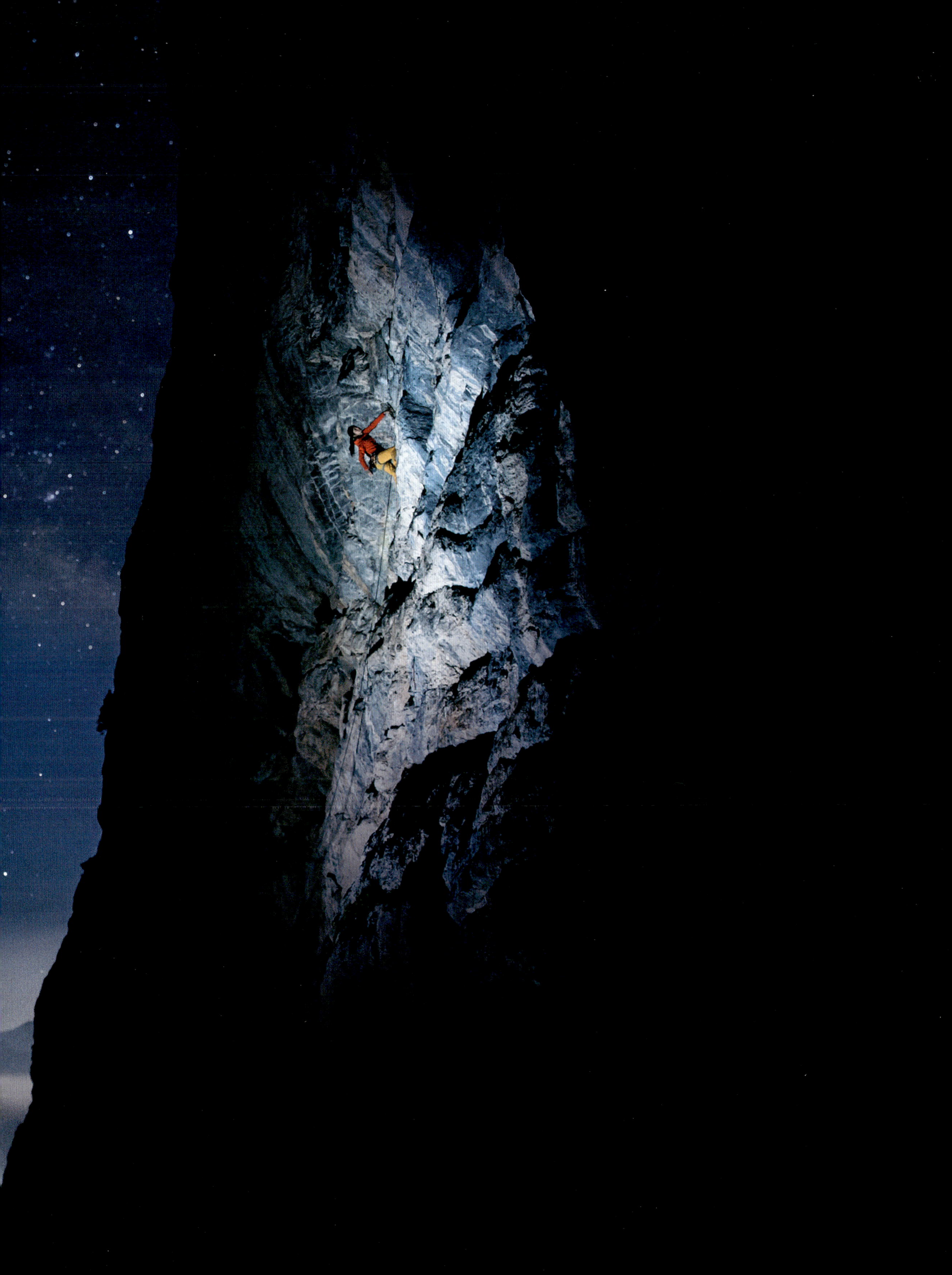

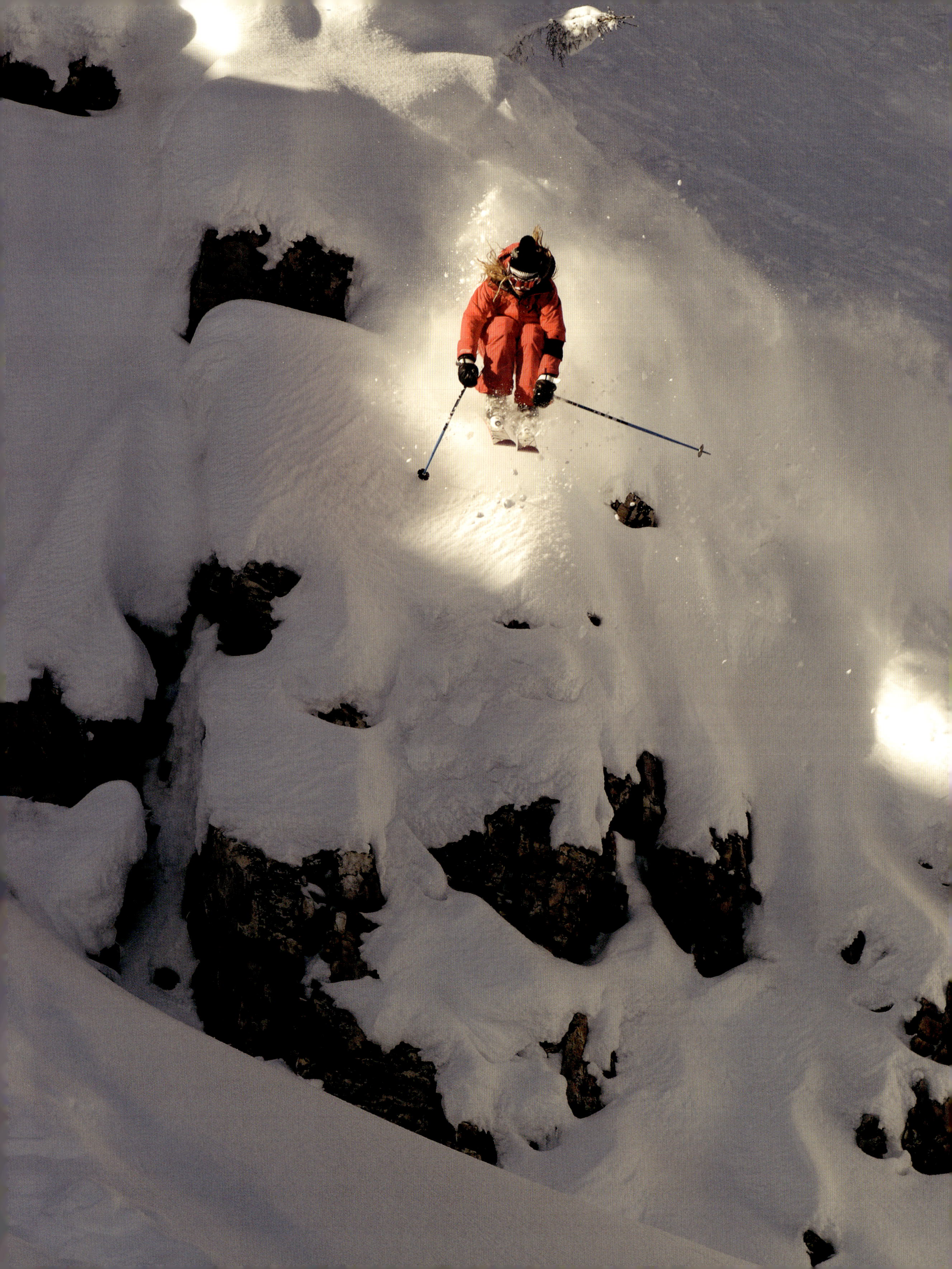

EXTREME LIKE A GIRL

Women in Adventure Sports

CAROLINA AMELL

PRESTEL

Munich · London · New York

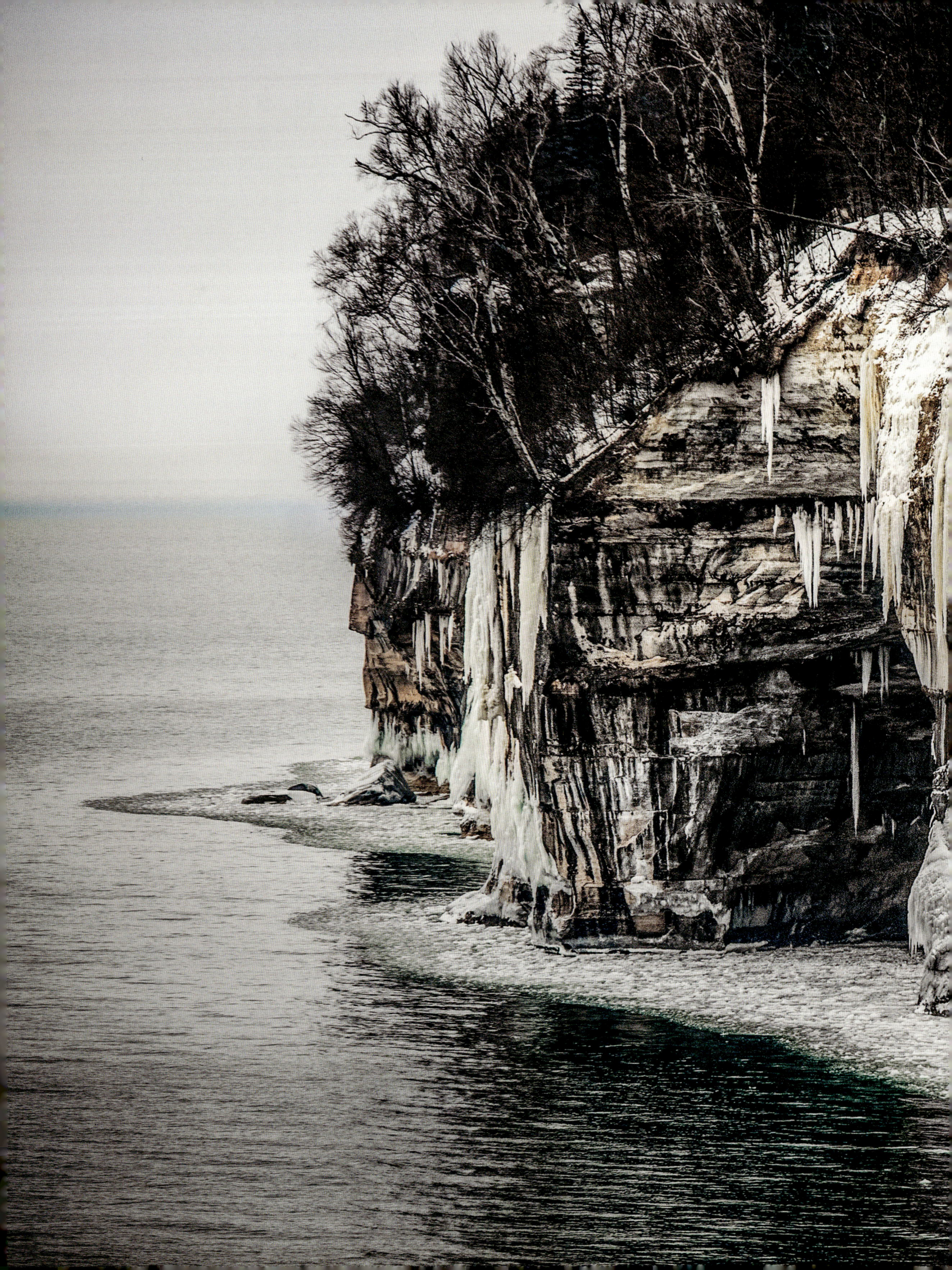

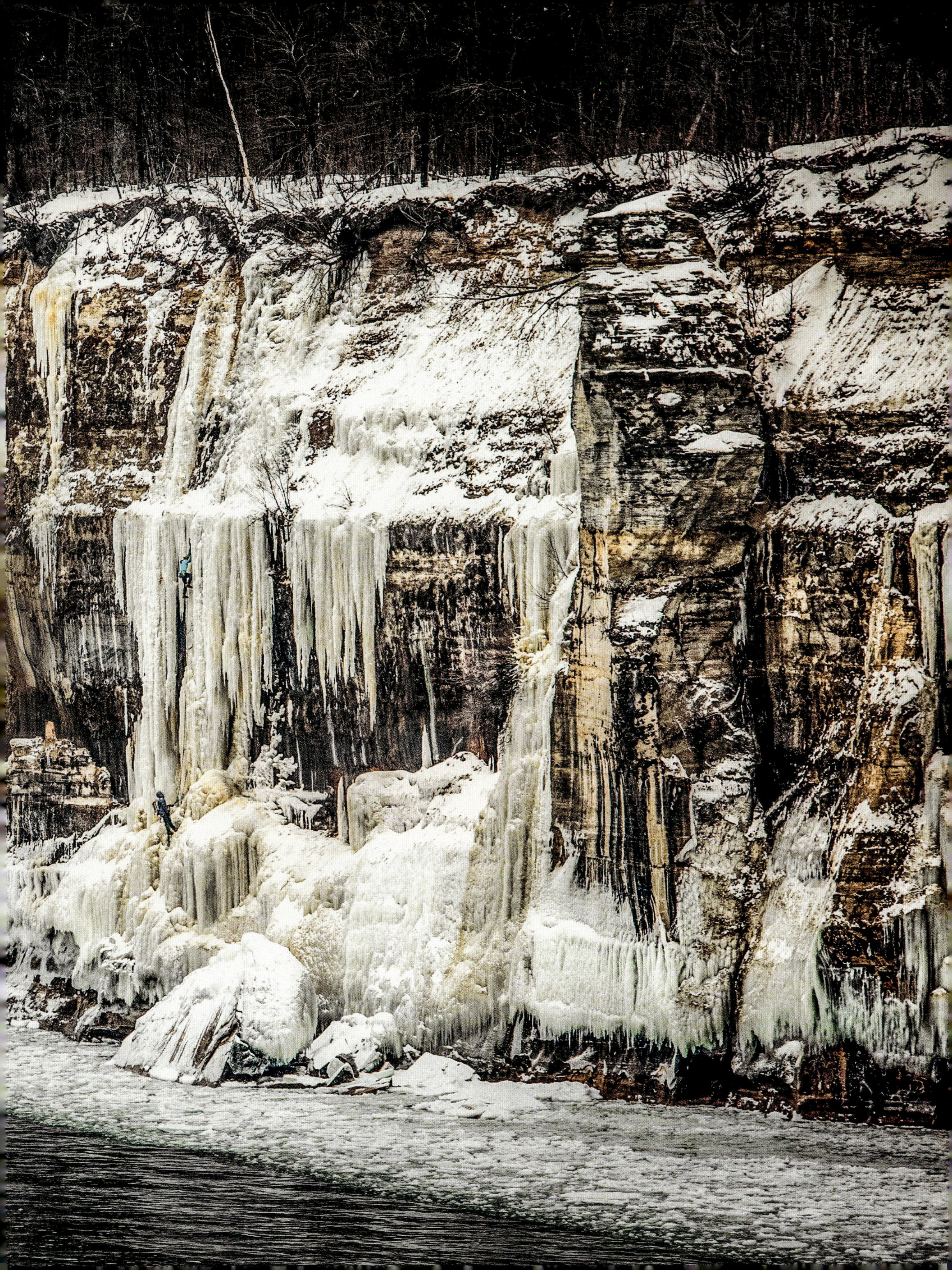

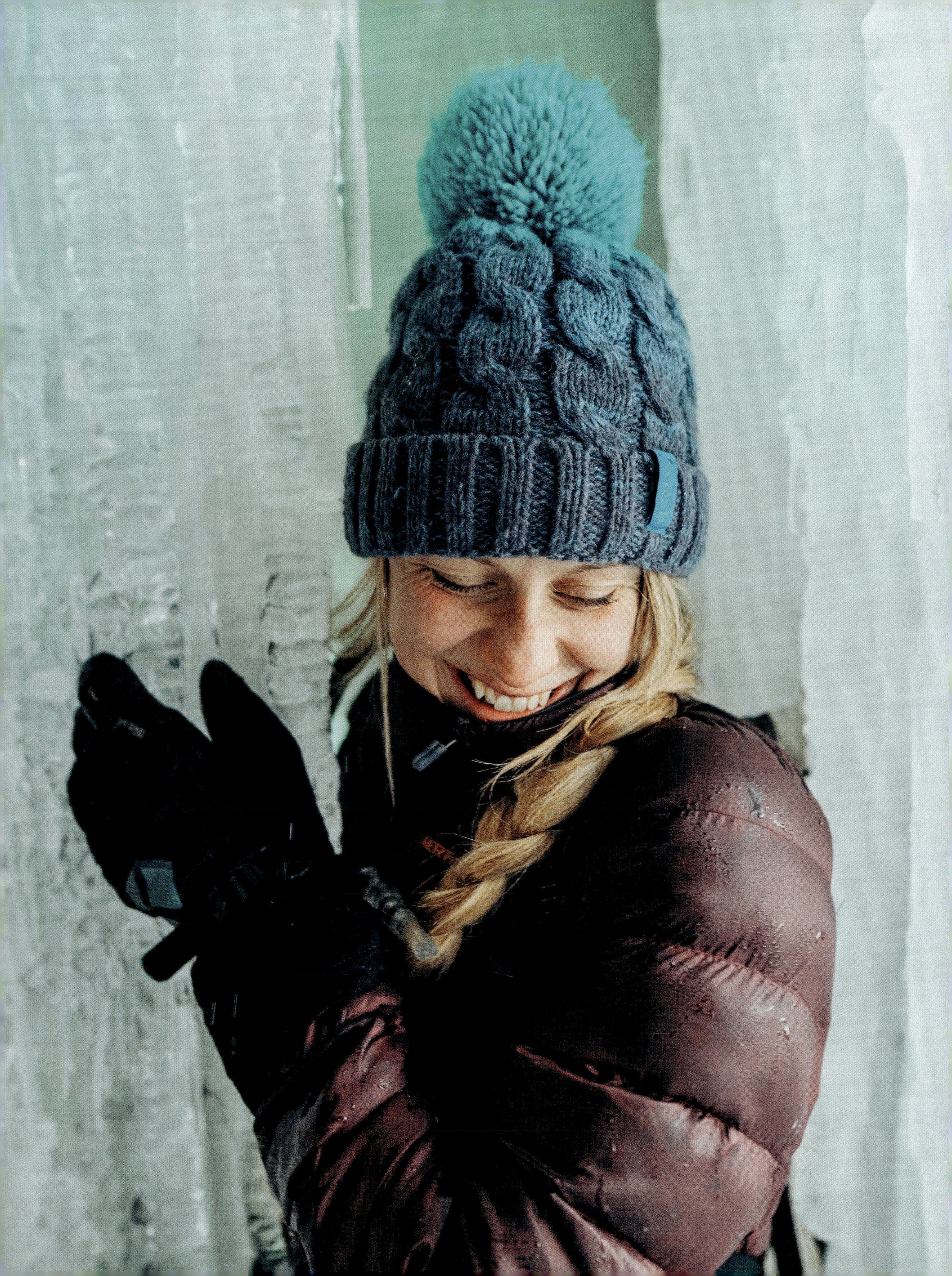

Angela Vanwiemeersch
Ice climber

@angela_vanwiemeersch

I grew up as a competitive ice skater in Detroit, Michigan, where I danced across the horizontal ice until my late teens. Following a few years as a fashion design major in college, I embarked on a life-changing bike tour that recalibrated my life. After selling all my fashion supplies, I hitchhiked, paddled, and sailed my way through all of North America from the Arctic Ocean to the Panama Canal.

While hitchhiking through California, I heard of a place called Ouray, Colorado, where people wore spikes on their feet and held axes in their hands to climb frozen waterfalls. I was enamored. I took every last dollar I had and spent it on a month's worth of rent in Ouray and a bag full of used climbing gear. I found the beauty and inspiration I was looking for and I am now fueled by the challenge that climbing offers.

I love big, aesthetic objectives in faraway places; remote locations with different cultures where my life seems to be in great contrast. I revel in the unknowns. I can't wait to go into a new zone, to touch ice that's never been climbed before. Climbing has given me so much beauty in my life. It provides me with a daily purpose, a sense of exploration. It is the thing that brings me to far corners of the world, the thing that drives me to experience otherworldly sunrises.

Climbing even brought me the love of my life, and the community I deem family. I can't imagine a life without climbing. It's something that will never leave me.

Lake Superior, Michigan, USA

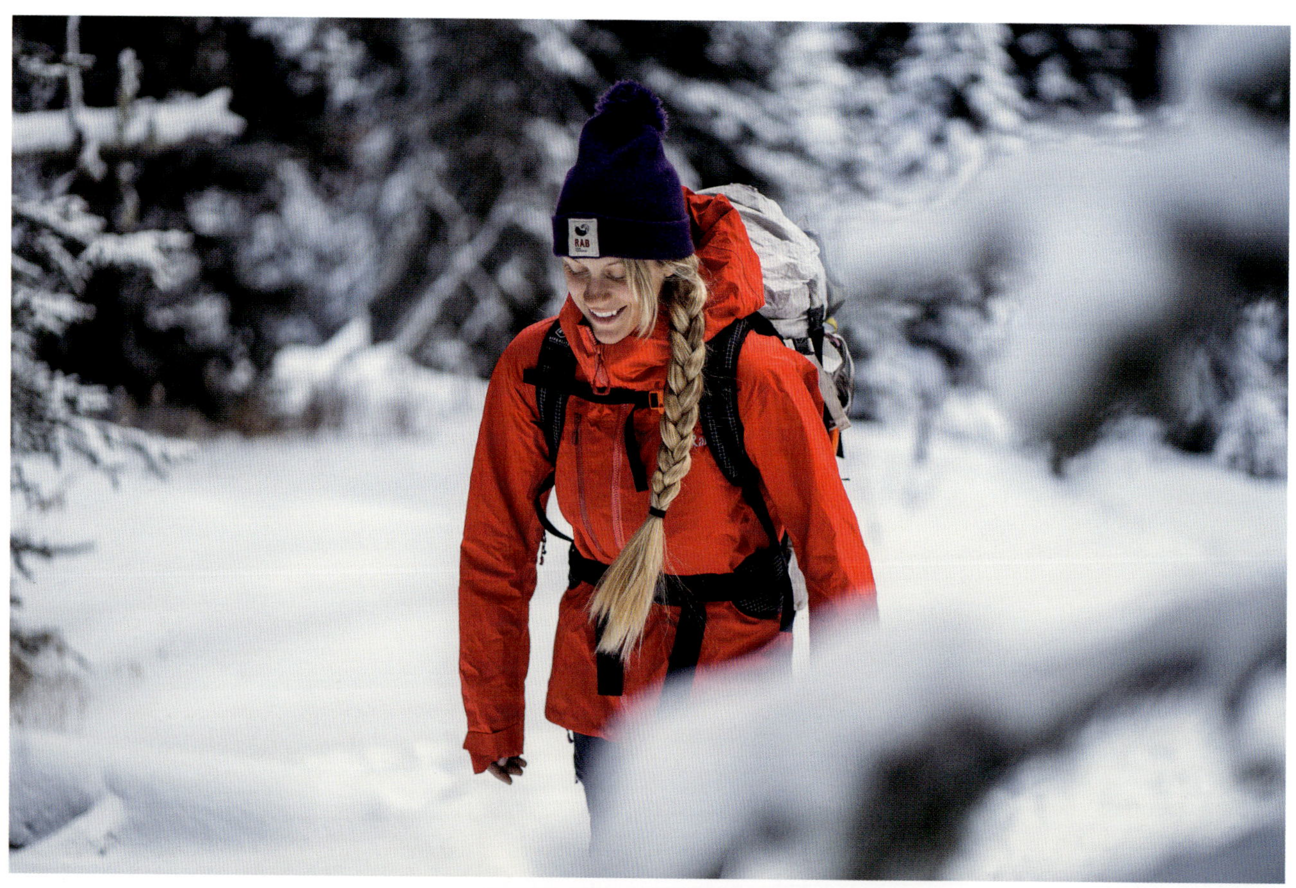

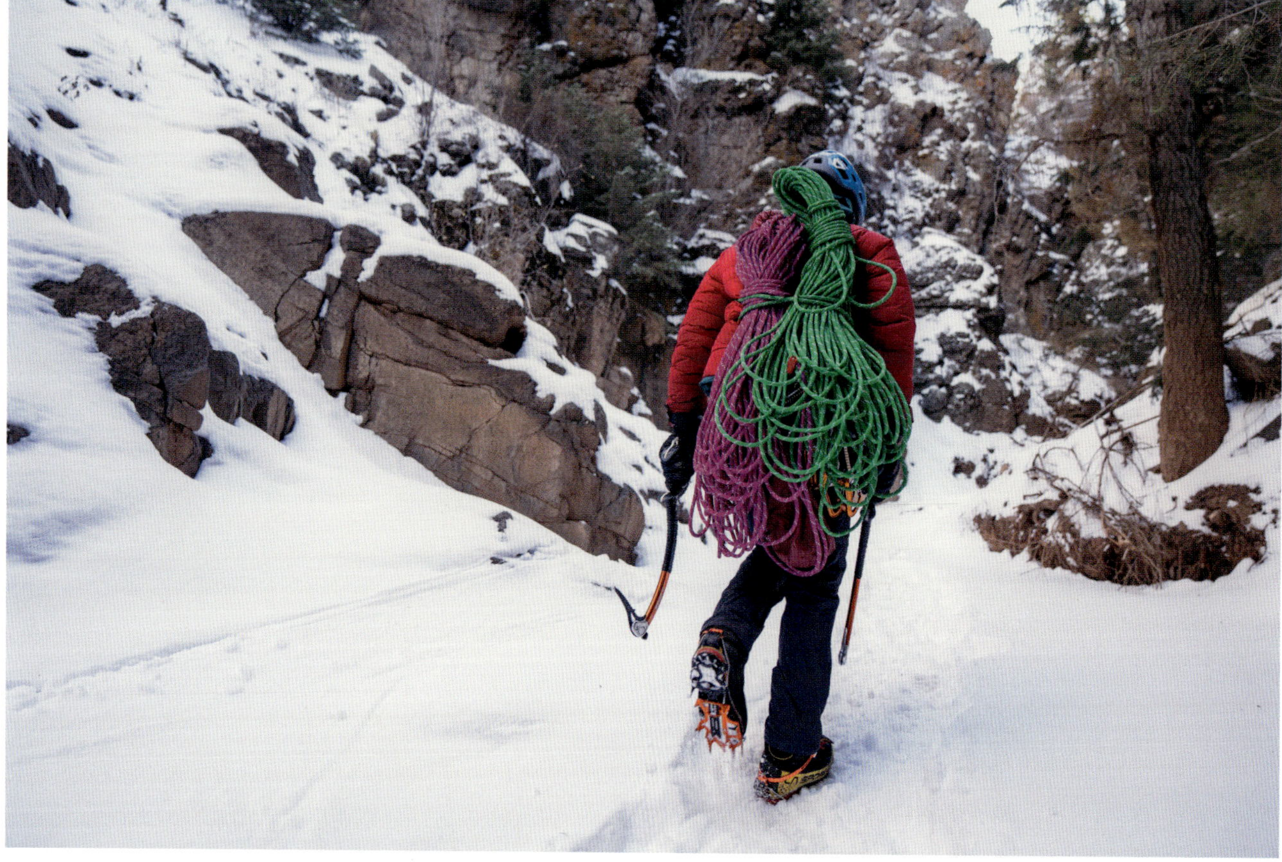

  △△ Hyalite Canyon, Montana   △ Parowan   ▷ Zion National Park | Utah, USA

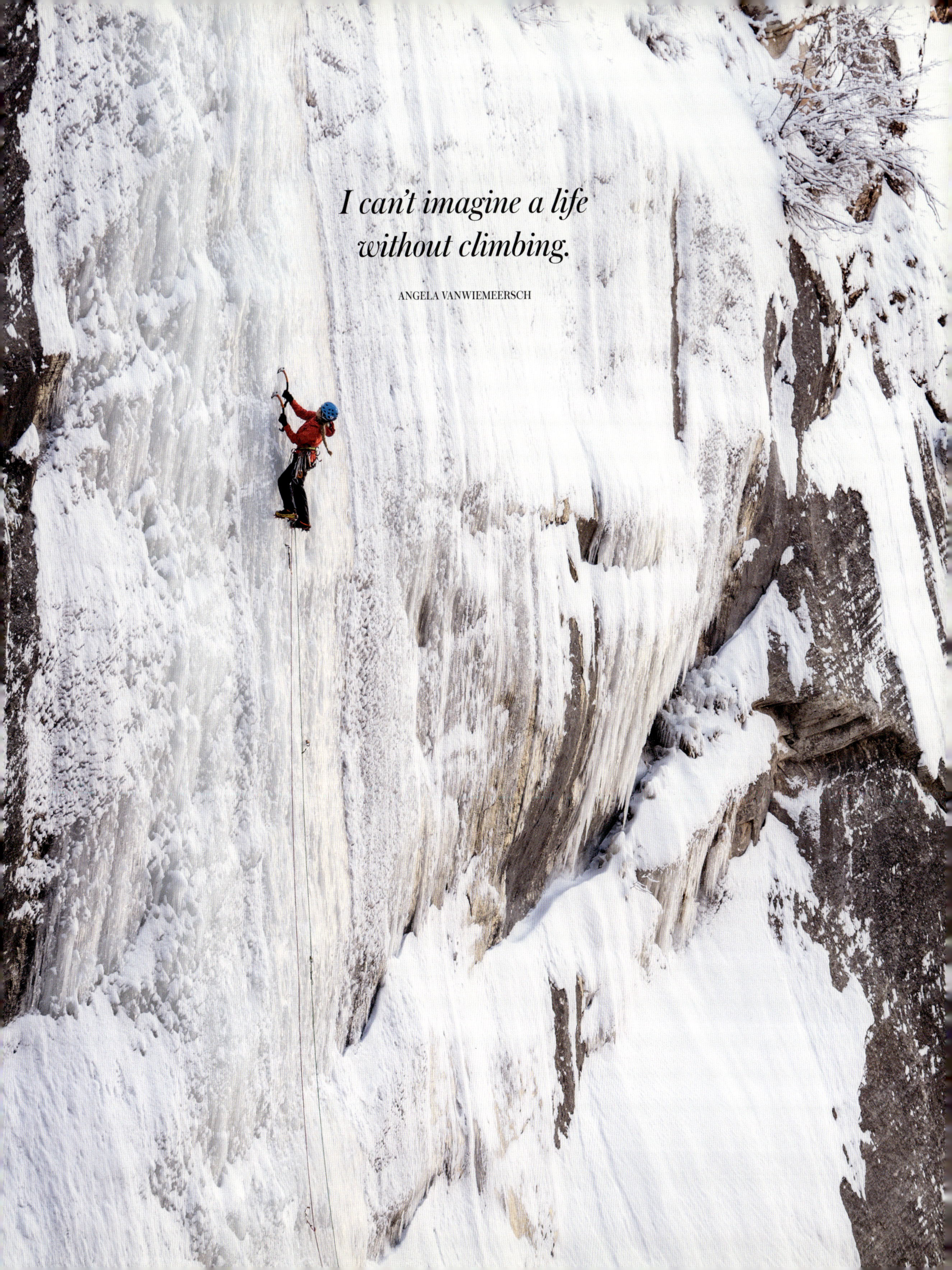

I can't imagine a life
without climbing.

ANGELA VANWIEMEERSCH

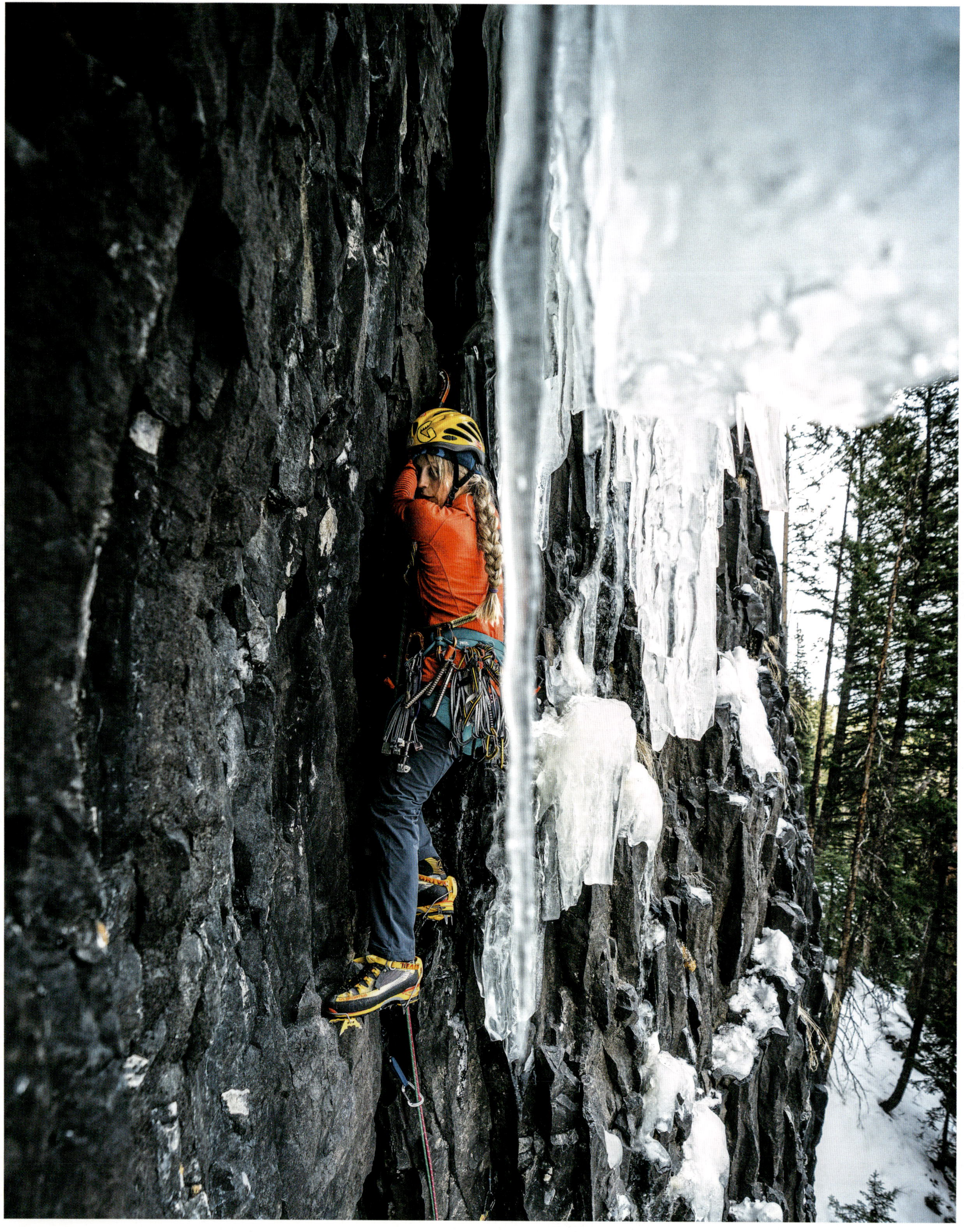

△ Hyalite Canyon, Montana   ▷ △△ Santaquin Canyon, Utah   ▷ △ New Hampshire   ▷▷ Zion National Park, Utah | USA

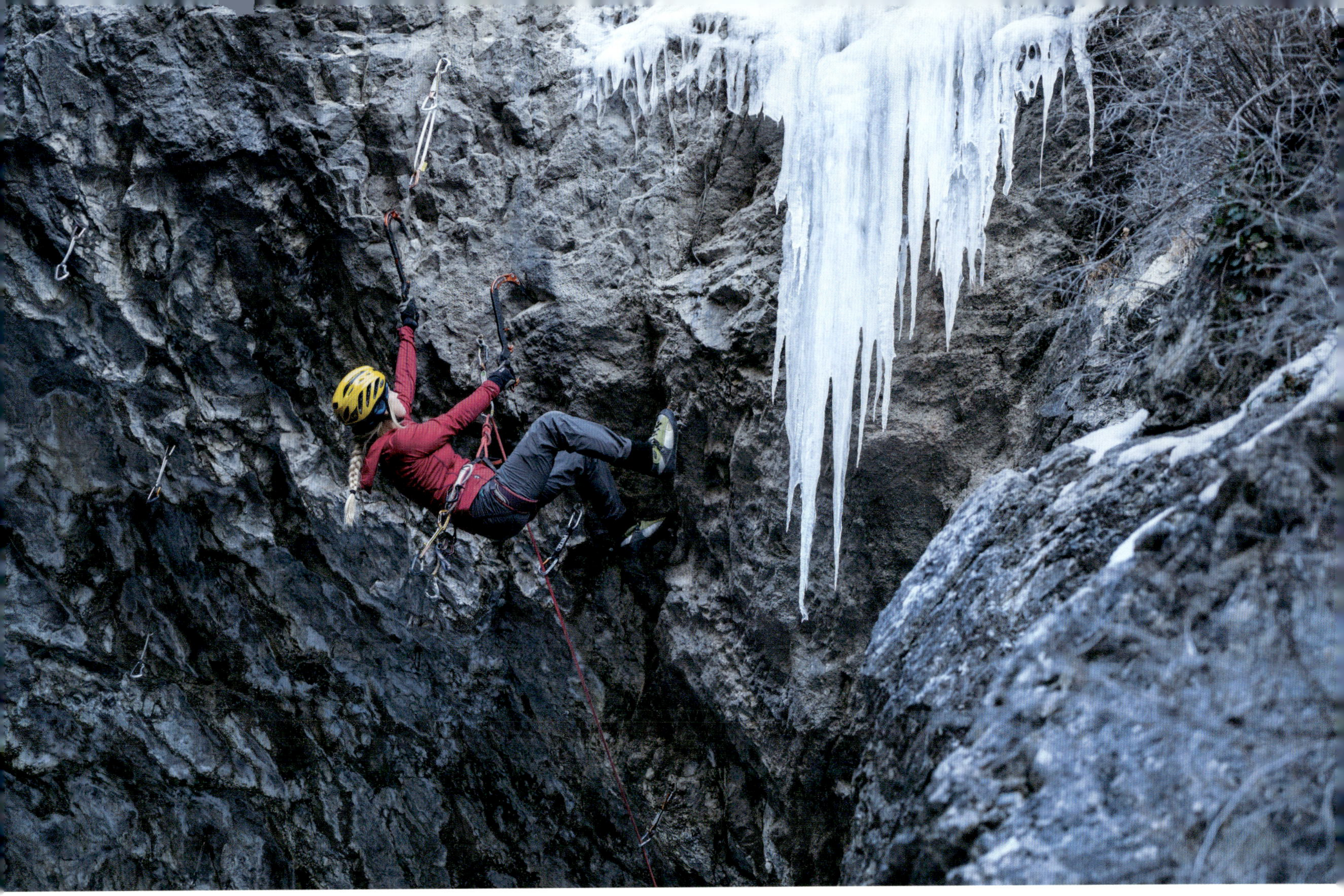

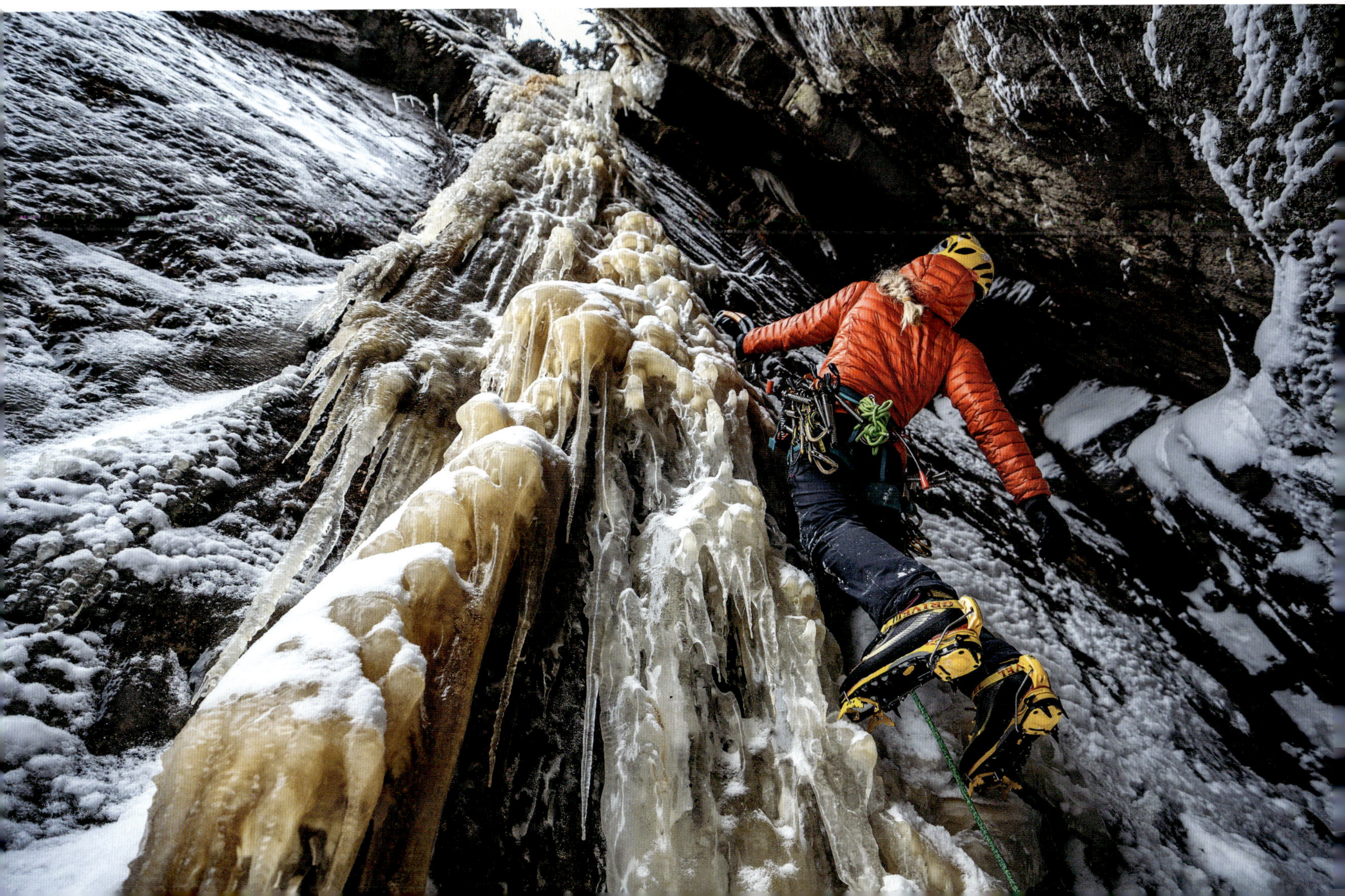

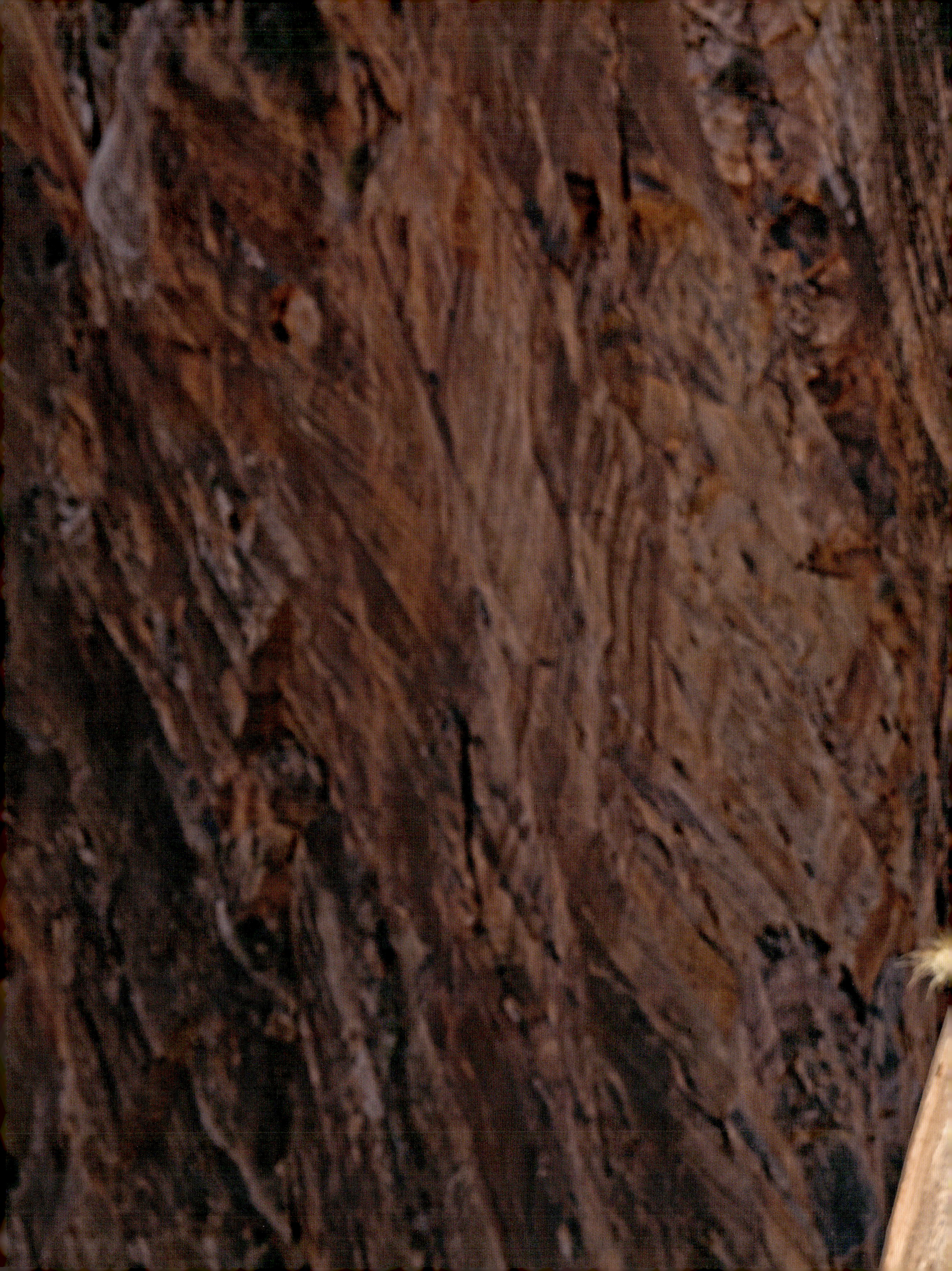

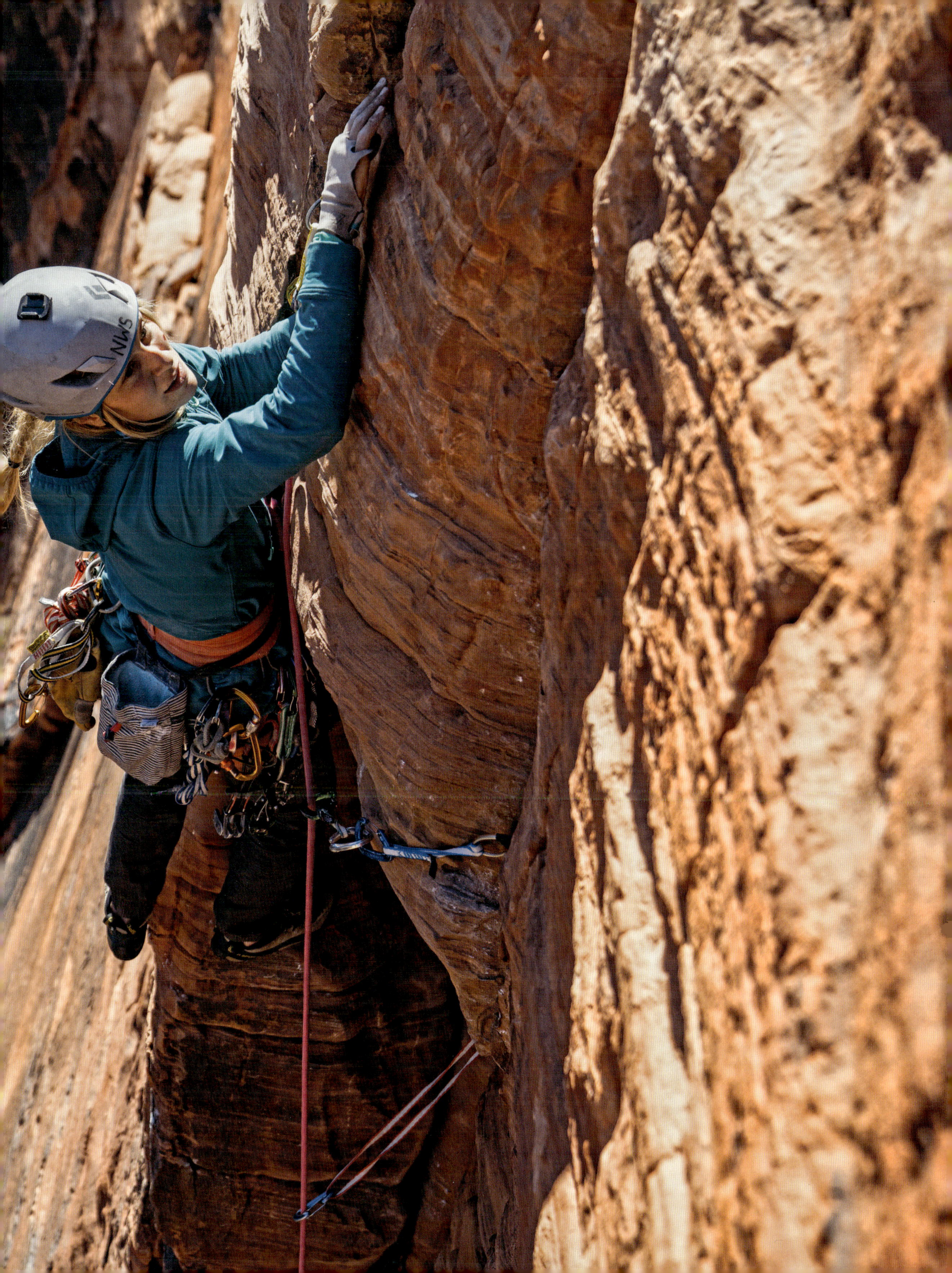

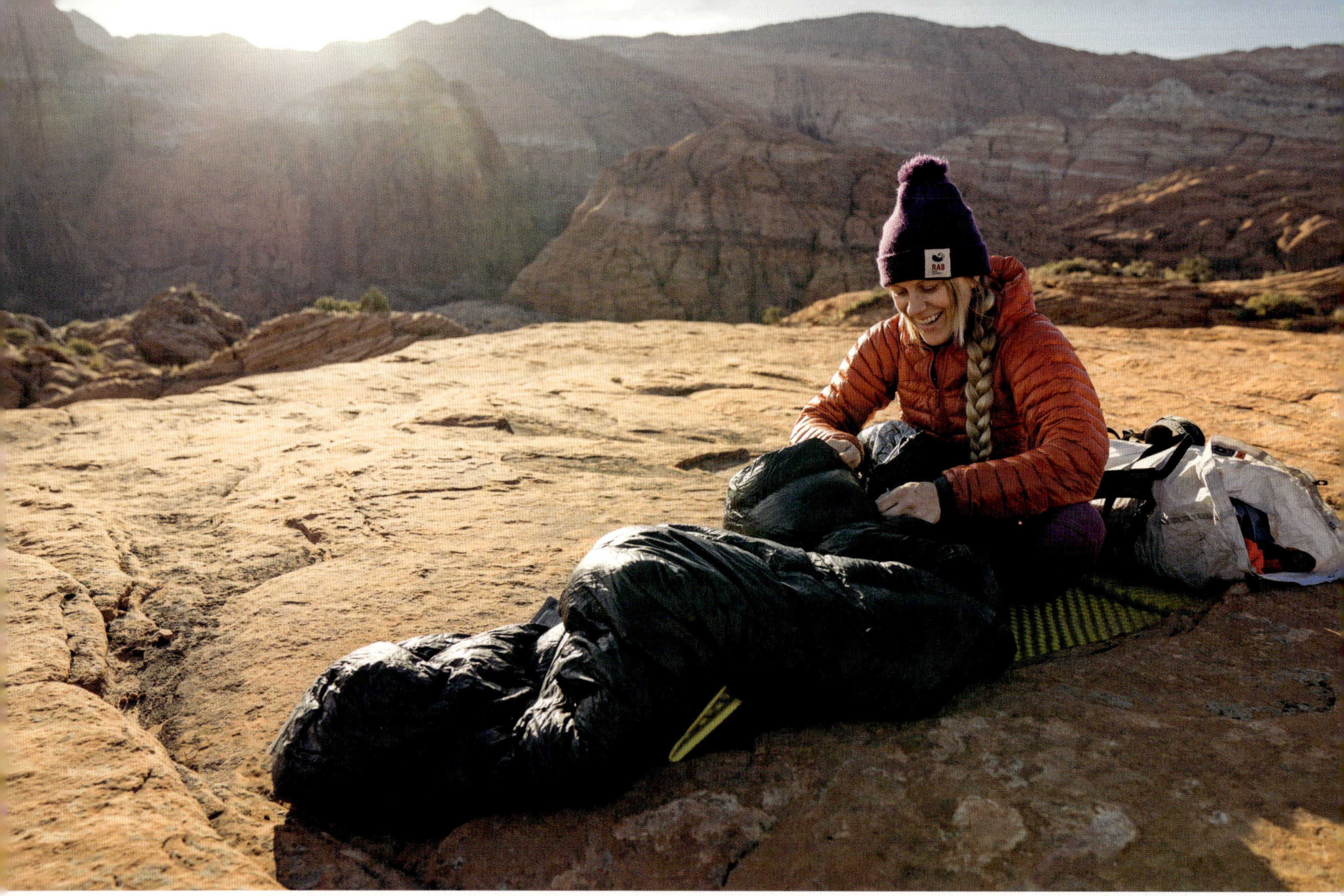

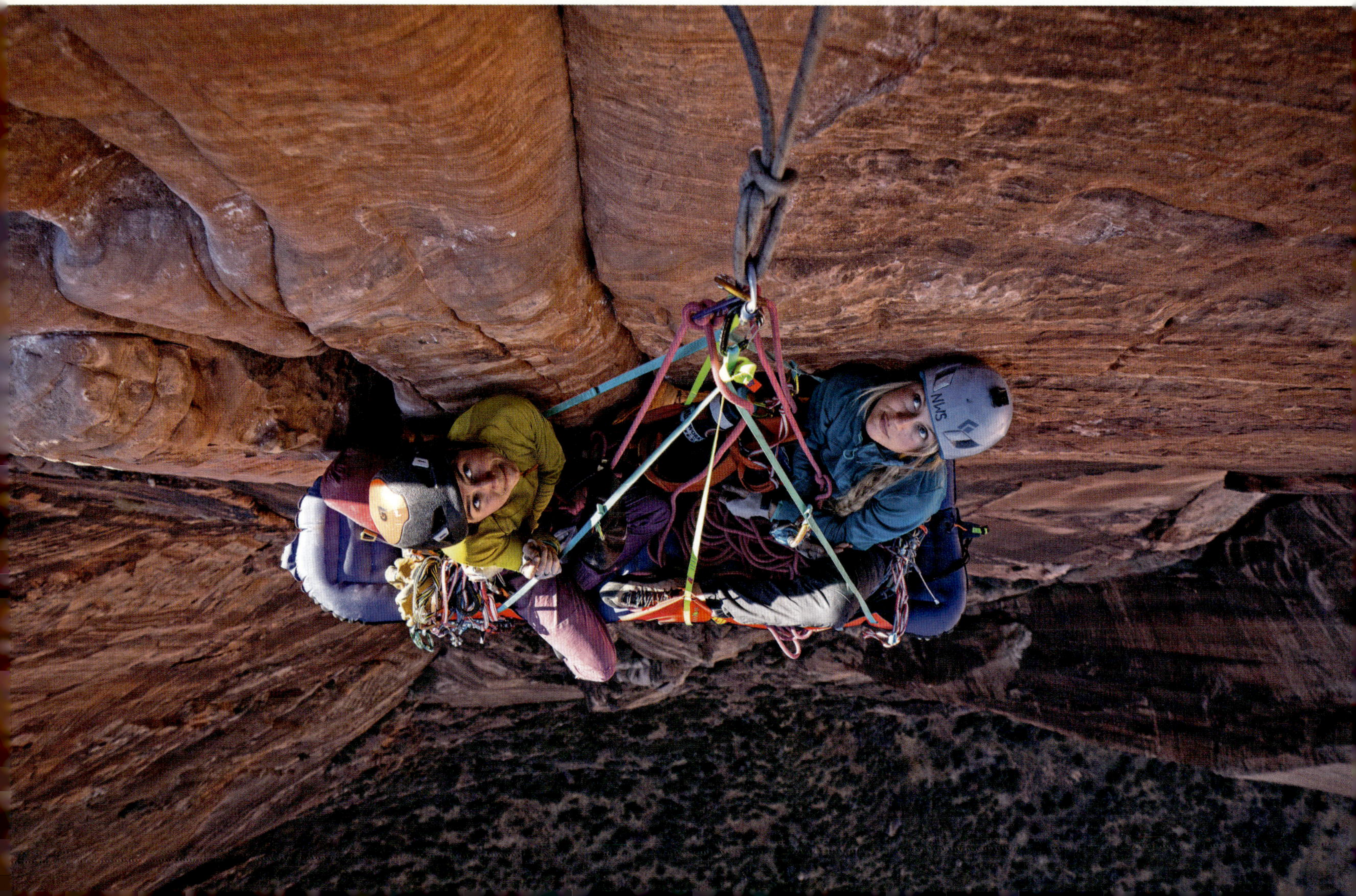

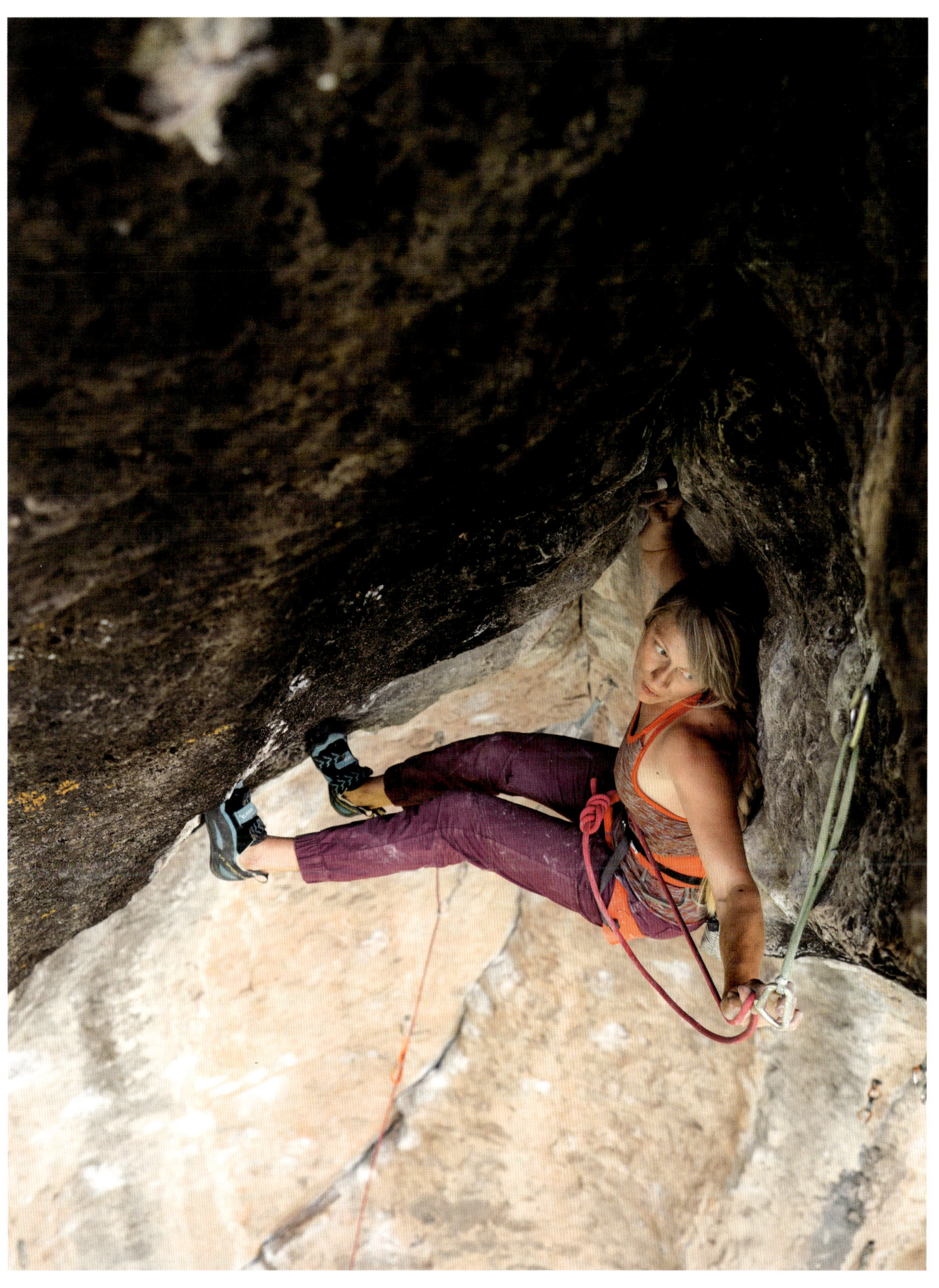

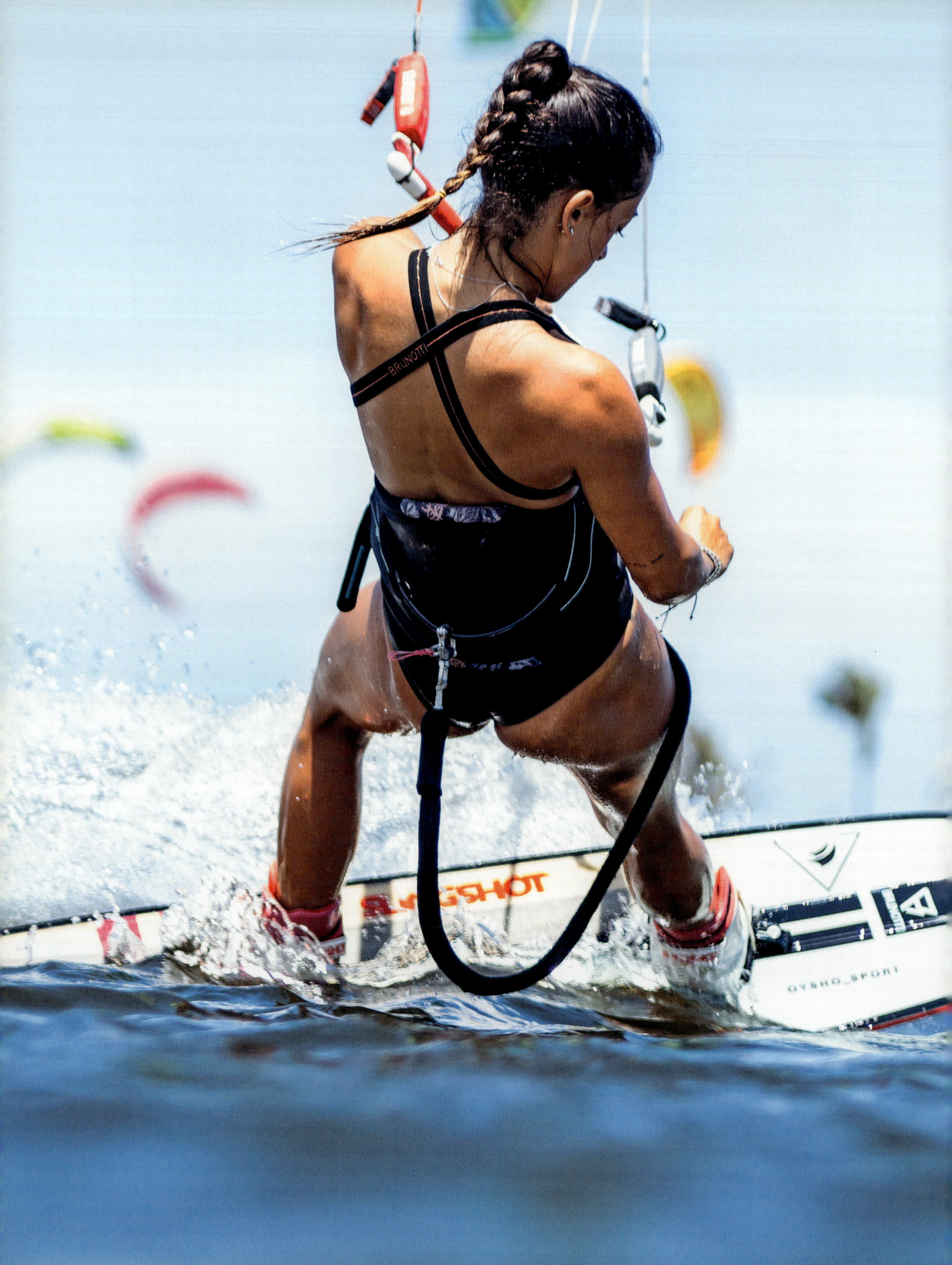

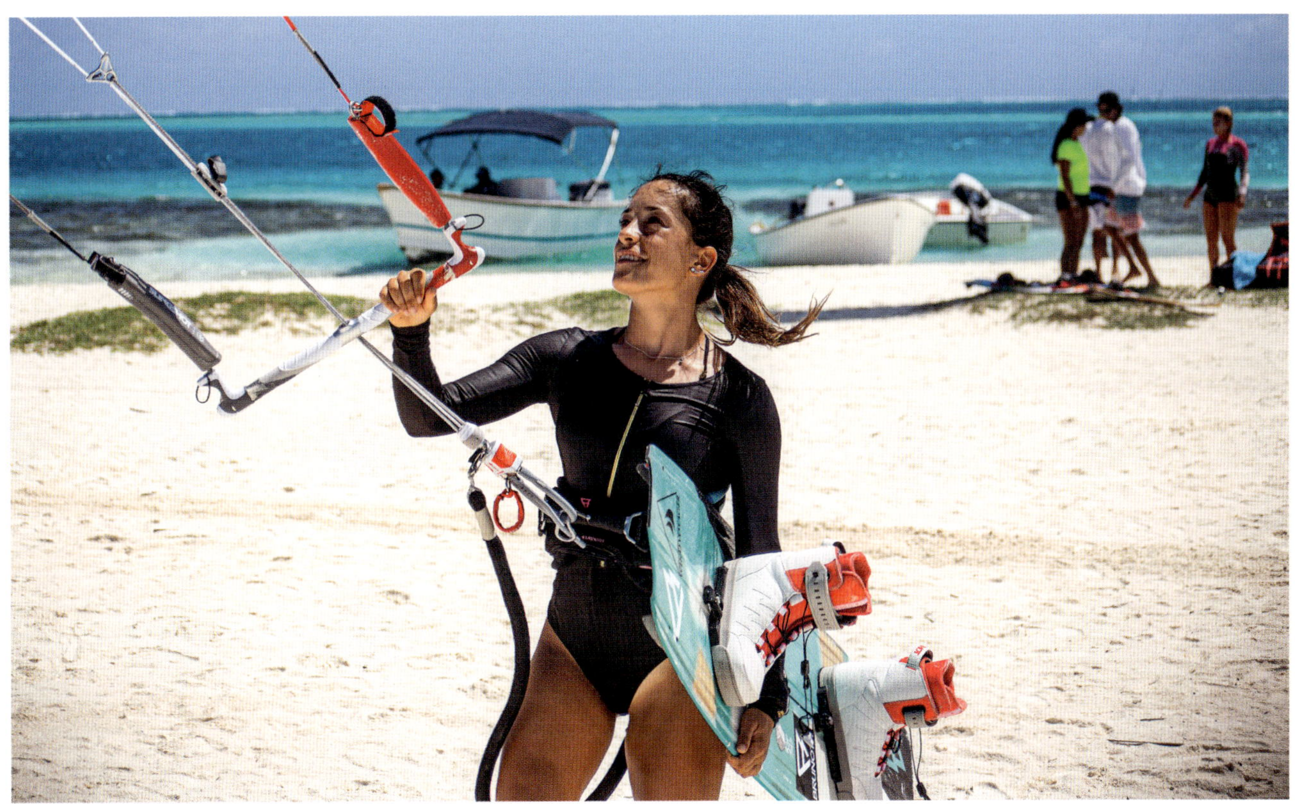

Rita Arnaus

Kiteboarder

@ritaarnaus
ritaarnaus.com

I was born in Barcelona in September 1995, into a very sporty family. Both my parents were Windsurf Spanish Champions and my dad was among the first people to start kiteboarding in Spain. At the age of ten I began windsurfing and sailing. My parents never pushed me to do any sports; they always respected my learning process and let me take my time, and I'm really glad they did! It wasn't until I was fifteen years old that I started kiteboarding.

My passion for it ignited, the windy days got even better, and after a month of kiting, I started doing my first backrolls. After each session I was even more hooked on the sport, and after two years the desire to be a professional kiteboarder started to burn inside me, so I knew I had to go for it. I began to study online and to pursue my dreams. With a lot of effort and dedication, I entered my very first world competitions and started creating content for social media. I got my first sponsorship deals and kept traveling around the world to train in the best conditions and to compete in the kiteboarding World Tour.

Do not give up. When times get tough, you do too, so long as you stick to your goals and dreams. Consistency, persistence, and discipline, combined with fun times, are all you need to become successful. Always enjoy the ride!

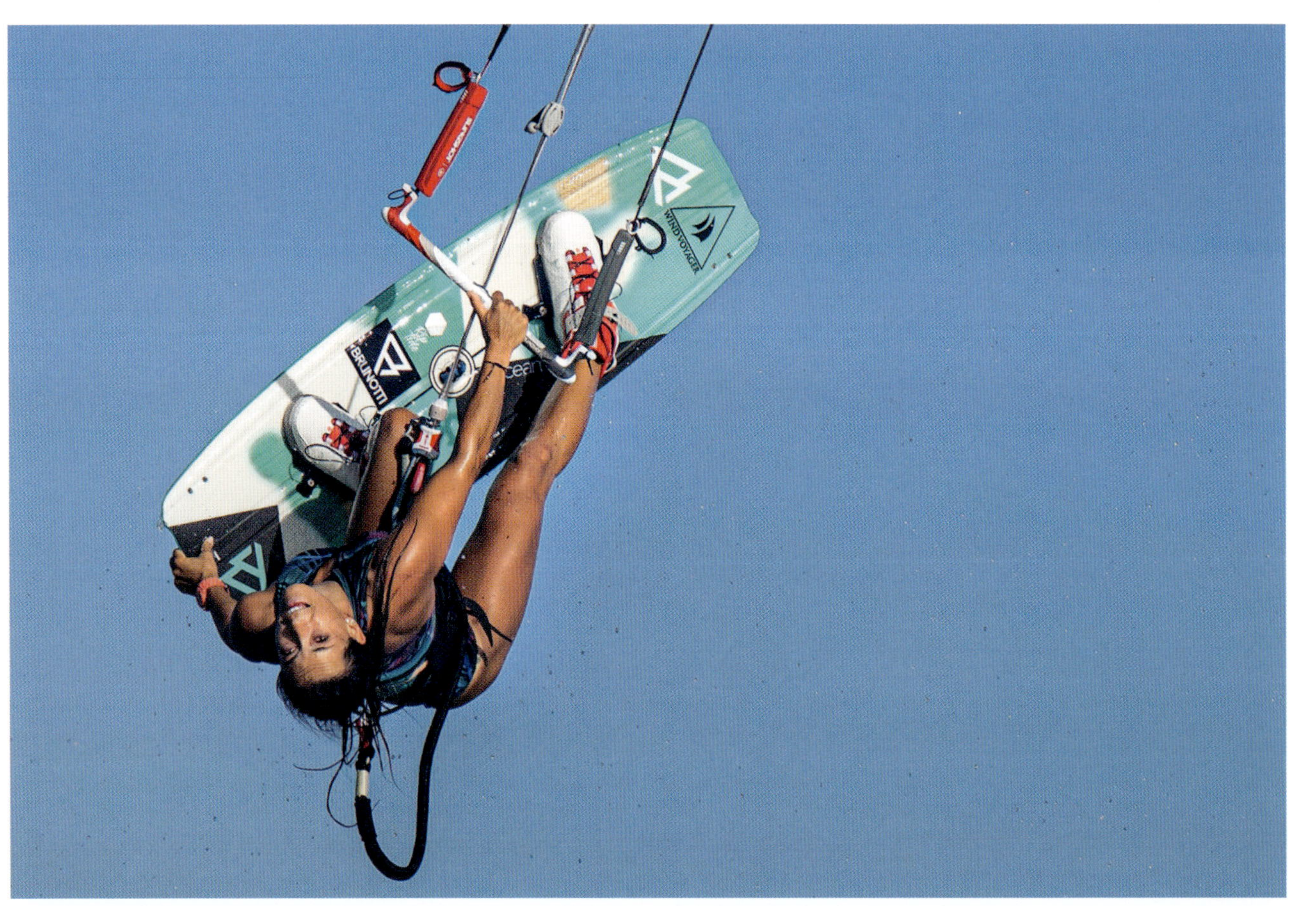

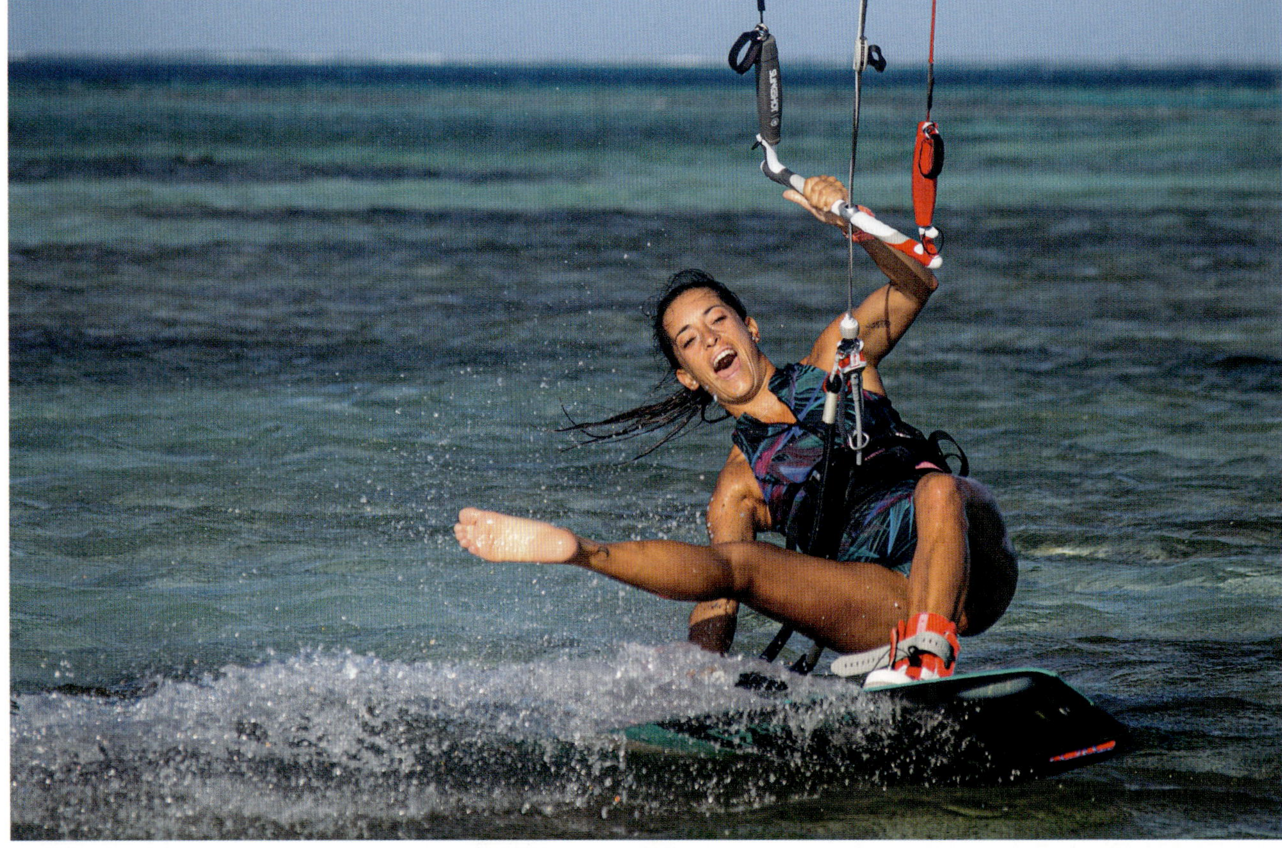

  △ Los Roques, Venezuela ▷ Lagoa do Cauipe, Brazil ▷▷ Cabarete, Dominican Republic

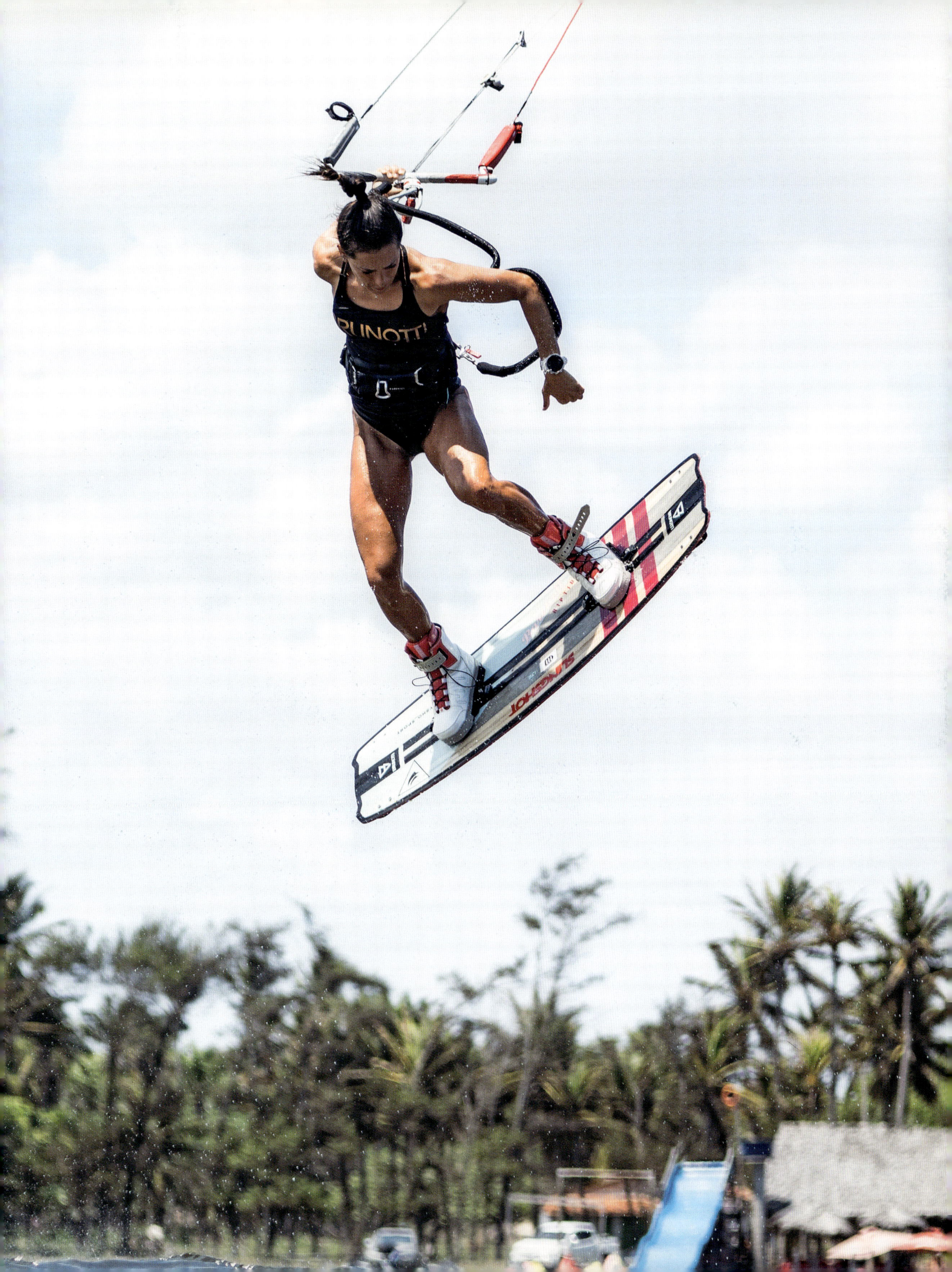

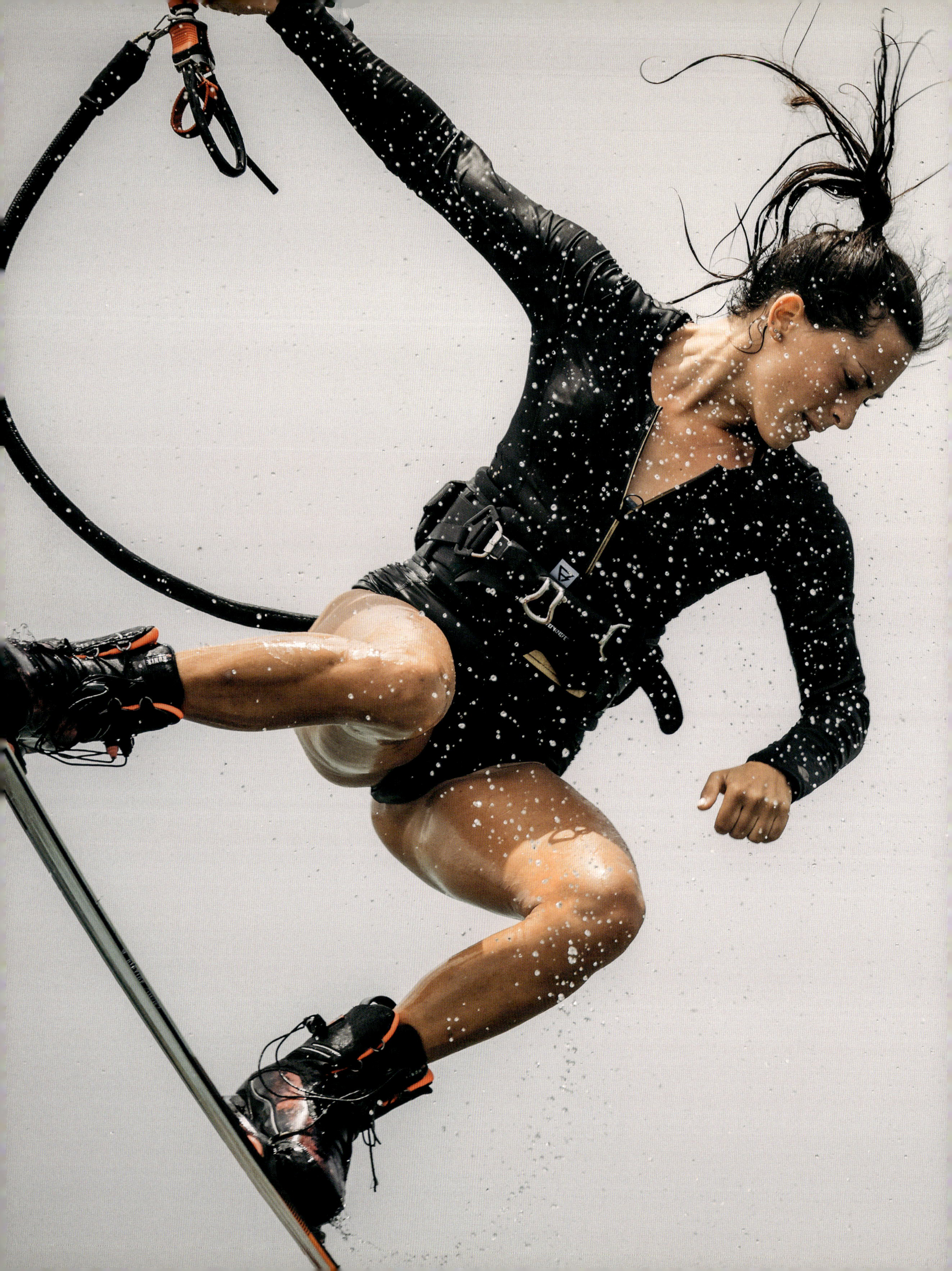

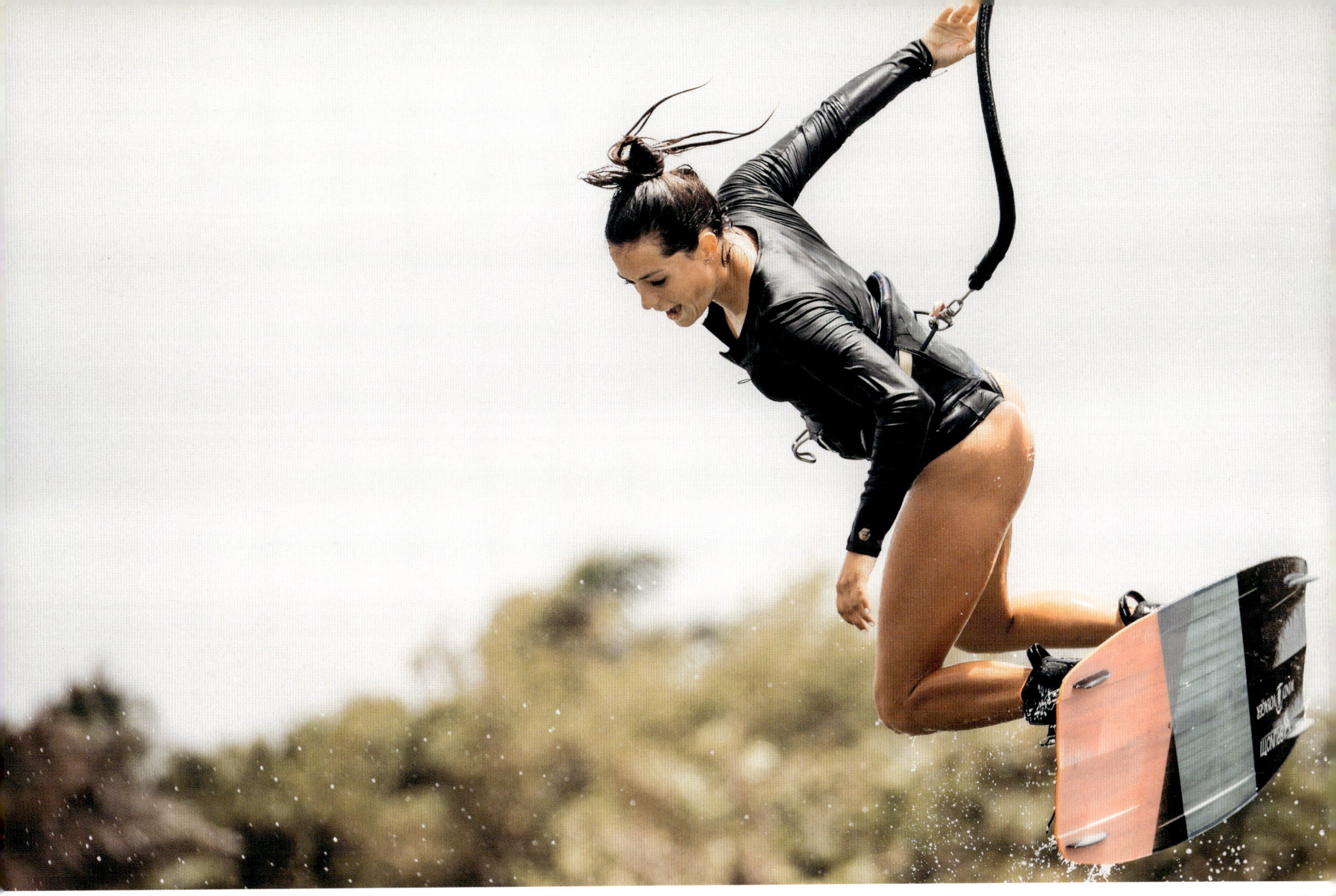

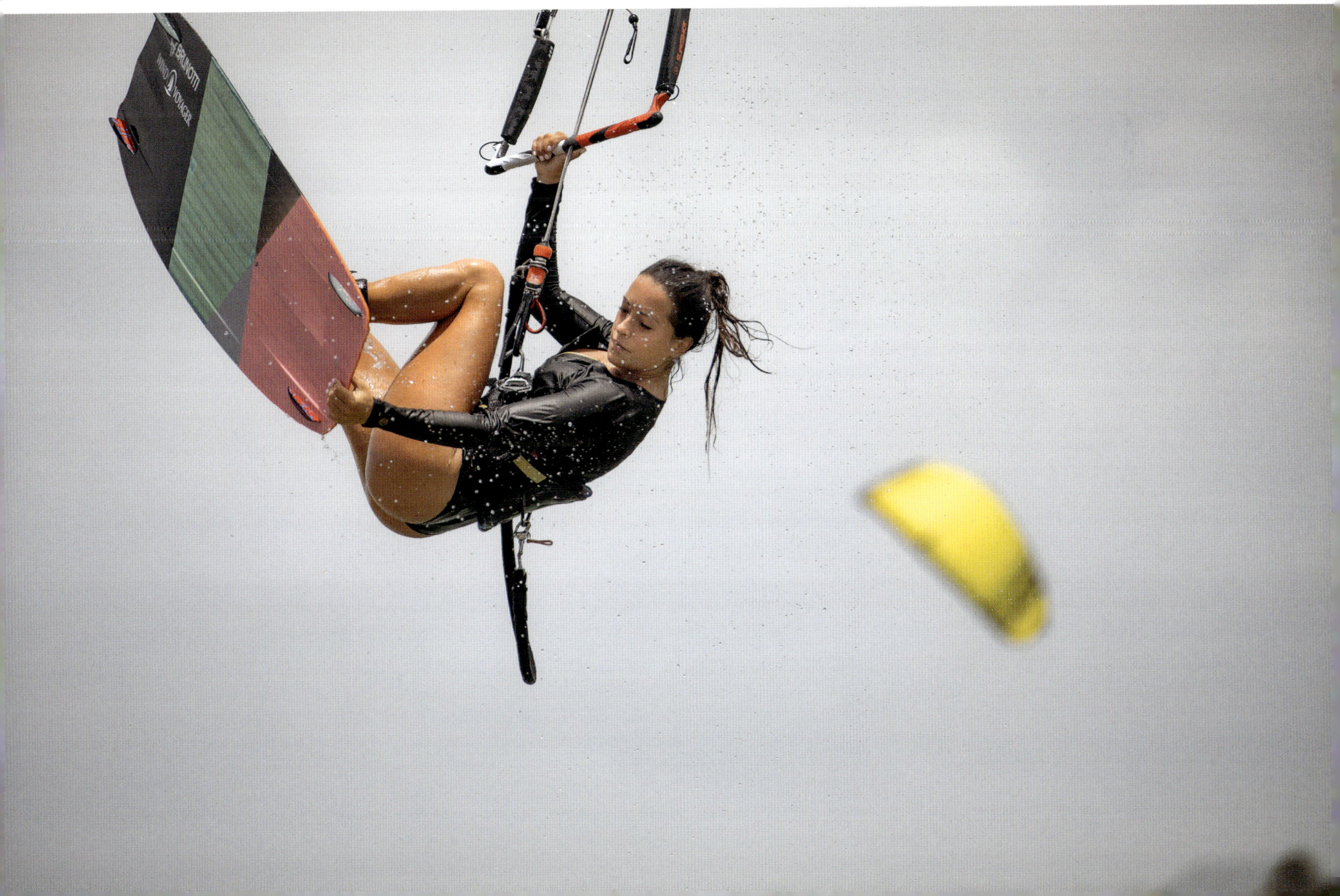

BRUNOTTI
WIND VOYAGER

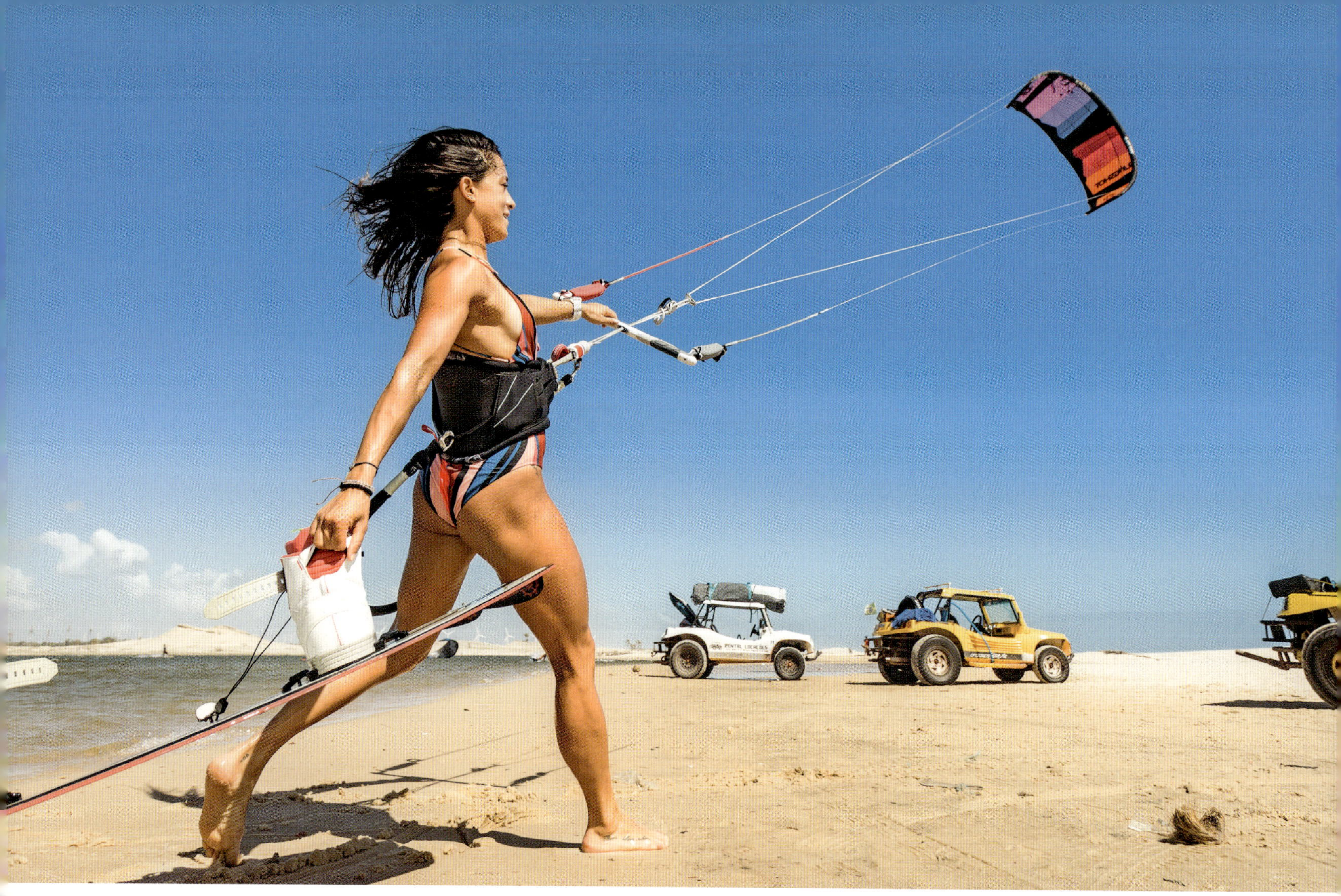

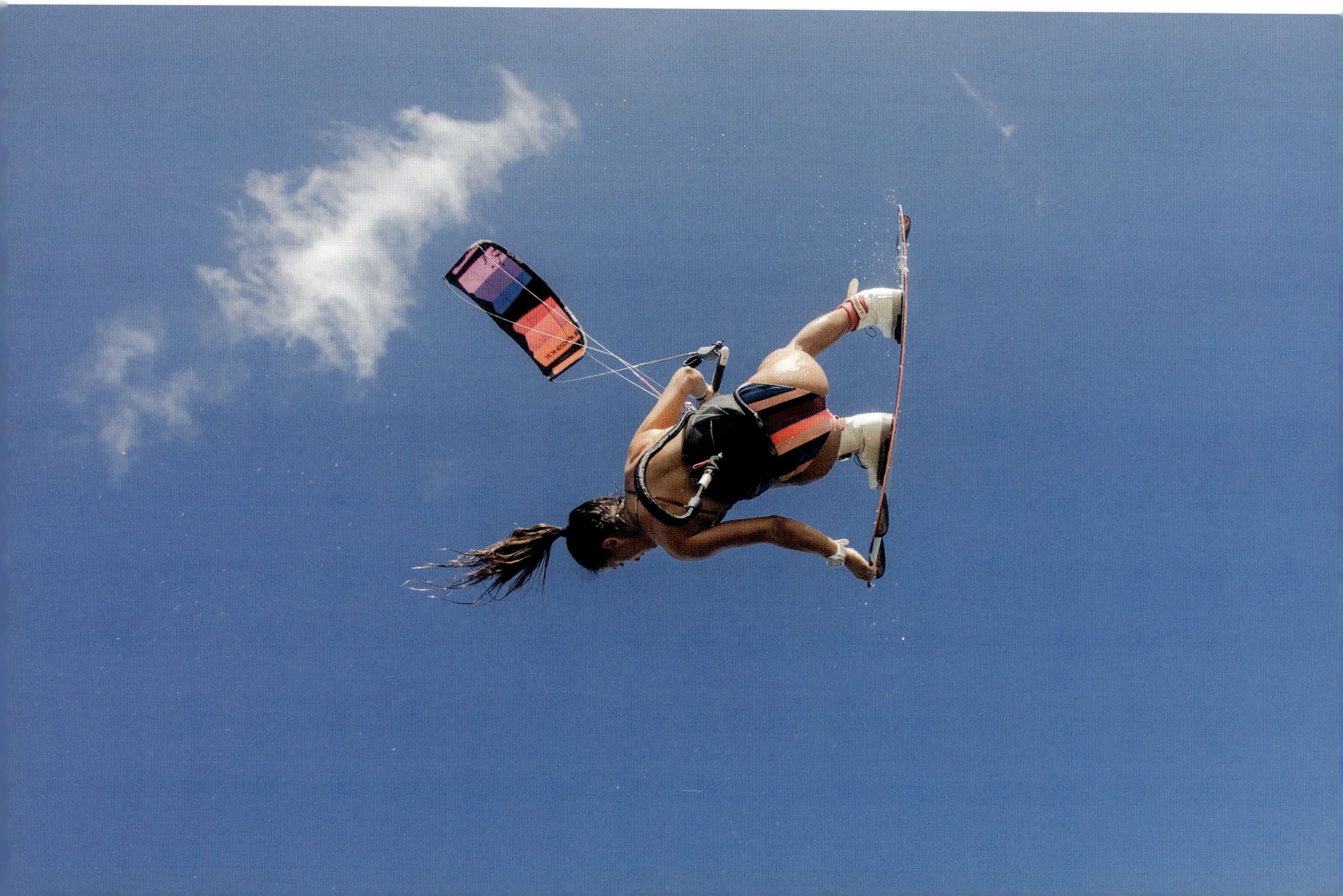

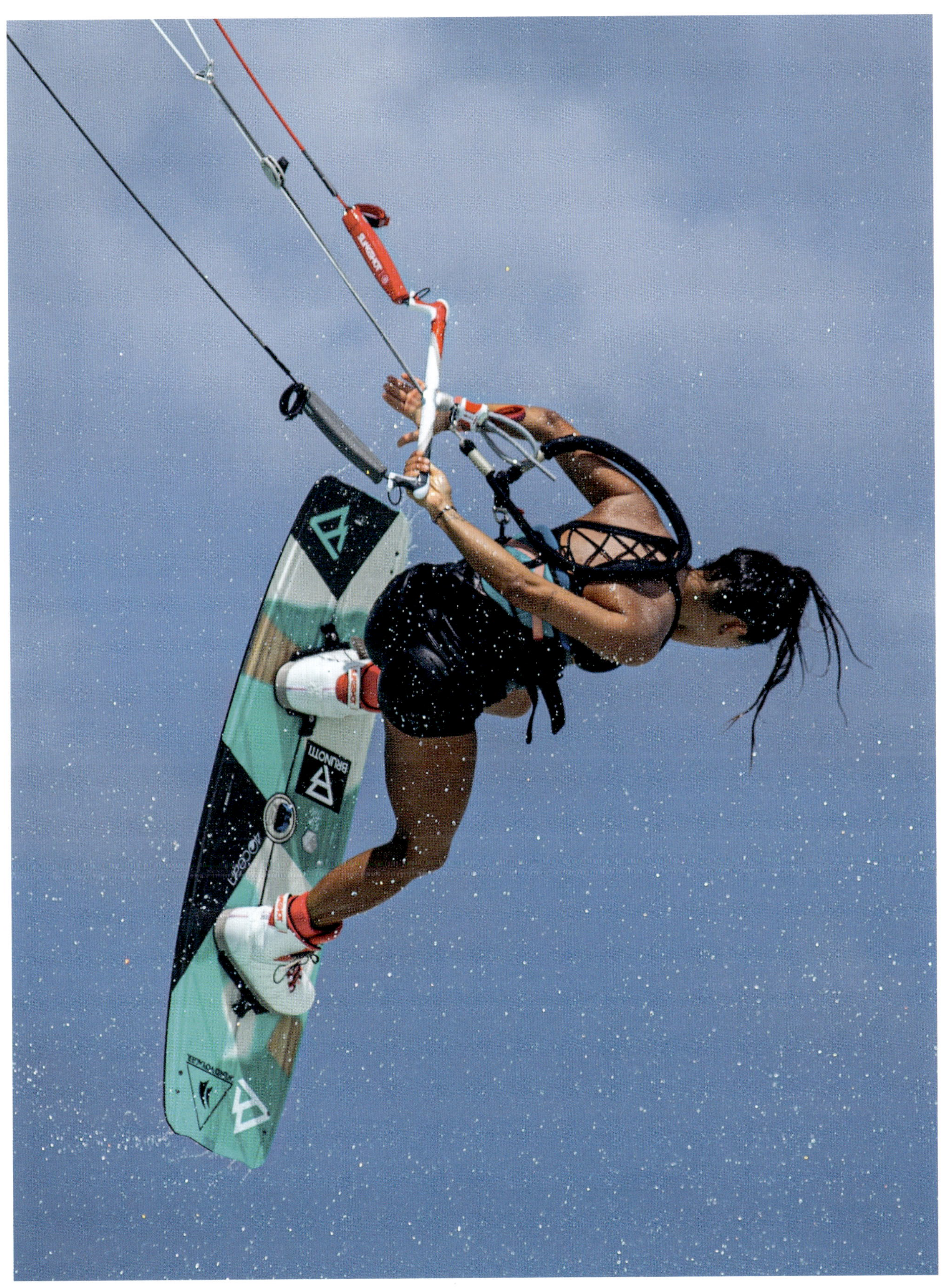

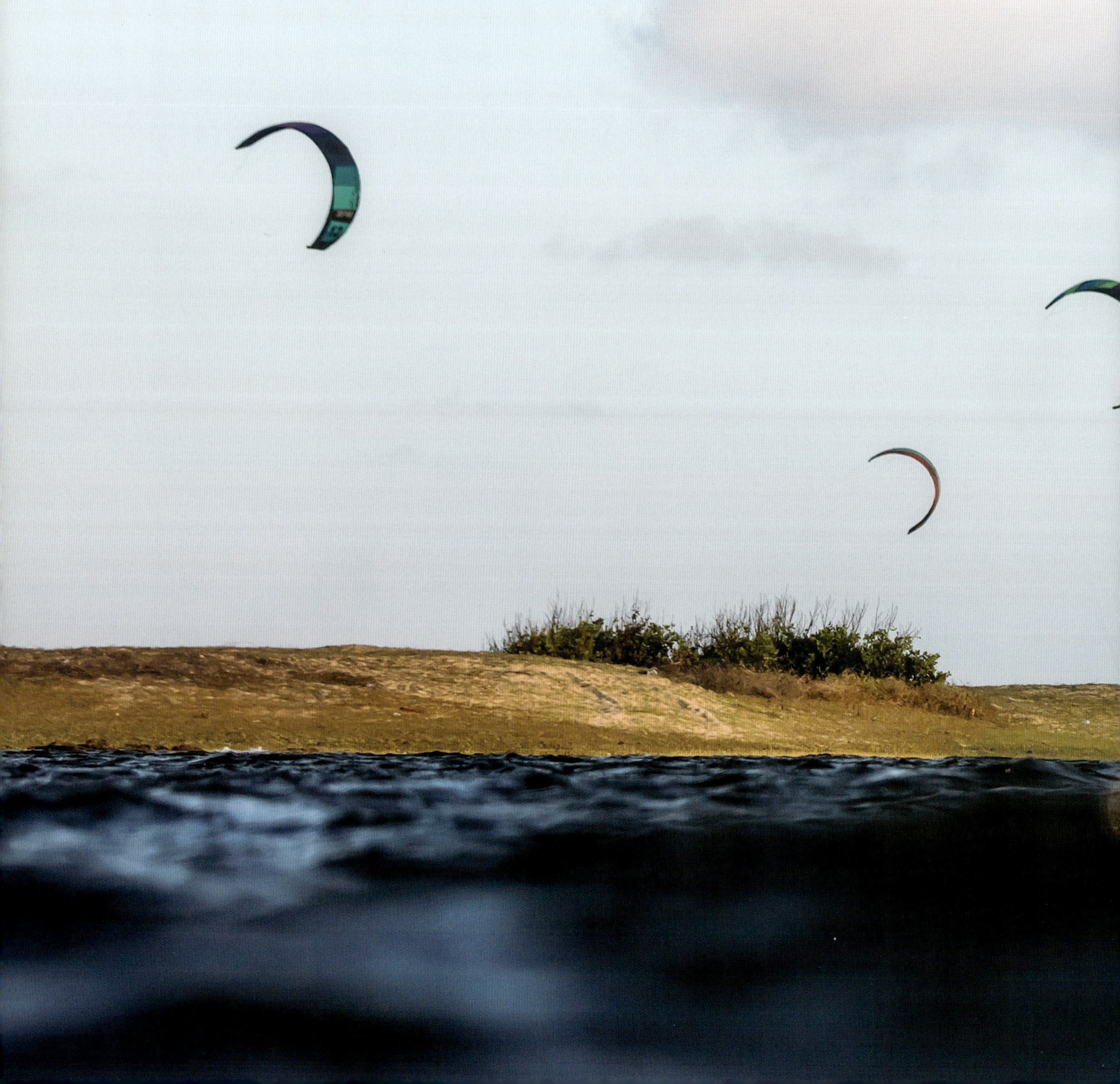

Consistency, persistence, and discipline, combined with fun times, are all you need.

RITA ARNAUS

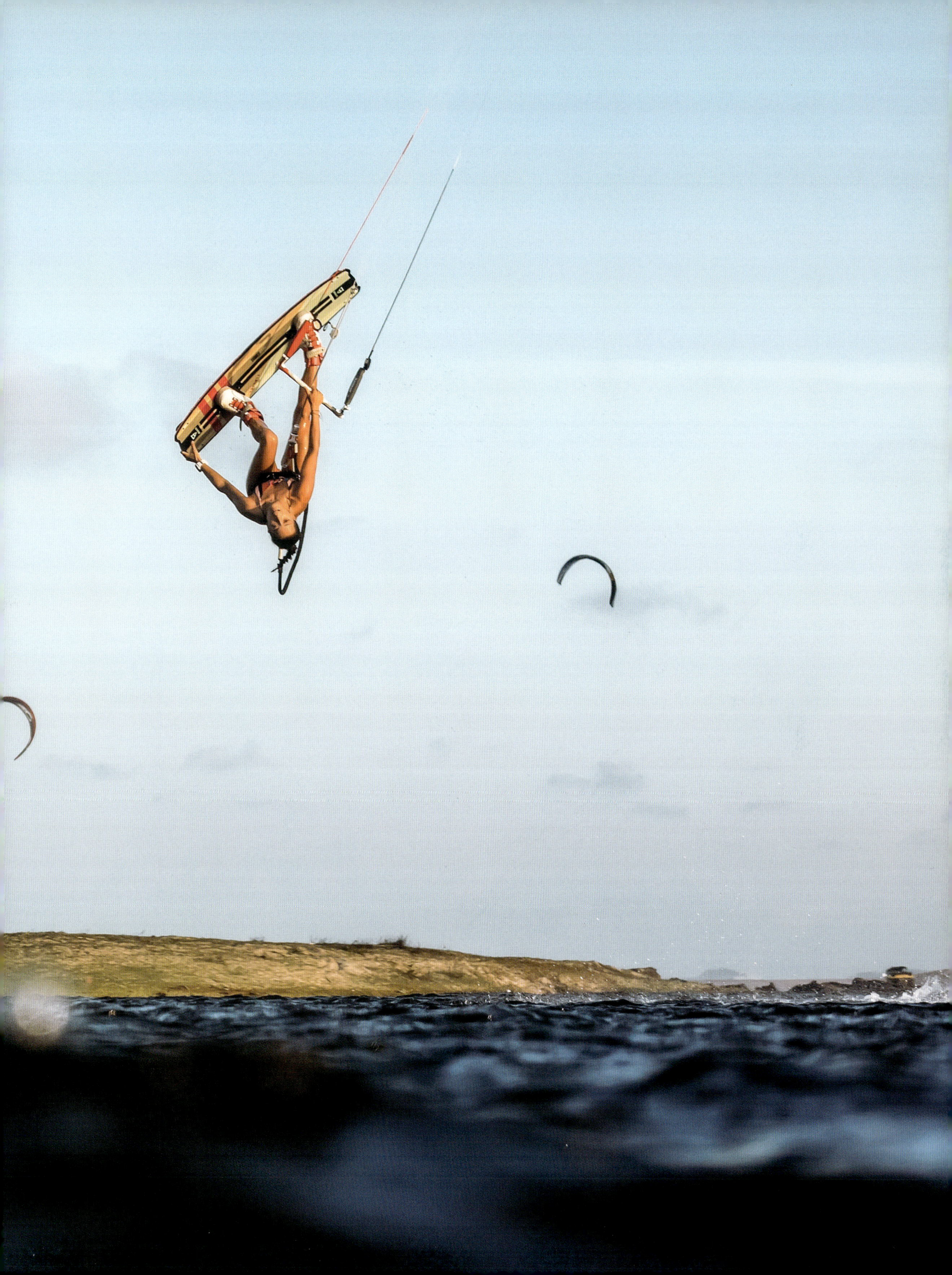

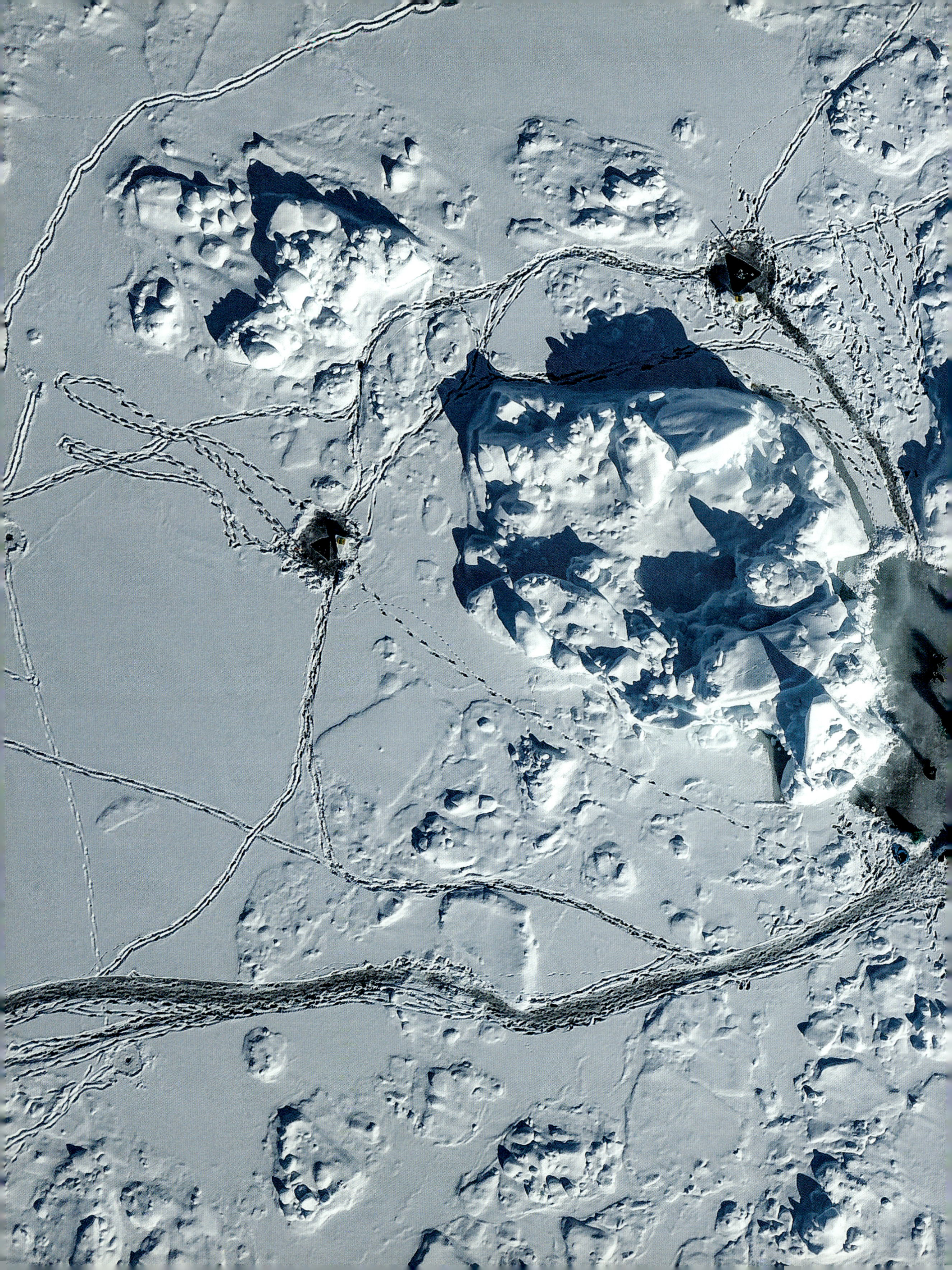

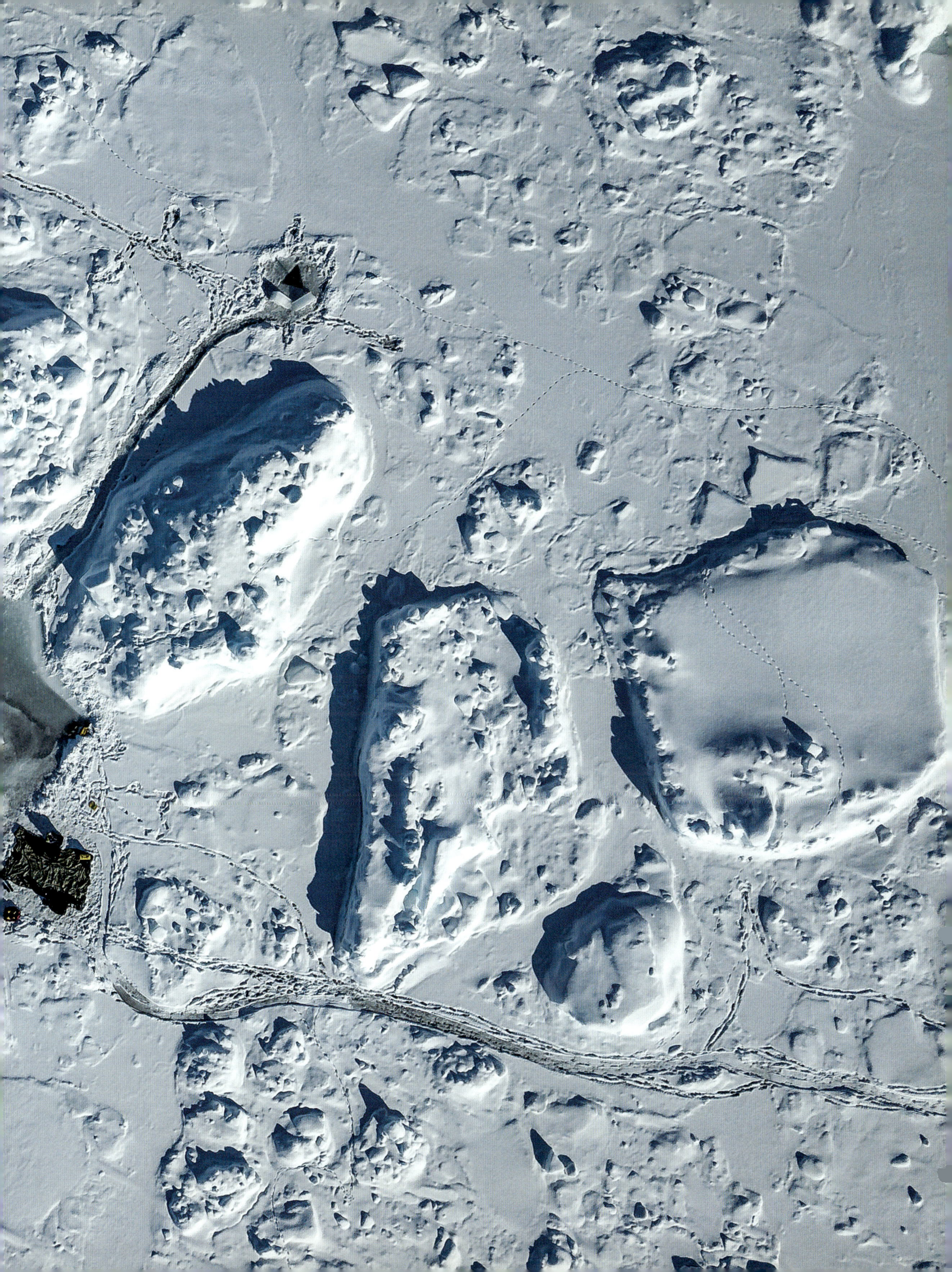

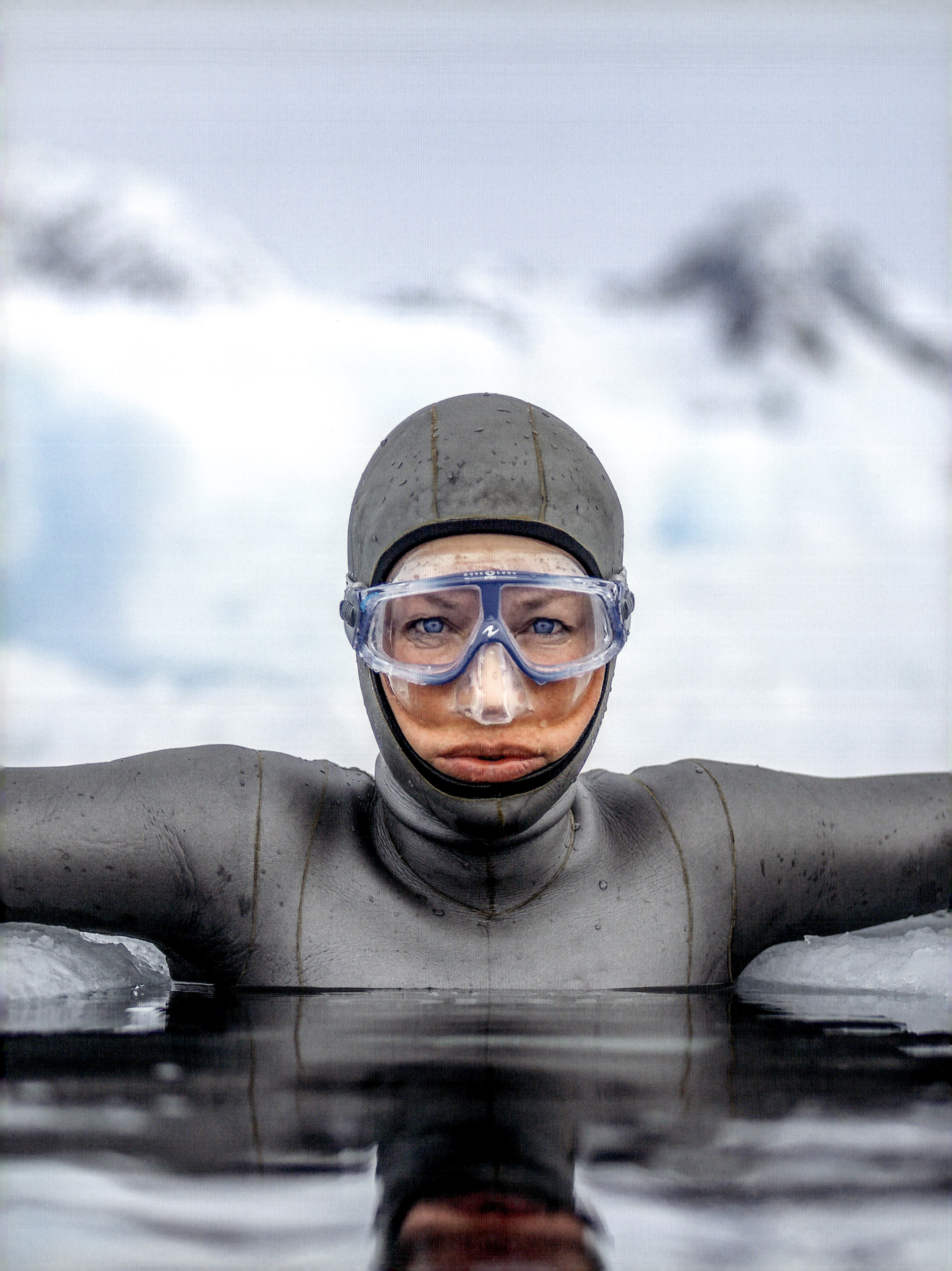

Anna von Boetticher
Freediver

@freediveanna
annavonboetticher.com

Ever since I was a child, I've been filled with a great sense of curiosity and a longing to discover the world and my place in it. I wanted to fly to Mars, to see the Alaskan wilderness and the highest mountains, to travel to the bottom of the sea in a submarine. This fascination with the unknown has stayed with me my whole life. The underwater realm was more accessible than space, and so I started to explore the deep places out there and to look below the surface, wherever and whenever I could.

"Why do you dive?" people ask me, and "Did you see anything?" To them, what I do can only make sense if there is a specific goal in it, something worthwhile. To me, to be there is enough. And to me, there is something to discover, always.

What did I see? I saw the light of the deep. Three hundred feet below in the Mediterranean sea, I saw the intense blue of the water fade to almost black in the nothingness beneath me. In the deep twilight zone next to a Caribbean coral reef, I opened my eyes and found myself surrounded by a school of fish that had followed me down from the surface. On my way up from a record dive in Greece, I saw a visible layer of warmer water extend into the distance, like a cloudy sky fading to an endless horizon, a sight that made me pause for a moment, record or no, and simply wonder. I watched a tiny crab climb on to my hand out in the blue,

far from land, and I saw a huge orca come close to take a look at me in the dark, freezing waters of the Norwegian polar night. Under the thick ice of a frozen fjord in East Greenland, I saw a stark, monochrome universe of light and shadow, of water and ice. I saw mesmerizing shapes formed hundreds of years ago, ice so old and clear that it was shimmering turquoise when everything around was in shades of black and white.

"How deep did you go?" people ask, and "How long did you stay?" Sometimes, I dive to find out how far I can go, and I compete with others. But most of the time, I dive only to look. I dive to explore, and to expose myself to the unknown spaces of this world. I dive to see beyond obvious beauty. I seek out the challenging places, to find their hidden magic. We cannot measure this world in feet and minutes alone. To discover it means to go through it with open eyes and to be willing to be surprised and fascinated by it, over and over, wherever you are. Although it may be satisfying and can be an accomplishment in itself, in the end it's not important how fast we run, how high we climb, or how far we travel. What's important is that we choose to look, and truly see.

How deep did I go? How long did I stay? I don't know. Does it matter? I saw the world below the surface, and it filled me with wonder.

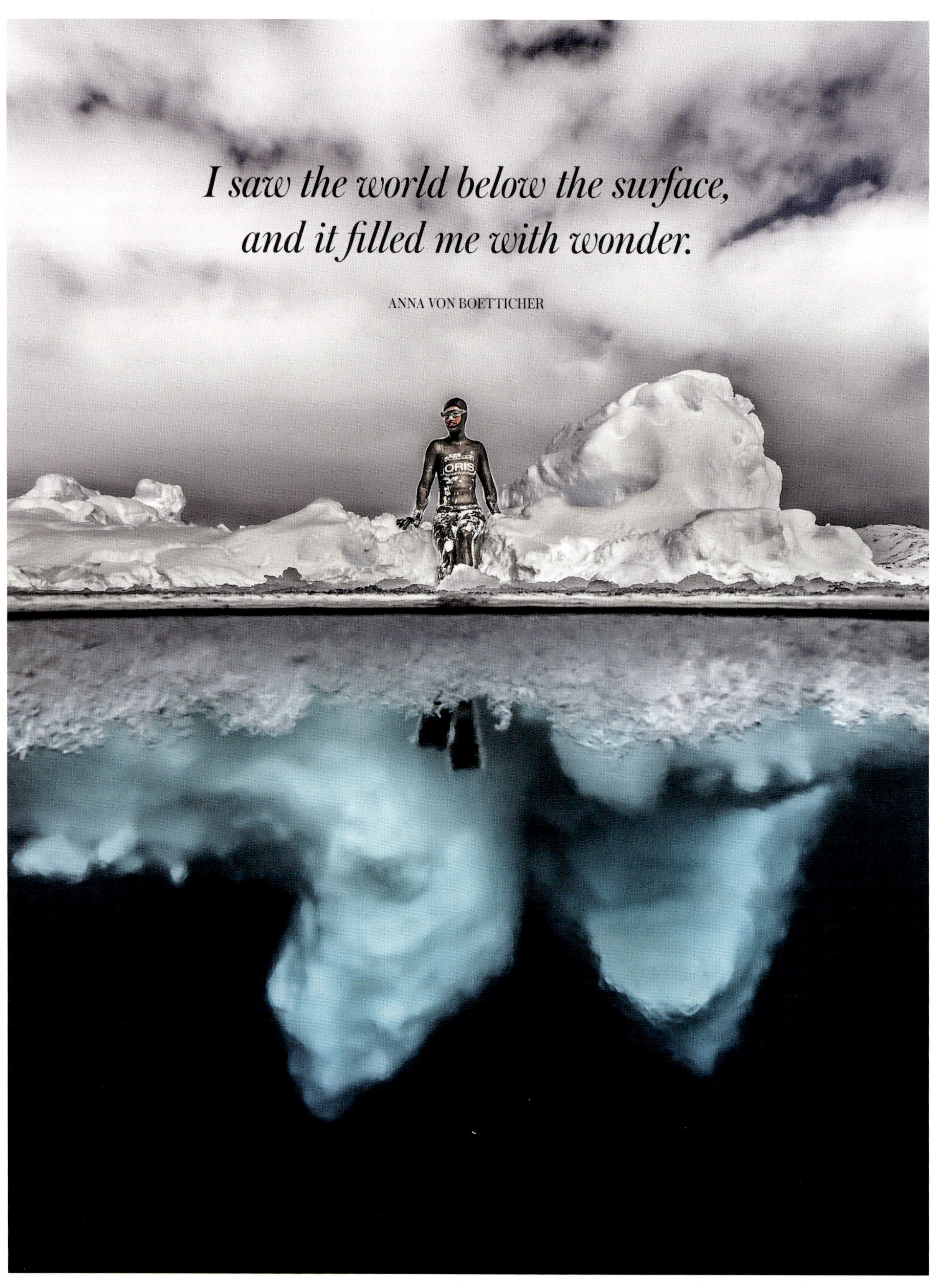

I saw the world below the surface,
and it filled me with wonder.

ANNA VON BOETTICHER

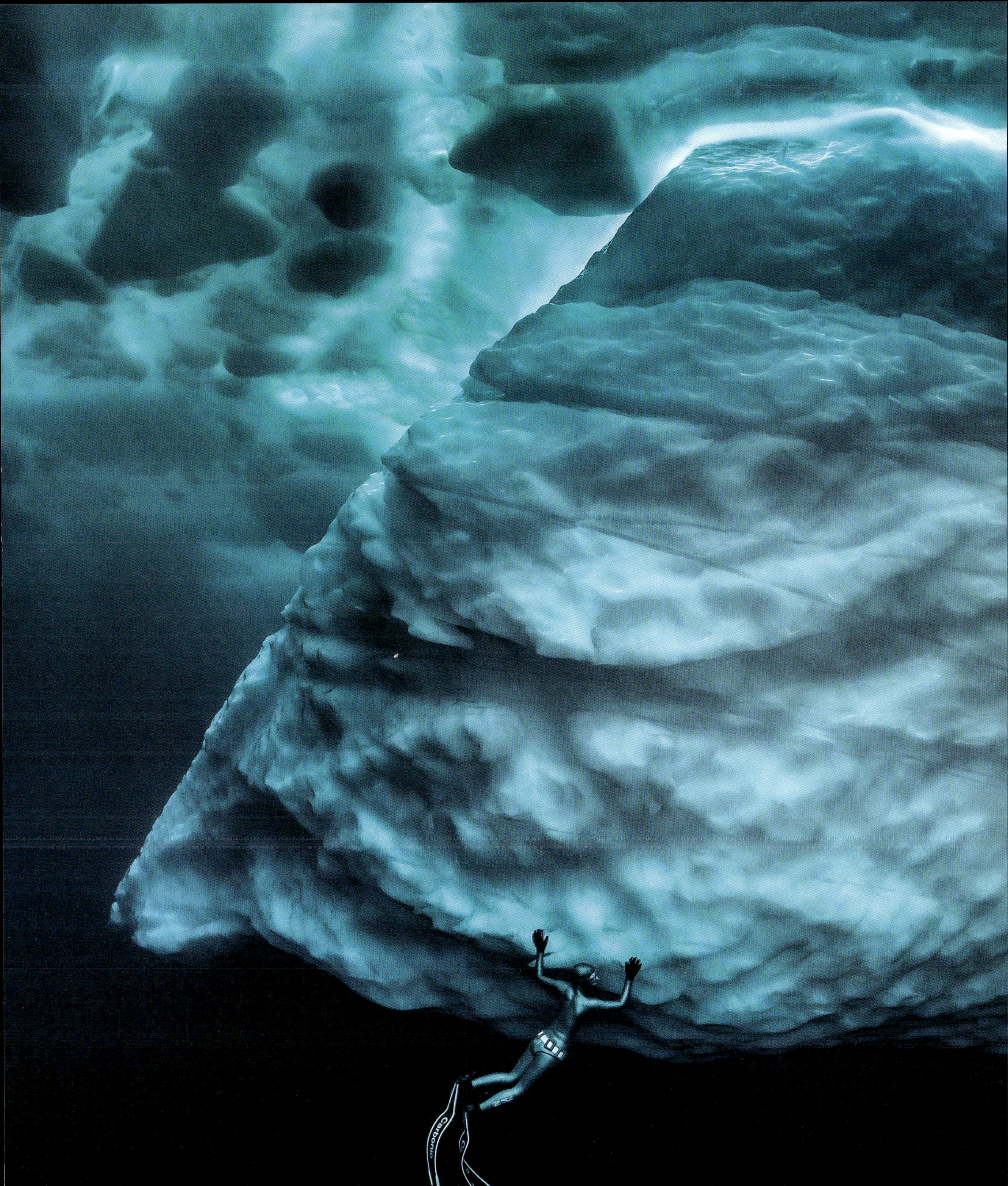

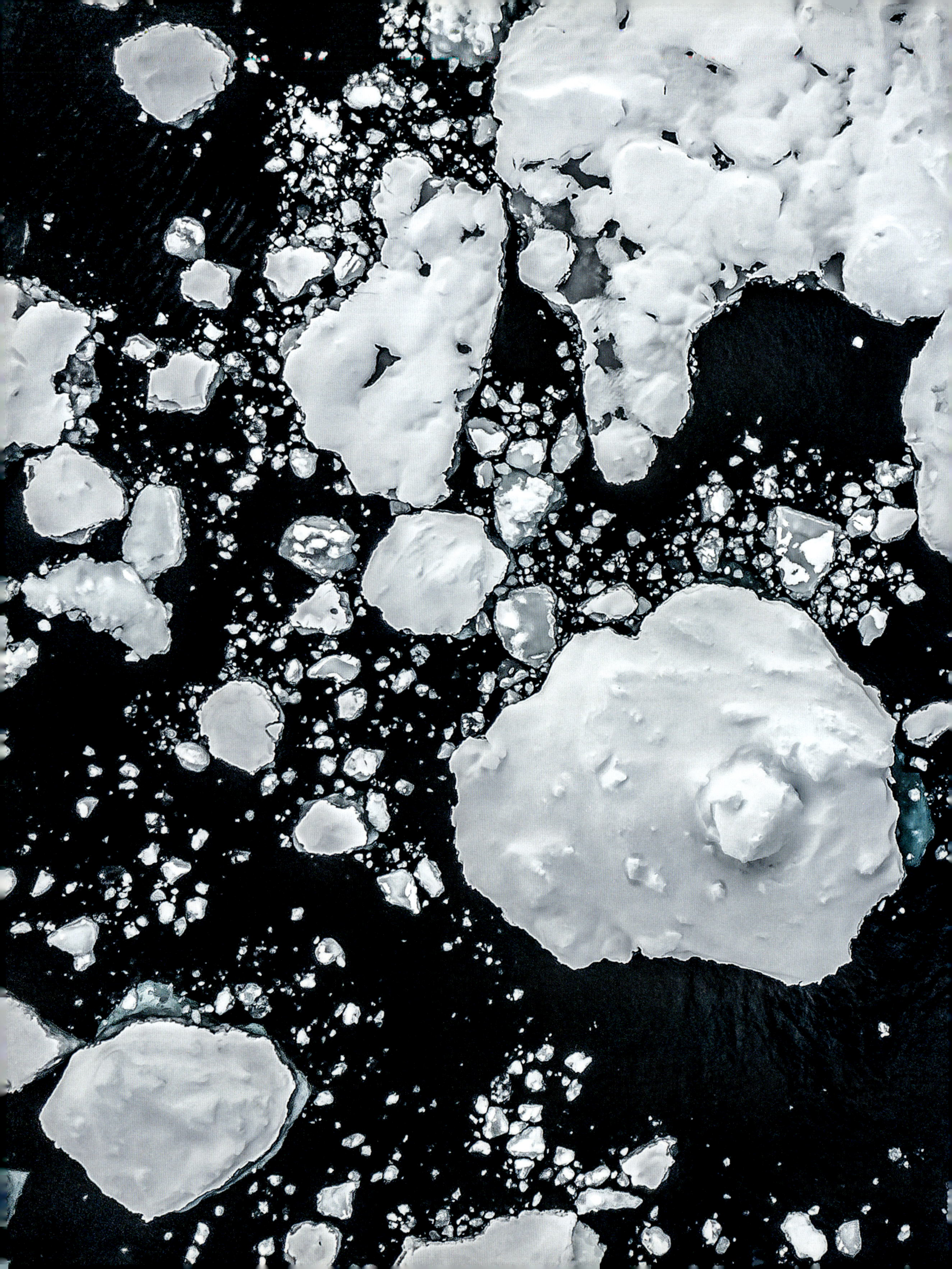

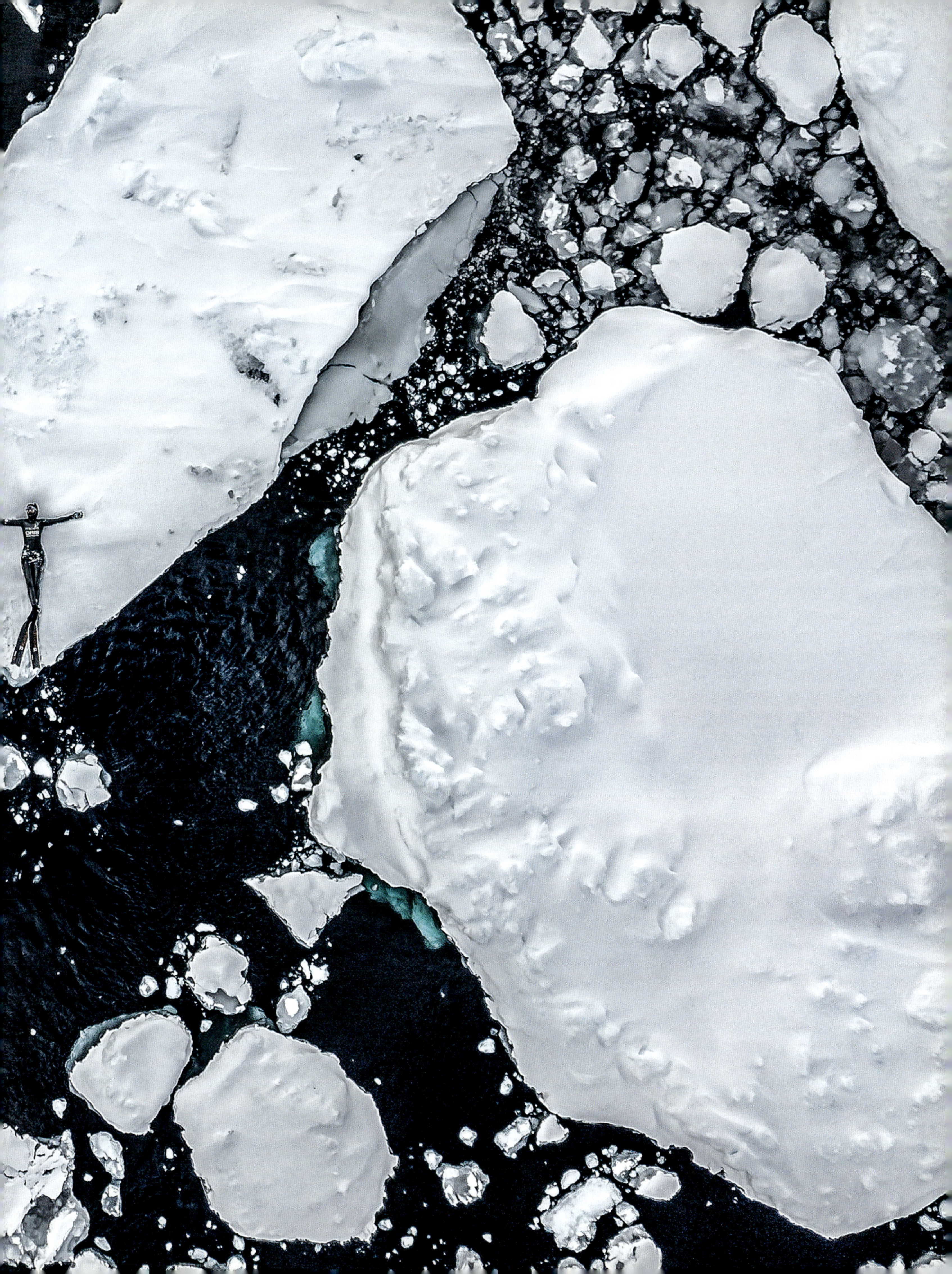

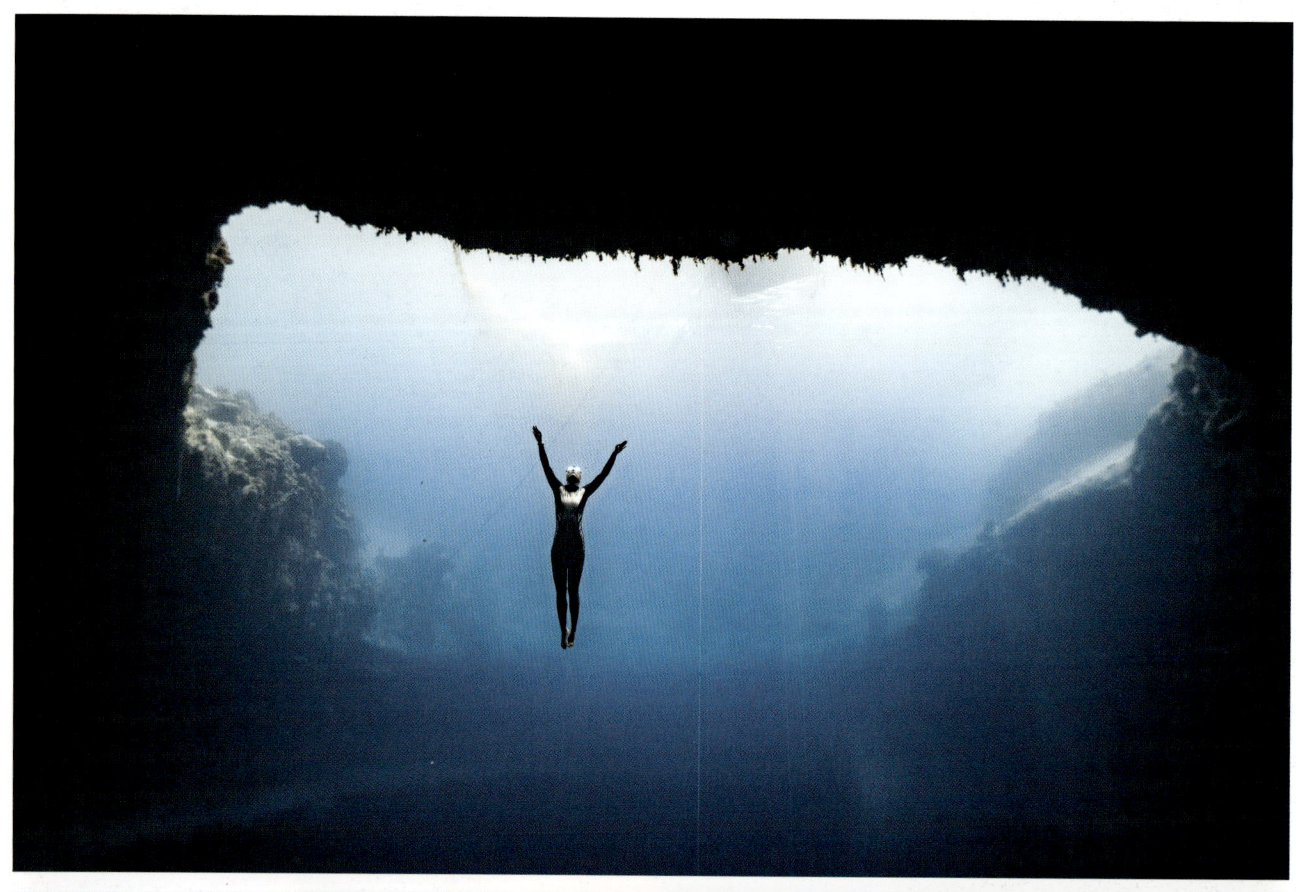

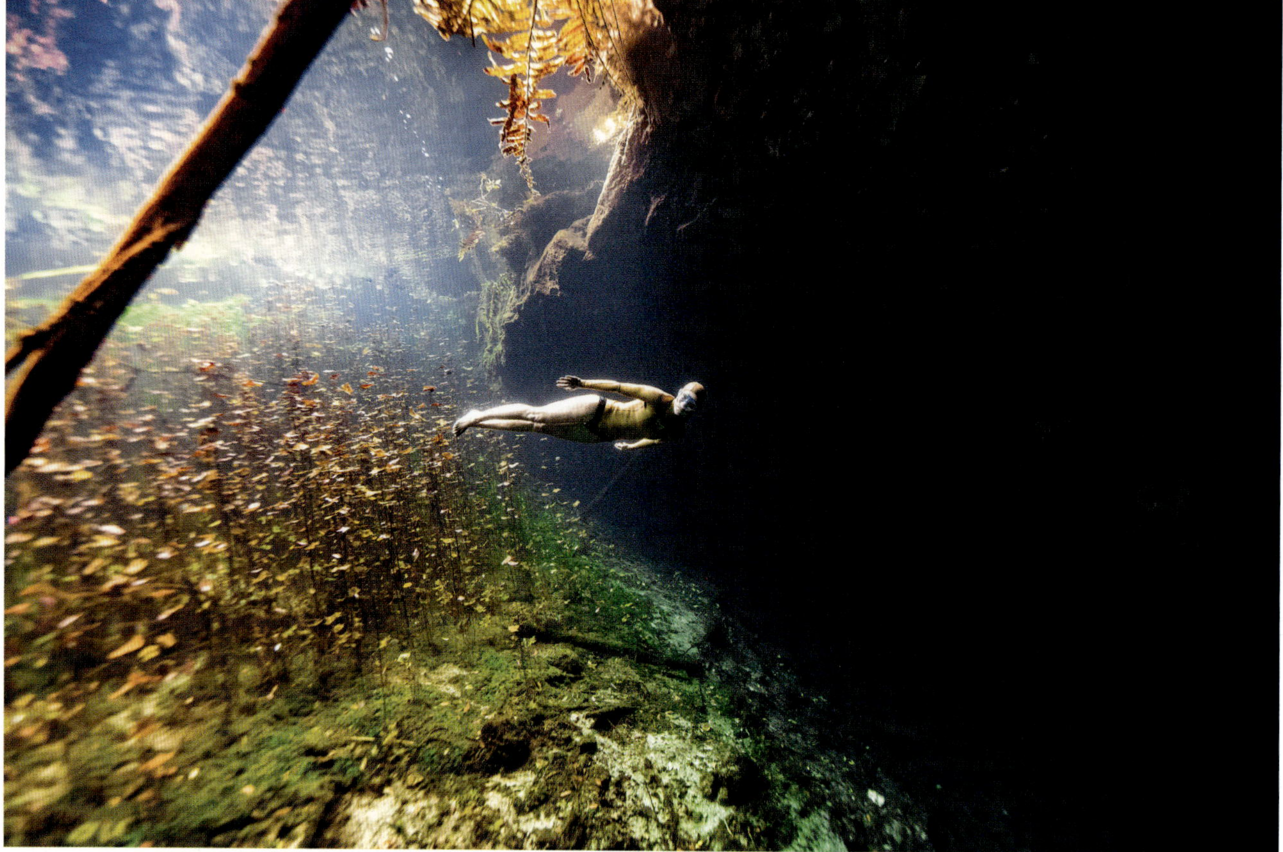

 △△ Dean's Blue Hole, Long Island, Bahamas   △ Cenote Carwash   ▷ Cenote Maravilla | Mexico

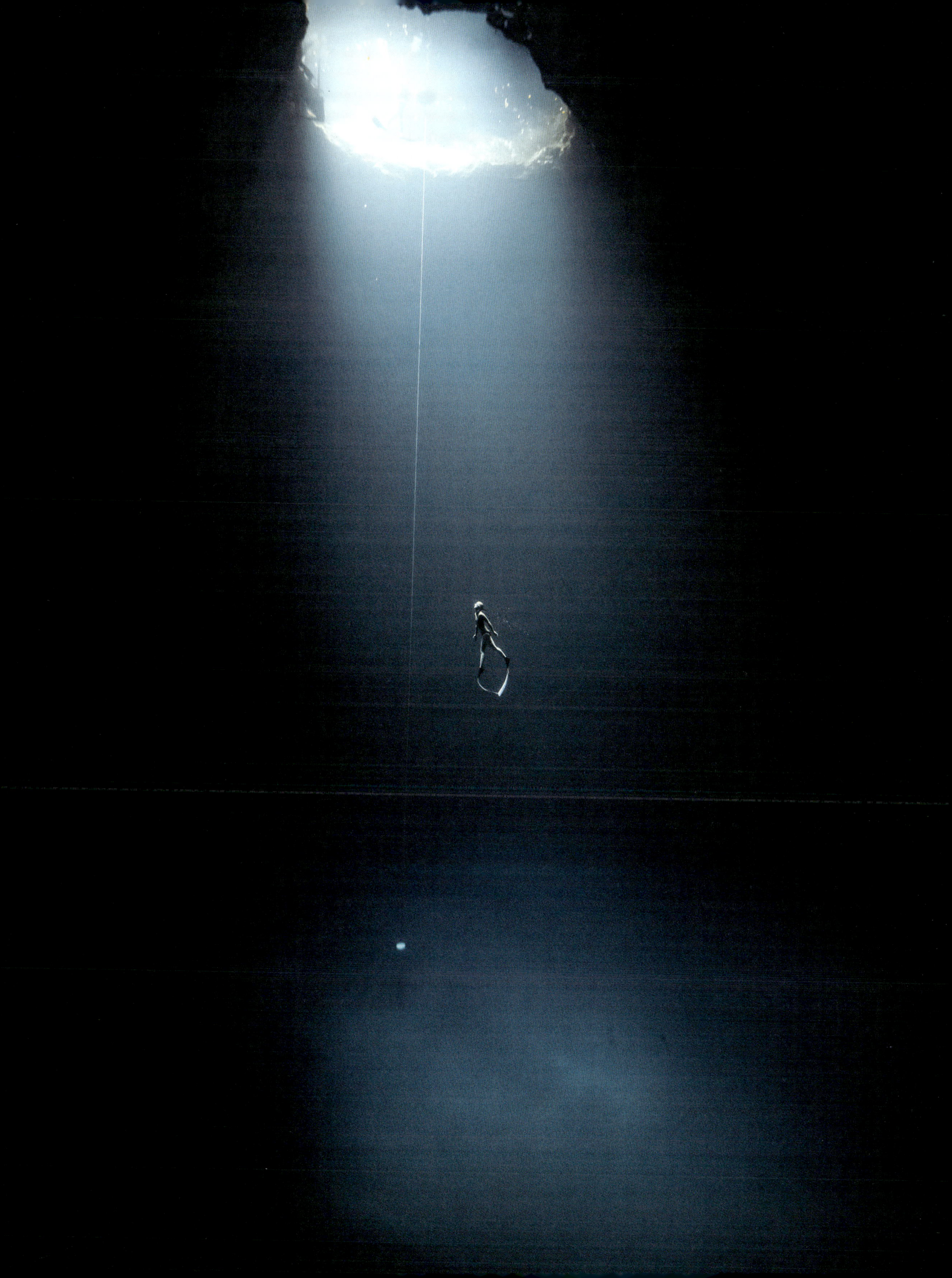

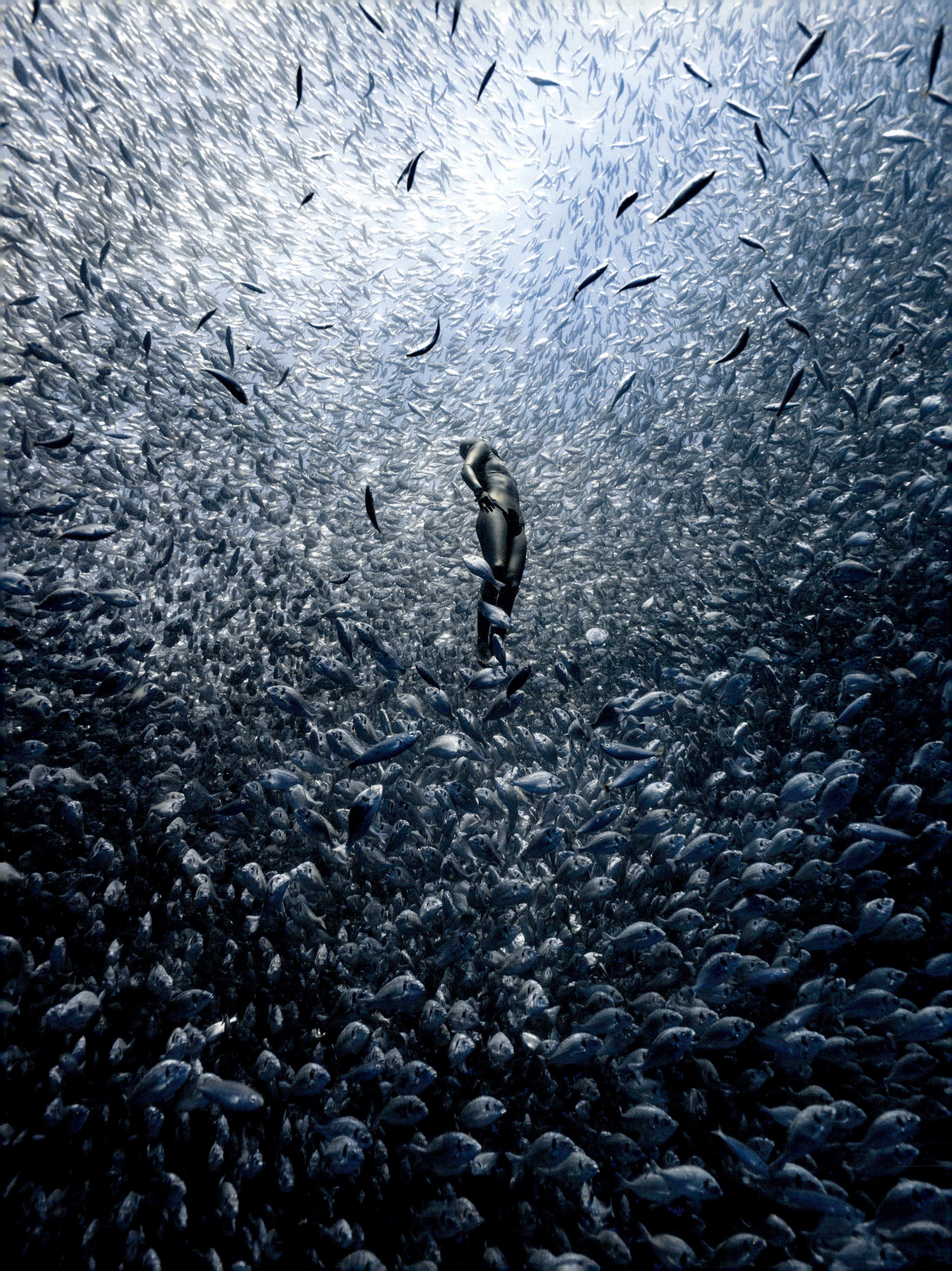

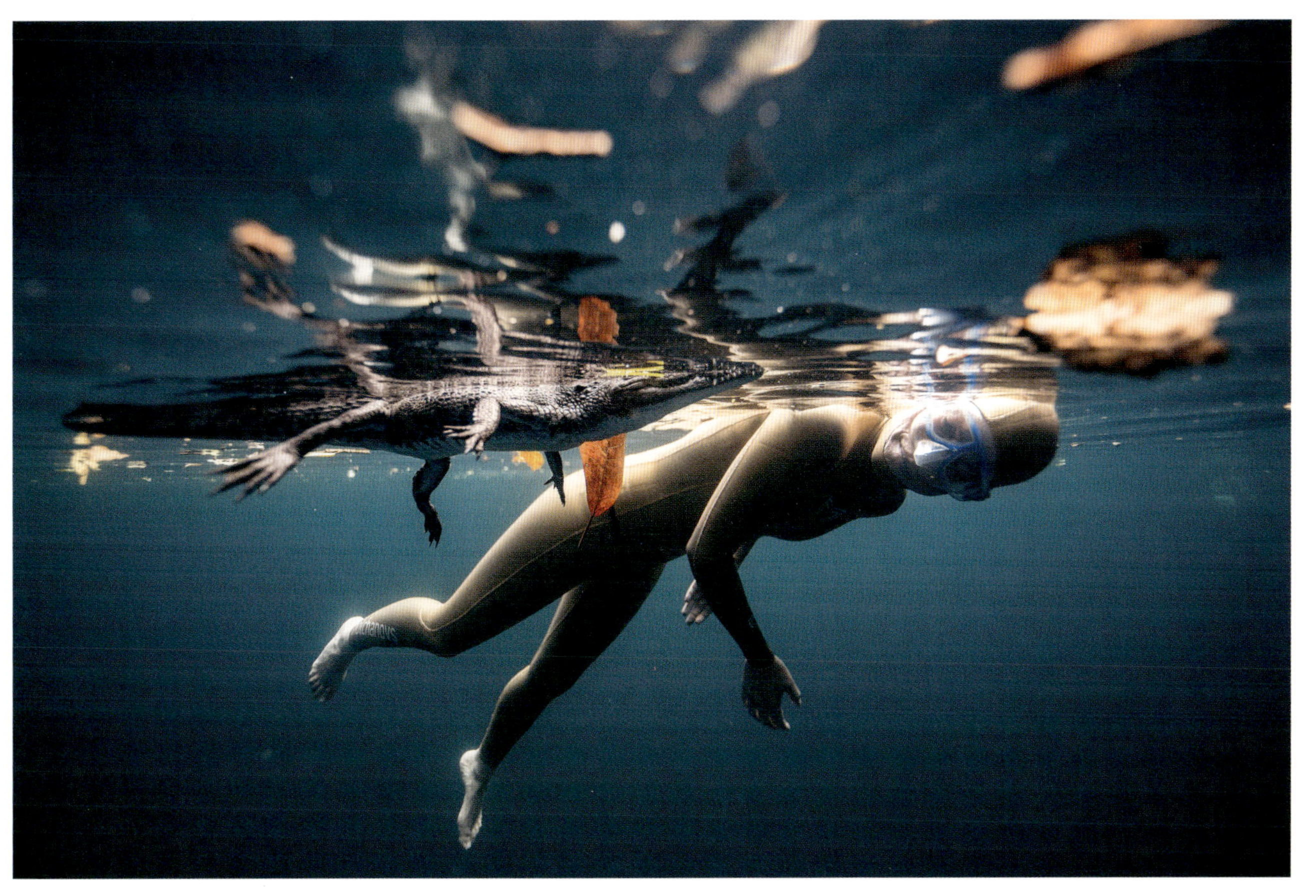

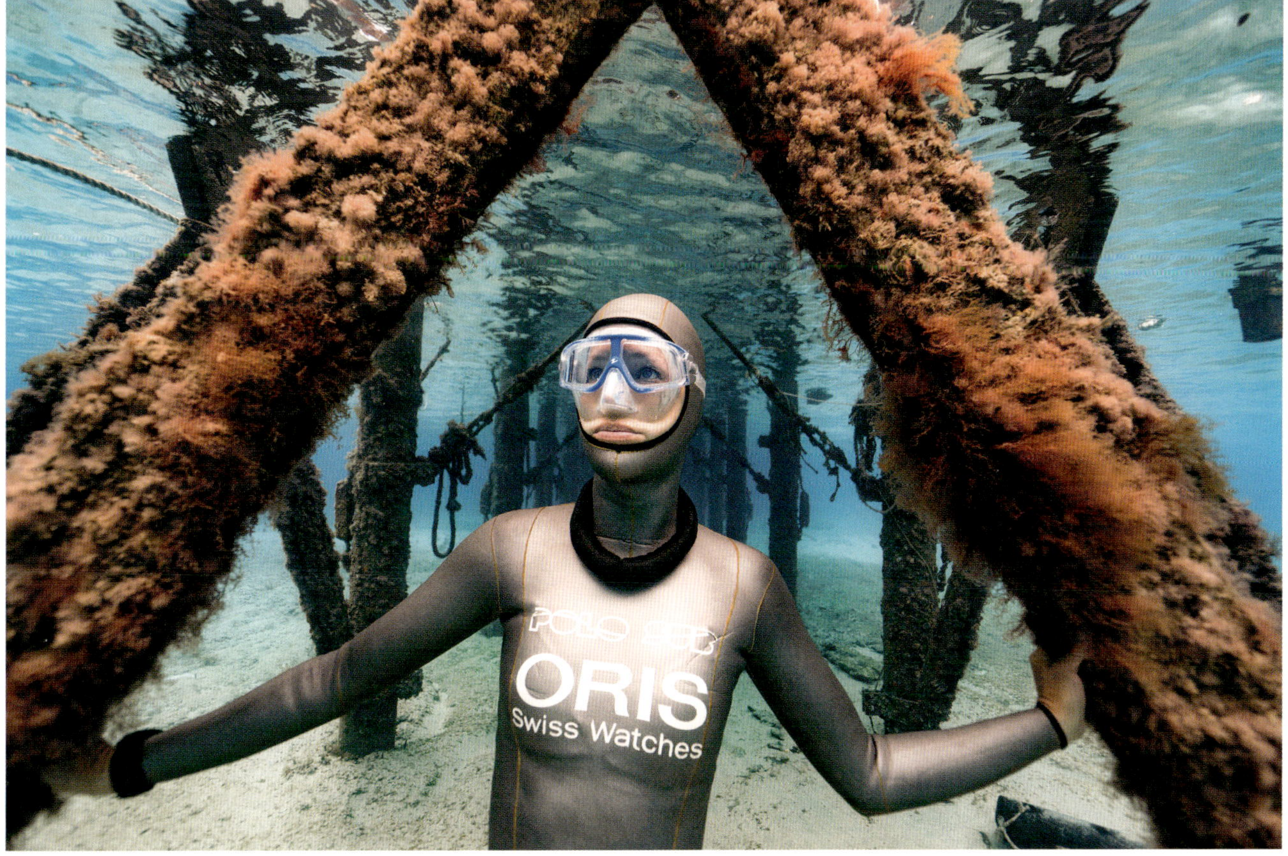

Noa Diorgina

Freerunner and parkour athlete

@noa_diorgina

My name is Noa Diorgina Man and I am a parkour girl. I am sixteen years old and started to train in parkour when I was seven, so I've been doing it more than half of my life now. I literally live parkour. I was never the type of girl who played with dolls: I was always running and climbing. My surf coach when I was seven years old told my parents that it would be wise to put me into parkour lessons because I was constantly jumping and flipping around during the surf sessions. My parents took me to the Jump Freerun Gym in The Hague and I was hooked the minute I stepped inside. I've practically never left—I'm still training there! It didn't bother me at all that I was the only girl training; the boys took me in like I was one of them. When I was thirteen, I was the youngest competitor in one of the biggest parkour World Cups. I made a qualifier video to show my skills to the judges and they decided to let me into the adult female competition in Sweden, where I took second place. That moment was the start of my life as a pro athlete.

Why I love this sport so much? The fact that you constantly challenge yourself to push your limits gives me such an adrenaline rush, especially when I do something I never thought I could. Like when I jumped over a canal 14.5 feet wide—I thought I would definitely fall into the water but I made it without getting my clothes wet. That feeling was indescribably good. Or the feeling I had when I won second place at my first World Cup on a set-up with drops more than 10 feet high. The evening before the competition started, when we got to check out the giant Air Wipp challenge set-up, I almost quit—I'm glad I had the courage to push through! Parkour might be introduced at the Olympics in Paris 2024. If it gets approved as an Olympic sport it will definitely be my next challenge to take part. I'm already training for it!

Don't underestimate what you're capable of, and never let anyone tell you you can't do something. If you have a challenge in front of you, no matter what the situation, at least try it. It's better to regret doing it than regret not doing it. You might surprise yourself, at least. That's the great thing parkour does for me—surprises me how much I'm capable of.

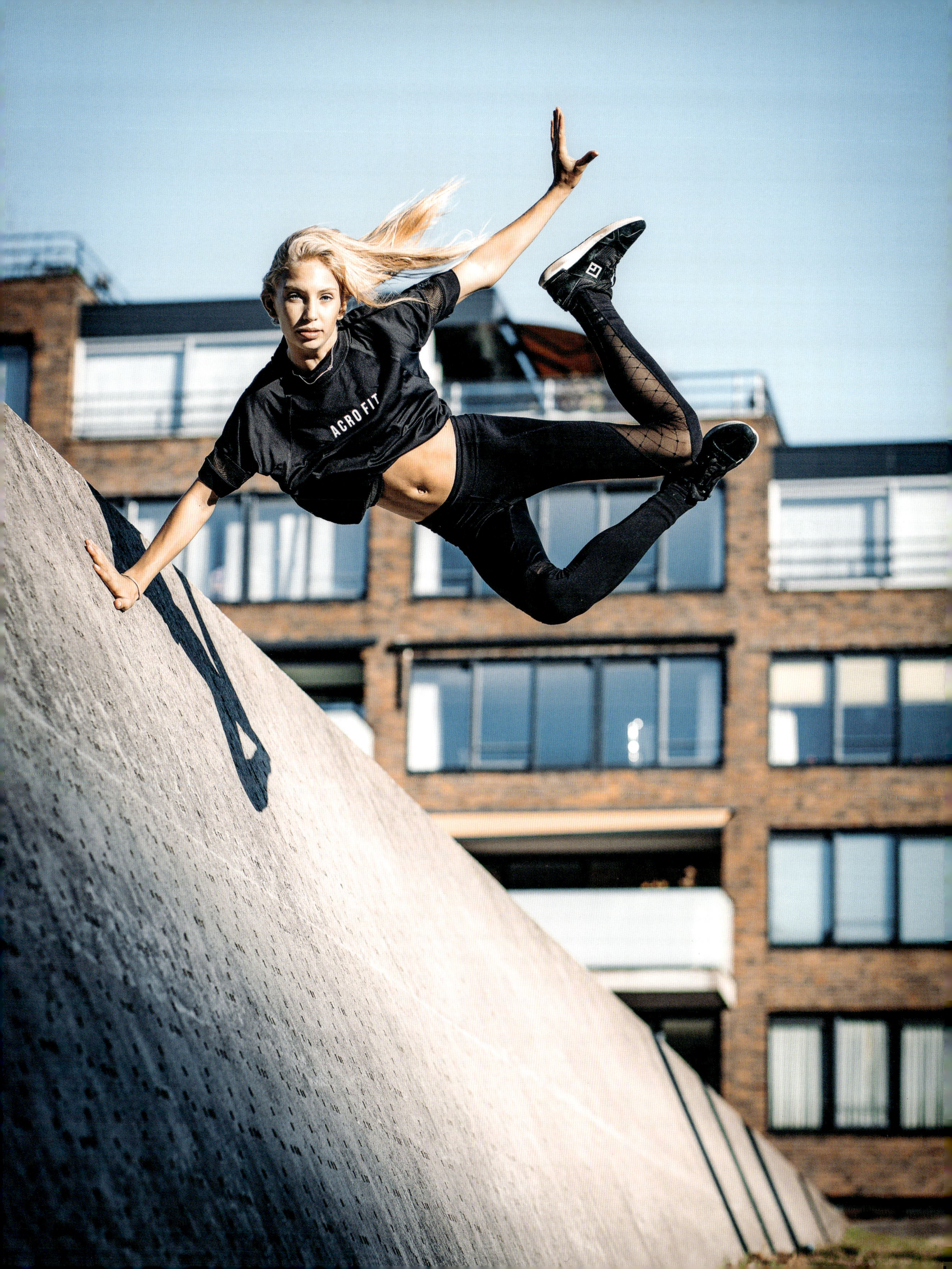
ACRO FIT

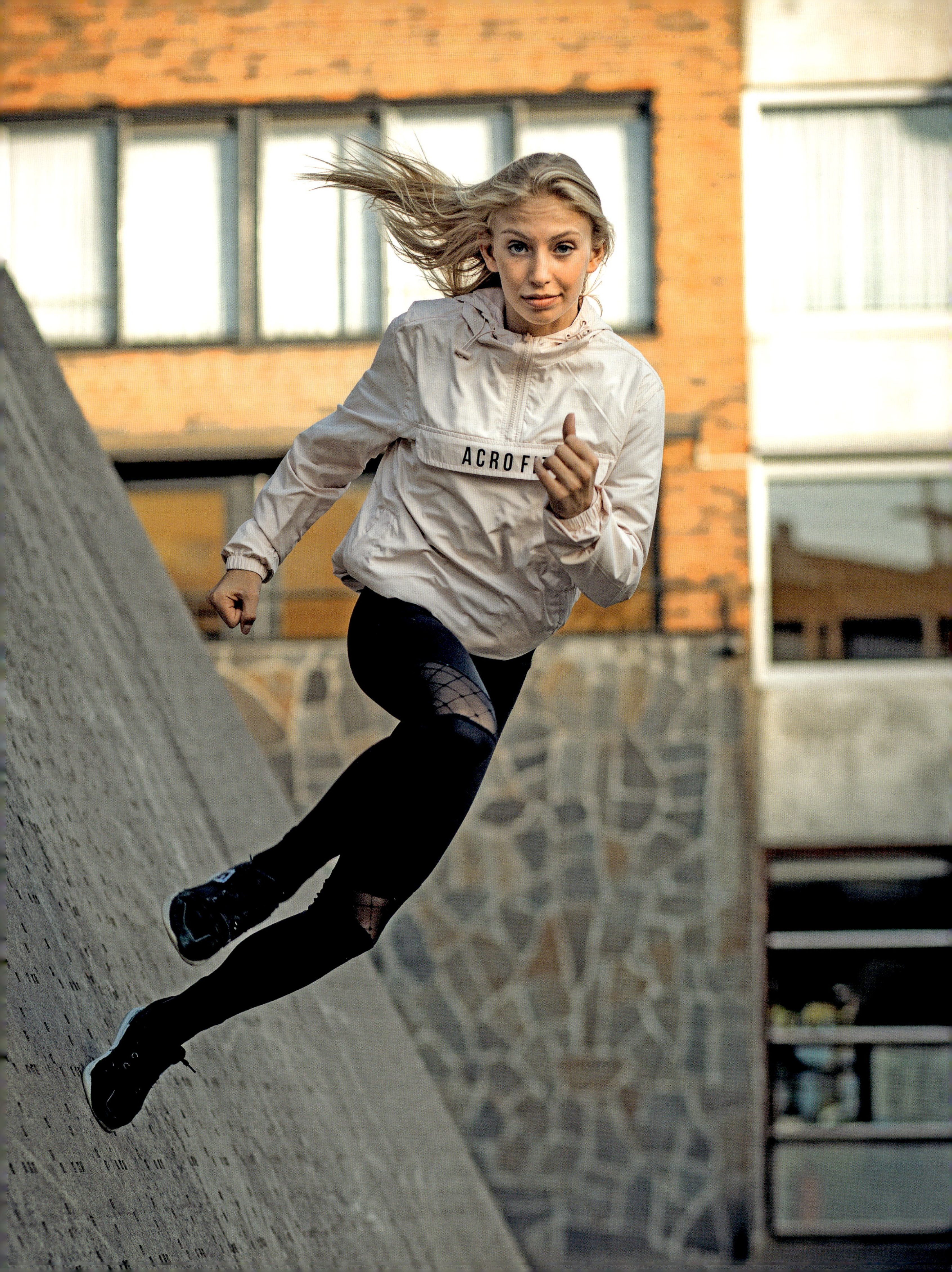
ACRO FIT

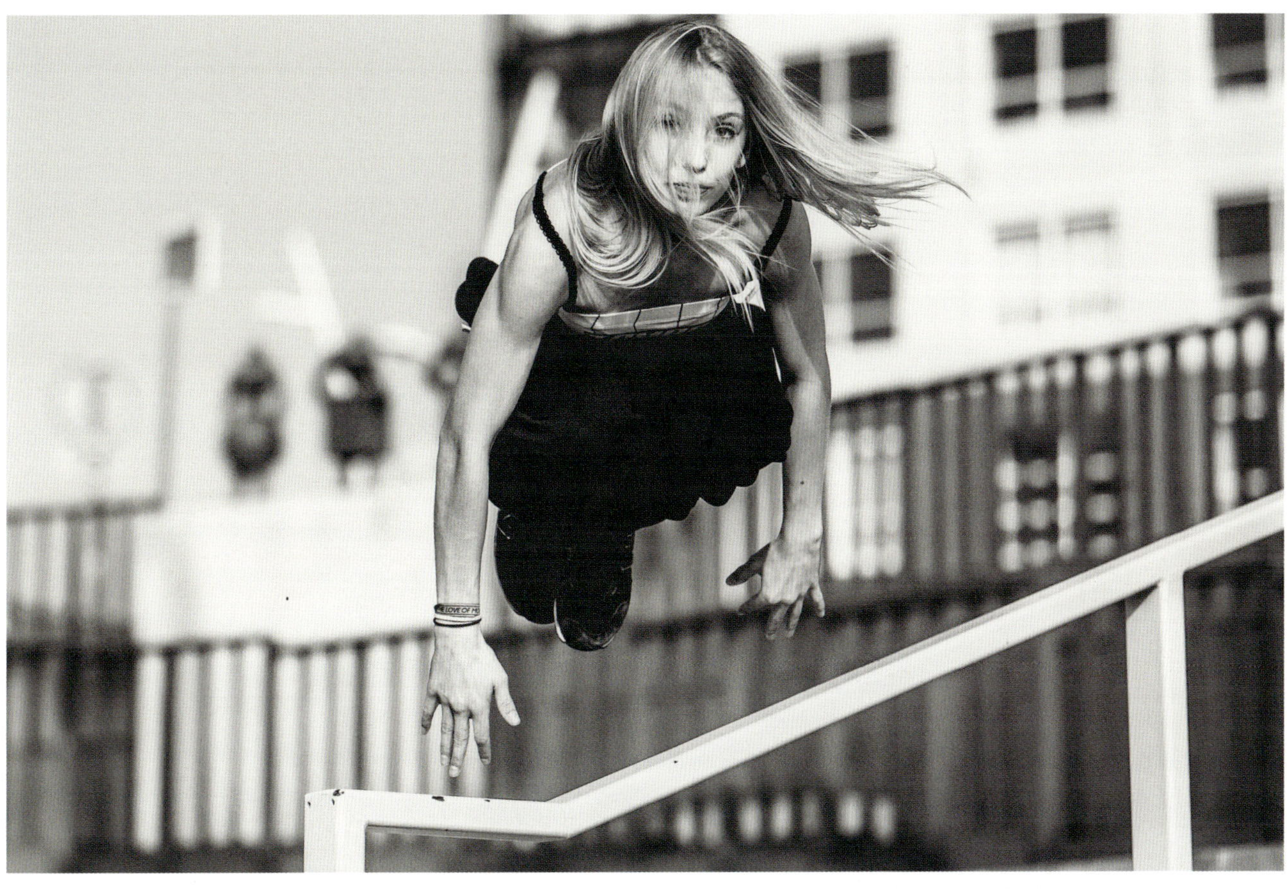

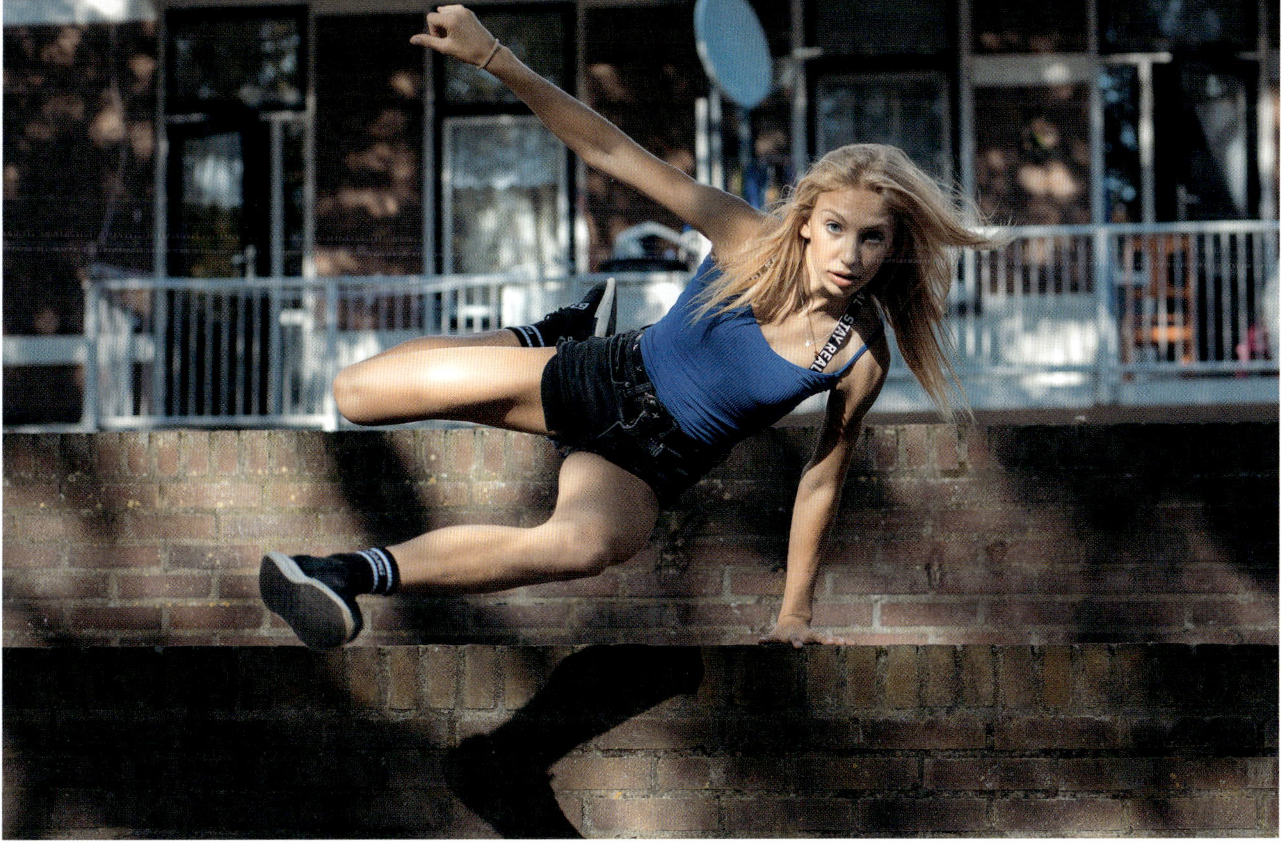

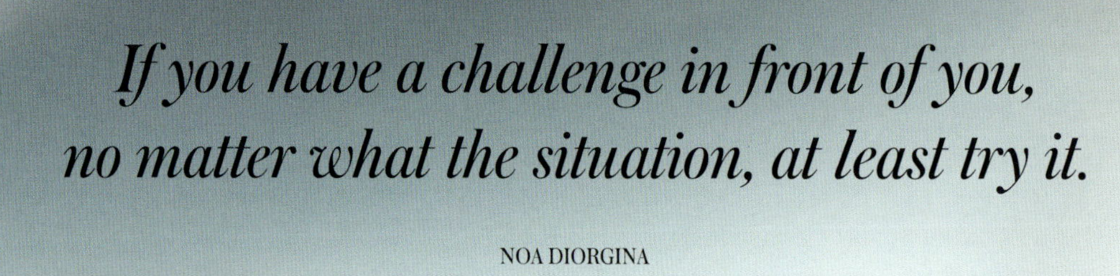

If you have a challenge in front of you,
no matter what the situation, at least try it.

NOA DIORGINA

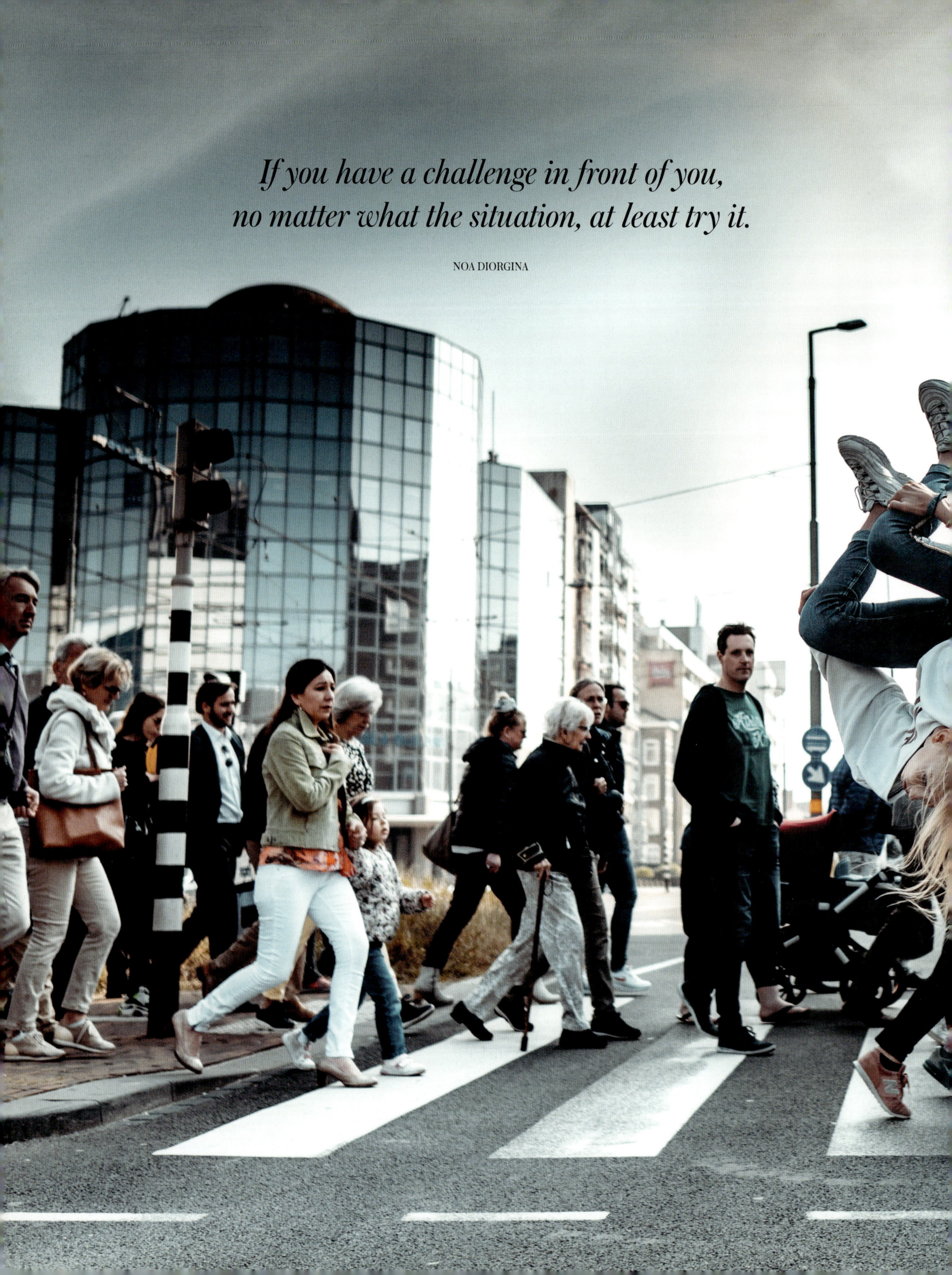

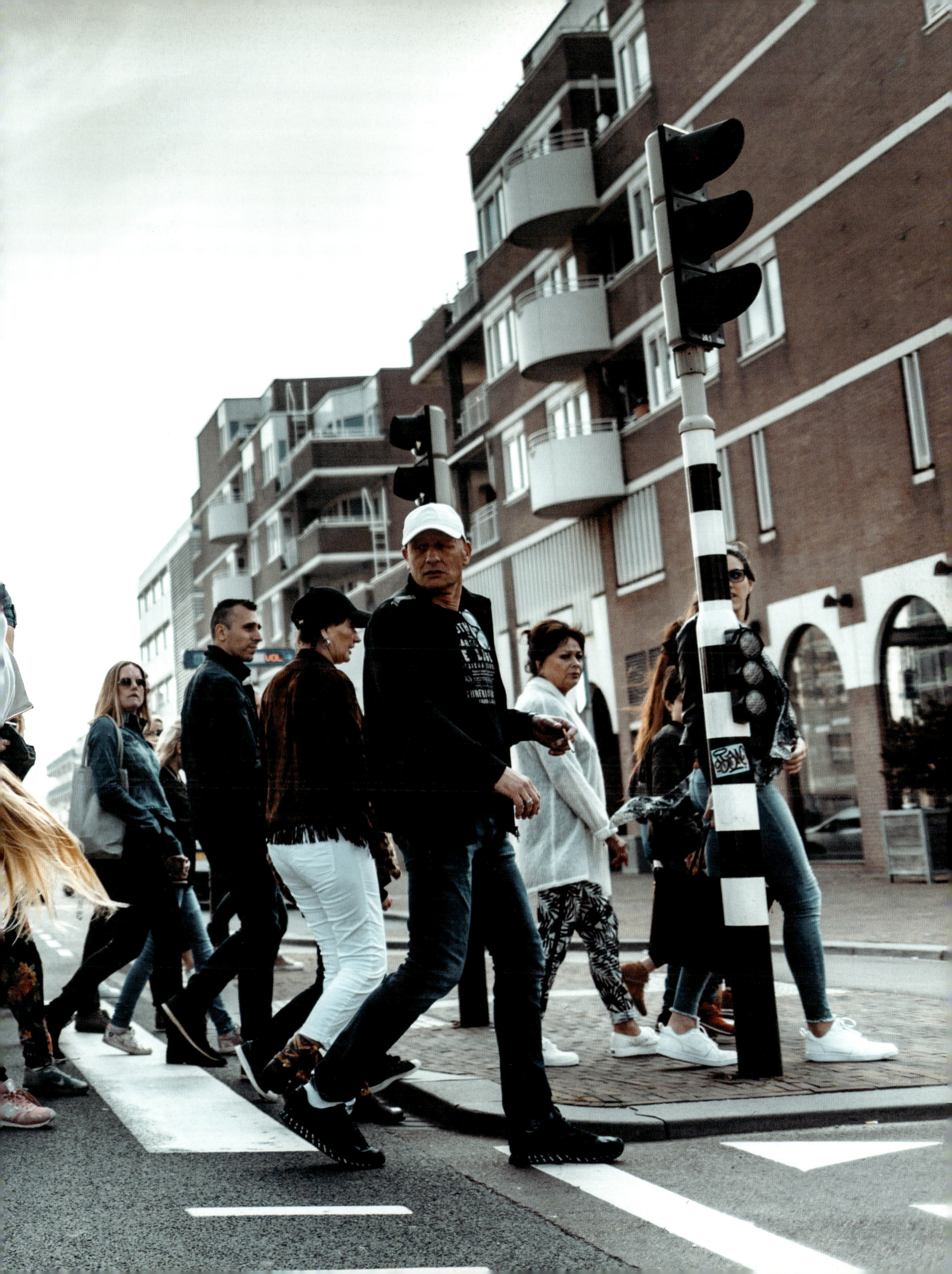

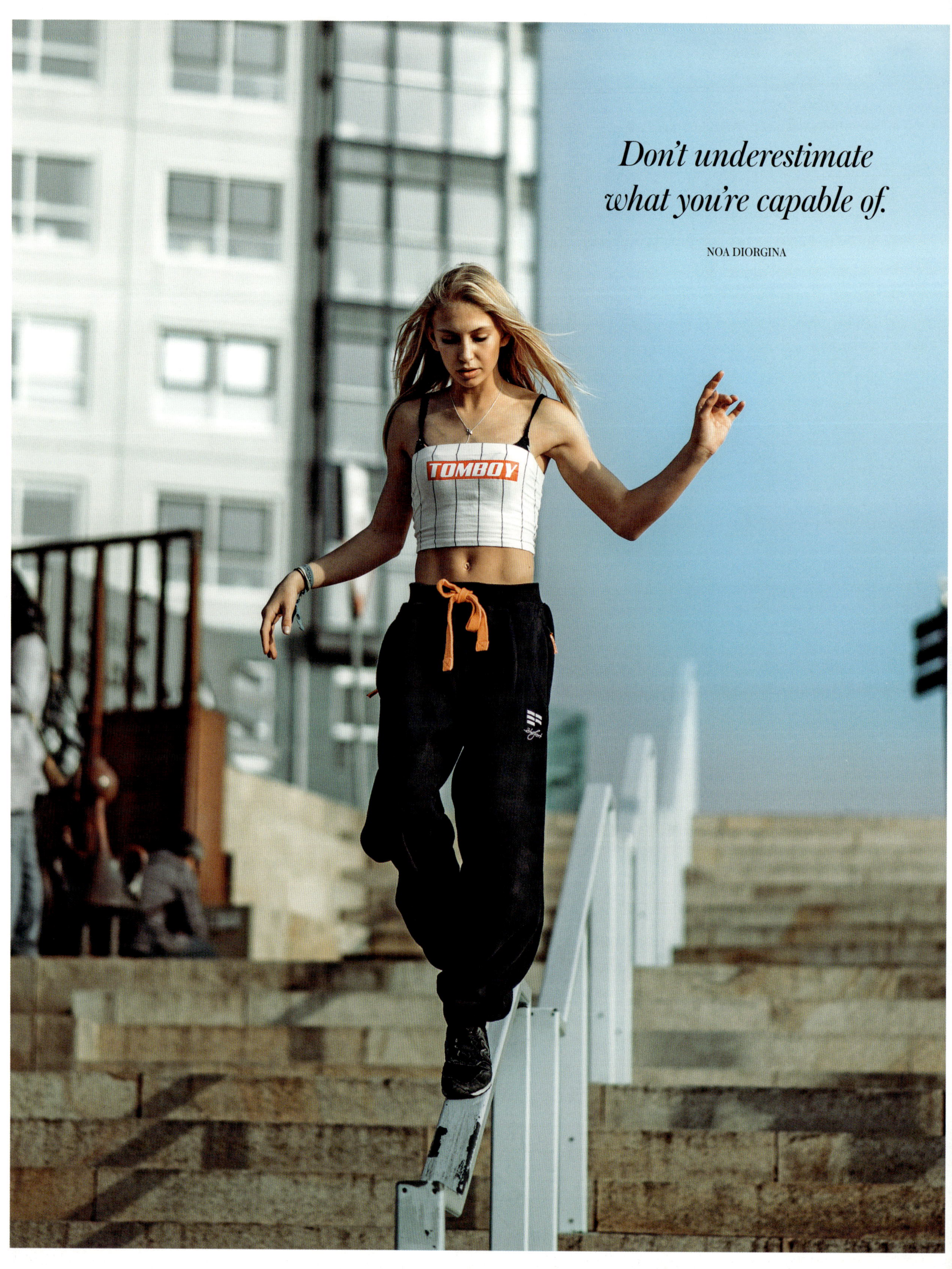

Don't underestimate
what you're capable of.
NOA DIORGINA
TOMBOY

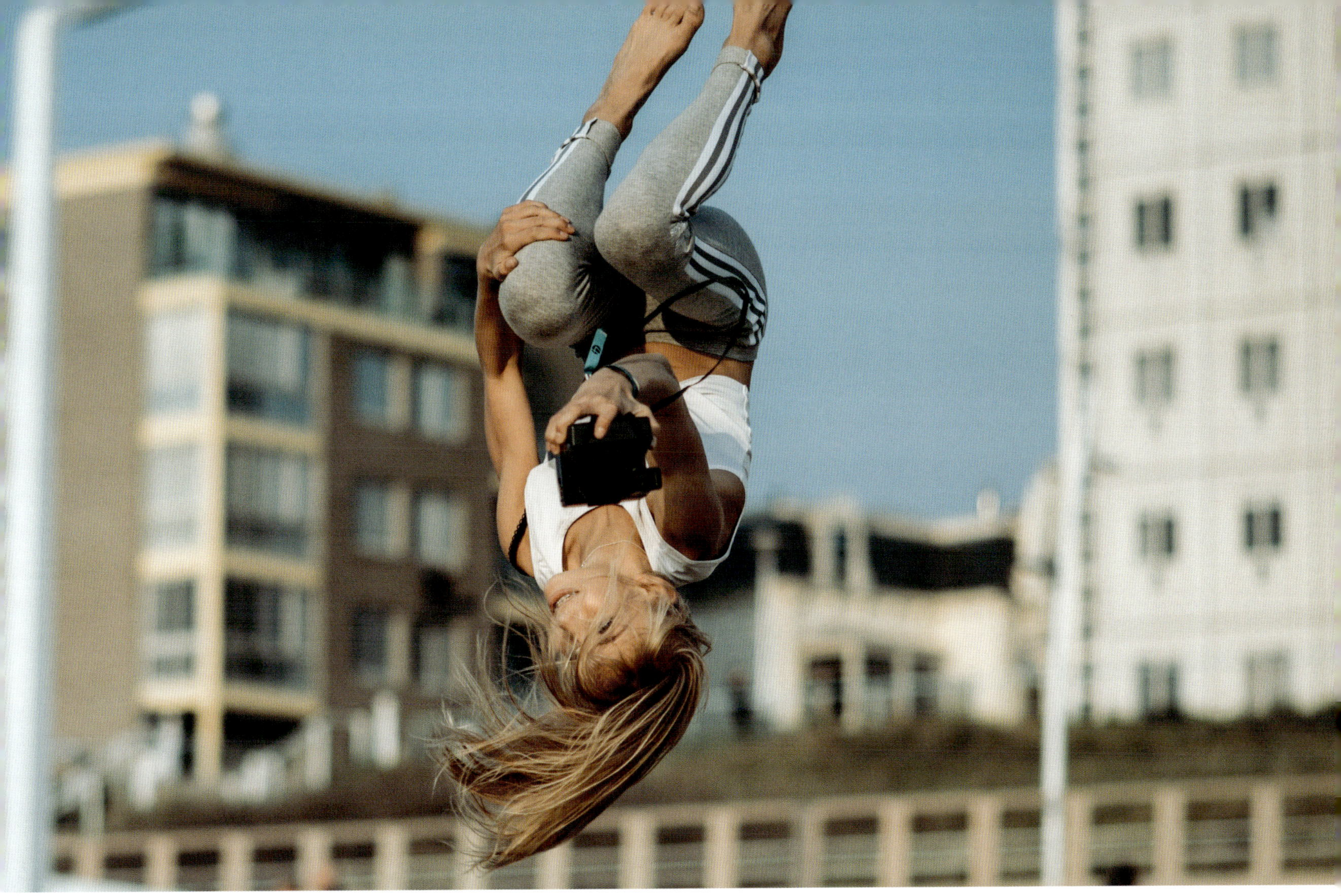

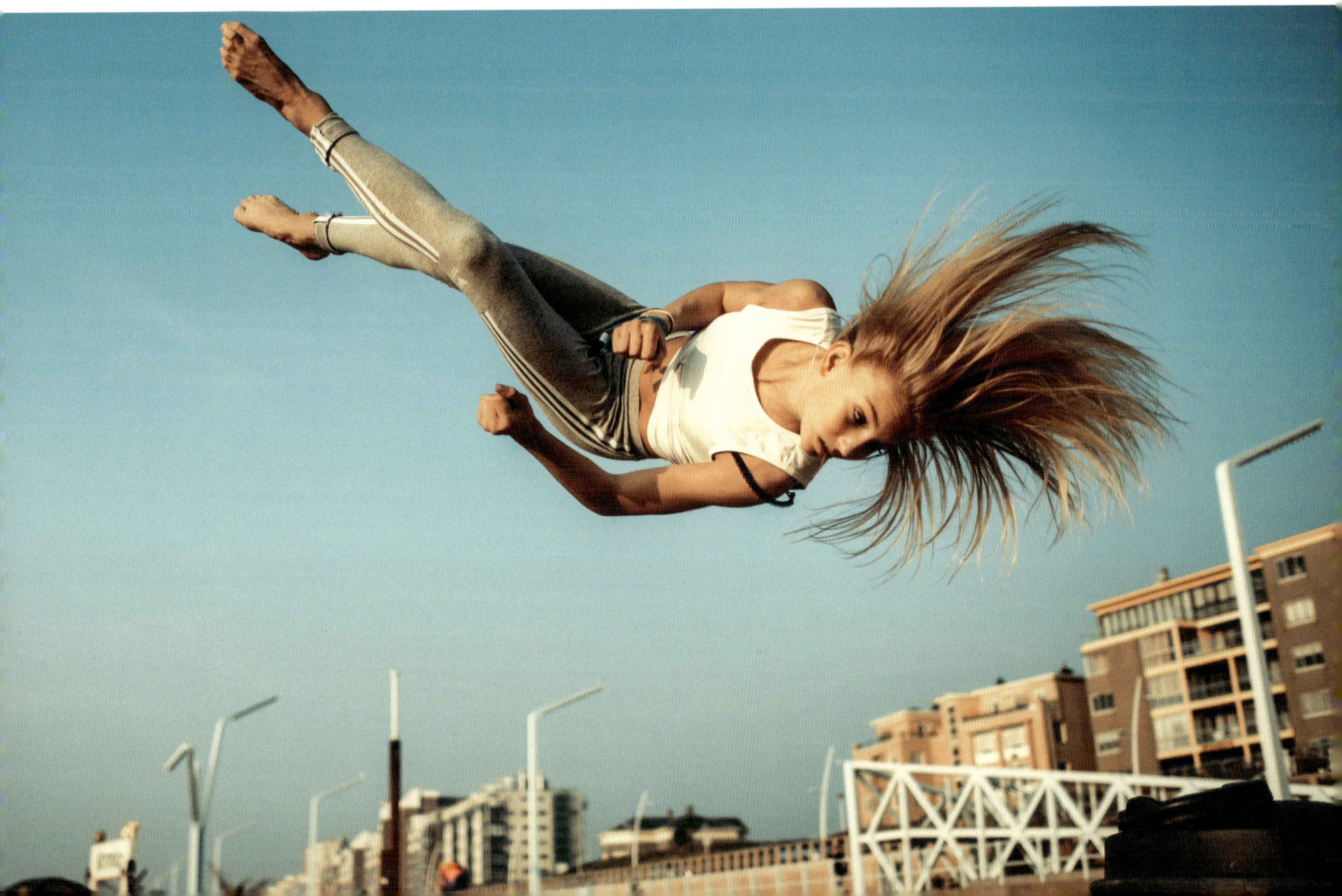

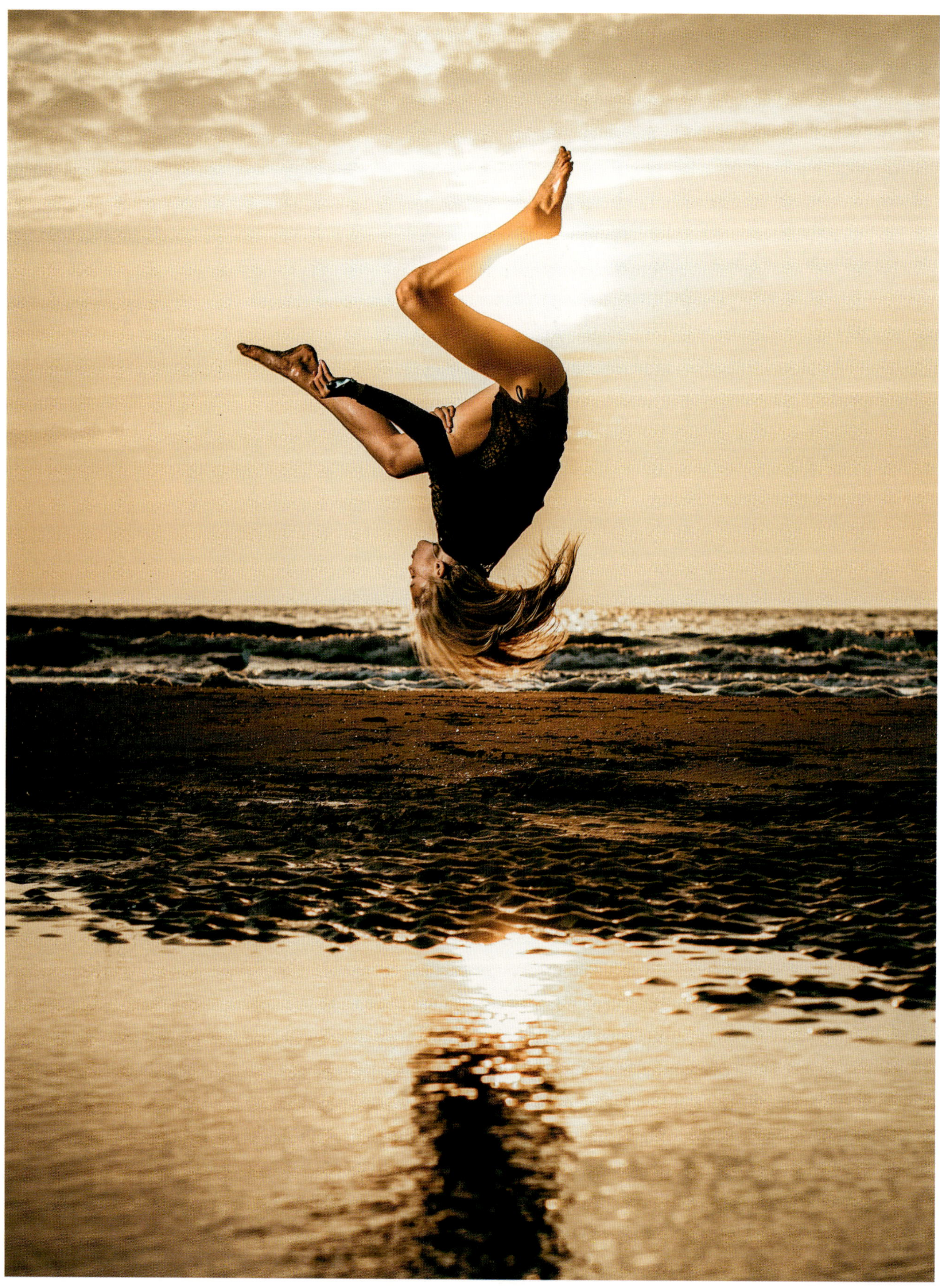

 Scheveningen, The Hague, Netherlands

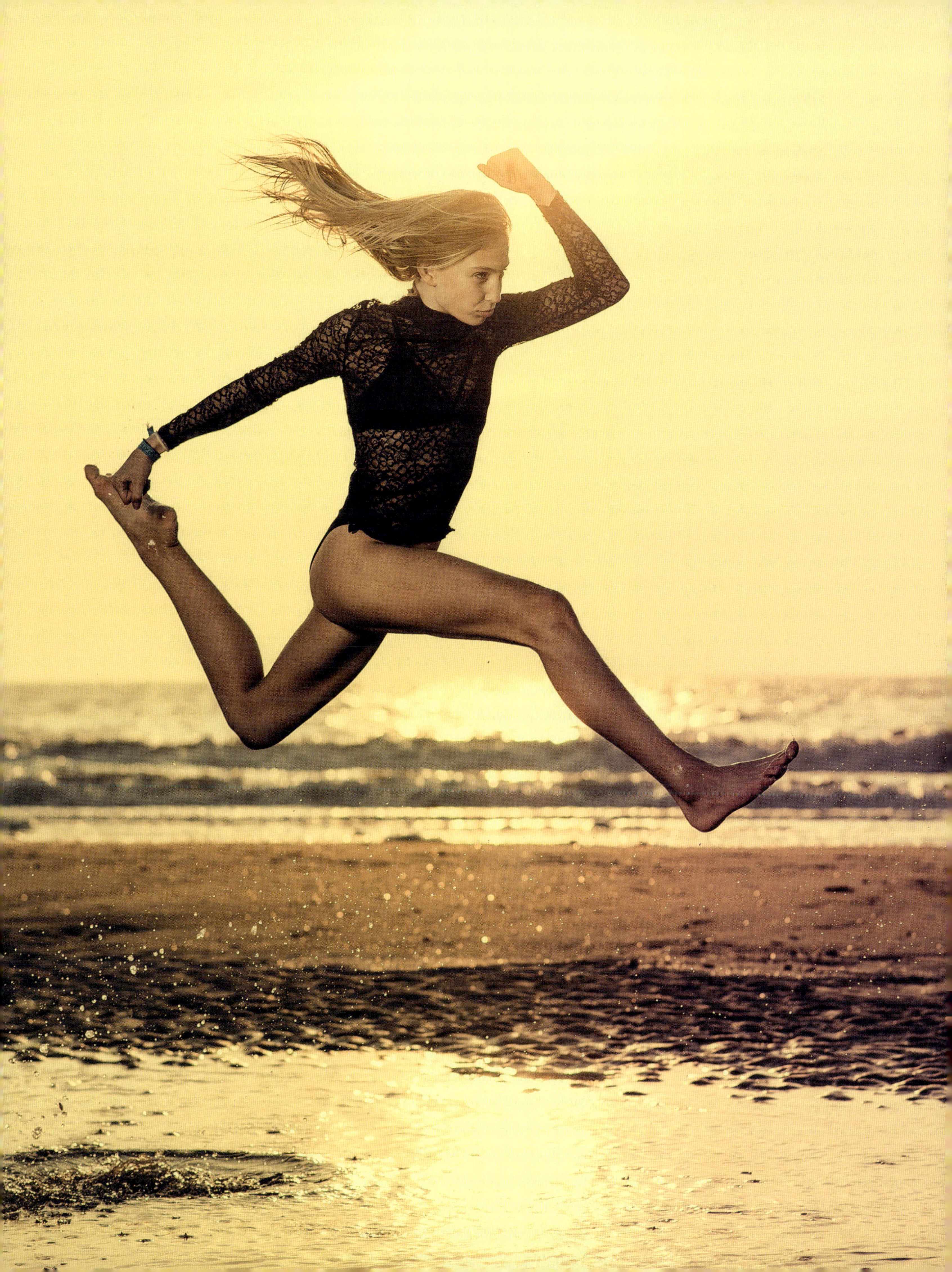

Jennie Milton
Snowkiter

@adrenajen

My parents had a sports store, so I started skiing, sailing, and skating at a very young age, together with my brother Michael. Our winter holidays were spent skiing and our summer holidays sailing up the coast of Australia. Before the age of fifteen I had already competed in figure skating, freestyle skiing, and windsurfing. One of my first jobs was as a ski instructor at the Thredbo resort at the age of fourteen.

Michael got cancer when he was nine. His leg was amputated but he survived the odds to live on and become one of the world's most awarded athletes with a disability. He holds multiple World and Olympic Records in skiing, speed skiing, cycling, running on crutches, and more.

That was a traumatic time for our family, and we all still live with the scars. But we also have the incredible motivation that comes from Michael overcoming the obstacles and becoming a sporting hero! He's the biggest inspiration in my life.

My school years were spent studying art, advertising, and graphic design. After a few years in advertising, I went back to the family business to start Adrenalin Sports. This was a retail business selling snowboards, rollerblades, skateboards, and more. During this time I competed in, taught, and demonstrated rollerblading and skiing, and even represented Australia in downhill mountain biking in Canada.

I was gifted my first traction kite in the early 1990s and in '98 discovered and bought one of the first inflatable kites in Australia. It took me many years to figure it all out back then, but going to Maui for lessons was a huge step in the right direction.

Since 2003 I've been flying kites on snow and discovering how awesome they are for traveling up and down mountains. Due to my teaching background as a ski instructor I made the transition to snowkite instructor very quickly. My skills were used by the heli-ski operators in Alaska to provide an activity when the weather was not suitable to fly helicopters.

In 2012 I was invited to attend the North American Snowkite Tour. The goal was to film, teach, and compete in multiple locations to help grow the sport. I competed with other women every weekend for fun, but at the final event in Alaska I got to race seriously against men from around the world, who were very competitive. Partly due to local knowledge of terrain and winds, I went on to take the first place open title.

My passion for running women's kite clinics started in Alaska in 2010 and I've run one or two every year since. It's amazing to get women together who have a mutual fear of learning a new sport and to teach them to overcome it while flying a kite. It's very empowering for both myself and every woman who has ever been to one.

In 2015 I started a snowkite school in Australia, with full permits and permission from Kosciuszko National Park. Since then I've taken over 200 people snowkiting in Australia. Some come with kiteboarding experience, but many have never flown a kite before. I've worked on providing a safe progression in snowkite instruction, which has given me a 100 percent success rate of getting every student up and riding with the kite in the first lesson. Because the snowkite terrain is in the backcountry behind the resort, it's also my job to teach backcountry skills, such as skinning and snow safety. I also work as a backcountry guide for the Thredbo resort and K7 Adventures.

My love of riding waves with the kite has dominated my style, and I'm lucky to have wave spots with wind at both my Aussie home and my adopted home of the USA.

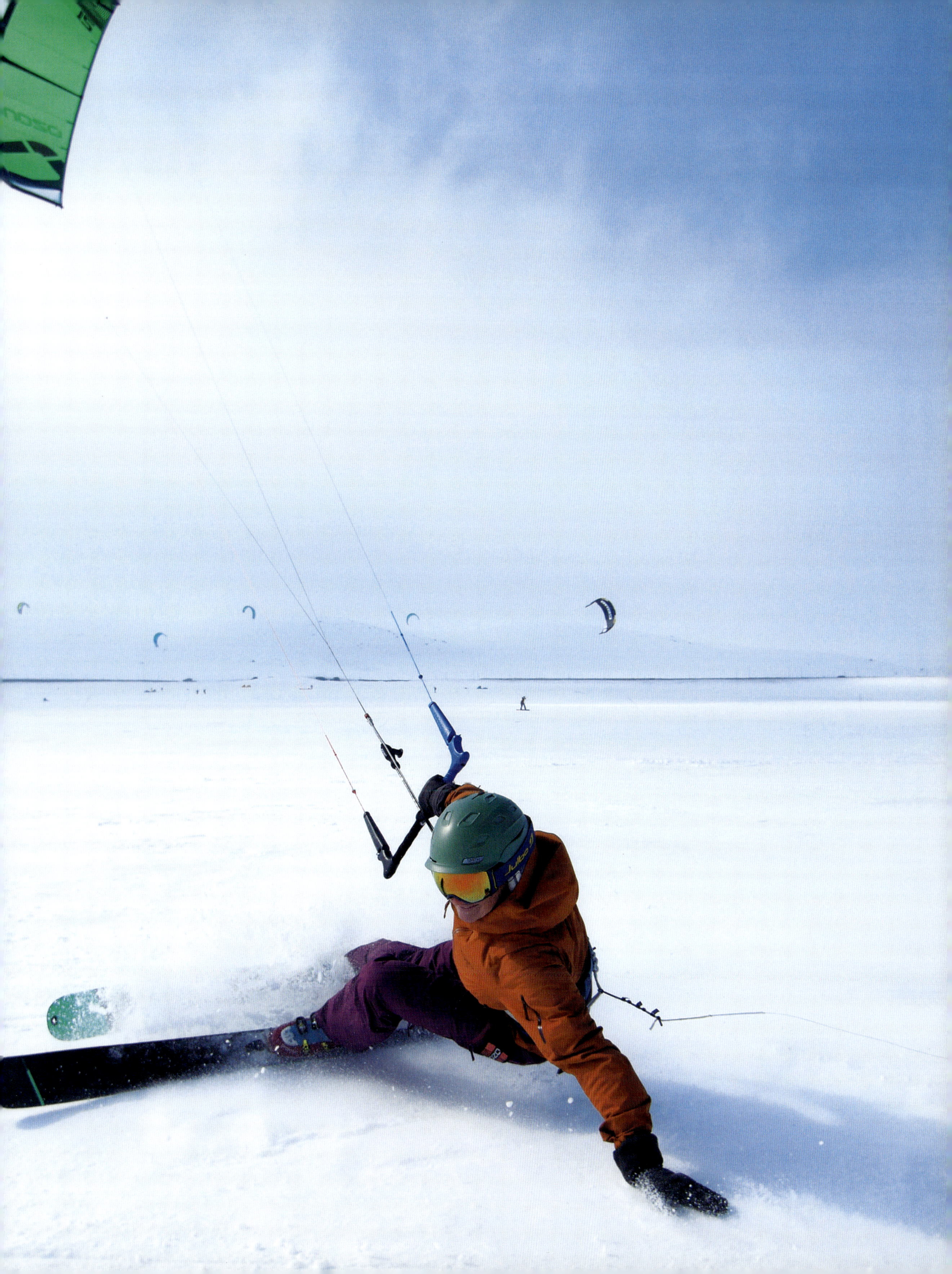

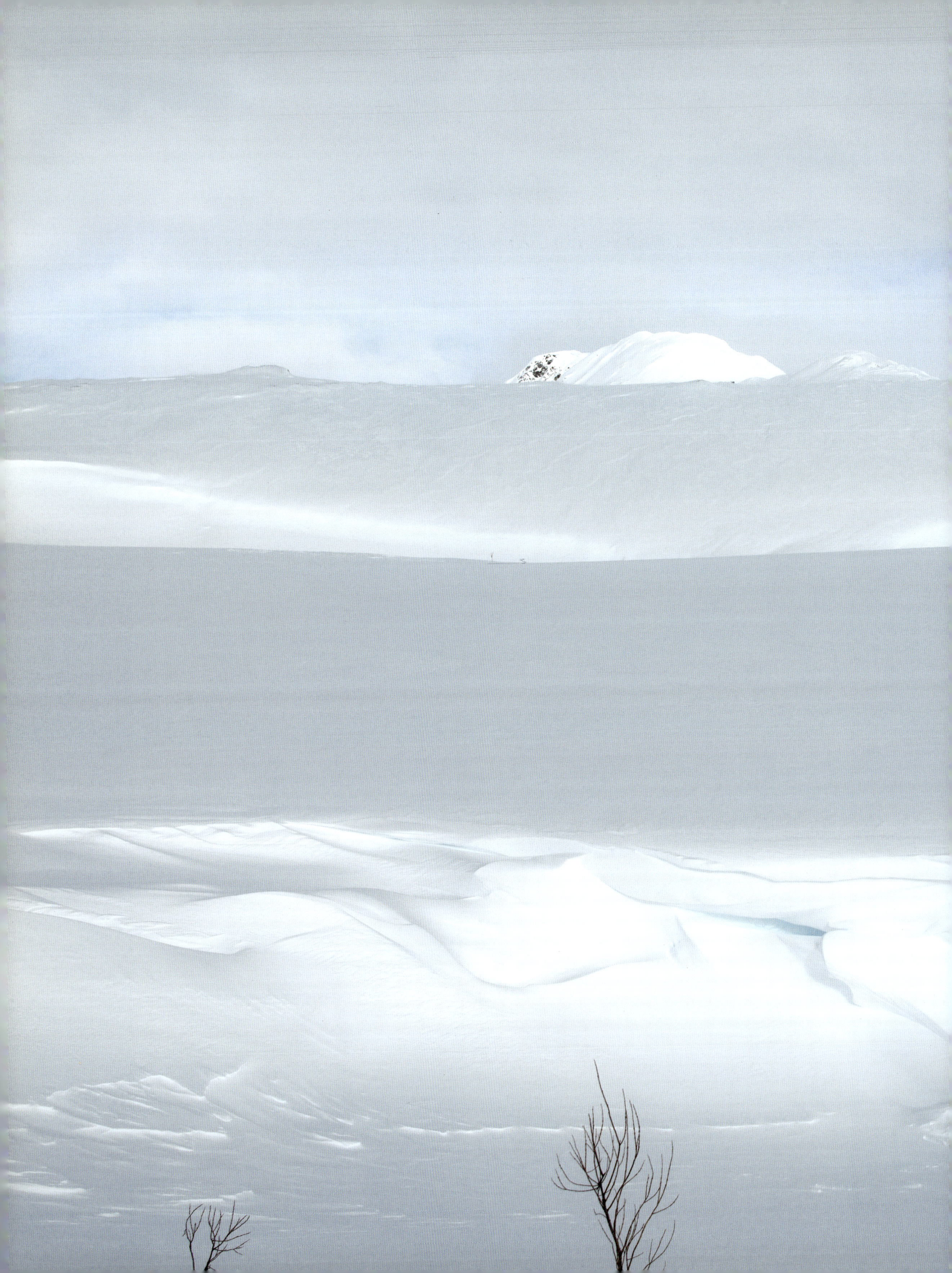

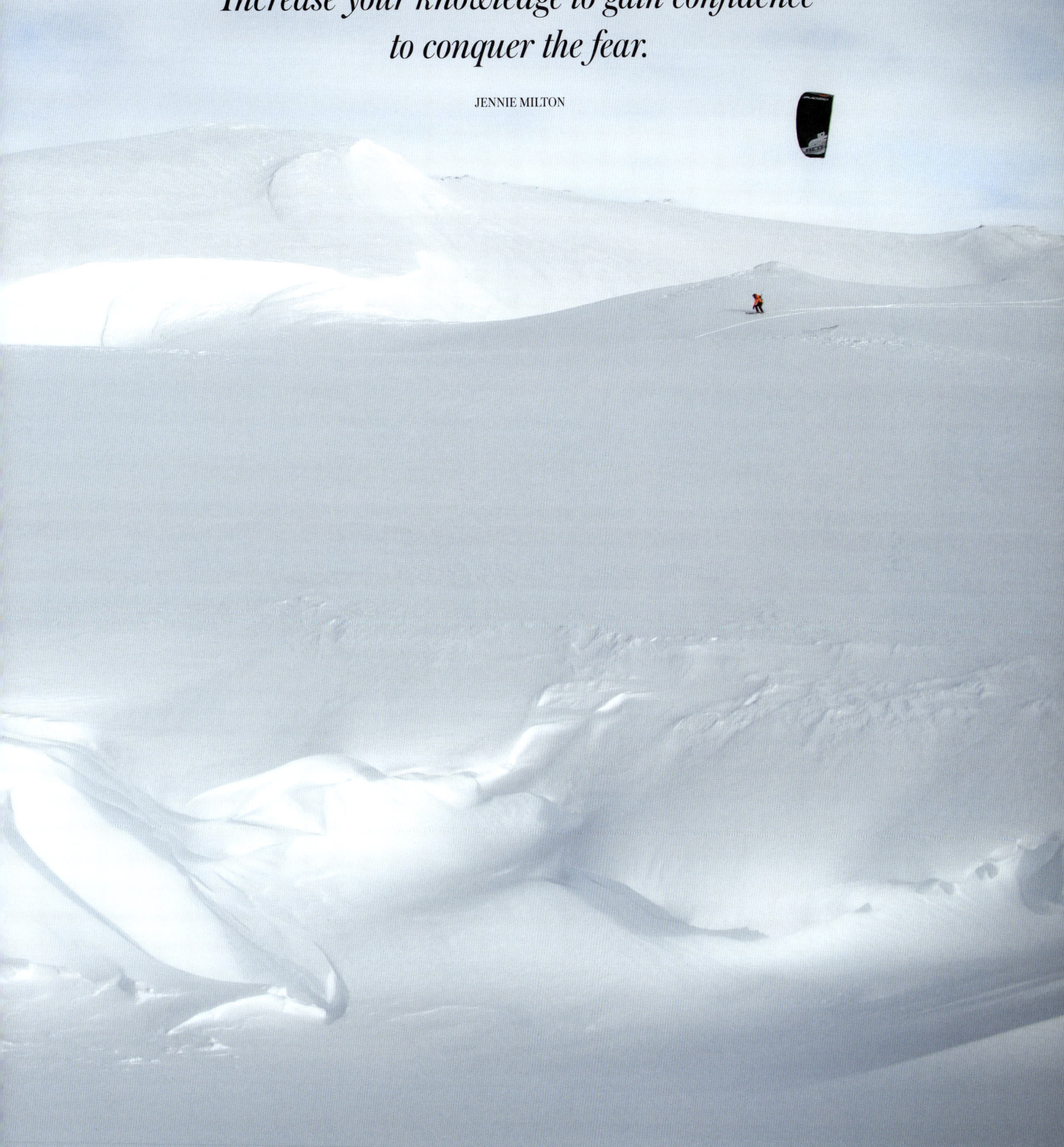

Fear is created by the unknown.
Increase your knowledge to gain confidence
to conquer the fear.

JENNIE MILTON

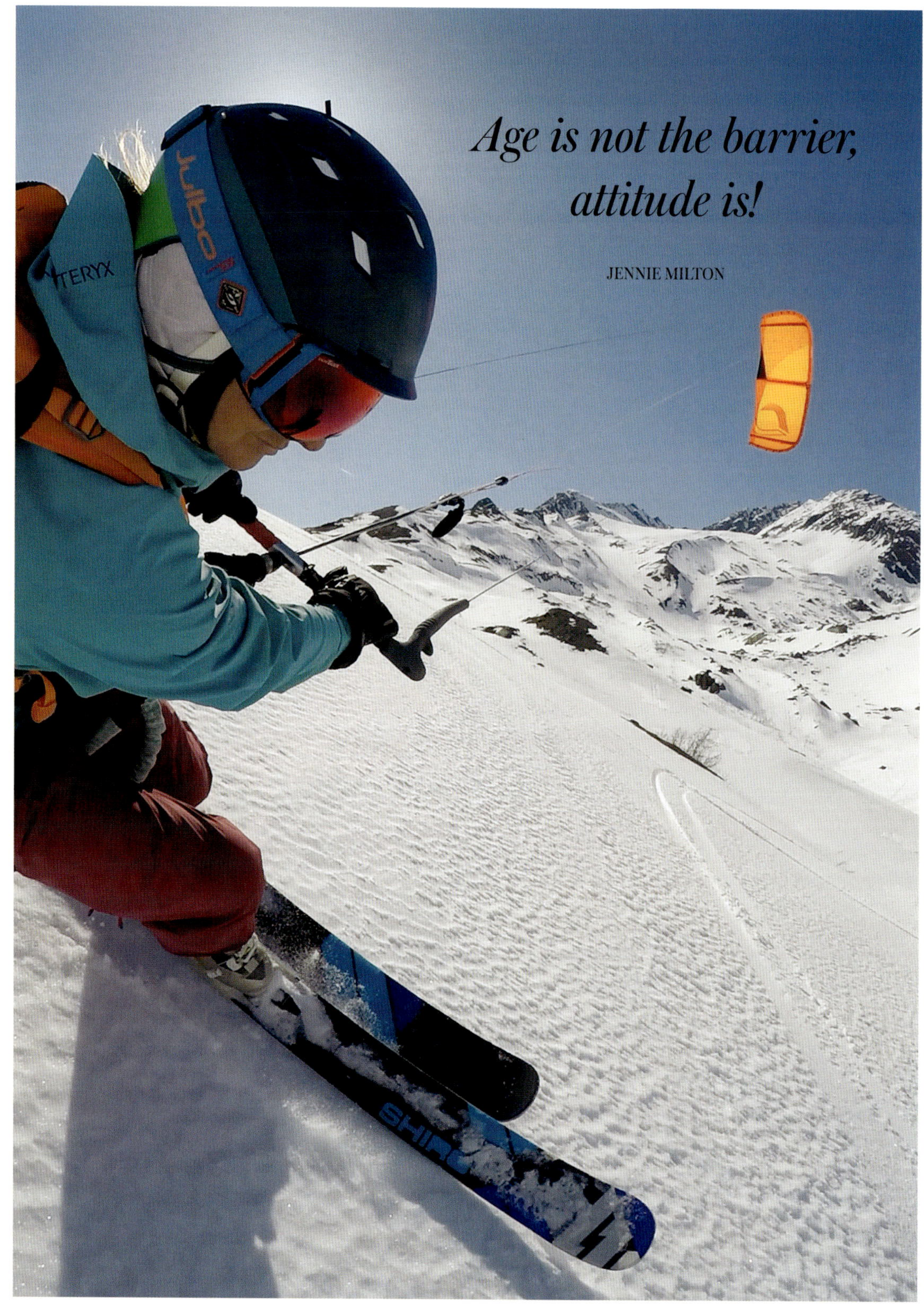

Age is not the barrier,
attitude is!

JENNIE MILTON

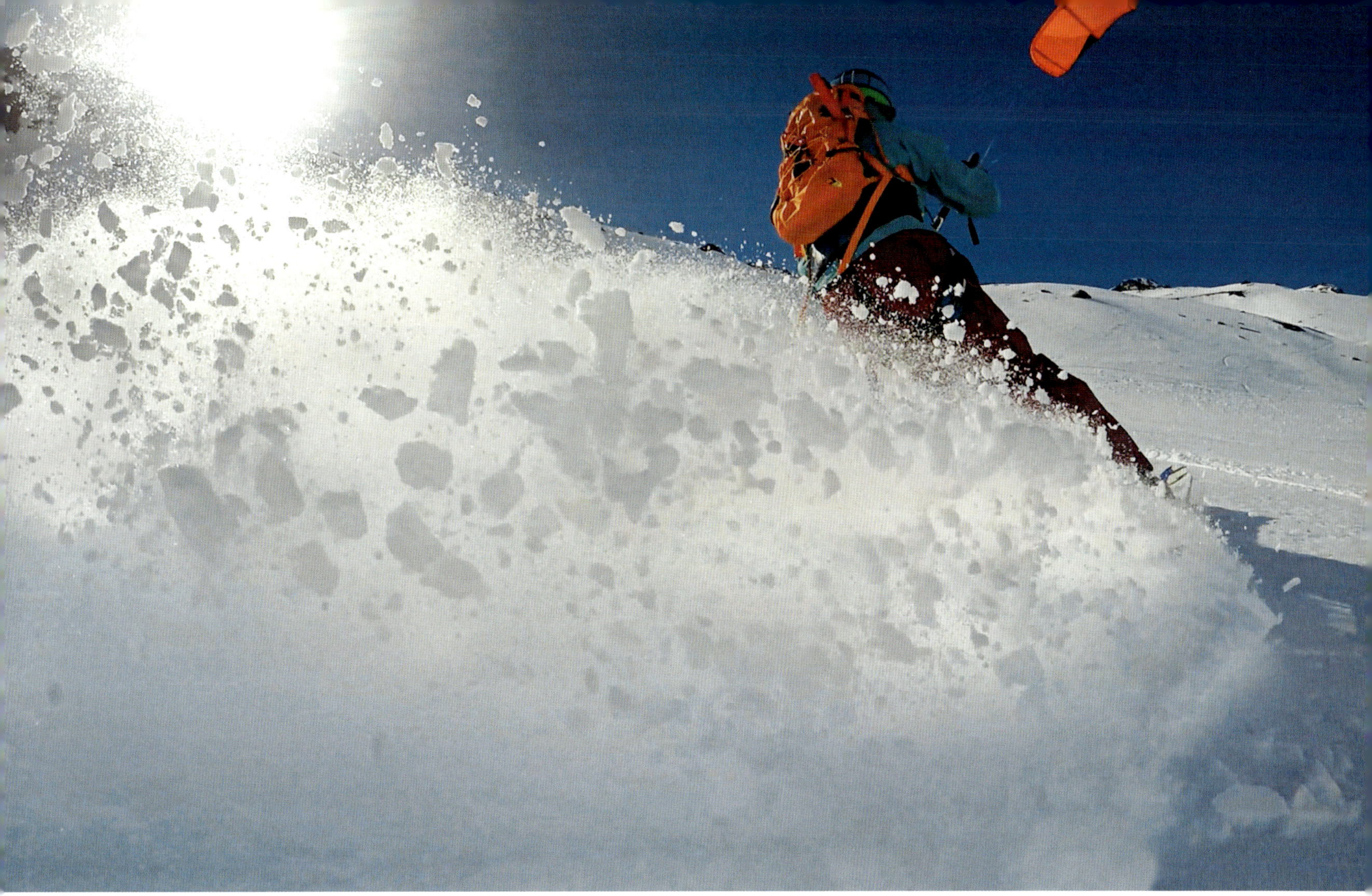

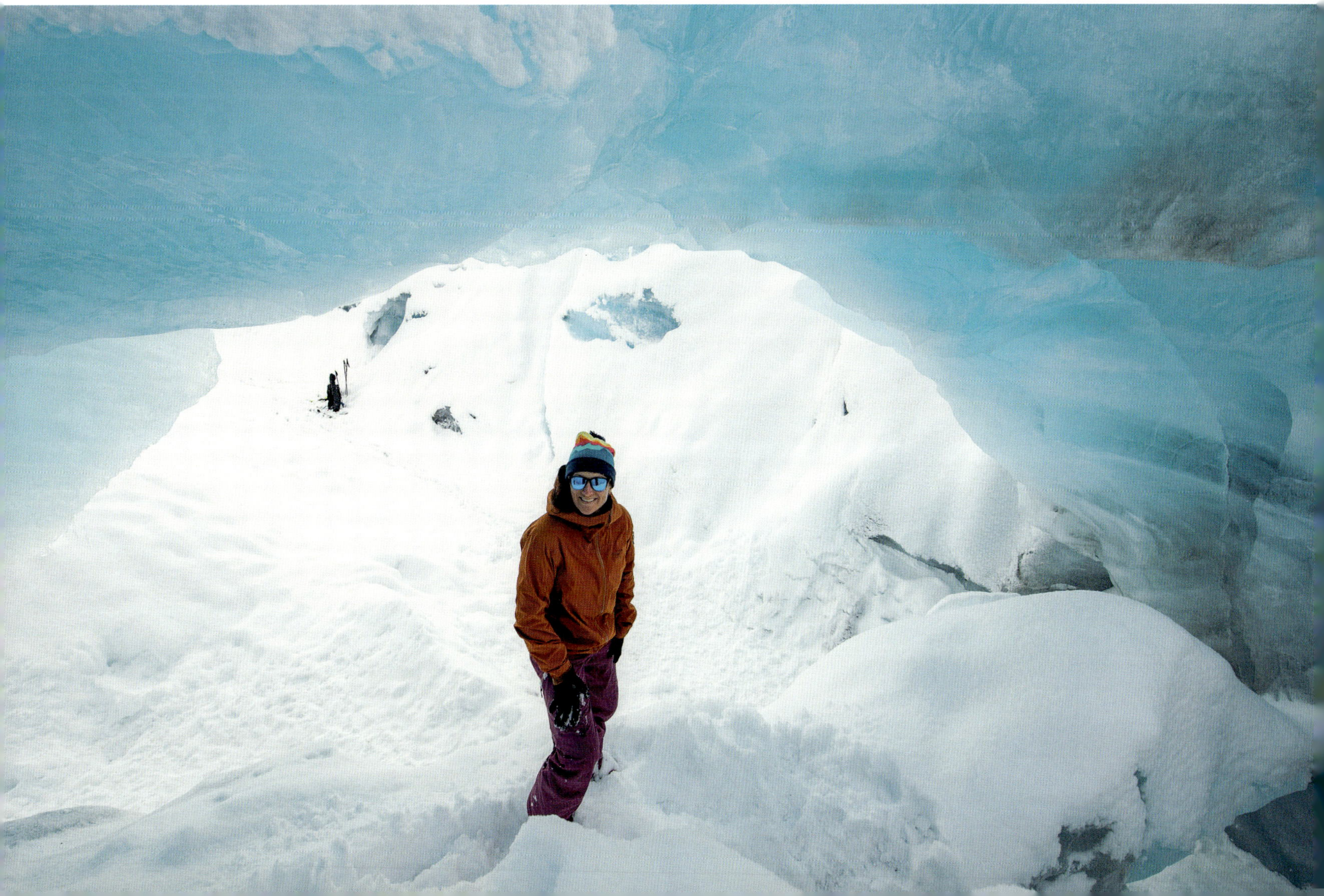

Marion Haerty
Snowboarder

@marion_haerty
marionhaerty.com

My passion for snowboarding started because I needed to create my own bubble. The situation at home was not easy: my family was working for a carpentry company and our finances were unstable. Bailiffs wanted to evict us from our home and there was lots of stress around all the time. Snowboarding, and the freedom to go outside with my friends in the mountains, was my key to happiness.

My dream of being World Champion started out of the desire to help my family stop this vicious circle and to have a job I will love for ever. I've been 2017 Freeride World Champion, 2018 Vice World Champion, and World Champion again in 2019 and 2020. For several years I was able to express myself at the World Championships, on the snow parks of the World Cup slopestyle circuit. From Alaska to Japan, I am now looking for the best lines to draw around the world for video projects with my sponsors or during competitions on the Freeride World Tour. My driving force is the exploration of new horizons; I aim to immerse myself in new cultures and to surpass what I've done already, but also to start from the discovery of others and of myself.

Freeride allowed me to enter into symbiosis with the mountain to understand the elements that surround us. Going off the beaten track, always in search of sensations of freedom, snowboarding gives me an infinite field of creativity where I can live my next adventures.

Thanks to my board, I've grown up with so many good memories. I've gotten more self-confident, I've met different people around the world, and I've realized that my dream makes me more at peace with myself and the world around me. Thanks snowboarding <3

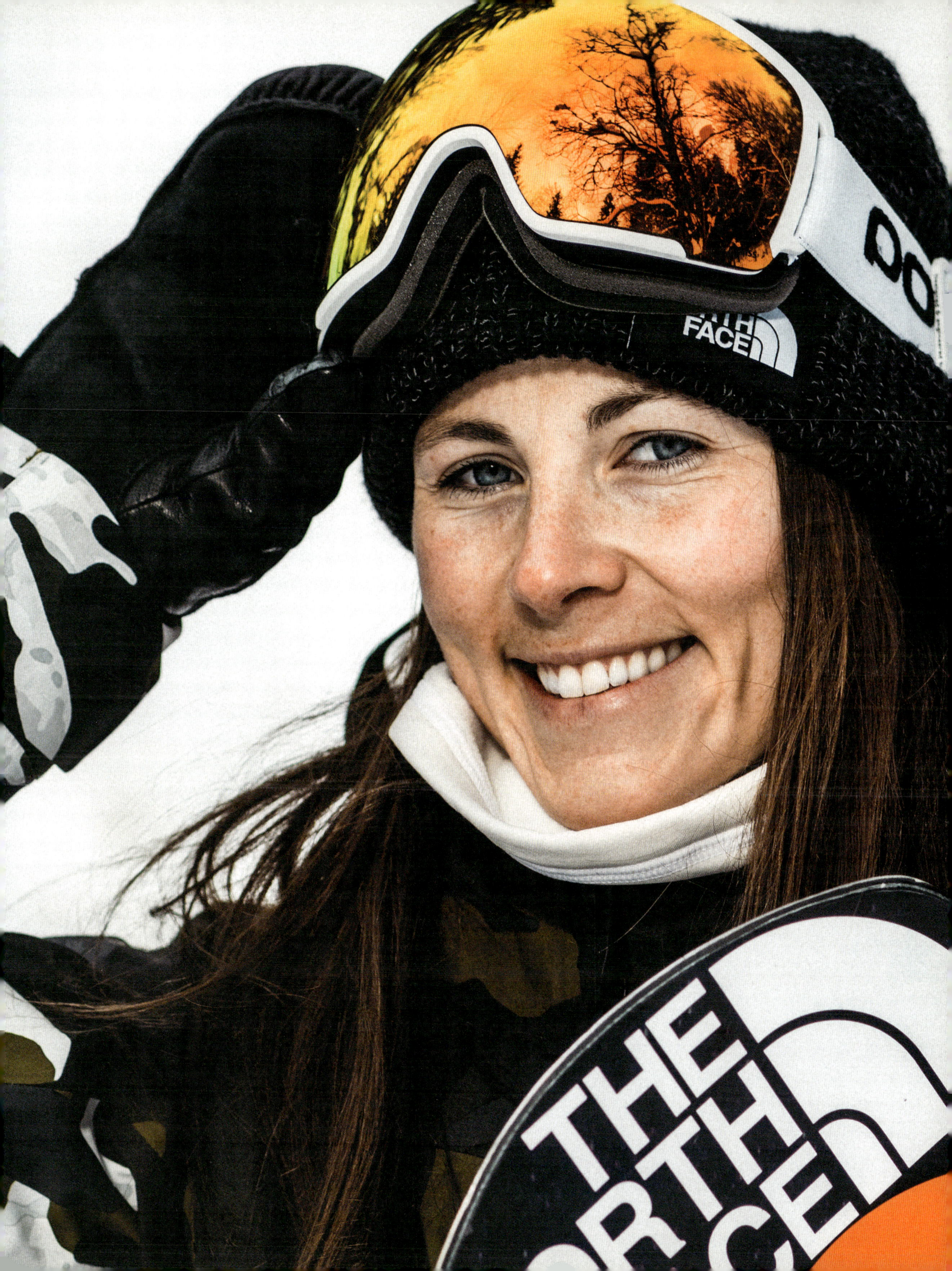

NTH
FACE
THE
ORTH
RCE

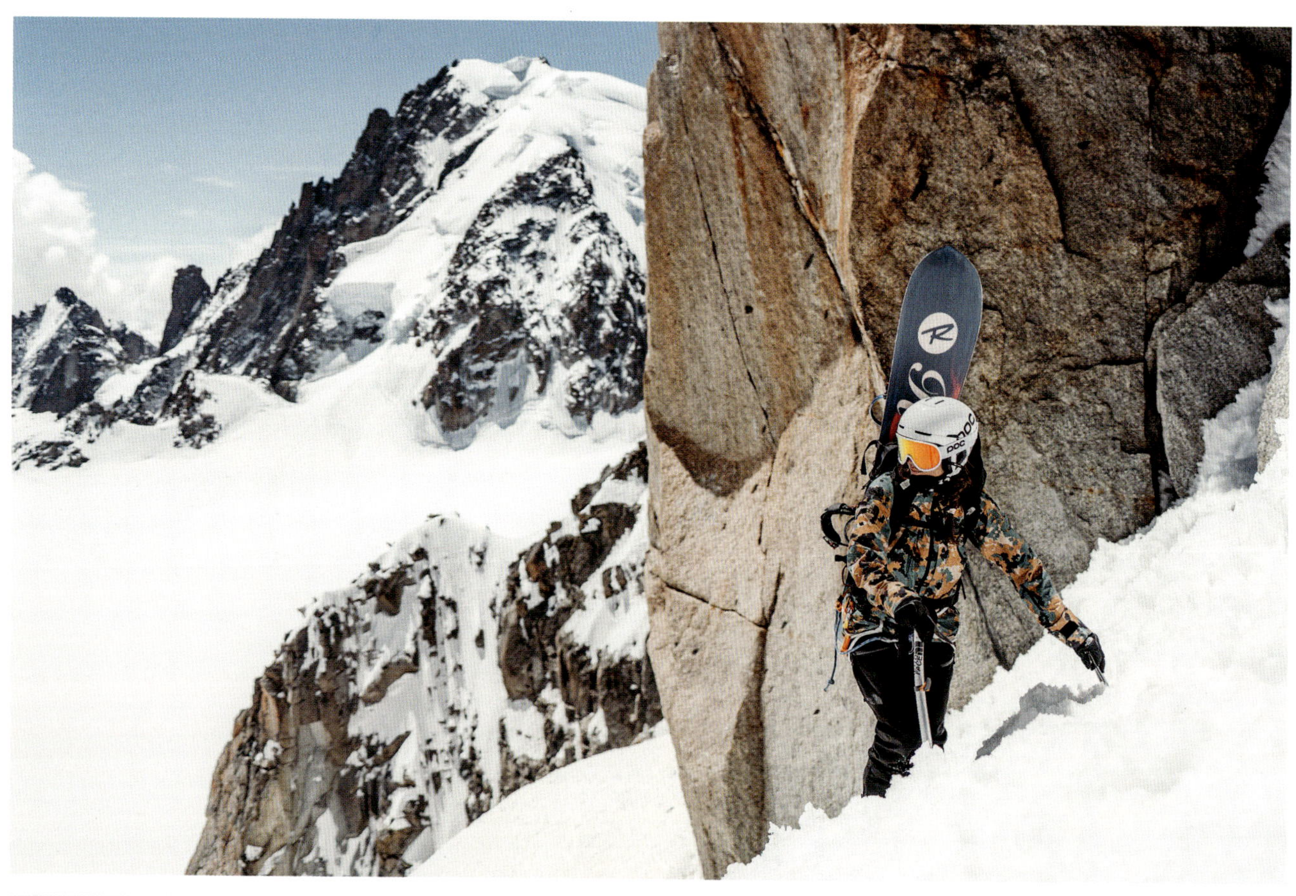

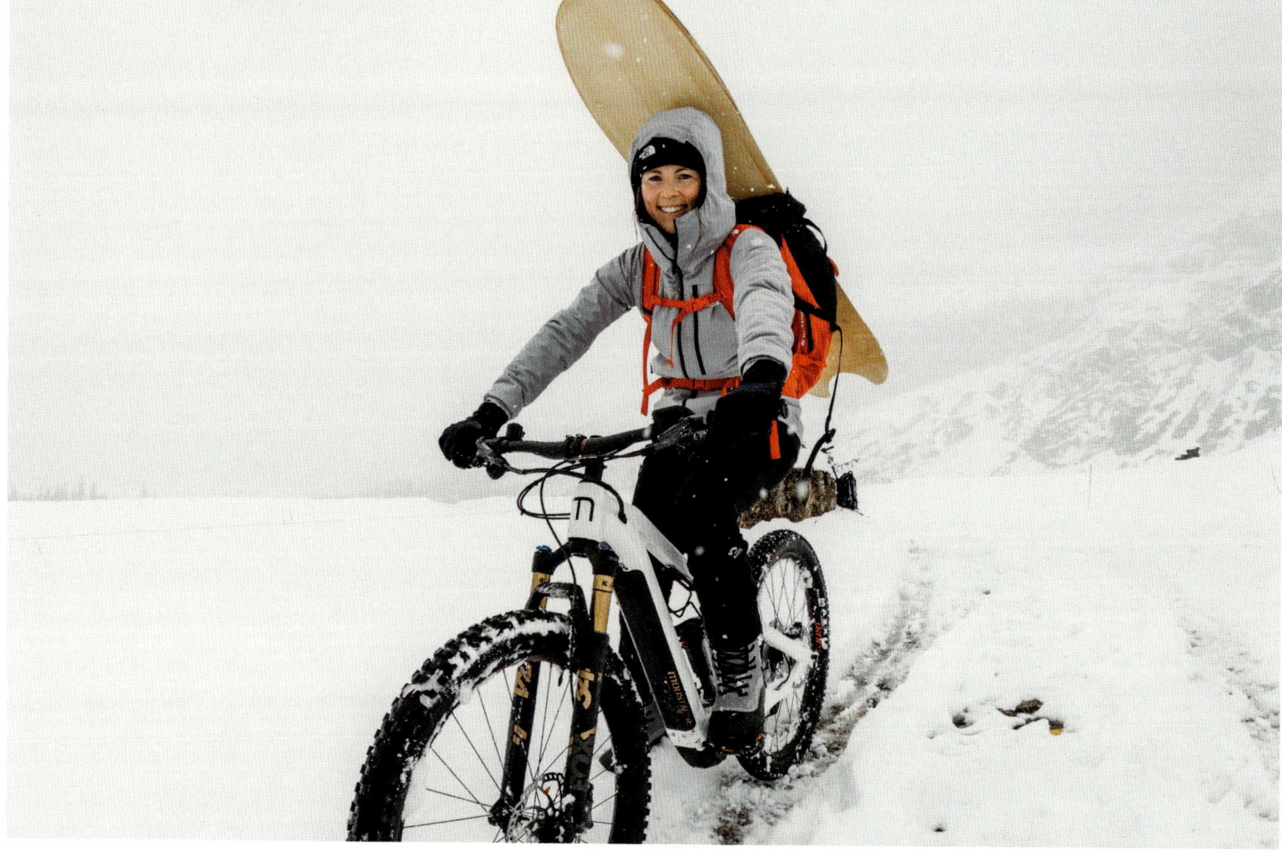

 △ Chamonix   ▷ Passy | France   ▷▷ Aiguille de l'Amône, Switzerland

*A flower doesn't think of
competing against the flowers next to it,
it just blooms.*

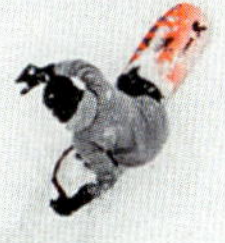

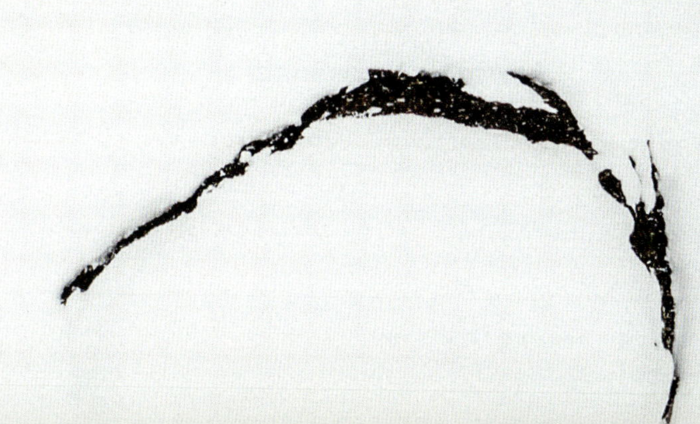

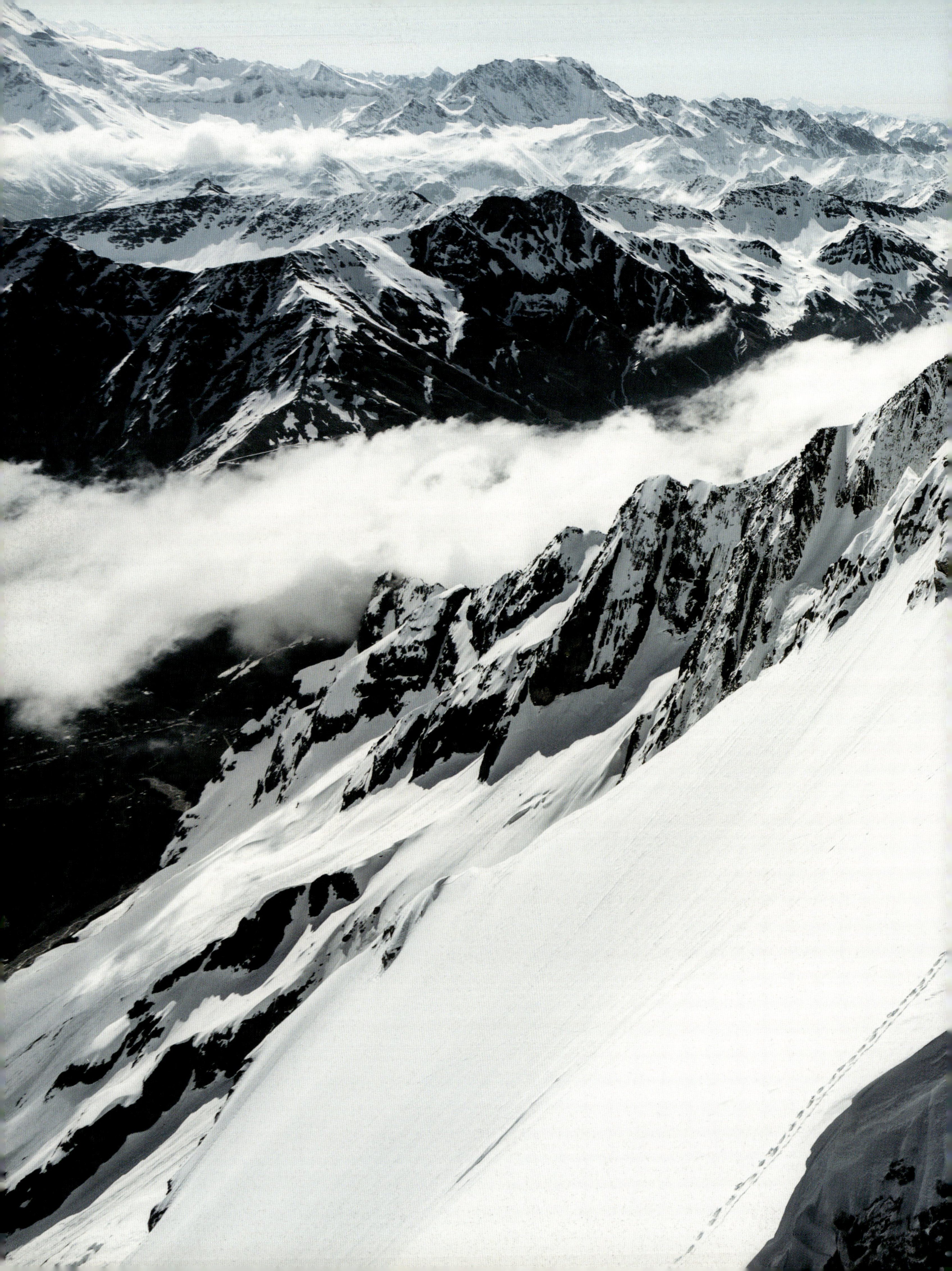

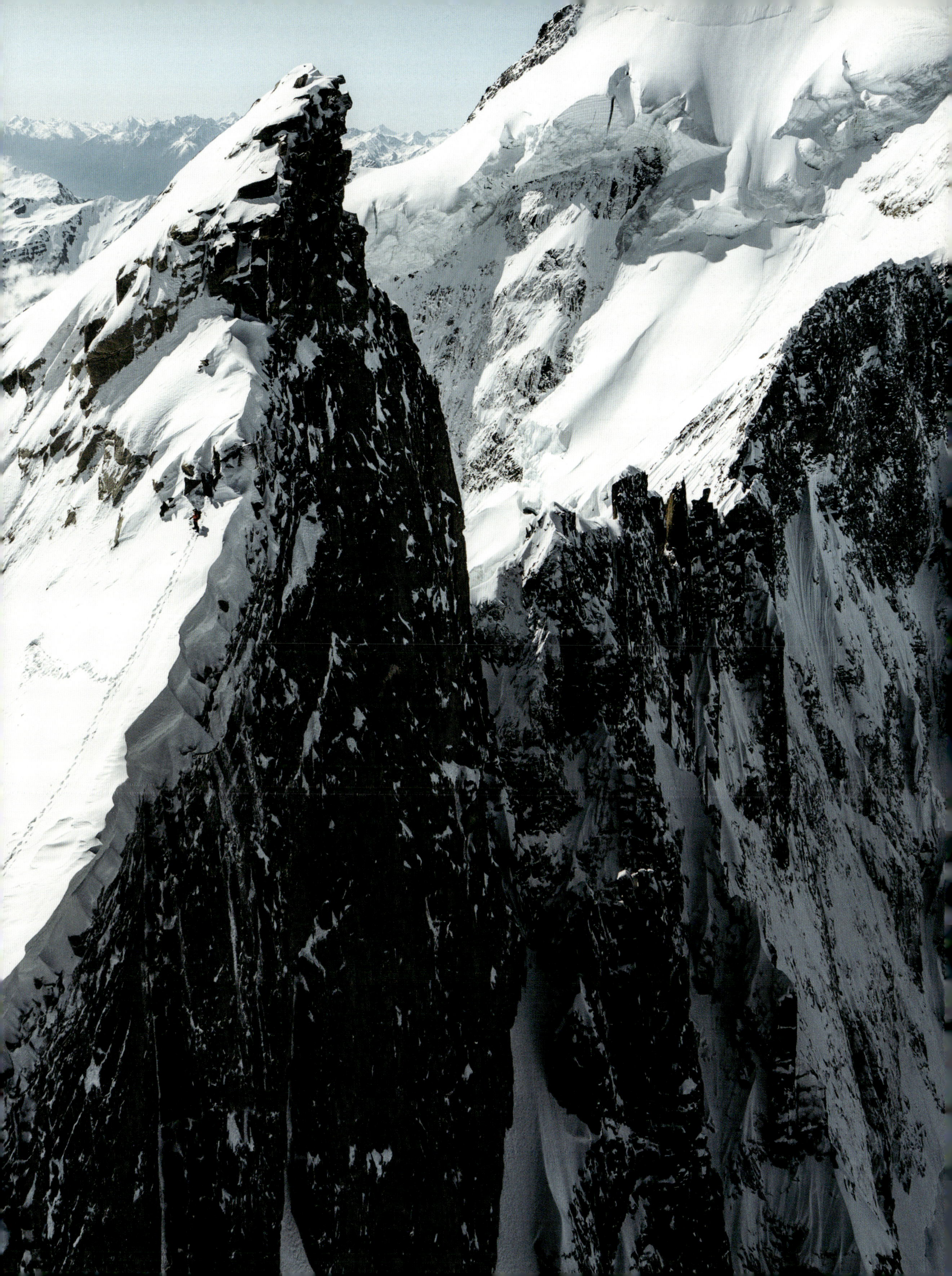

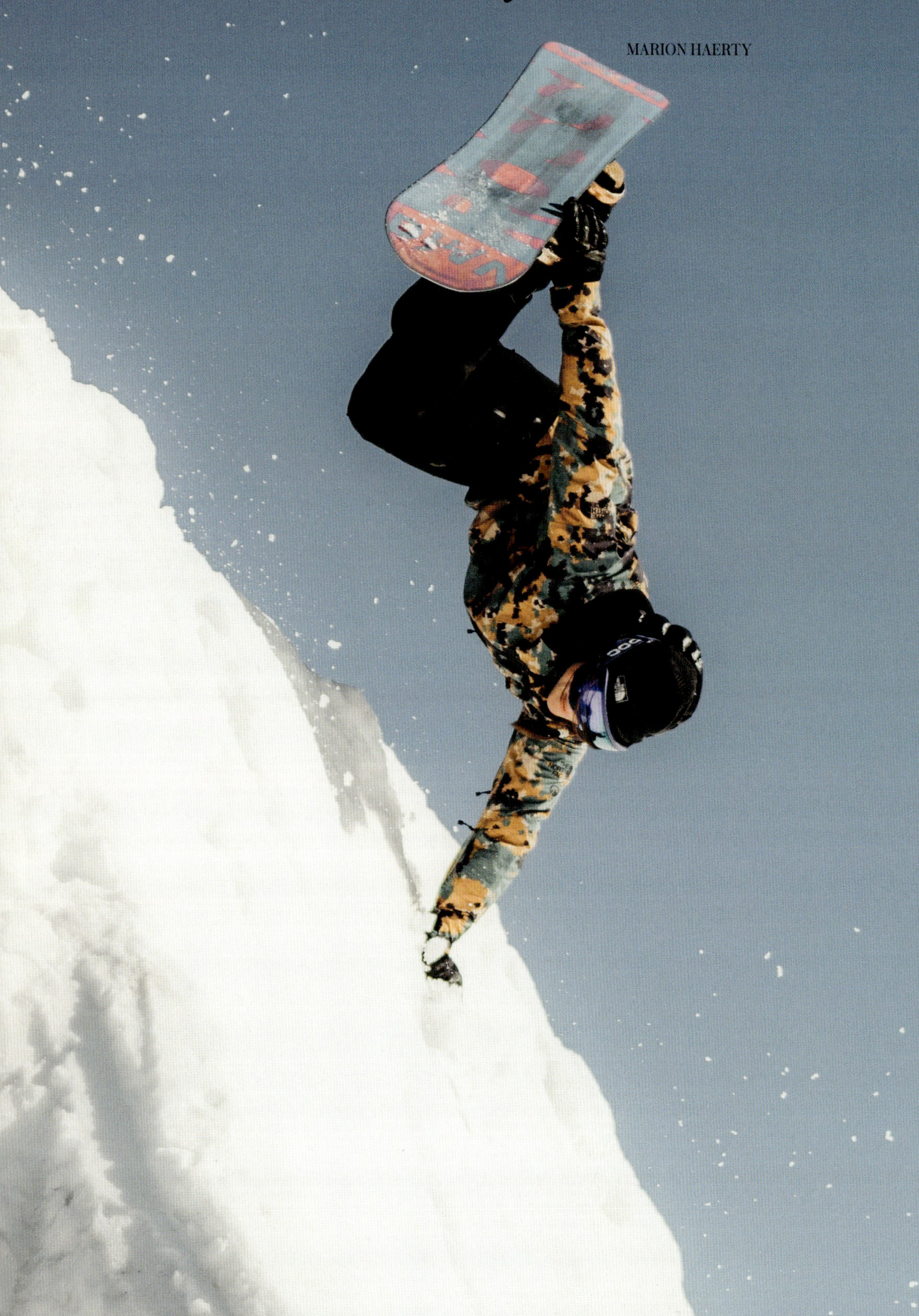
If you don't test it
you will never know.

MARION HAERTY

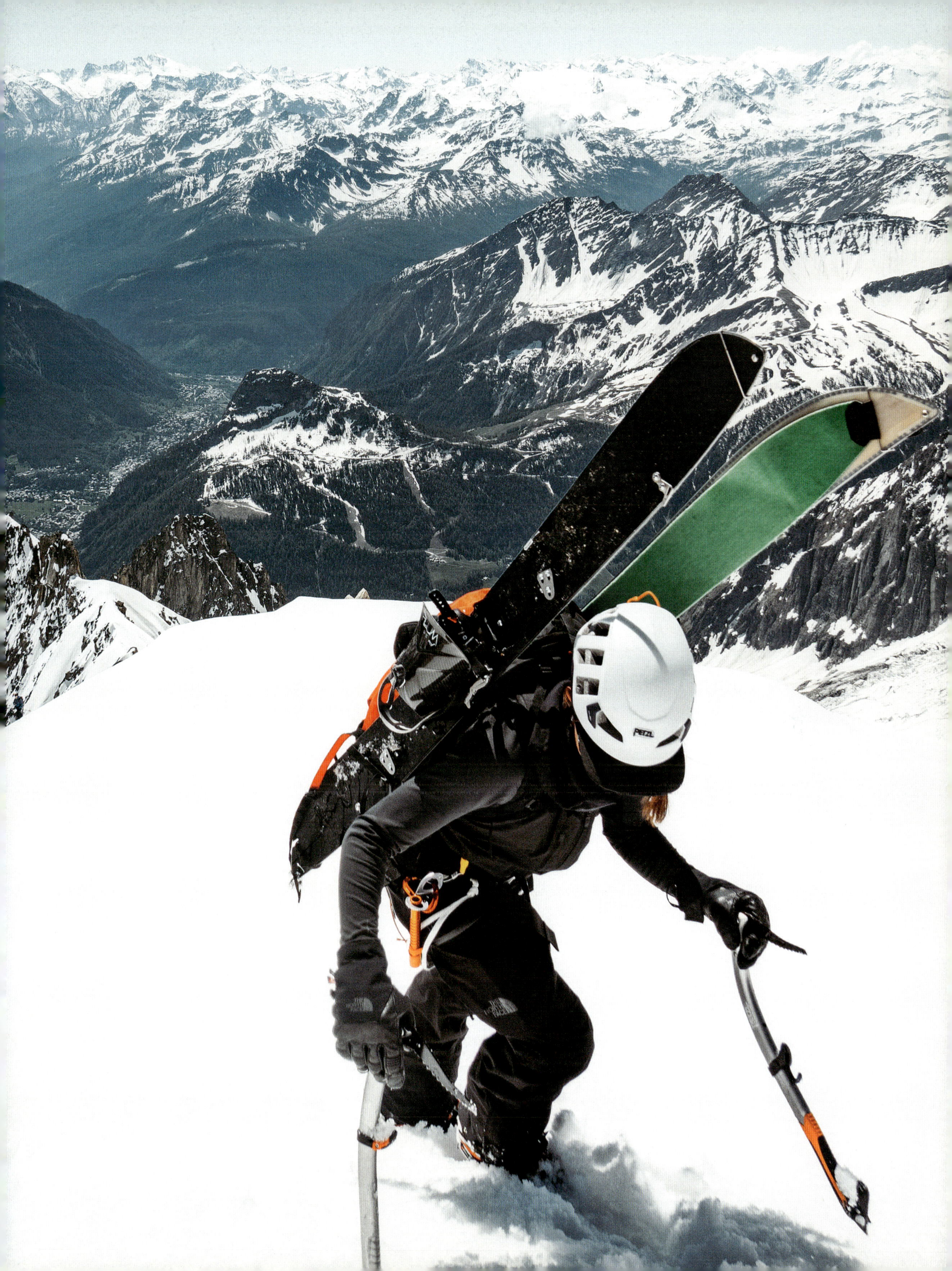

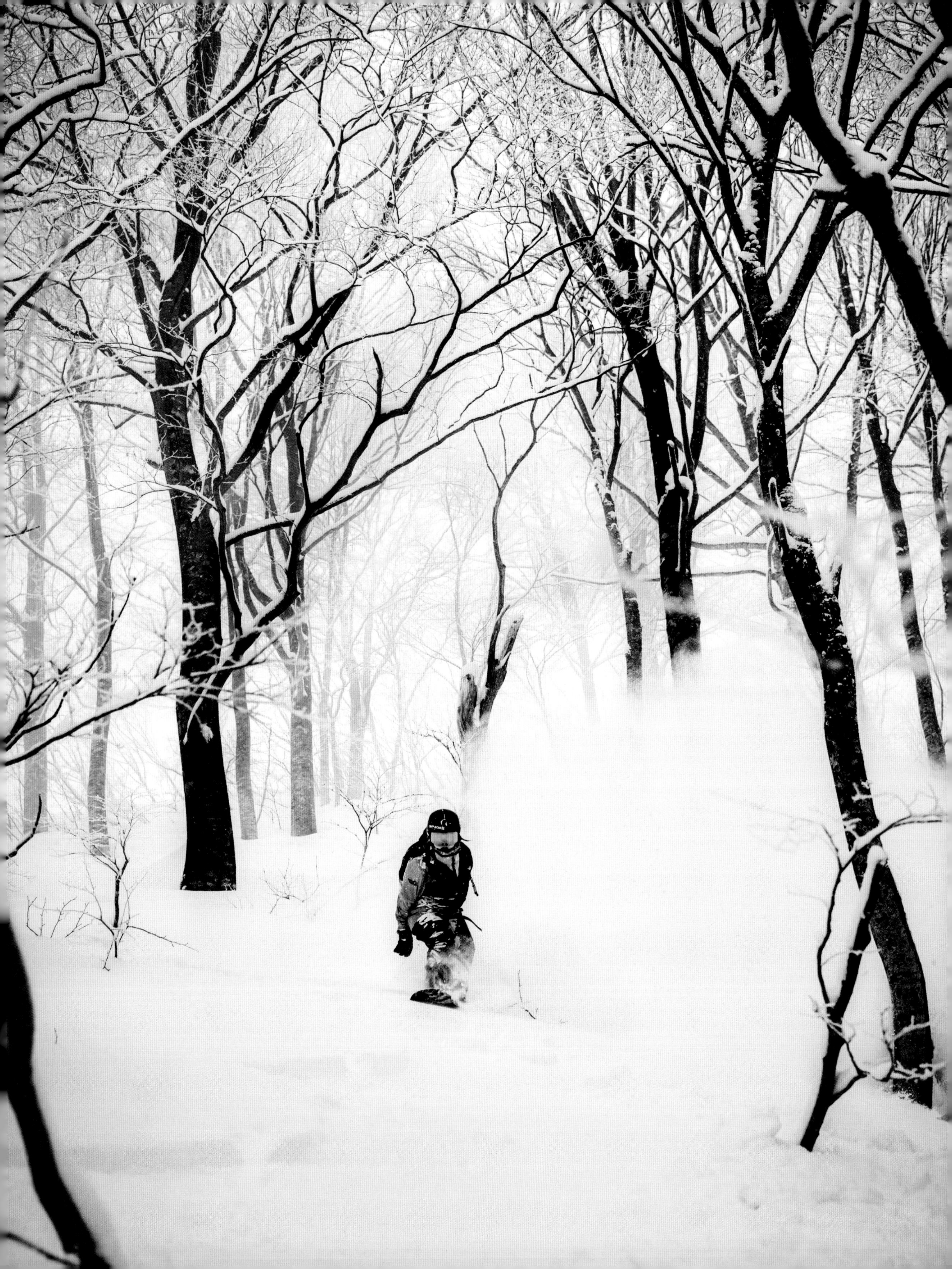

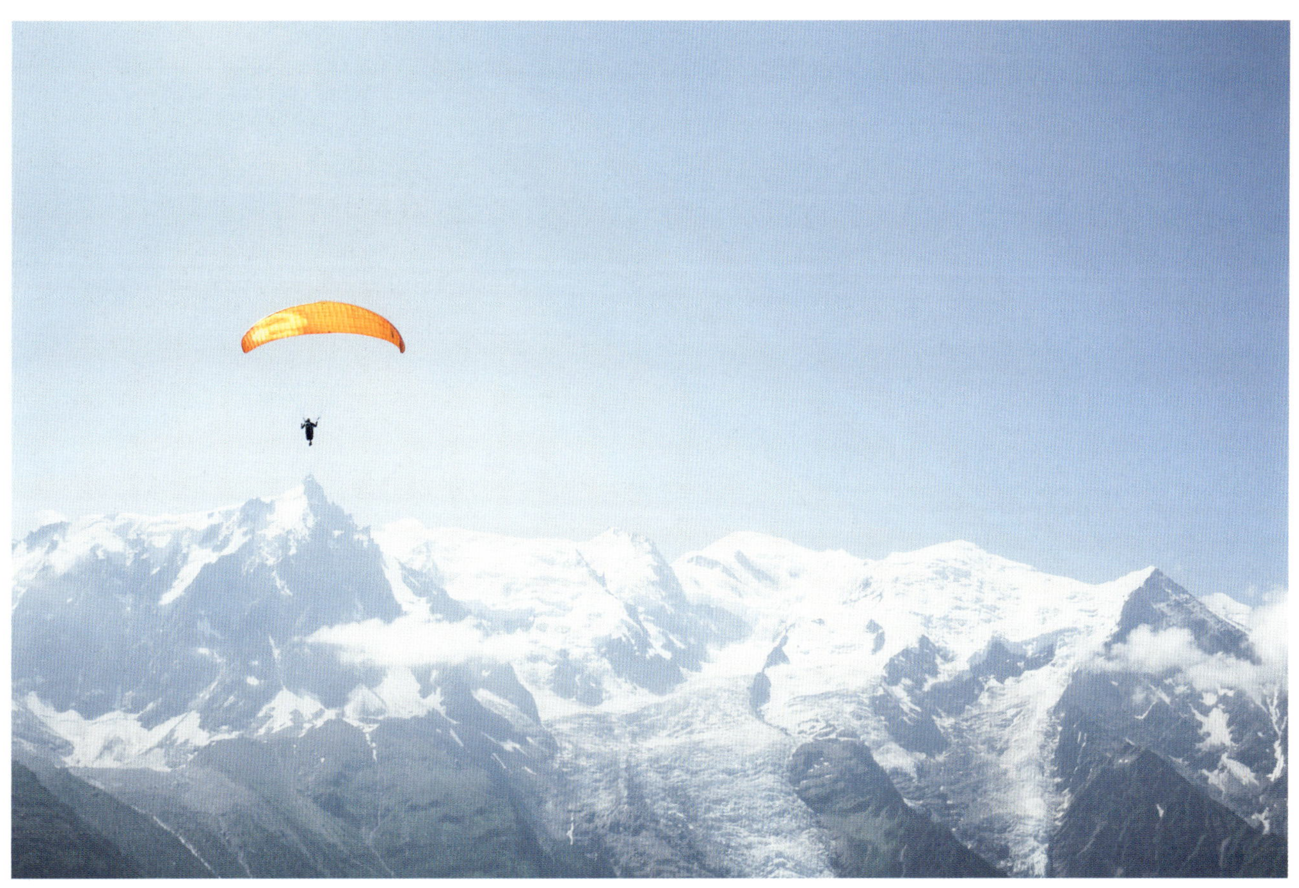

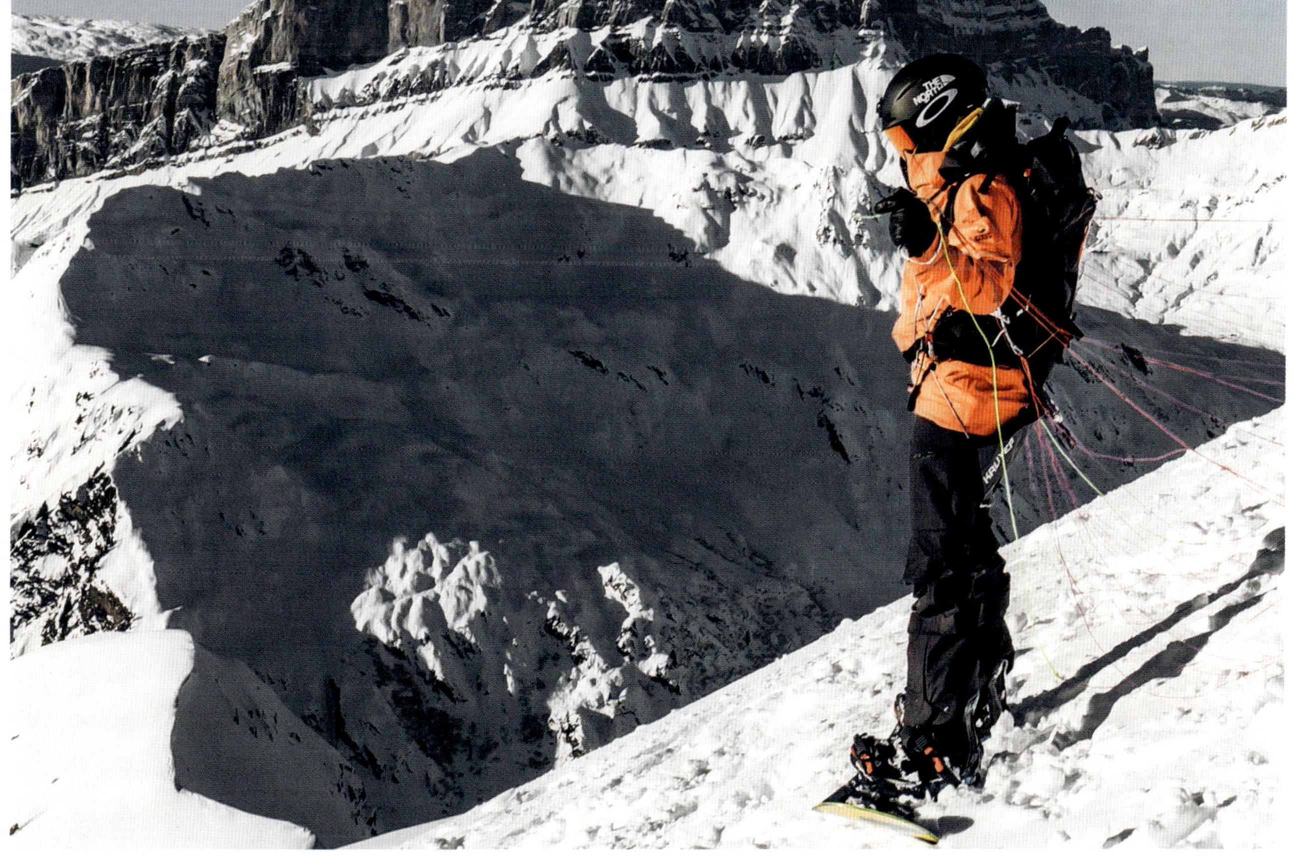

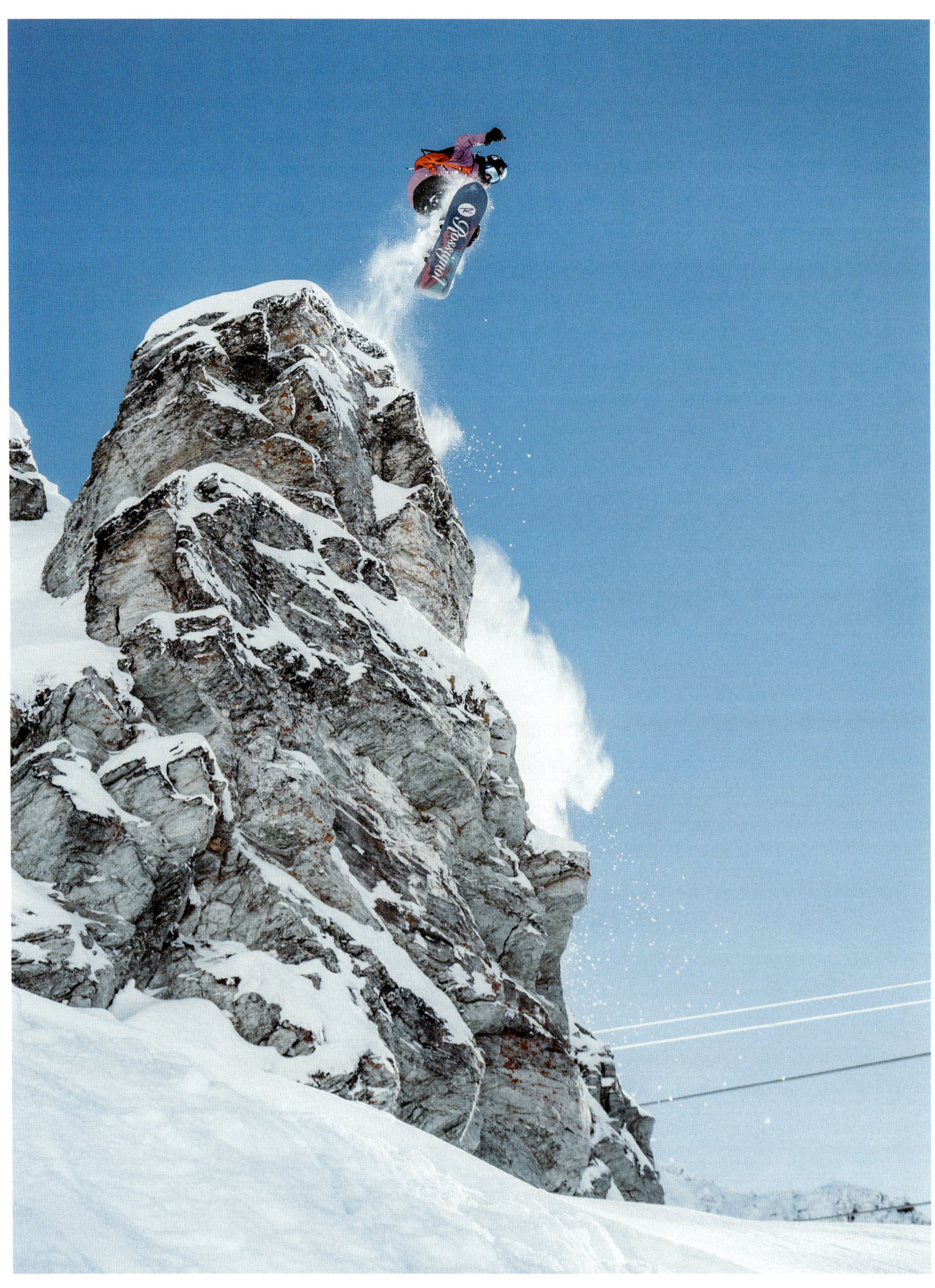

 △ Verbier ▷ Aiguille de l'Amône | Switzerland

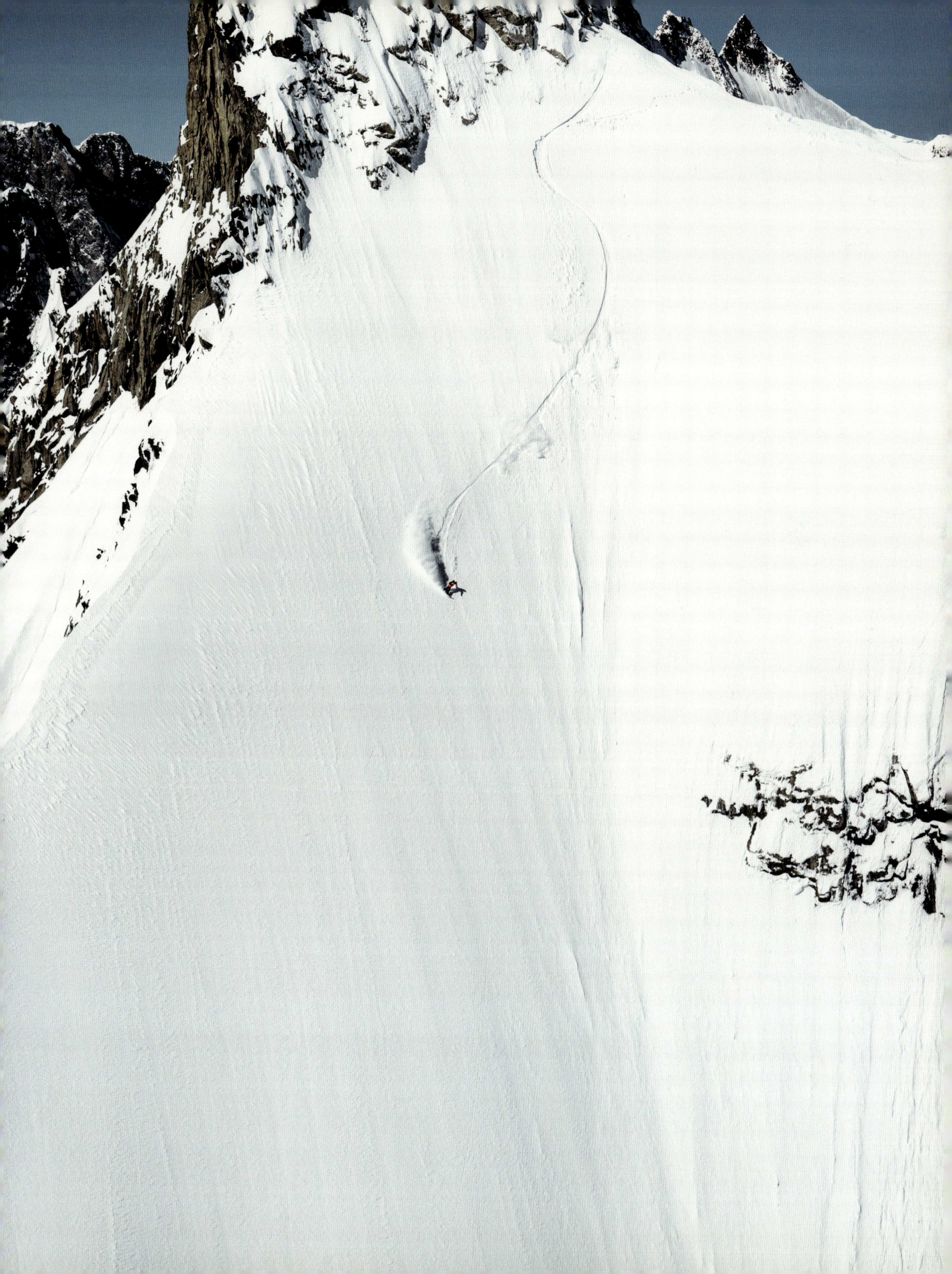

Géraldine Fasnacht

Snowboarder, BASE jumper,
and wingsuit pilot

@geraldinefasnacht

I grew up surrounded by nature. I learned to slide on skis at the age of two, as soon as I could walk. In a country covered with mountains, like Switzerland, this is quite normal. But it was when I discovered snowboarding at the age of nine that I found my true passion. This passion made me want to explore the mountains and to draw lines to new heights.

At twenty-one I was invited to participate in the most extreme competition in the world, Xtreme Verbier, which I won the first time I entered. After that, I left my city life working at Geneva airport for Freeride snowboarding. I made my dream a reality!

Along with my snowboarding career, I discovered first parachuting and then BASE jumping. For me, flying from a mountain was more natural than jumping from a plane. Thanks to my snowboarding experience, with my wingsuit I was able to open up the most legendary peaks in the world, in Antarctica, the Arctic, and the Alps, such as the summit of the Matterhorn (Switzerland) or the Drus (France).

Each line is a quest—I analyze it, imagine it, memorize it, and prepare it. It's like gently taming the mountain so that she invites me to draw my line in the best conditions. I've learned to be humble in front of her and to know my limits.

In my sports I have no leeway to make mistakes, and to have fun I need to do flawless preparation in order to always be ahead of the game and to be in top physical condition.

In the mountains I feel connected with the elements; I live and breathe, and I feel present. They inspire me and always make me want to evolve, to achieve the perfect line. The only limits that exist are those that nature imposes on me. On my snowboard I feel as if I'm flying on the snow, just as I fly in the air from the peaks with my wingsuit.

I have always had faith in life and have followed my path. It is thanks to my passion for the mountains that even during a very difficult time in my life, I managed to find the strength to continue. When I was little in school, my teachers often had trouble getting my attention. I preferred to watch the snow falling through the window or the sun shining rather than listen to them. I dreamed that I was flying! They told me to stop dreaming, and that if I didn't start working I would never get anywhere in life.

They were right. Achieving the goals we set for ourselves takes a lot of work, but what I'm sure of today is that we must never stop dreaming, because in life even the wildest dreams can come true. Today I fly with my own wings from the most beautiful peaks in the world!

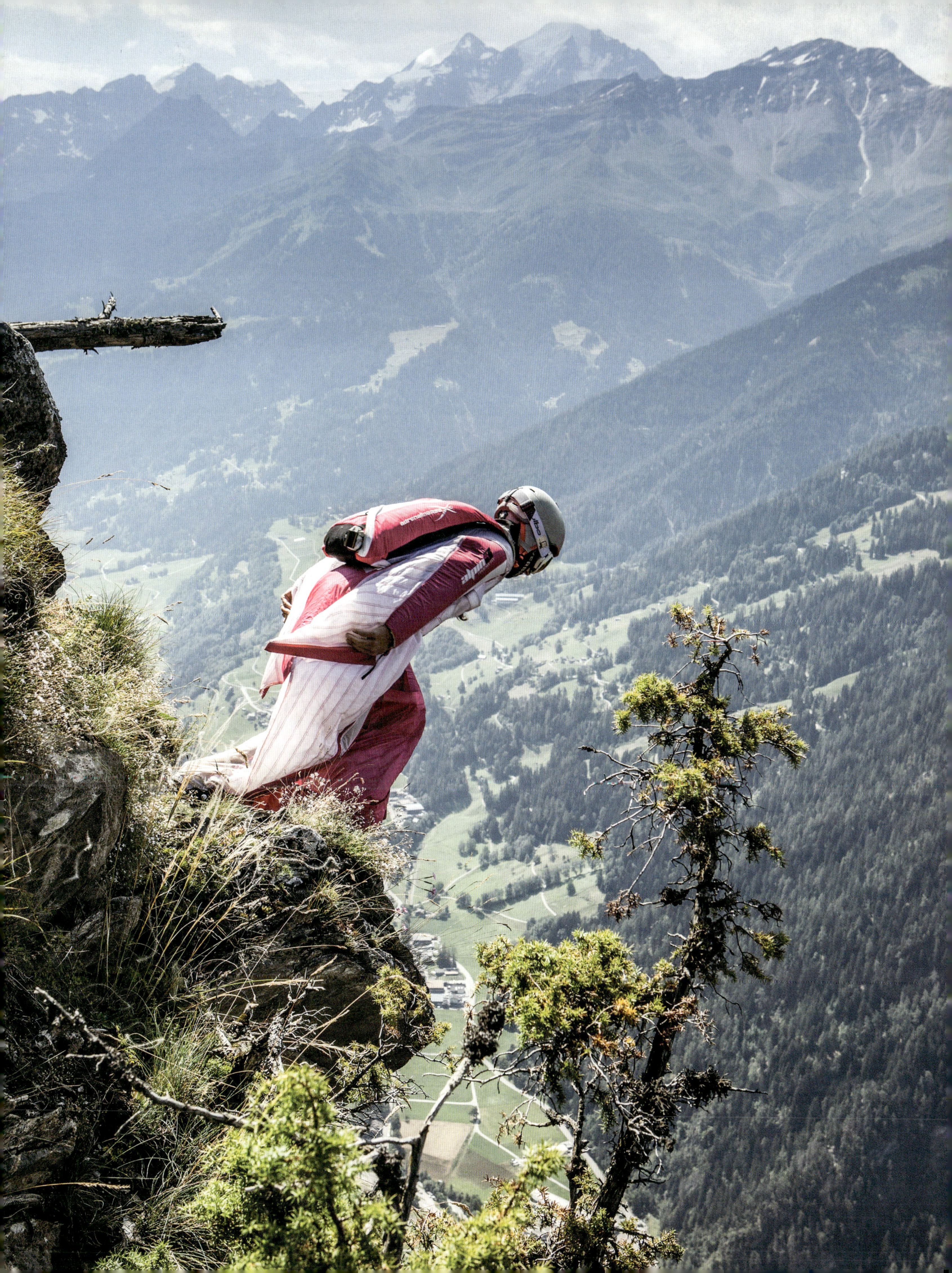

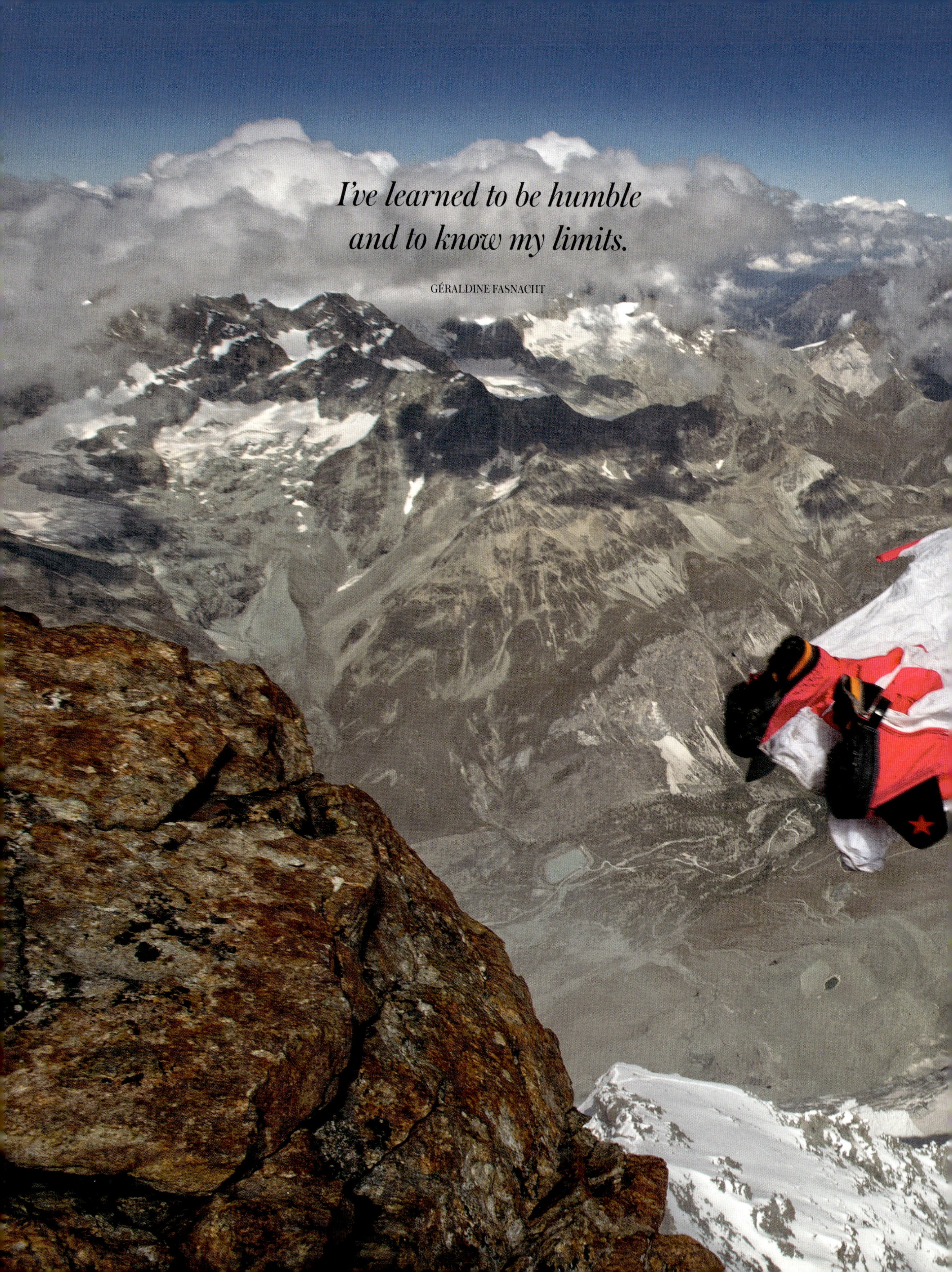

I've learned to be humble
and to know my limits.
GÉRALDINE FASNACHT

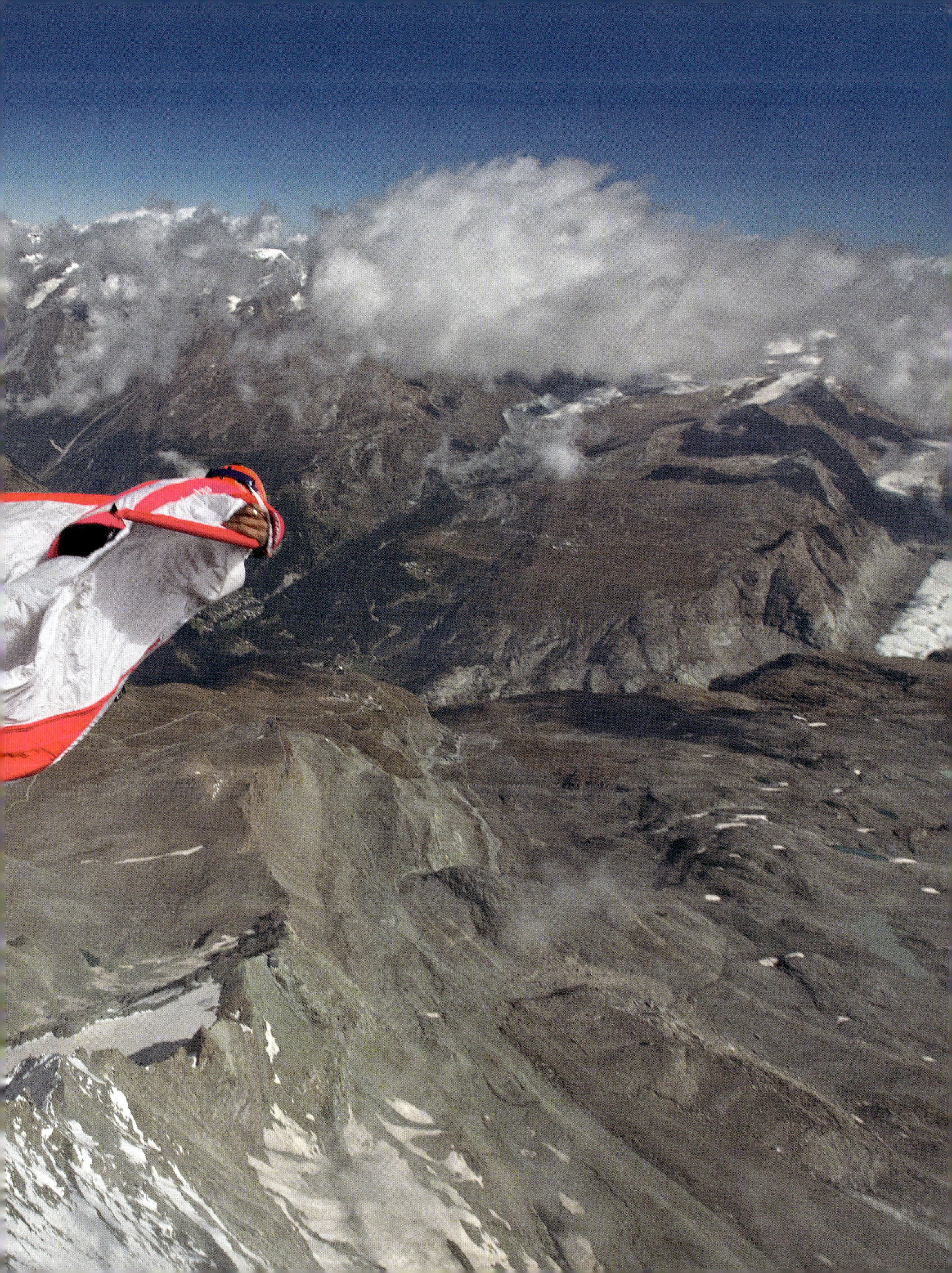

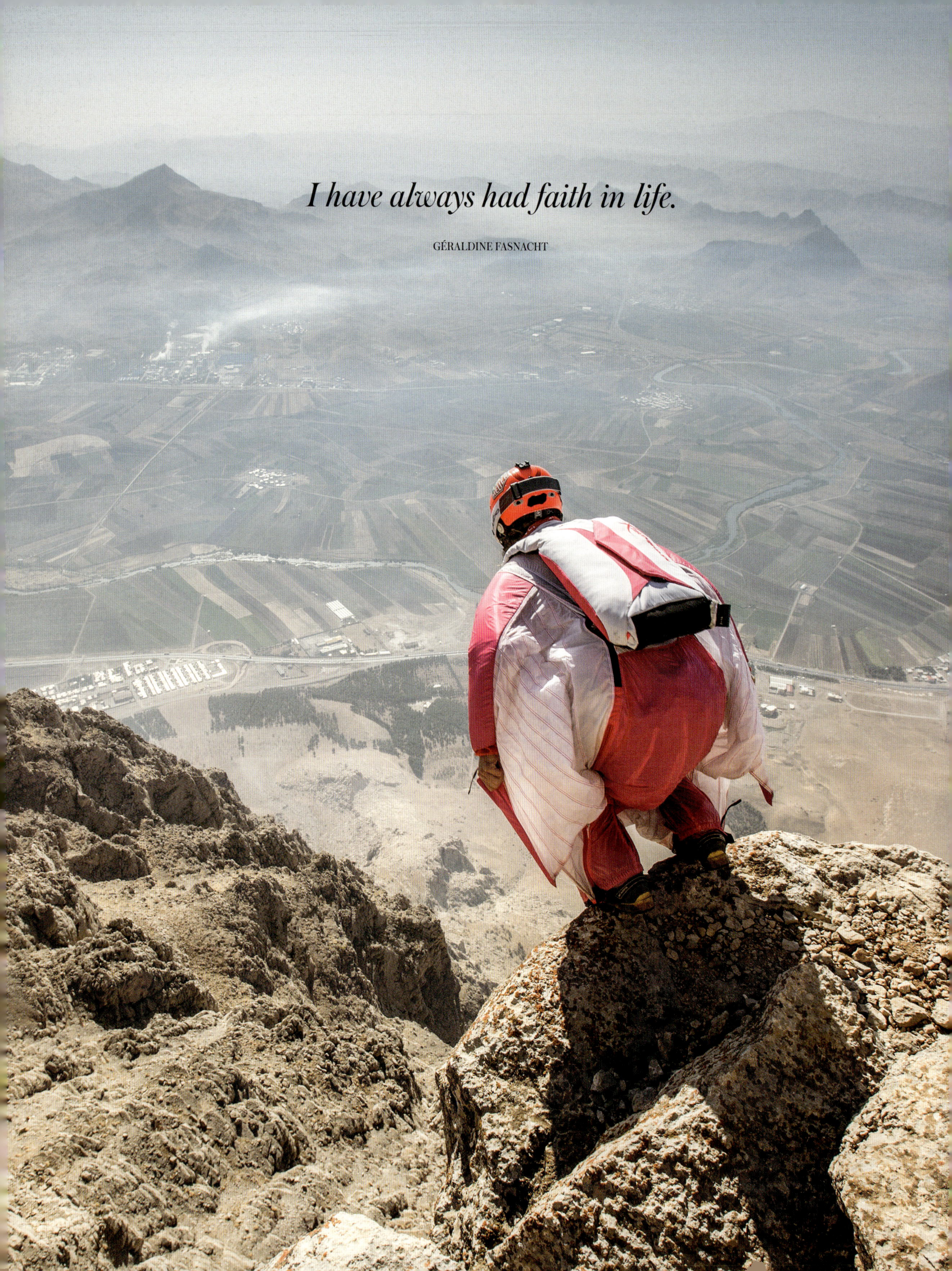

I have always had faith in life.
GÉRALDINE FASNACHT

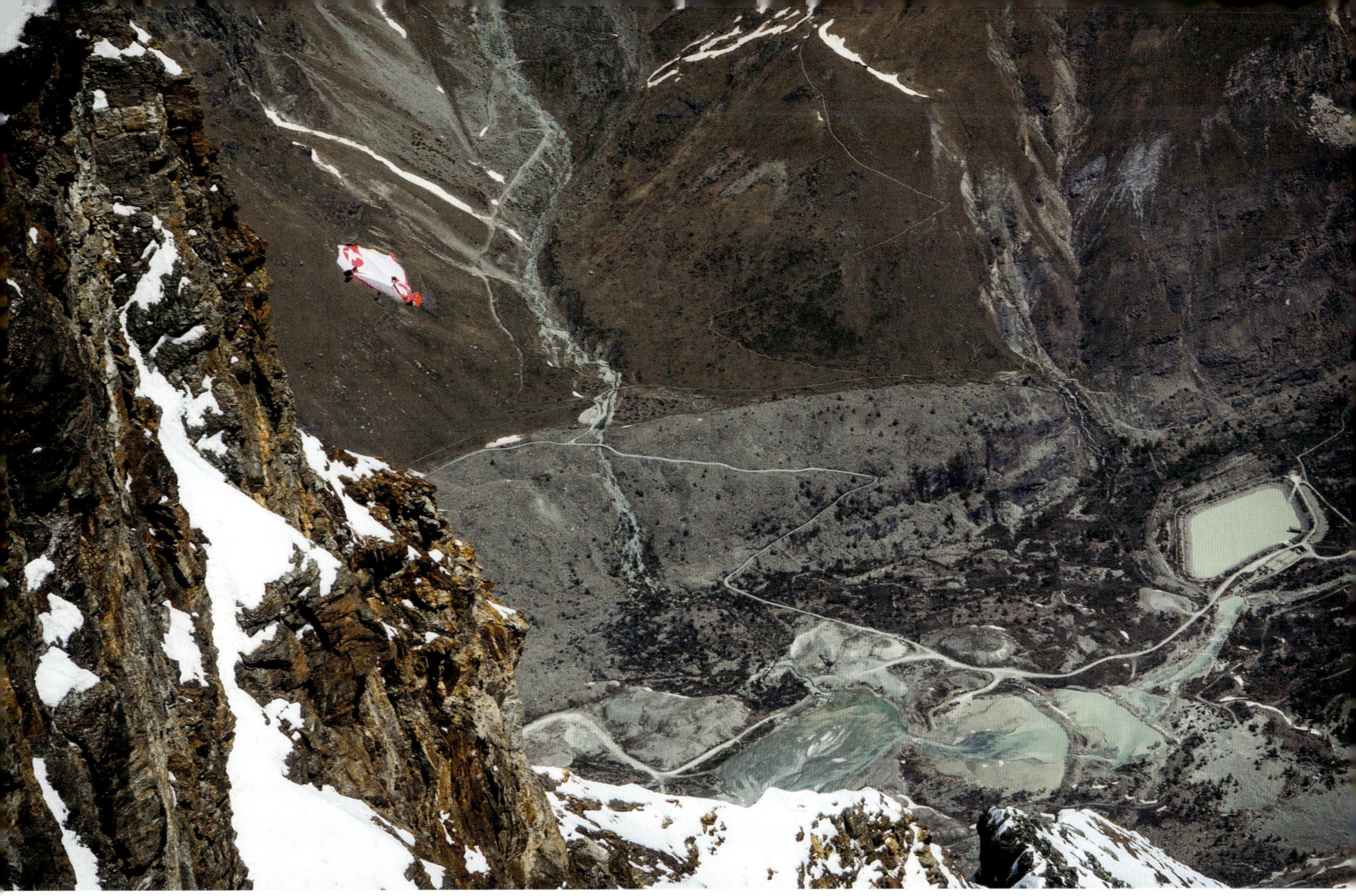

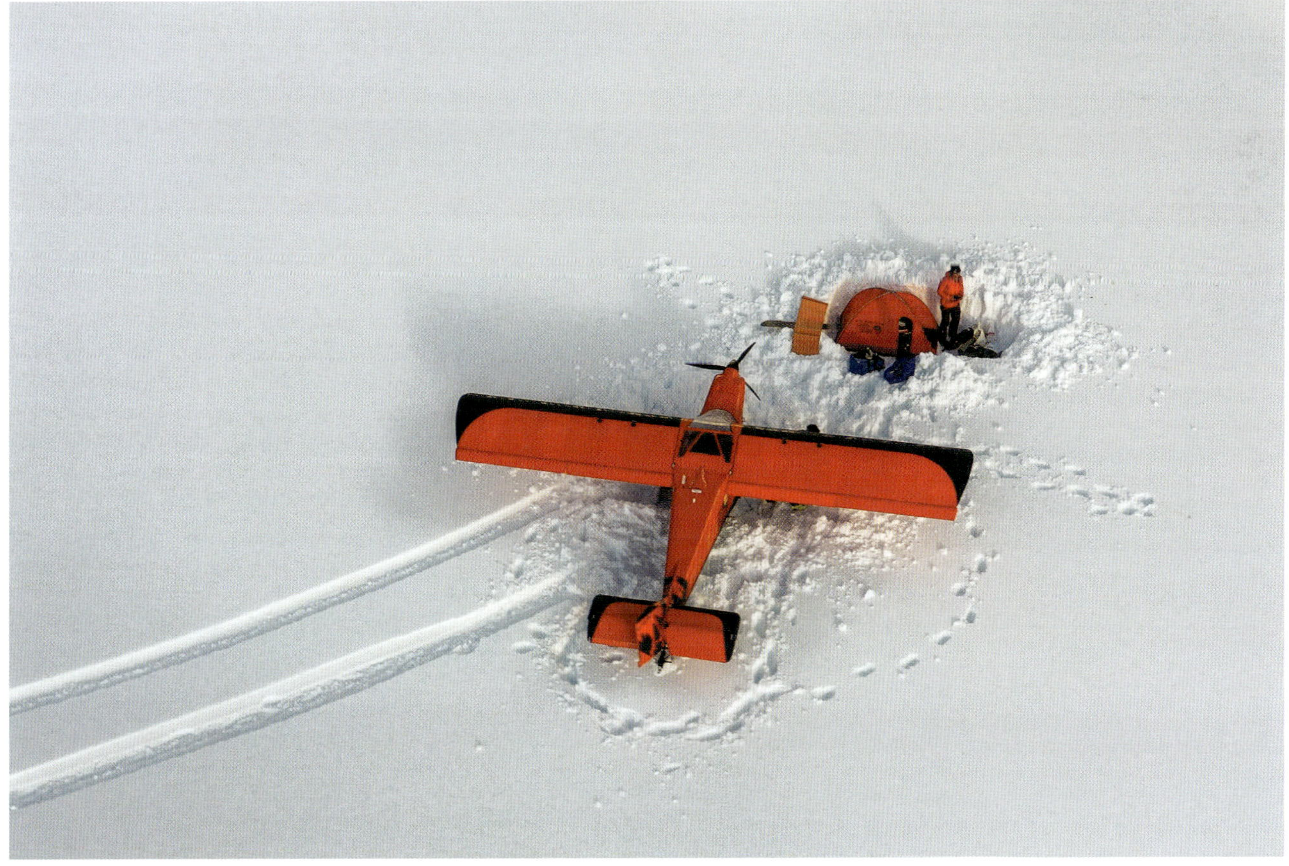

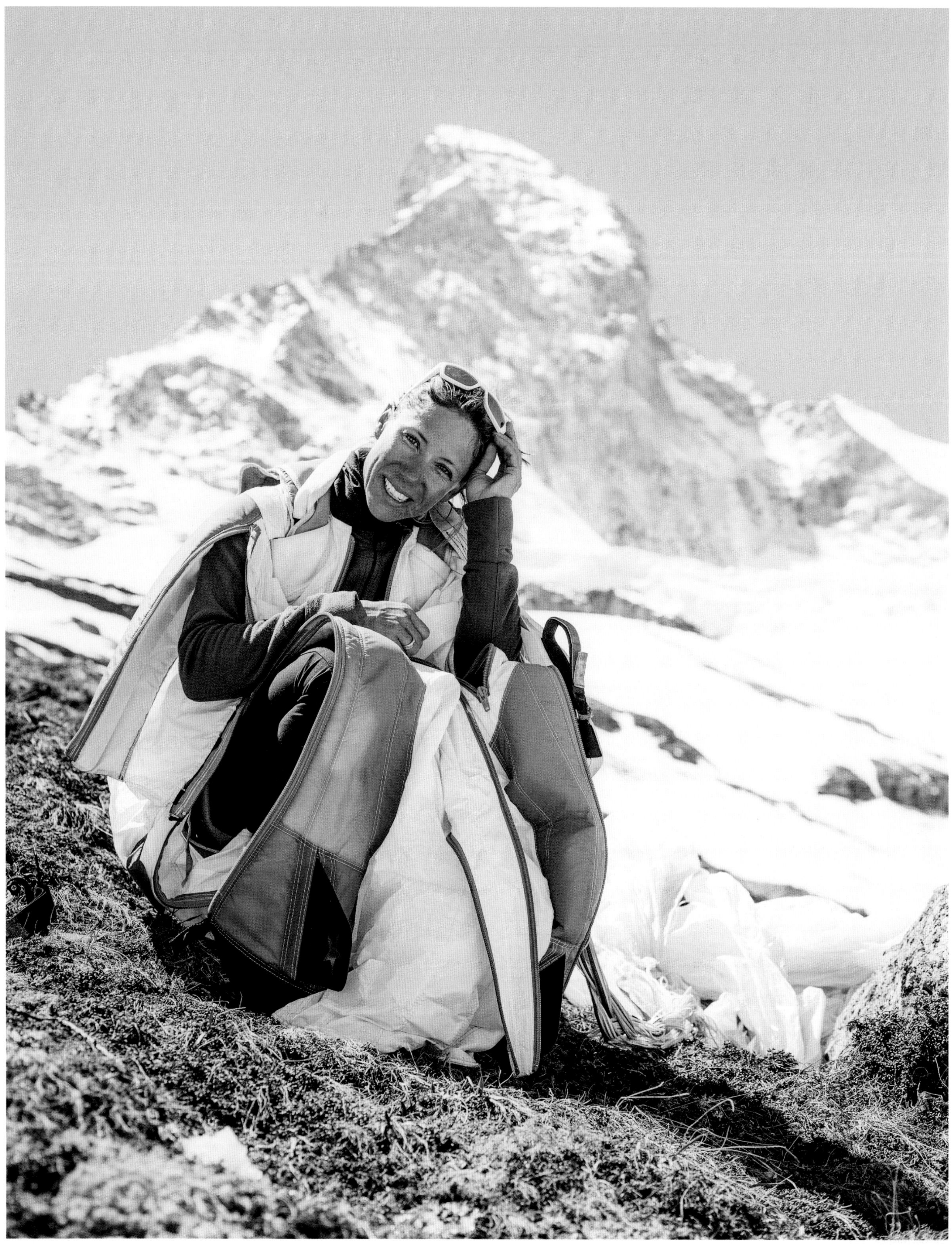

△ Matterhorn, Valais, Switzerland   ▷ △△ Bisotun Wall, Kermanshah, Iran   ▷ △ Verbier, Switzerland

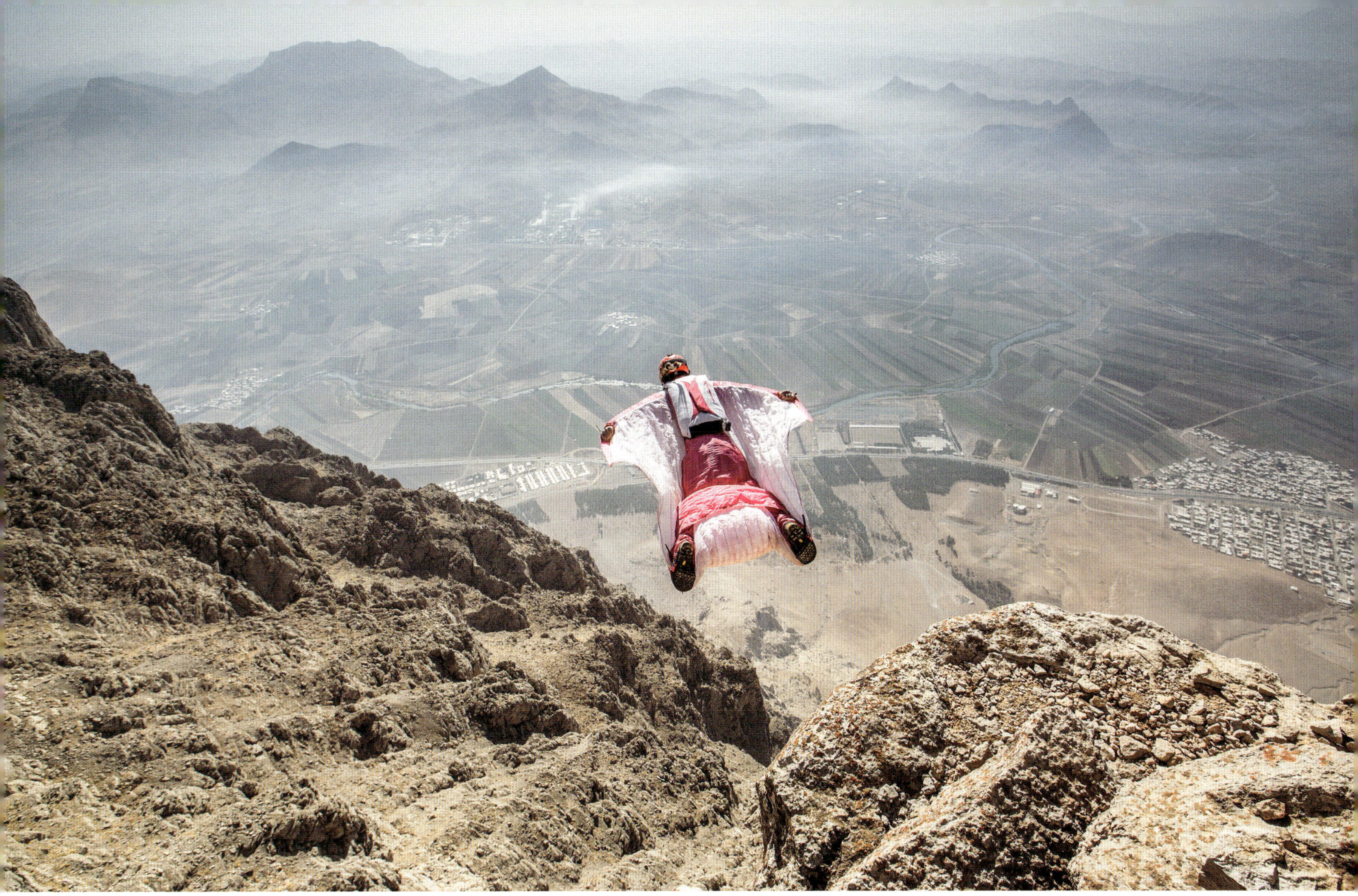

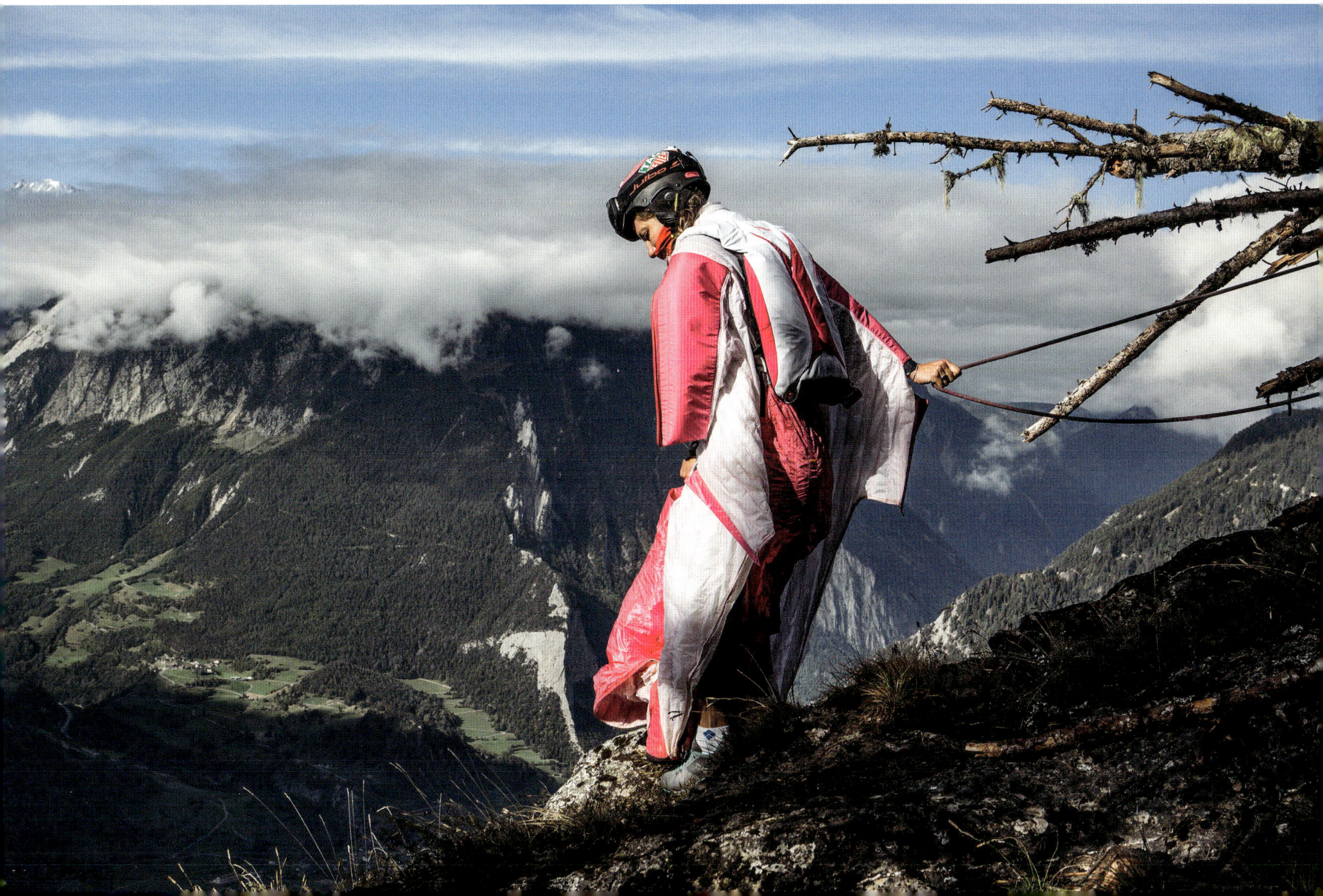

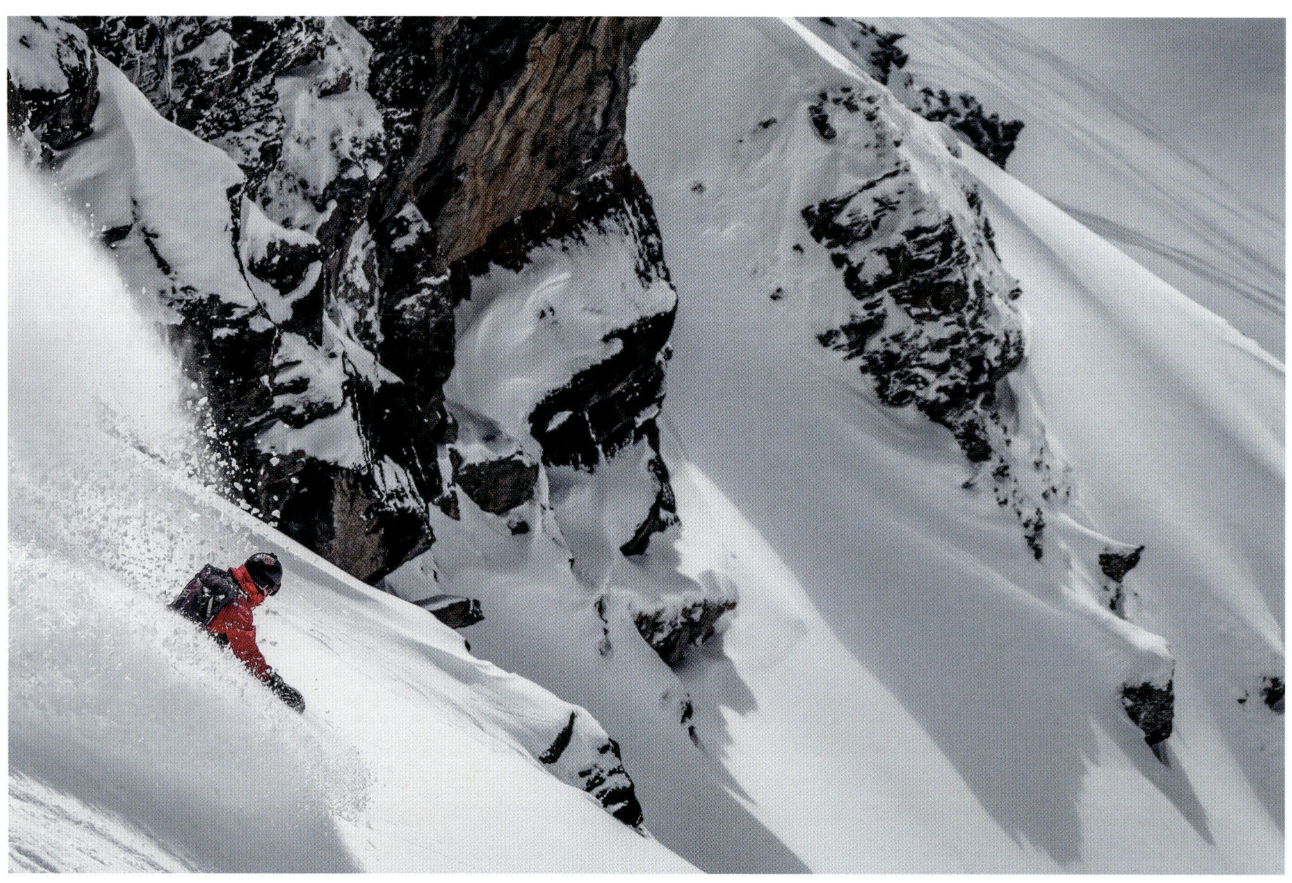

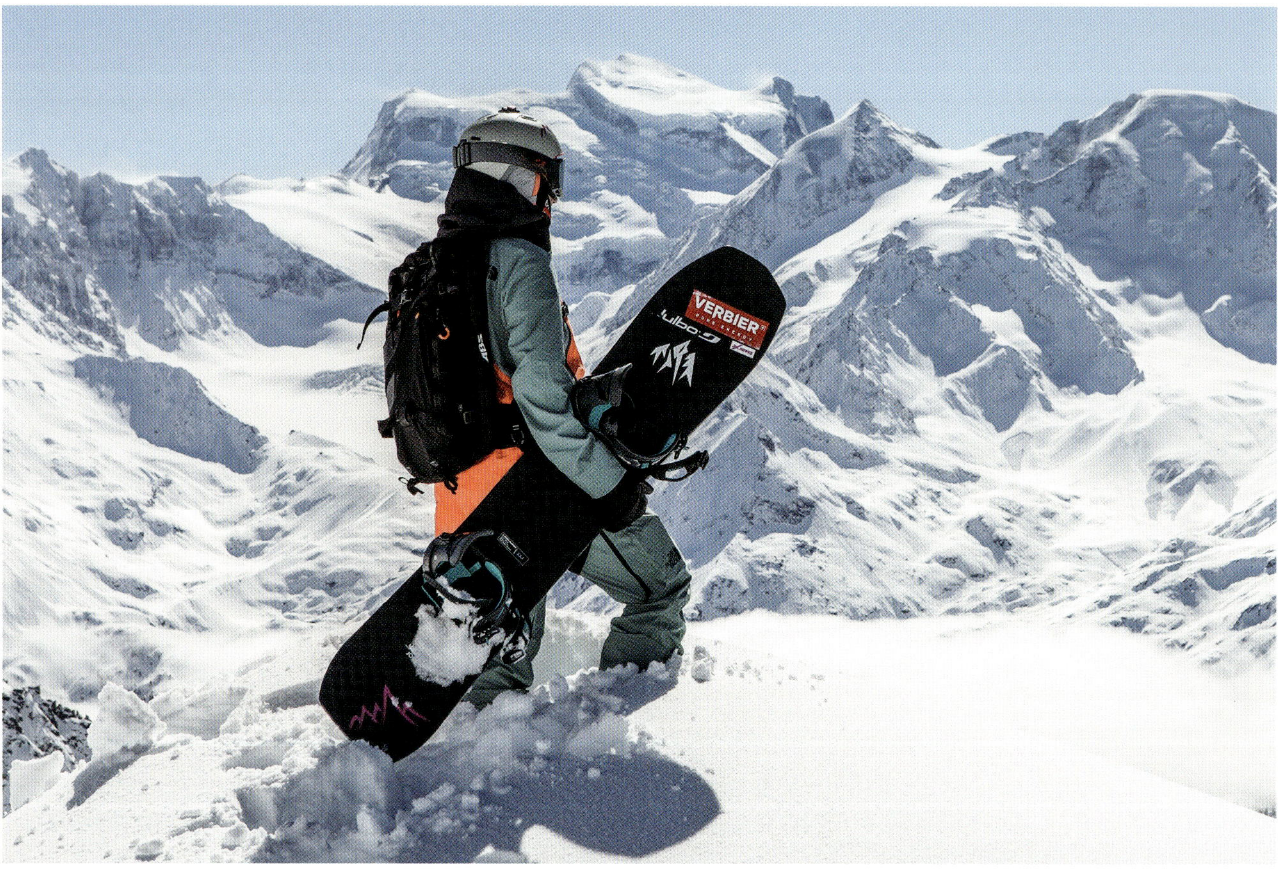

   Verbier, Switzerland

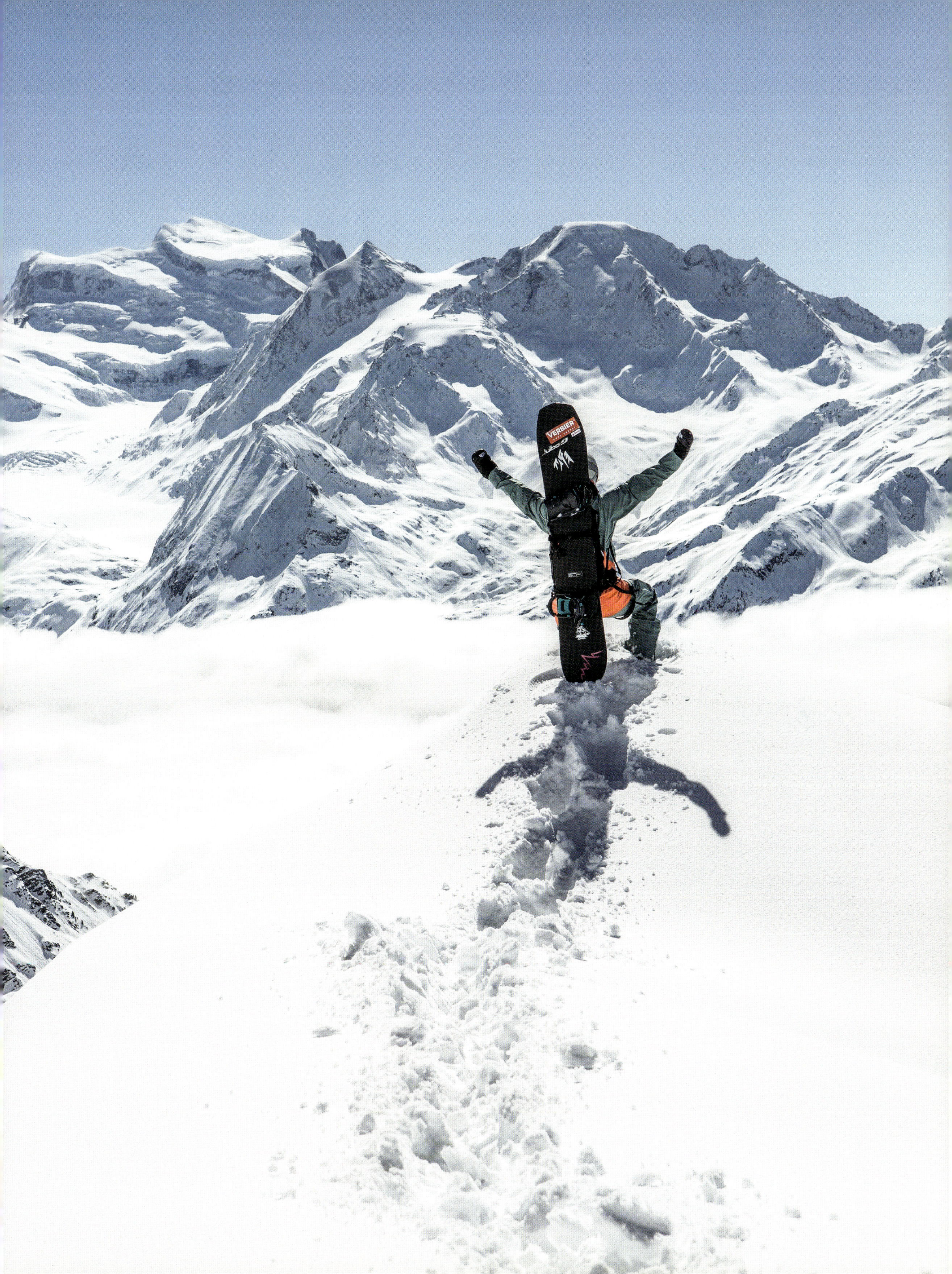

VERBIER
Julbo
JONES

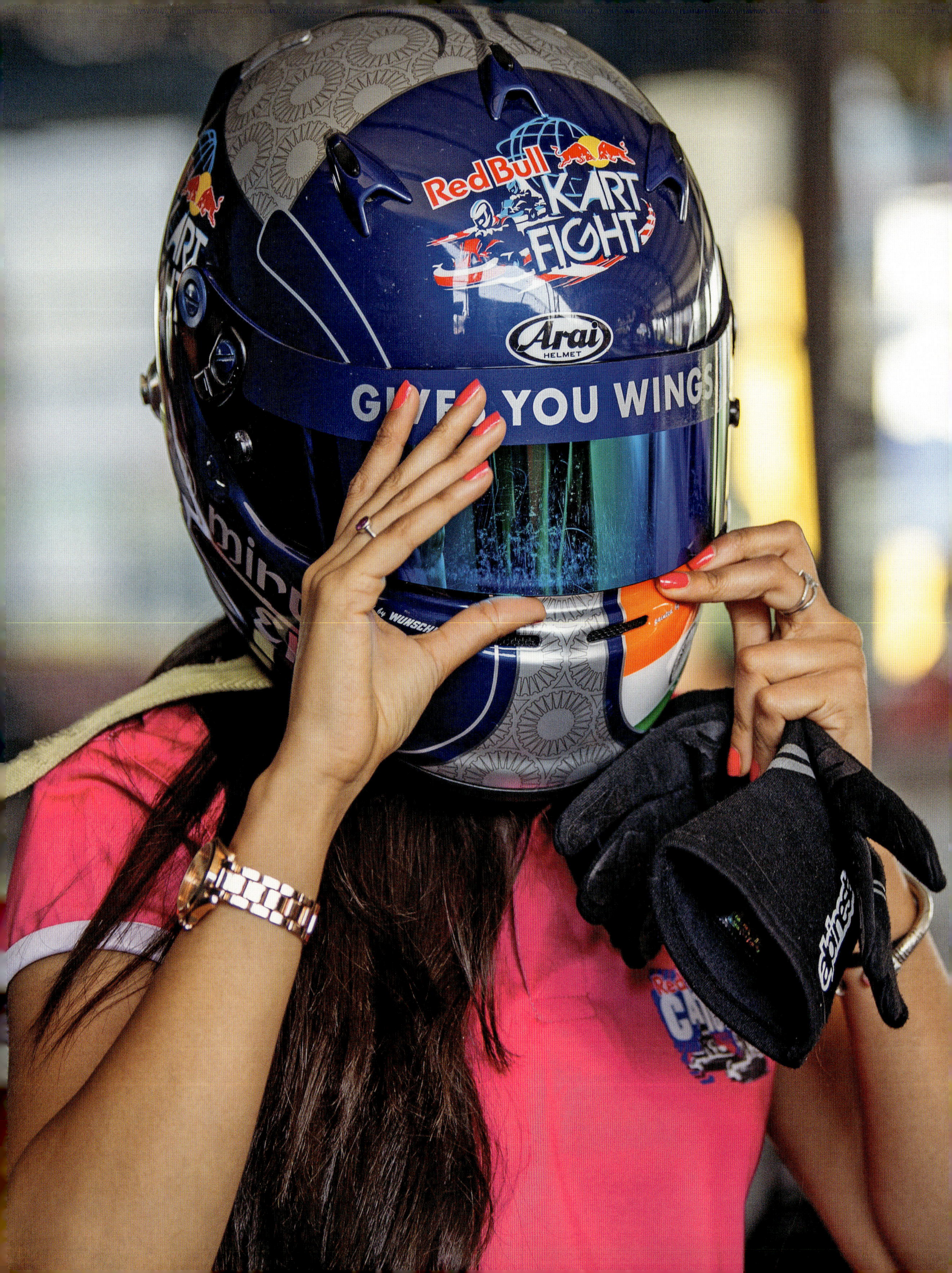

Red Bull KART FIGHT
Arai HELMET
GIVES YOU WINGS

Mira Erda
Racing driver

@mira_erda

My racing journey began when I was eight, when my father set up a Go Karting track out of his passion for speed. After ramming the Go Kart into the wall my first time driving, I started practicing with my brothers and eventually beat them. That's when Dad popped the question: "Are you interested in motorsports?" I was completely clueless as to what he meant, but said yes nevertheless, because I knew it involved travel and would get me out of going to school and doing homework!

I remember I'd gone to Pune to watch my first ever race and realized that this was a male-dominated sport. Dad told me we would all be competing with each other and I got really excited at the thought of getting to race with the guys! And so, I went to Kolhapur to train professionally, and within 25 days, I was in Hyderabad for my first national race.

The first time I got pole position, I was disqualified due to some technical issues; time and again, in 2017 and 2018, I finished last in races. My parents were my rock through it all. While Dad backed me up financially, Mom arranged notes for me and helped me study when we got back to the hotel, as we were always traveling.

Success came, and after winning multiple races in Go Karting, I shifted to driving Formula cars and became the youngest girl to participate in Formula racing in India. It's funny that I shake and shiver while delivering a fifteen-minute TED talk or even when sitting a driving license test, and yet when a race is about to start, I'm as calm as a millpond. I'm twenty now, and am working on a degree in journalism alongside motorsports. I believe it's time for me to go international and compete in F3 races; I'm already racing at the highest level in India.

What makes me most proud, however, is when I take off my helmet and people say, "Oh look, it's a girl." Just those five words justify what I've worked to prove for most of my life, and they're an answer to all the people who questioned my father's decision to believe in my dreams.

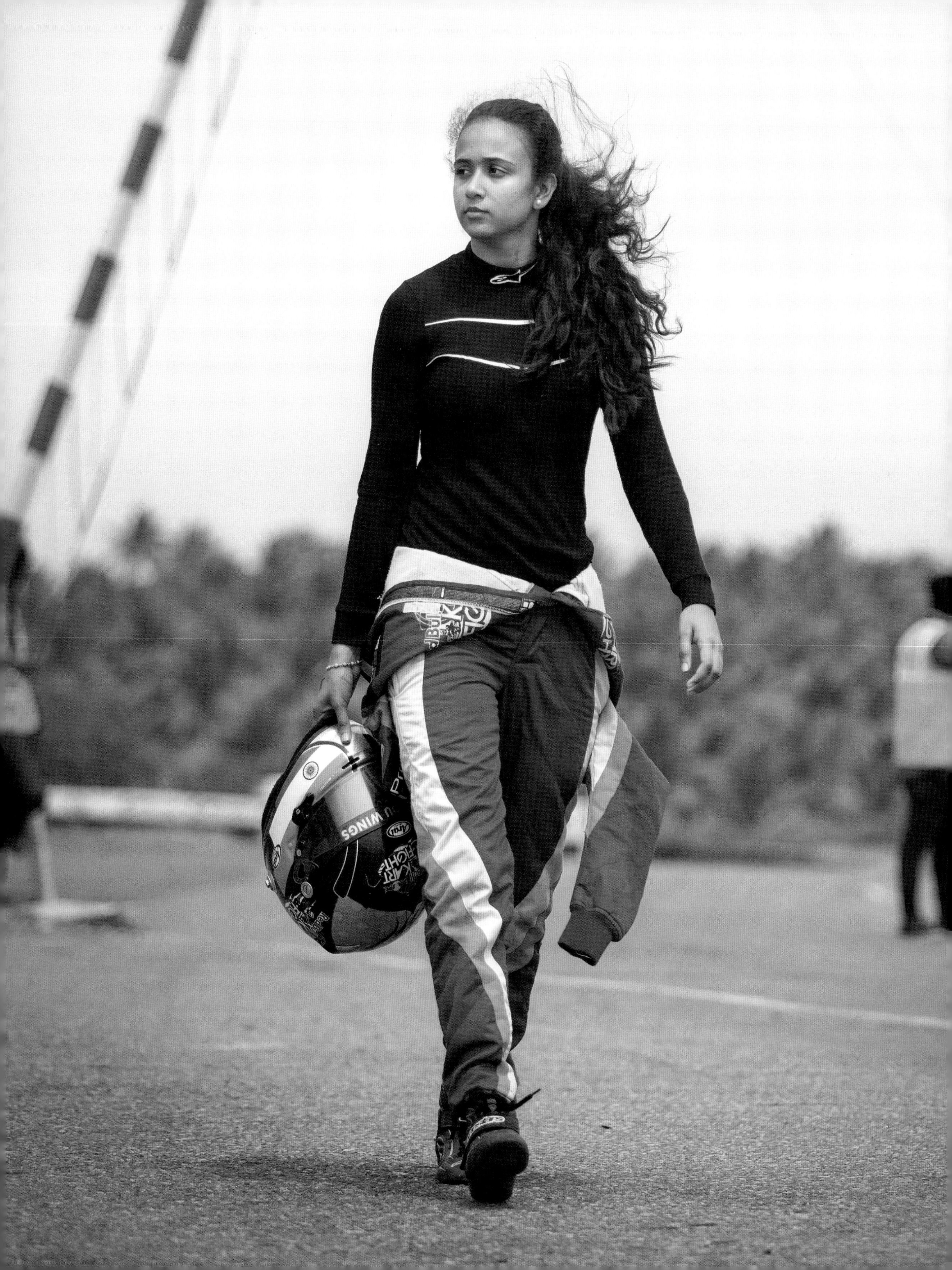

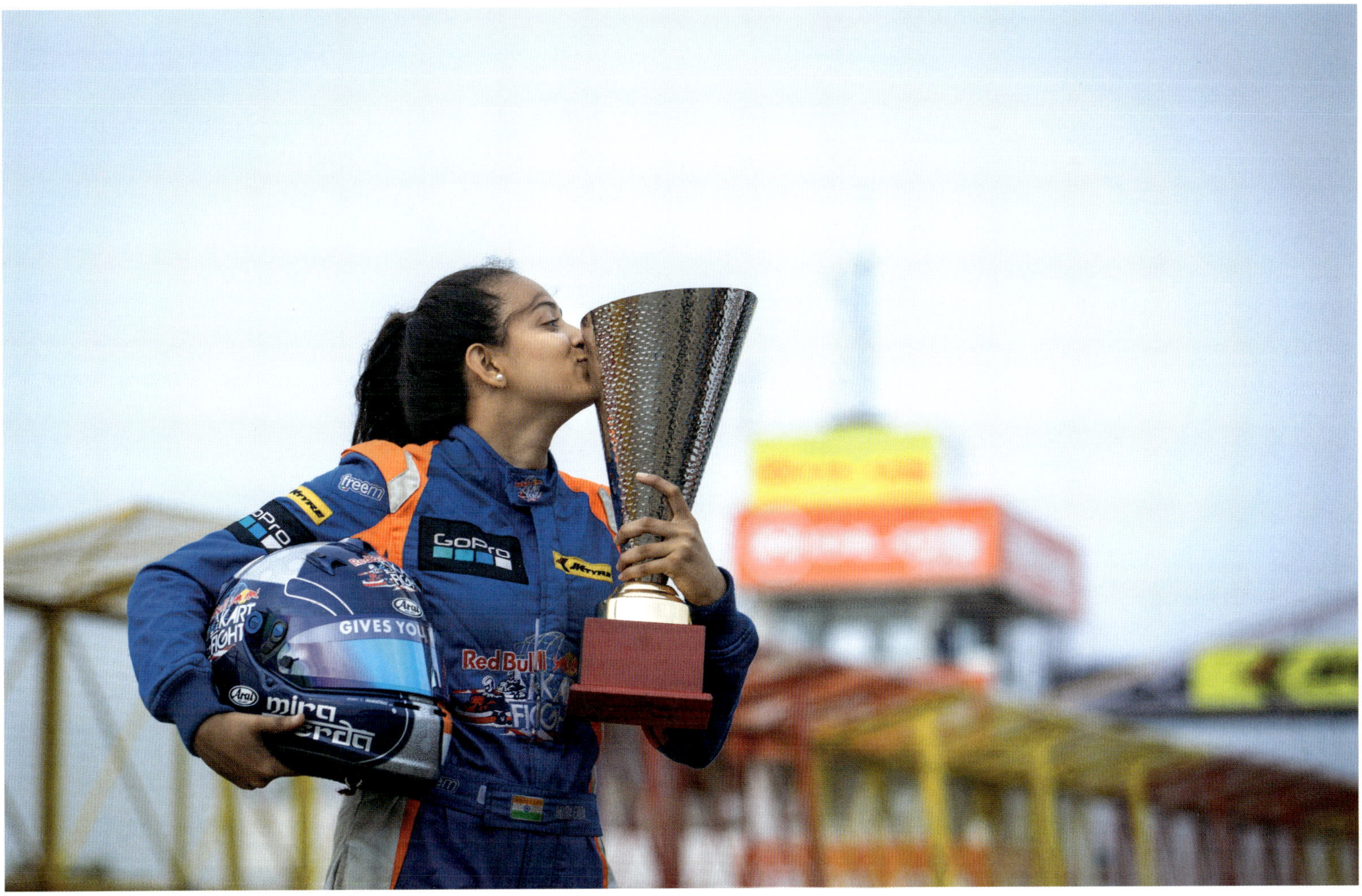
GoPro
Red Bull
GIVES YOU
mira erda

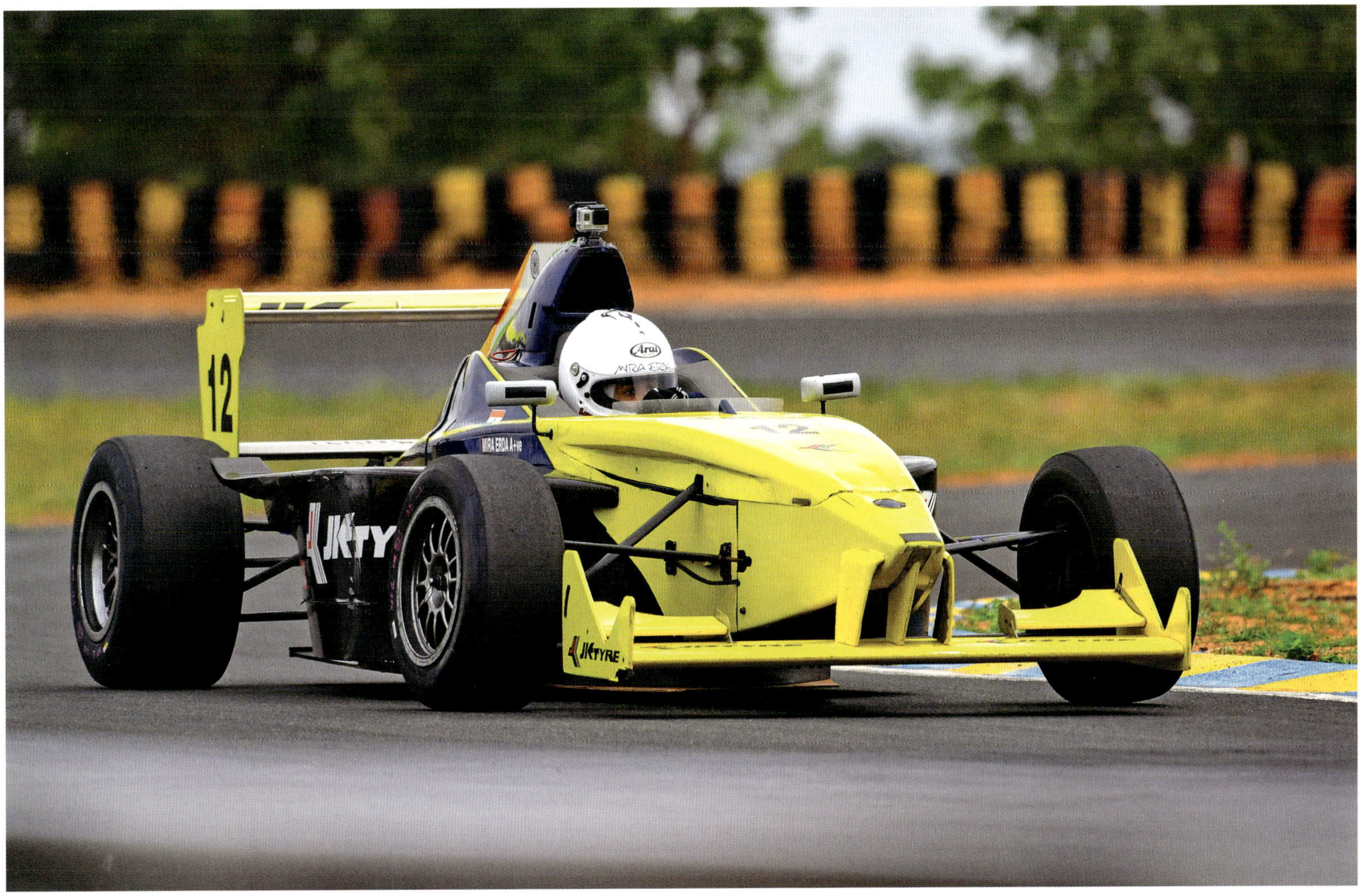
12
JKTY
JKTYRE

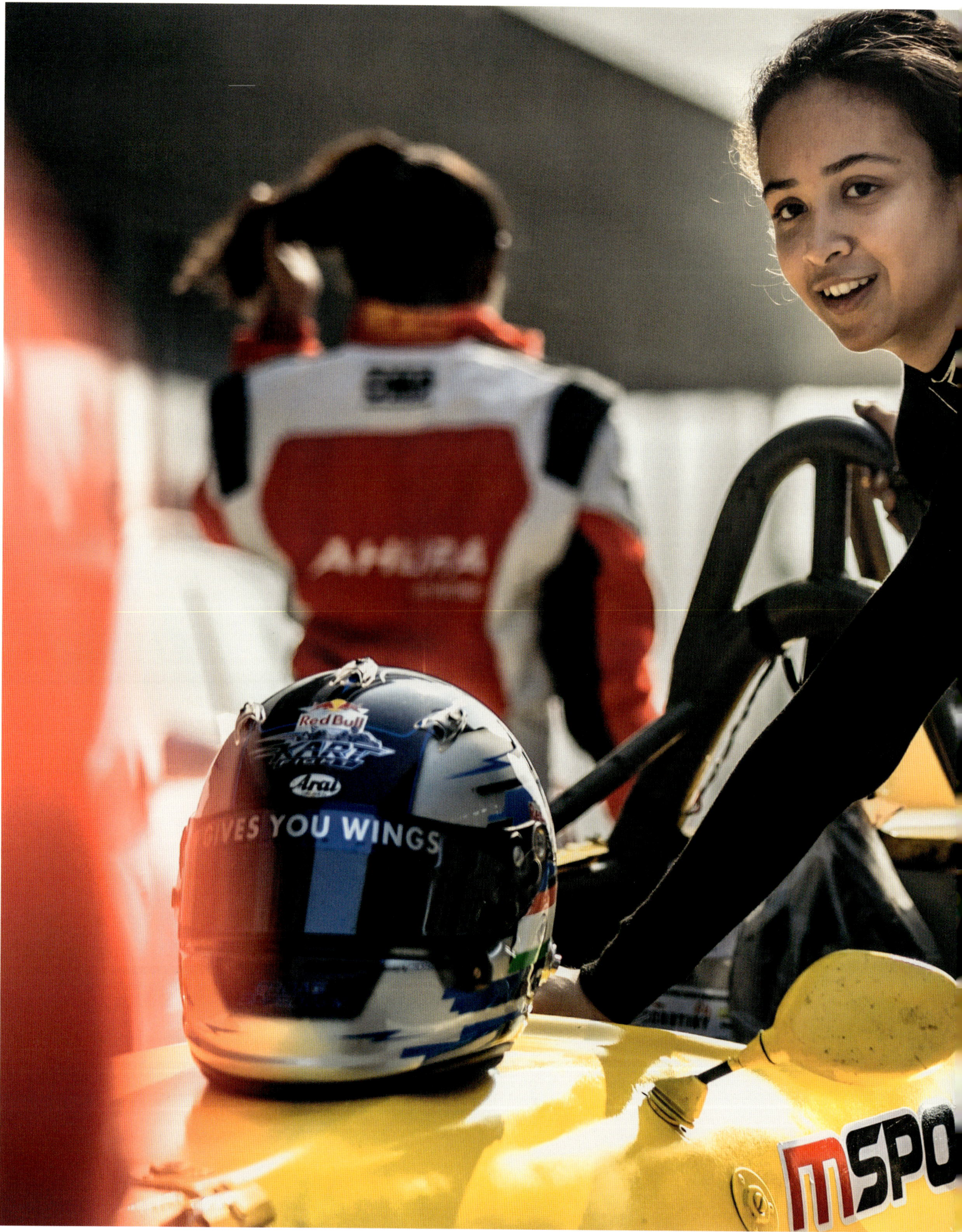

Red Bull
KART FIGHT
Arai
GIVES YOU WINGS
mSPO

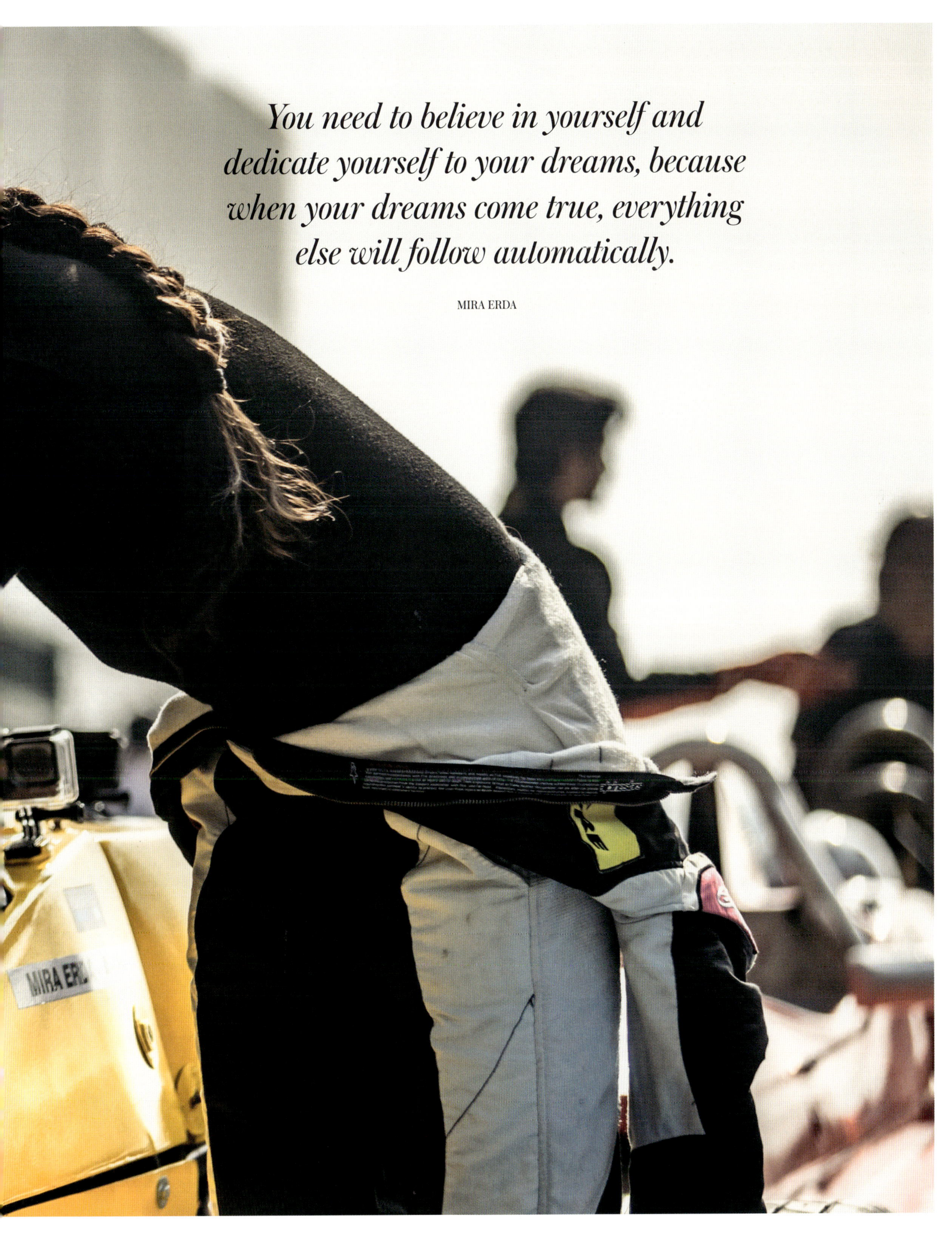

You need to believe in yourself and dedicate yourself to your dreams, because when your dreams come true, everything else will follow automatically.

MIRA ERDA

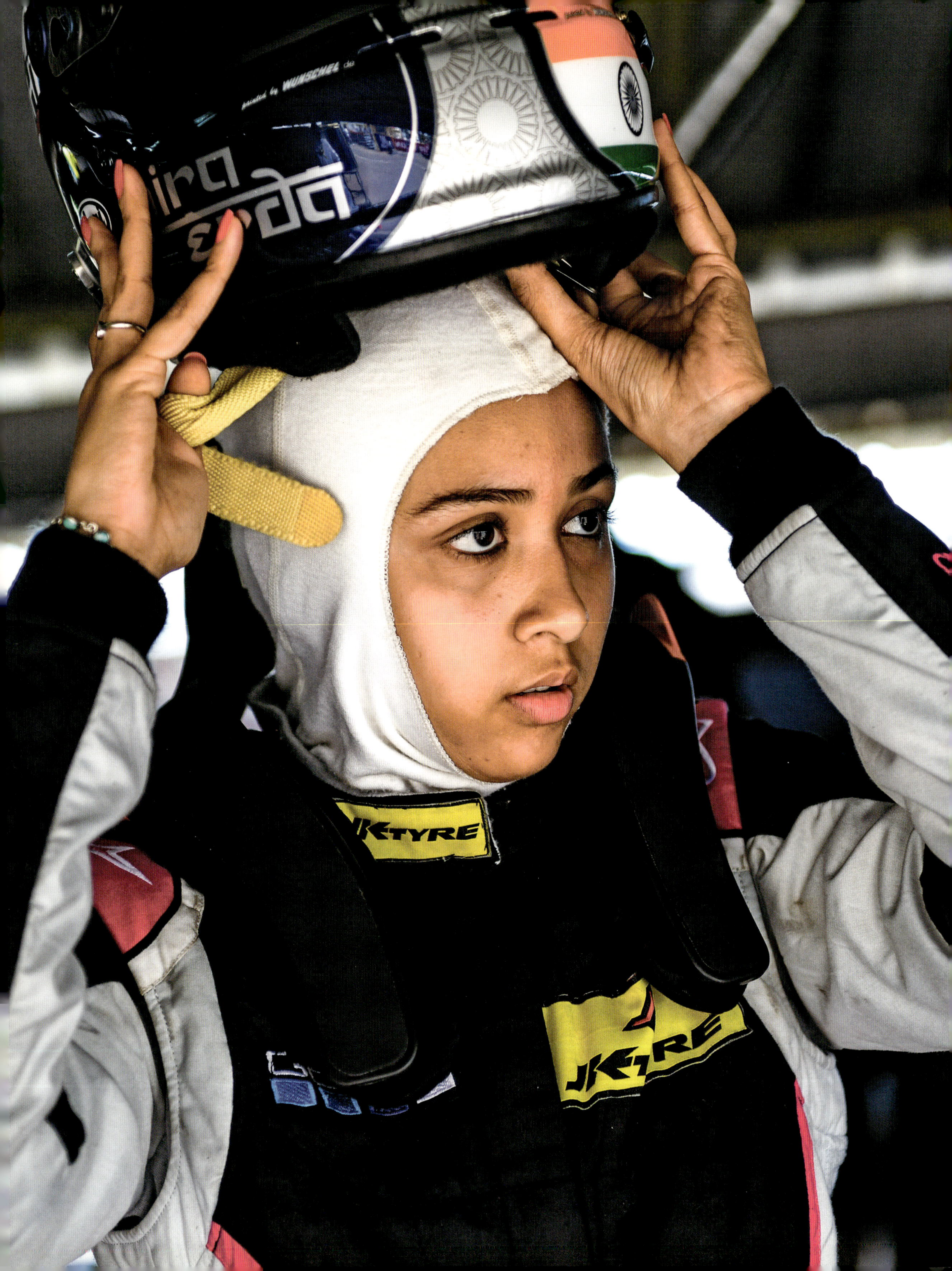
ira
nda
JK TYRE
JK TYRE

*What makes me most proud
is when I take off my helmet and
people say, "Oh look, it's a girl."*

MIRA ERDA

Iris Schmidbauer

Cliff diver

@irisschmidbauer
iris-schmidbauer.com

My favorite part of cliff diving is when I feel the rocks underneath my feet before I dive into the foaming ocean. That's when I feel connected with nature; that is real cliff diving.

My name is Iris Schmidbauer and I am a professional cliff diver. I am the best cliff diver in Germany. I'm also in the top eight in the world and one of only three athletes who compete in the hardest dives. What makes me stand out in my cliff diving career is the fact that when I started this sport, I was more or less self-taught, with no athletic background. I was only diving for fun at first, but then it got more serious. I had never seen the inside of a gym until I was nearly twenty. And it wasn't until then that I realized that much more was involved in this sport, and that most of the training is done on dry land.

Only five months after I started training for cliff diving and working with coaches, I competed at my first World Cup. I'm convinced that with the right support, diligence, and hard training, I will become the next World Champion!

When I'm up there, I have to overcome my fear every single time. But if I take the risk and jump, when I hit the water, swim my way up to the surface, and take a very fast breath, it is the best feeling ever and I want to do it all over again. When I'm not training in the pool, I'm on adventurous road trips to find cliff diving spots, or going surfing, skateboarding, mountain biking, climbing, or snowboarding. I hope to inspire people to embrace their free spirit and live an adventurous life.

  ▷ Azores, Portugal ▷▷ Sisikon, Switzerland

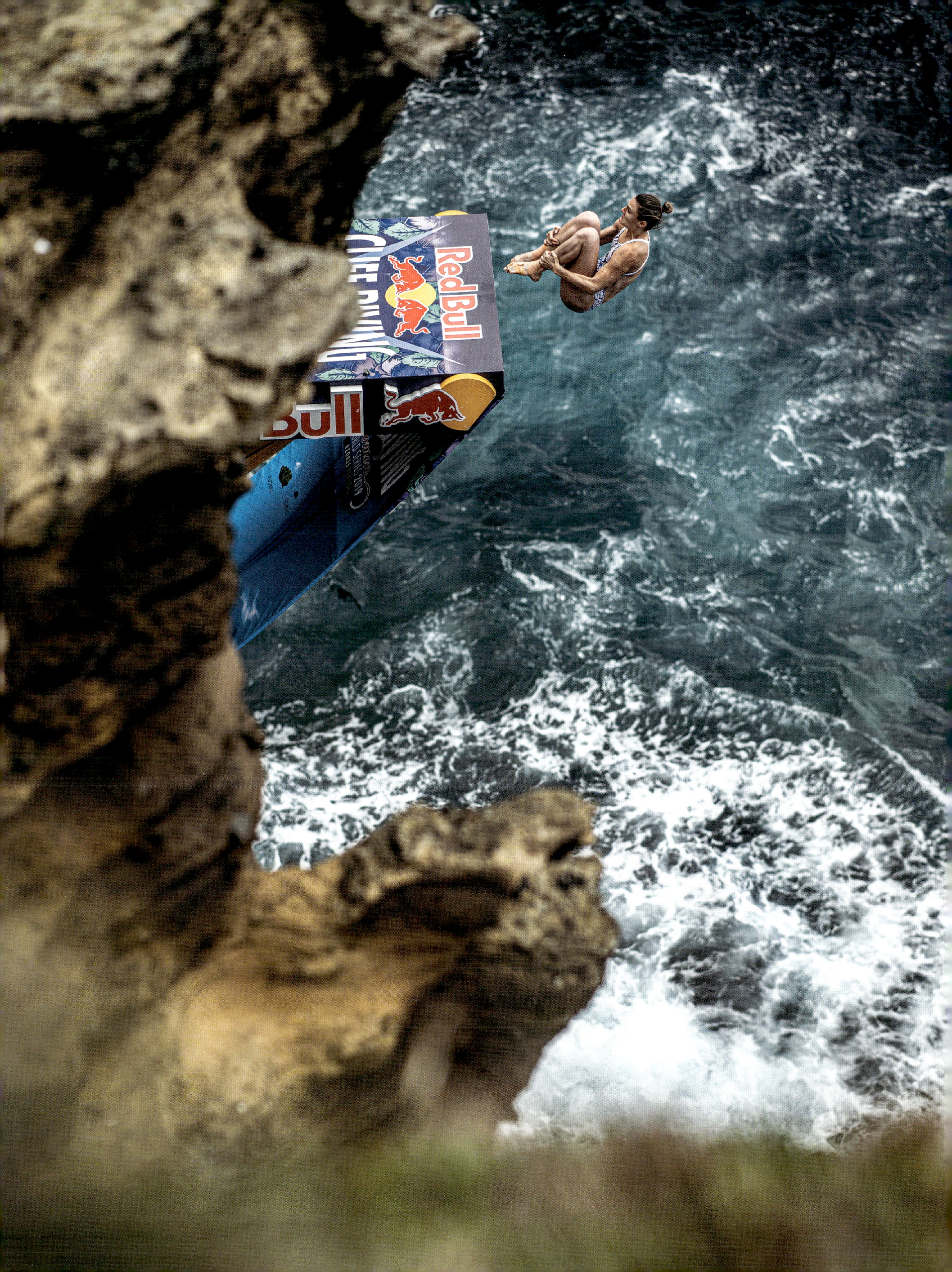

Red Bull
CLIFF DIVING
Bull

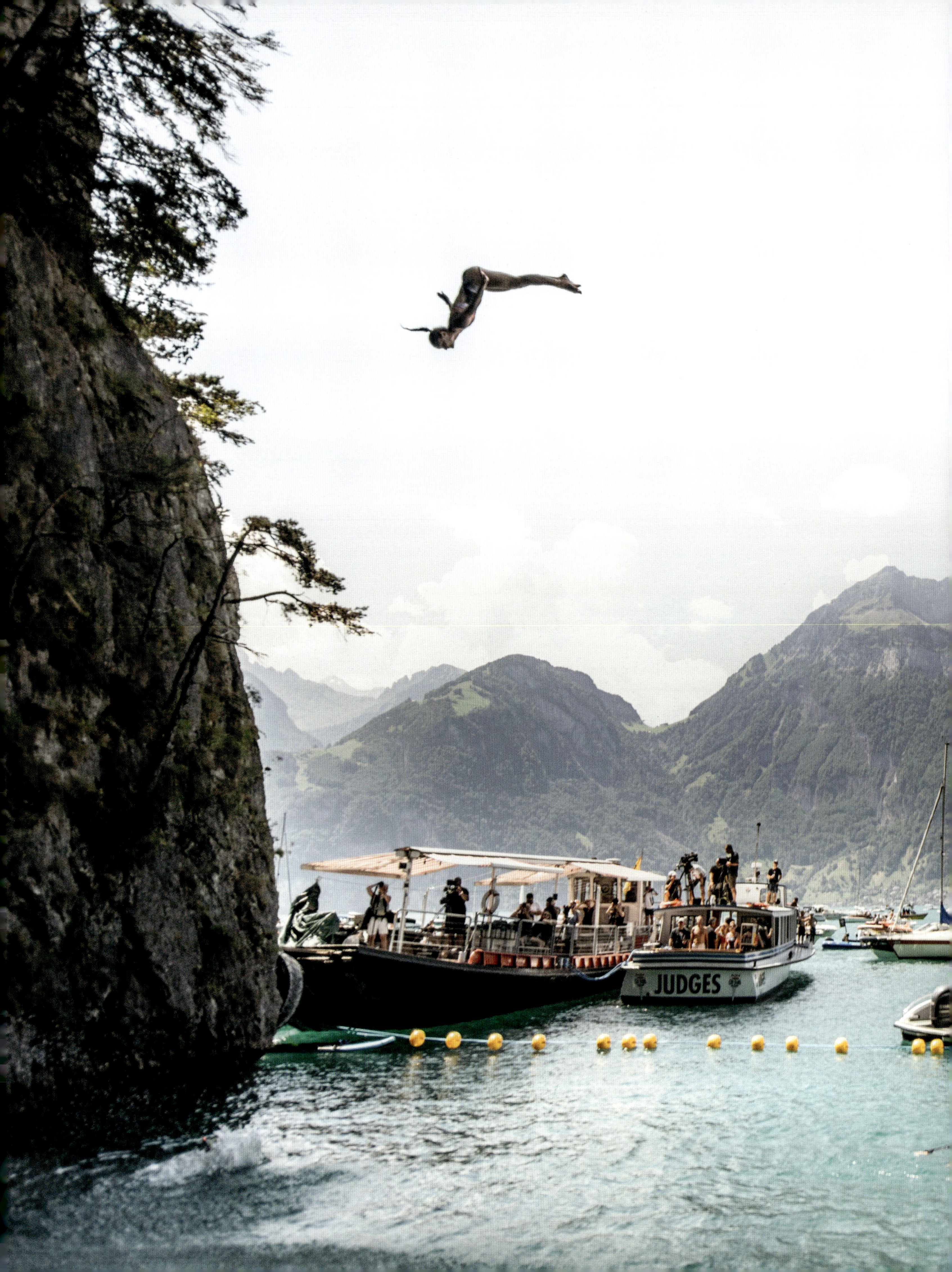
JUDGES

When I'm up there,
I have to overcome my fear
every single time.

IRIS SCHMIDBAUER

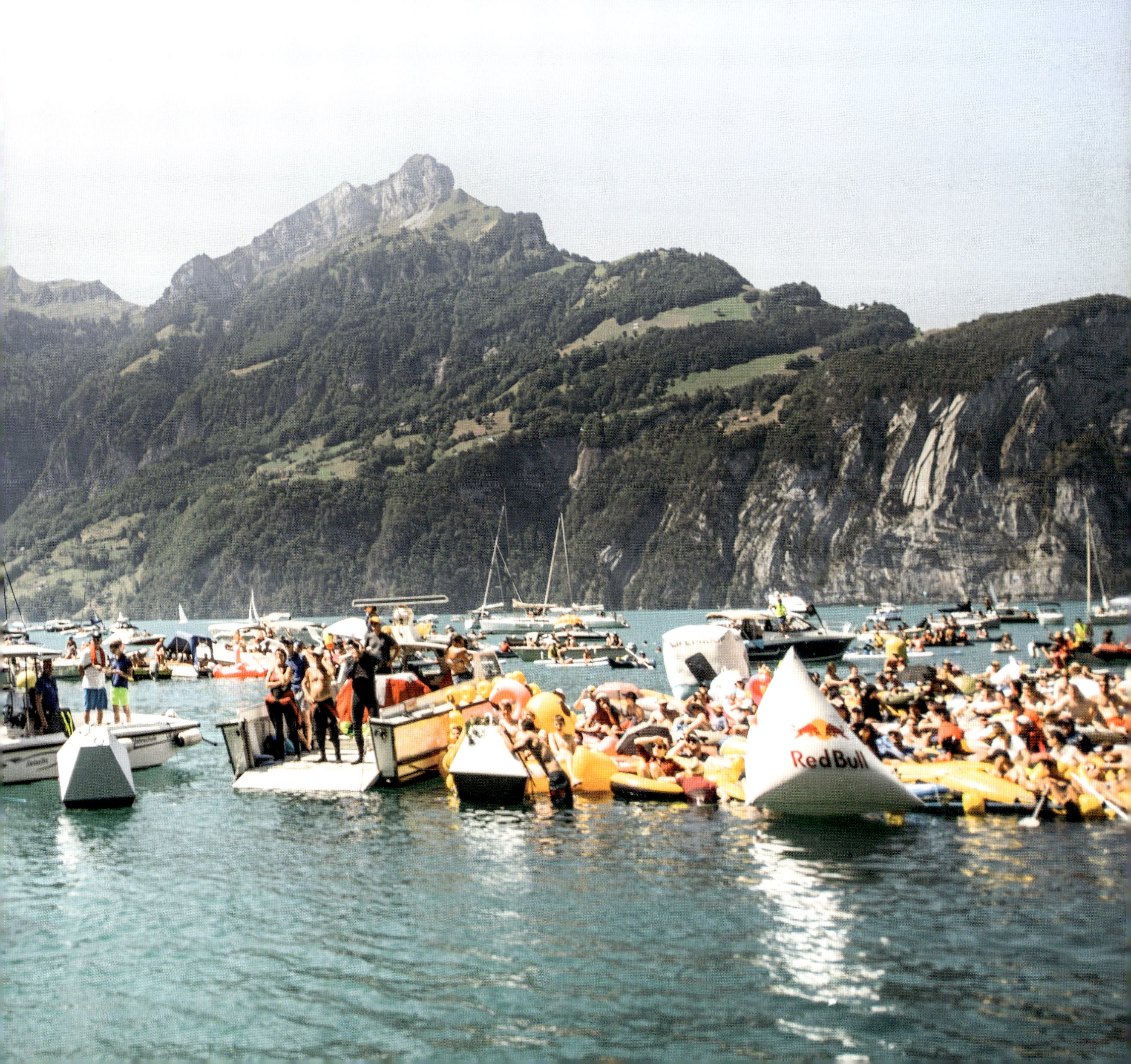

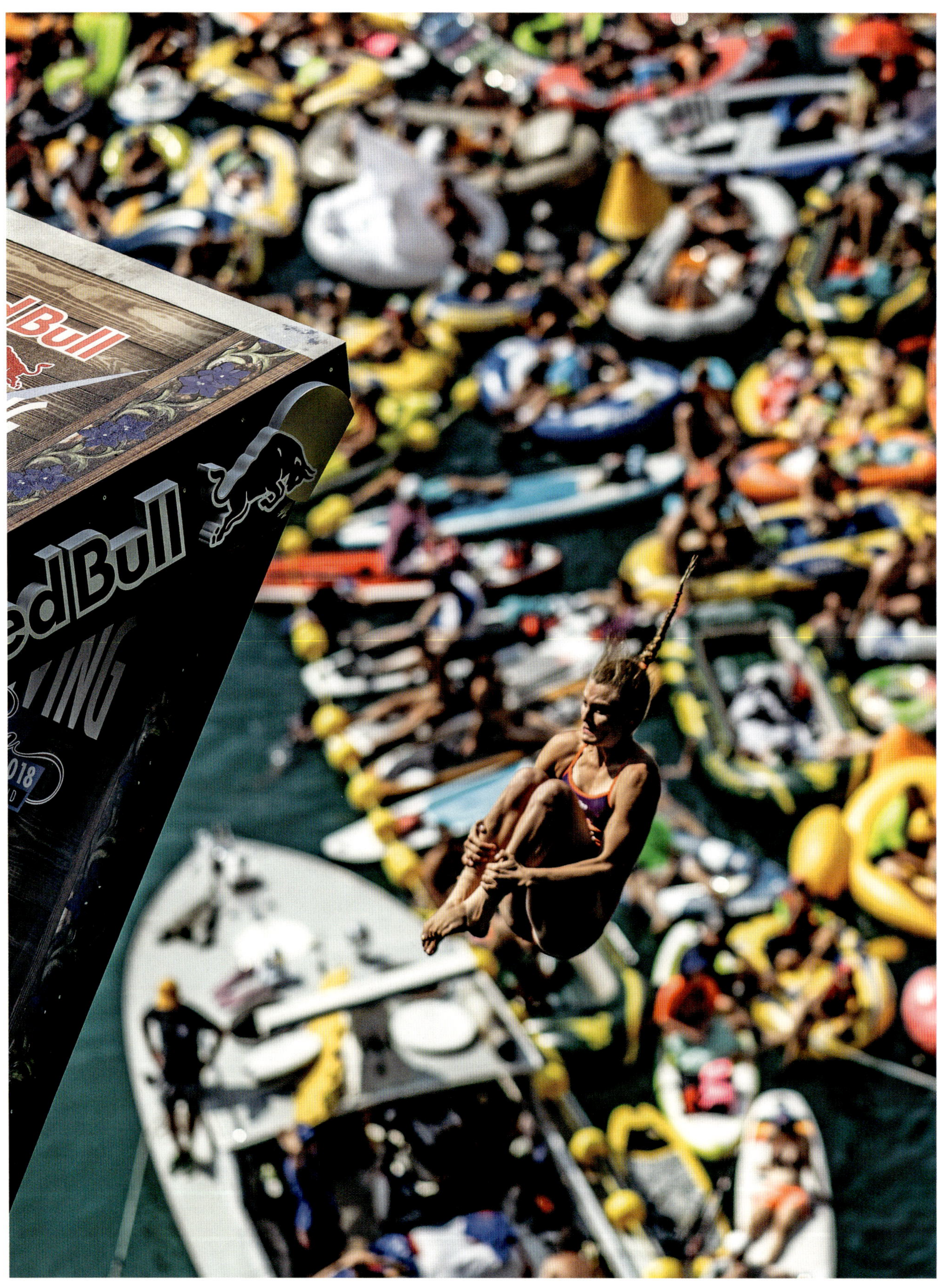

  △ Sisikon, Switzerland   ▷ Azores, Portugal

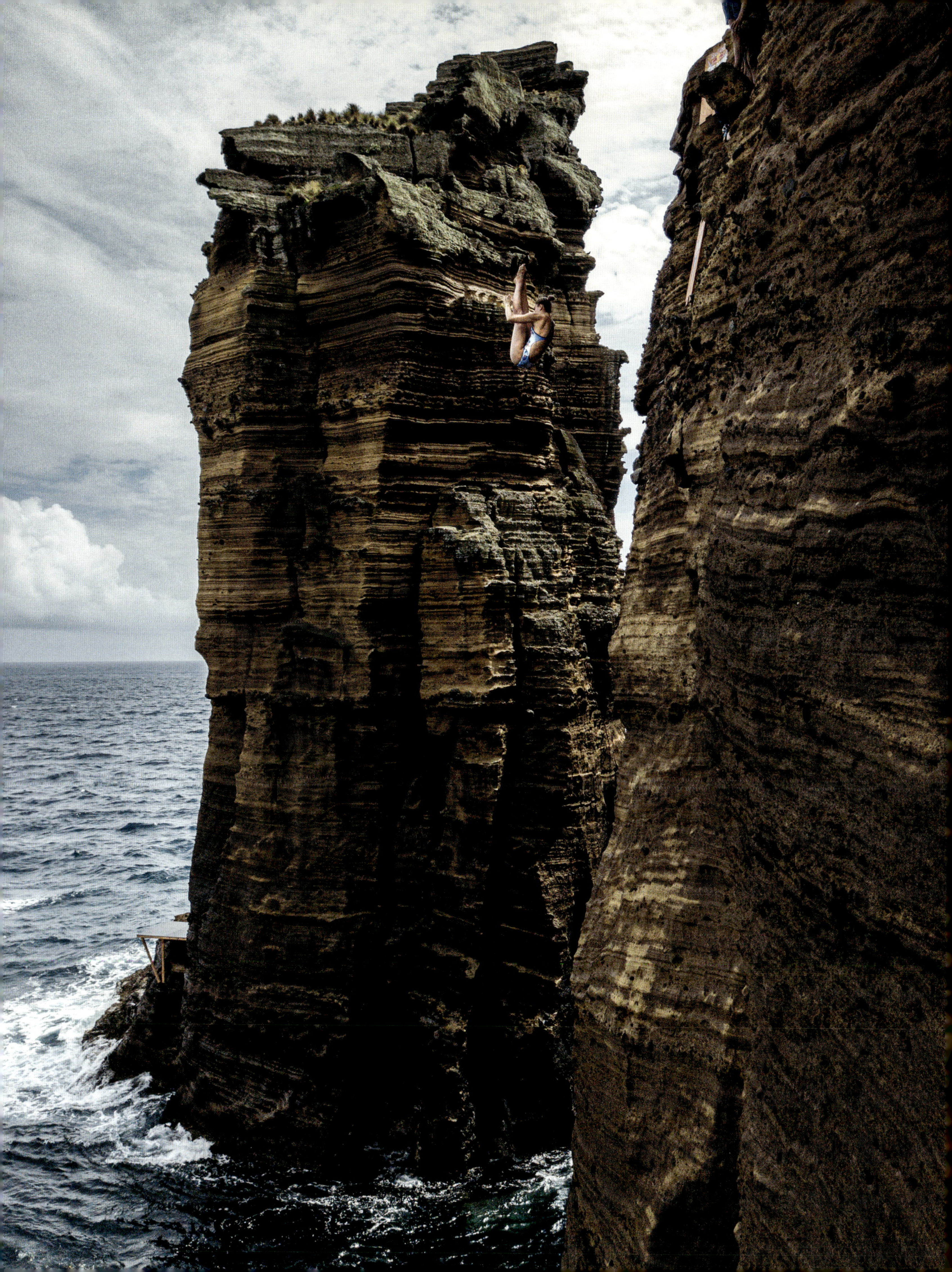

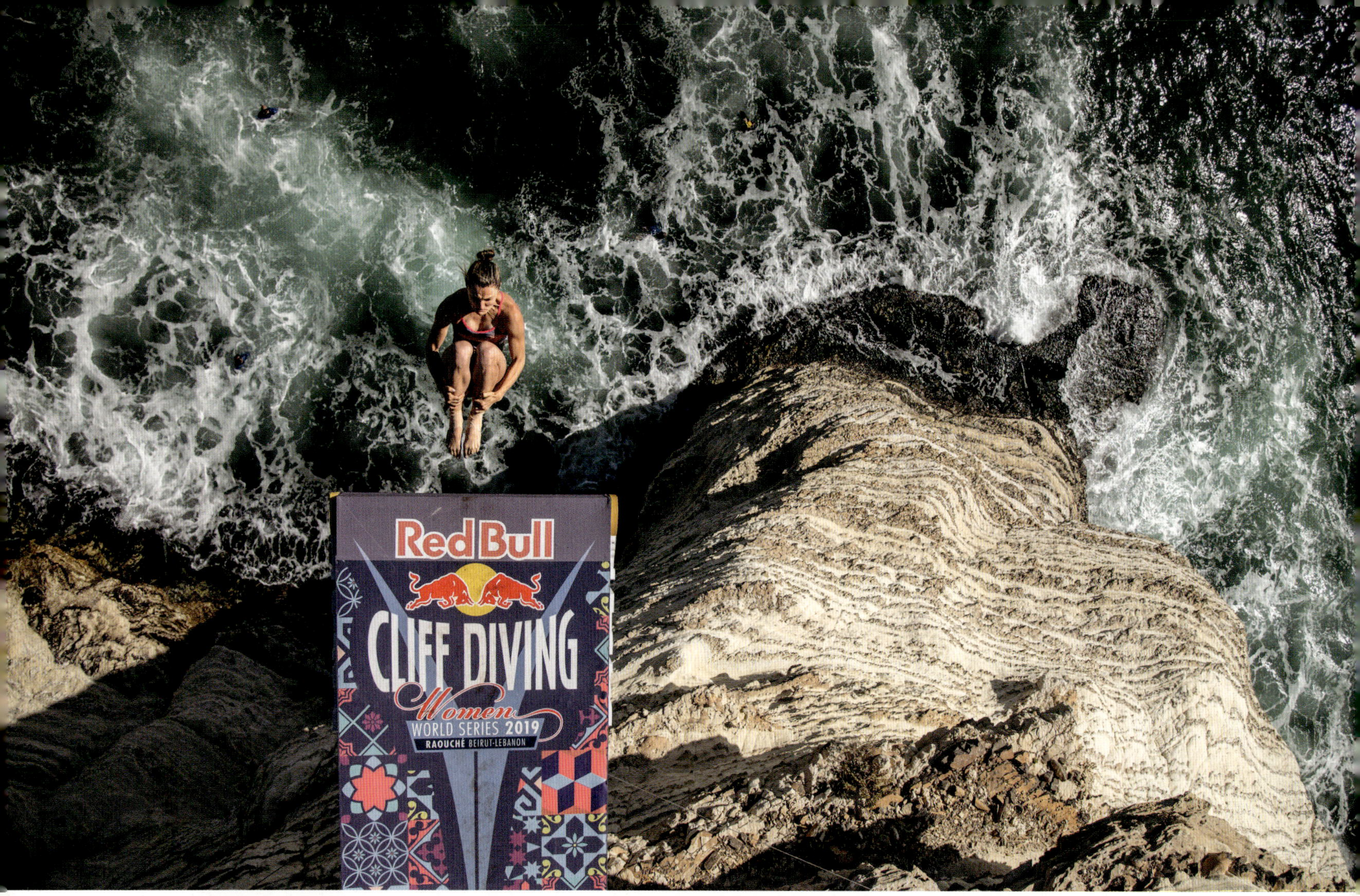

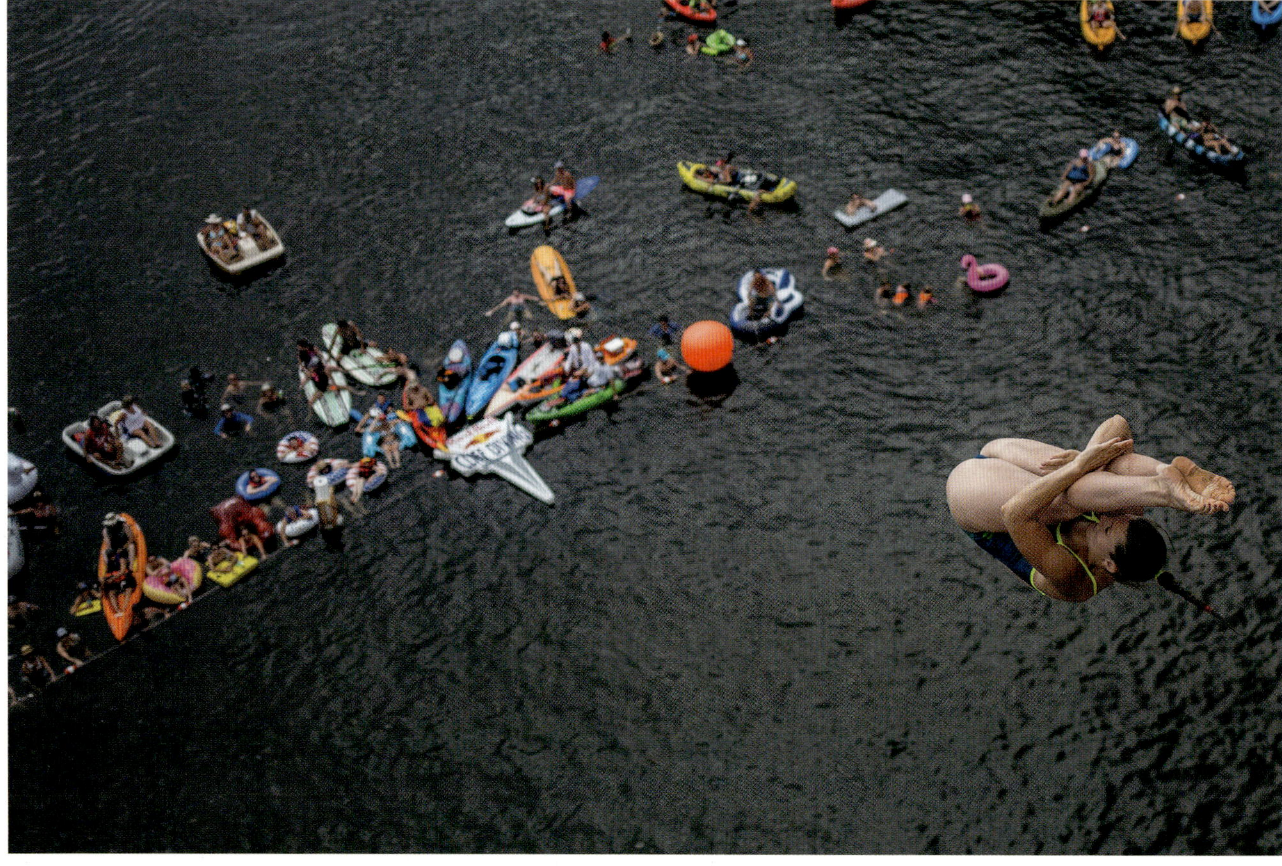

   △△ Beirut, Lebanon   △ Possum Kingdom Lake, Texas, USA   ▷ Azores, Portugal

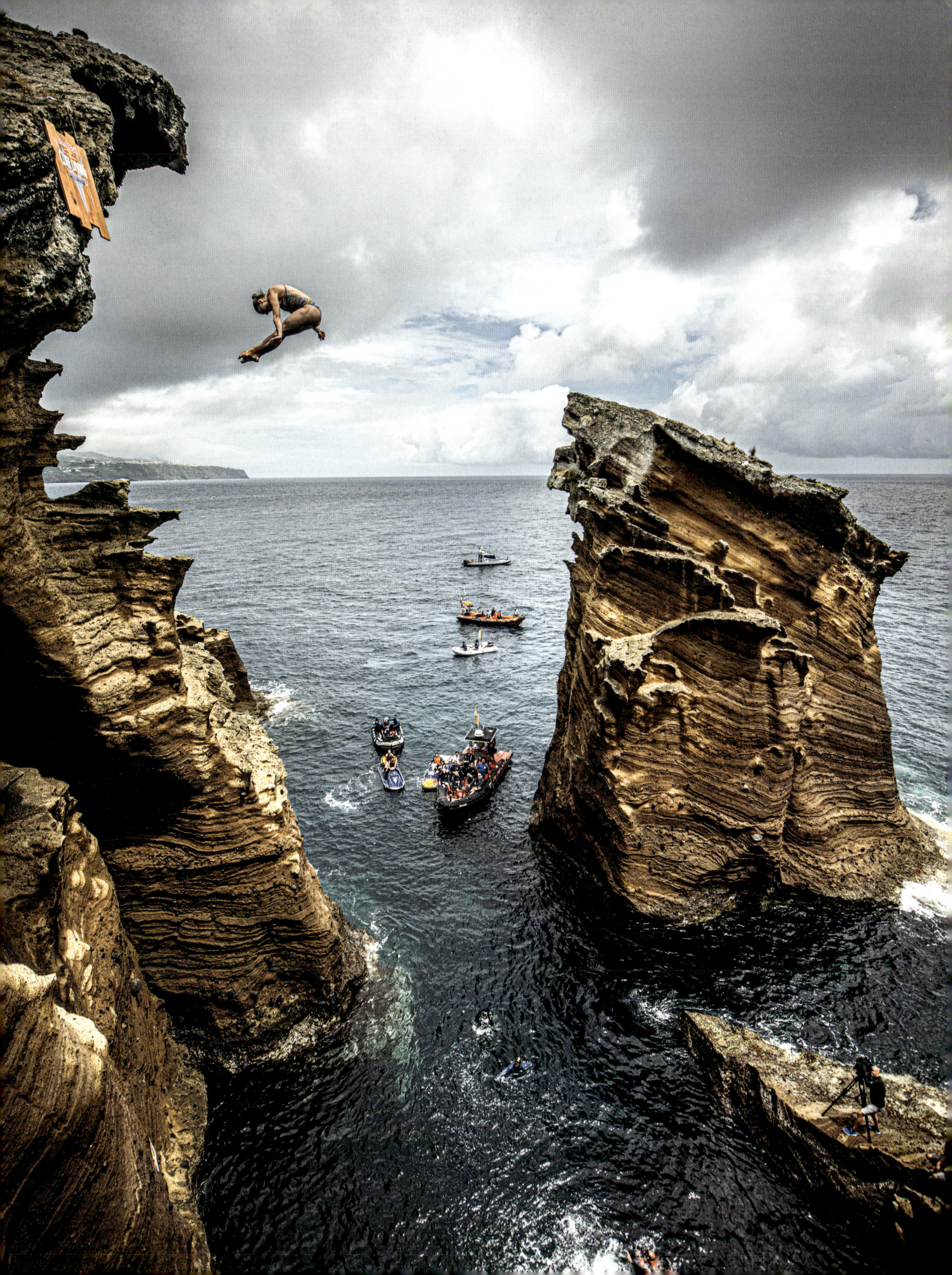

Red Bull
Cliff Diving

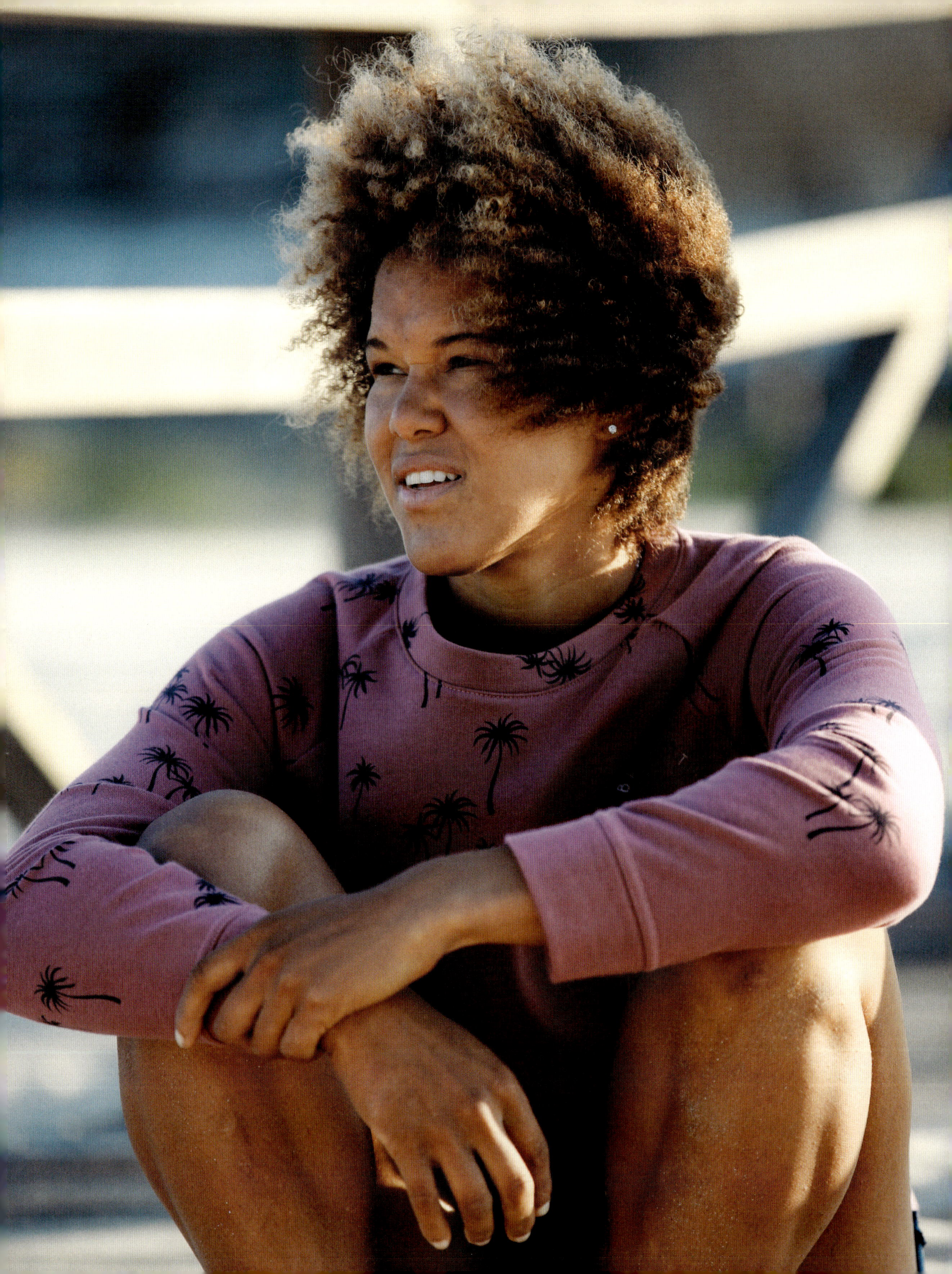

Sarah-Quita Offringa
Windsurfer

@cabeibusha
sarah-quita.com

Hi! I'm Sarah-Quita Offringa and I'm twenty-nine years old. I was born and raised on Aruba, a small island pertaining to the Netherlands right off the coast of Venezuela in the Caribbean. I am a professional windsurfer and have been competing on the Professional Windsurfers Association (PWA) tour since 2005. I've won twelve freestyle world titles consecutively since 2008, four slalom world titles, and one wave world title.

It's like I fall in love with the sport more and more every year. In the end it's just my biggest hobby and passion. To progress is my biggest goal. There's always a bigger wave to ride, a new freestyle trick to learn, or a way to go that bit faster on the slalom gear, and the better you get at it, the more fun it becomes.

I've been windsurfing for twenty years now and there is always something new to learn. I love the little adventures I get to experience while windsurfing. Not just learning new tricks, but also sailing in different waters, experiencing different scenery: How crazy is it to sail in Iceland surrounded by snowy mountain tops? Or to see the Haleakala volcano from the water while sailing in Maui, with whales breaching in the distance and turtles popping up right next to you? Windsurfing has been and is one grand adventure for me. In terms of traveling it can be quite tough, but I love all the different people and cultures I get to experience.

We're always being compared to men. I think for me that has been a big driver to push harder and show what we are capable of as women. I have to say that I am as inspired by men as I am by women. The men are at a higher level and for me that just serves as an example of what is possible as a human. I'm motivated and inspired by the women around me because I can relate better to them.

Windsurfing is quite a small sport and there aren't many women in it. So I feel like the only way to move forward and grow the sport is to encourage and help each other. When I compete or train anywhere, I try to motivate the women around me by creating a friendly competitive environment. On the water it's fun and games trying to outdo each other, and on land we have a positive camaraderie where we look out for each other. Even during competitions we do our own thing, but still end up looking out for each other. And I think that's a cool vibe.

Wave sailing is the most challenging discipline I have done, as fear is a big aspect as well. I come from a fairly waveless island, so getting over my fear of waves is challenging, and jumping high requires a lot of willpower from my side. But I've taken it step by step by competing at different contests, and that's how I keep pushing my boundaries. I often let go and do things I wouldn't do in freesailing, and that is such a freeing feeling.

It's one of the hardest things to do, to push past your fear, but the feeling afterwards when you do is so euphoric. I know I will keep on windsurfing for the rest of my life because of the rush it gives me. Just stepping on my board and speeding across the water gives me so much joy and a sense of freedom, as I am the one who gets to decide what direction I am going in, what wave I want to catch, how high I want to jump. The rush I get from this sport just keeps me coming back for more.

Family is very important to me, so when I can, I try to fly back home for big events like birthdays and family gatherings. When I first started traveling I wouldn't come home much. But I learned that coming home even for four or five days really grounds me and re-energizes me for upcoming travels. My parents have been and still are my biggest support system and it's thanks to them I have the life I do now. They were the ones driving me back and forth to the beach and watching me train, and they traveled with me to my first contests. So I'm very grateful to them for putting so much time and energy into me.

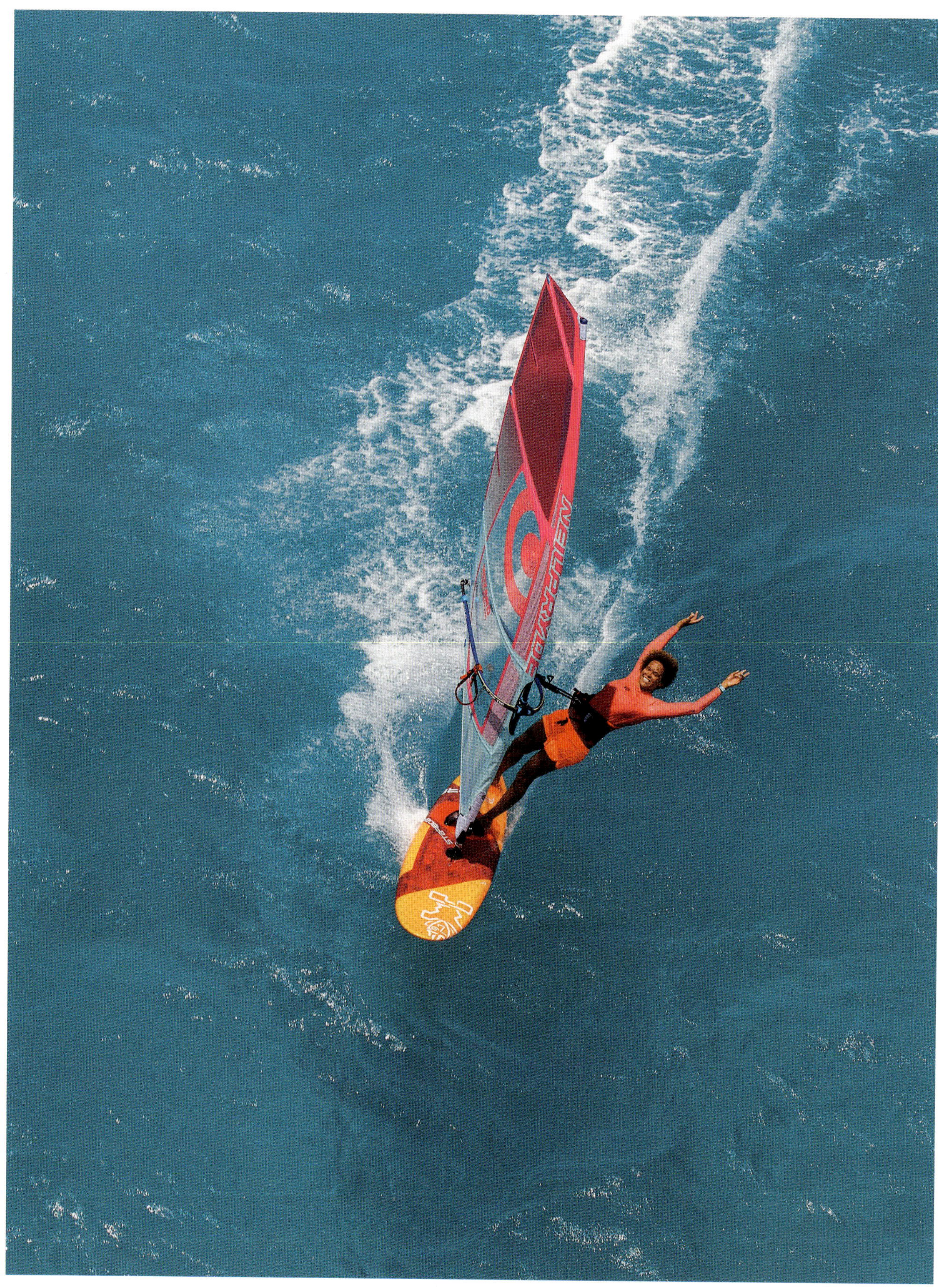

 △ Nouméa, New Caledonia   ▷ Esperance, Australia   ▷▷ Nouméa, New Caledonia

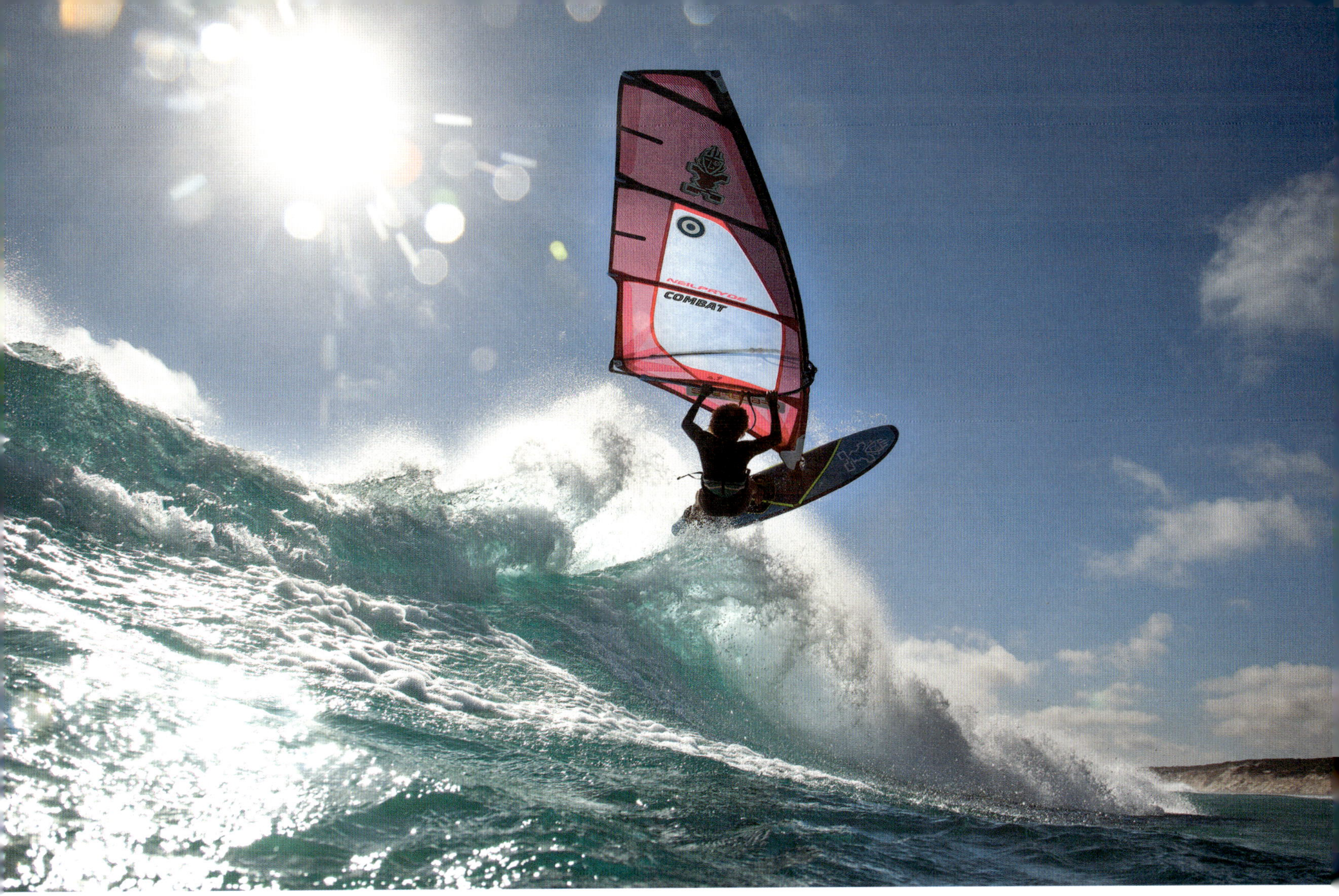

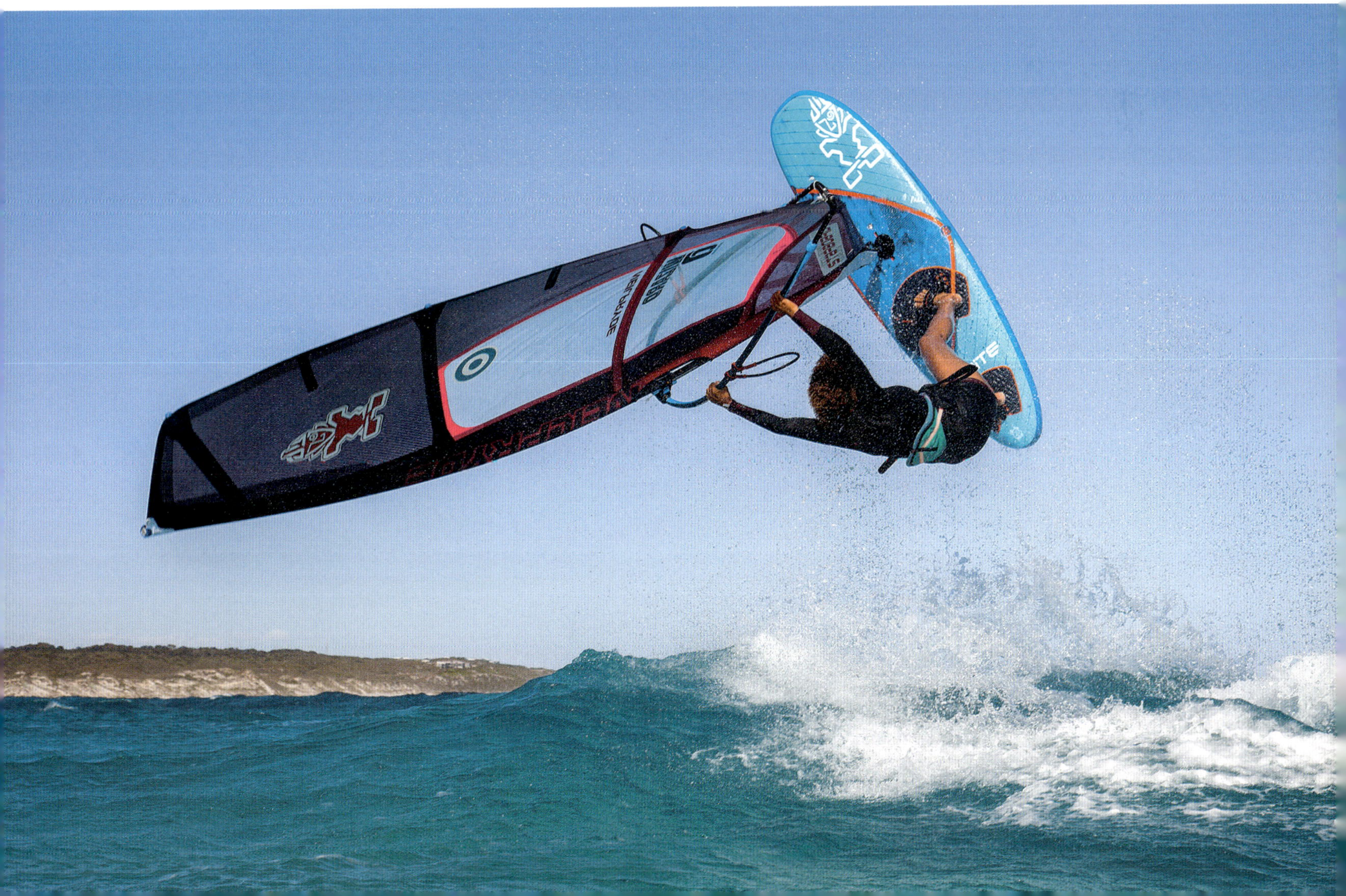

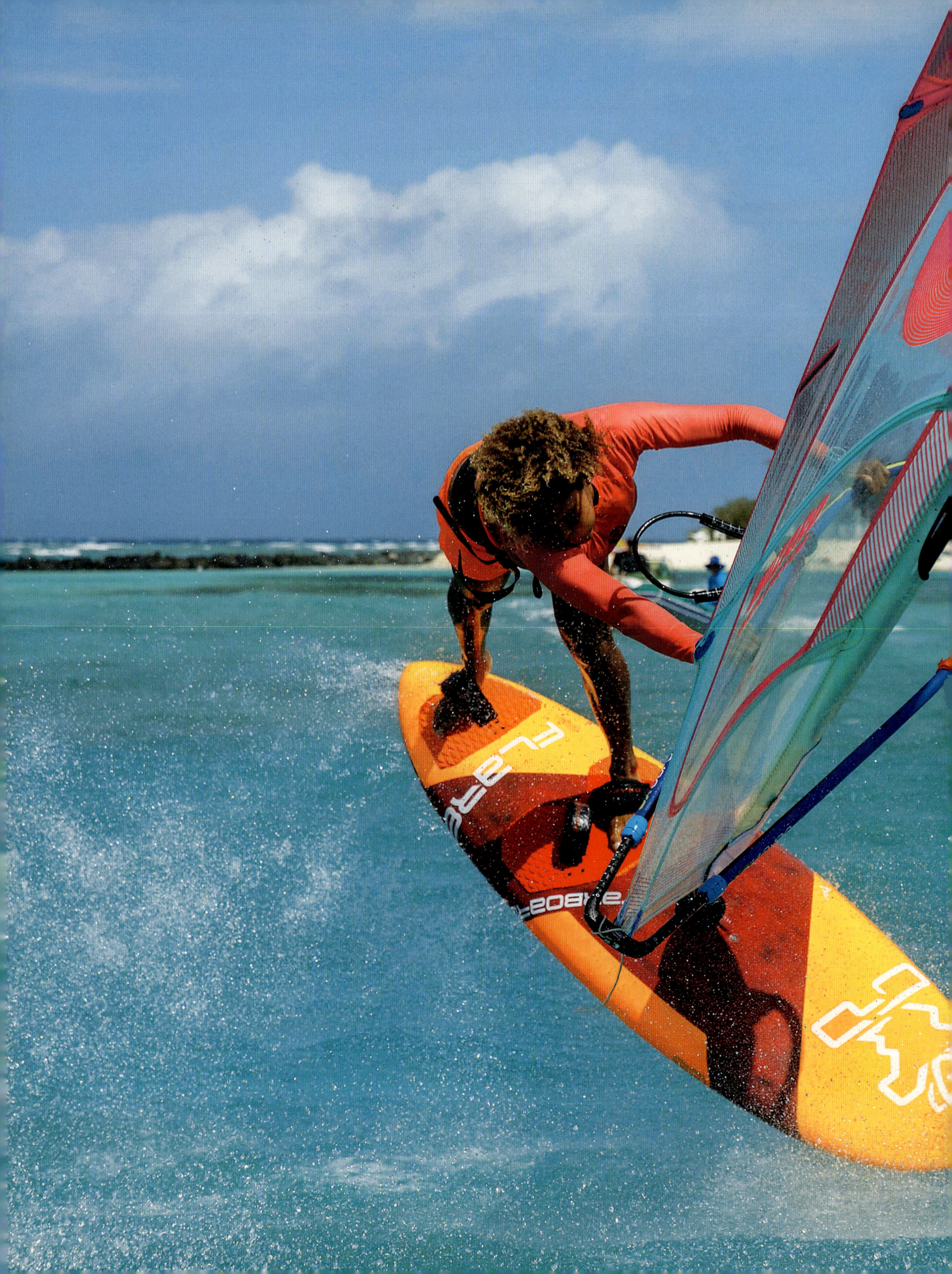

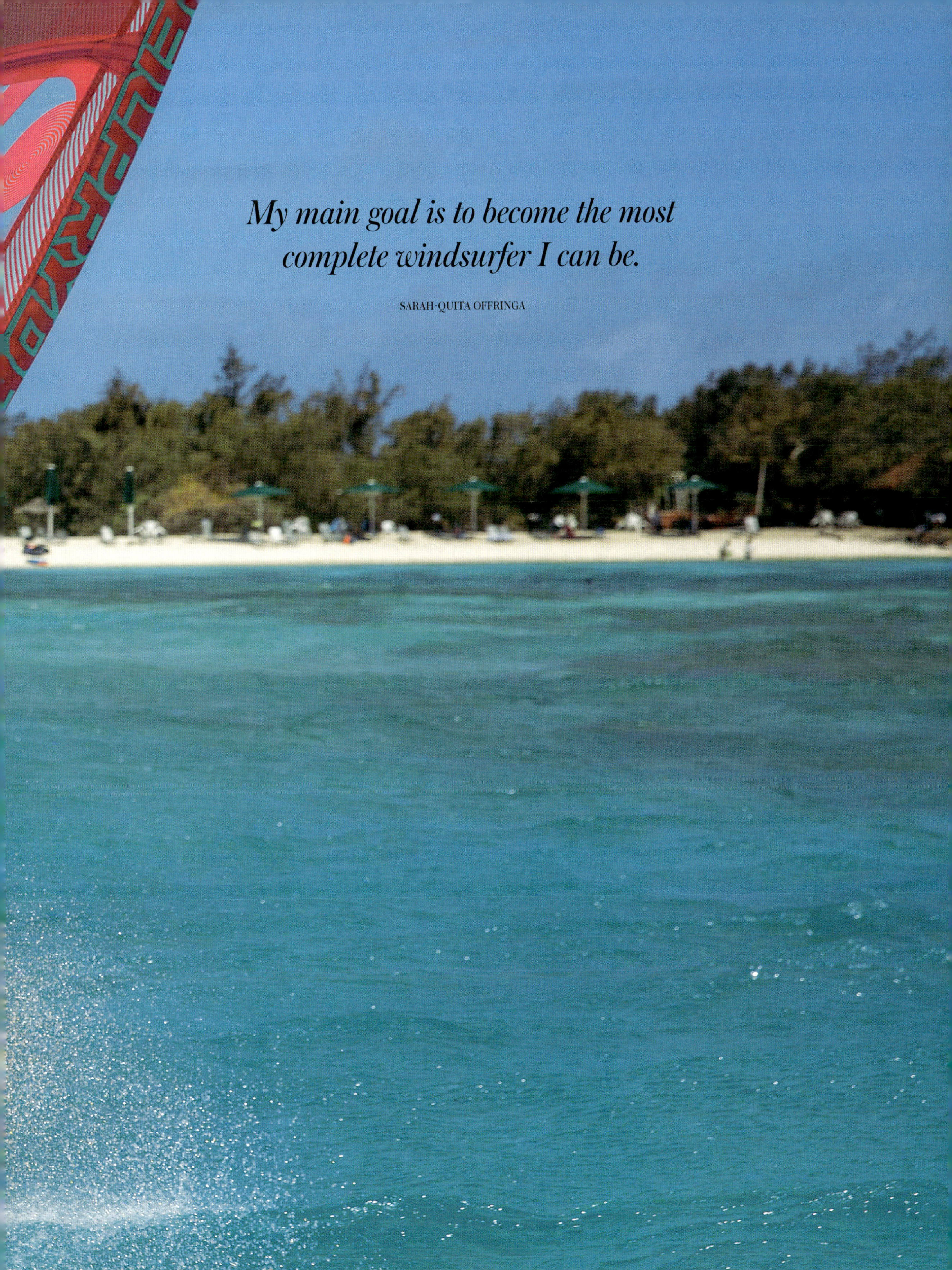
My main goal is to become the most complete windsurfer I can be.

SARAH-QUITA OFFRINGA

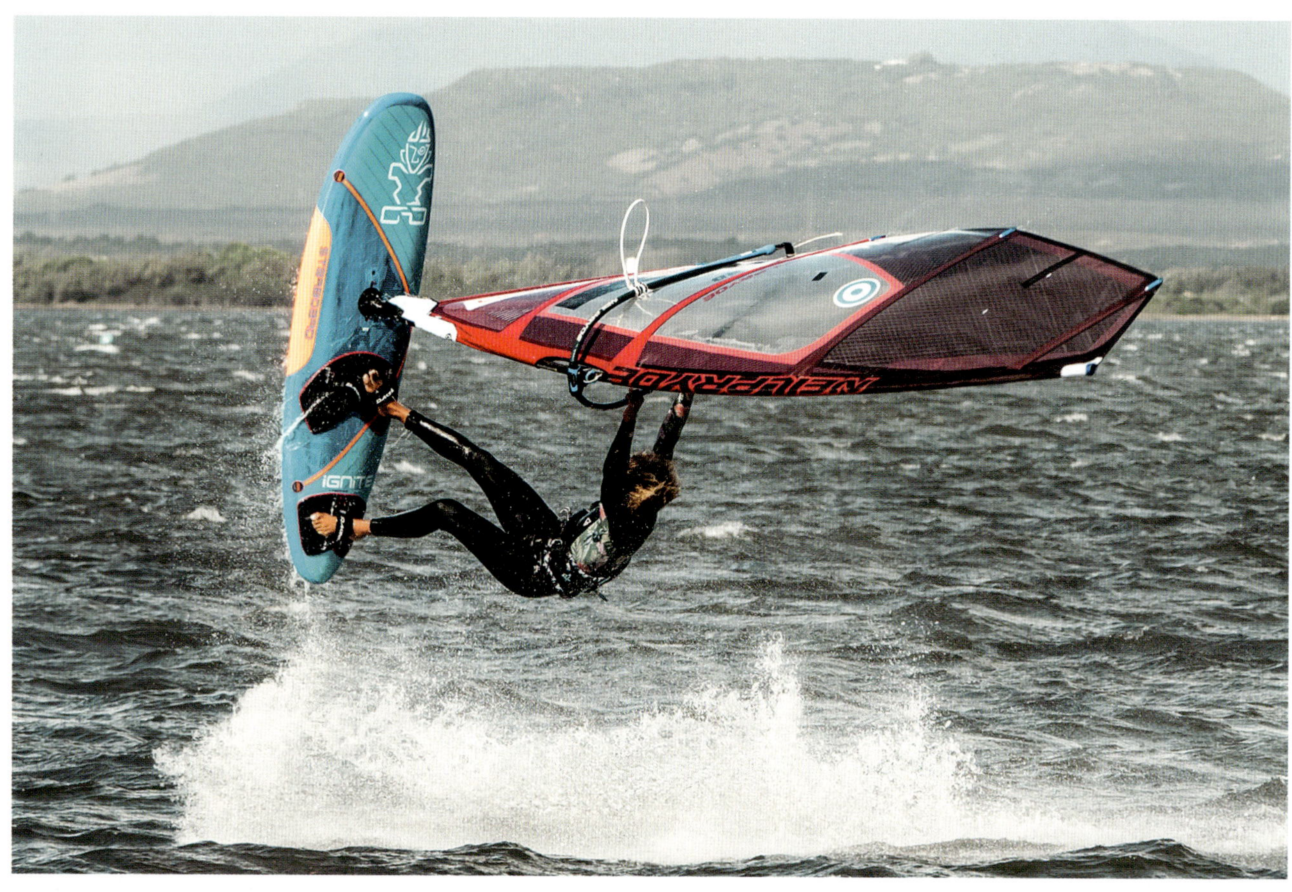

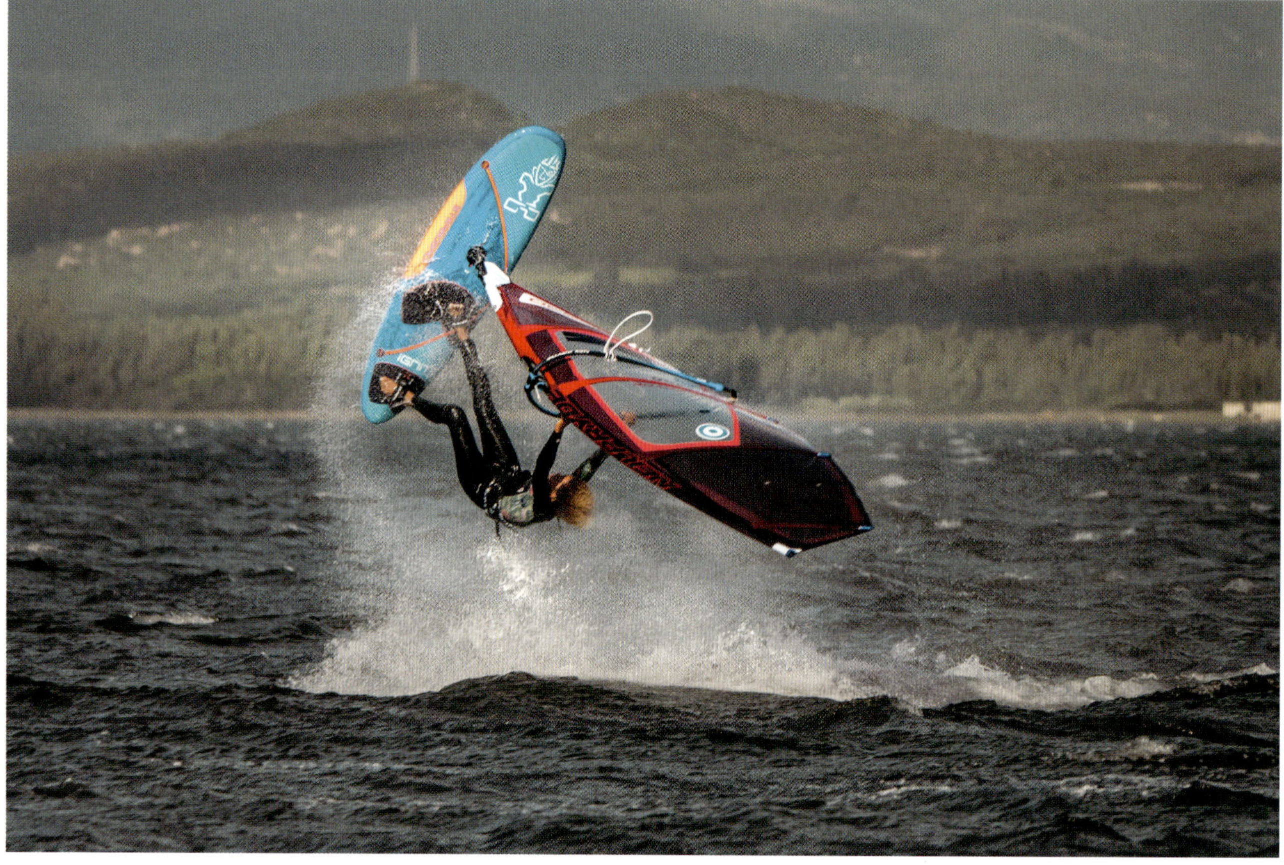

    Sa Barra, Sardinia

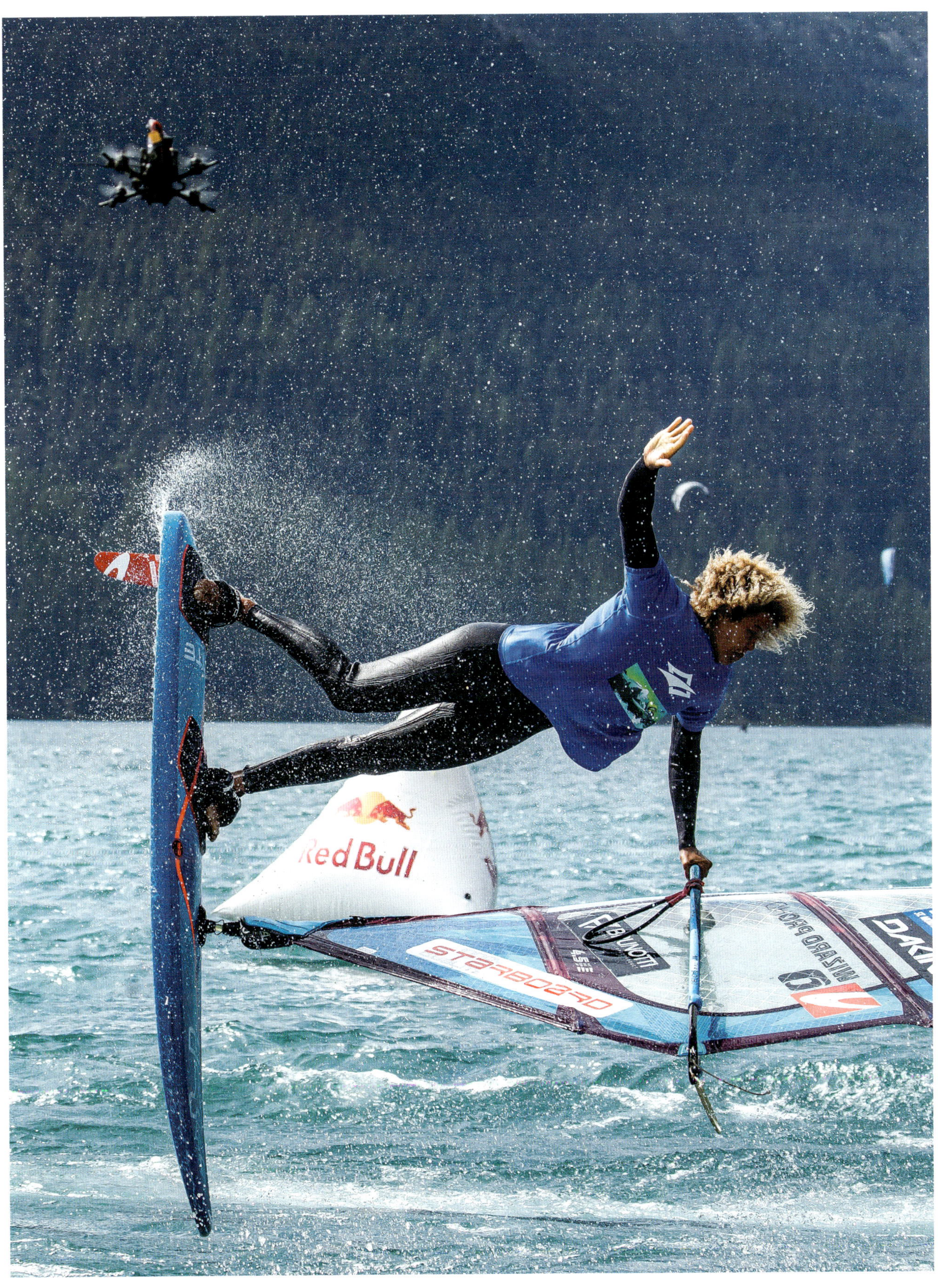

Red Bull
STARBOARD

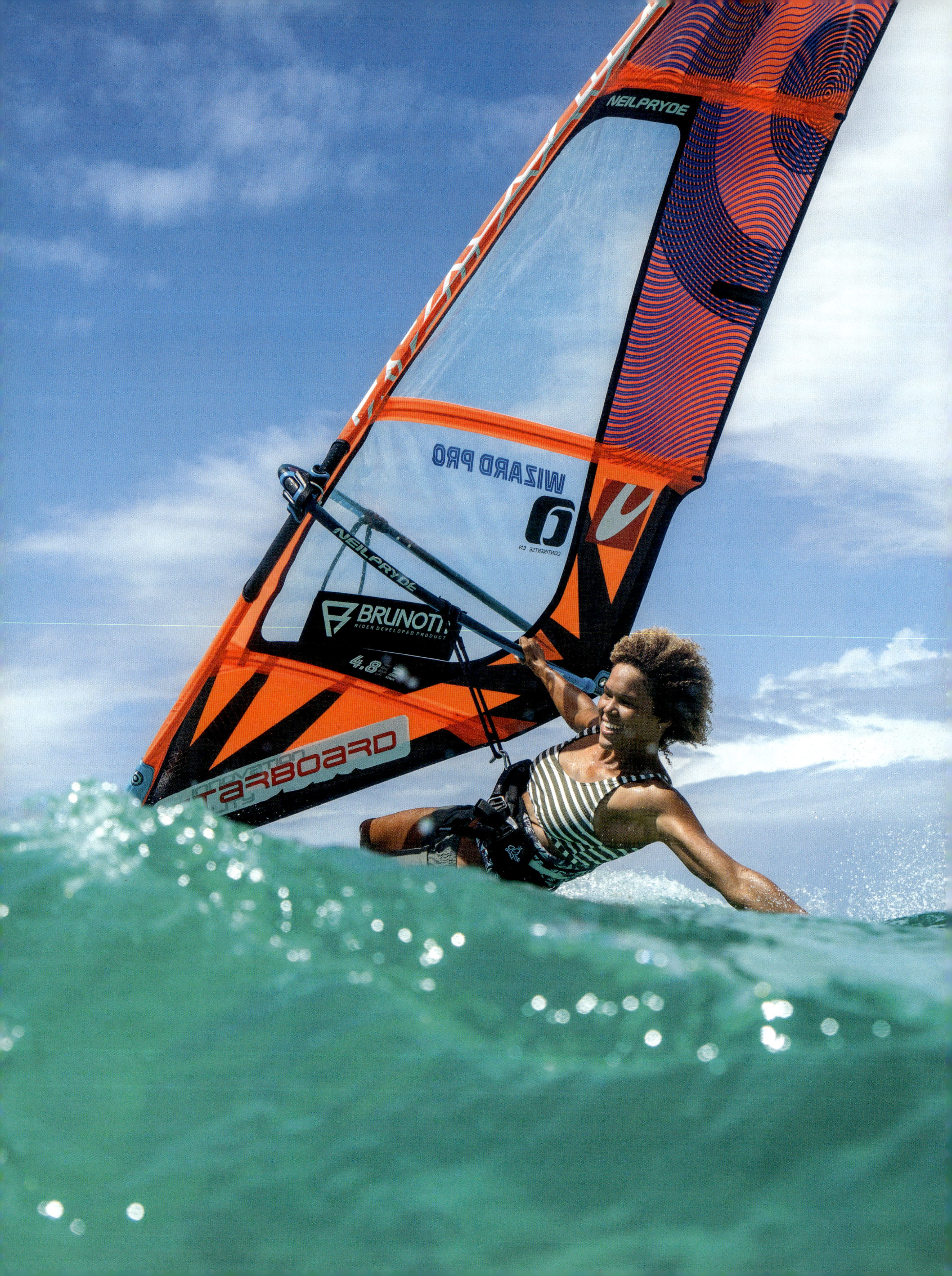

NEILPRYDE
WIZARD PRO
CONTINENTSE EN
NEILPRYDE
BRUNOTTI
RIDER DEVELOPED PRODUCT
4.8
STARBOARD

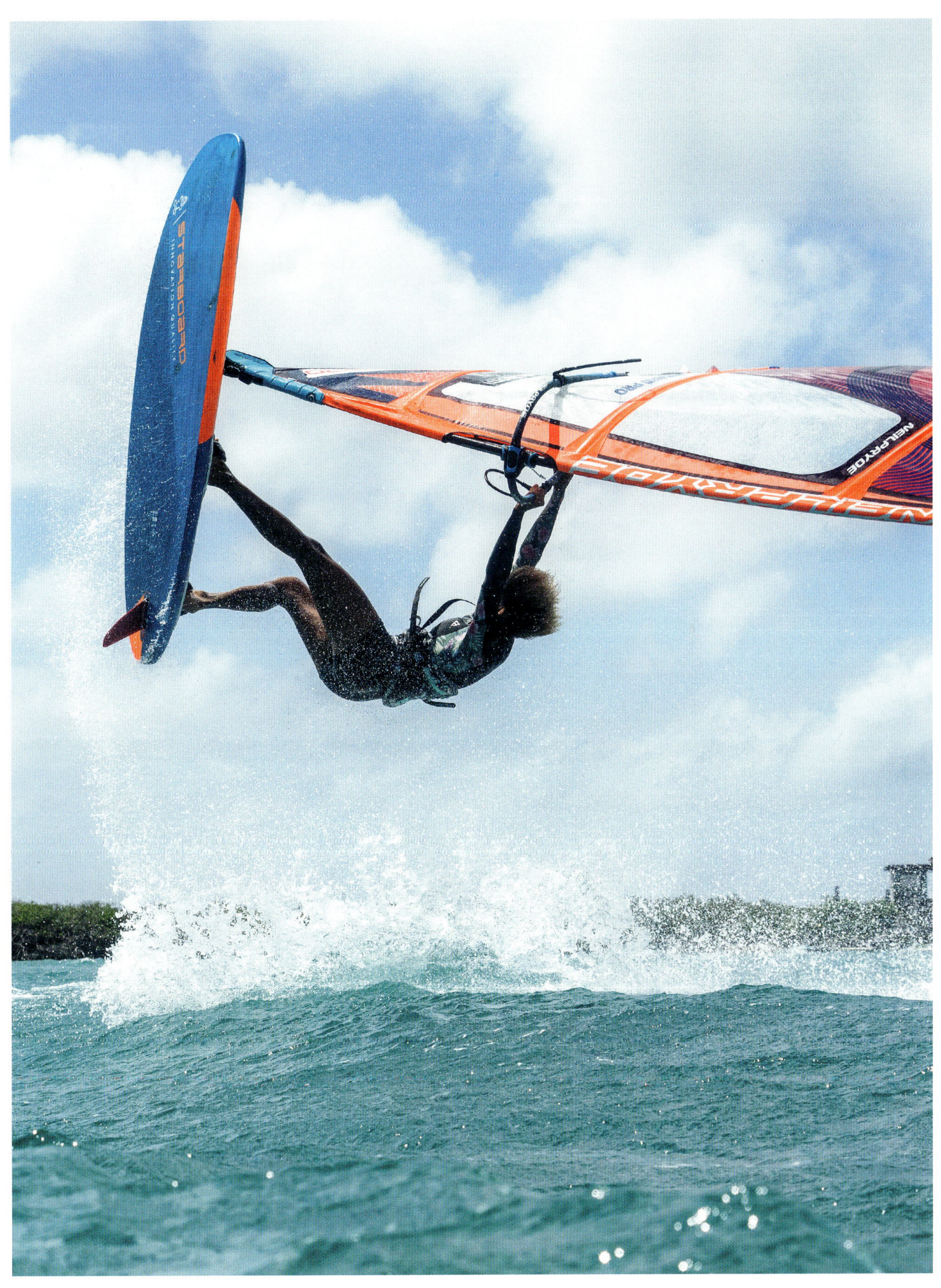

Kyra Poh
Indoor skydiver

@kyrapoh

Flight has always seemed like an unattainable goal for humans, but I've been fascinated by flight from a young age. Ever since I was a child, I wanted to become an astronaut, as to me that was the only way to be airborne. However, when I discovered indoor skydiving, I realized that it was my true passion and the adrenaline and feeling of freedom it gave me were unimaginable. Being only nine years old, female, and Asian in a sport dominated by American and European males at that time, it was truly a struggle to try and place my tiny country on the world map in the extreme sports scene. I'm glad it all worked out and I am able to fly my Singaporean flag high.

I thrive off the feeling of freedom, letting my body flow with the wind and using my creativity to express myself through my tricks and movements. To me, competing in this extreme sport is the best feeling in the world. My eagerness to succeed in competitions drives me to push myself harder every time I step into the wind tunnel, and the excitement I get when I perform in front of an audience is unlike any other feeling: it is a mixture of nervousness, pride, and happiness that I am sharing something that I have created and love with others. To me, flying is my passion, my love, and my life. It has shaped me into the person I am today. I hope everyone can find their own spark: flying is mine.

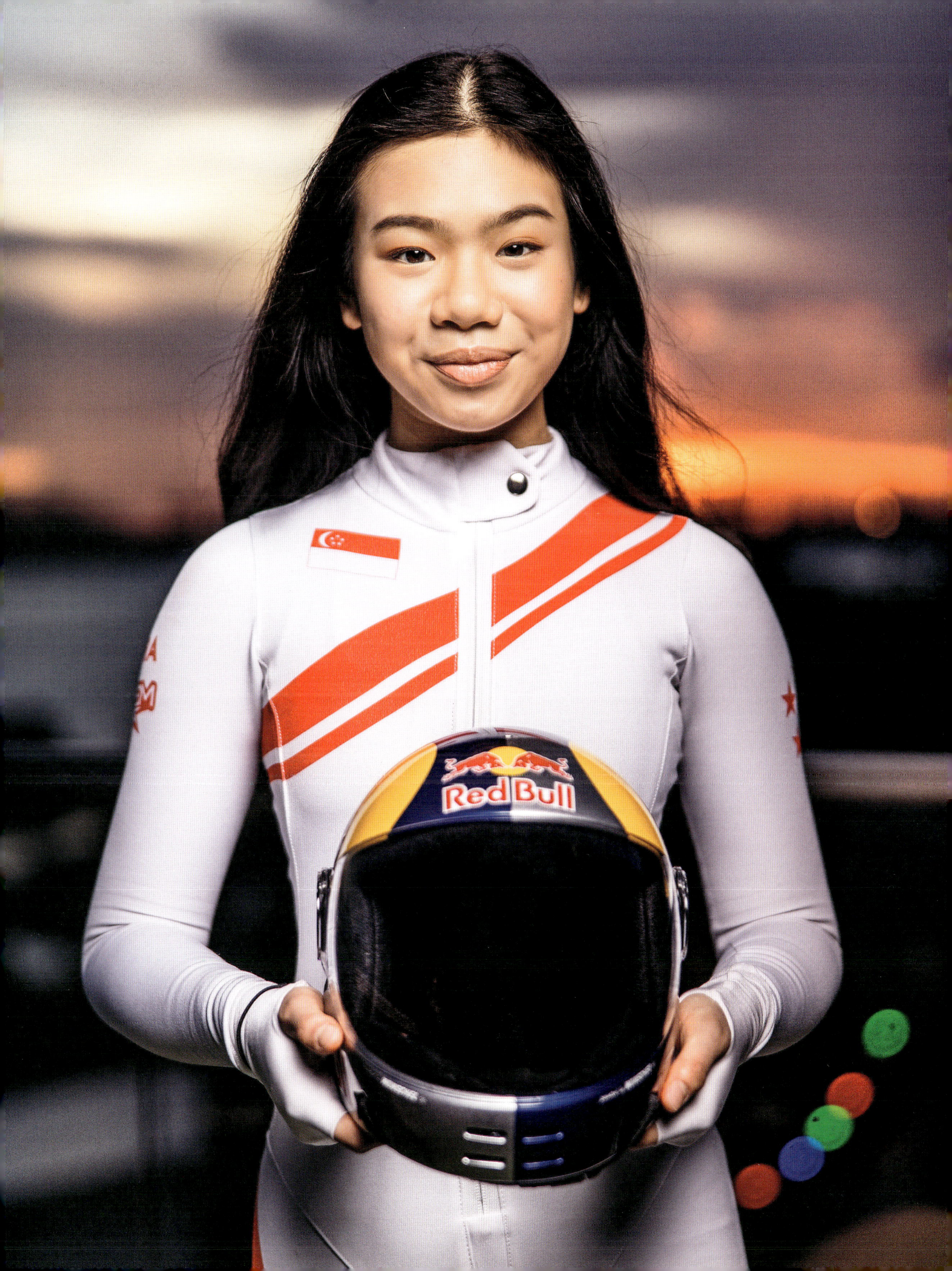

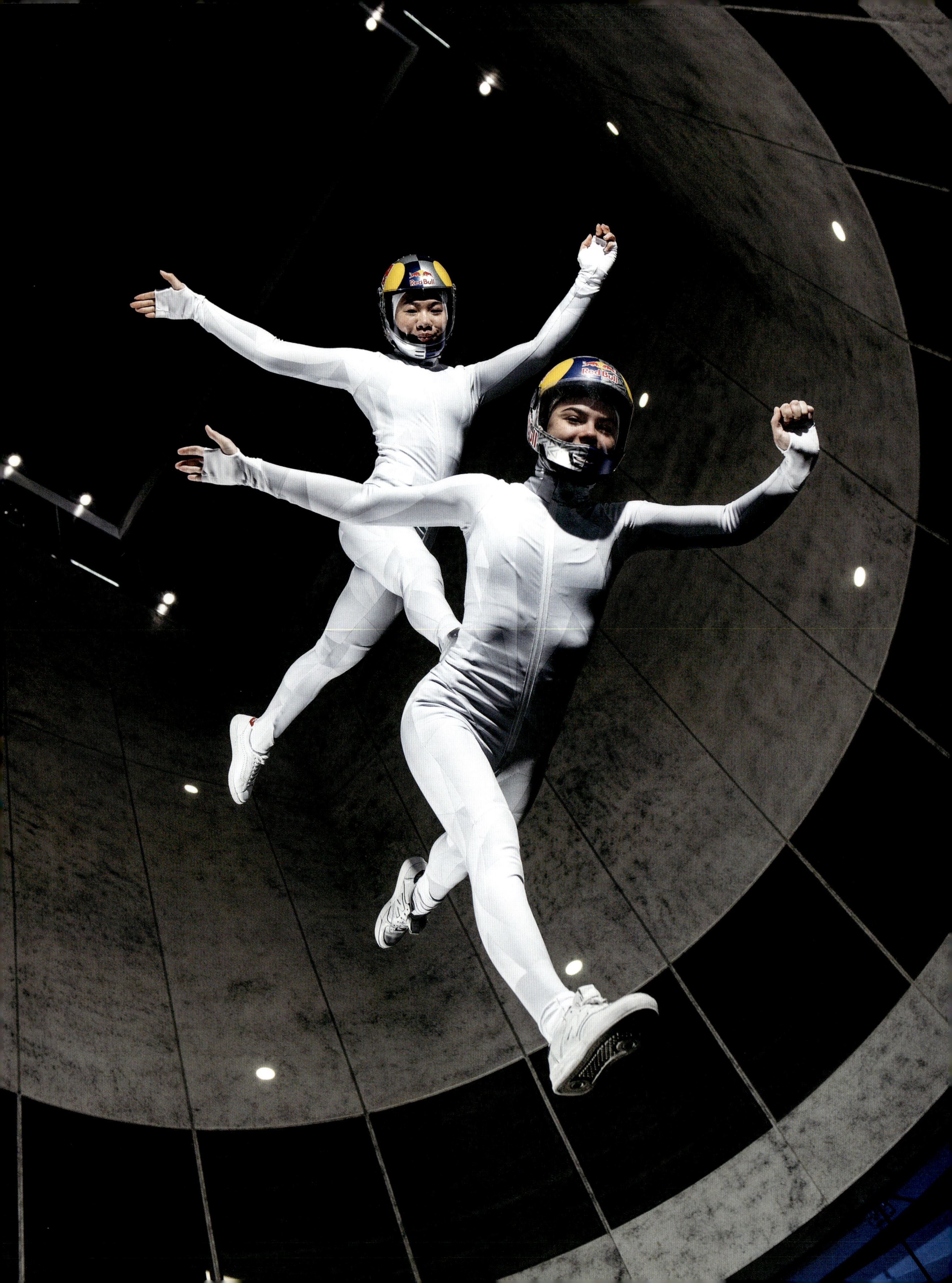

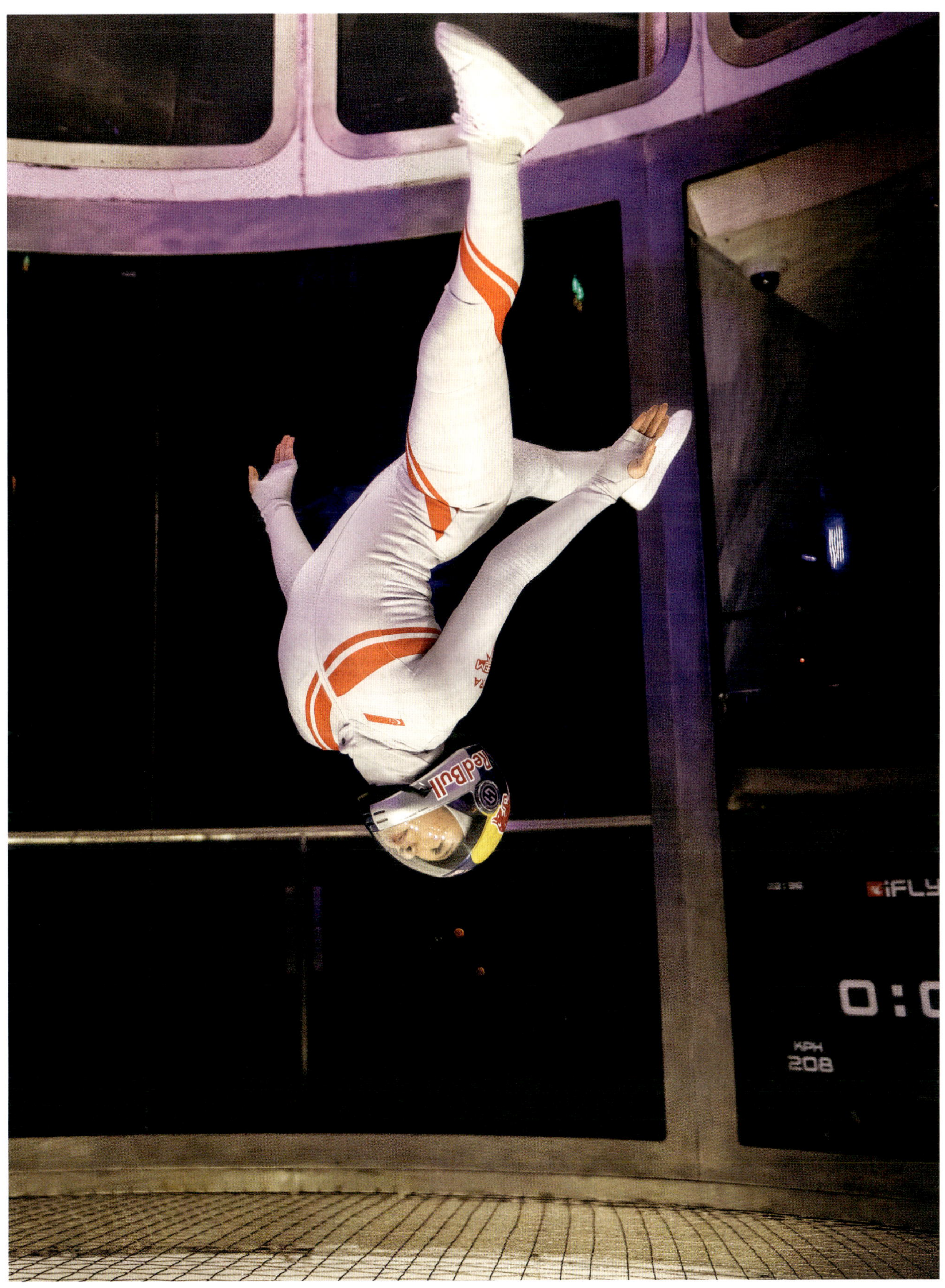

Red Bull
iFLY
208
KPH
0:0

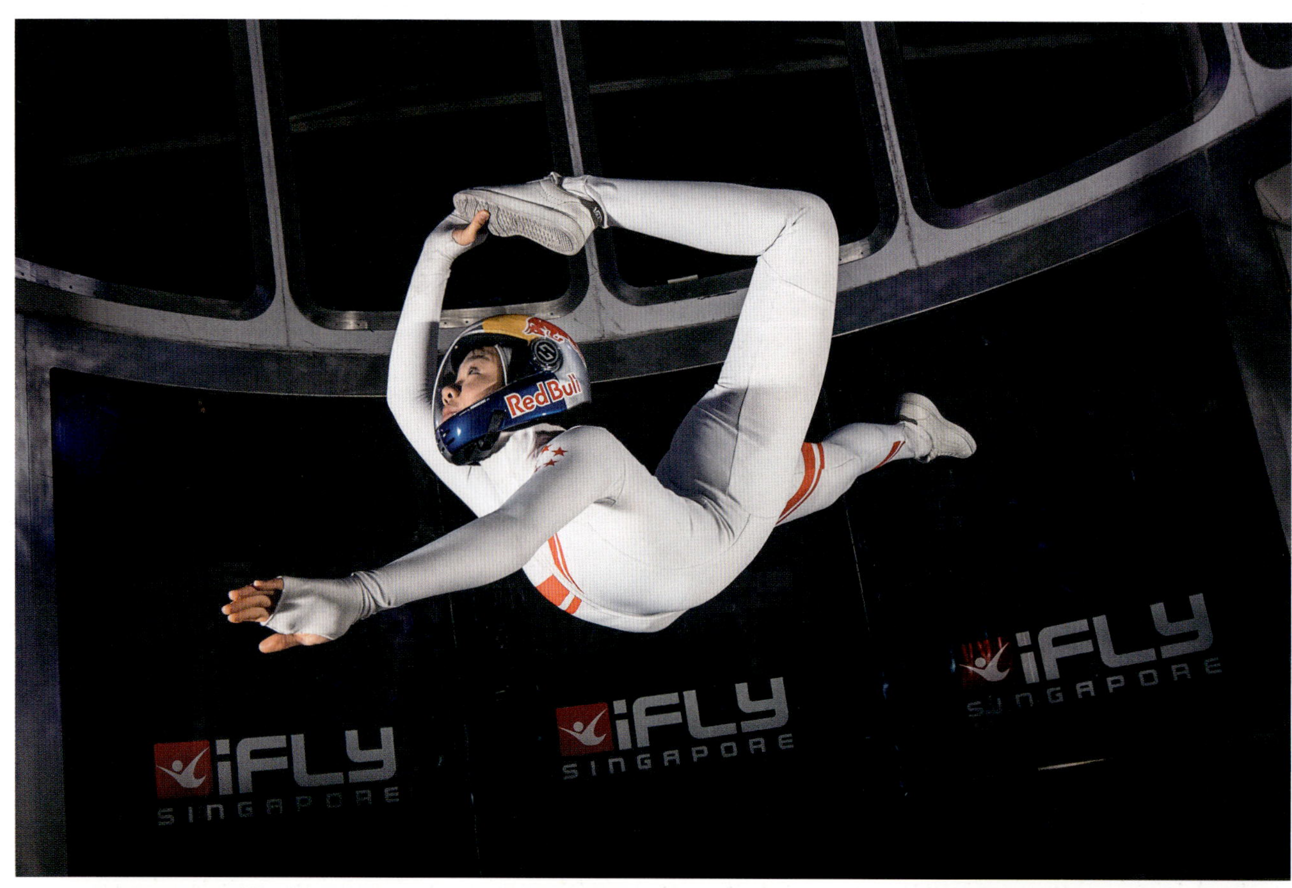

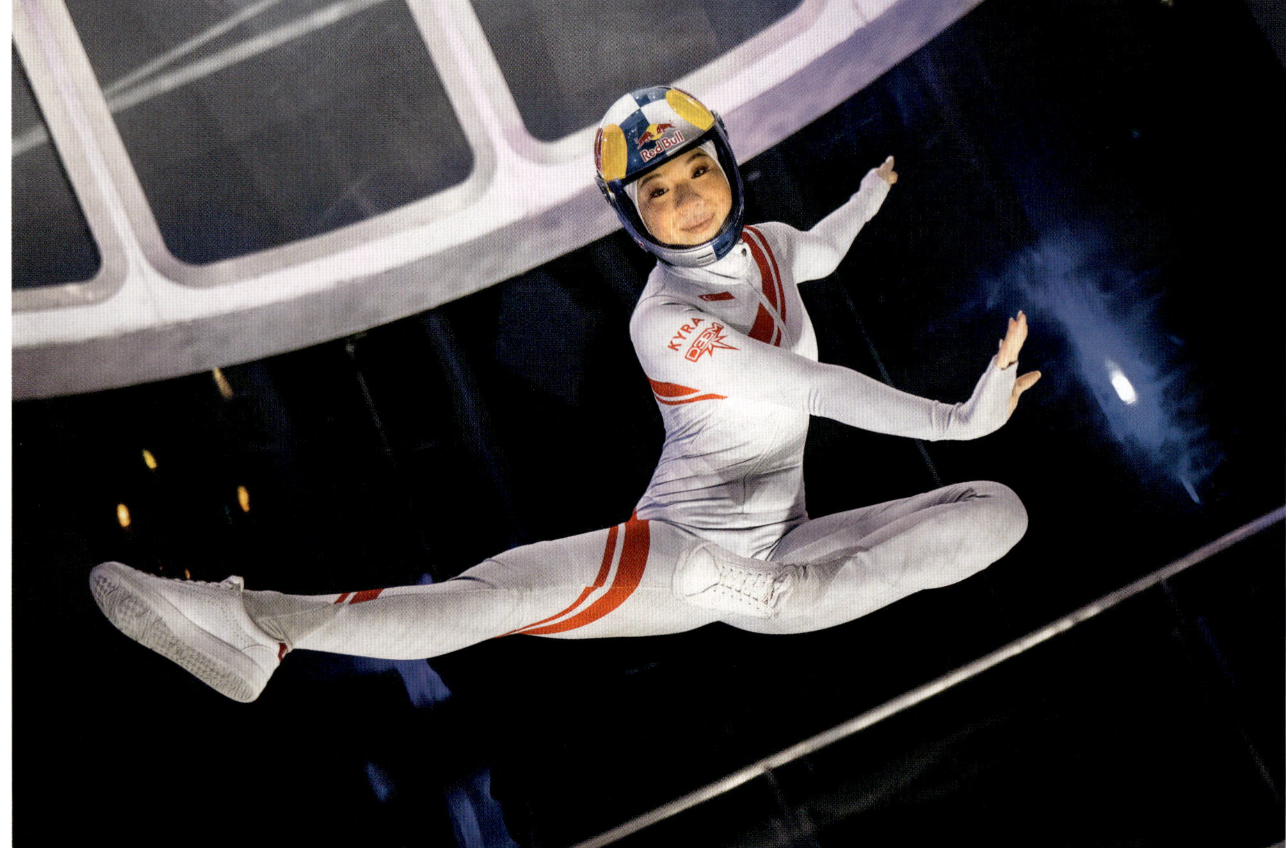

 △ iFly Sentosa, Singapore   ▷ CLYMB, Abu Dhabi, United Arab Emirates

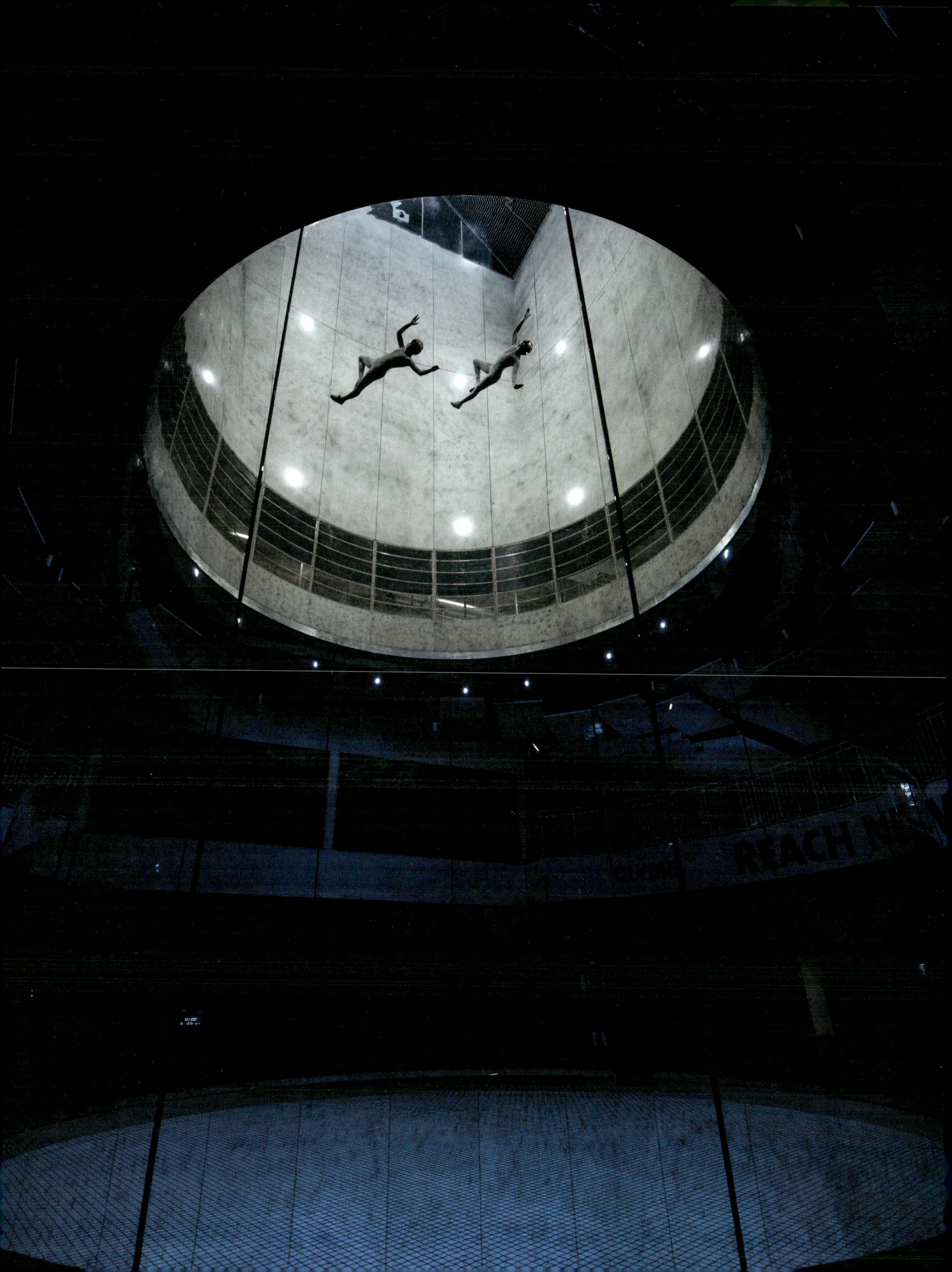
REACH

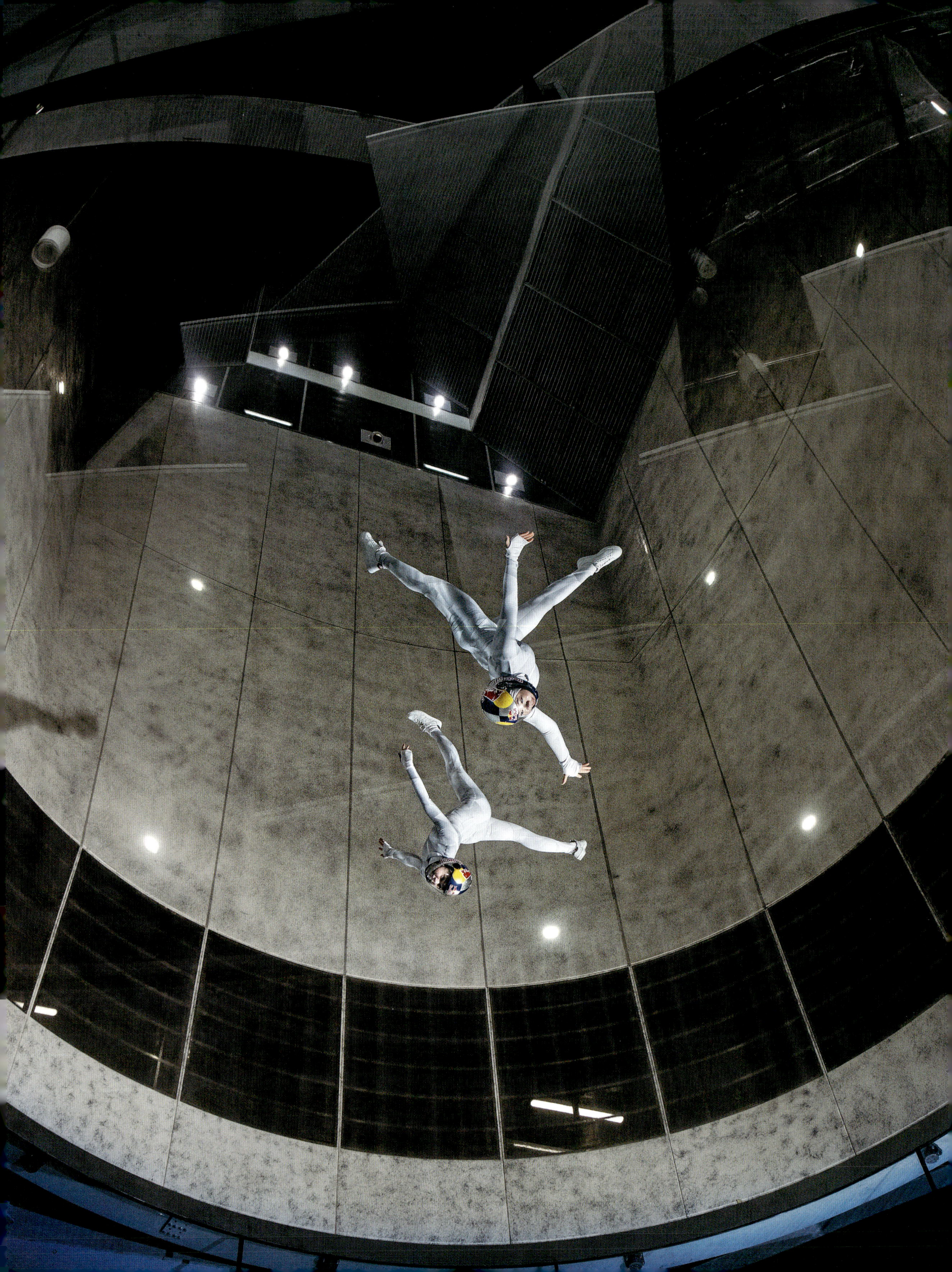

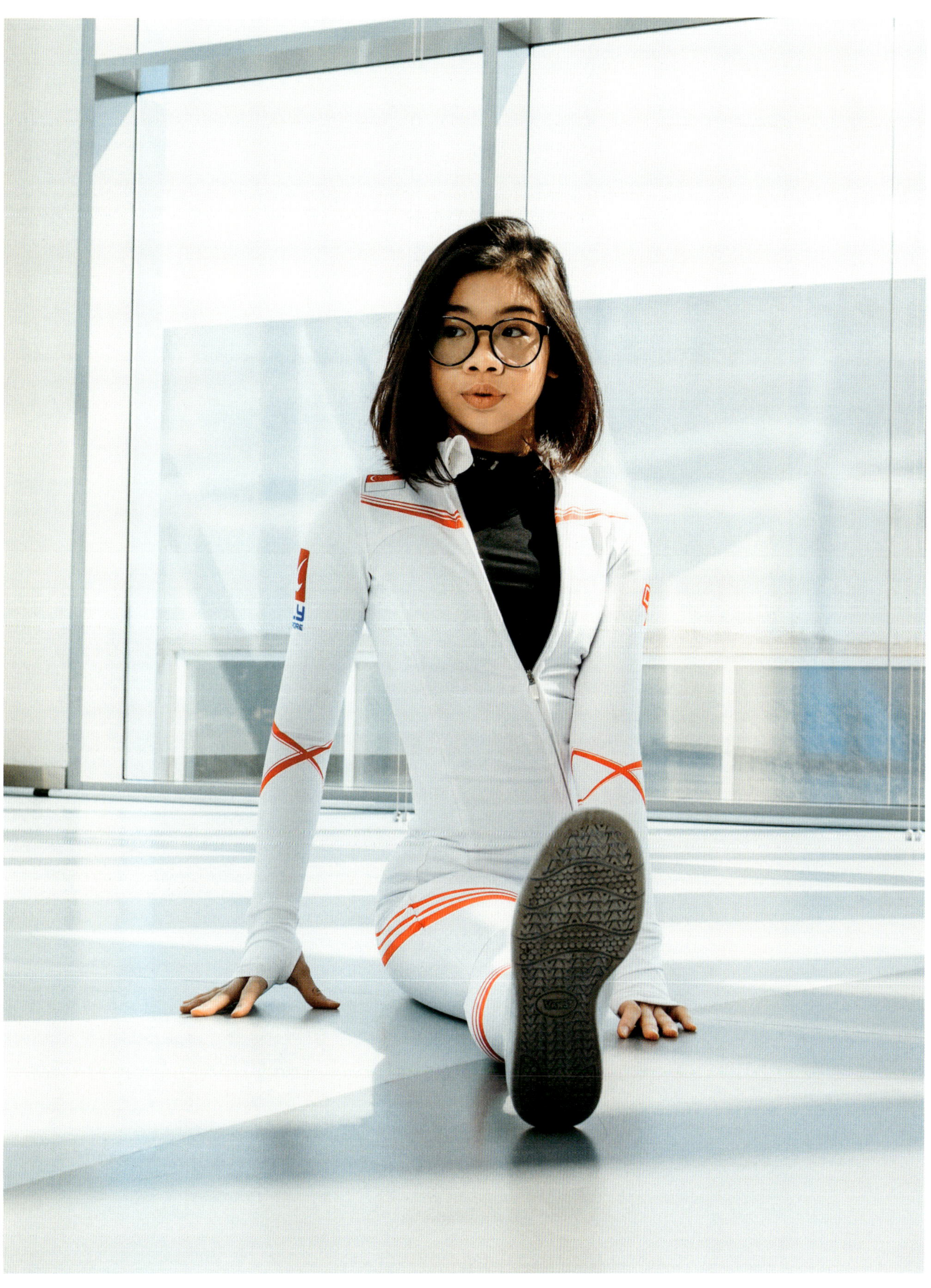

Liloo Fourré

Kiteboarder

@liloofourre

I was born in France and grew up in Venezuela. I began my kiteboarding career after obtaining a specialized Masters in International Sport and Event Management. I started to compete on the national scene and became double Venezuelan champion in 2014. In 2015 I started a new cycle as the team rider leader of Crazy Fly Kiteboarding and competed in the Kiteboarding World Tour. I managed to be ranked in the World Top Ten.

In 2019 I decided to stop competing to focus on other kite disciplines and travel the world for my sponsors to get the best footage and videos. I have created Waraos Beachwear, a beachwear brand for men and women specializing in watersports. I am also a kiteboarding instructor and organize kite coaching around the world.

I'd like to share something with you and hopefully inspire you. In life, I'm not someone to whom things have come easily—I've always had to work hard to make it, and in all areas. But my lack of natural ability turned out to be a strength because it means I always work hard and never give up, no matter what. My dad always taught me, "Querer es poder," "When we want, we can," even if we are not talented at something.

When I started kiteboarding, I never would have thought I could get where I am today. I remember that my mom, even though she is my number one supporter, thought that I'd never even get on the board! But I've never stopped fighting and will always continue to do so. Faith, determination, and hard work are stronger than anything.

Kiteboarding represents most of my life, and all the punches, the crashes, the tears that fall into the sea, and the sacrifices are definitely worth it. Never let anyone tell you what you can or can't do, who you can or can't be. Live your dreams, no matter what other people think about you, because nobody knows the difficulties you've faced to get where you are.

Fight for what you love, and never give up. If life puts walls in front of you, just break them!

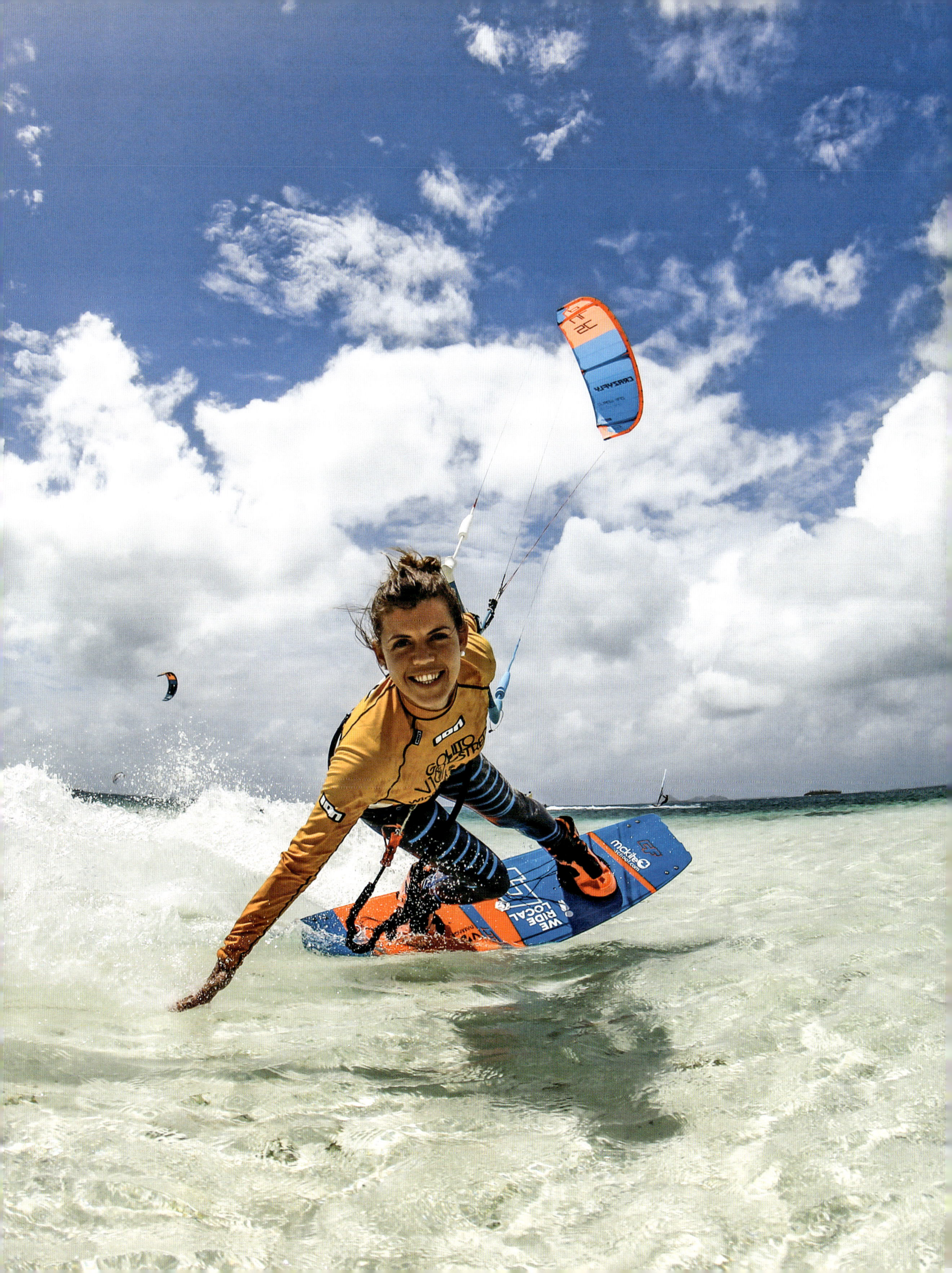

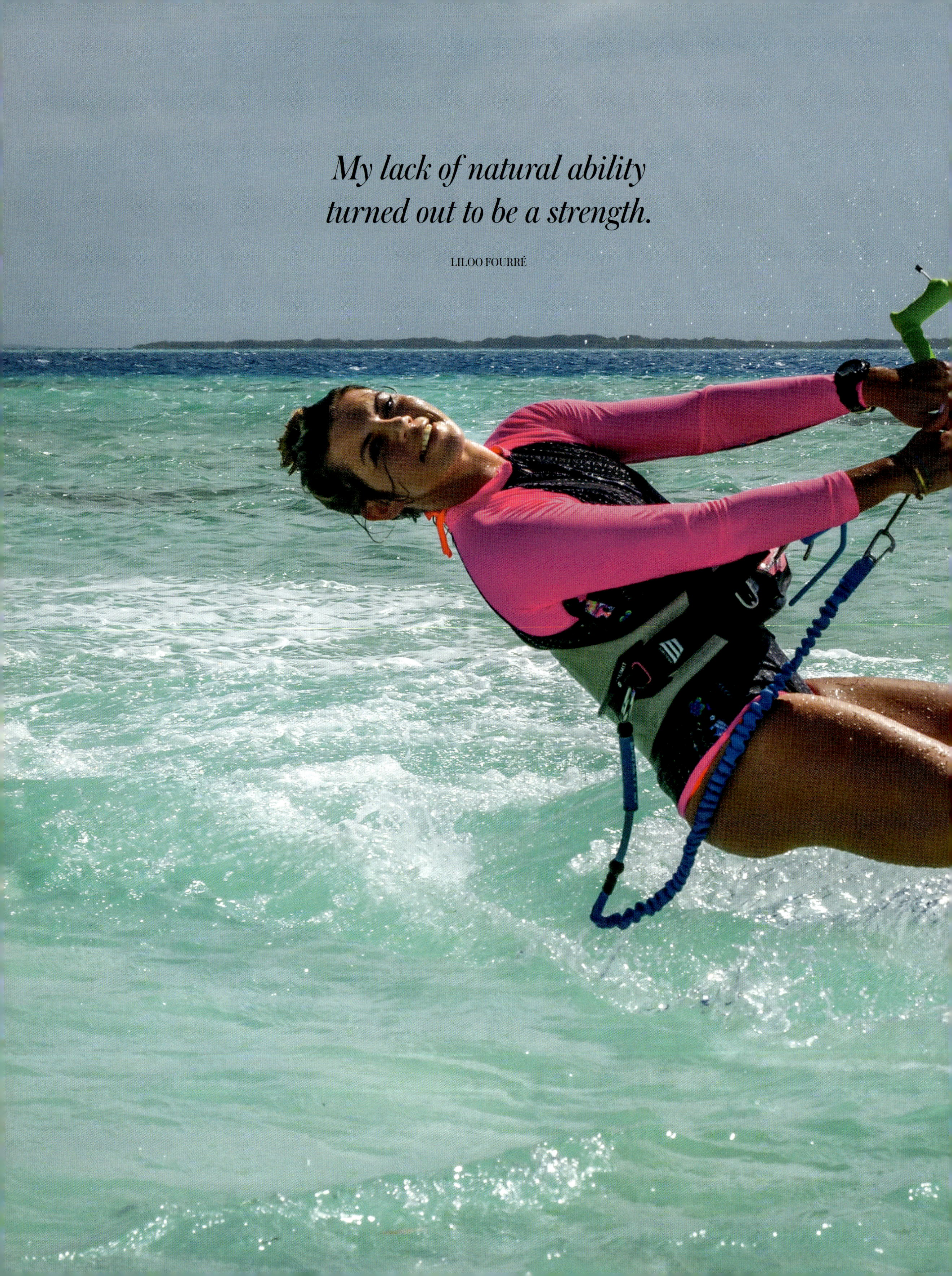

My lack of natural ability
turned out to be a strength.

LILOO FOURRÉ

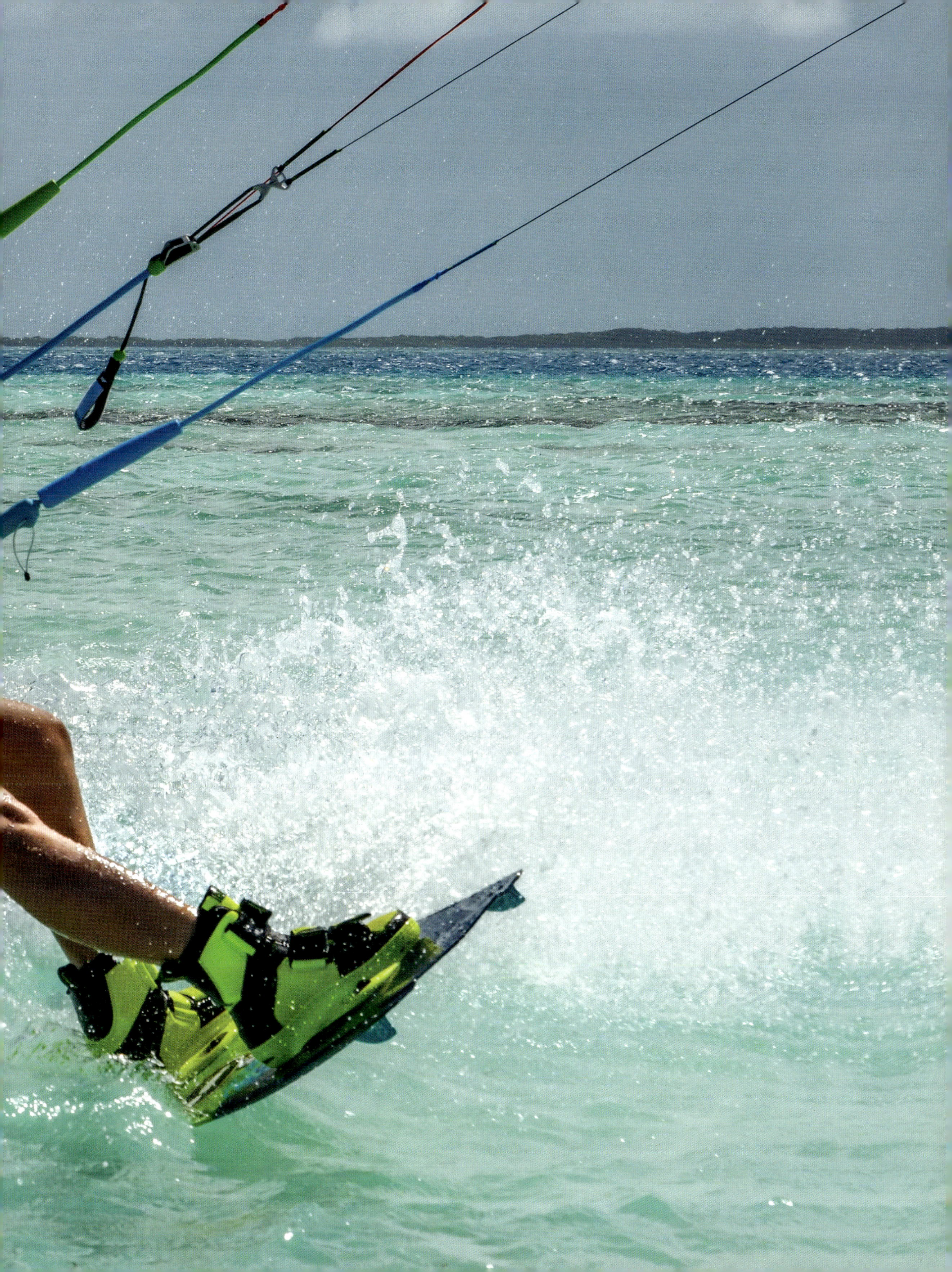

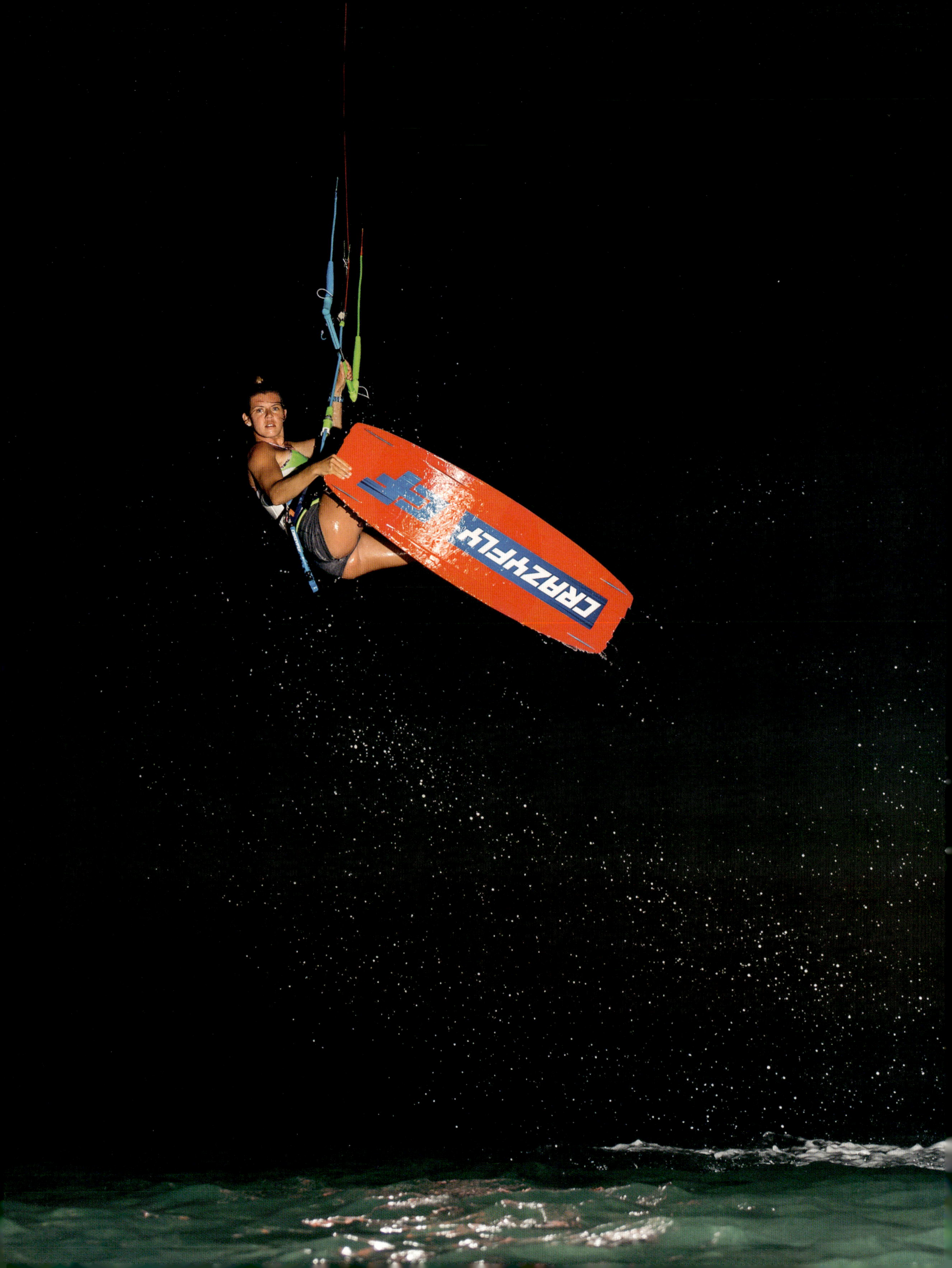
CRAZYFLY

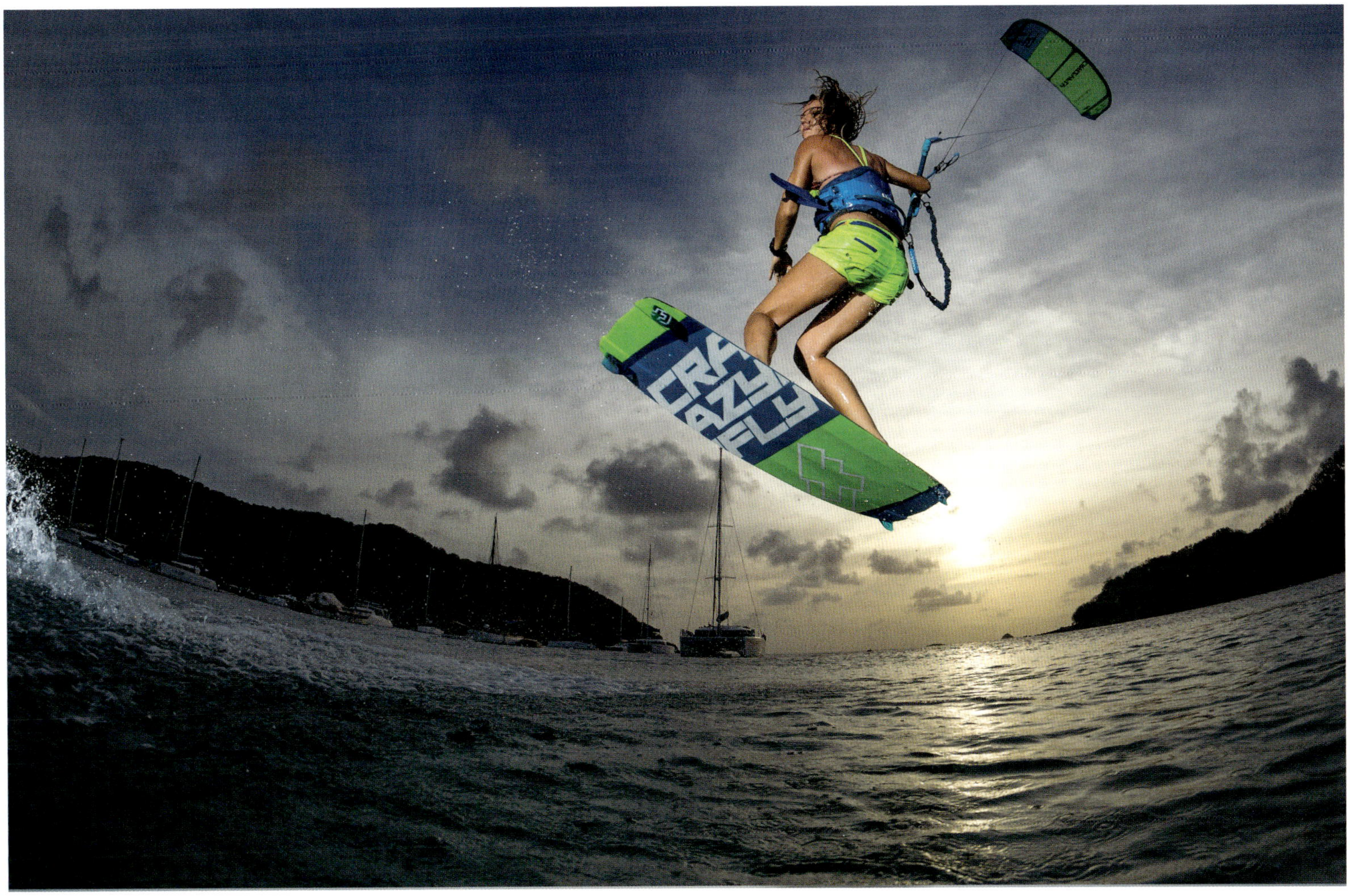

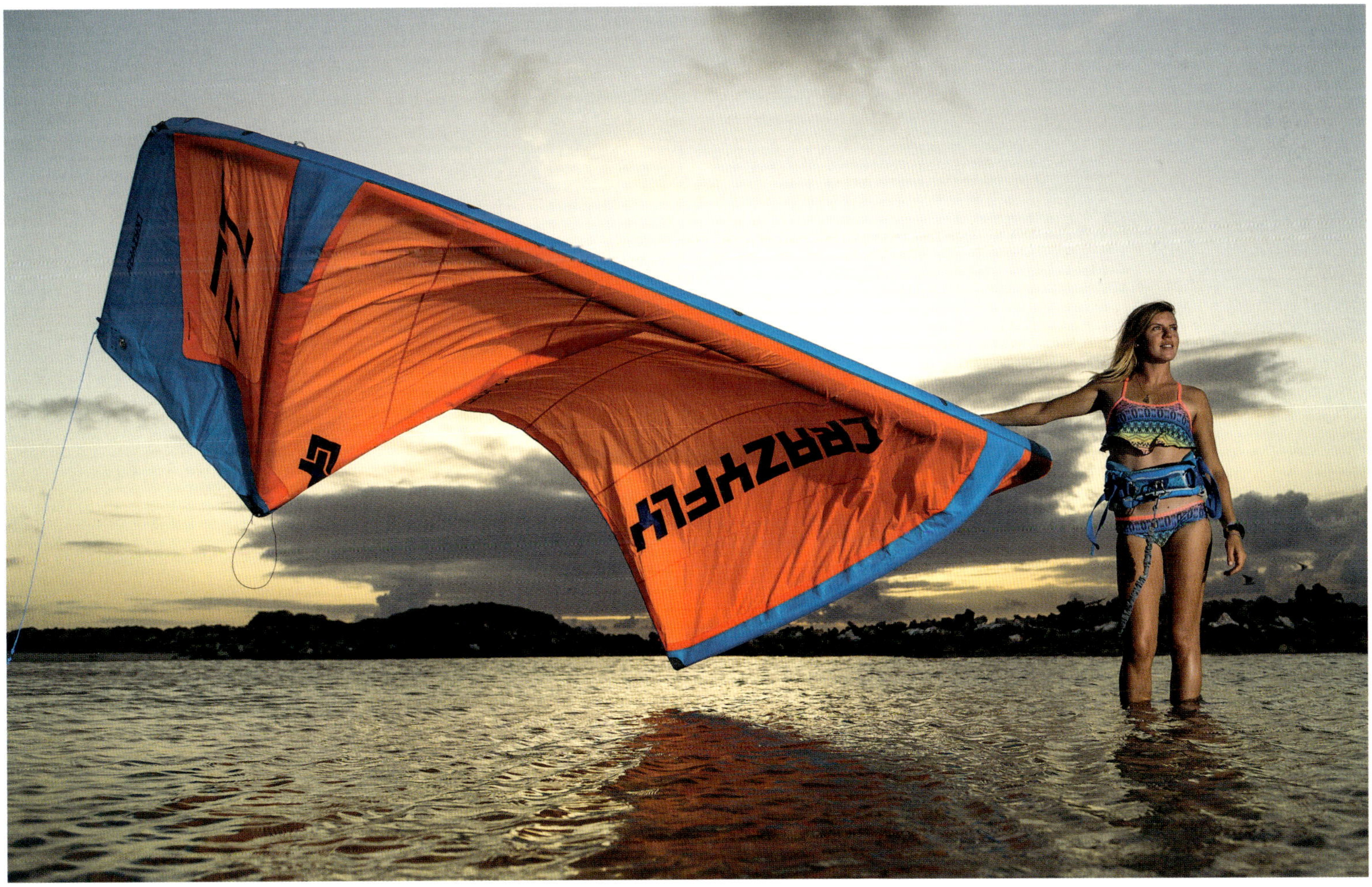

◁ Turks & Caicos △ St. Vincent & the Grenadines | Caribbean

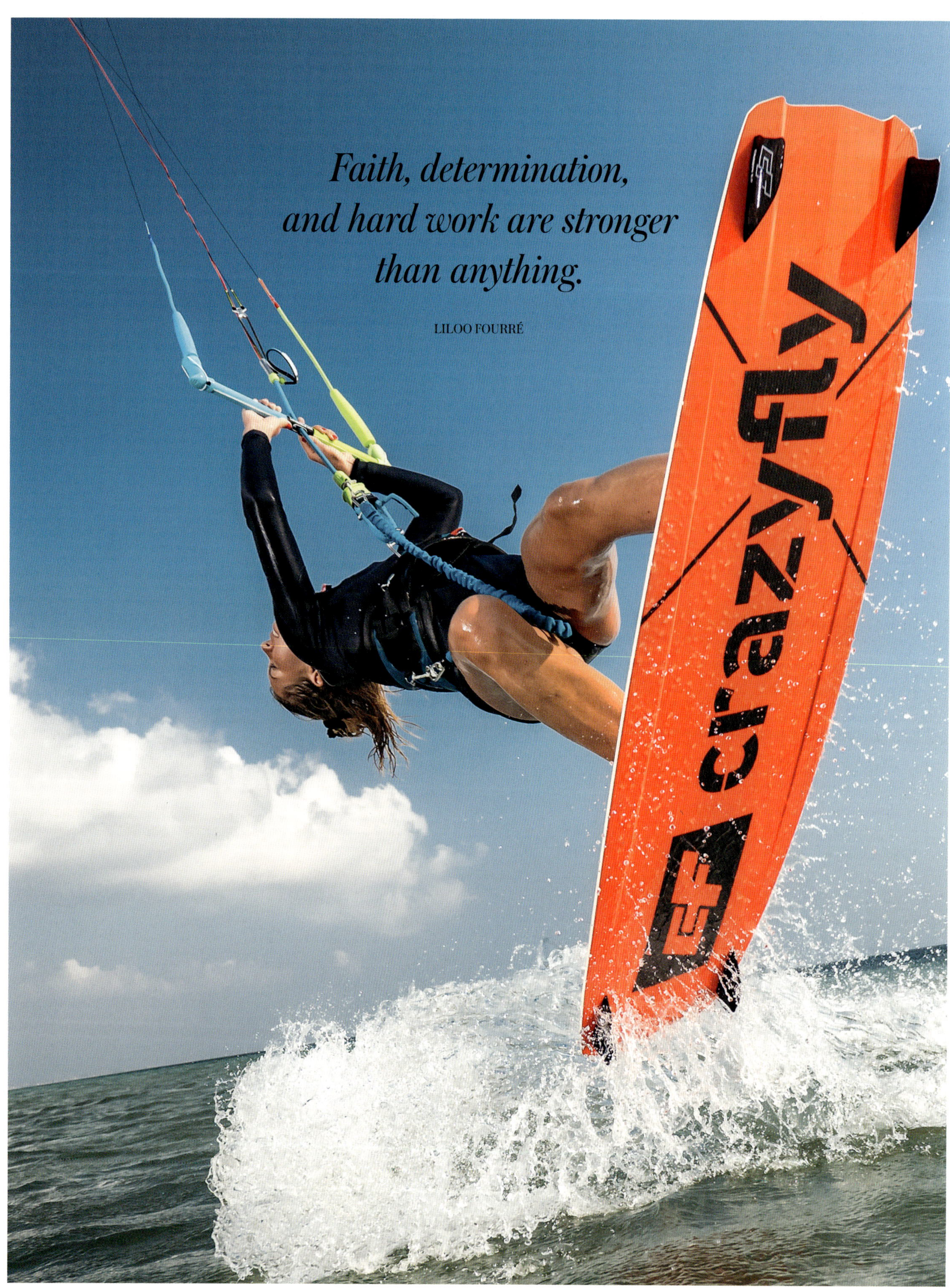

Faith, determination,
and hard work are stronger
than anything.

LILOO FOURRÉ

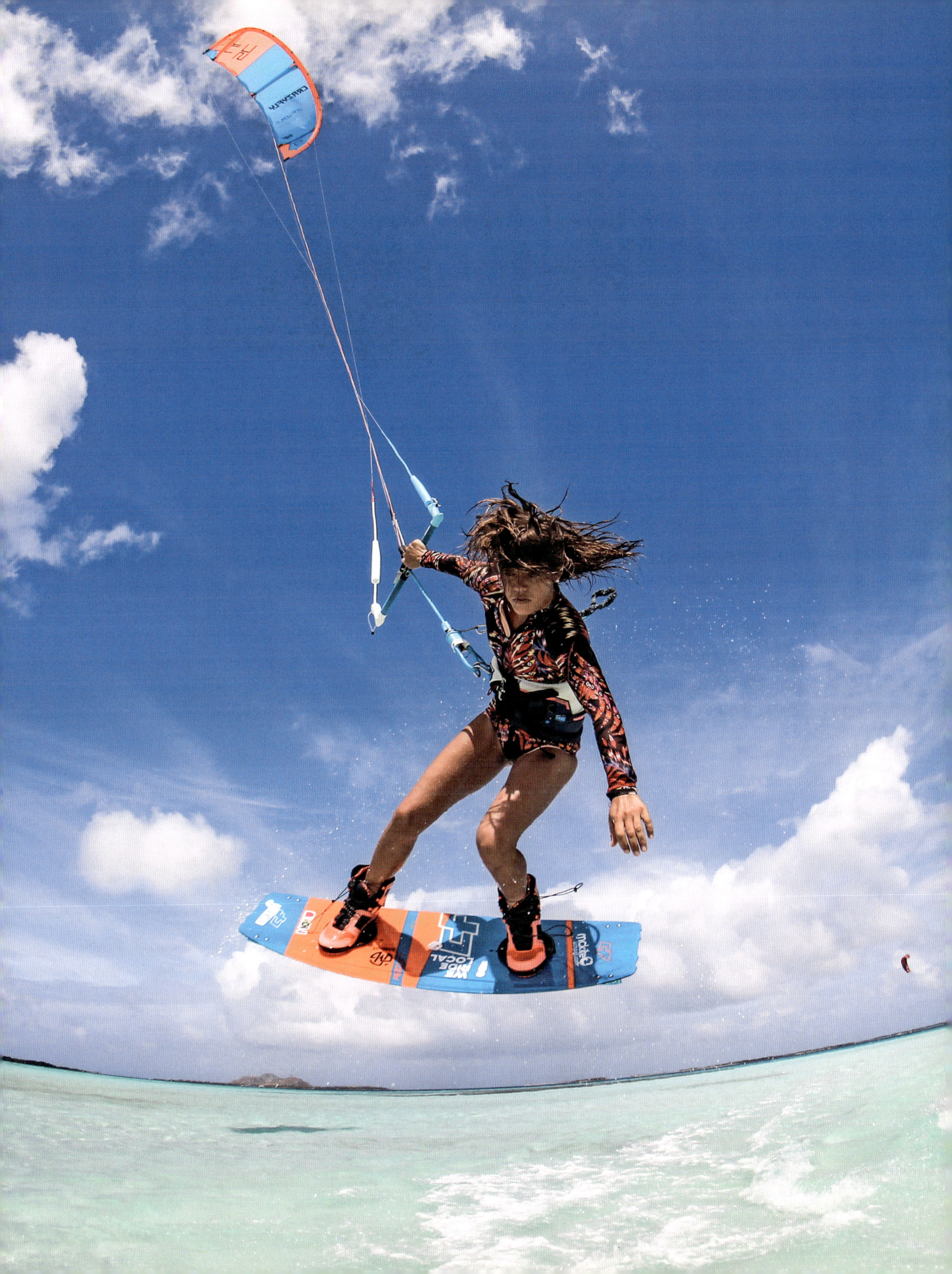

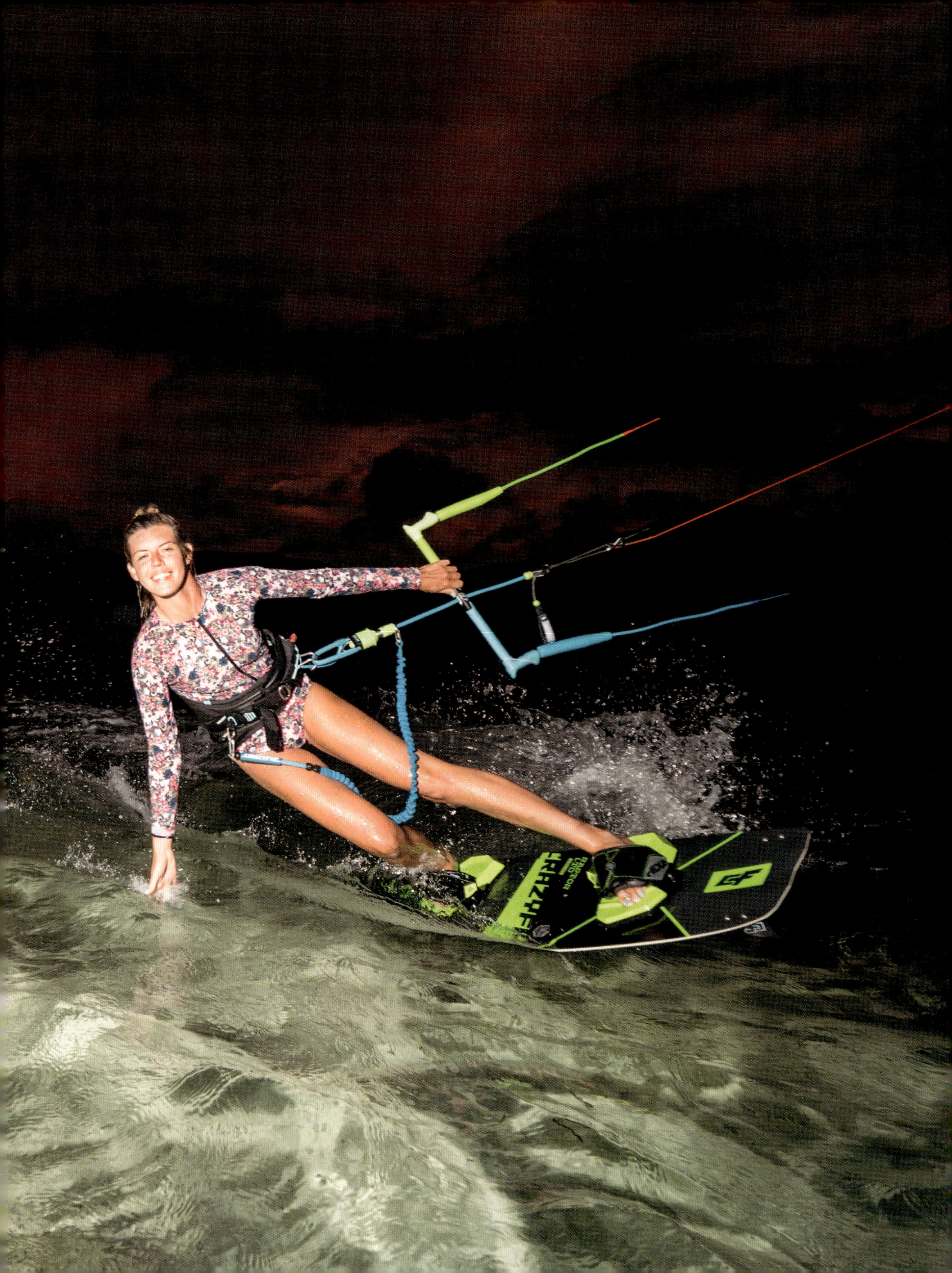

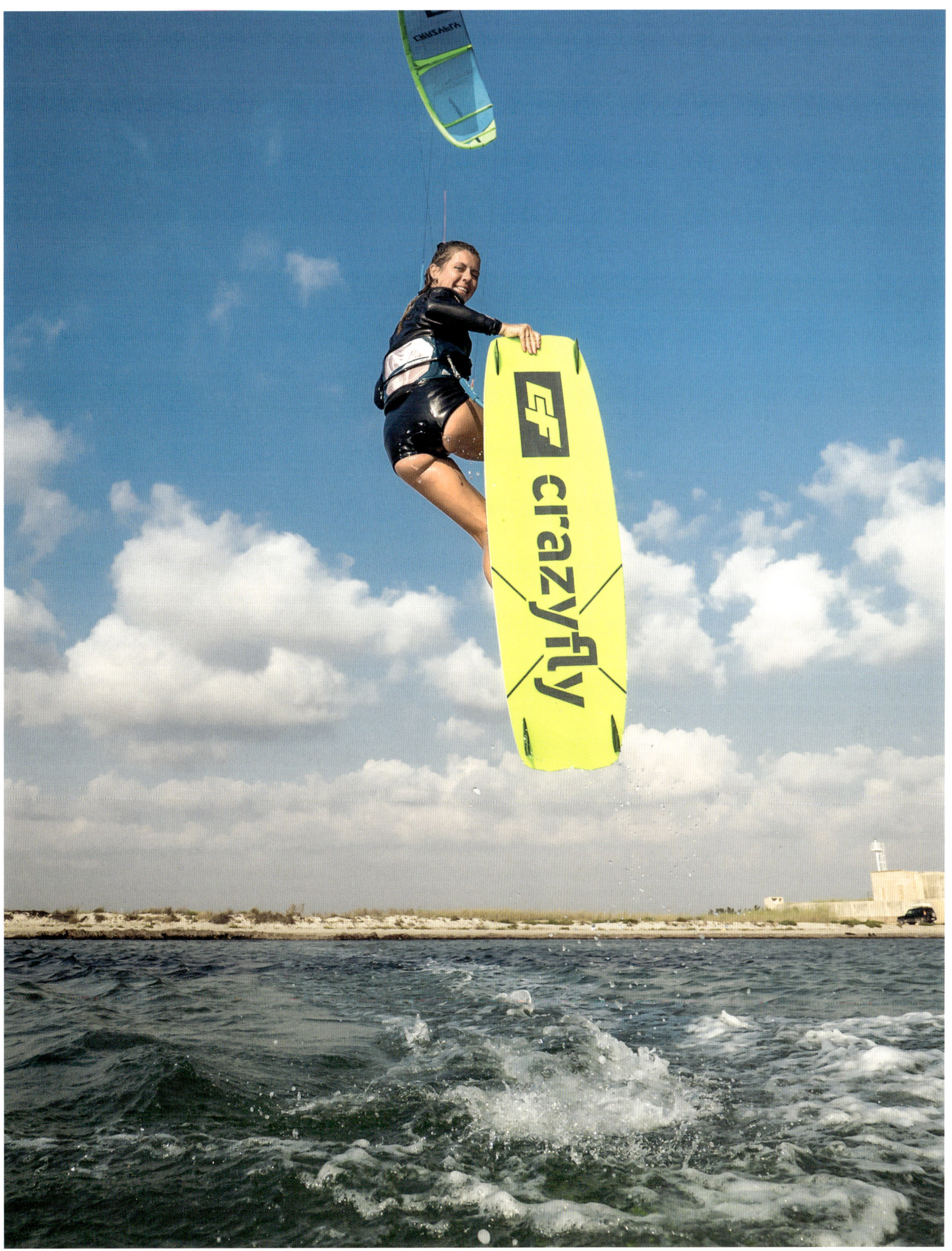

Carro Djupsjö
Wakeboarder

@wakecarro
wakecarro.com

Wakeboarding makes all my thoughts disappear. I only focus on what is right in front of me, whether it is a World Cup event, a new trick, or just that incredible feeling of carving through warm, glassy water. In a way it's instant mindfulness, as I forget about any anxiety or worries I may have and focus on the now.

I grew up wakeboarding in Sweden, where the summer is so short that there was usually still a thin layer of ice on the water when we started riding in the spring. I loved it so much that even the cold was just a sacrifice that had to be made. After I finished high school, I decided to take a leap and left my safe path of university studies to pursue my dream of becoming a professional wakeboarder. I was training hard, traveling all over the globe, and working by cleaning boats, or whatever I could do, in order to pour all the money I made back into my journey toward a pro life. I believed that I could do anything I set my mind to, and I am extremely stubborn.

A few years into my journey, I was starting to question my choices. Somewhere along the road, I had forgotten about why I was doing this and other people's opinions were clouding my judgment. Somehow the industry, stress, and worries about prestige were taking over and that pure joy of me and my board had taken a backseat. I think that's when life decided I needed a break, which literally translated into breaking my body. My career came to an abrupt halt as I went through two major knee injuries, both requiring years of rehab.

There were many nights I was terrified of never being able to wakeboard again, or never even being able to walk without pain again. My injuries forced me to deal with all the emotions I'd been running from and to take a step back and see the bigger picture. They also made me reconnect with the deep longing of just being back in my element again, regardless of skill level, contest results, or sponsor contracts.

During my darkest times I never thought I would write this, but I am grateful for my injuries as they sparked the most unexpected personal growth. Sometimes when we are in the middle of a bad situation we don't understand why it happened to us. But as time passes, we discover that what has happened is the best thing that could have happened.

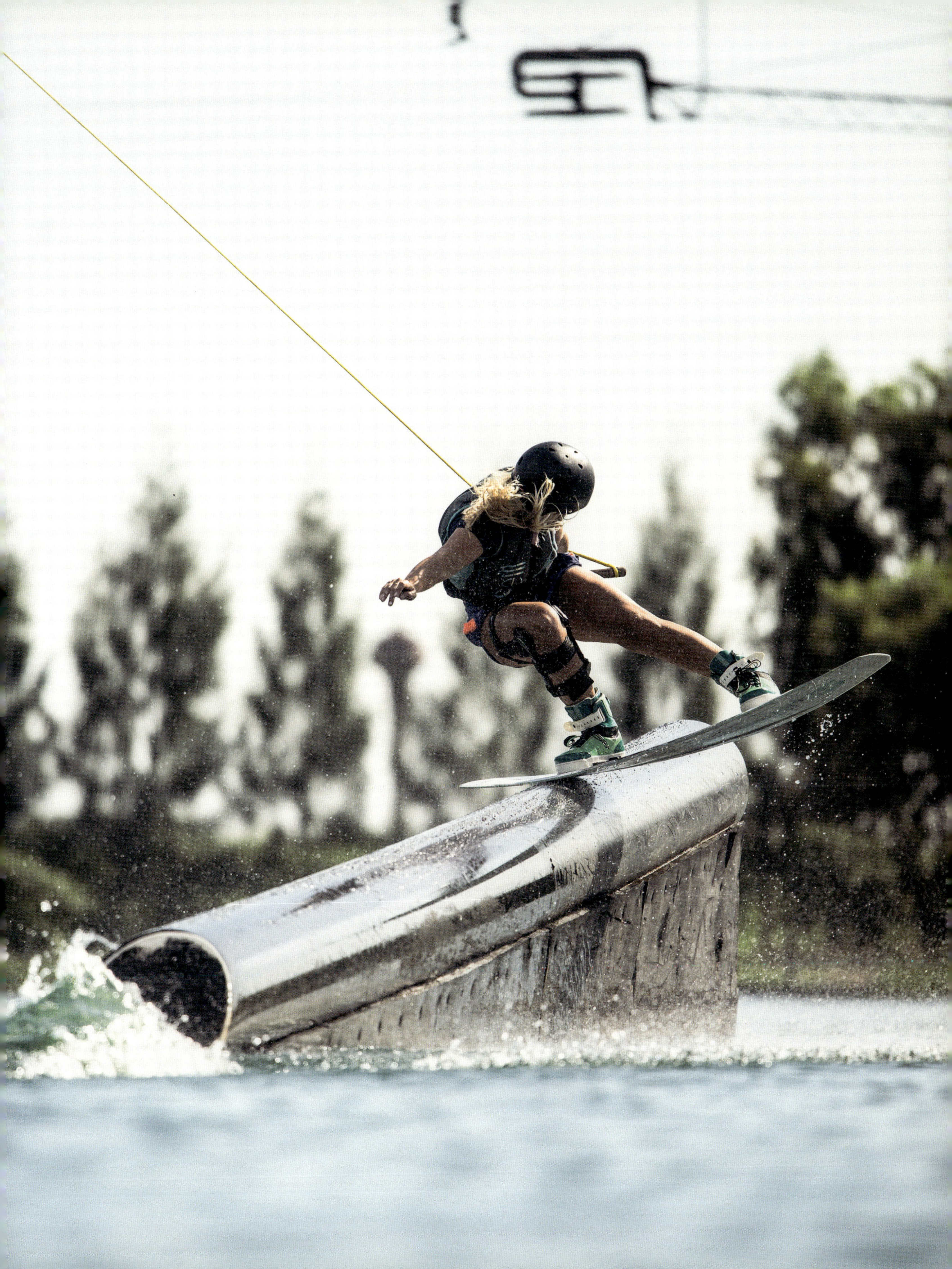

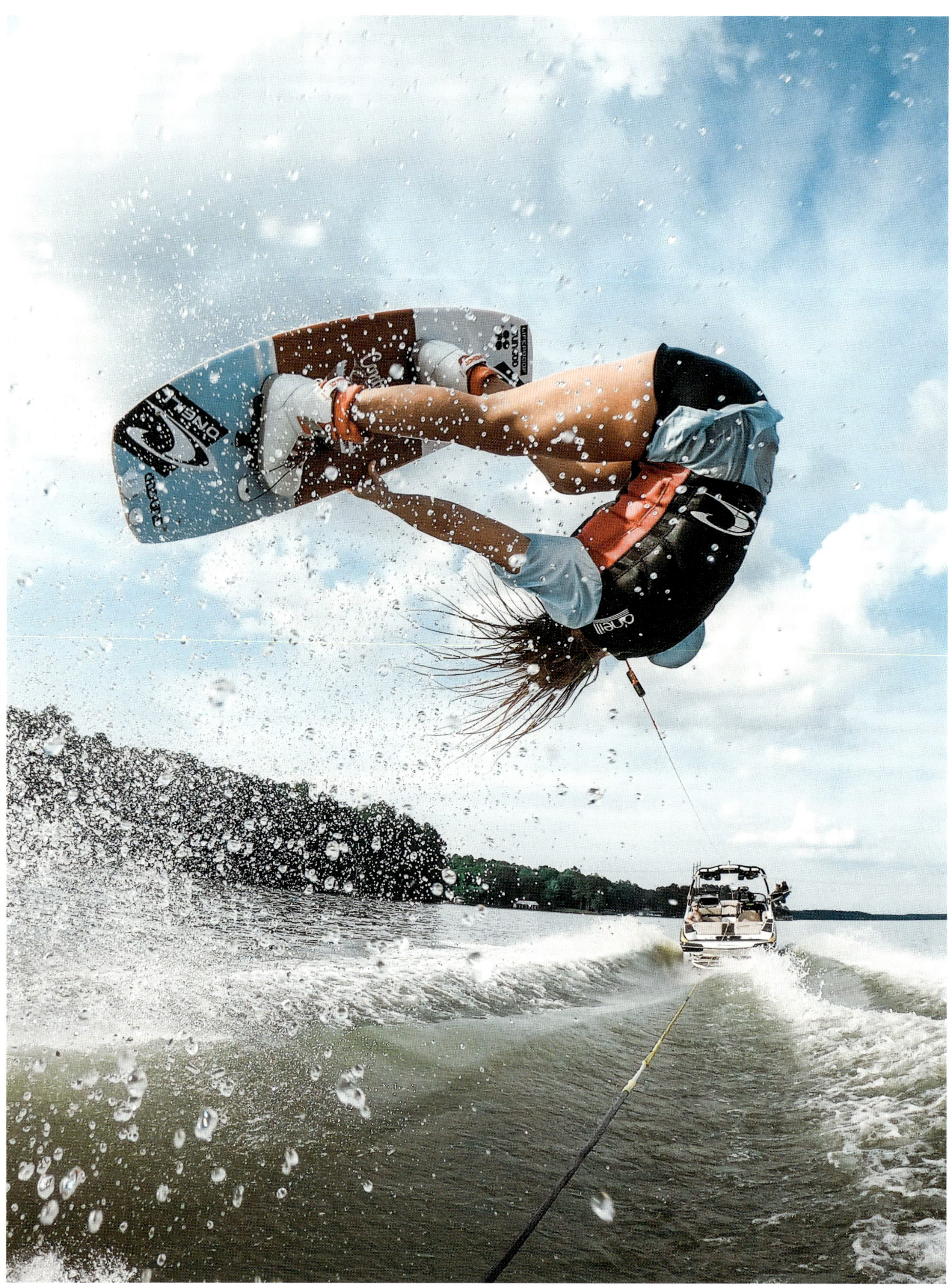

 △ Lake Gaston, North Carolina, USA

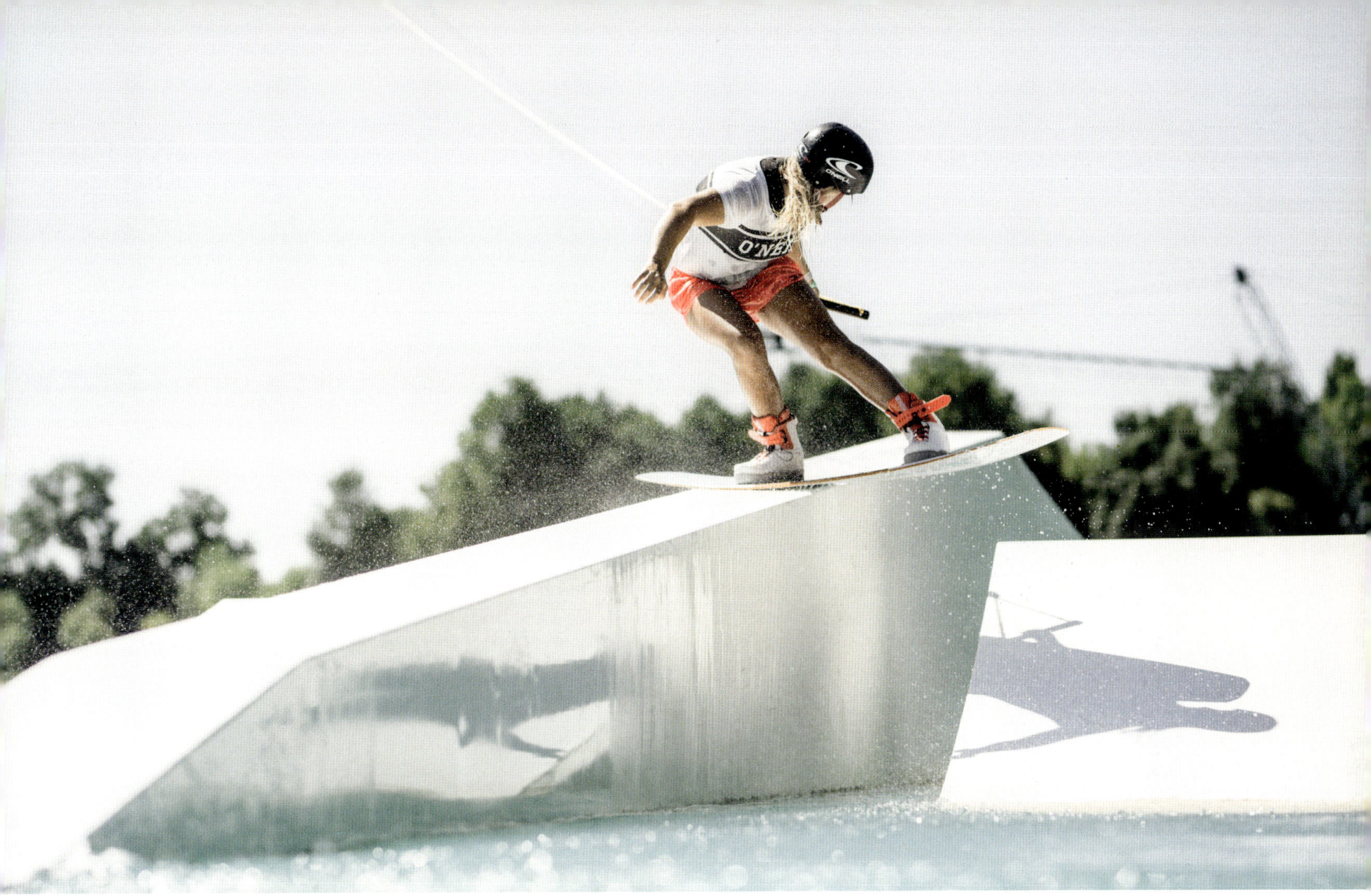

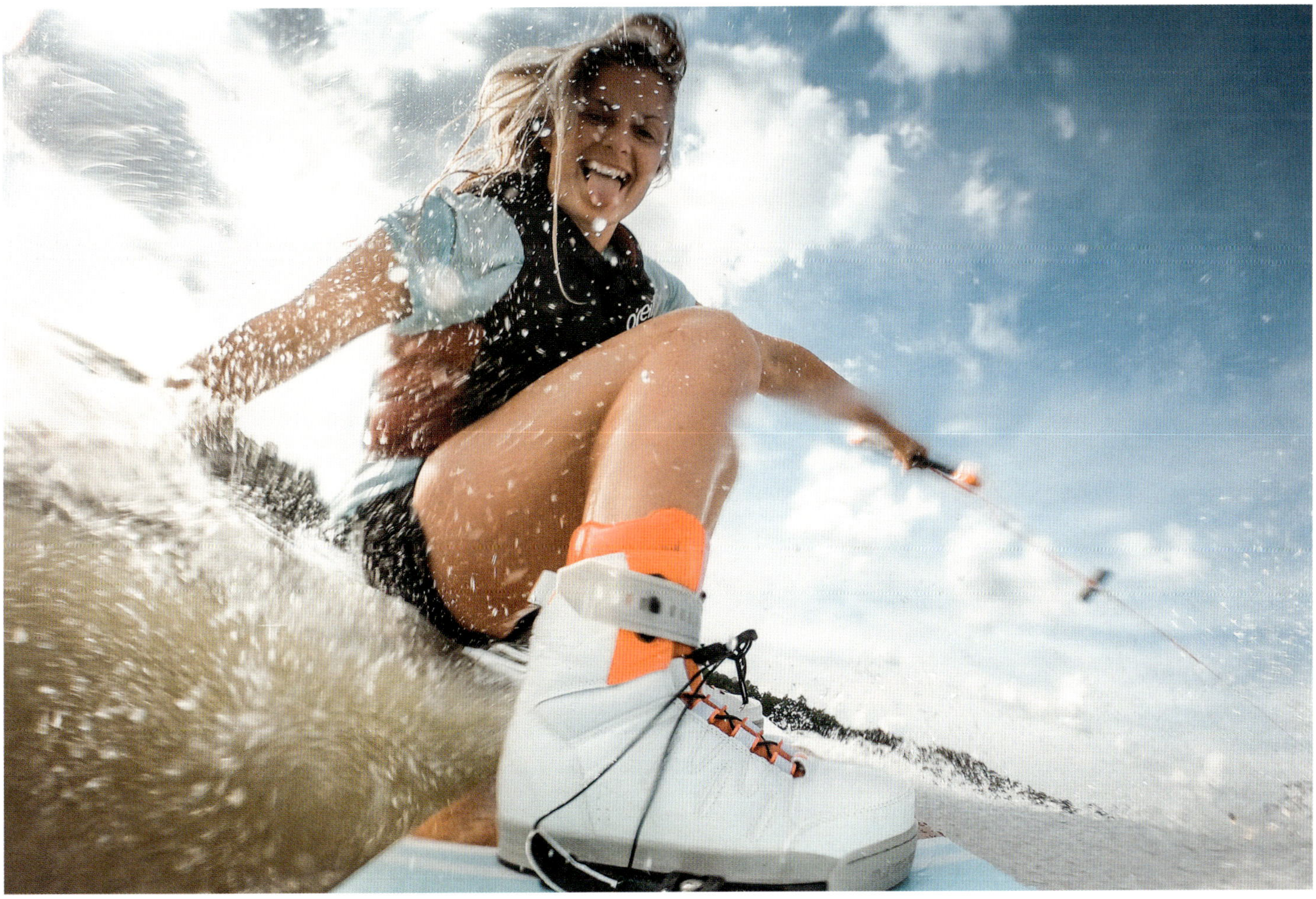

△△ Wake Park Cable 7, Venice, Italy △ Lake Gaston, North Carolina, USA

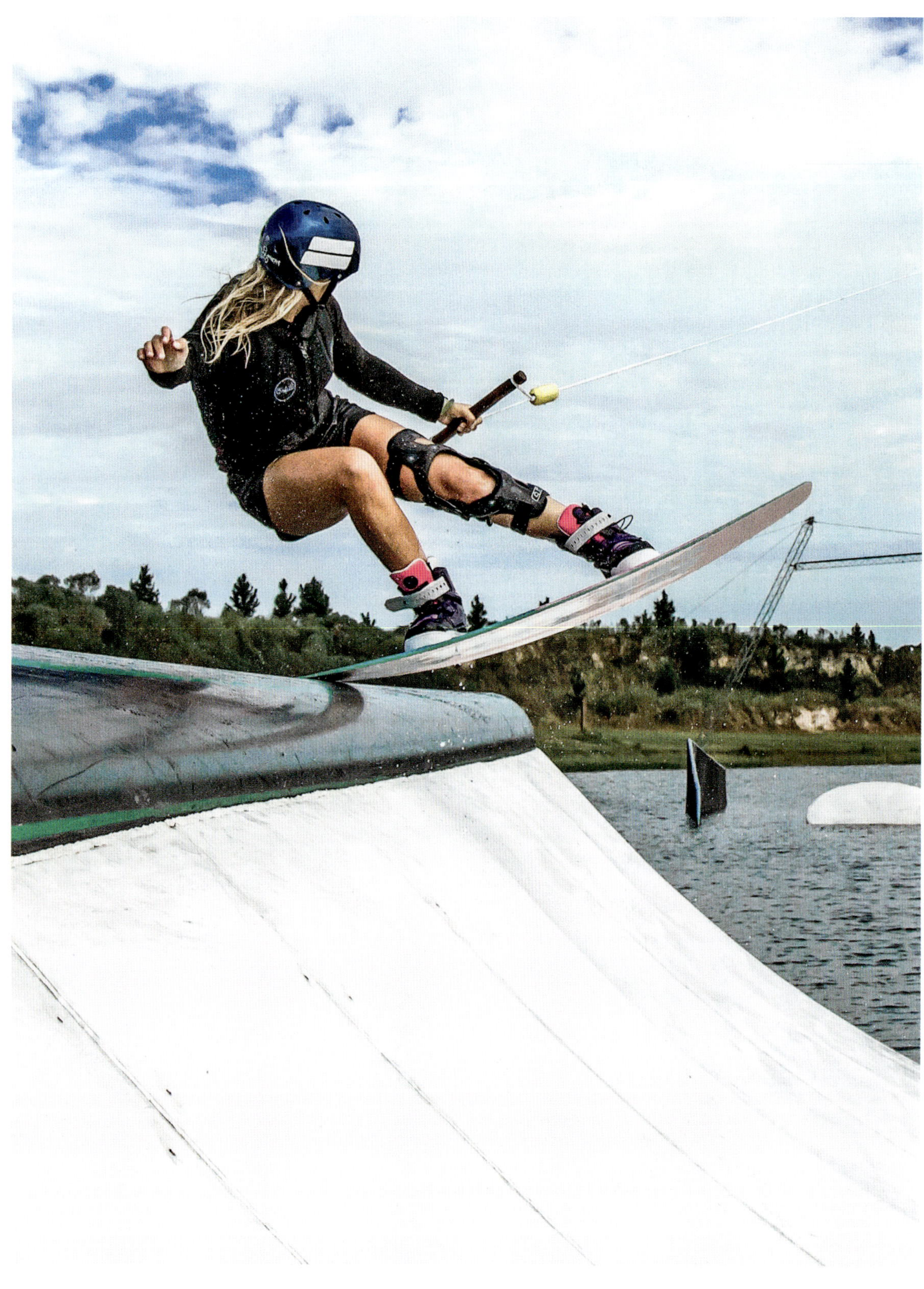

△ Valdosta Wake Compound, Georgia, USA   ▷ Munich, Germany   ▷▷ WakeWay, Vilnius, Lithuania   ▷▷▷ Orlando, Florida, USA

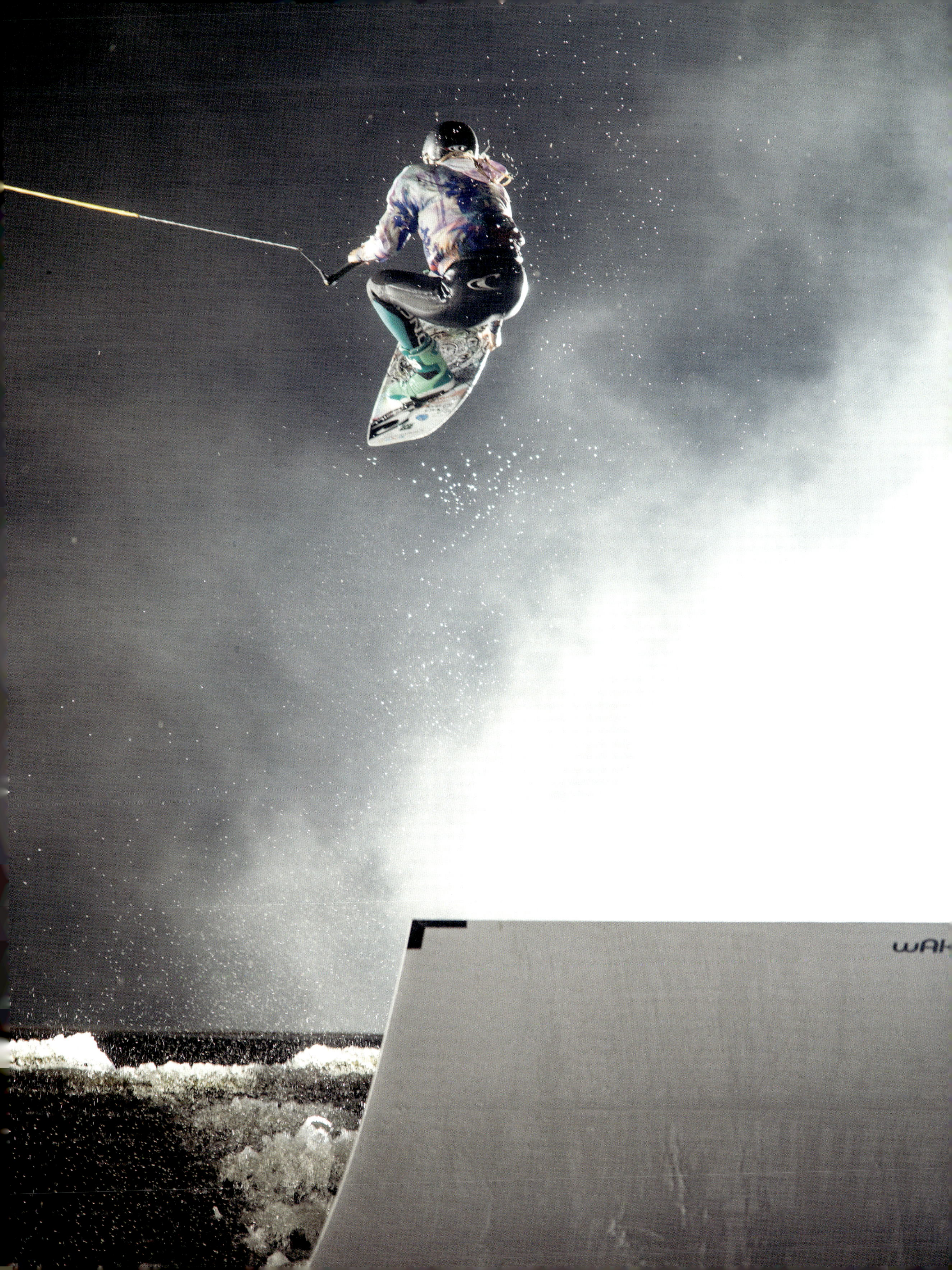
wAK

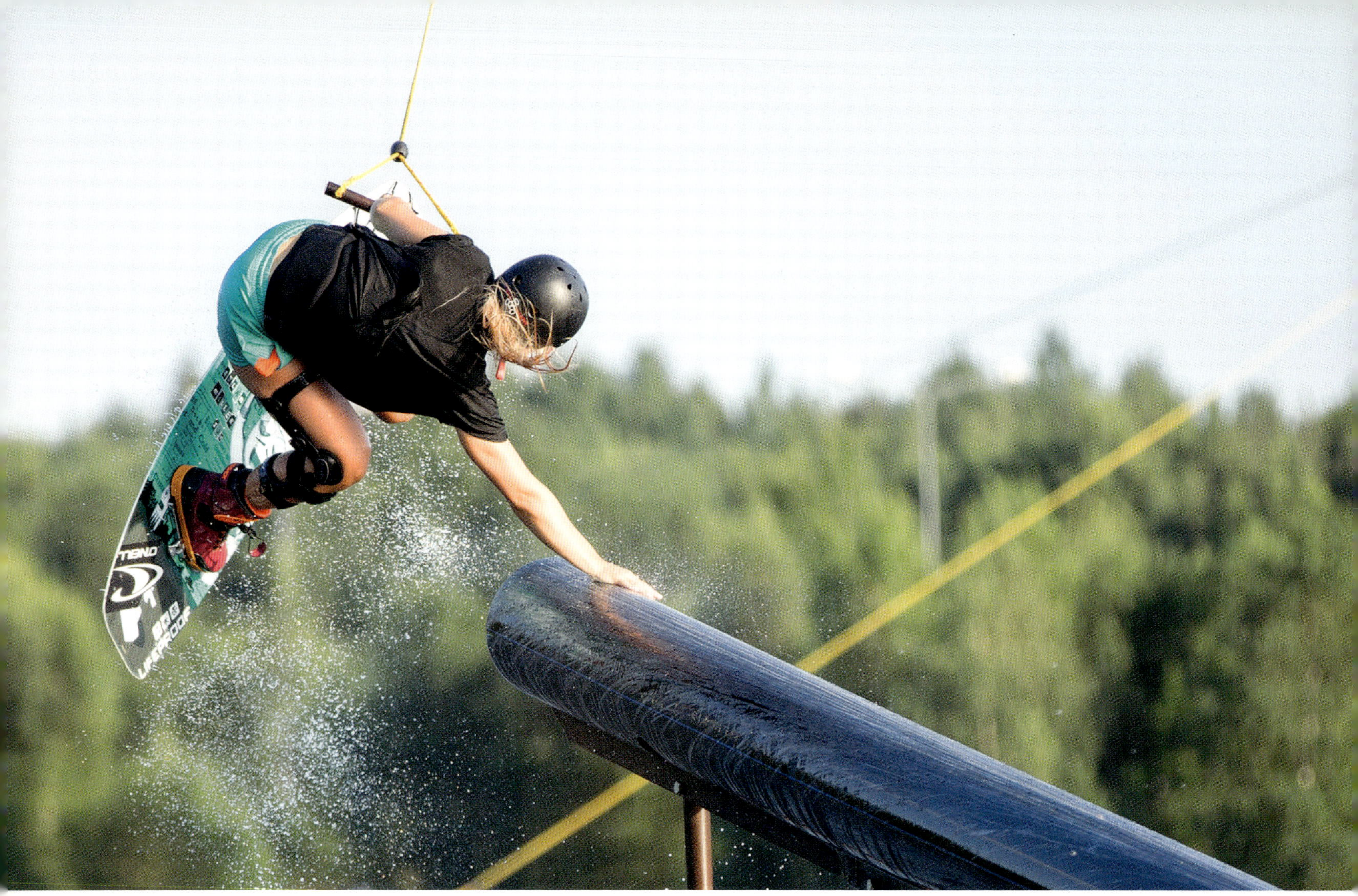

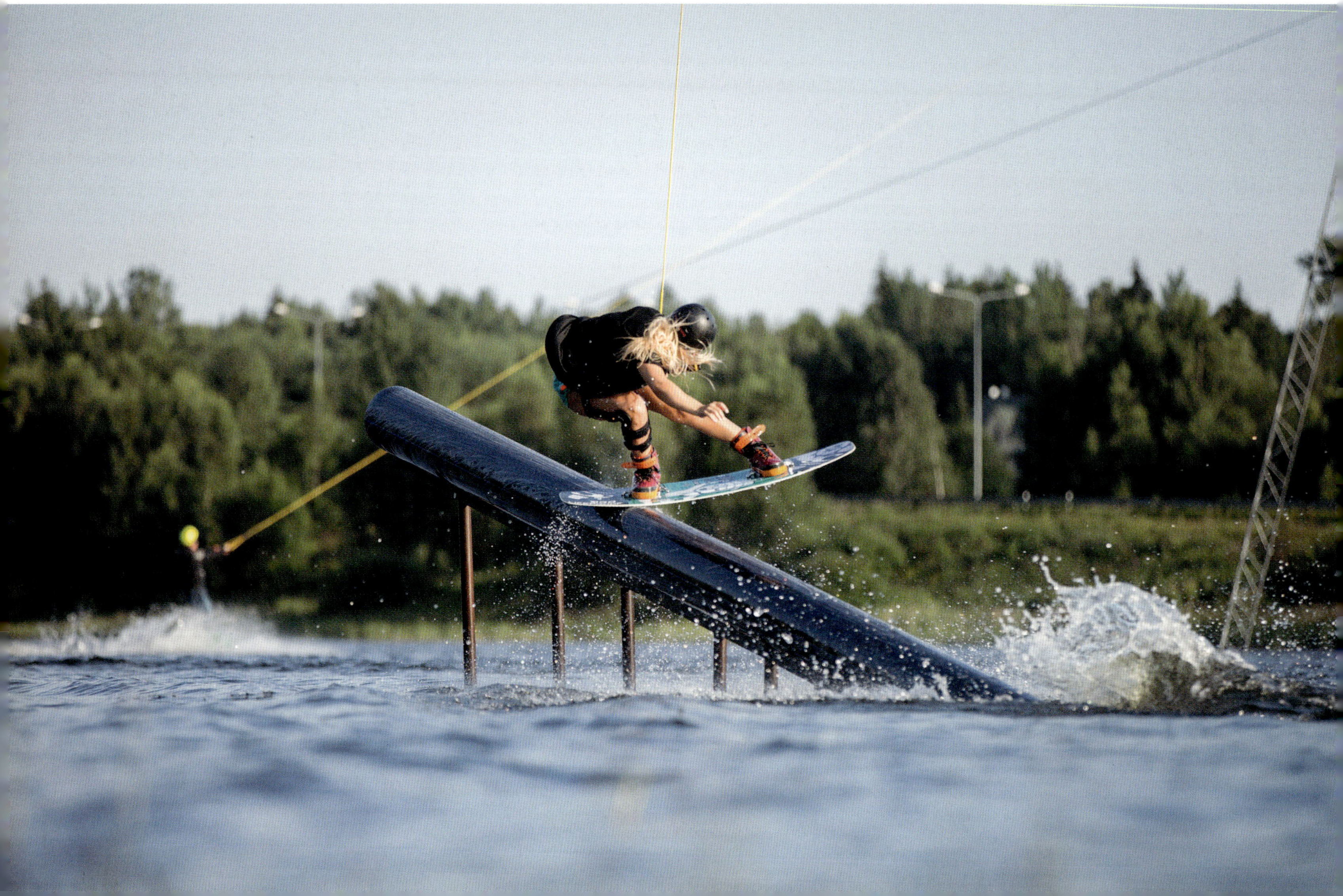

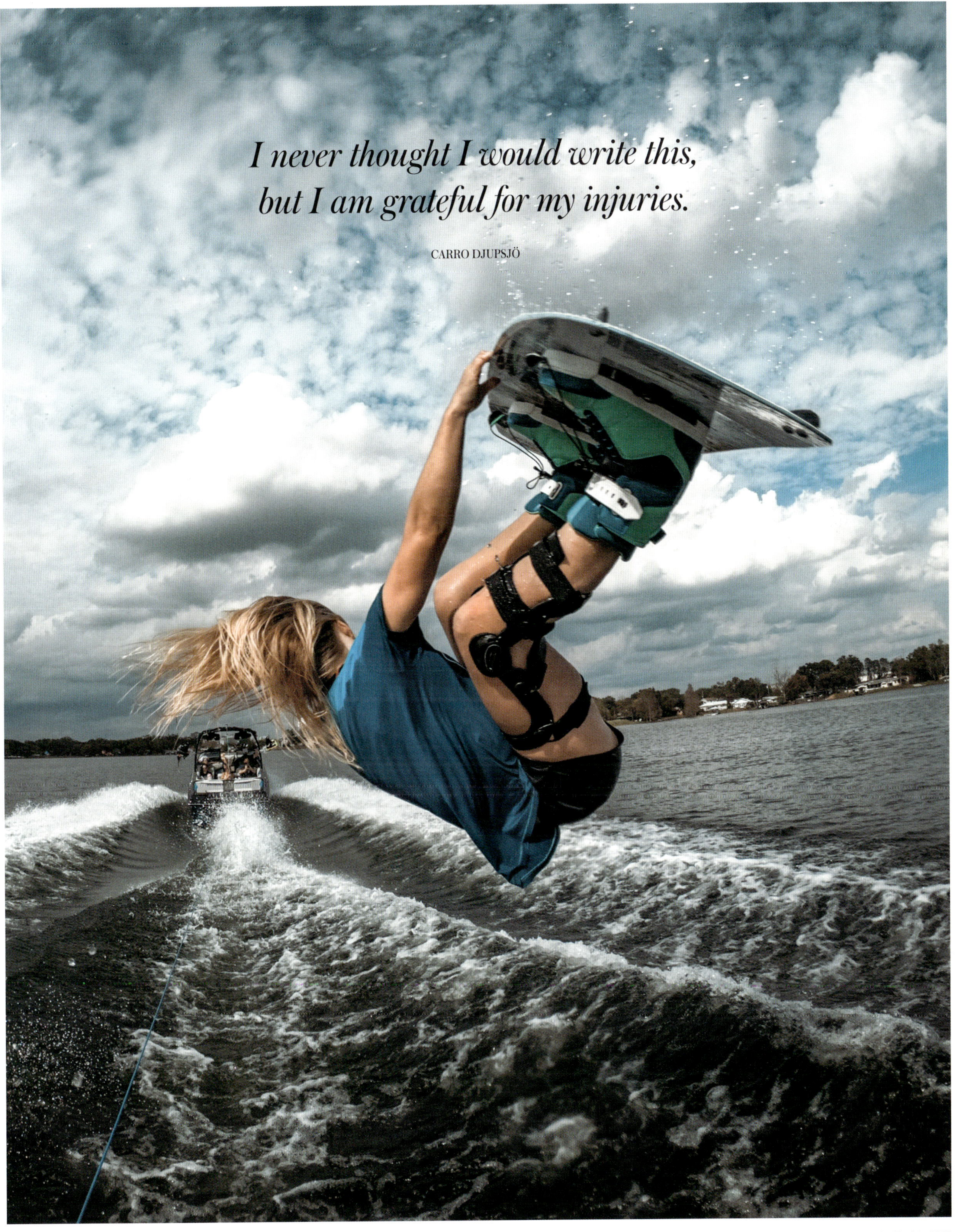

◁ WakeWay, Vilnius, Lithuania   △ Orlando, Florida, USA

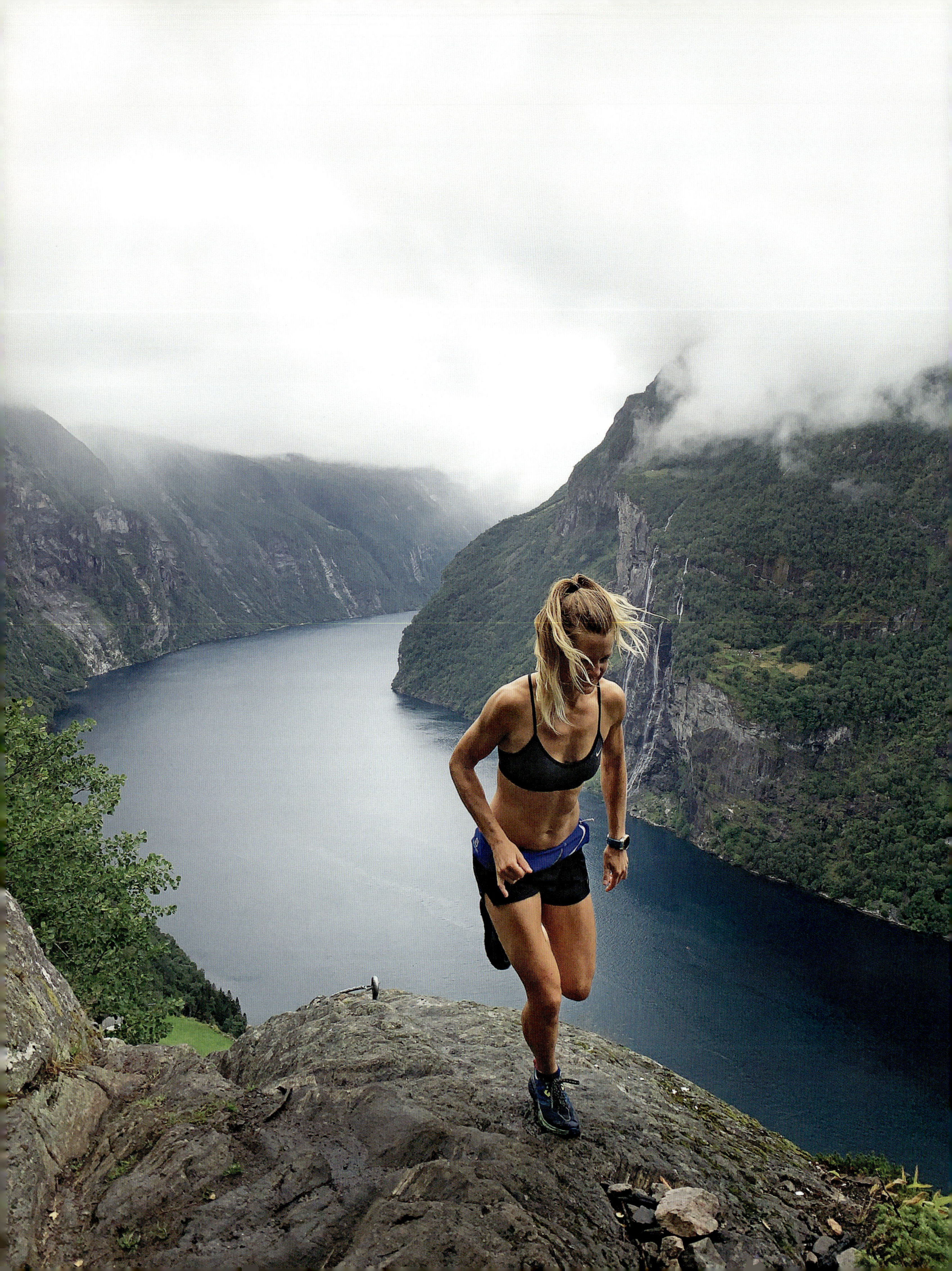

Karin Karlsson

Obstacle course racer

@ocrkarin
karinosteopat.se

I started with the sport of obstacle racing at the age of 24 after four years of traveling and working around the world. Before that I did gymnastics as a kid, football/soccer as a teen, and snowboarding as an adult. When I moved back to Gothenburg, Sweden, for my studies I started to train more again after years of exploring the world and who I wanted to be in life. After a year of intense and fun training at the gym I wanted a challenge and found an obstacle race that I just had to try. It was love at first sight—it's a sport that encourages you to be creative, to move your body forward and conquer obstacles on your way, in a way that works for you. I enjoyed it so much that a thought crossed my mind: "I wonder just how good I could be!?" That was when I started to explore the sport of OCR as well as physical and mental training.

For me it has always been about doing what I love, about living and enjoying life. If you want to be the best at something, you need to do it a lot. You need to make sacrifices and decide on your priorities in life. At the same time I wanted to make my training fun and enjoyable— after all, it was still a hobby. So I started analyzing what was required to improve in the sport of OCR—strength, technique, having guts, and being fierce—and spent most of my time running trails in the forest and mountains, and climbing for grip and upper body strength. The work to become the best in the world has been tough but every day for five years I've been doing something that I love. That led to two World Champion titles.

I've always had big and small dreams, or big and small goals. I started thinking early in life about how I want to spend my days and live my life. And I've worked hard to make it happen. I've thought a lot about where this comes from, why I have this drive. I believe that some of it comes from when I was a kid, when I lost a sibling at an early age,

a sibling with severe disabilities. Growing up and seeing what she wasn't able to do, I realized how fragile and short life is. It needs to be spent doing what you enjoy and with the people you love—not tomorrow, but today.

When it comes to motivation, I believe that you need to start with discipline. It's always hard in the beginning, hard to be motivated to do something you're not comfortable with. But with time, whatever you want to achieve will be easier. The motivation will always come and go and that's when you need a good plan.

When I lose my motivation I always ask myself why. What's the problem today—am I tired or lazy? If I feel that I'm actually tired, I will rest for a day or two. If it's not about energy levels but lack of motivation, I make it harder for me to skip what it is I want to do by scheduling with a friend, booking a class, putting my clothes on. And if I need to, I change my plan and do something similar instead. If you constantly do something you don't want to do, it will break you down. Then it's time to revise the plan.

To become the best at something you need to be fierce, stand up tall, and believe in yourself. Being brave doesn't mean you're never scared; it means being scared but doing it anyway.

Obstacle racing is a lot like life: you need to give it 100 percent when you're out racing because even 1 percent of doubt will cause you to fail. "Fake it till you make it" is a cliché but it actually works. Dare to believe, dare to fail, dare to stand up and try again. Make your dream a plan and start working on how to make it happen. It took me five years to turn my dream into reality because I dared to believe in it, I dared to say I was going to do it, and I did it. I freaking did it!

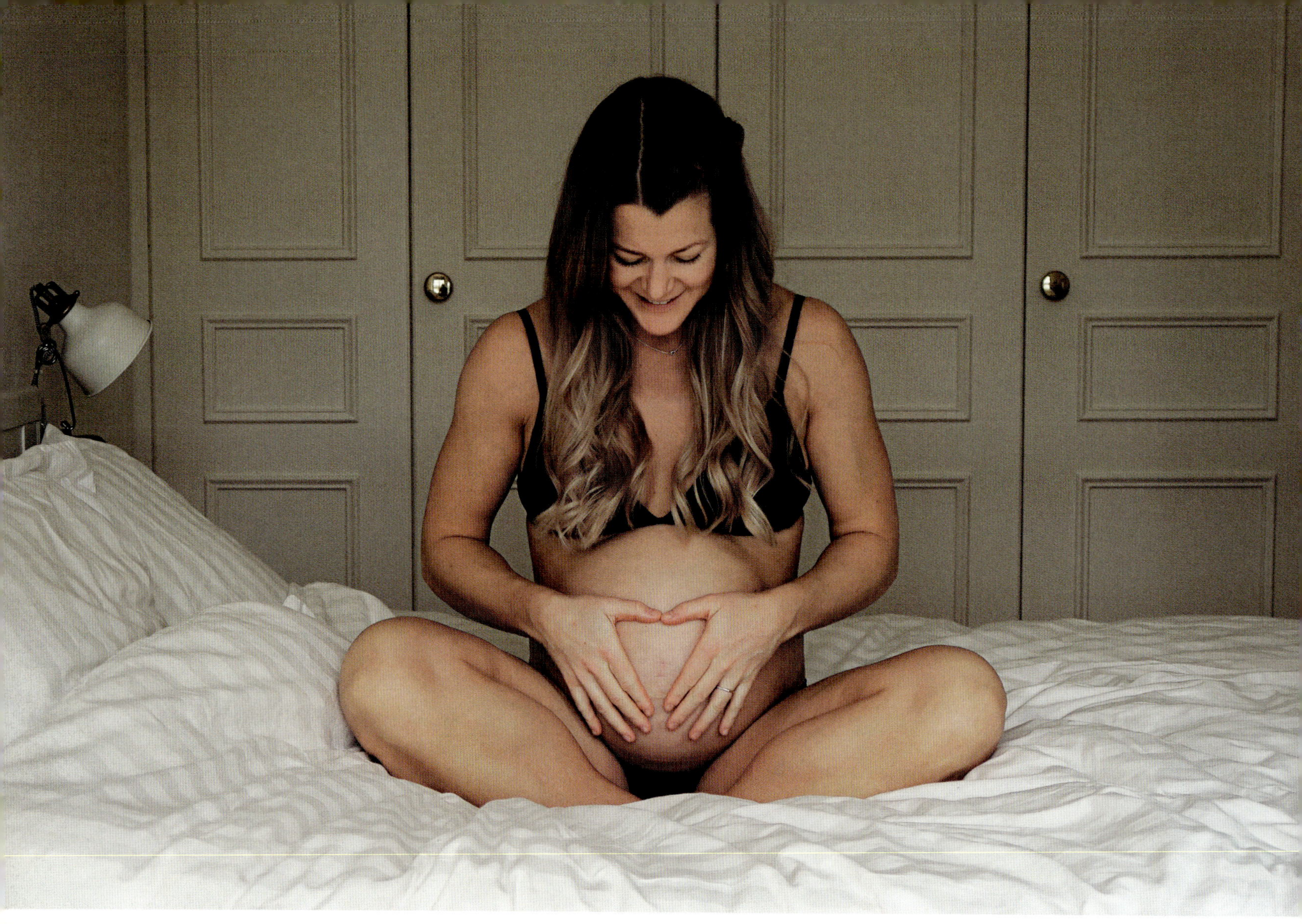

It's been a really exciting journey being pregnant and continuing with my hobby, training and exploring. People have so many opinions on what you should and shouldn't do while pregnant. I've focused on listening to science and most of all to my own body. The answer is always there. It does help of course that I'm a professional osteopath, with the knowledge and experience that brings. My expertise has helped me evaluate my weekly and even daily progress, my pains and my troubles, and to adjust my rehab and training accordingly.

I went into pregnancy with the mindset that I wanted to see what was possible for me to keep doing. I wanted to run and do pull-ups for as long as I could. The funny thing is, they were both among the first things I had to stop doing because they didn't feel good. When in week ten I experienced pelvic pain from running, I was very frustrated and sad. I was scared that not being able to do what I love from so early in the pregnancy would affect my mental state. But it only affected me negatively for as long as I held on to it tightly. As

soon as I accepted that it was just not going to work and that I needed to change how I was doing things, I barely missed it. I'm looking forward to doing it again, but for now I'm happy with where I am and what I can do.

The mental game of being pregnant is very similar to being injured. Instead of focusing on what you would've or could've done if you hadn't been injured, focus on the positive side: what you can do now. Maybe you can't run, but you can hike. Maybe you can't do pull-ups, but you can go to the gym. It will make the journey you're on way more fun and fulfilling.

Overall the pregnancy has been a well-needed break from an otherwise goal-oriented mind and life. It gave me some time to reflect on all the things I've accomplished and experienced in the last few years. Now I look forward to new adventures: making my body strong and healthy again, getting to know my daughter, and creating a new life together with her and Oscar.

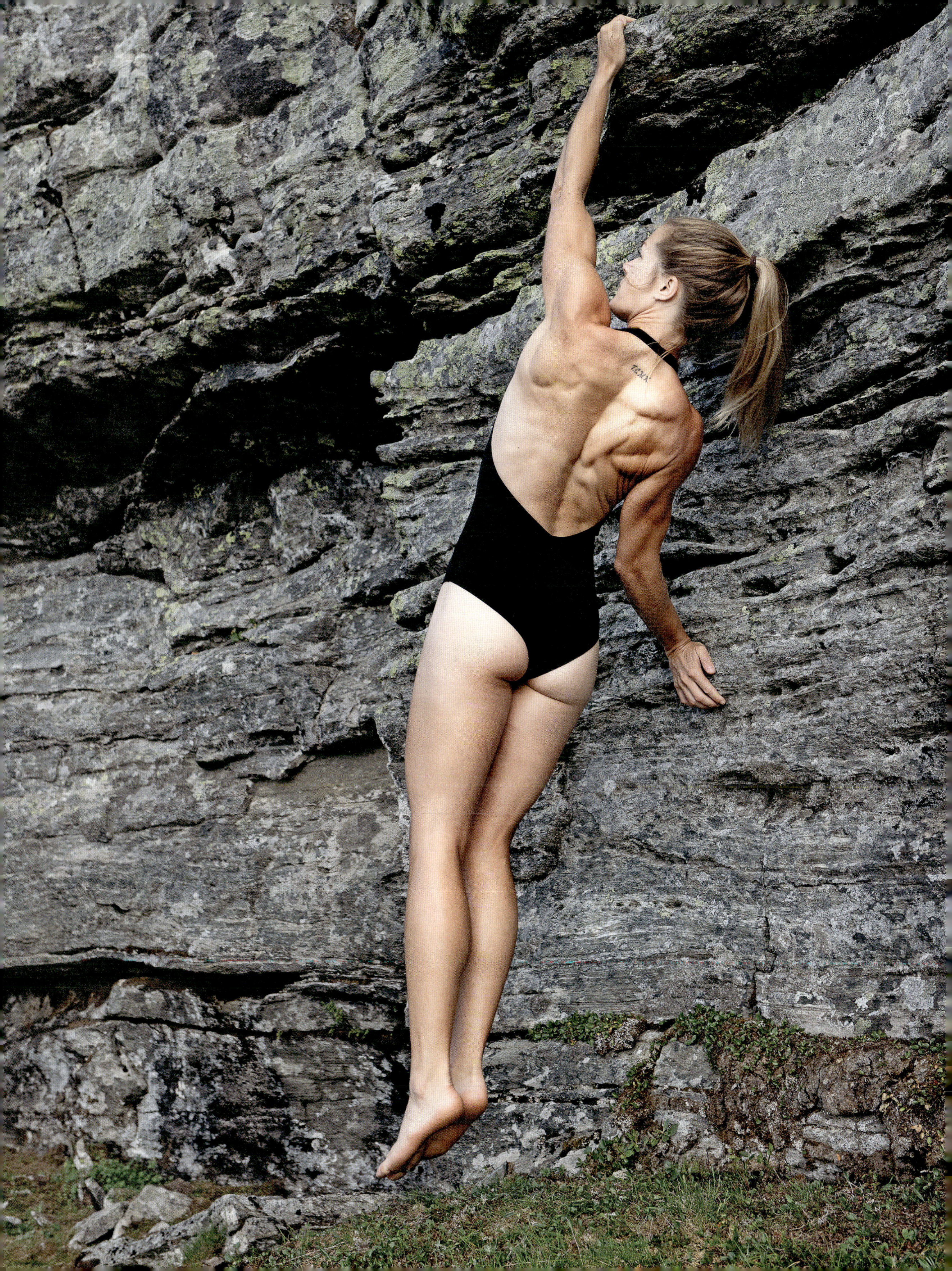

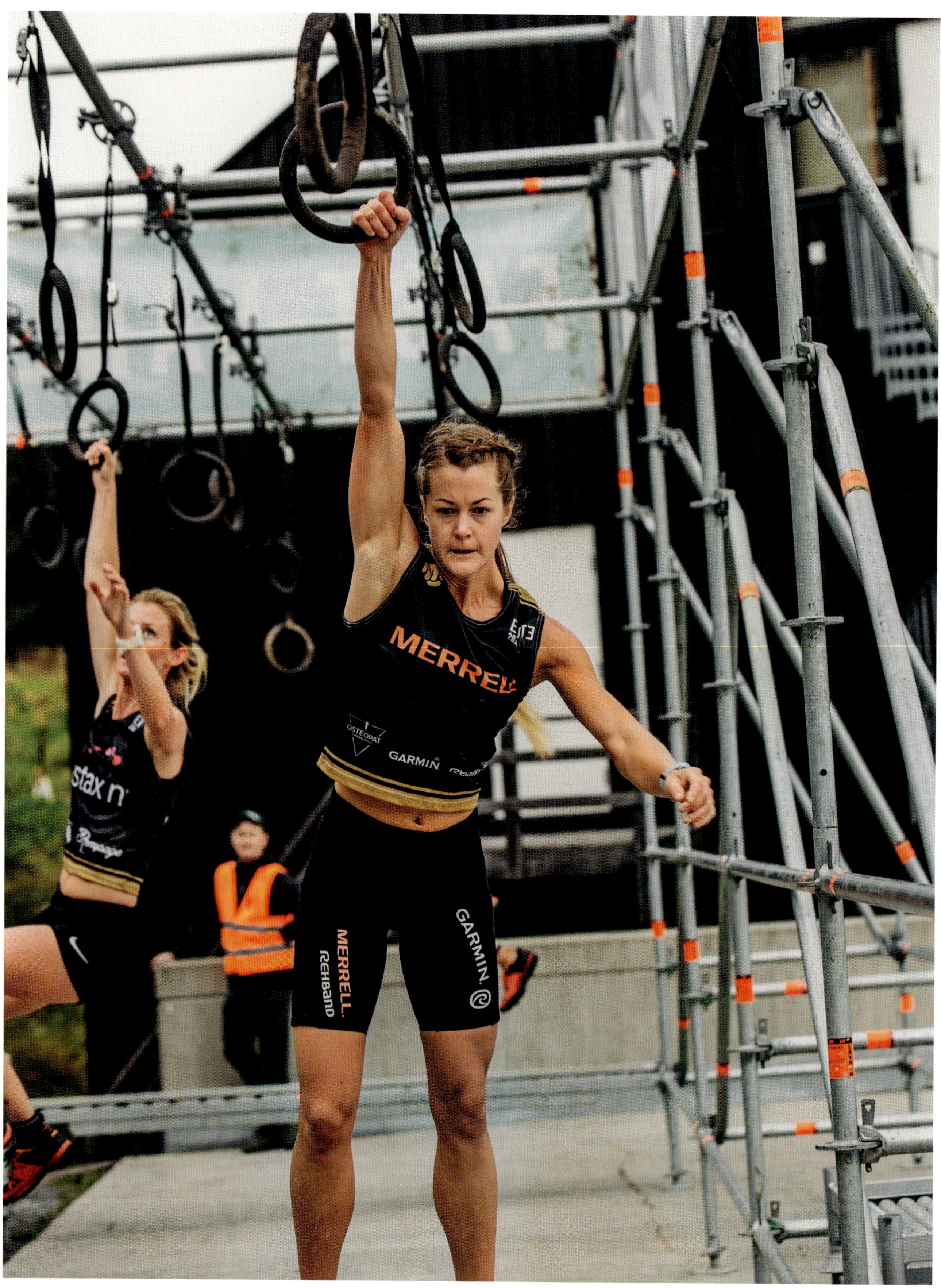

  △ Oslo, Norway   ▷ Malmö, Sweden

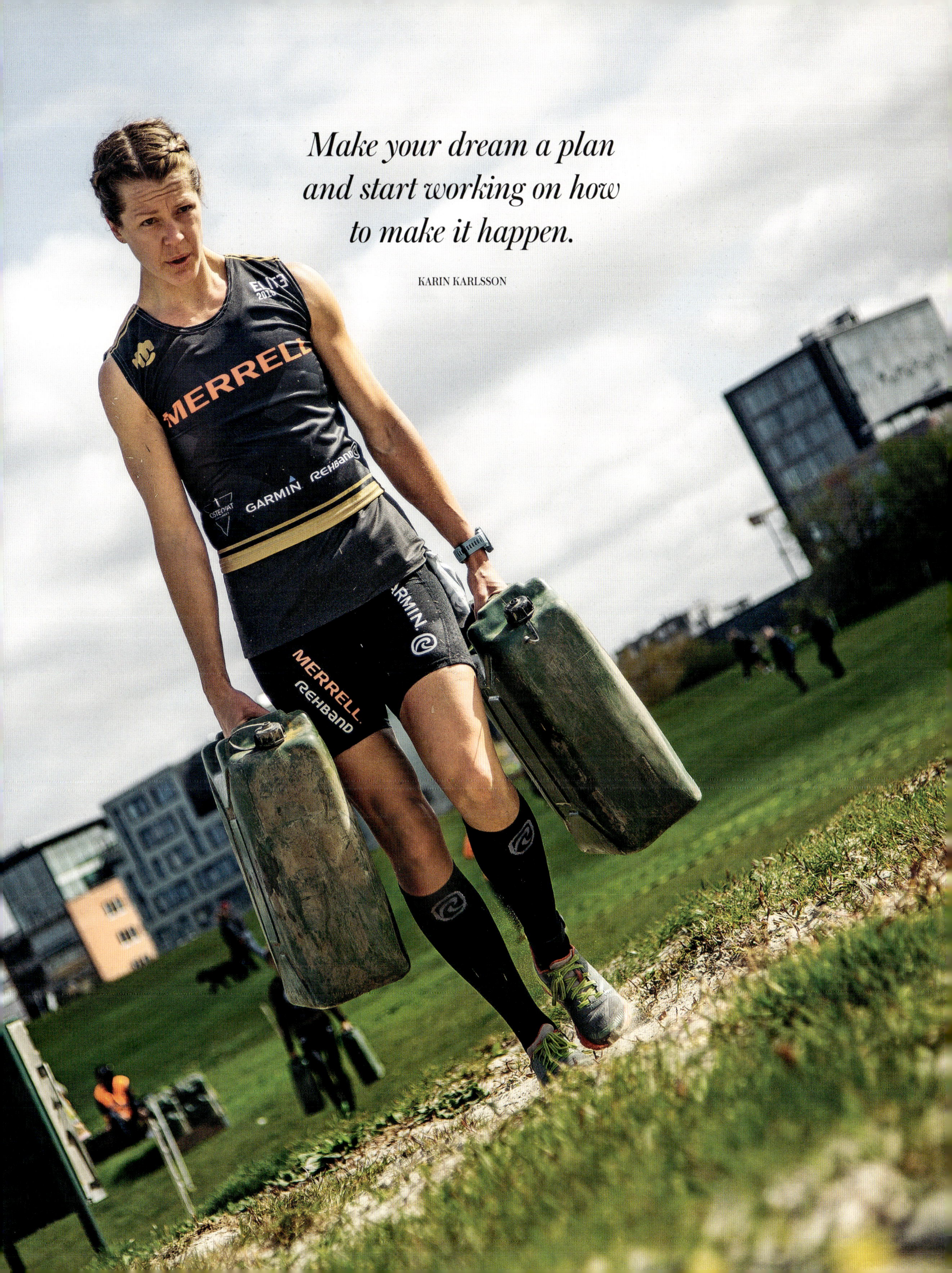

Make your dream a plan and start working on how to make it happen.

KARIN KARLSSON

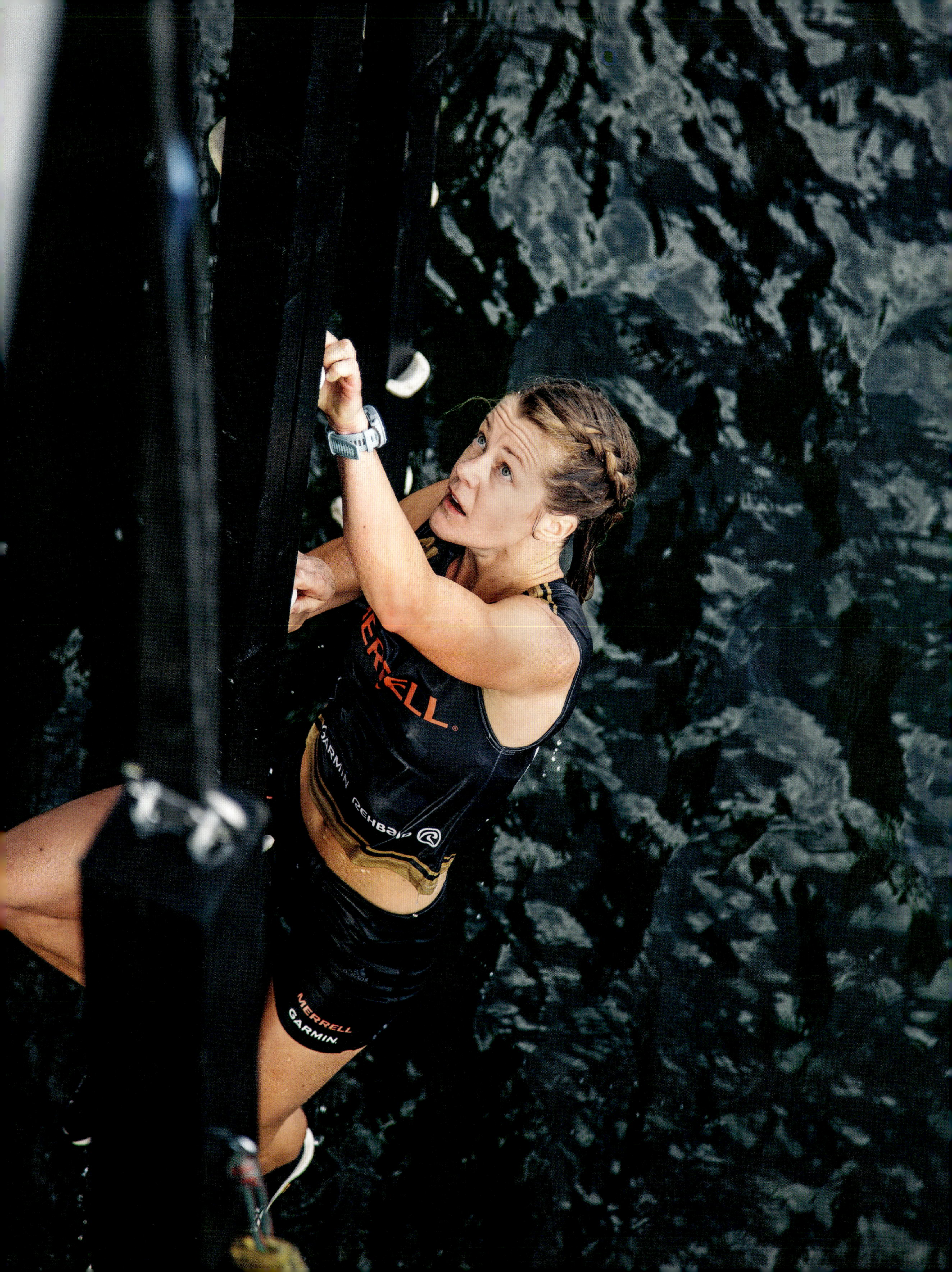

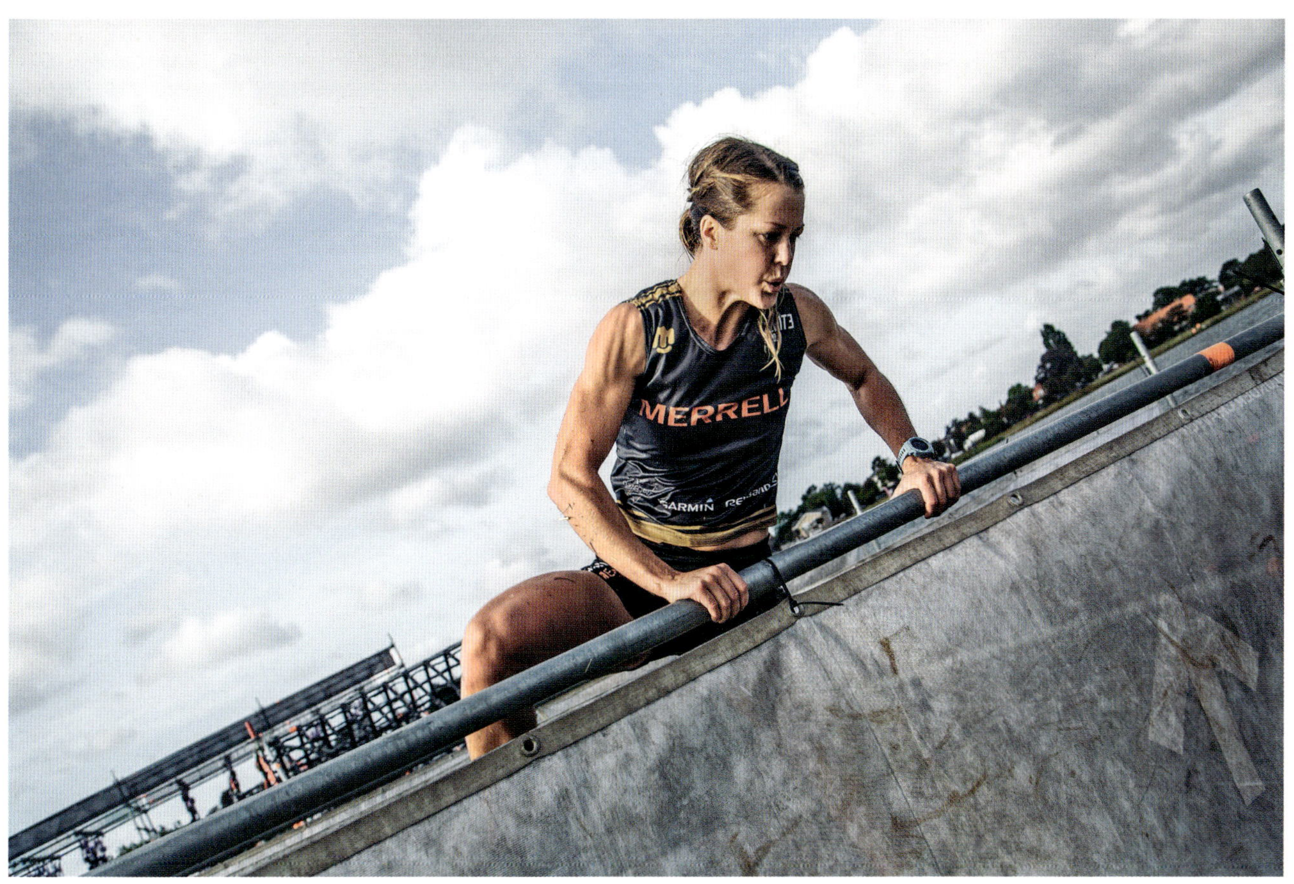

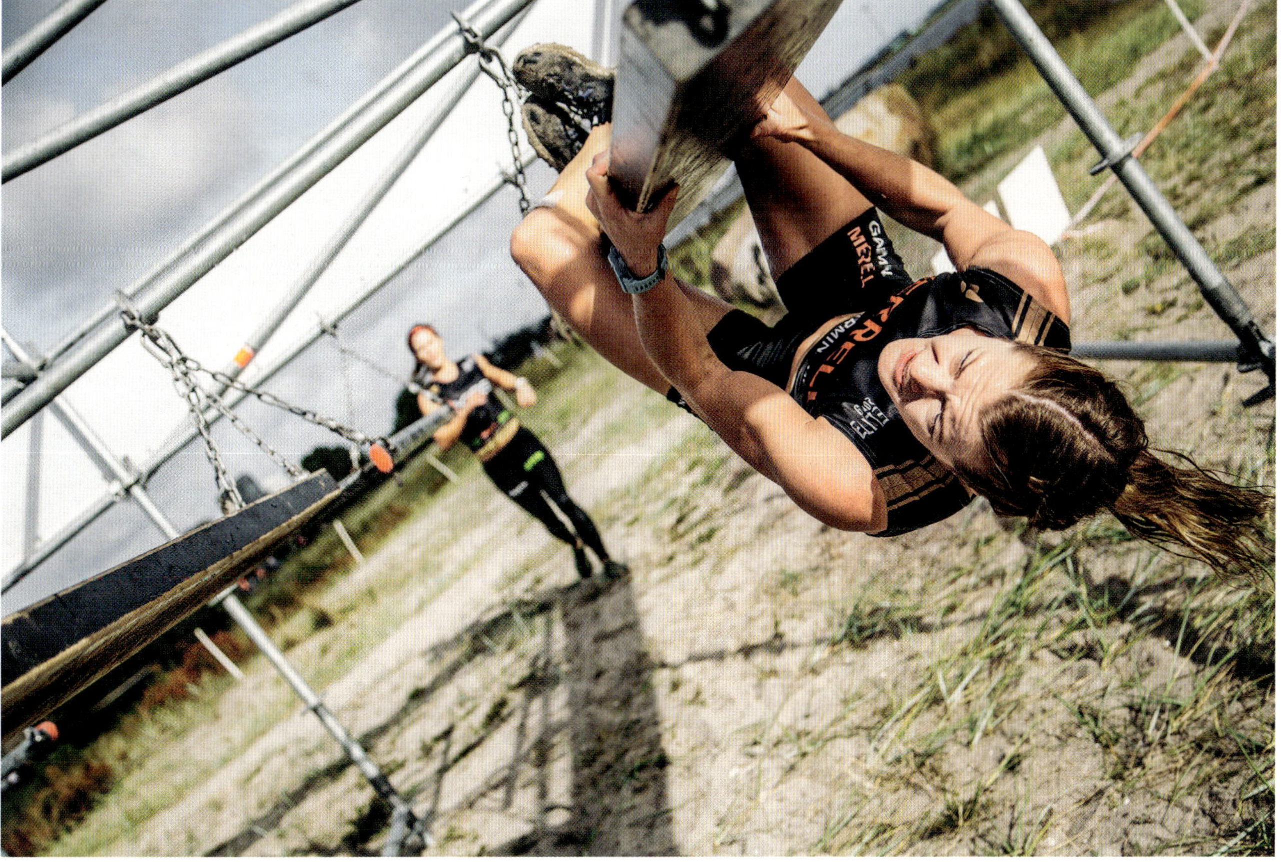

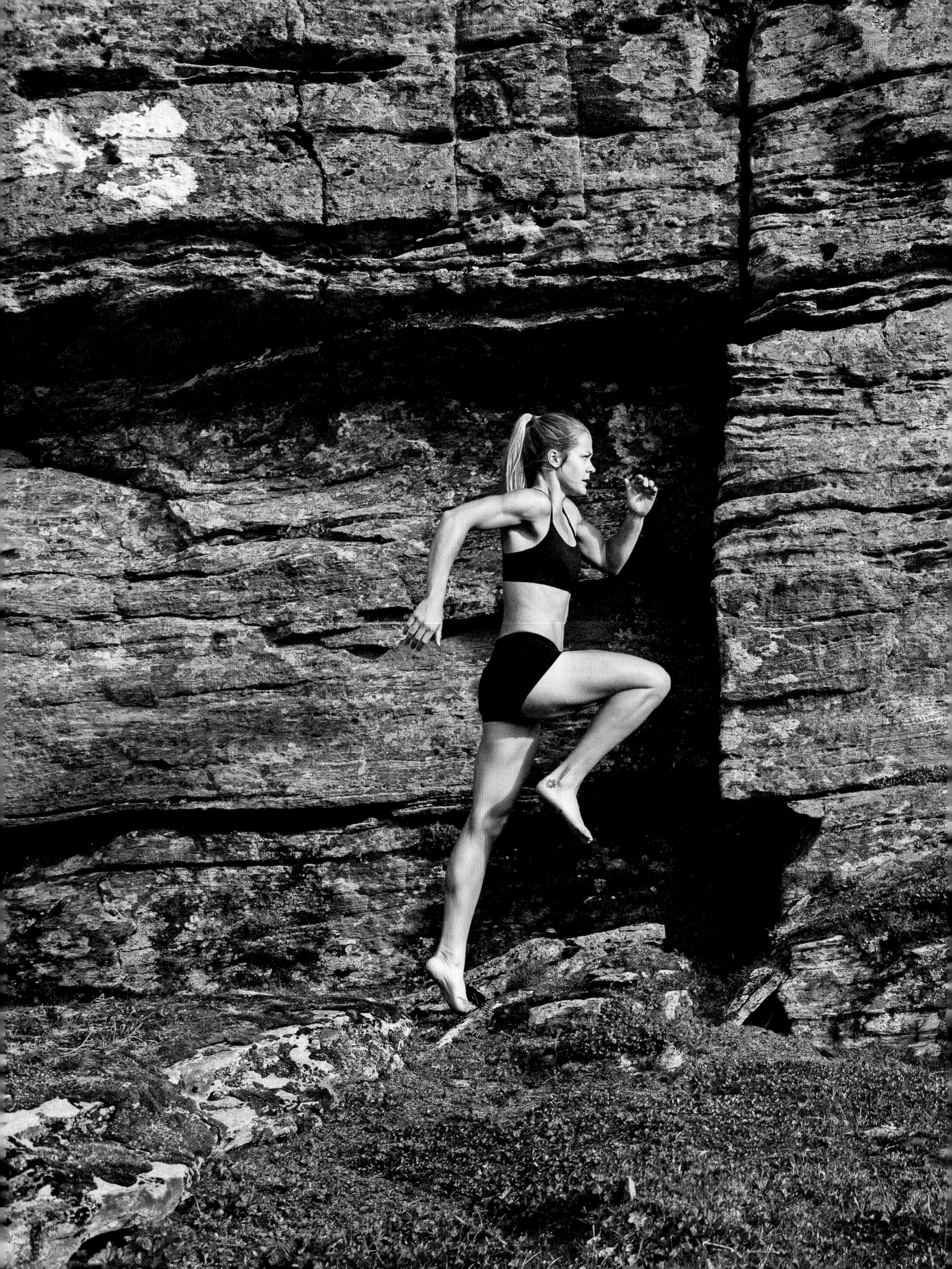

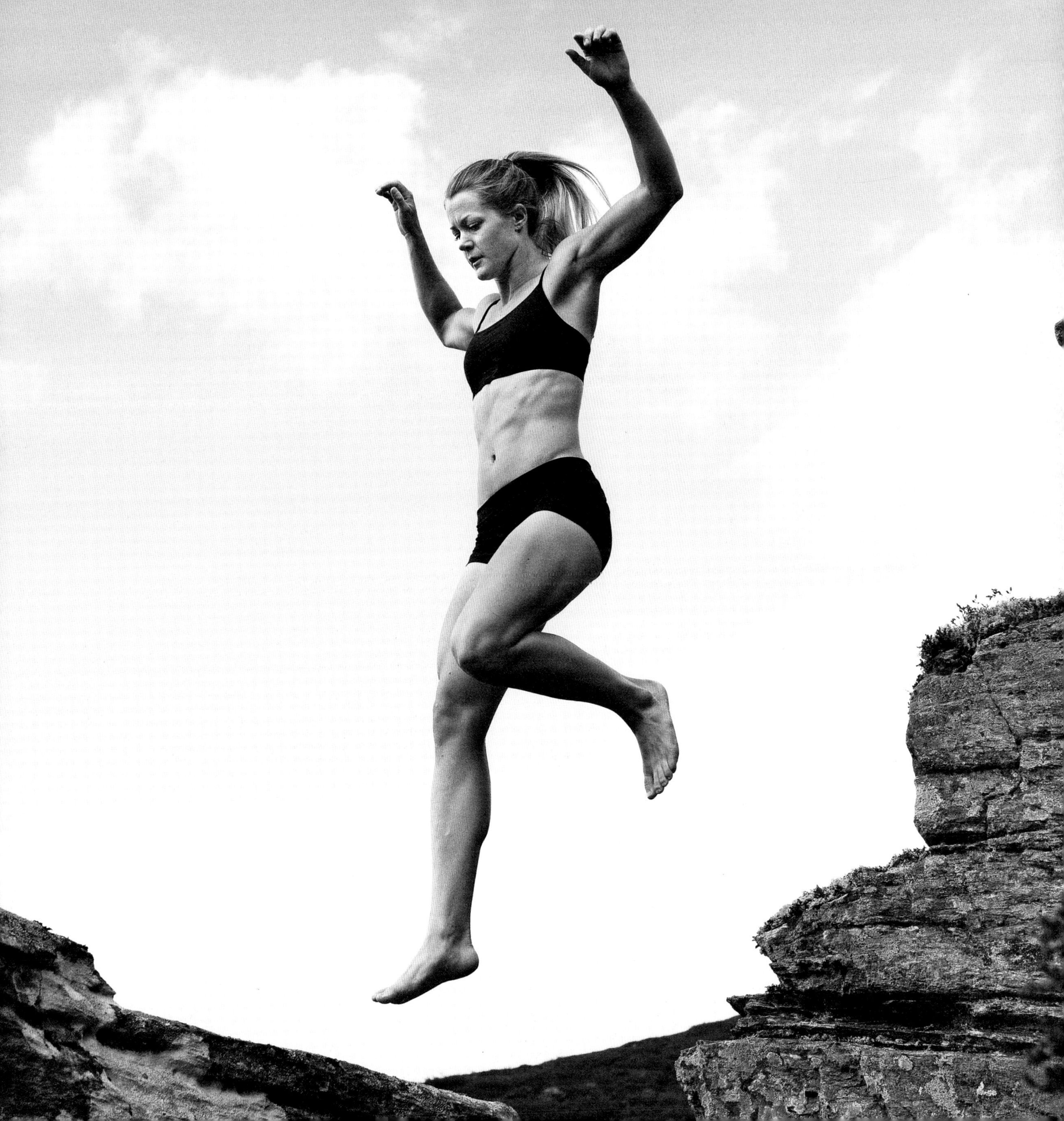

There is no magic
shortcut to results.

KARIN KARLSSON

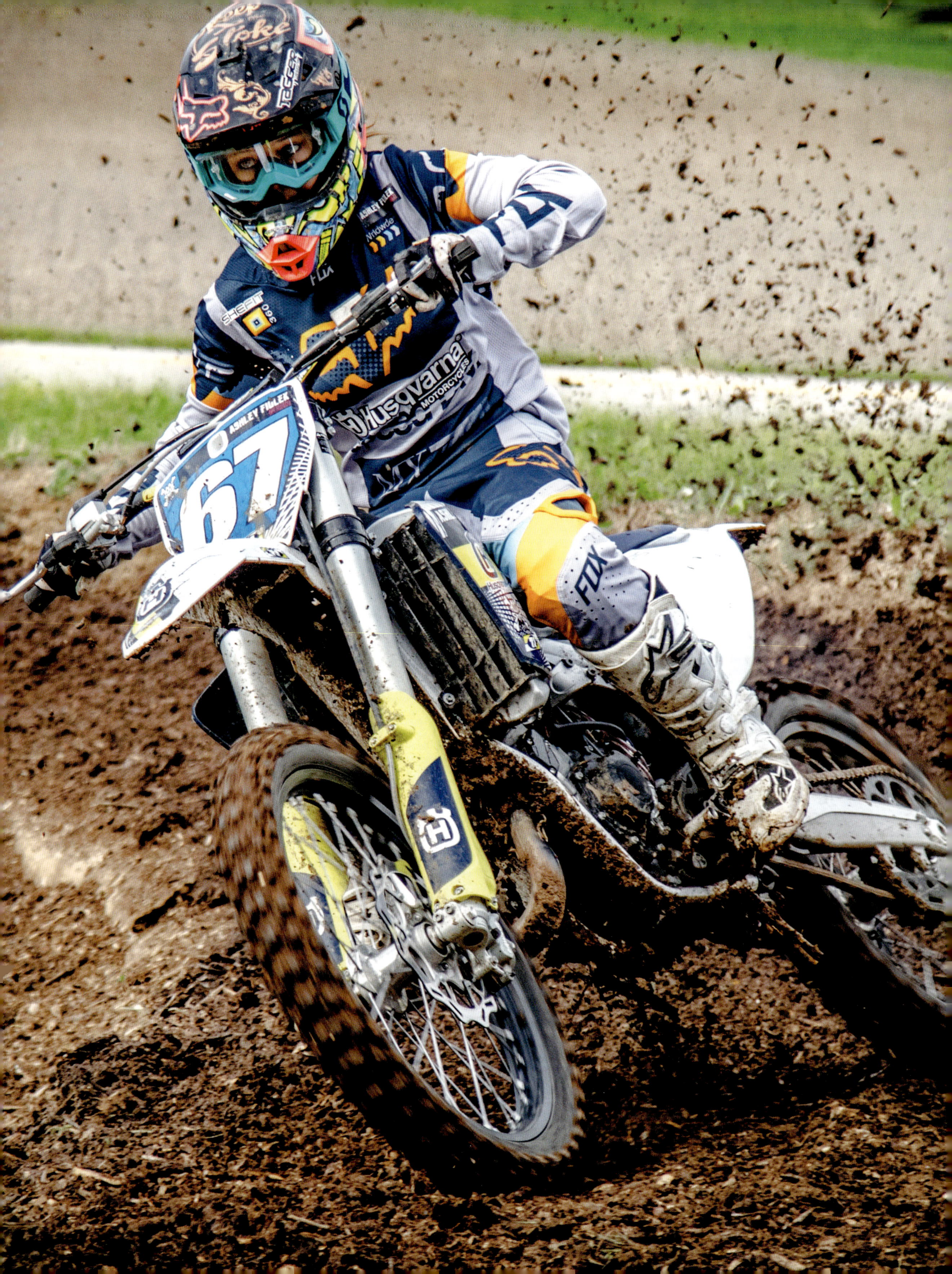
ASHLEY FINLEY
Worldwide
Husqvarna
MOTORCYCLES
MY
FOX
67

Ashley Fiolek
Motocross racer

@ashleyfiolek_67

I was born deaf. My parents didn't know that I was deaf until I was three years old. How did they find out? My mom dropped a bunch of pans in the kitchen one day by accident and she noticed that I didn't even flinch, so my parents immediately knew something was not right. They took me to the doctor's and after some tests, they found out I was deaf. My family moved to Florida to be close to schools for me. Florida is where I fell in love with dirt bikes. The first time my dad put me on his dirt bike I couldn't get enough. I wanted to ride on it all the time and I would scream to go faster. We grew up riding through woods and I would cry if we stopped.

A few years later, I got my own bike and began to enter amateur motocross events (mostly against boys). People asked my dad all the time how I knew when to shift my bike since I couldn't hear, but for me it seemed natural to shift by the feel of the vibrations.

At the time I was ready to race professionally, the women's professional motocross championship was coming on strong, and X Games added Women's Super X to the summer event the same year I went pro. My first year as a pro I won the championship. It was unreal because it was something I had dreamed about since I got on a dirt bike. The following year I earned my first X Games gold medal—my biggest accomplishment ever. Being the first deaf person to win an X Games medal will always be a huge honor for me.

I no longer race motocross, but I still ride dirt bikes for fun. Riding will always be my form of meditation. A few years ago, I started my own motocross school and I found a new love—teaching girls and kids how to ride and improve. I absolutely love seeing them having fun, learning new skills, and gaining confidence. I hope to show them that anything is possible.

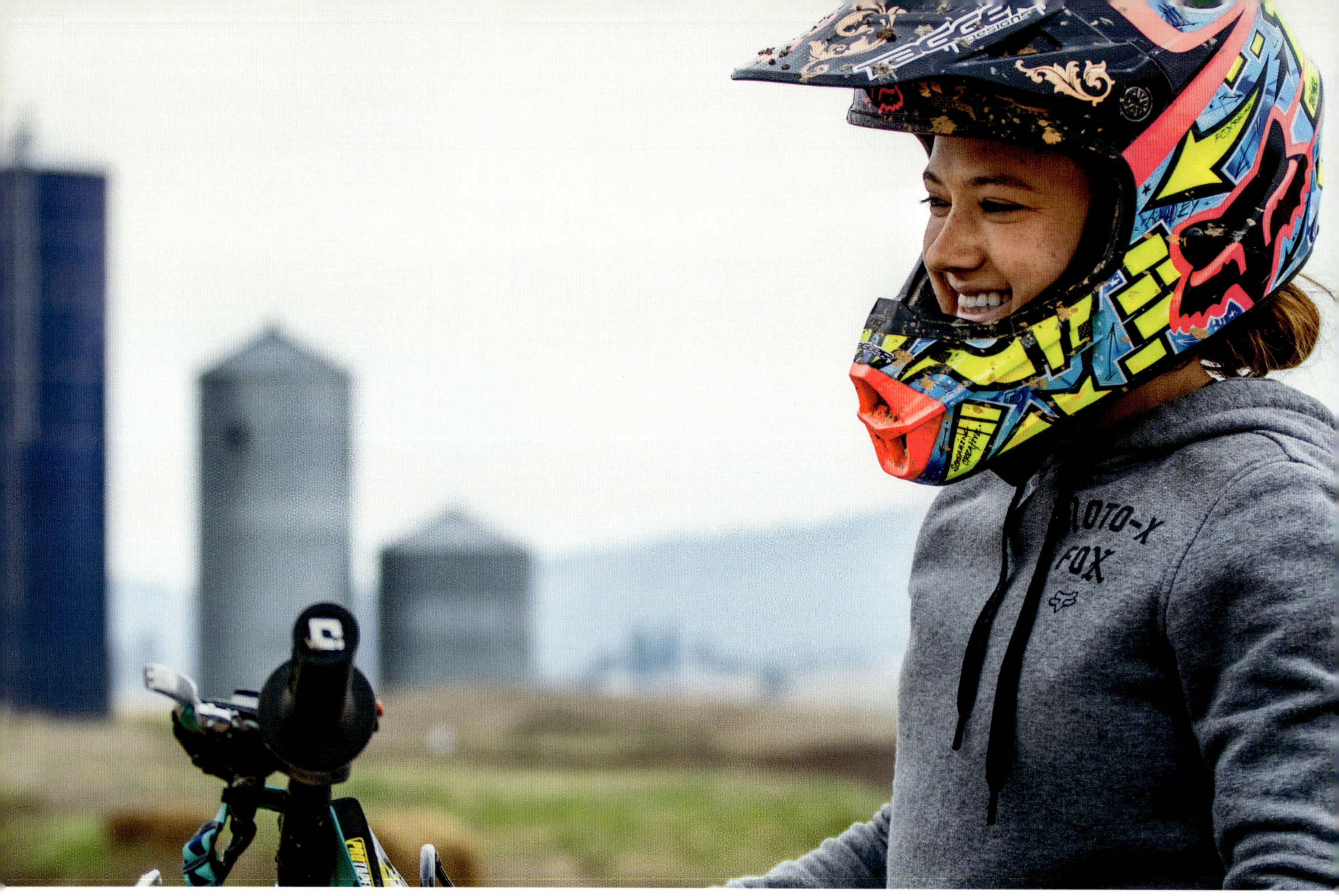

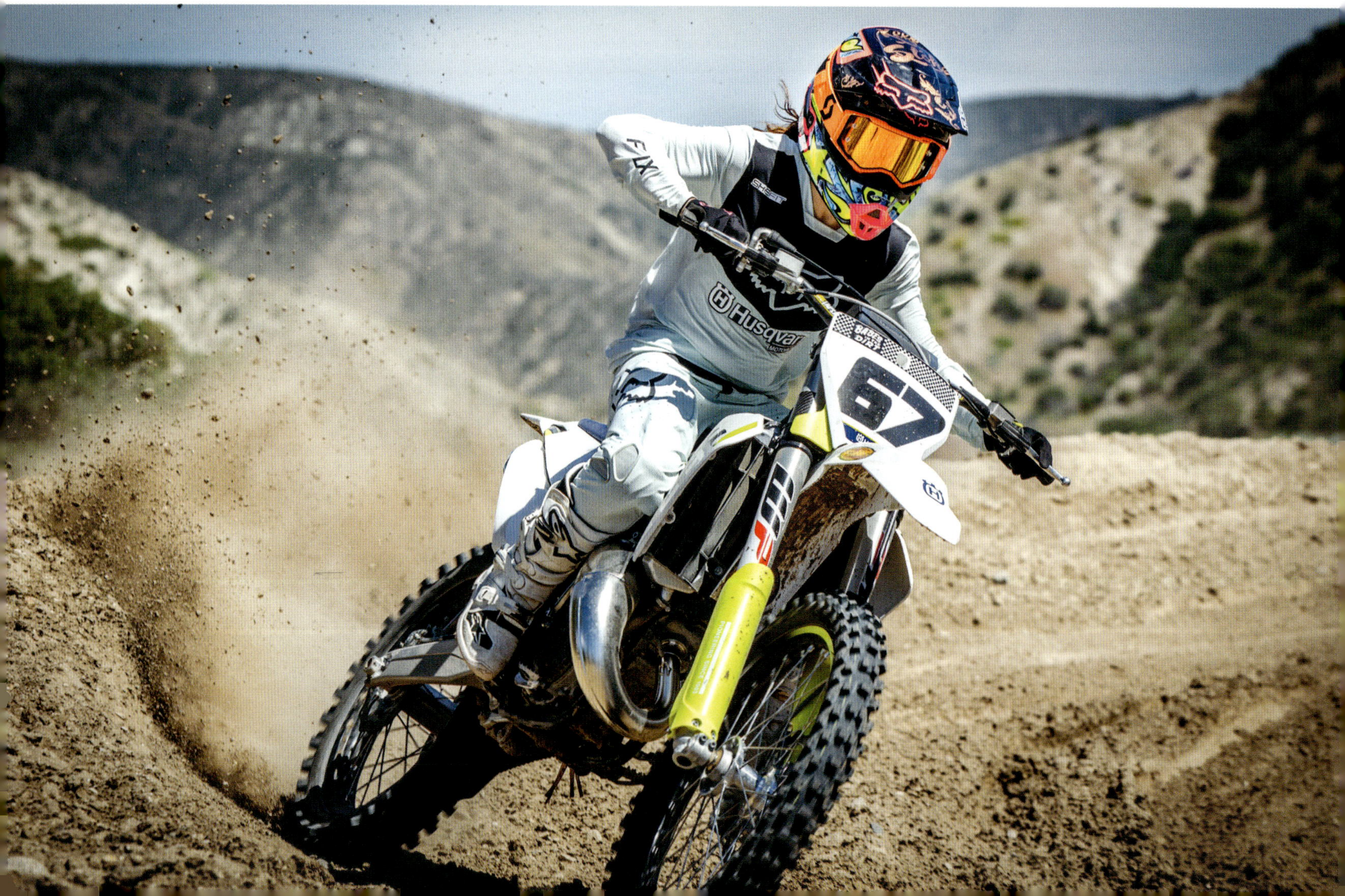

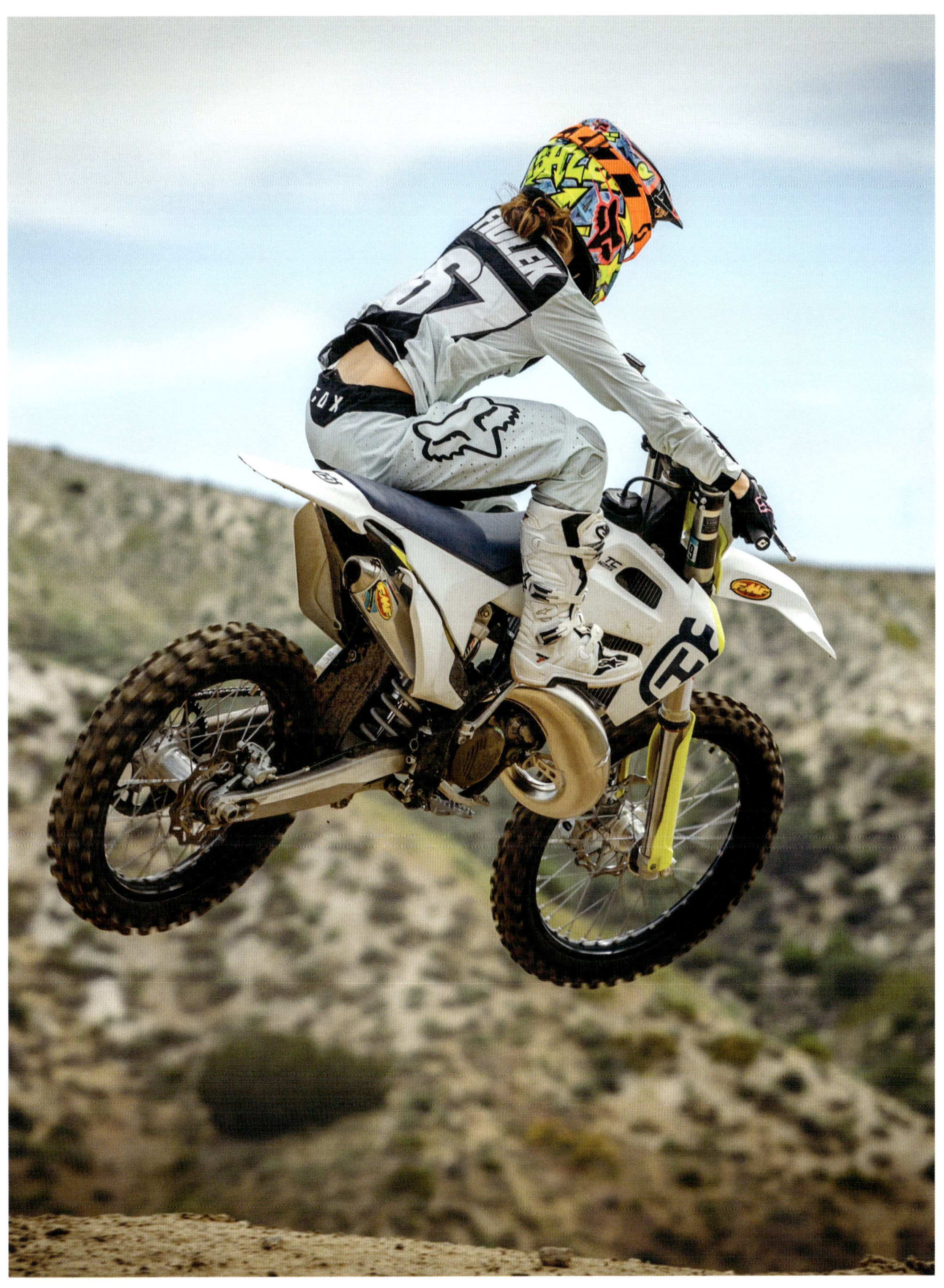

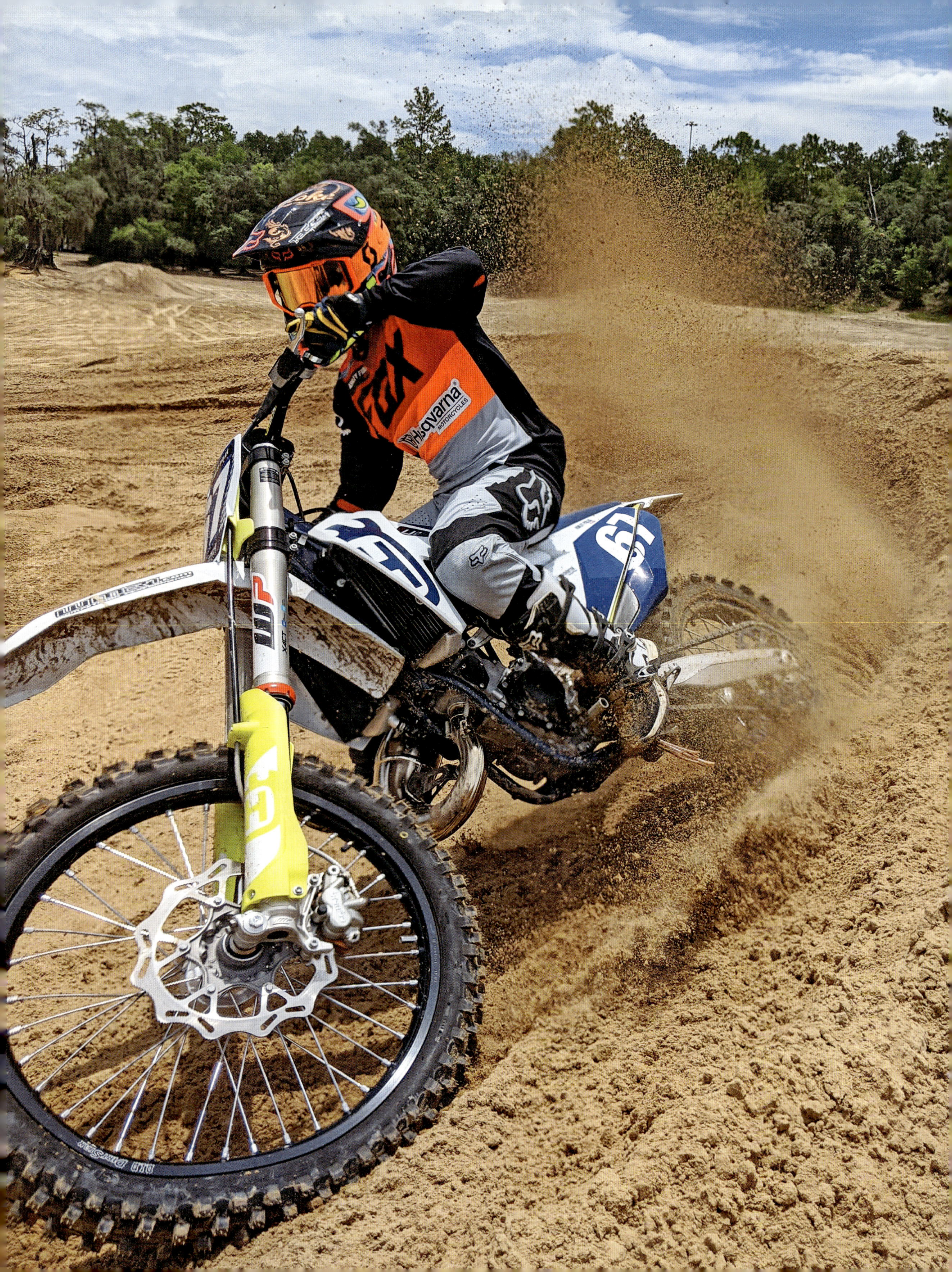

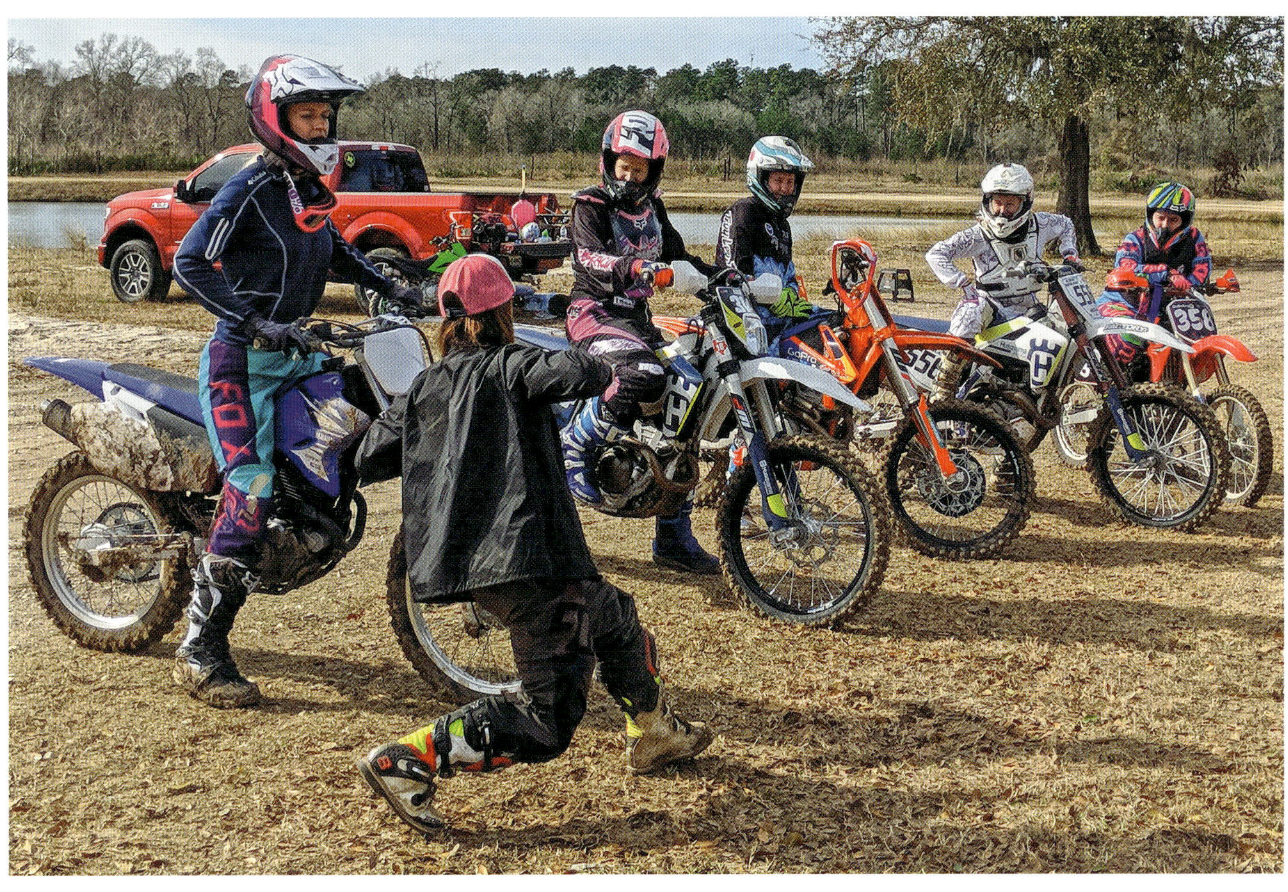

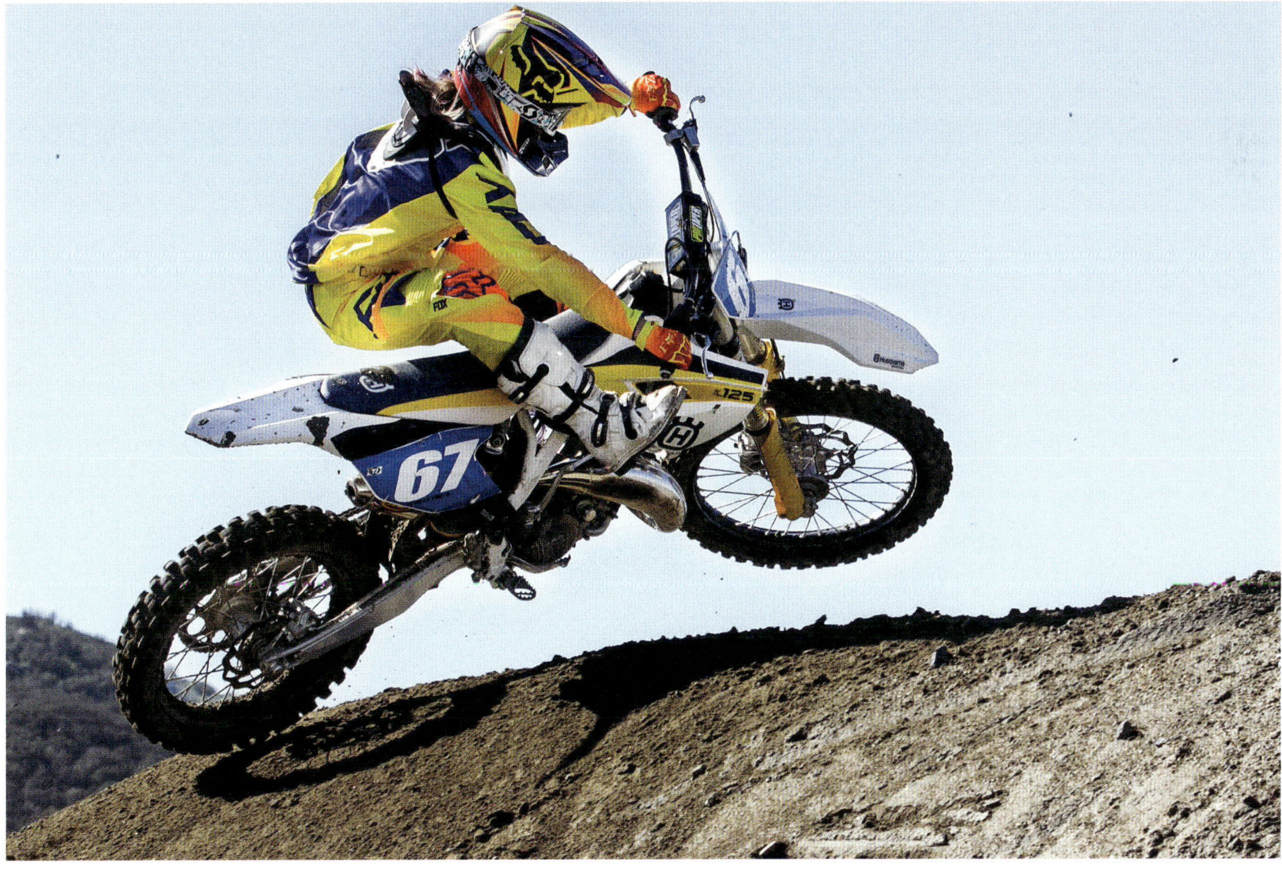

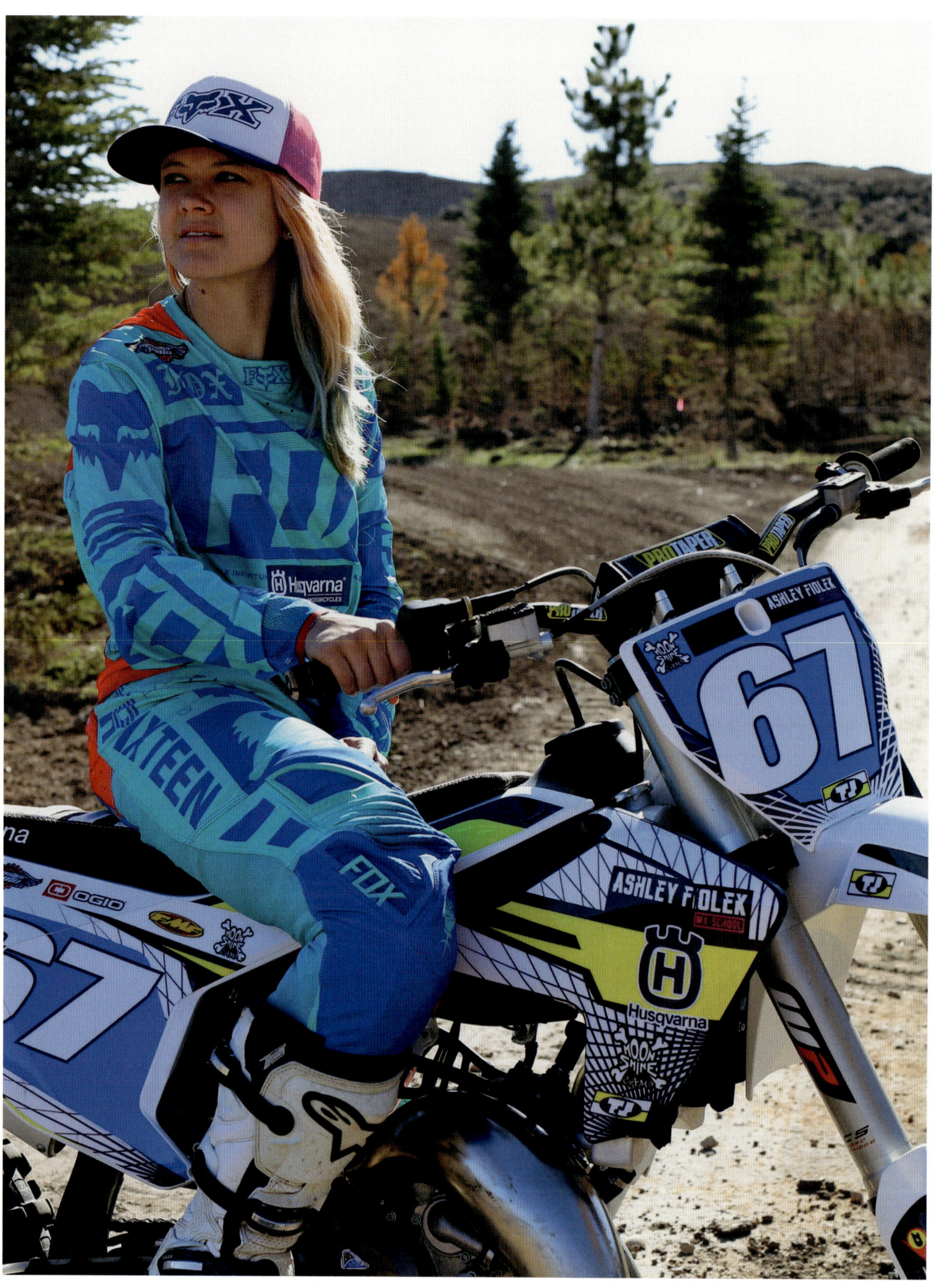FOX
FOX
FOX
Husqvarna
MOTORCYCLES
SIXTEEN
FOX
OGIO
FMF
PRO TAPER
PRO TAPER
ASHLEY FIOLEK
67
ASHLEY FIOLEK
MX SCHOOL
Husqvarna

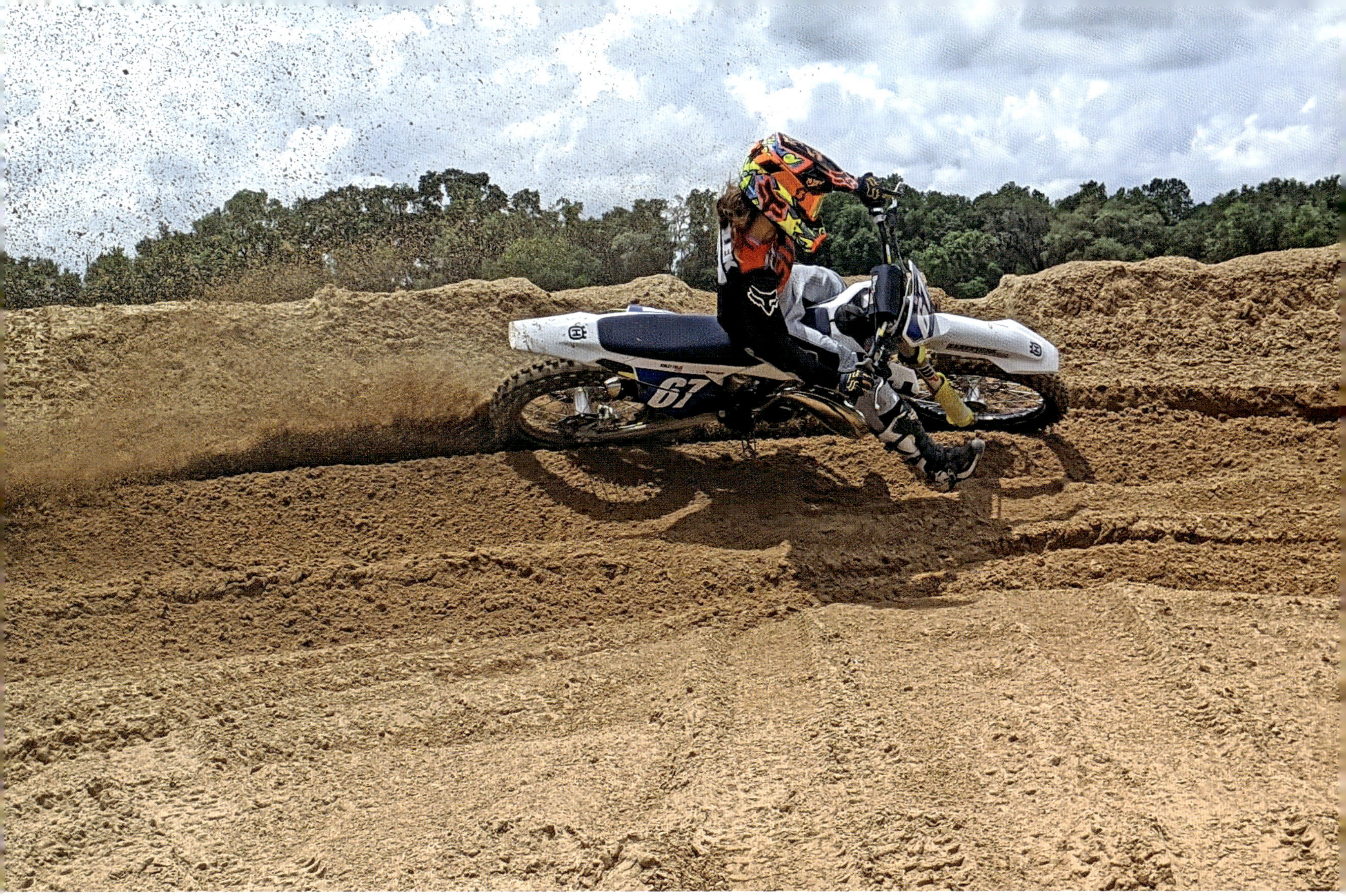

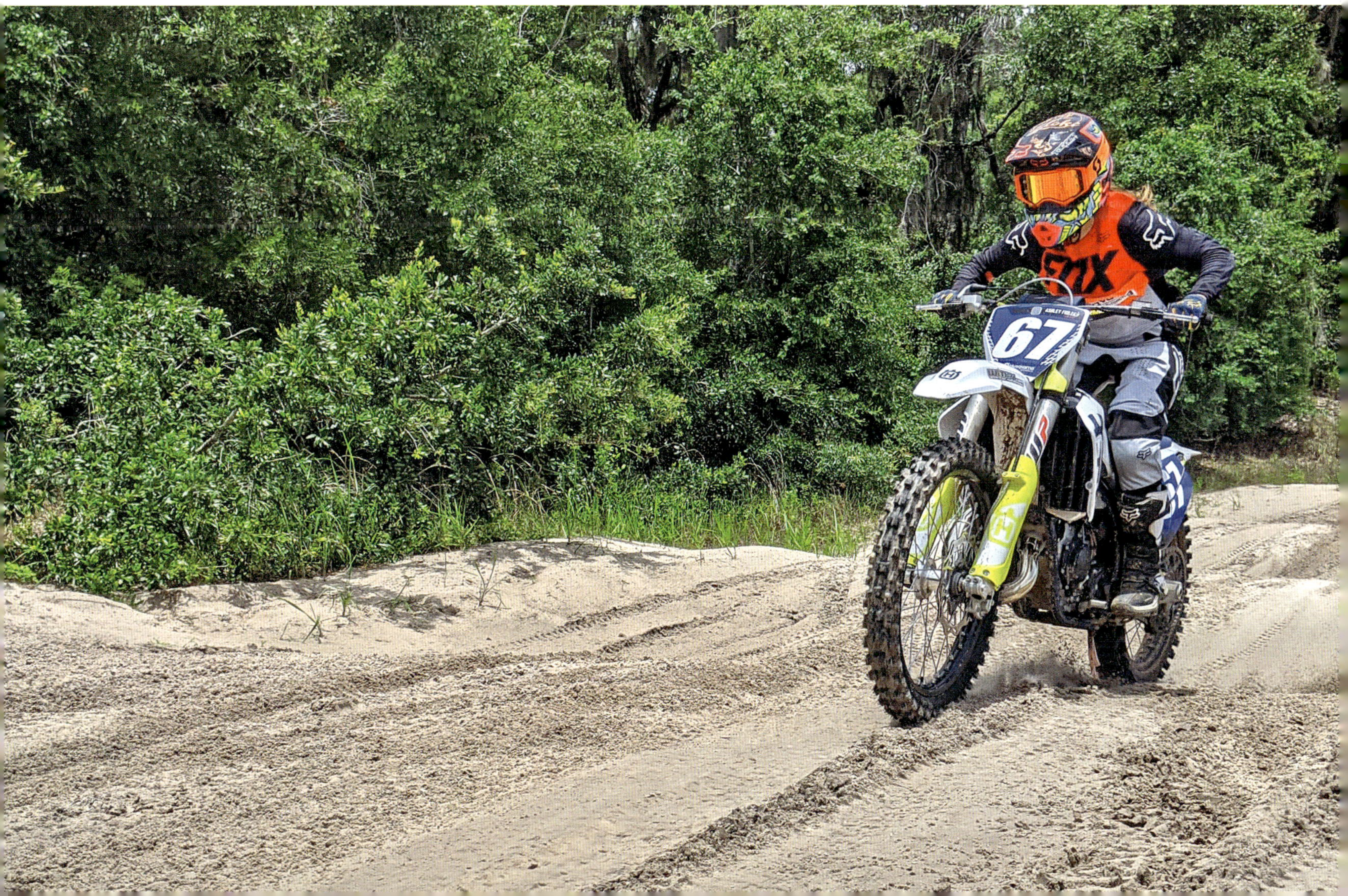

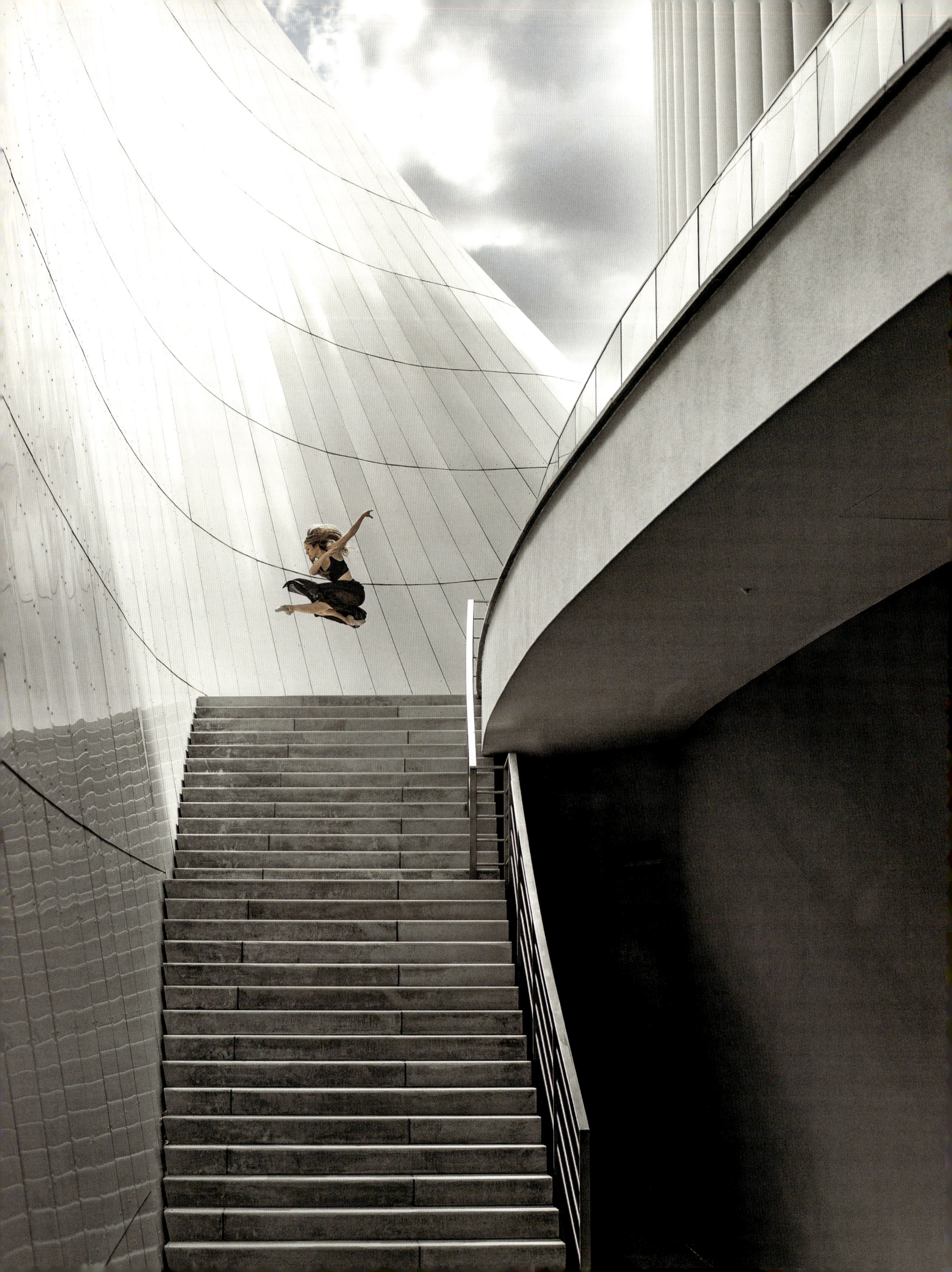

Lynn Jung
Freerunner and parkour athlete

@lynn_jung
www.lynnjung.net

Although I spent the majority of my childhood in gymnastics clubs and a considerable amount of my teenage years in dance studios, it wasn't until I was in my early twenties that I developed a passion for movement that would completely change the way I lived my life.

I lost my dad at the age of 23 and the experience of grief was an intensely physical one for me. Trapped in a constant state of restlessness, and as an introvert struggling to express my emotions verbally, I found comfort in movement. I immersed myself in the parkour and freerunning culture and started to dedicate most of my time and energy to my practice. Setting myself short-term training goals and working toward them gave me a sense of purpose and confidence that brought me out of my shell. The more I trained, the more passionate I became about parkour. At the time, I did not have the faintest idea about the incredible journey my practice would take me on.

I remember my very first parkour job and how amazed I was that someone would pay to watch me do parkour. It was for the opening of a local shopping mall and I was paid €20 for the day. I couldn't have been more excited. I was just as excited when I was invited to one of the biggest parkour jams in the world for the first time as a guest athlete, and slowly realized that parkour could be more than just a hobby. After I finished my studies in Austria and worked as a semi-professional athlete for a couple of years, I decided to move to the UK to pursue my dream of becoming a professional freerunner. I was terrified and mired in self-doubt but was lucky enough to have a strong network of friends who fully believed in me.

Being a professional freerunner isn't always smooth sailing and like most things in life, parkour jobs come in waves. It can be stressful not knowing when you will next be hired for a commercial job, a show, or a photo campaign, and having to rely on a healthy body to be able to work adds a little bit of stress on top of that. Looking back, though, I could not be happier with the life I have lived for the past ten years and wouldn't change a thing if I could.

The older I get, the more I want to explore my body's abilities, not just with parkour but any sort of movement that sparks my interest. One of the biggest drives for my training is gaining a deep understanding of my body. My years as a professional athlete have taught me to have patience and compassion toward my body and to listen to its signs and how it feels, to know when to rest and how to work within my abilities in order to extend them. My training has shifted from looking outward for recognition to fully turning this focus inward and listening to what it is that I want to do with my body and what direction I want to take my training in.

Having dealt with some severe injuries in the past, I now understand the importance of being aware of what is going on inside my body and mind and knowing when my head is not in the right space for jumping off walls. I believe that one of the most important skills we can develop as parkour athletes is knowing our bodies' limits and being aware of when to step away from a challenge and come back to it at a later time. Having the confidence to acknowledge one's personal limits will only make you a better athlete in the long run.

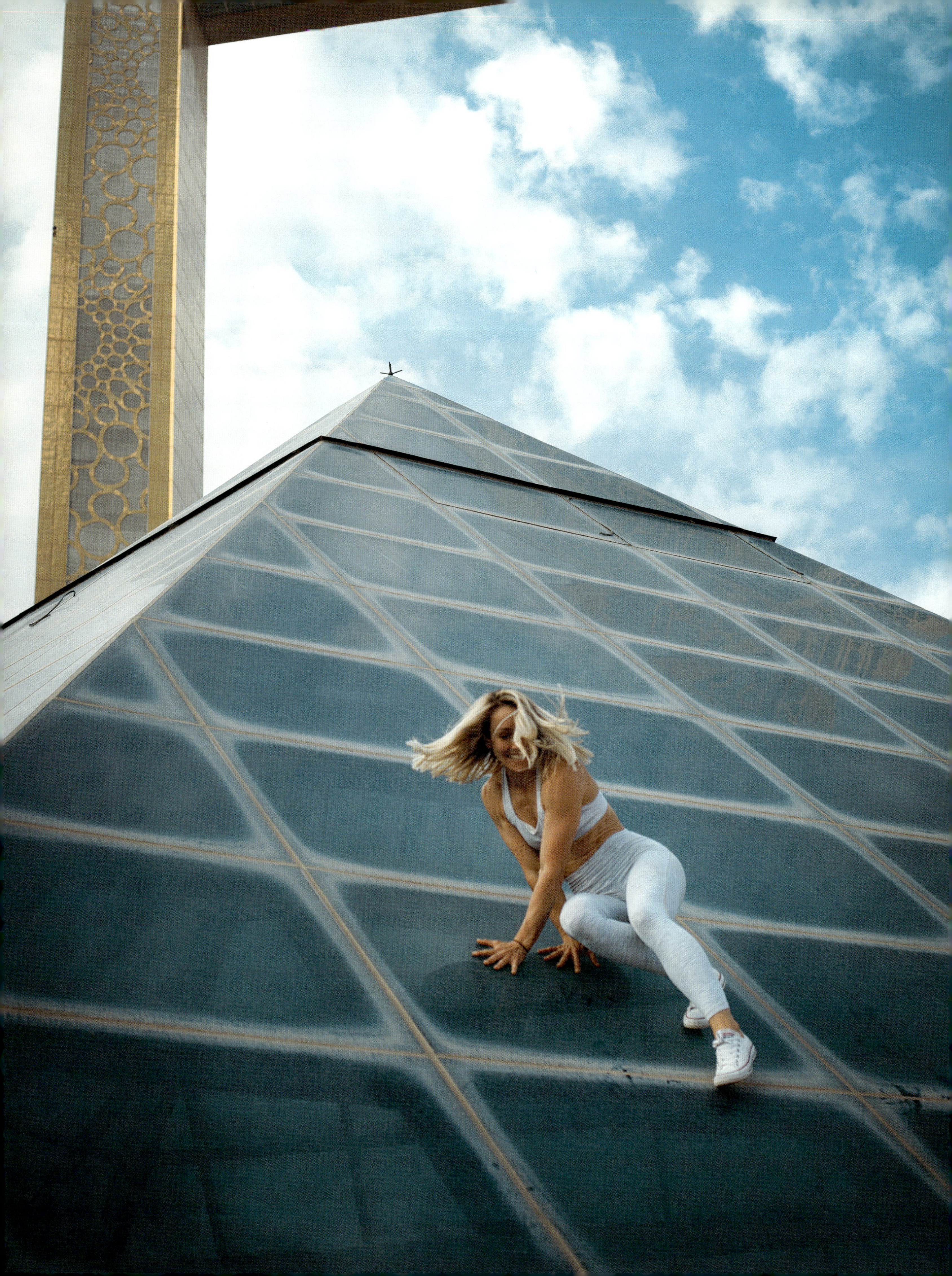

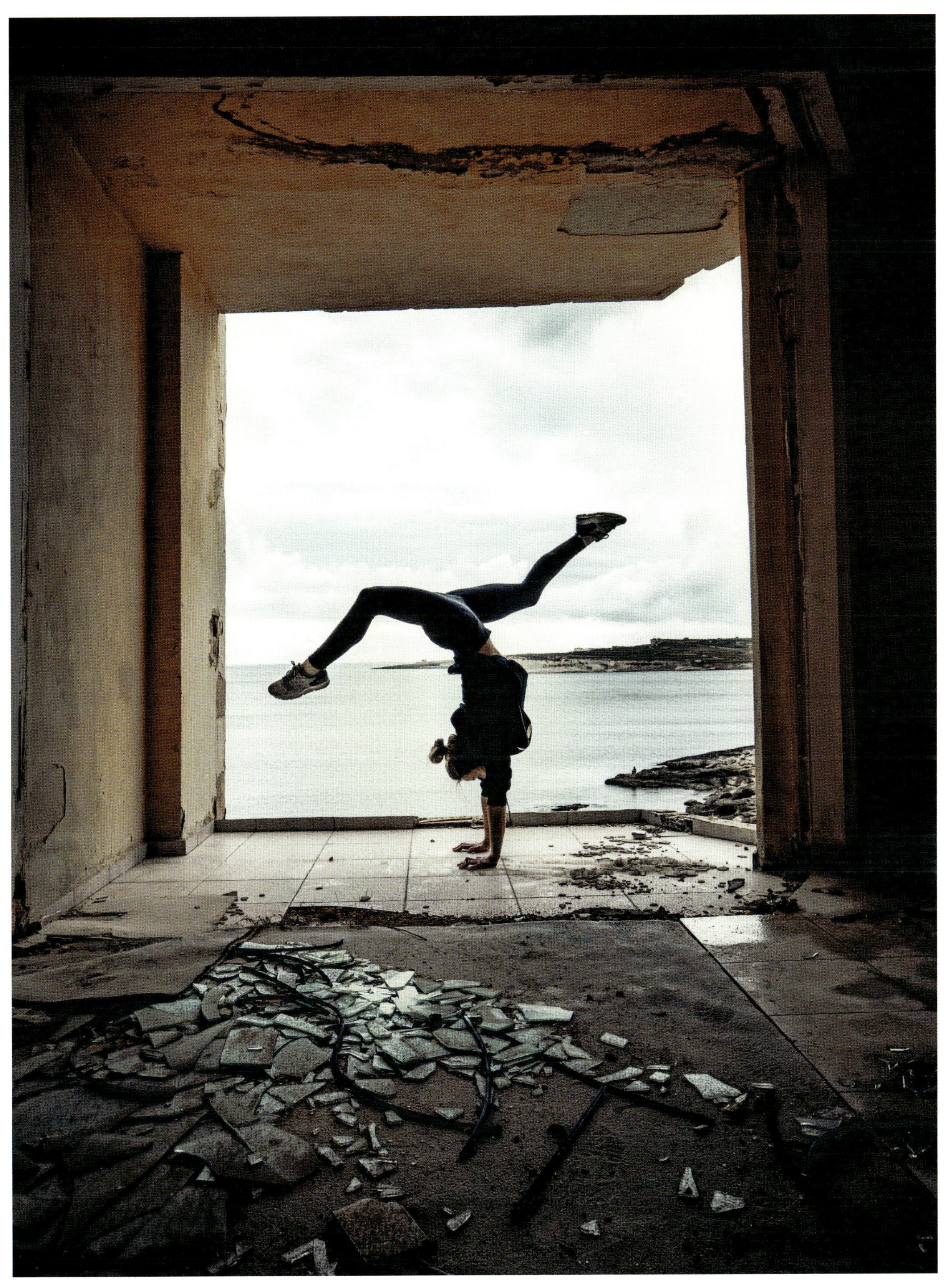

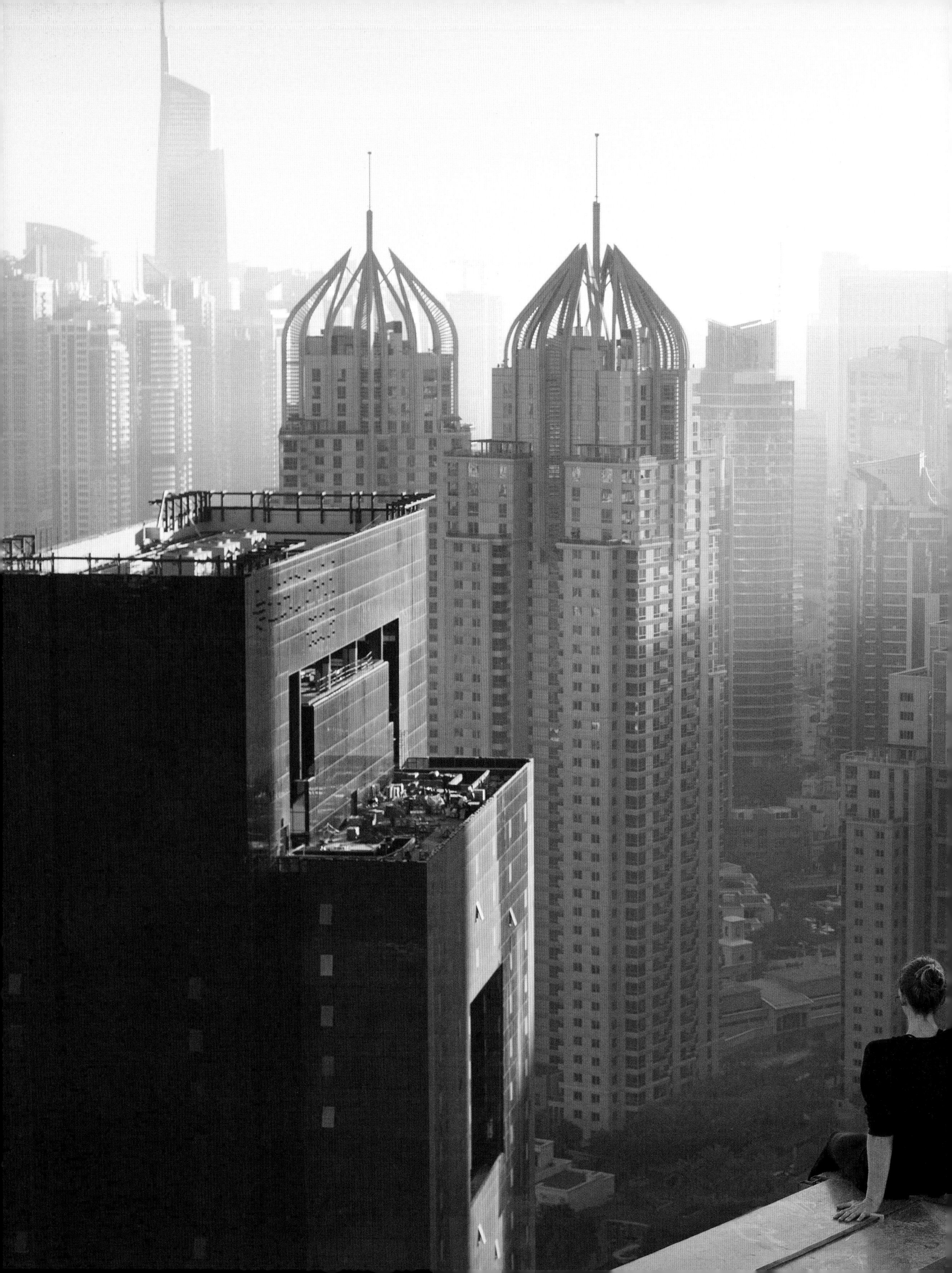

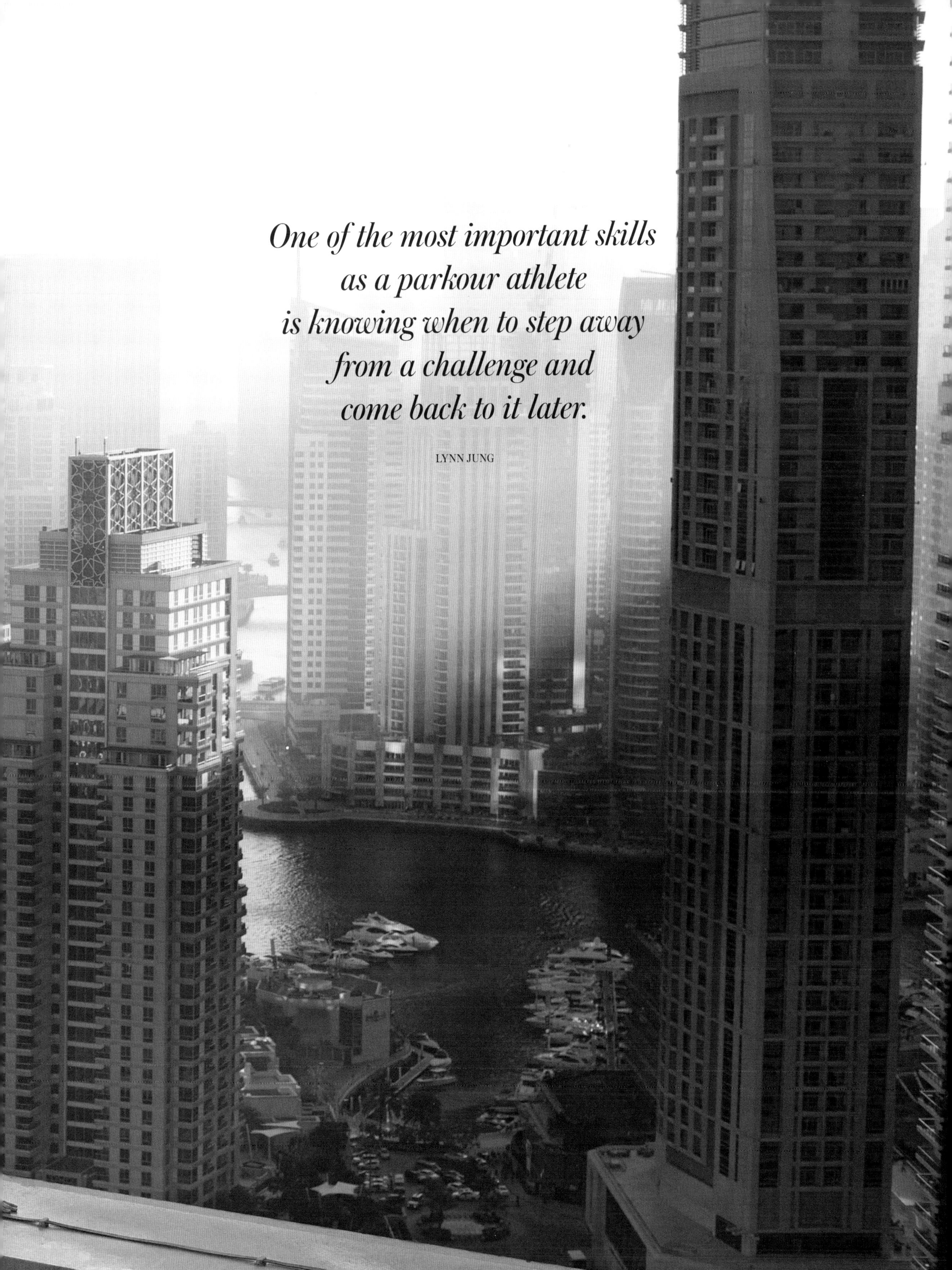

One of the most important skills
as a parkour athlete
is knowing when to step away
from a challenge and
come back to it later.

LYNN JUNG

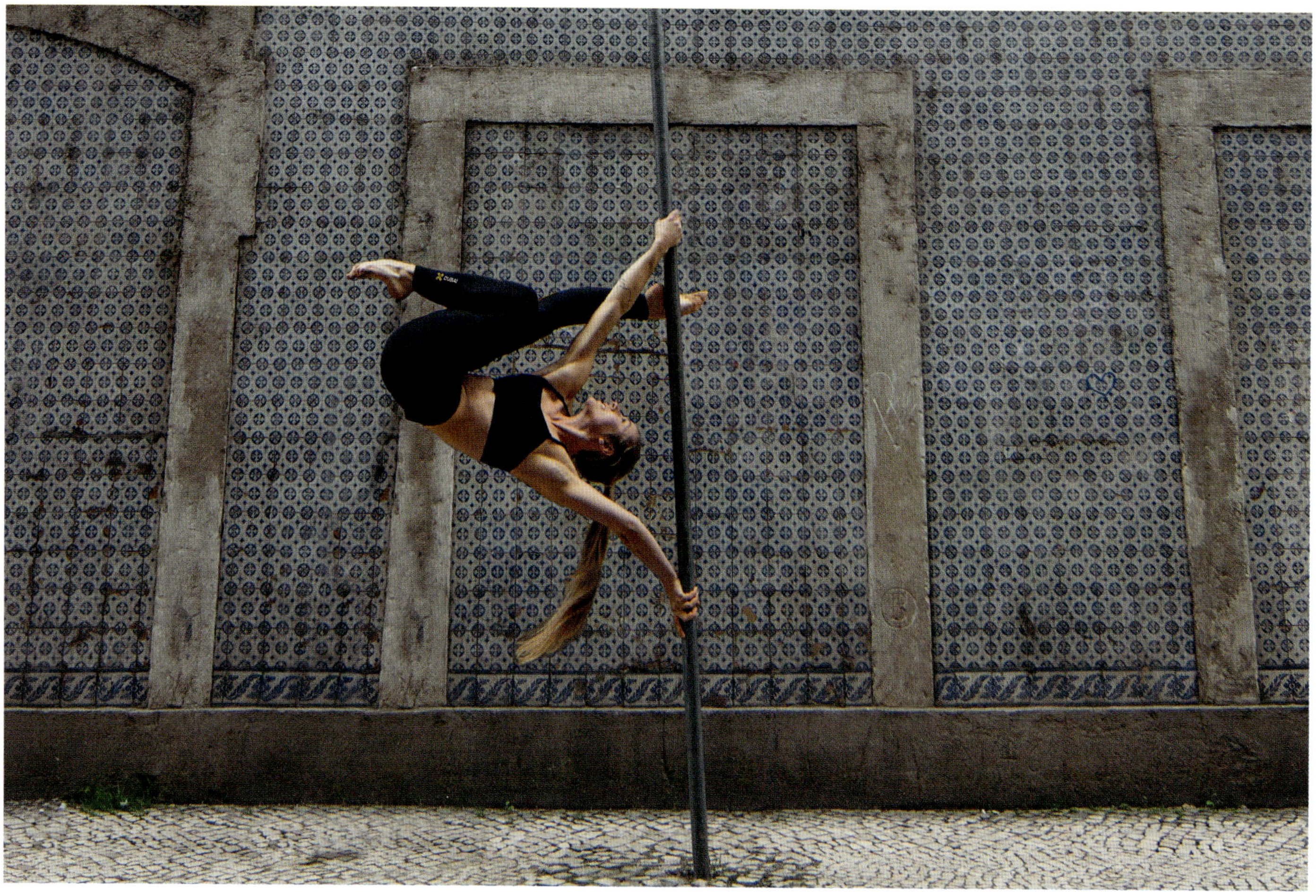

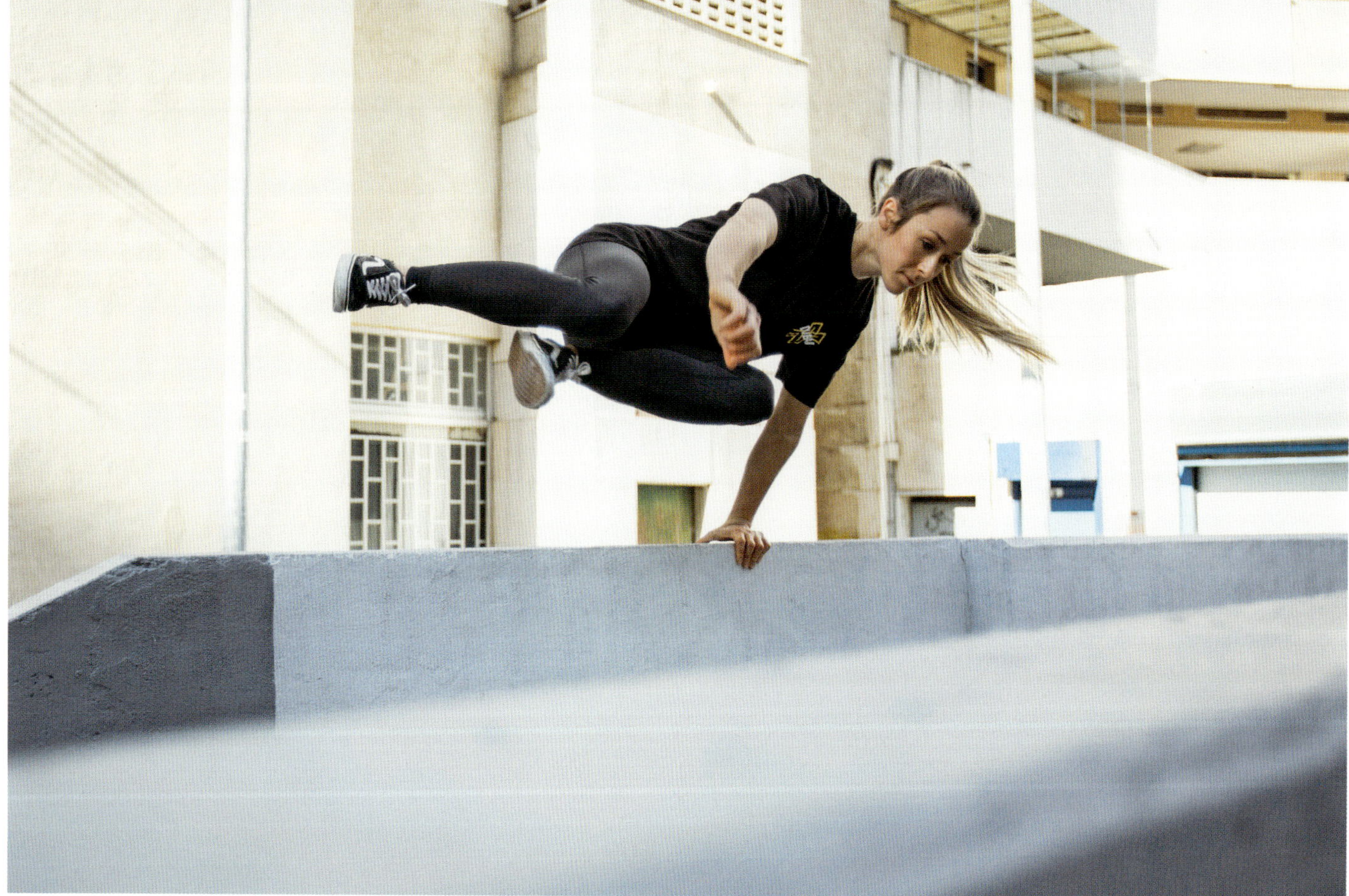

  △ Lisbon, Portugal   ▷ Brighton, UK

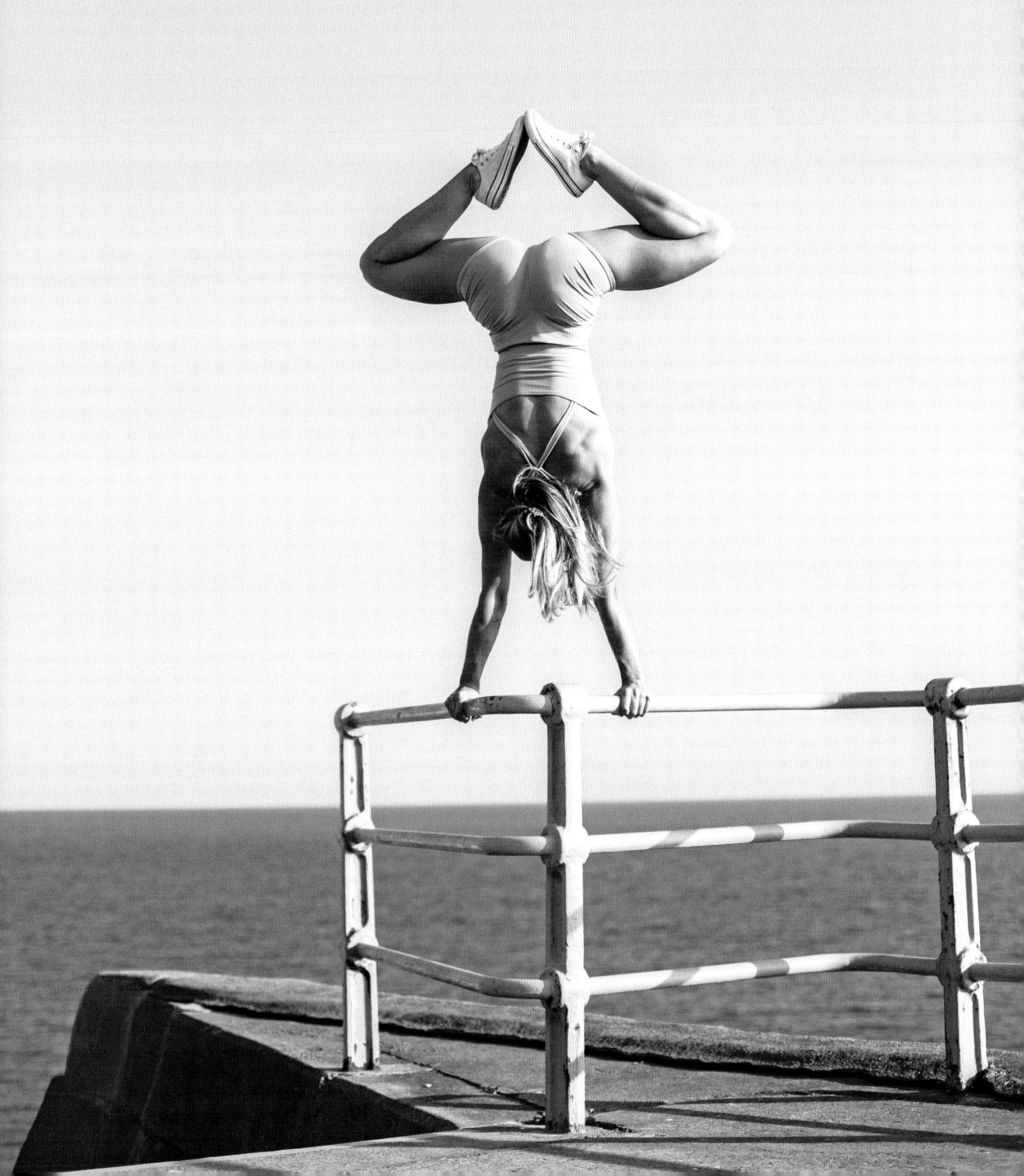

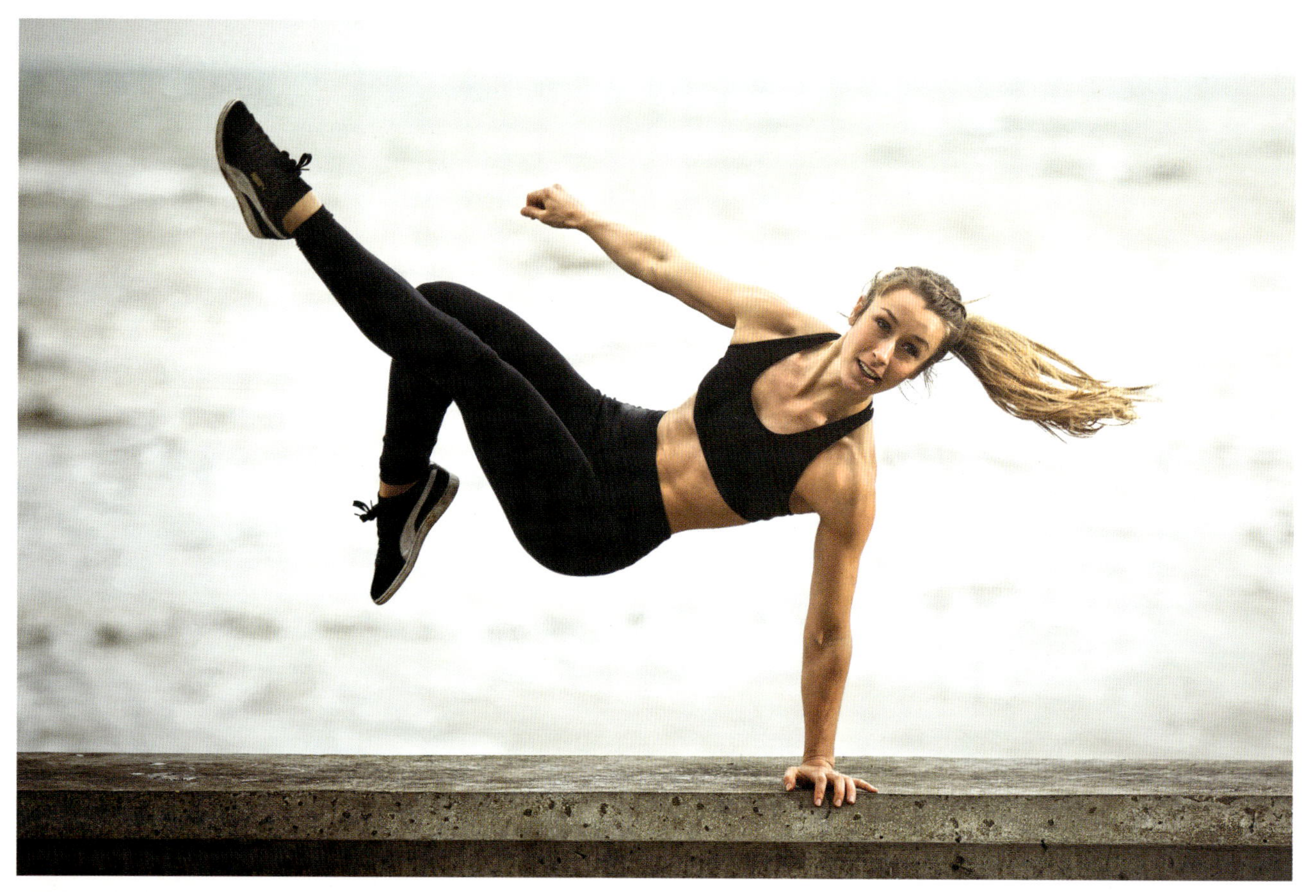

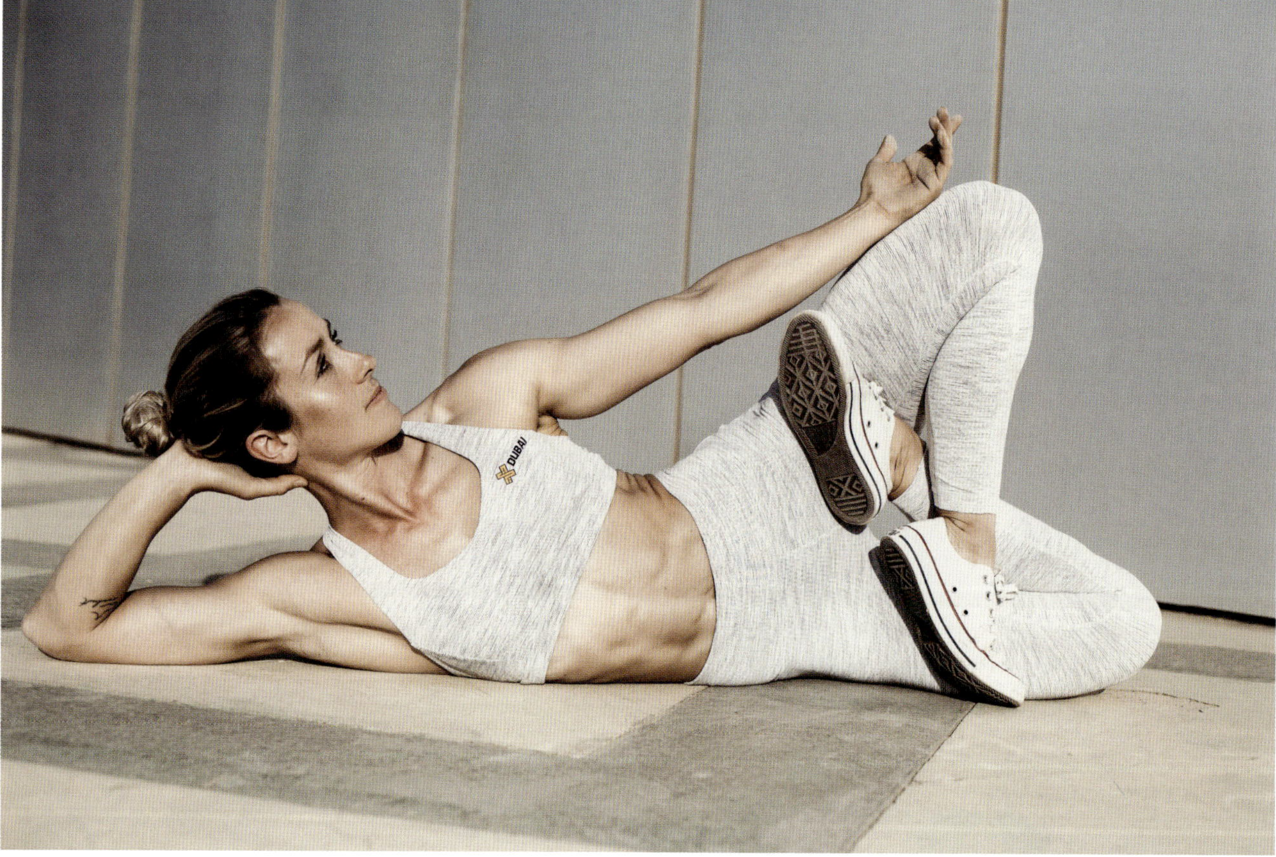

  △△ Brighton, UK   ∧ Dubai, United Arab Emirates   ▷ Santorini, Greece

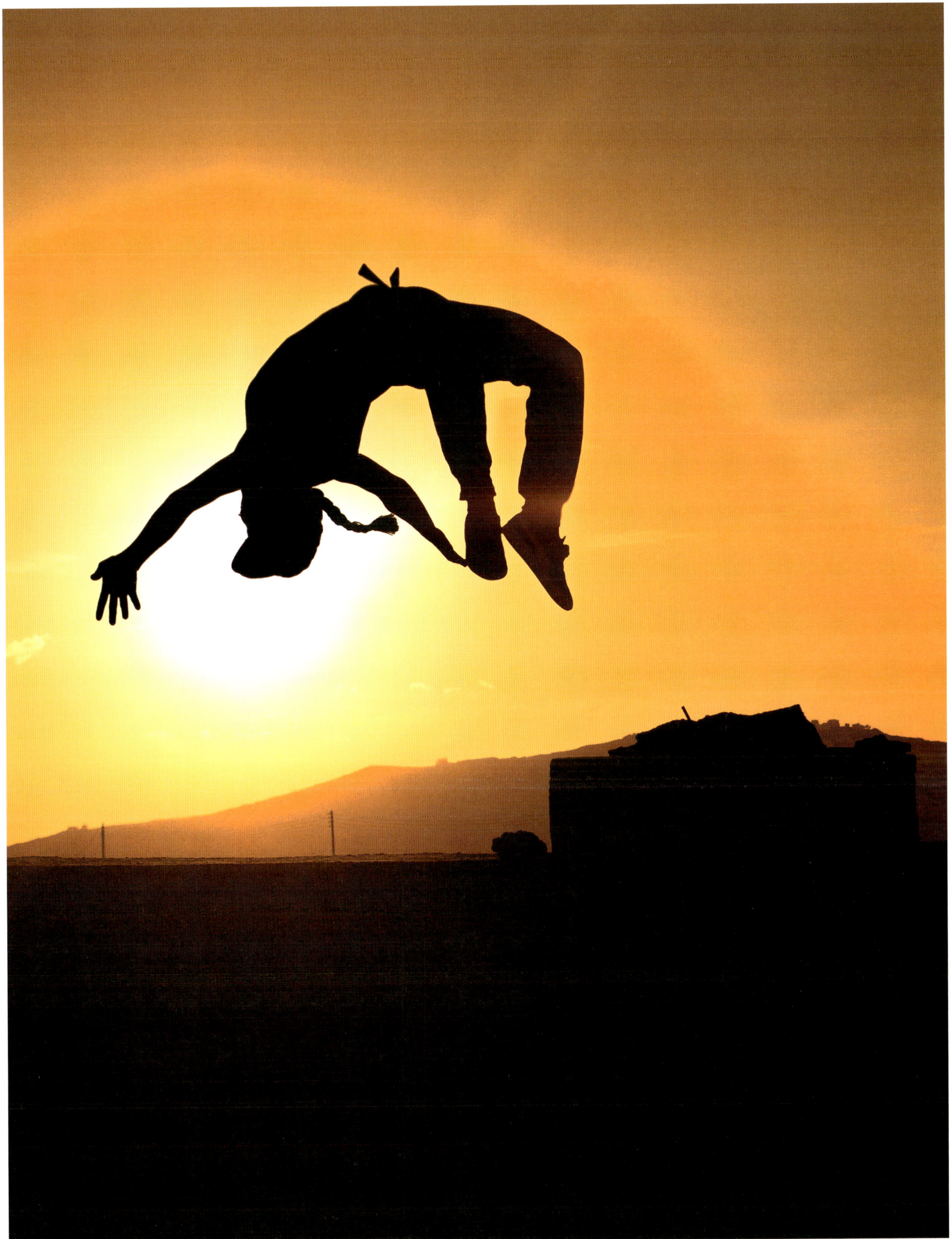

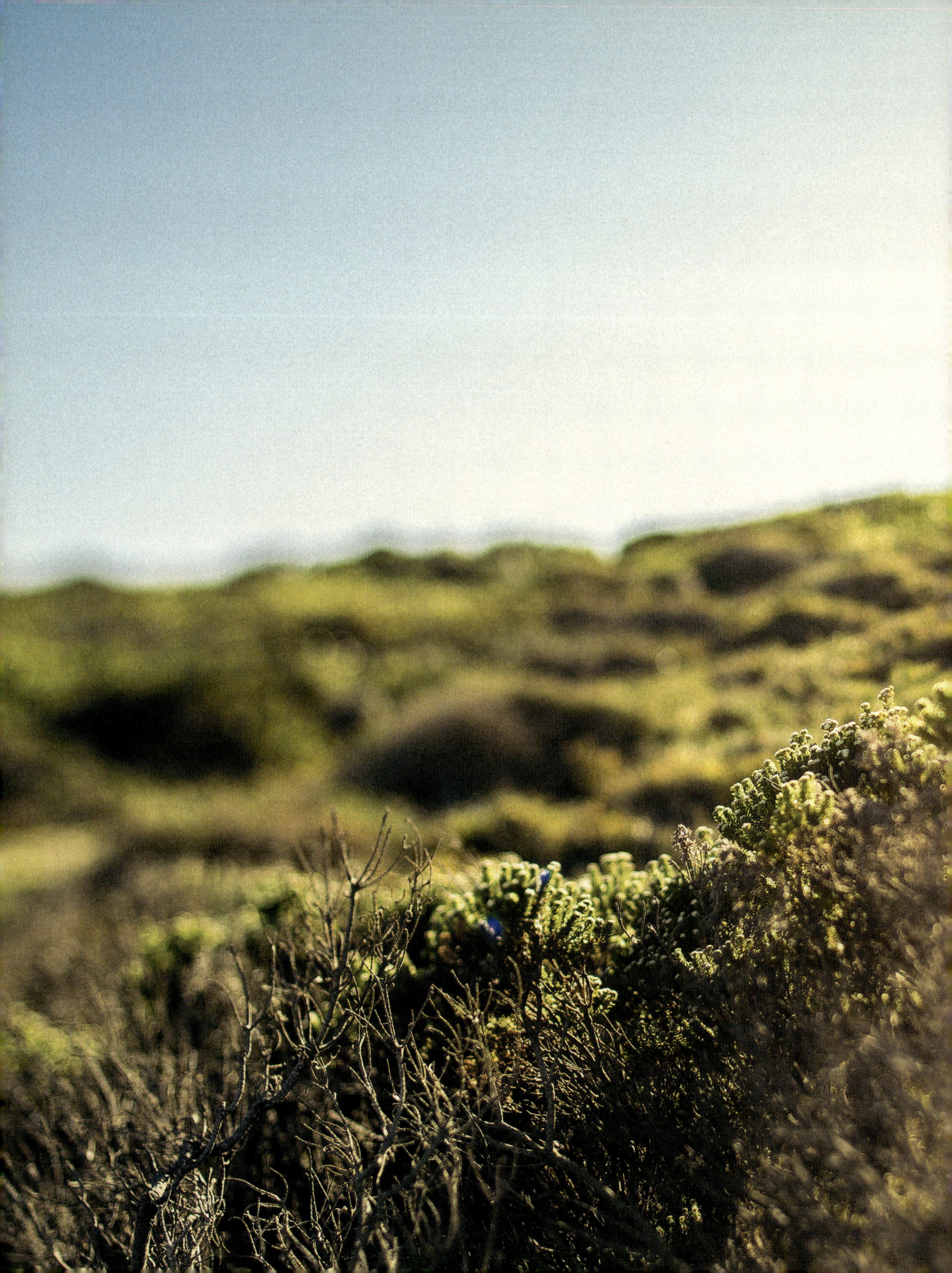

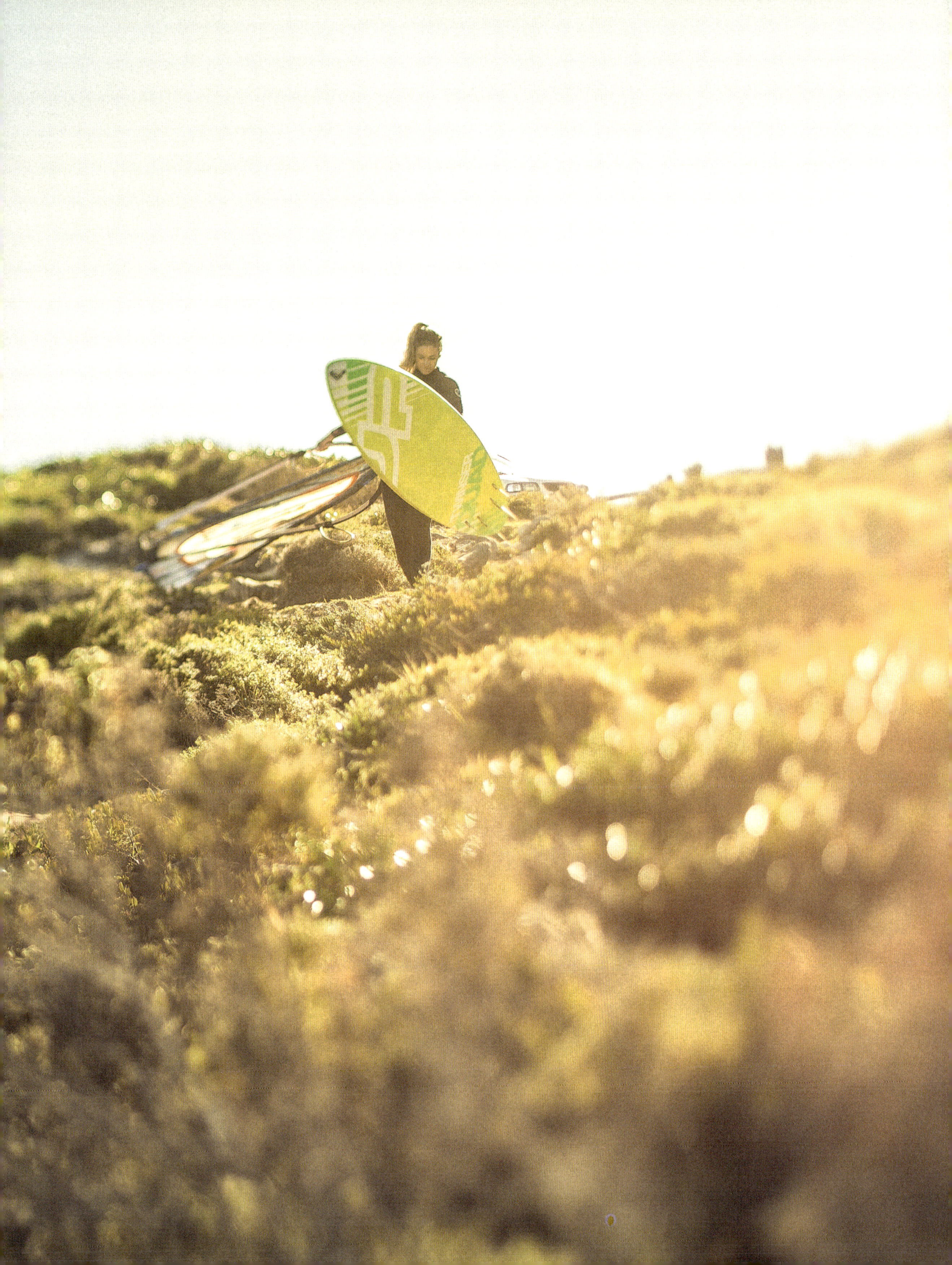

Olya Raskina
Windsurfer

@olyaraskina

I'm Olya Raskina, a professional windsurfer from Russia. Russia has a long history of windsurfing: in the days of the USSR we had two big factories producing our own windsurf gear and many people sailed on the lakes, rivers, and seas. After the 1990s, the windsurfing community shrank until it was very small, and the factories shut down. It began to grow again at the beginning of the 2000s, when modern freestyle and wave sailing started to spread.

I learned how to windsurf in 2005 in Dahab, Egypt, which was a Mecca of European windsurfing at that time. I'd just finished university in Moscow—I got a bachelor's degree in languages—and staying in Dahab for a while after a hard five years of studying seemed like a great idea to me. My hobby turned into my profession. After I learned basic freestyle in Dahab, I went around the world to compete in the World Cup and follow my passion—sailing in the waves and teaching windsurfing.

Now I have my own project, the Windsurf Beauties camp, where I teach ladies how to sail and stay fit. I also organize a big festival in Moscow—Boardriders Fest—where we give free lessons and workshops in windsurfing, long boarding, SUPing, and yoga. We also run kids' classes and have a great music line-up with DJs and bands. It's a free sports festival, so many people join us to learn watersports for the first time.

Being a pro windsurfer is very challenging and demanding. I've had many ups and downs—injuries, victories, two kids, and a long journey to get back into shape after I had them. Traveling, teaching, trying to find a balance between the things I do and being together with my family. I think we are very lucky to share windsurfing and meet great people—it's a small community, but people are very friendly and helpful. It's always a challenge to find sponsors, to earn enough to practice, travel, and improve. It has never been easy, but I would say that if you know it's your thing and you love it, don't let anything stop you. Try, explore, don't be scared, and trust yourself. Like they say, a smooth sea never made a skilled sailor, so you'll get a few beatings, but it will be good at the end. I know you can do it!

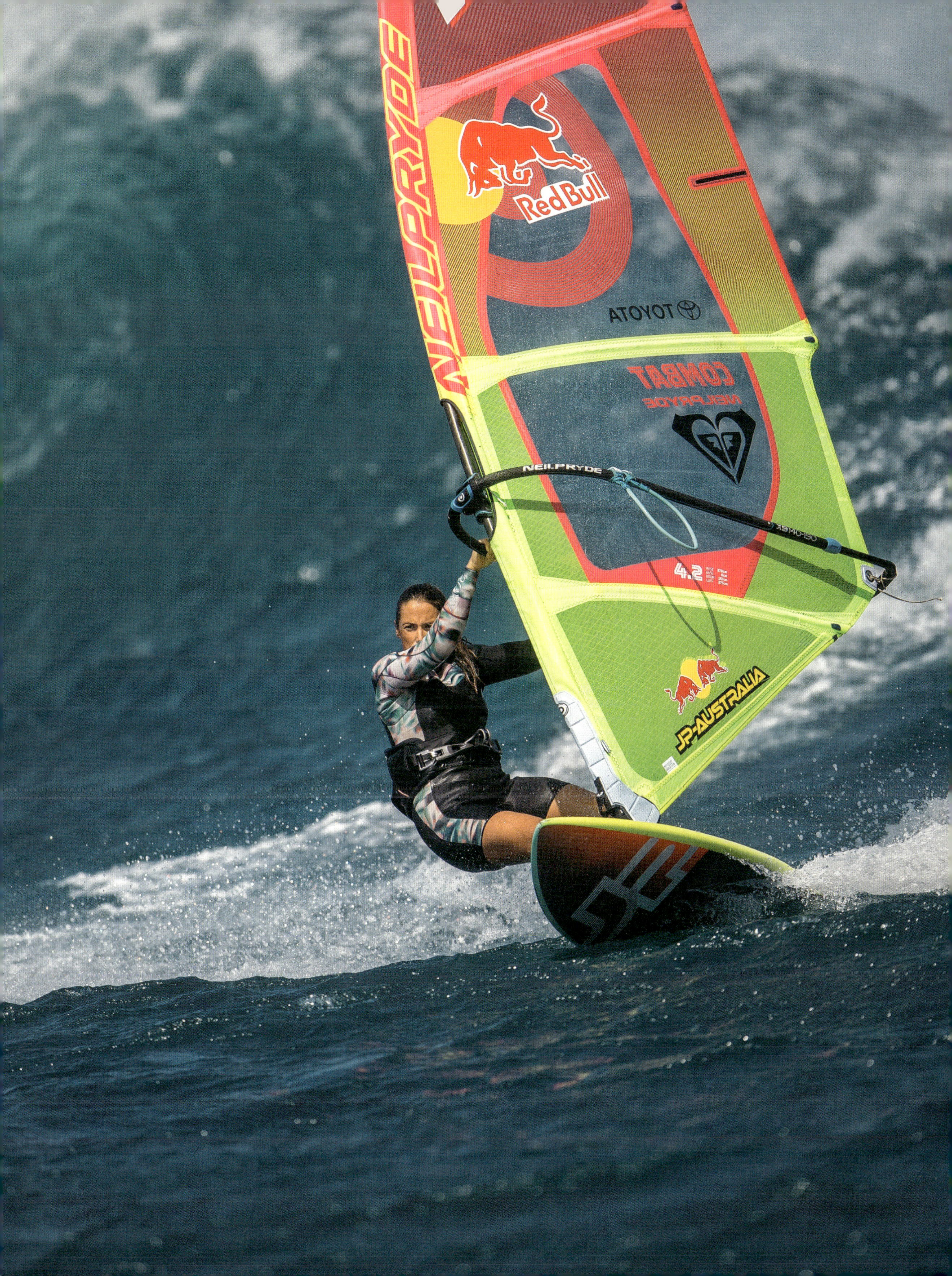

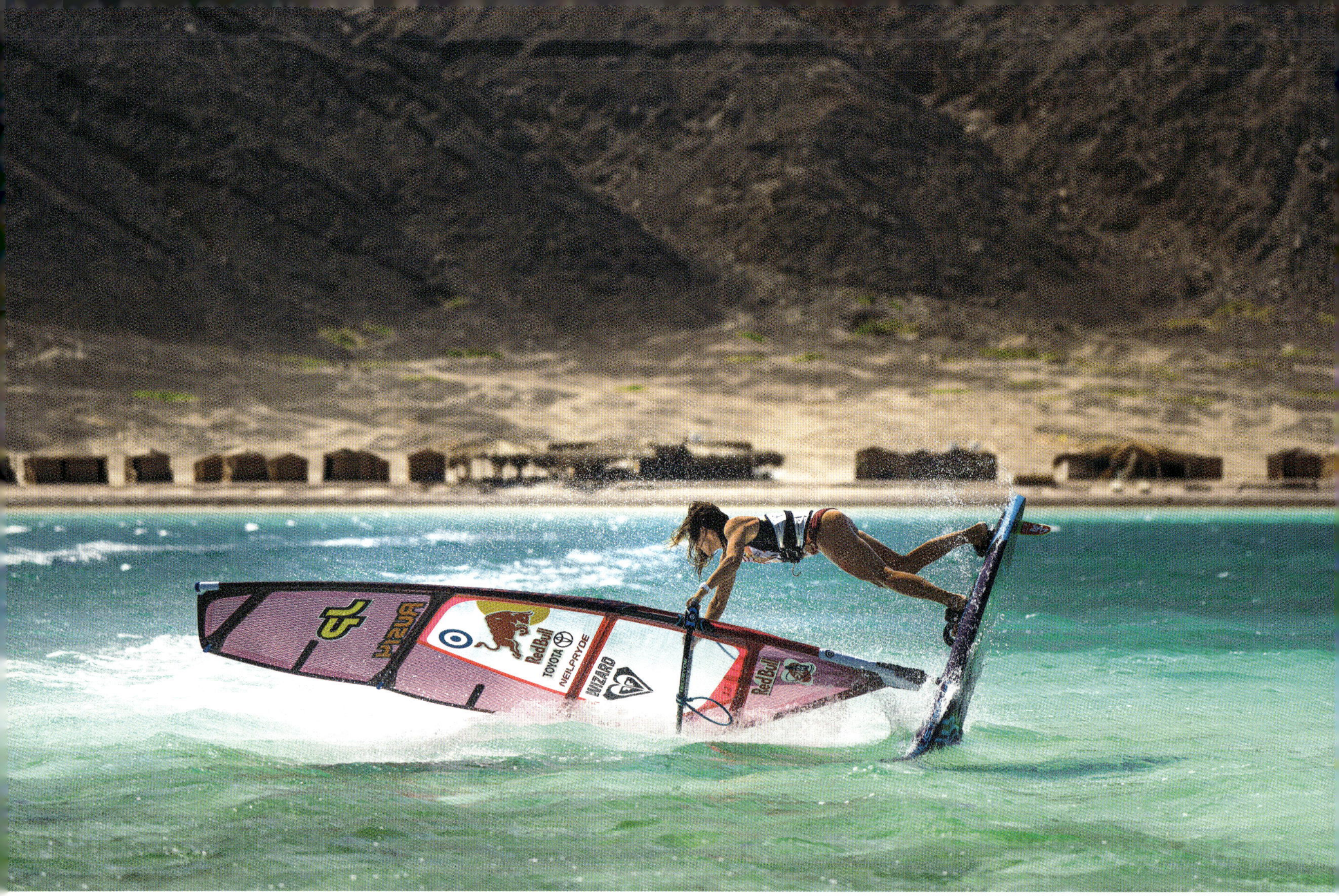
Red Bull
TOYOTA
NEILPRYDE
WIZARD
Red Bull

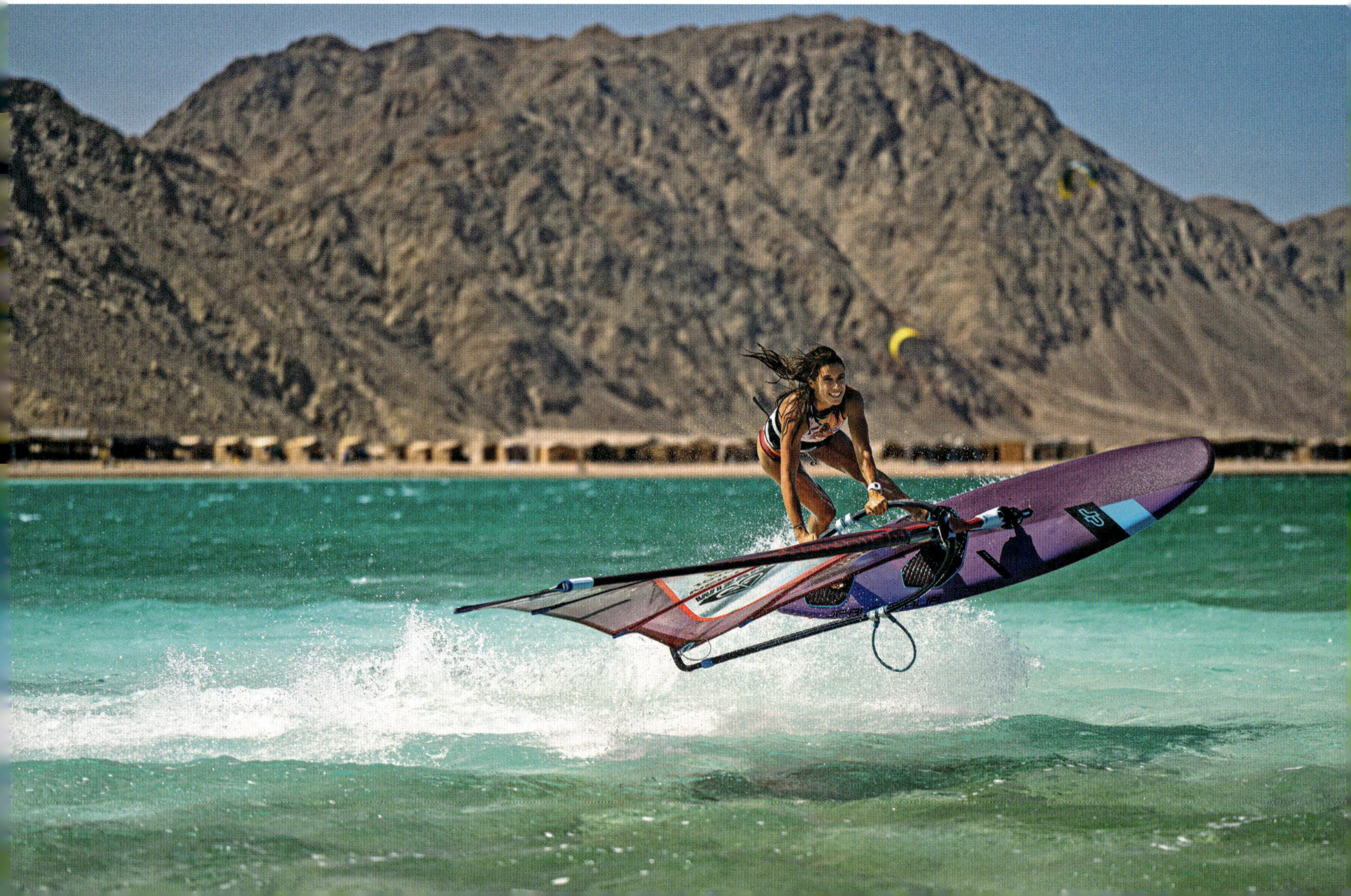

I've had many ups and downs—injuries, victories, two kids, and a long journey to get back into shape after I had them.

OLYA RASKINA

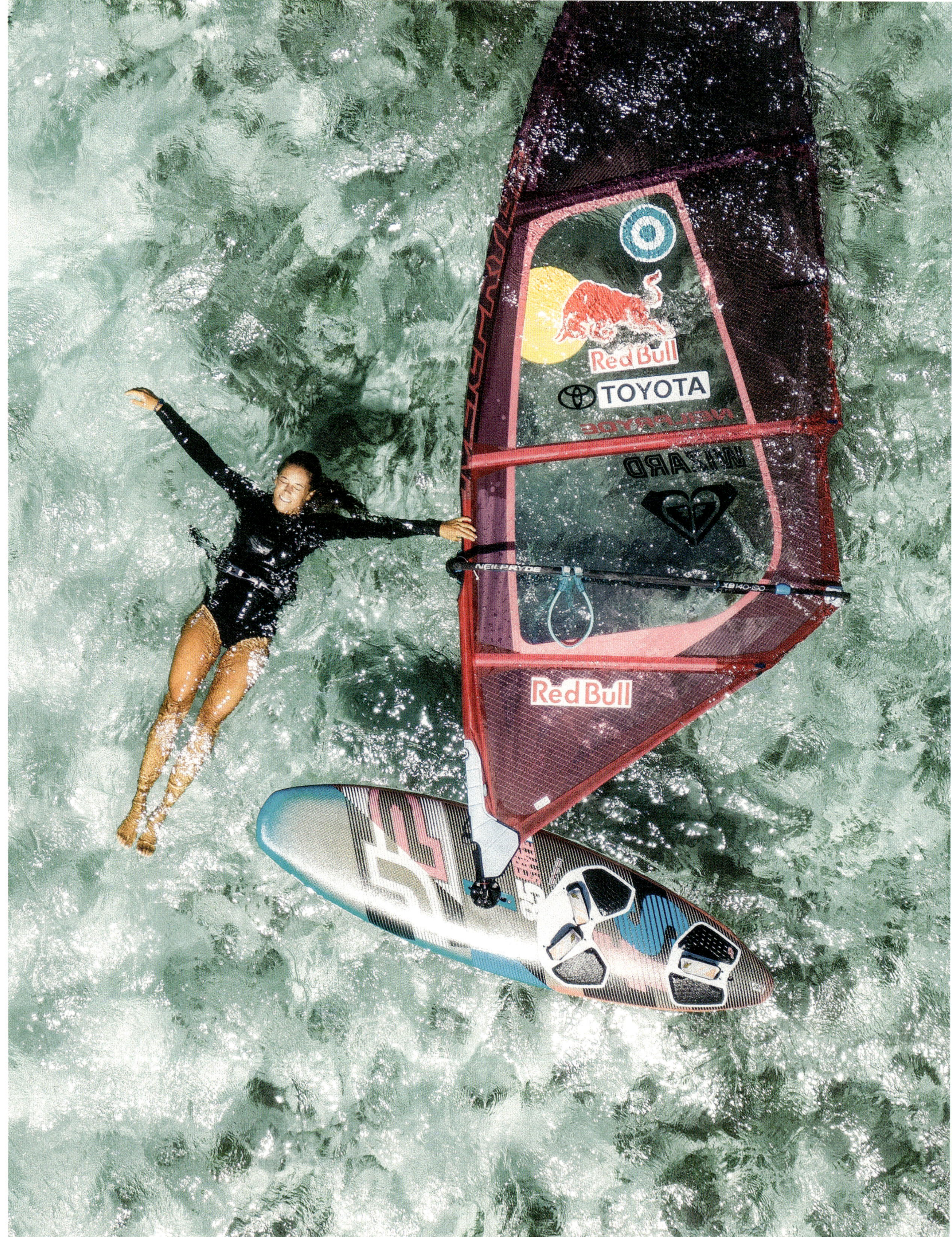

Red Bull
TOYOTA
NEILPRYDE
NITARD
Red Bull
NEILPRYDE
XB 140-150

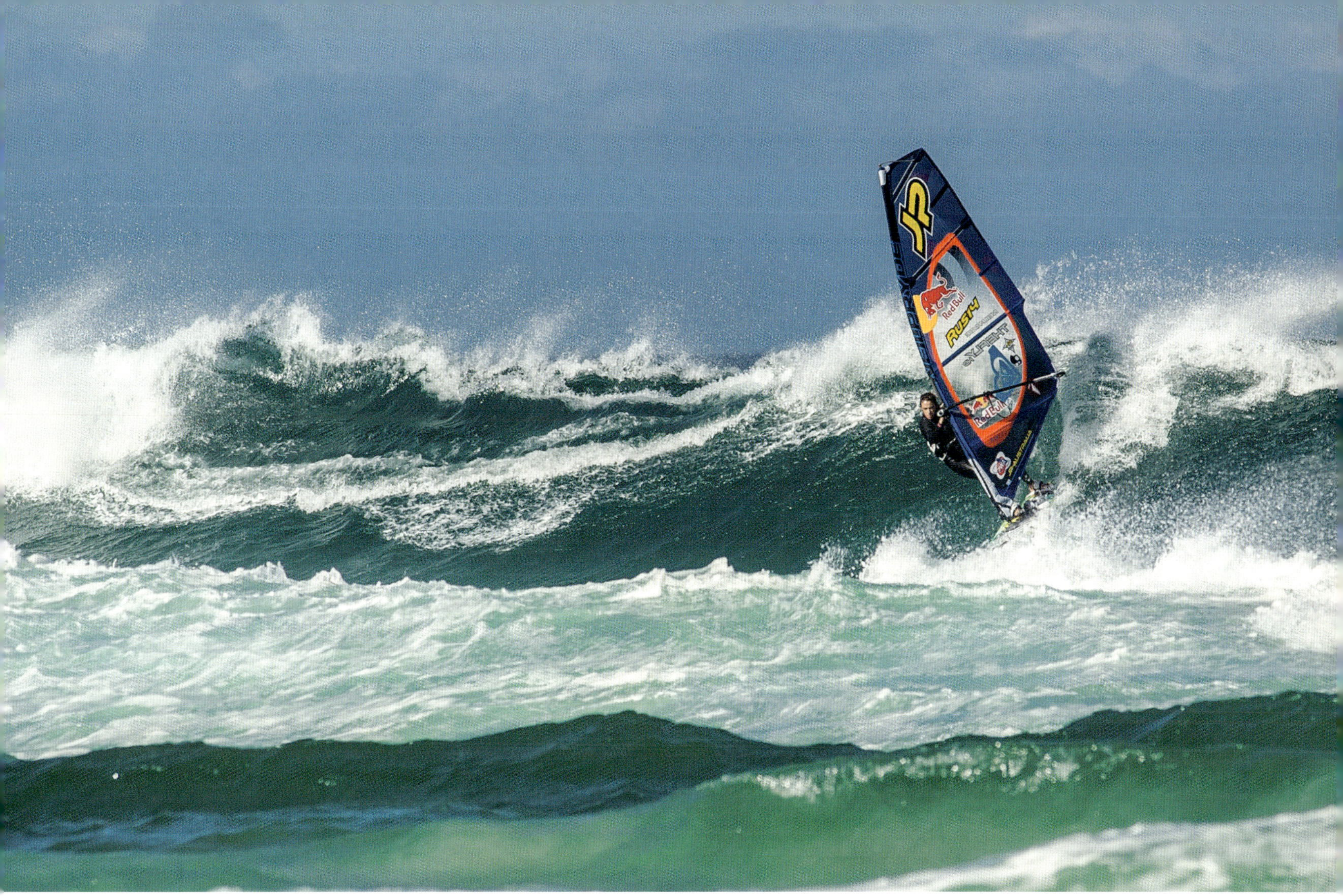

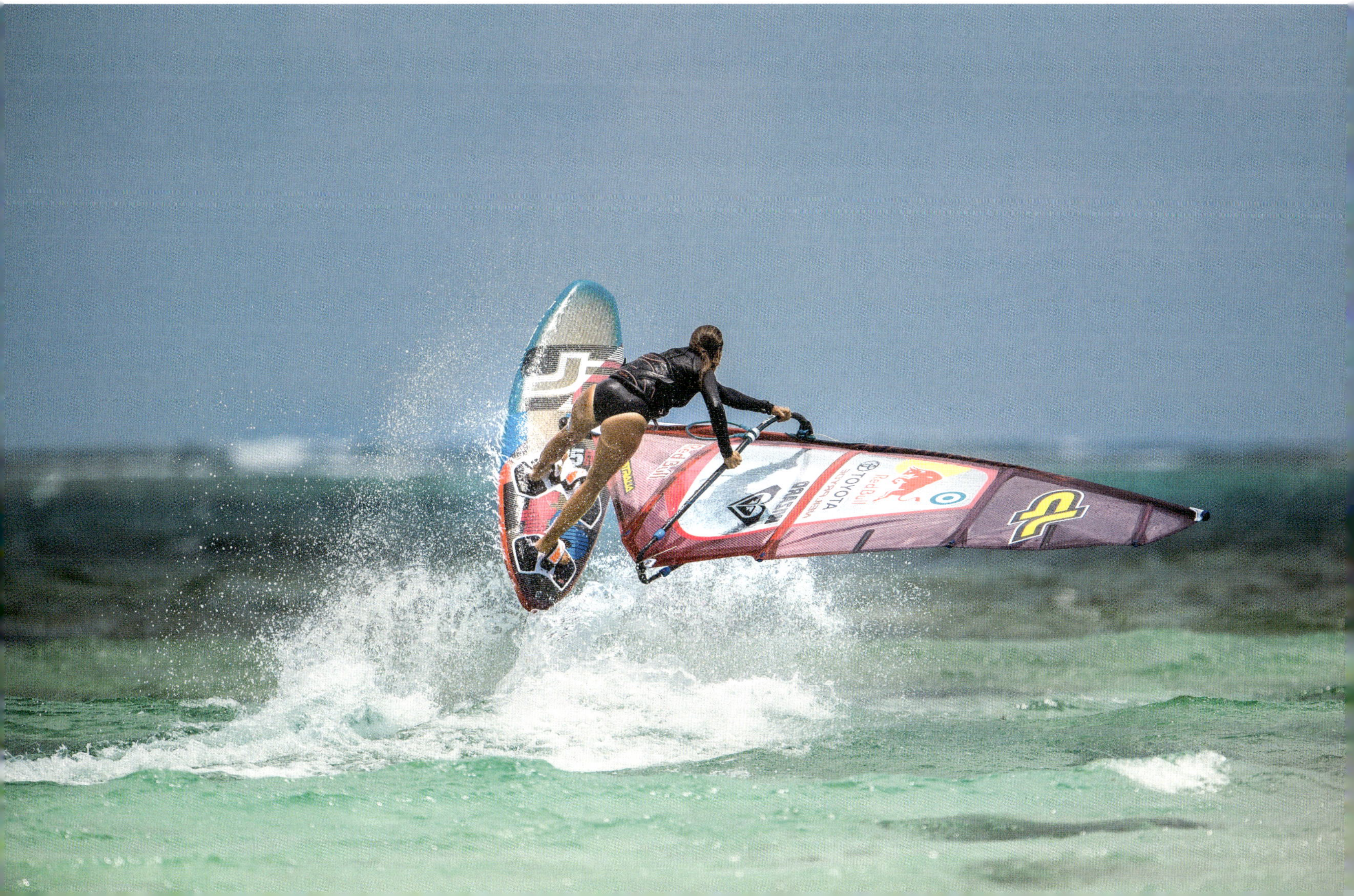

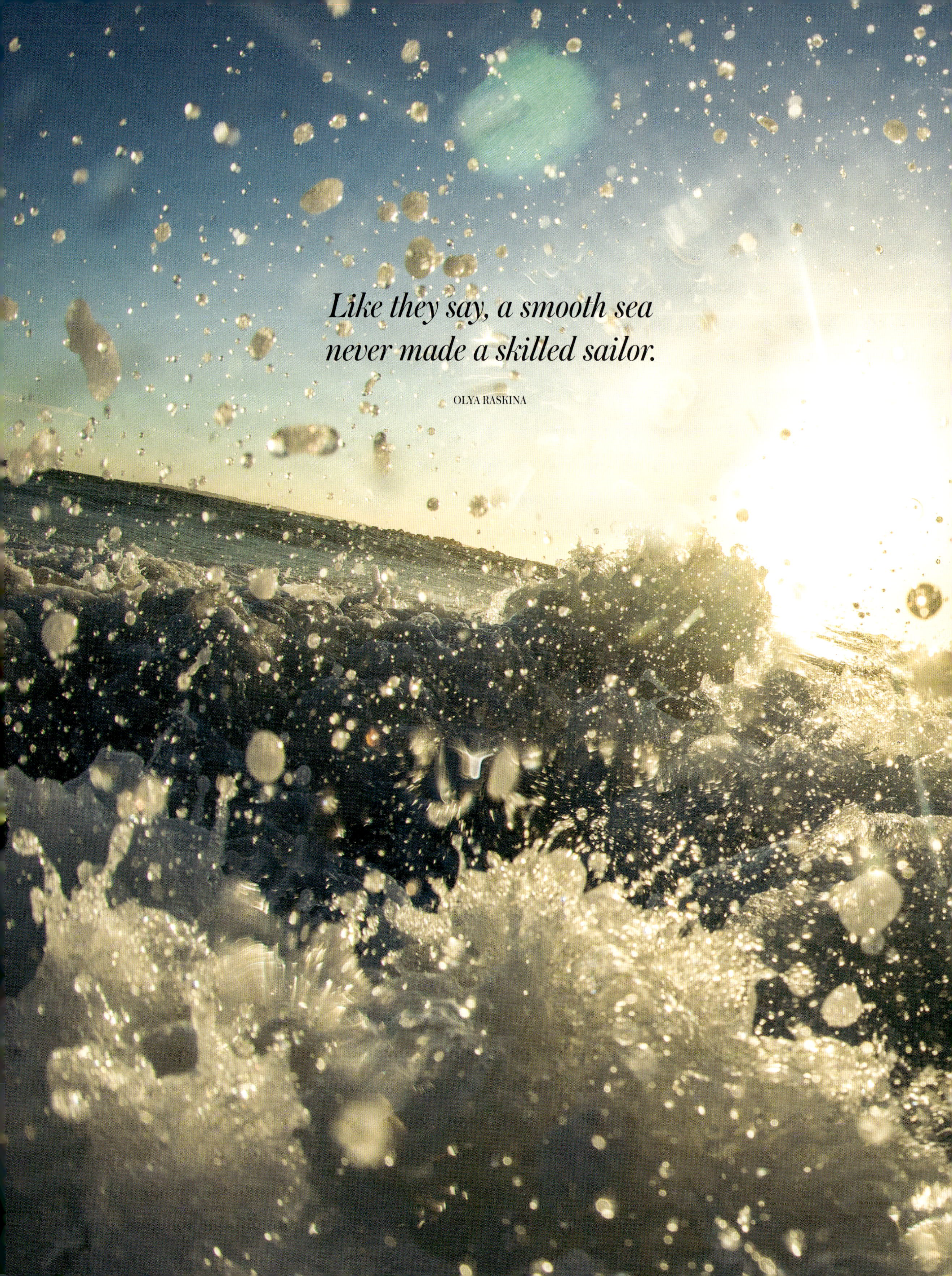
Like they say, a smooth sea
never made a skilled sailor.

OLYA RASKINA

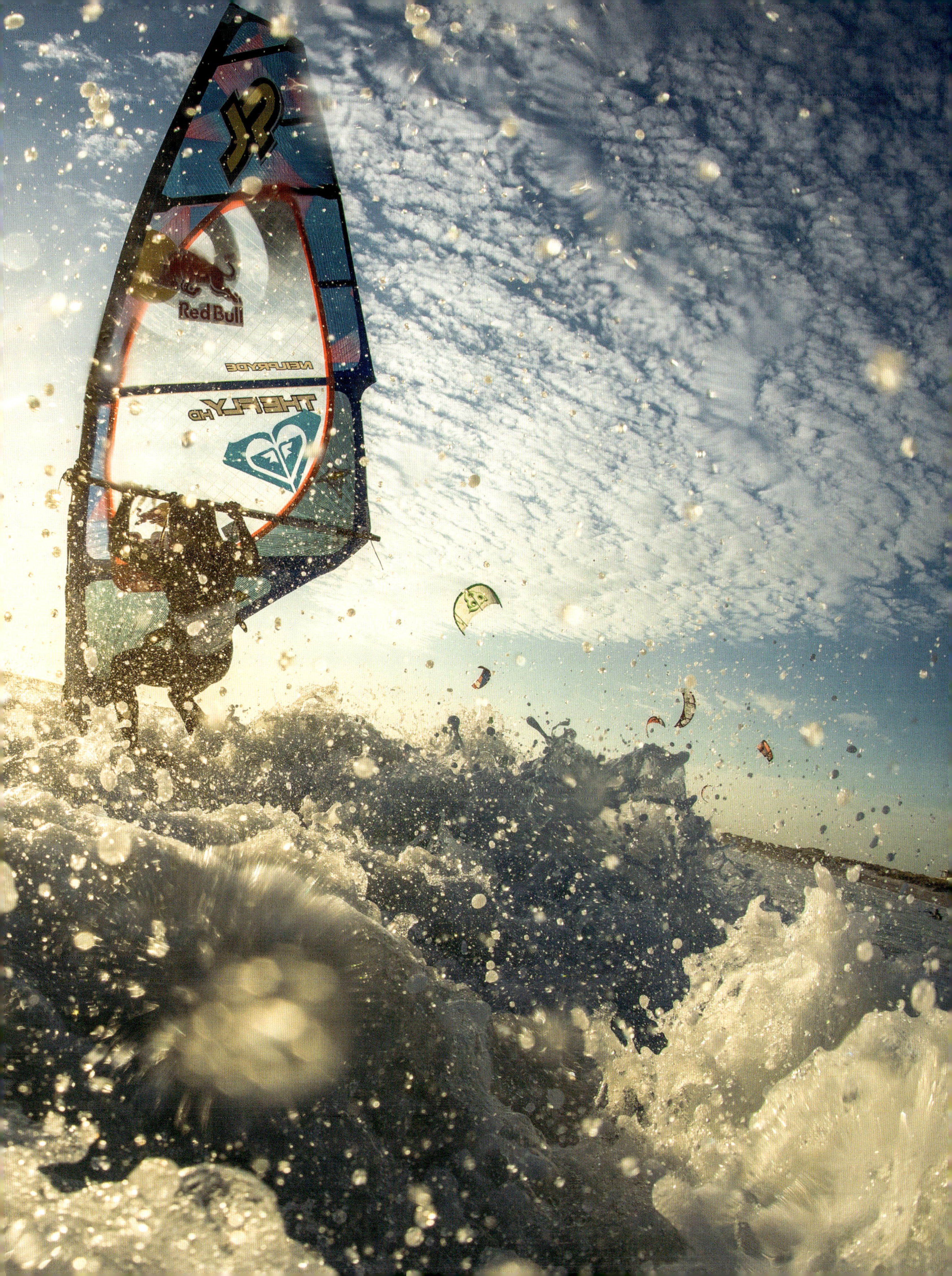

Red Bull
NEILPRYDE
THE FLY HD

Fernanda Maciel
Ultra runner

@fernandamaciel_oficial

I'm Fernanda Maciel, a Brazilian ultra runner. I was born in Belo Horizonte, a big city of five million people surrounded by mountains. I live in the French Alps now, in Chamonix. I chose to live here in order to be a better ultra runner. I love to run long distances in the mountains, to feel the freedom, the simplicity, and the silence that this sport provide me. Here in Chamonix I'm able to run in high mountains, as well as on glaciers, peaks, and beautiful single tracks, which inspires me to keep pushing my mind and body.

I've lived in Brazil, New Zealand, Spain, and France. I've always been looking for a way to run and to be close to nature in an extreme or wild environment. As a child, my passion was to play in the wild jungles and mountains close to home. I love to be outside, but training hard has also been part of my routine since I was eight.

My sporting career started with gymnastics. I stepped up on many podiums as a gymnast but my career finished when I was fifteen. Capoeira was my next sport. I learned capoeira and jiu jitsu, which helped me a lot, giving me the values to become a champion fighter. My dream was to protect nature and be part of it. I graduated in law and started to work as an environmental lawyer. At the same time I became a runner. I was running in my free time and I couldn't ignore my passion.

Running is part of my life today. I live for running, which has given me the opportunity to spend hours outside exploring extreme places, emotions, and sensations. I became Vice World Champion in ultra trails, racing 100 kilometre and 100 mile races around the world, but running high mountains impacted me a lot. I did a great project running the 550 mile Camino de Santiago de Compostela, which goes from France to Spain, as a pilgrim without support; I was the first female runner to do it. It took me ten days. I became the first woman on the planet to run up and down the highest mountain in the Americas, the Aconcagua; it is 22,840 feet from the base of the mountain to the top and back (22 hours and 52 minutes up and down). I've also run up Kilimanjaro, the highest mountain in Africa (10 hours and 6 minutes up and down), and the Elbrus, the highest mountain in Europe (7 hours and 8 minutes up and down), as well as Gran Paradiso in Italy (4 hours and 3 minutes up and down), and many more.

I face the fear when I run. I have learned to live with the fear; it is part of my emotions and I like it because when I feel it I get stronger, more focused, and more prudent in each step and decision I make. I can't control my fears, but I can control my mind.

At Vipassana meditation retreats I learned to observe my bodily sensations and my thoughts and to see them as separate from myself. I became able to remove some sensations and bad thoughts from my mind. That helped me a lot in my daily life and also as an athlete.

Some years ago I spent 200 days sleeping on the mountains. The stars were my roof and I experienced the real spirit of the wild and the simplicity of life. We don't need much to be happy and to be grateful for what we have. When we are out of our comfort zone, that's when we grow.

Being a woman and a runner of extreme routes teaches me to work in the present moment and not to think too much. When I run I'm training my body and also my mind: to think positive or not think at all, to experience the atmosphere and the sounds of the snow falling. Our minds have all the control. Mental training is super important.

I don't have children yet. I'm divorced and I froze my eggs three years ago so I'll be able to be pregnant one day without experiencing fertility issues. When the time is right for me to be a mom, I will.

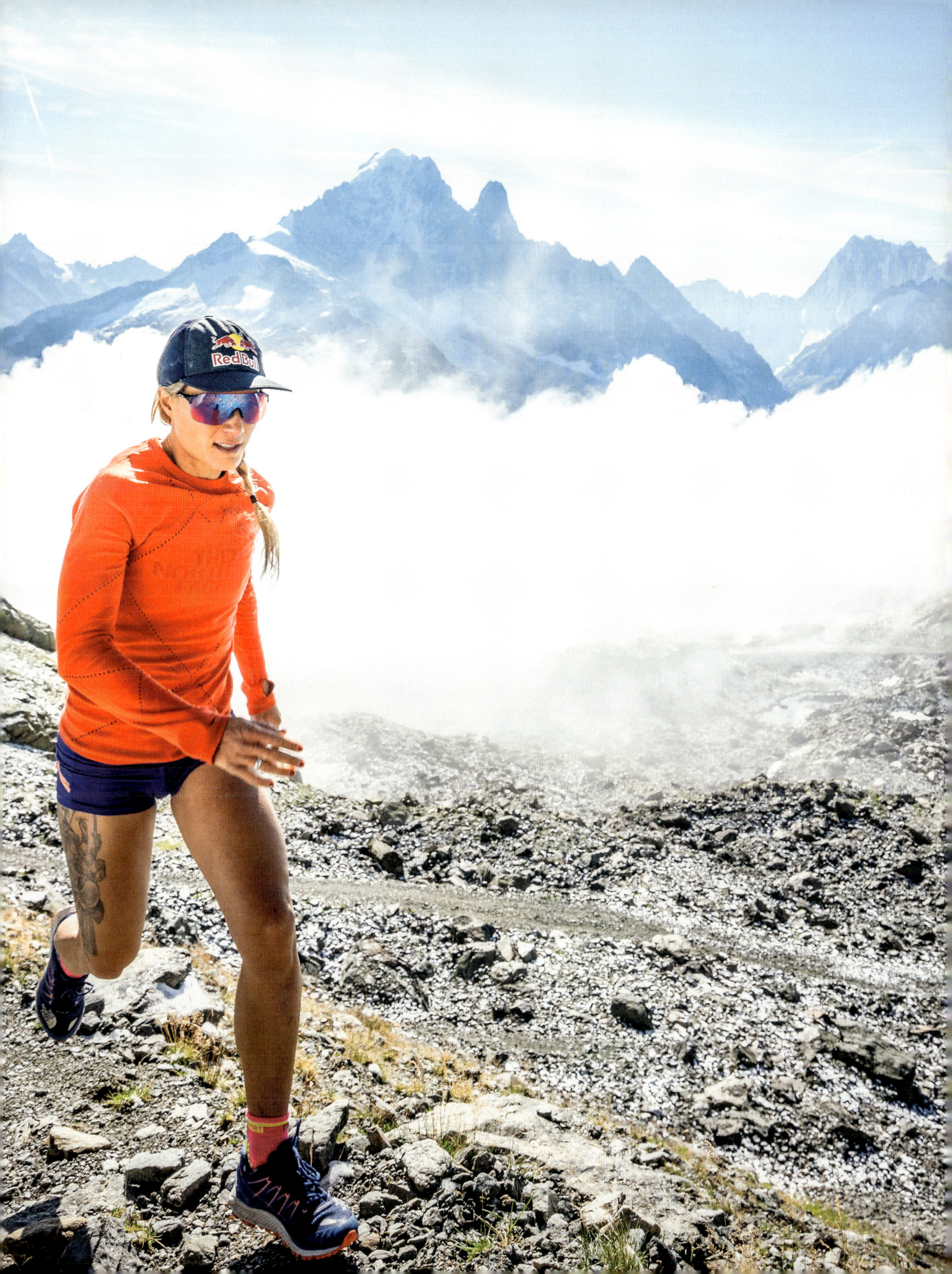

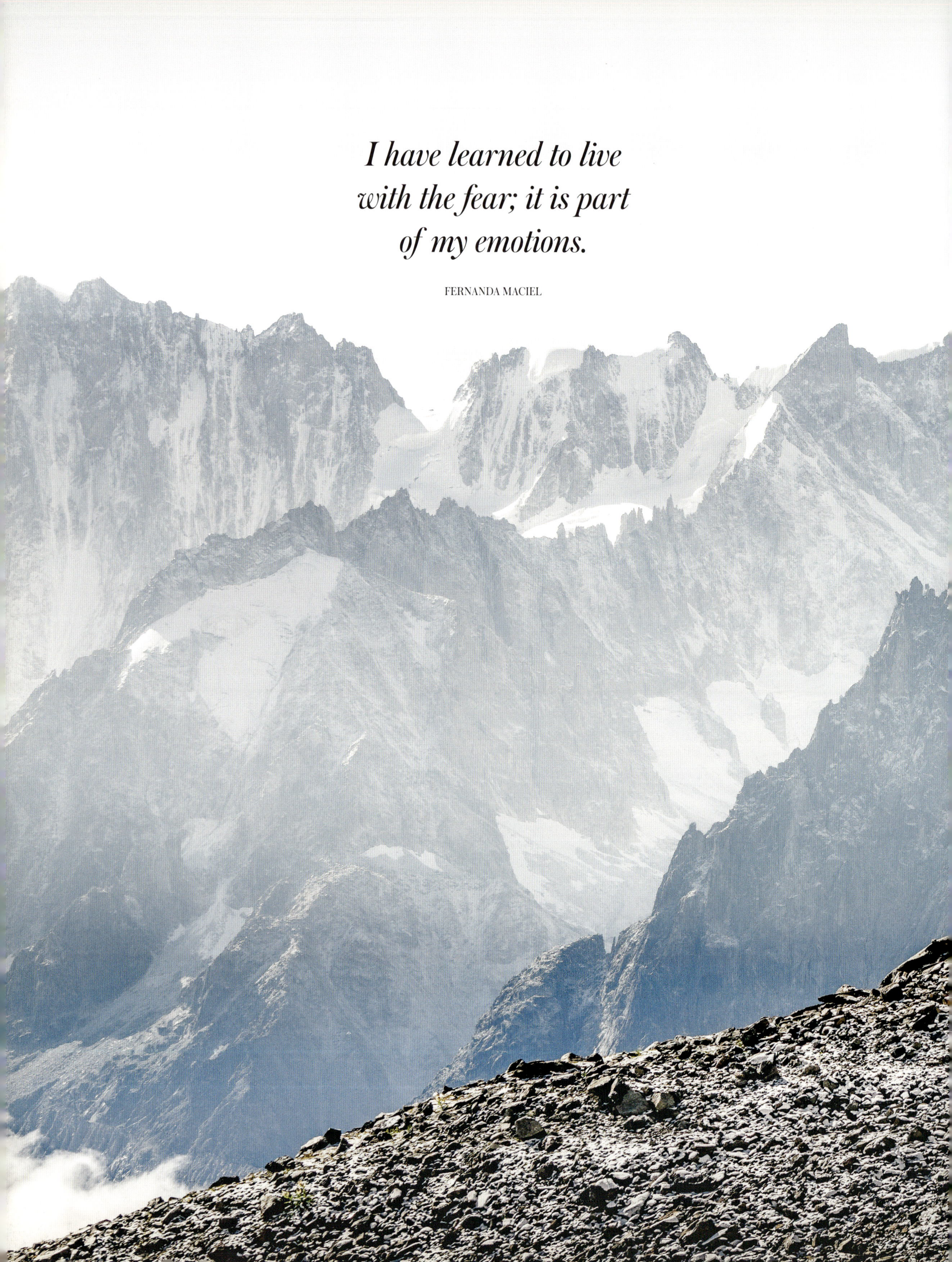
I have learned to live
with the fear; it is part
of my emotions.

FERNANDA MACIEL

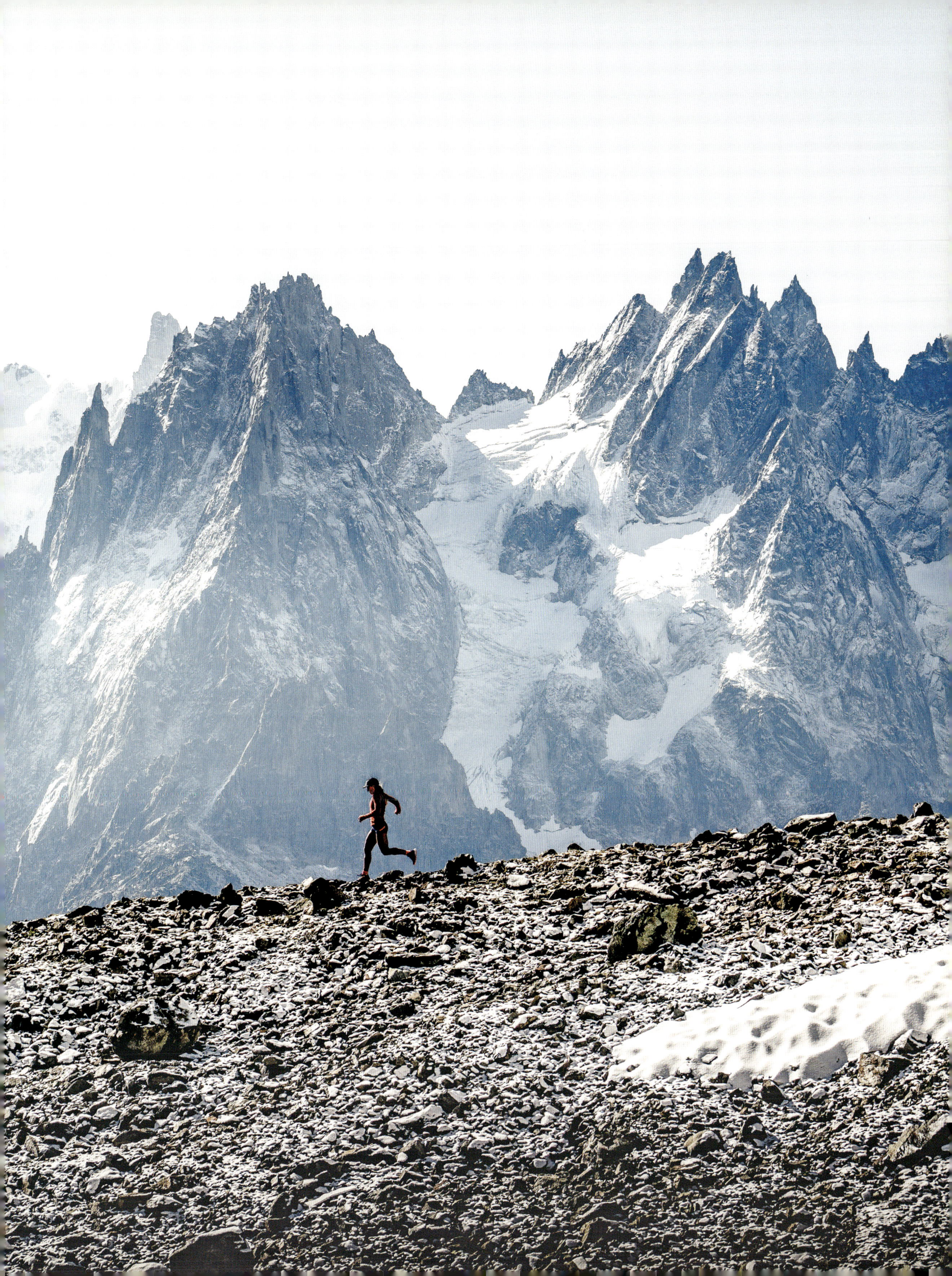

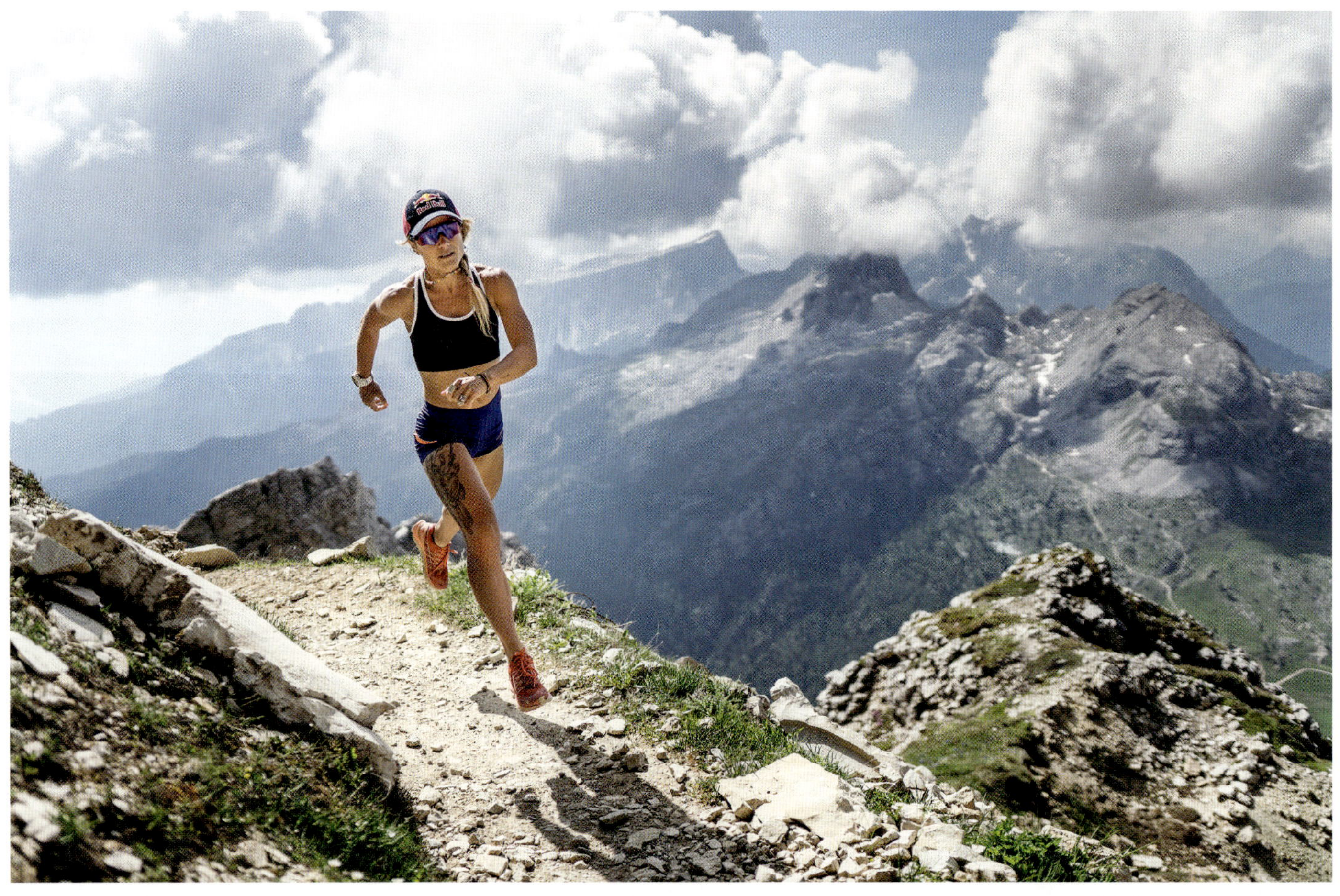

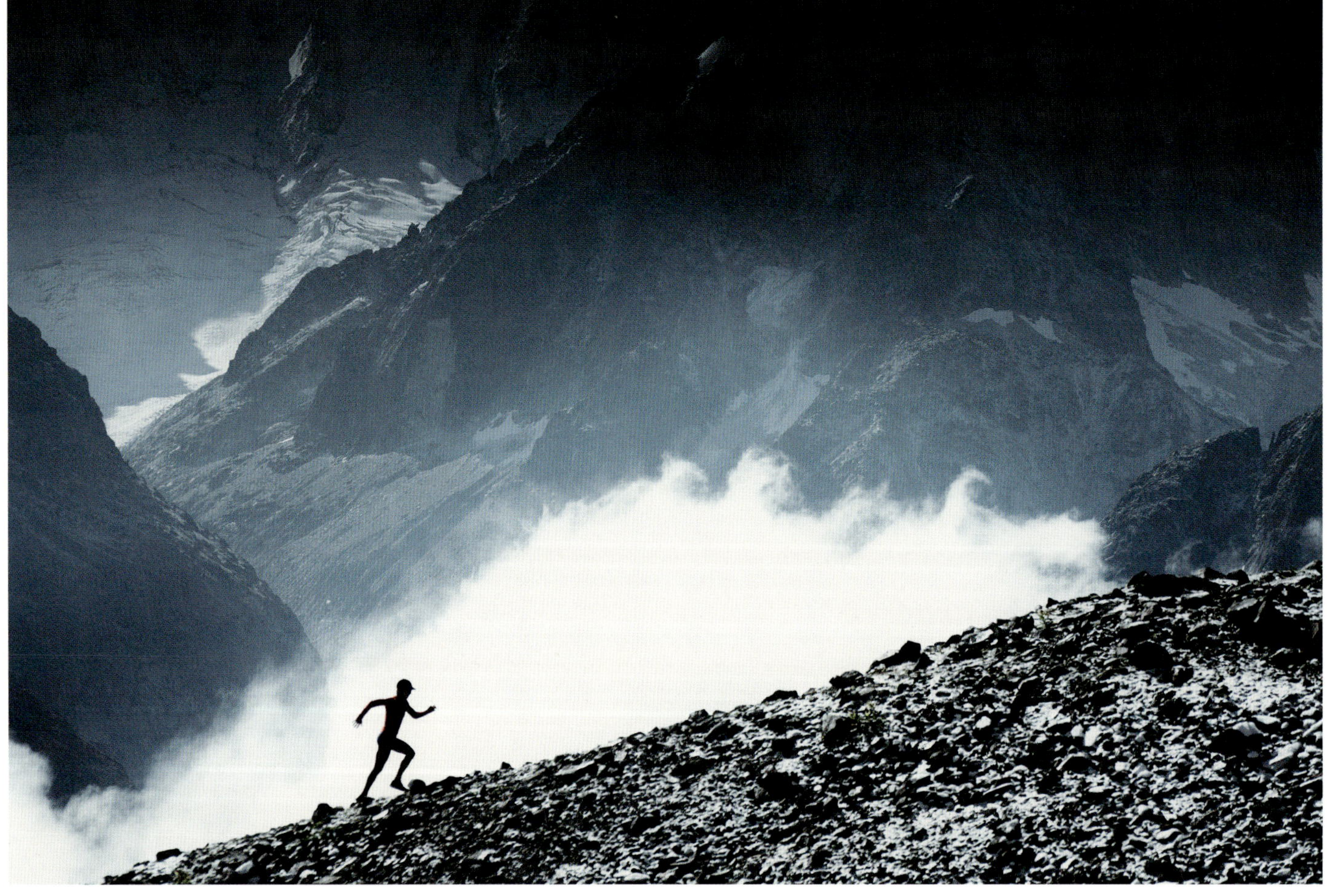

  △△ Dolomites, Italy   △ Chamonix, France   ▷ Estana, Catalonia, Spain   ▷▷ Chamonix, France   ▷▷▷ Dolomites, Italy

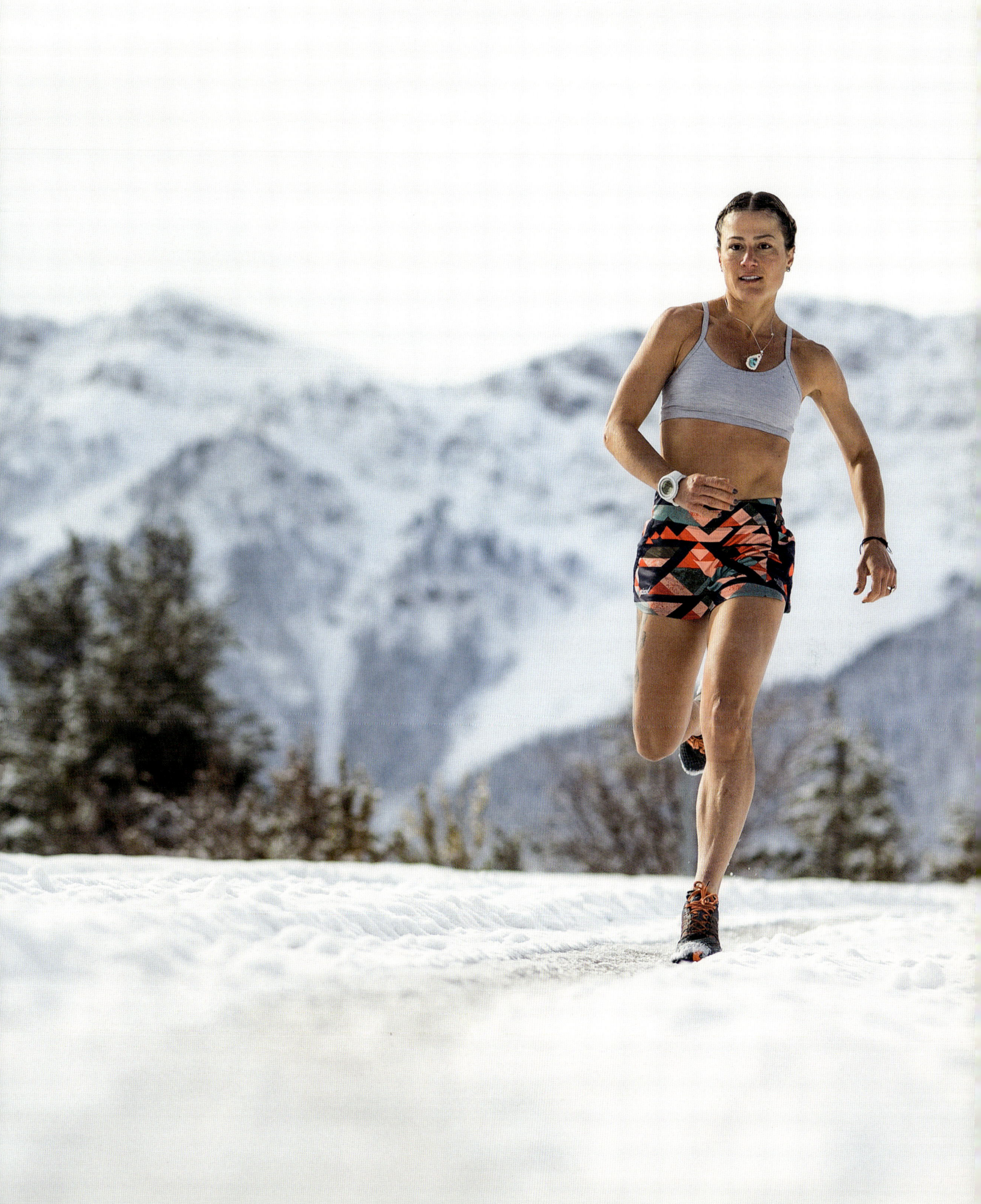

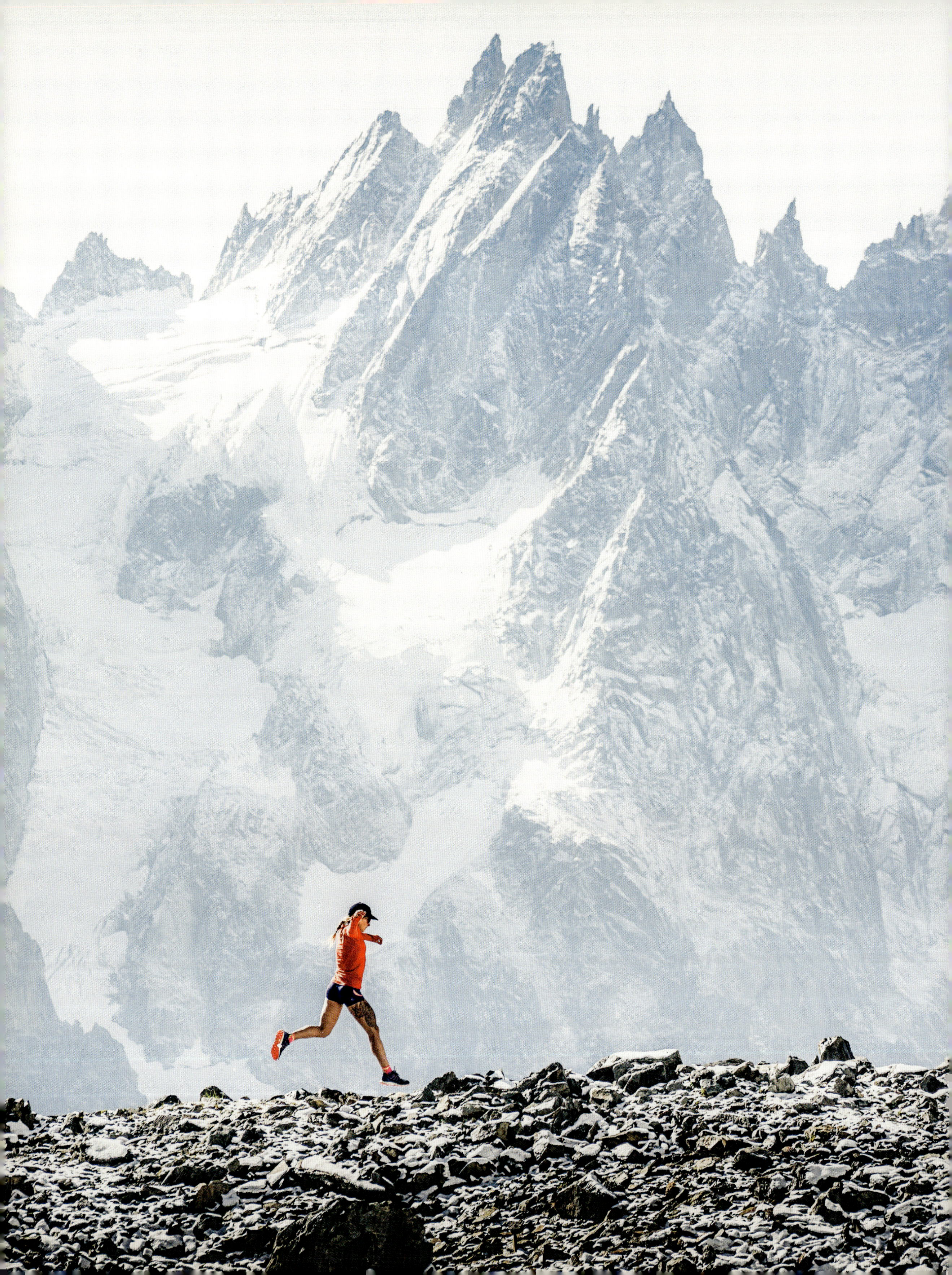

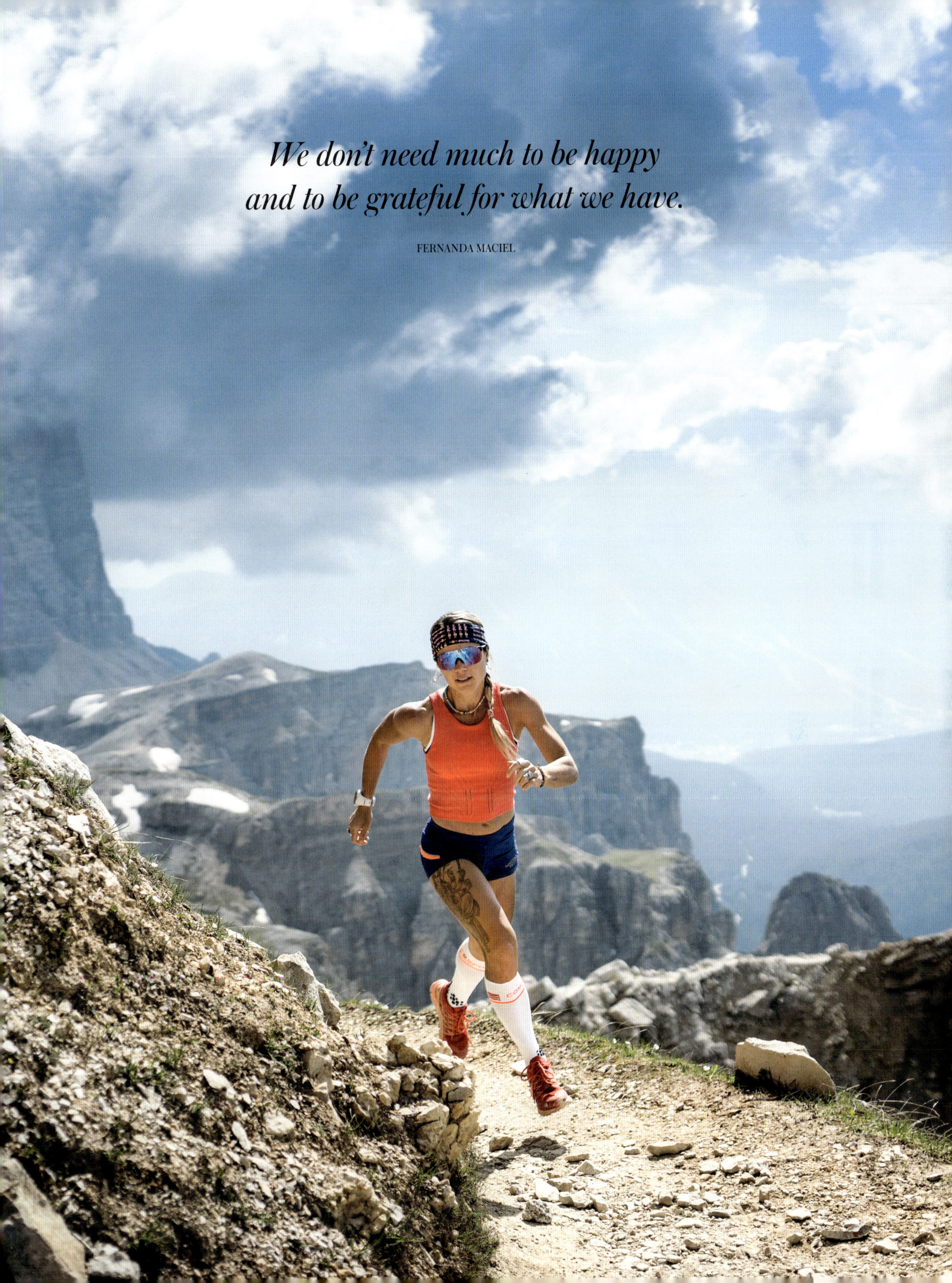

We don't need much to be happy
and to be grateful for what we have.

FERNANDA MACIEL

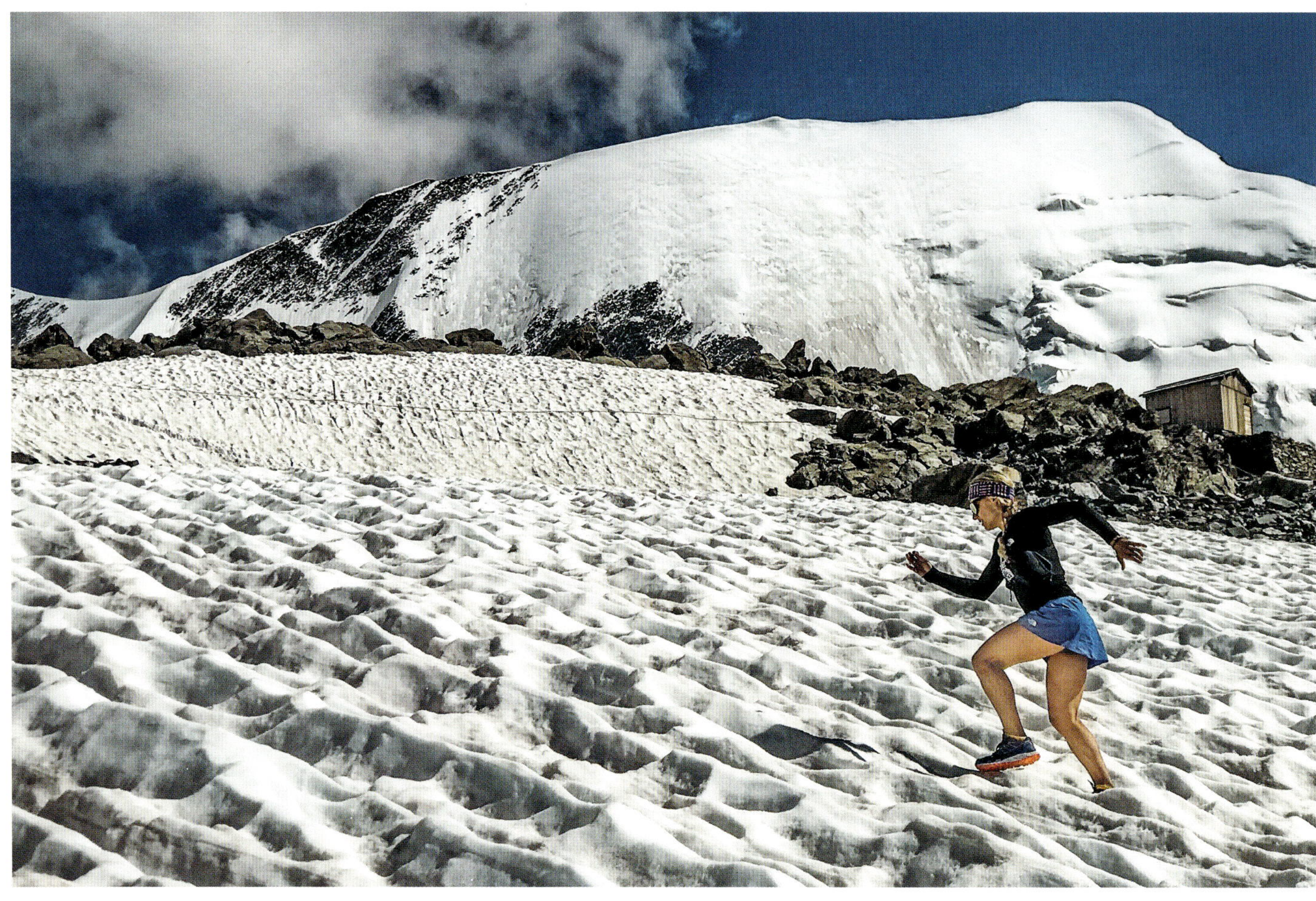

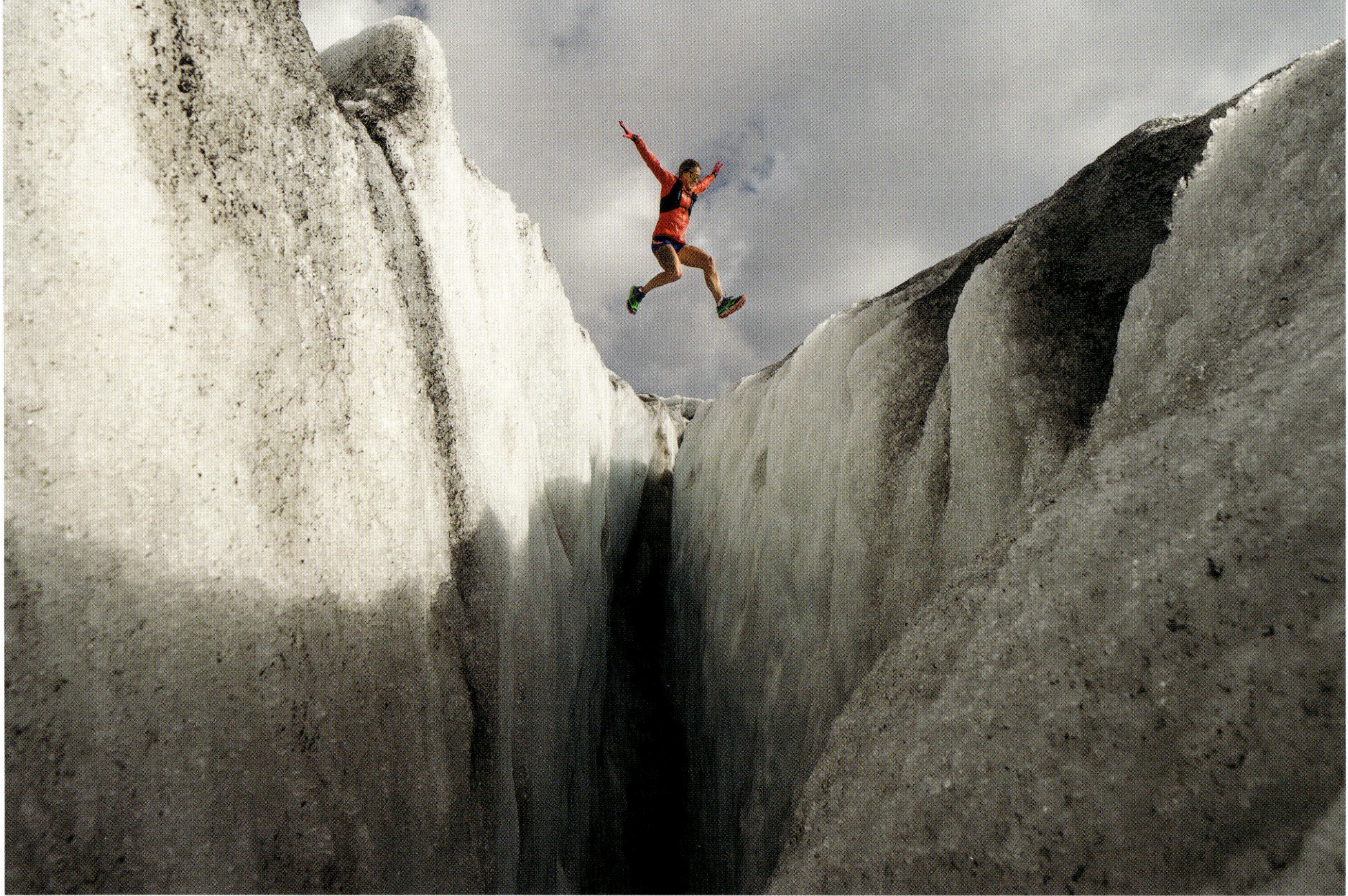

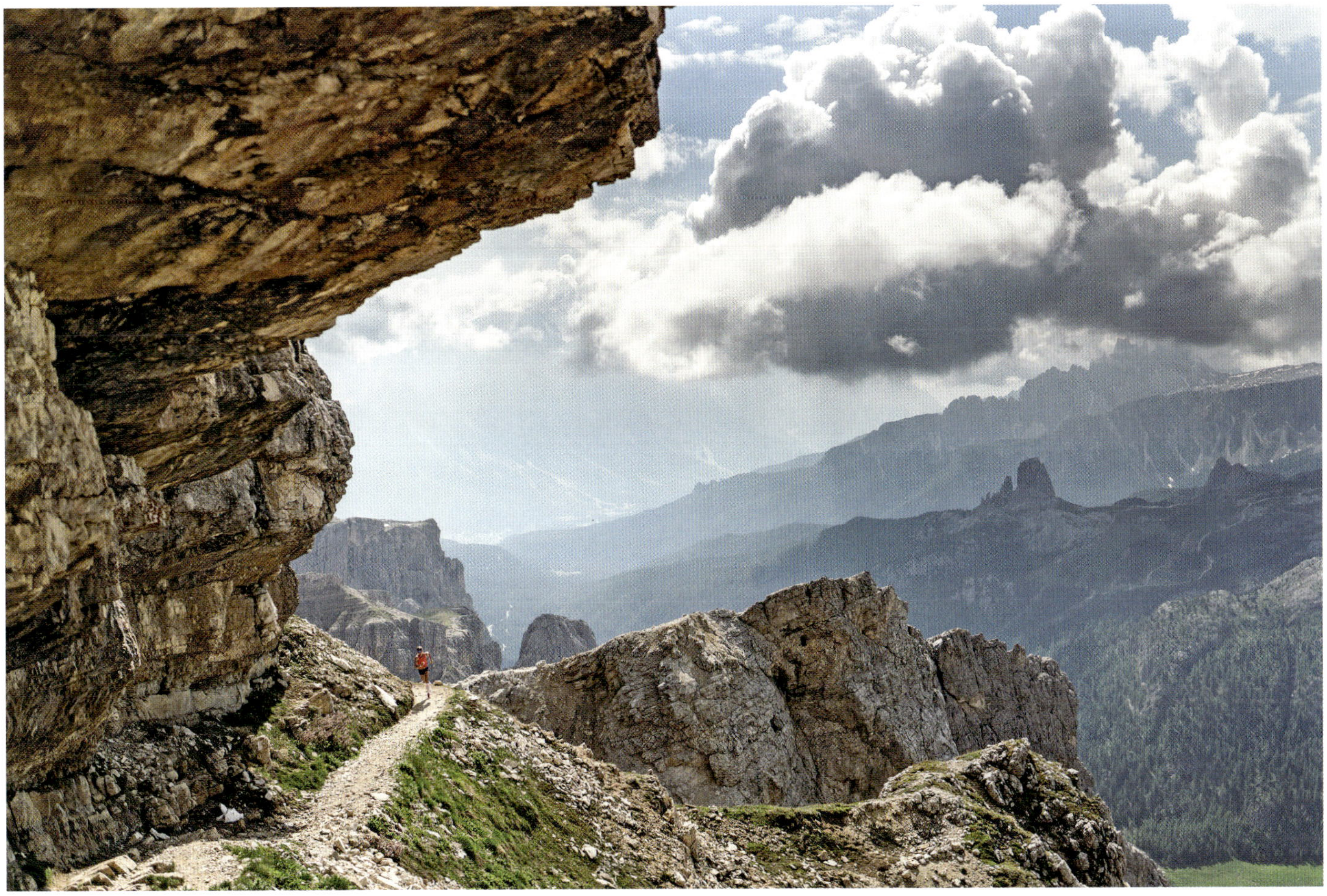

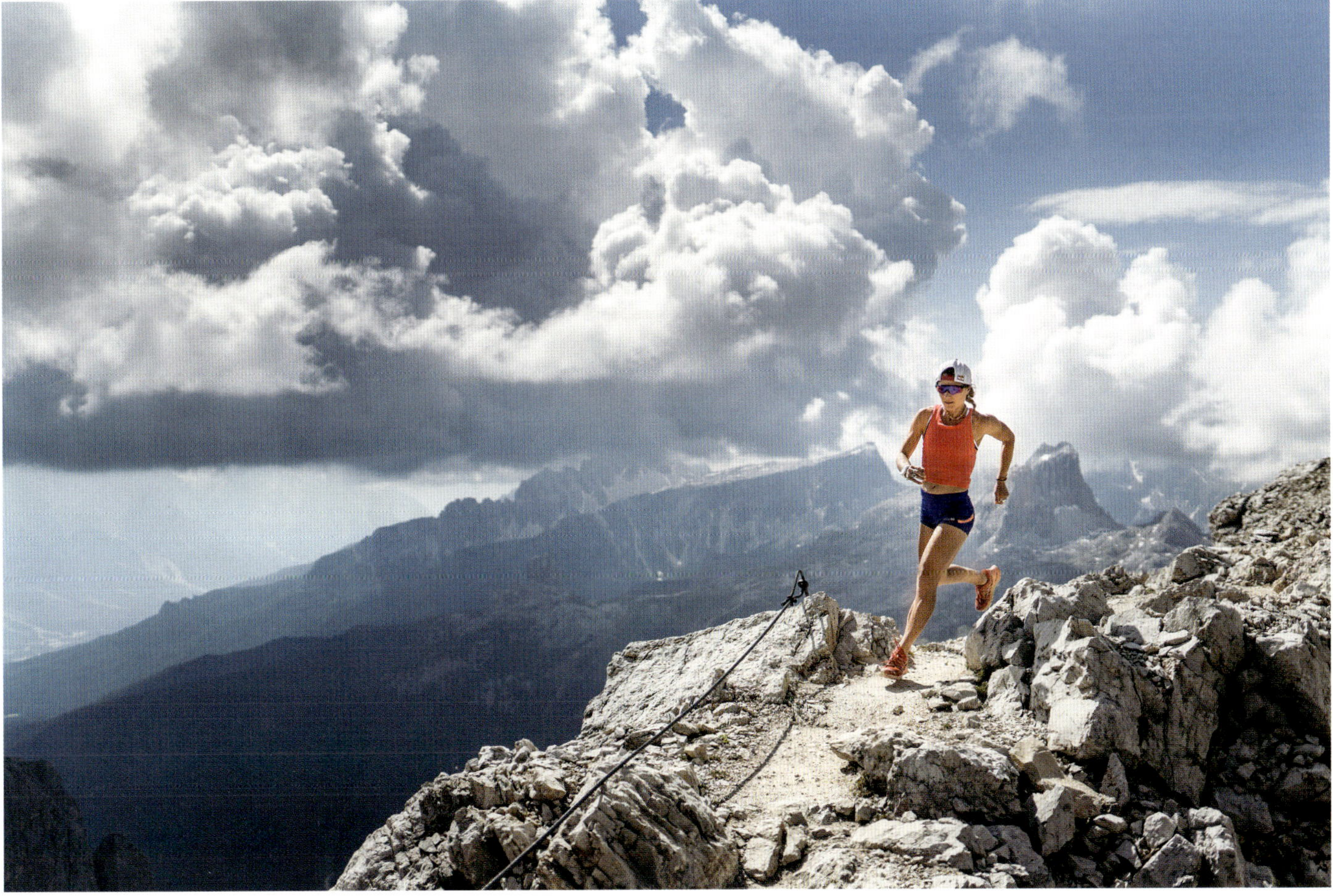

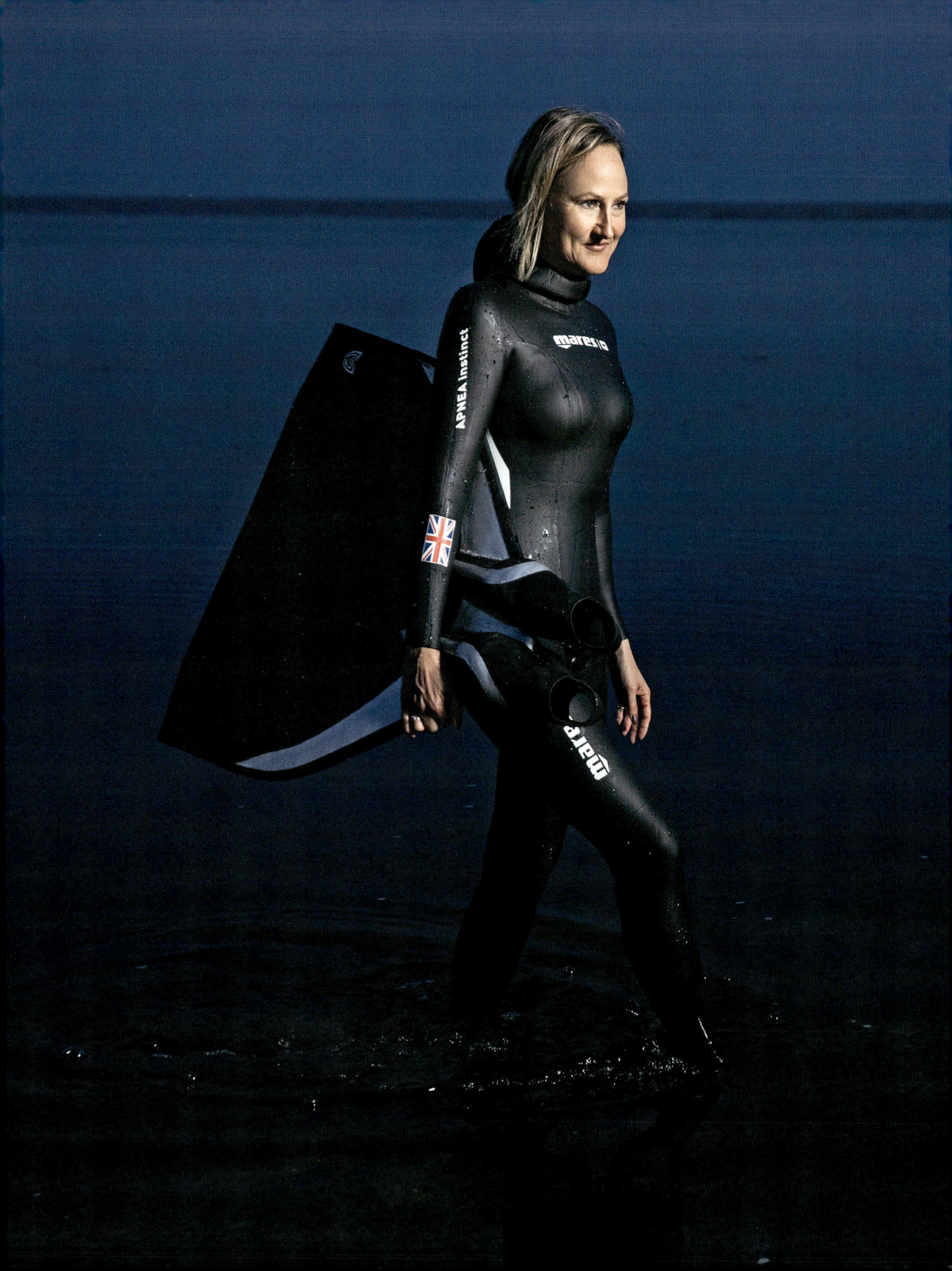

Helena Bourdillon

Freediver

@helena_bourdillon
www.HelenaBourdillon.com

I was born in 1974 and grew up in London, where I was a water baby from the start. I learned to scuba dive aged twelve and enjoyed it for many years, but always found it to be a bit noisy and cumbersome. I discovered freediving aged 39, and it was love at first dive! I put my head under the surface and found the peace and quiet mesmerizing. All the everyday chitchat that goes on in my head just vanished and I was calm and totally focused in that moment.

As well as being a freediver with several national records and representing the UK at four World Championships so far, I do public speaking, talking openly about my journey through chronic depression, which took me to the brink of suicide in 2000. I survived it by reaching out to loved ones, getting help from the National Health Service, and years of intense work with my therapist. Today I live a life that I could not have dreamed of twenty years ago.

Discovering freediving was an epiphany, as I realized that a lot of the training I need to do to compete at world-class level happens to be what I would recommend people do to promote good mental health: regular exercise, spending time in nature, meditation, good breathing habits, nutrition, hydration, and sleep.

I am also a breath trainer, helping people to use their breathing apparatus as effectively as possible to immediately start to gain the numerous health benefits, both physical and mental.

My message is one of hope, inspiration, and encouragement to those who suffer with mental illness as well as working toward dispelling the associated stigma. The deeper I dive, the further my message will carry—plus I also get to do something I love.

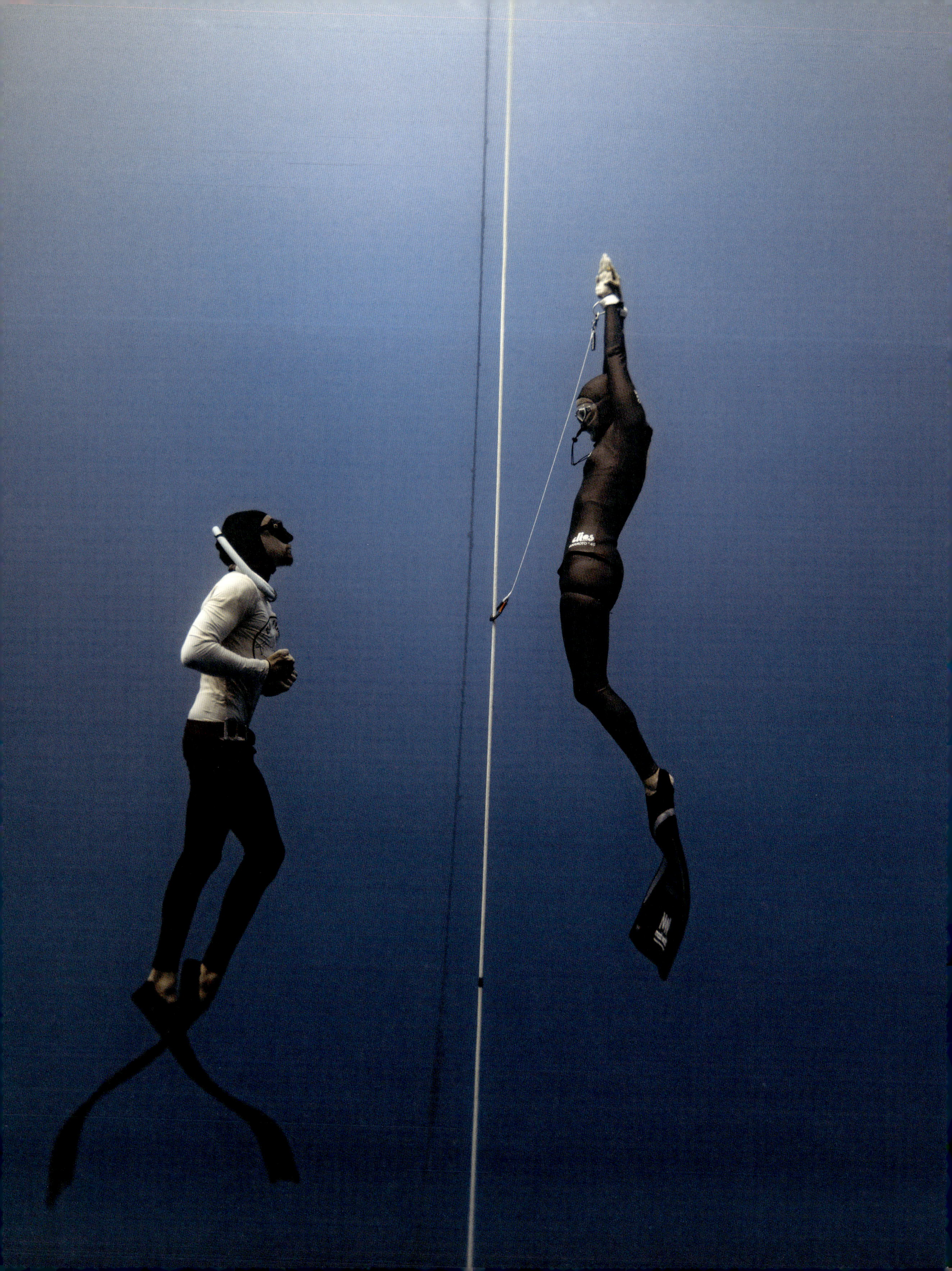

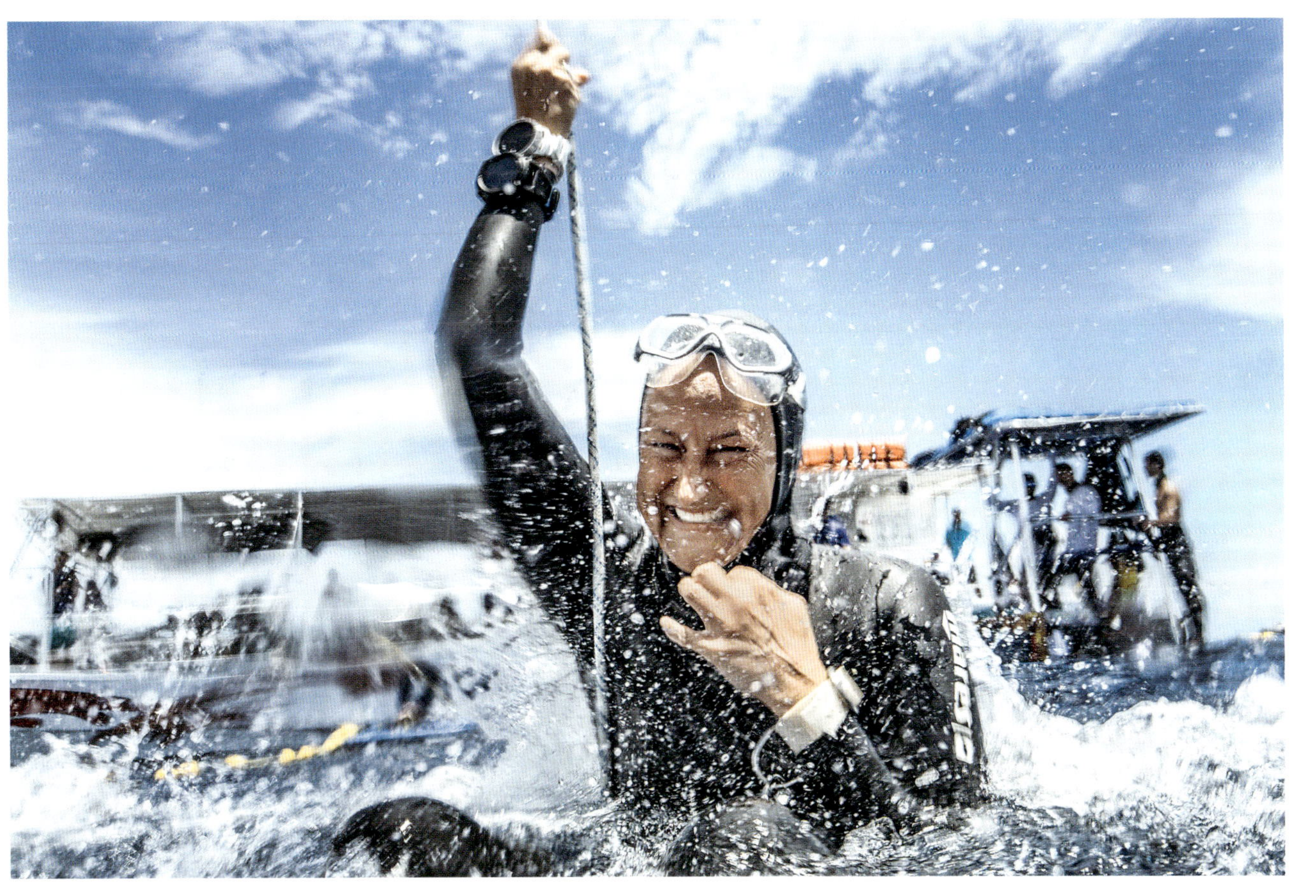

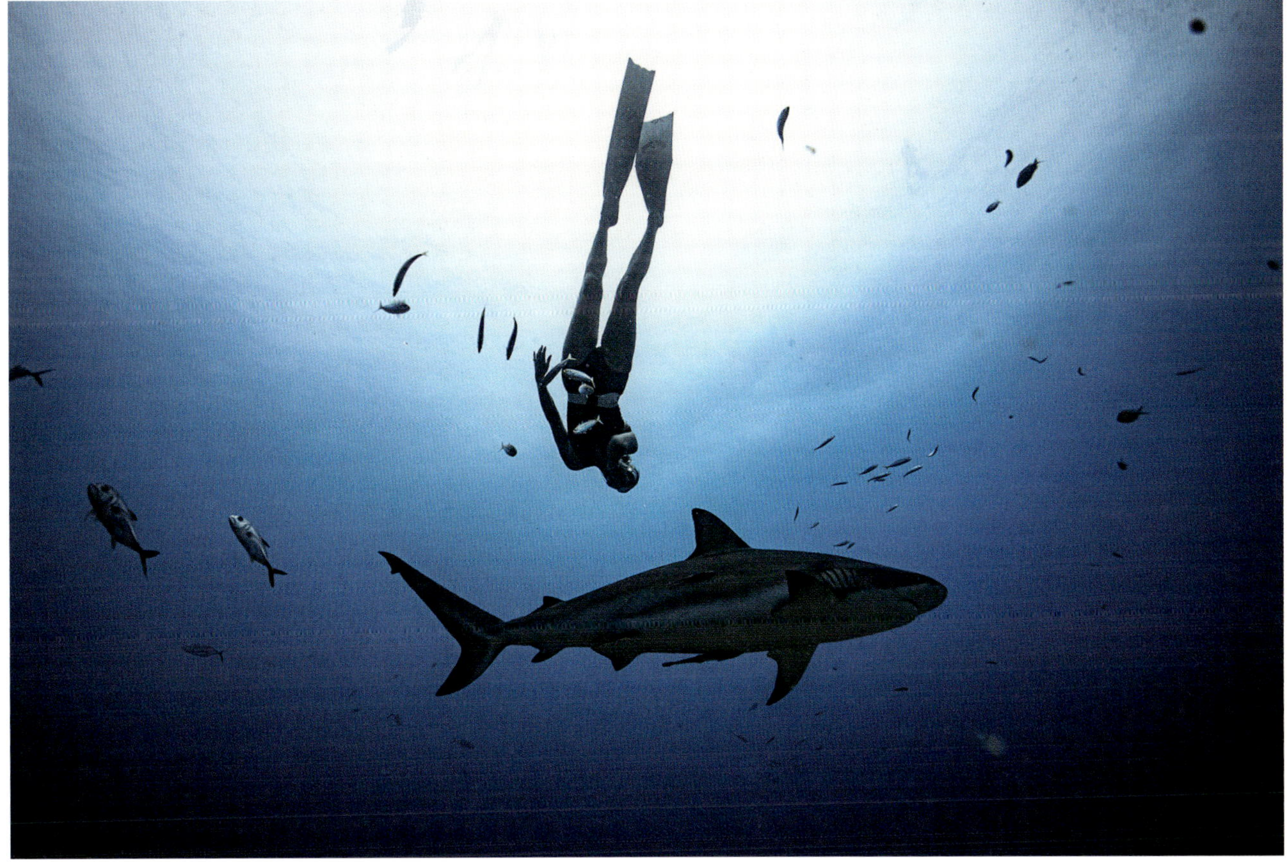

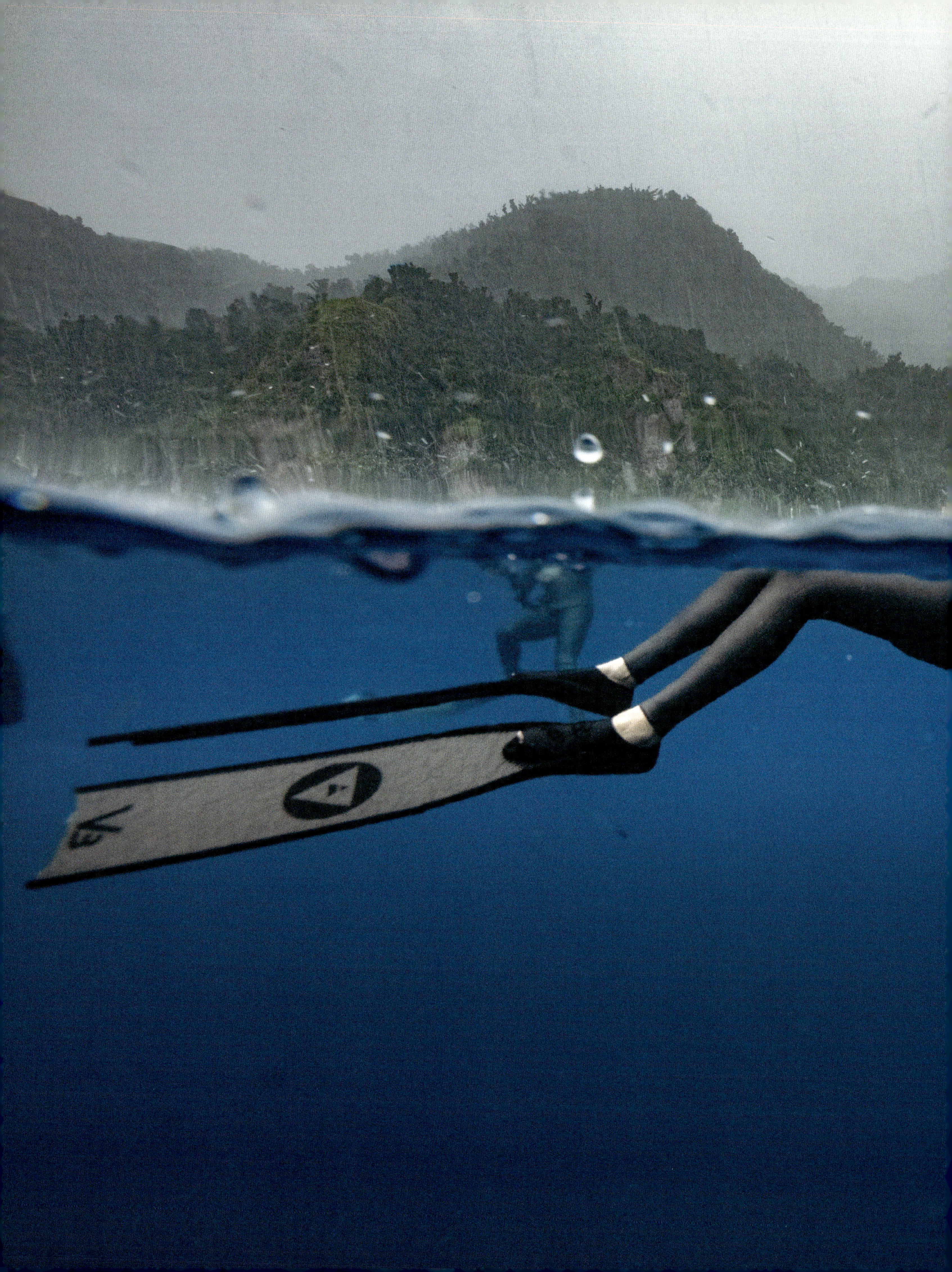

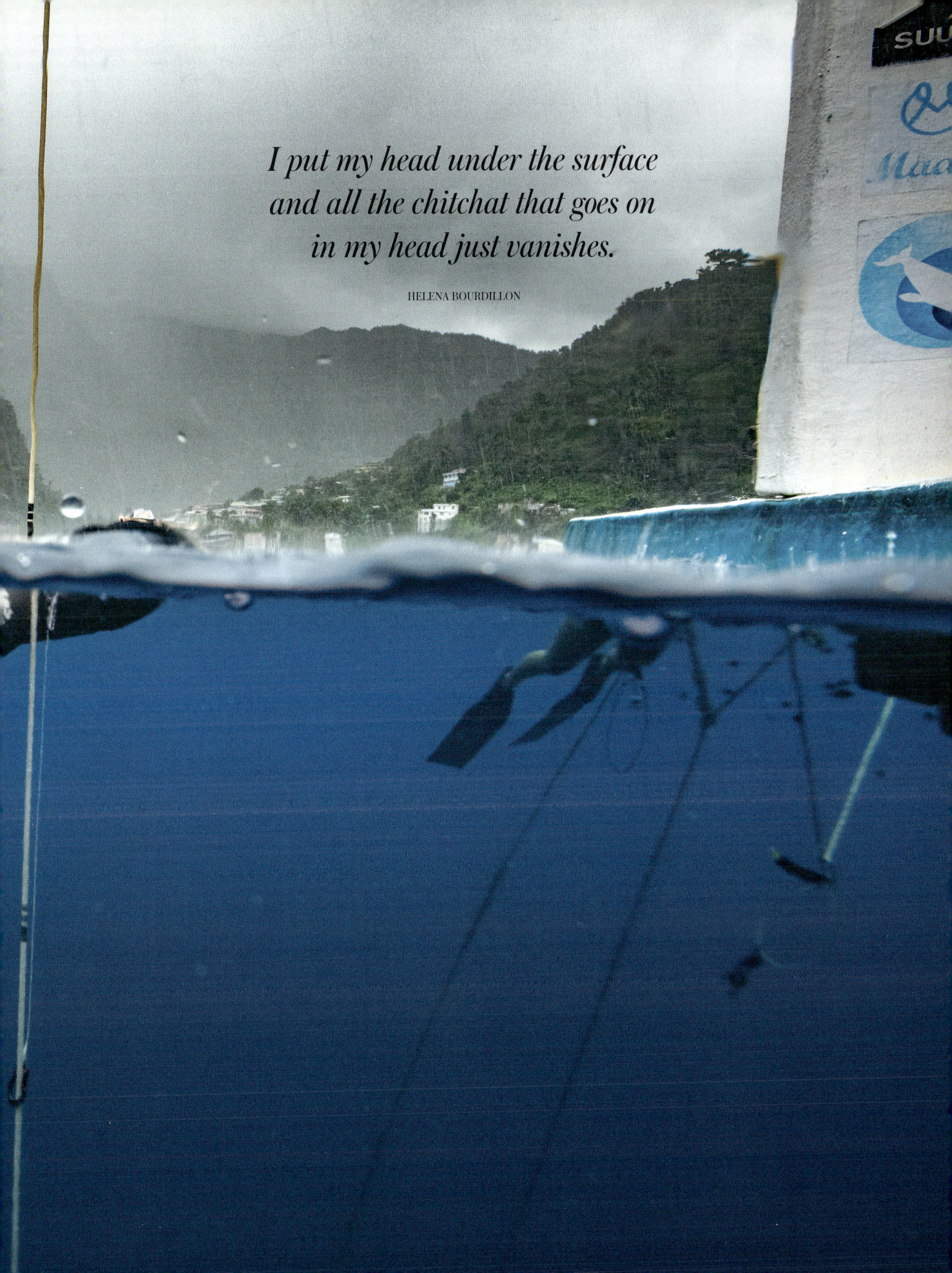

I put my head under the surface
and all the chitchat that goes on
in my head just vanishes.

HELENA BOURDILLON

Katherine Choong
Rock and competition climber

@choongkatherine
katherinechoong.ch

This is how I feel when I'm in the flow:

Squeeze, move forward, stay calm, breathe. My concentration is at its zenith, focusing on each hold, each placement, making move after move toward the top of the route. Nothing disturbs me anymore. I feel the texture of the rock under my fingers, my hands full of chalk, to find the hold I am looking for. I execute the movements to perfection. The smallest detail counts: a simple hesitation could lead to failure and in a thousandth of a second I would find myself hanging at the end of my rope. My arms hurt; my fingers open under the weight of fatigue and abandon me. The pressure rises and doubt assails me. But my head takes over again. A little voice screams at me from the depths of my guts to resist for a few more moments. My heart palpitates but my body continues to execute the movements dictated by my will in an increasingly precarious balance. I am getting closer to the impossible. Only a few more feet separate me from my objective. Then I reach the summit.

I started climbing when I was about eight years old and I haven't stopped since. Rock climbing is a facet of climbing that I particularly like, because it requires you to have the will to constantly surpass yourself. The relationship with nature is also very special and from my passion for this sport was born the passion to travel, to discover some of the most beautiful places on the planet, and to experience beautiful cultures and people.

Since I started, I've dreamed about climbing in the ninth degree. The level of the almost impossible, reserved for the elite and only a handful of women, it attracted me while also scaring me.

For this reason, after finishing my law studies at university, I decided to interrupt the internship I had undertaken in order to obtain a lawyer's license and devote myself 100 percent to my sport. It wasn't easy to make that decision in a country where it is difficult to make a living from sport, especially climbing, and where unconventional choices are sometimes looked on with disapproval. But it was essential for me to dare to live my passion, to trace my own path and not follow that of others, and to reconnect with nature and simple things. I believe that today's challenge is to be oneself—to be unique.

These objectives are my driving force, always higher, always harder. The most interesting thing about success is the process, the path you take to get there: being able to draw unimaginable resources from oneself, finding solutions to complex problems dictated by the rock and continuing to believe when nothing seems possible. It is above all the work of a perfectionist. There are no competitors: the challenge is to surpass oneself and give one's best. It requires a mix of methodical work and feeling—feeling your body in perfect symbiosis with your mind in order to accomplish feats that you didn't think you were capable of. Because strength does not come from physical ability but from the will.

Climbing for me is the school of life. Fear, doubt, and questioning work for me in my daily life. But in climbing, there is no room for doubt. You have to be 100 percent in the present moment. Each placement and each memorized hold has its importance. It's about getting rid of all the parasitic fears that prevent you from daring and succeeding. The real victory is this struggle against one's own failures, those that push us to give up.

There is a fine line between obsession and passion. Even if I am aware that I am risking failure, that the moment of clipping the anchor may not come quickly, I am convinced that I will succeed one day. Climbing has also taught me to accept that I will not achieve success immediately, to turn frustration into patience, and to learn from every experience. Failing is always more productive than not trying. Above all, climbing is just a game; life is too short to take yourself too seriously.

  ▷ Hintisberg, Lütschental   ▷▷ Jungfrau Marathon 9a, Gimmelwald, Bern | Switzerland

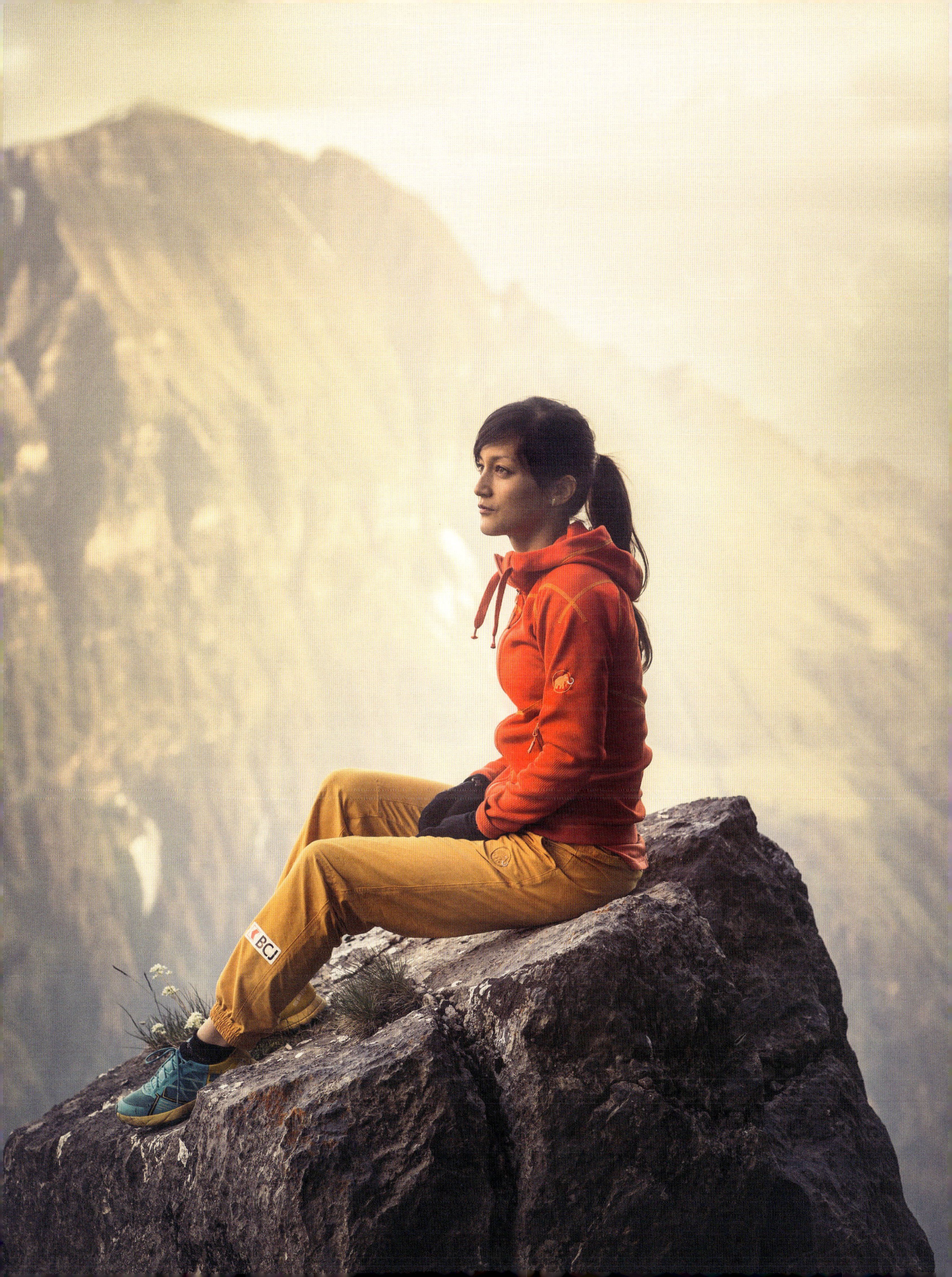

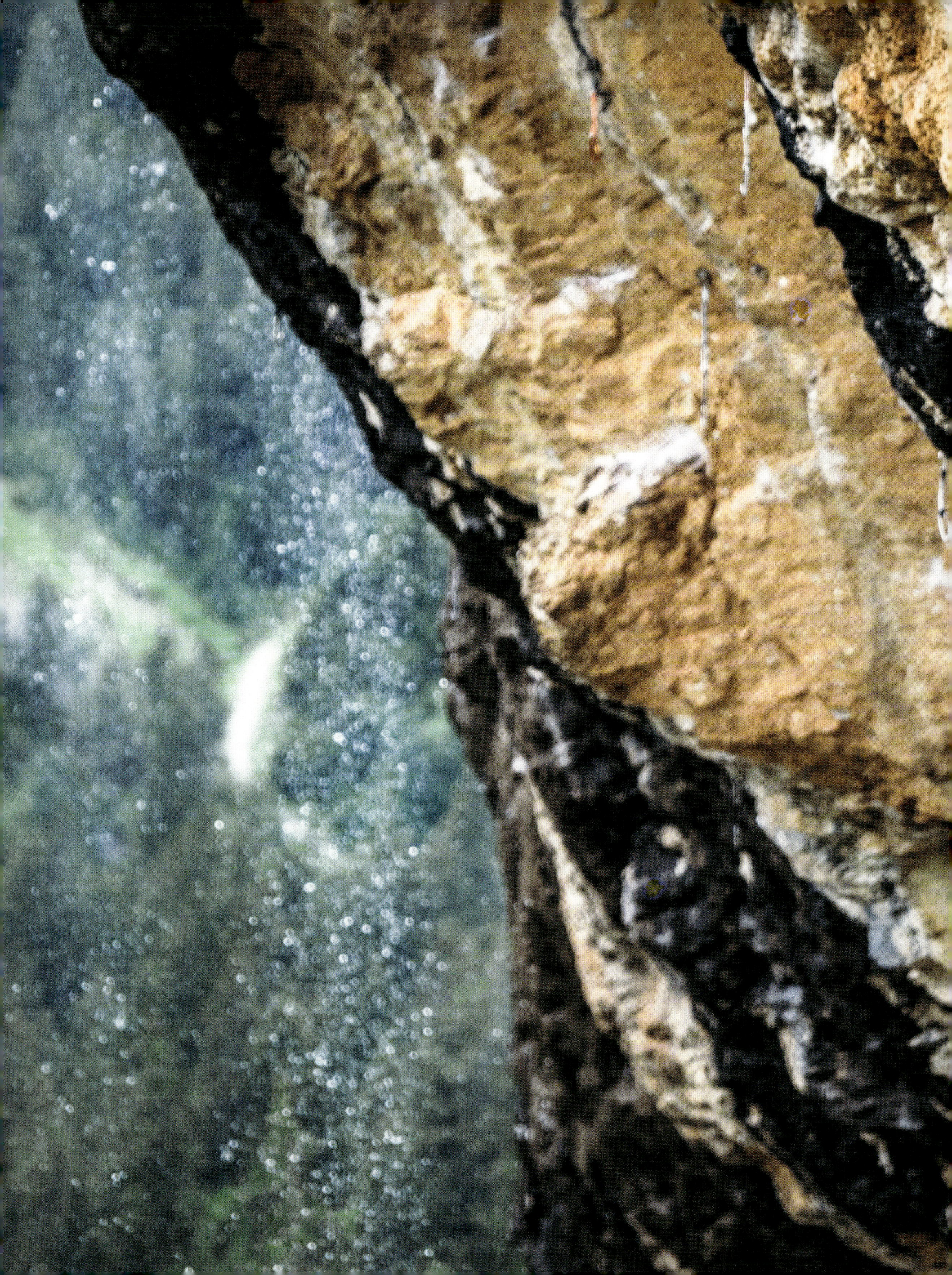

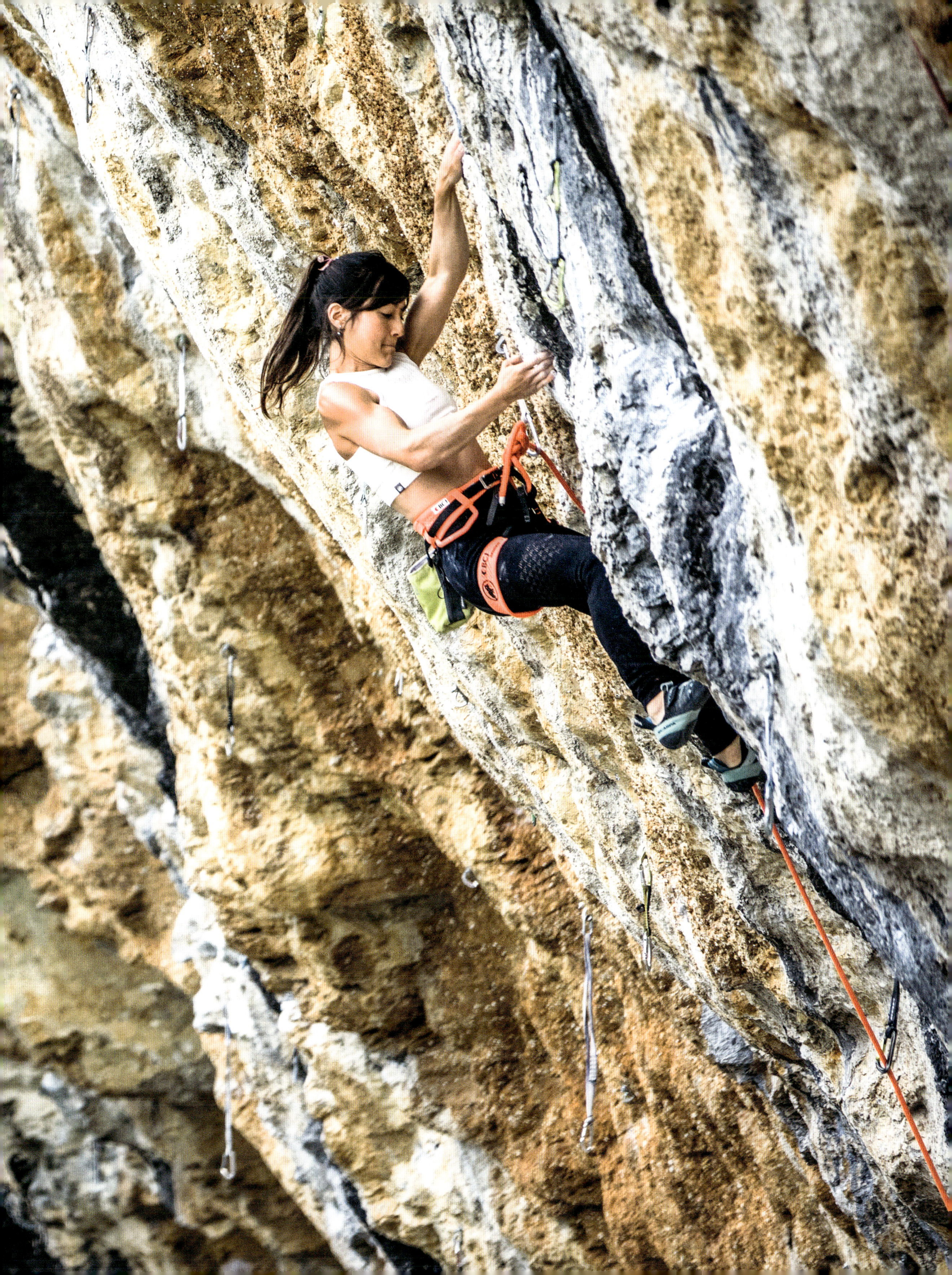

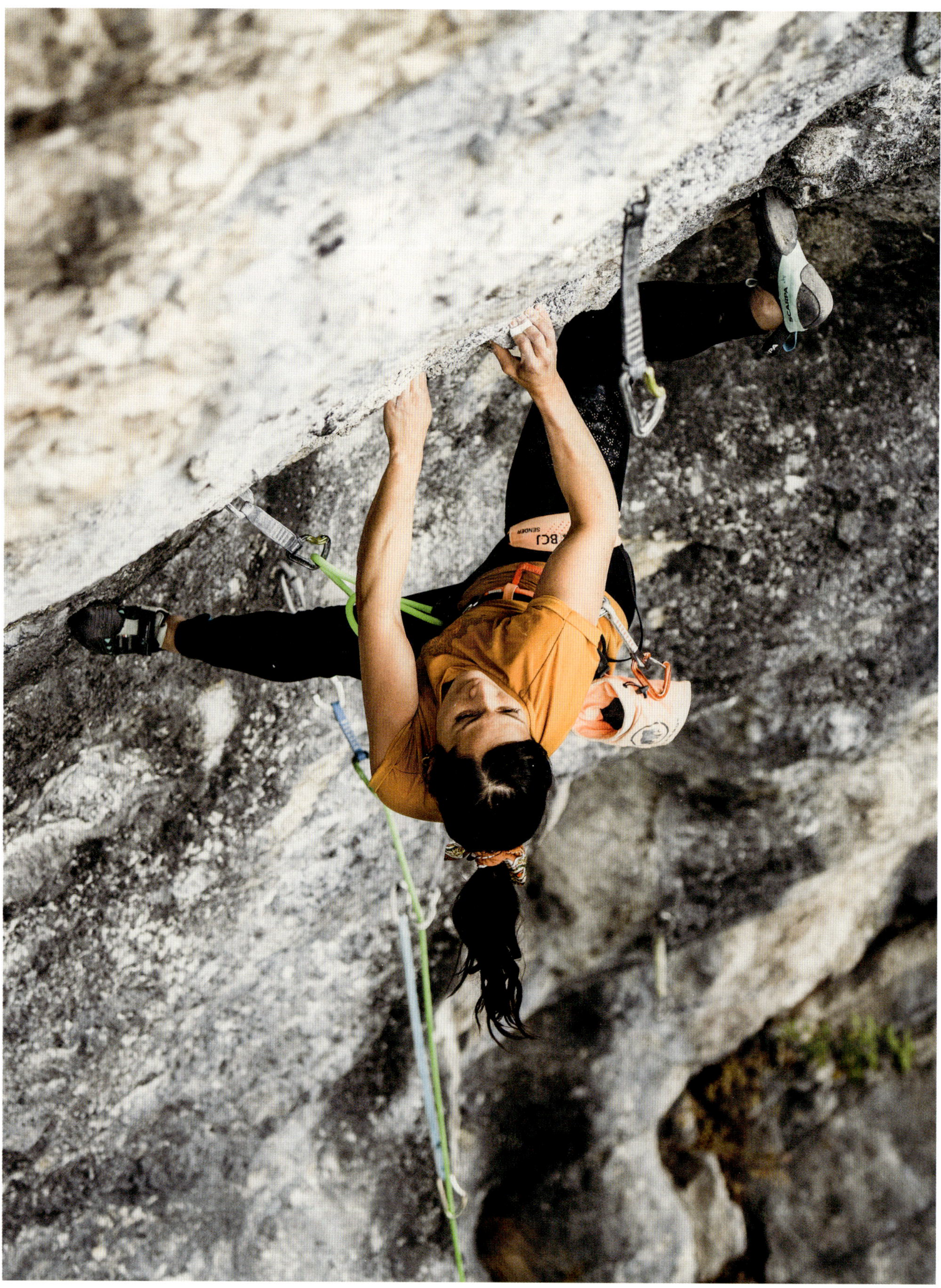

   △ The Back of Beyond 9a, Soyhières   ▷ Tornado Power 8c, Gimmelwald, Bern | Switzerland

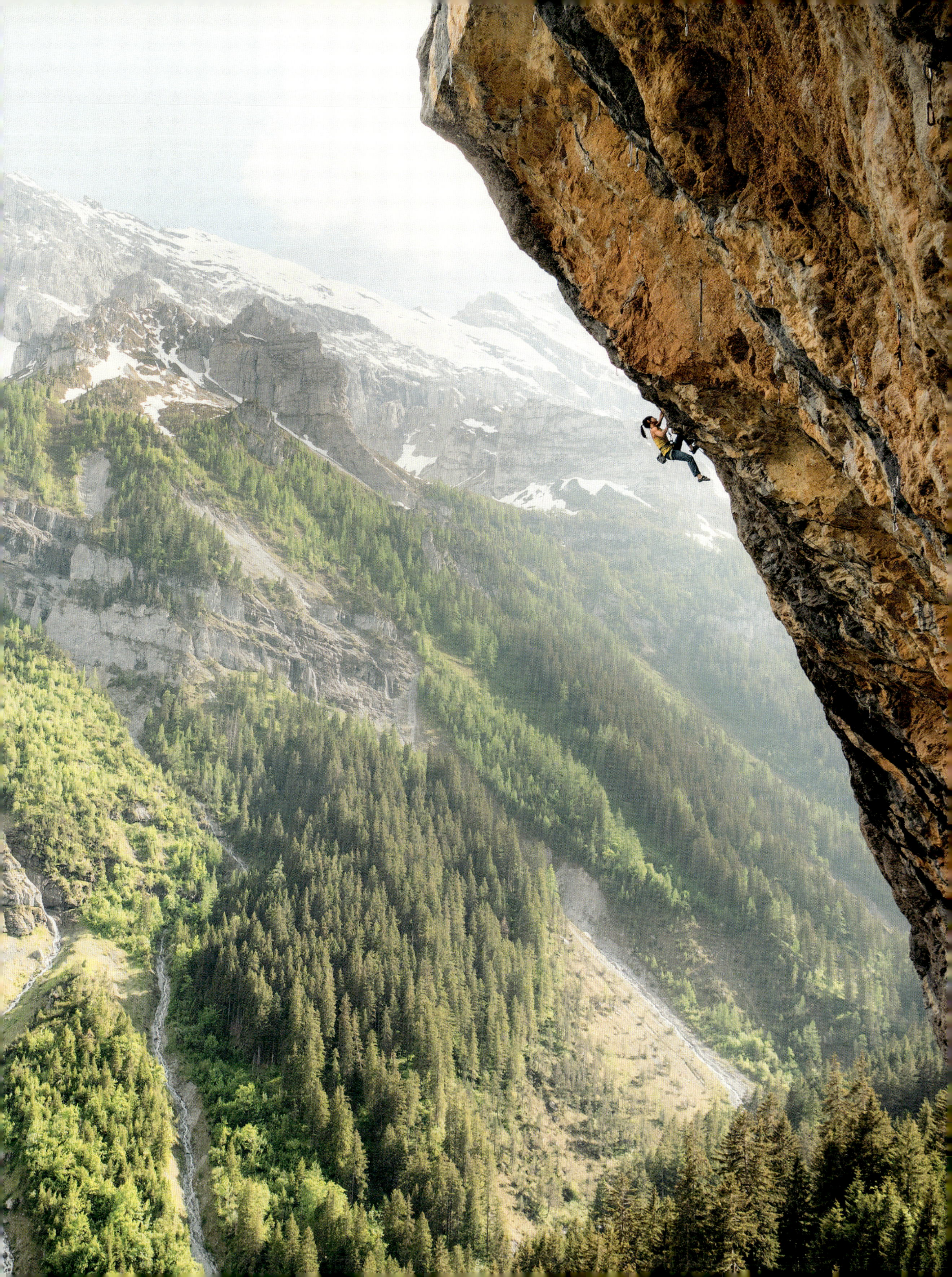

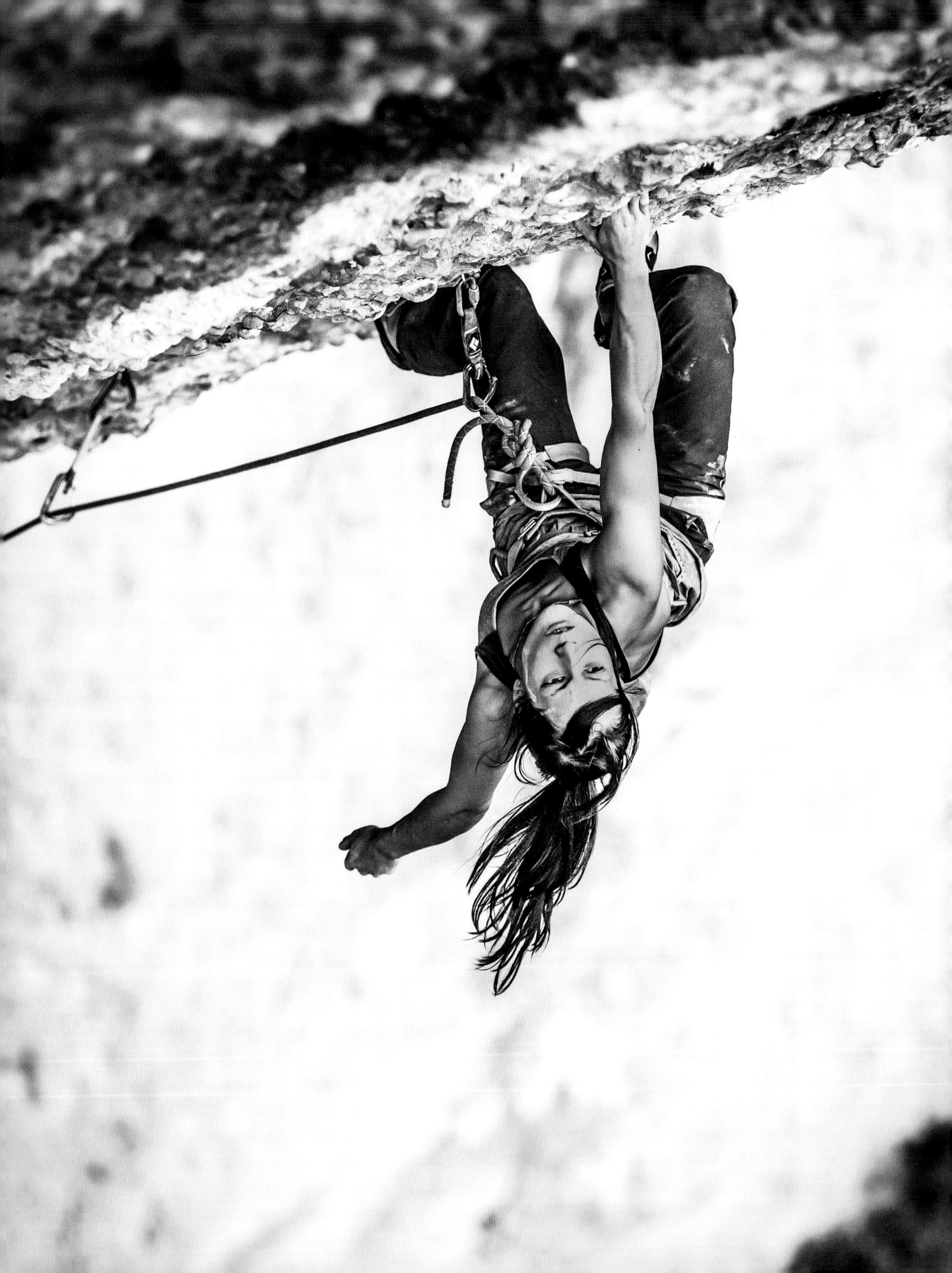

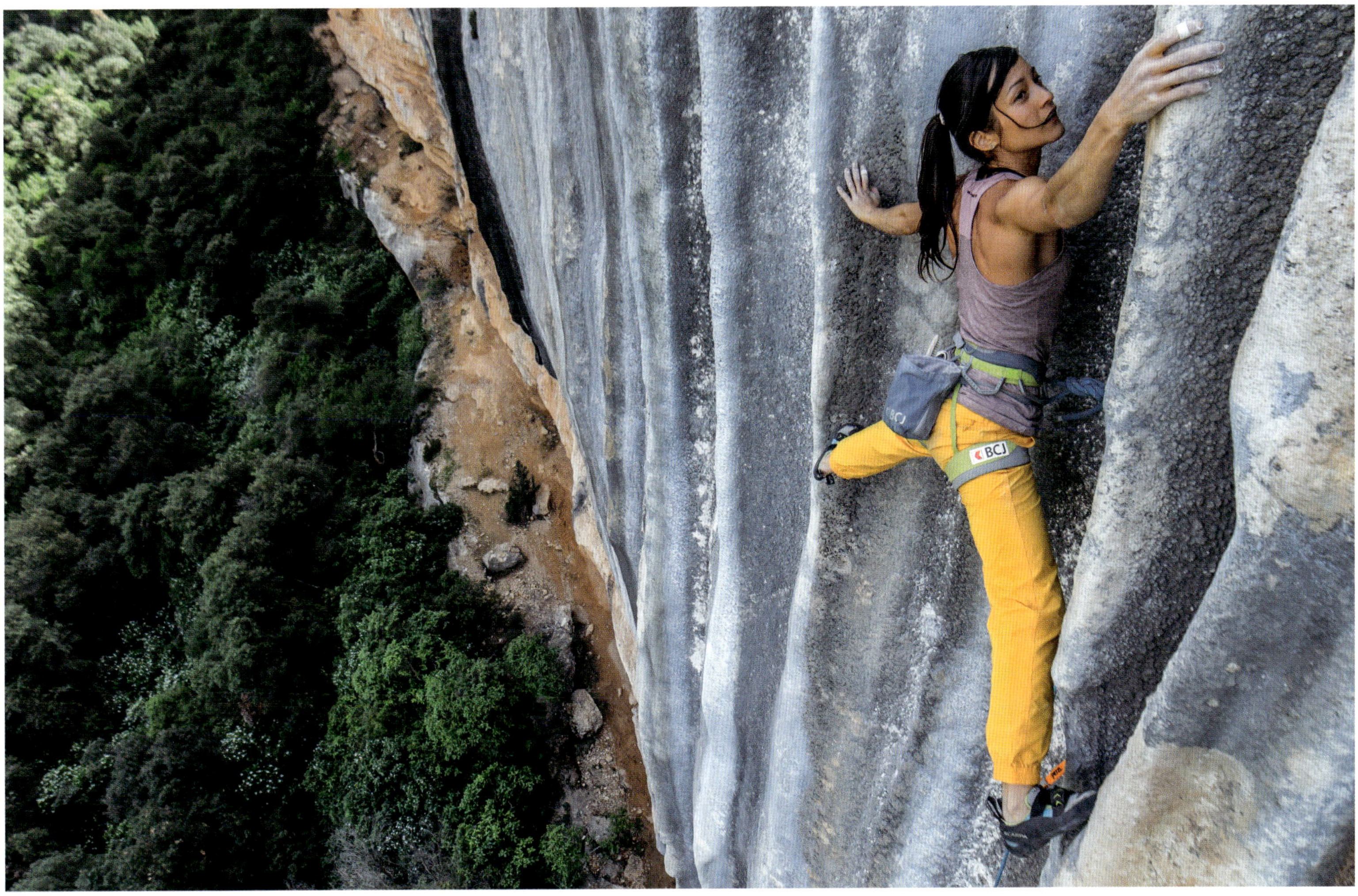

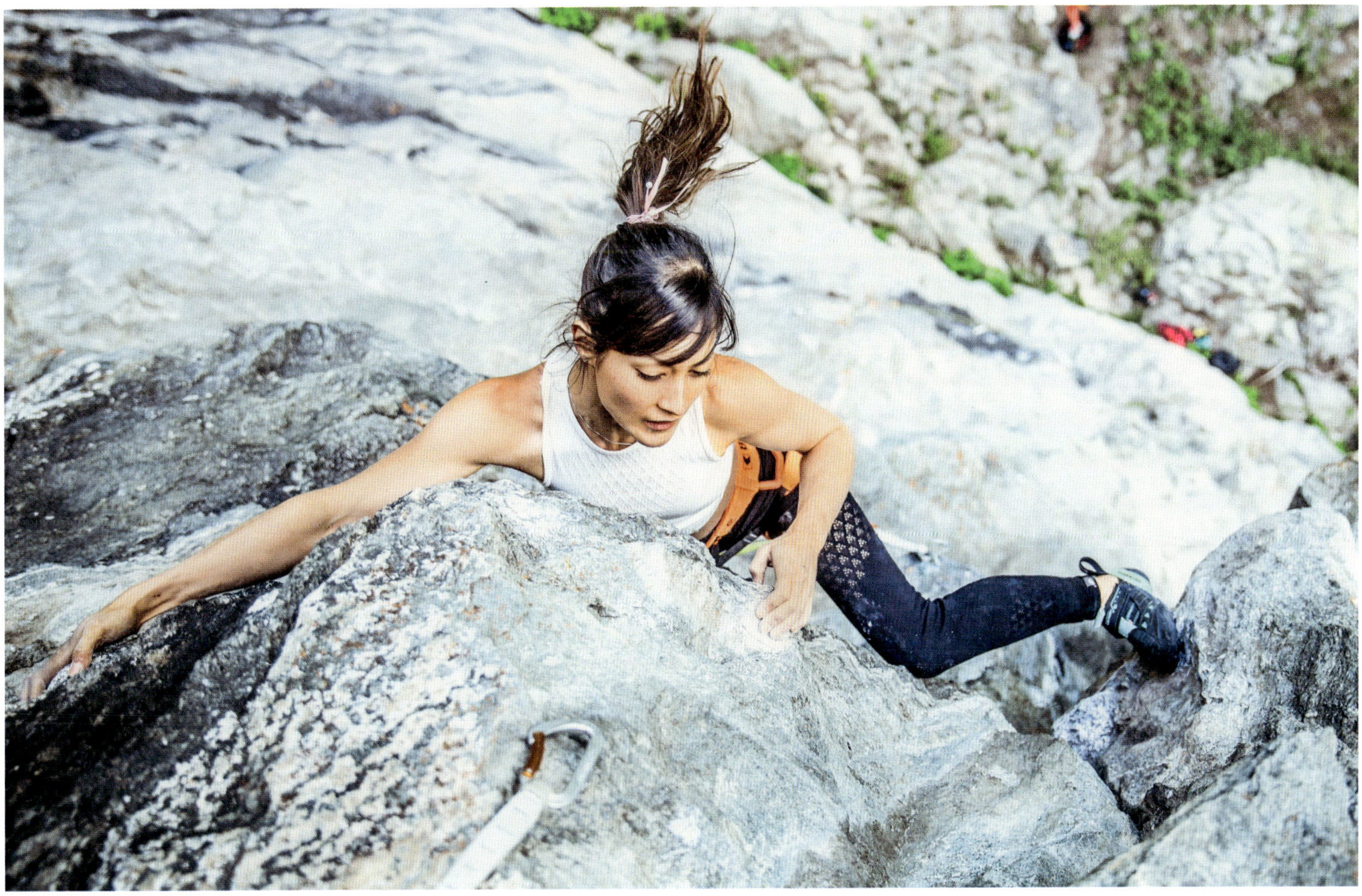

◁ Era Vella 8c+/9a   △△ Via del Joan 8a/8a+ | Margalef, Spain   △ L' Argentière, France

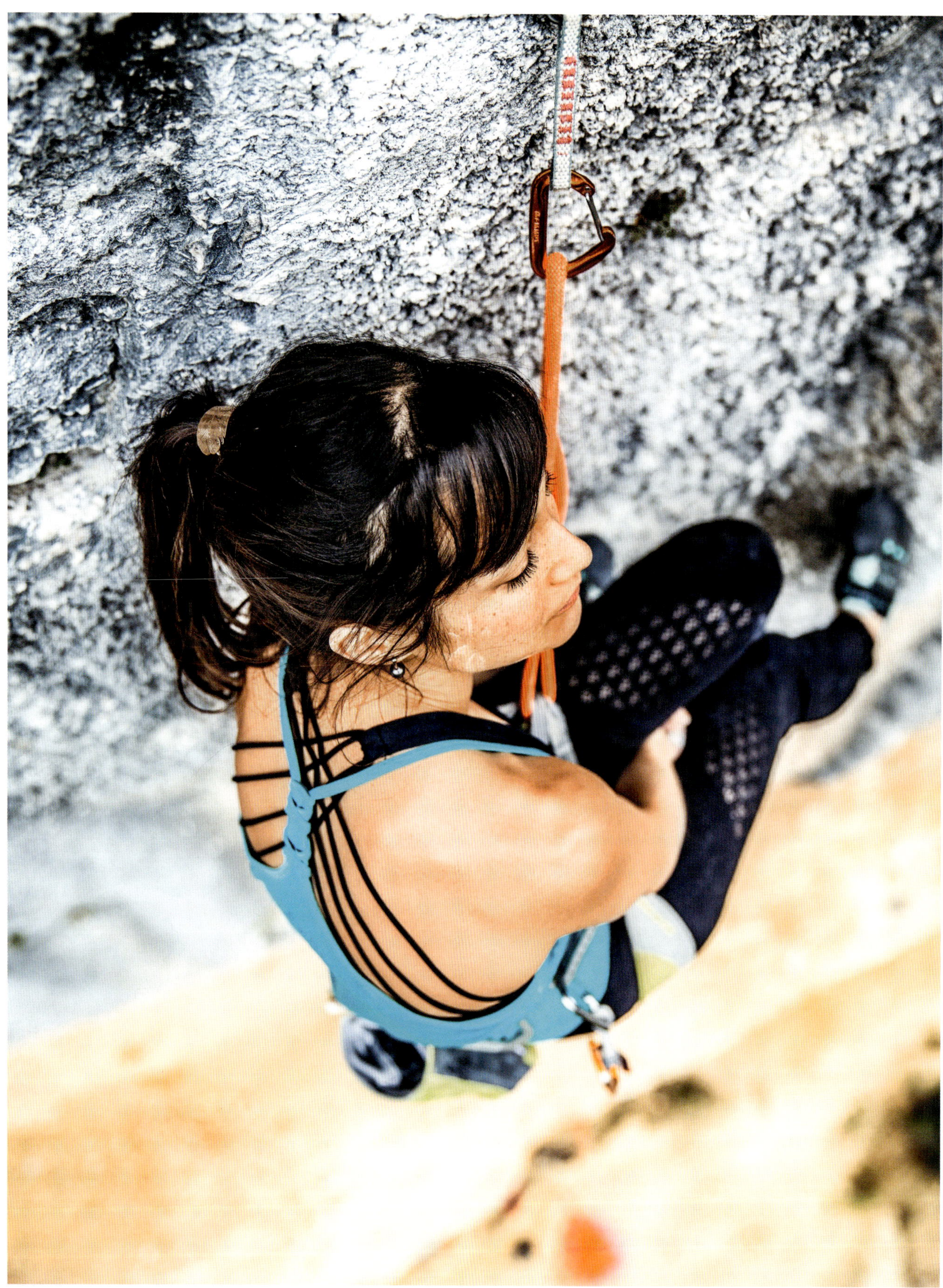

   △ Margalef, Spain   ▷ Ultime démence, 150m, 8a max., Gorges du Verdon, France

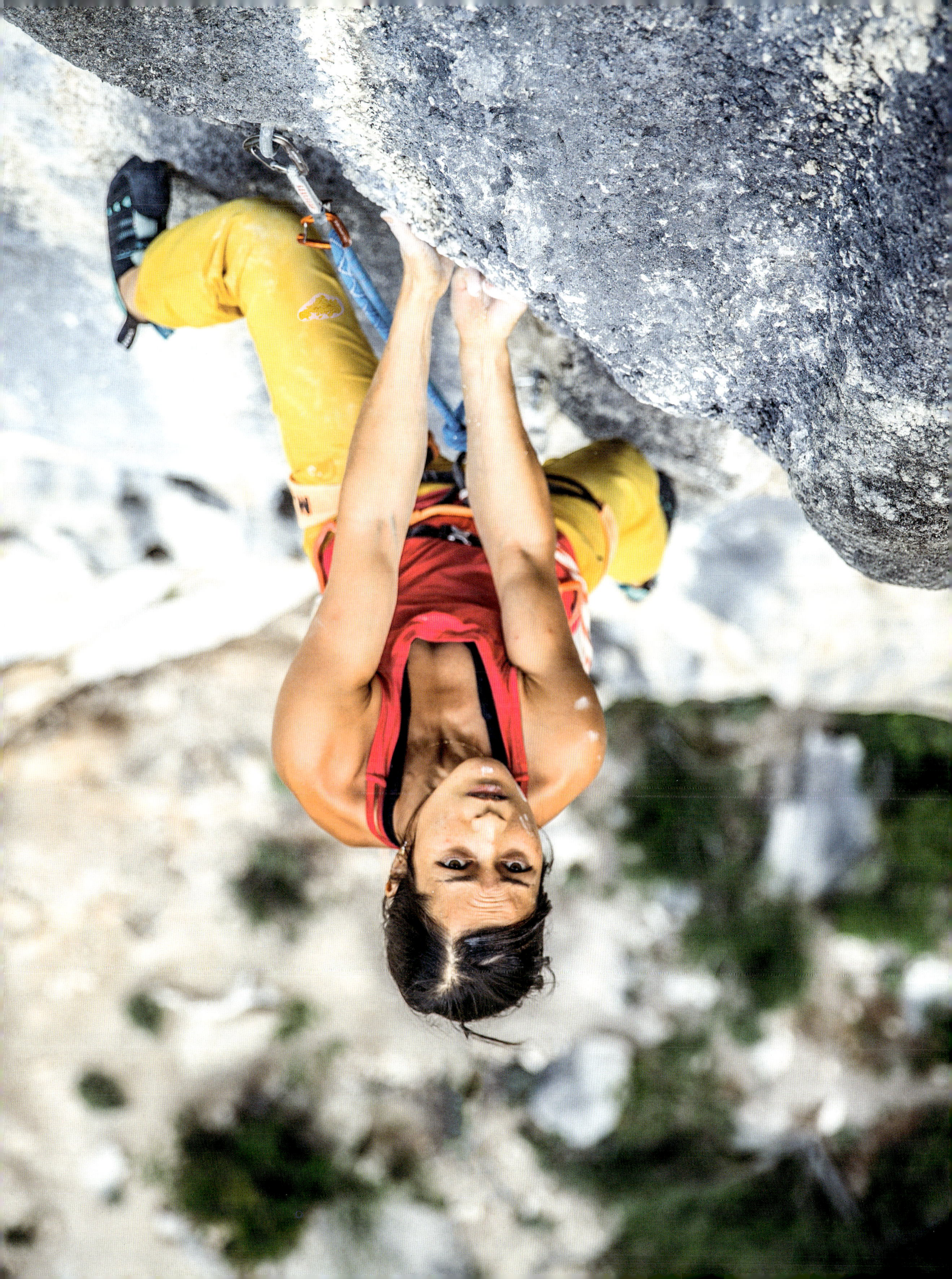

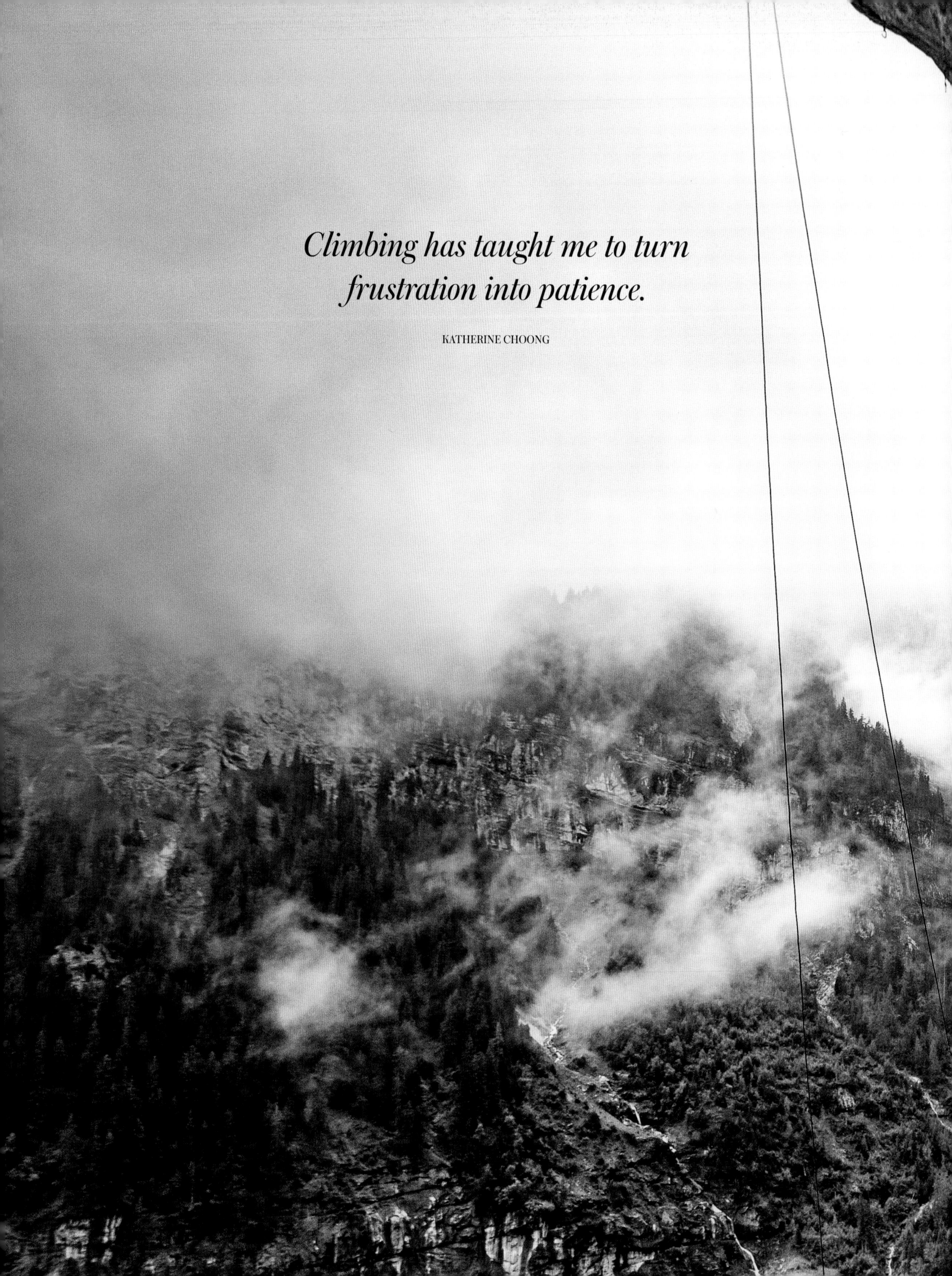

Climbing has taught me to turn
frustration into patience.

KATHERINE CHOONG

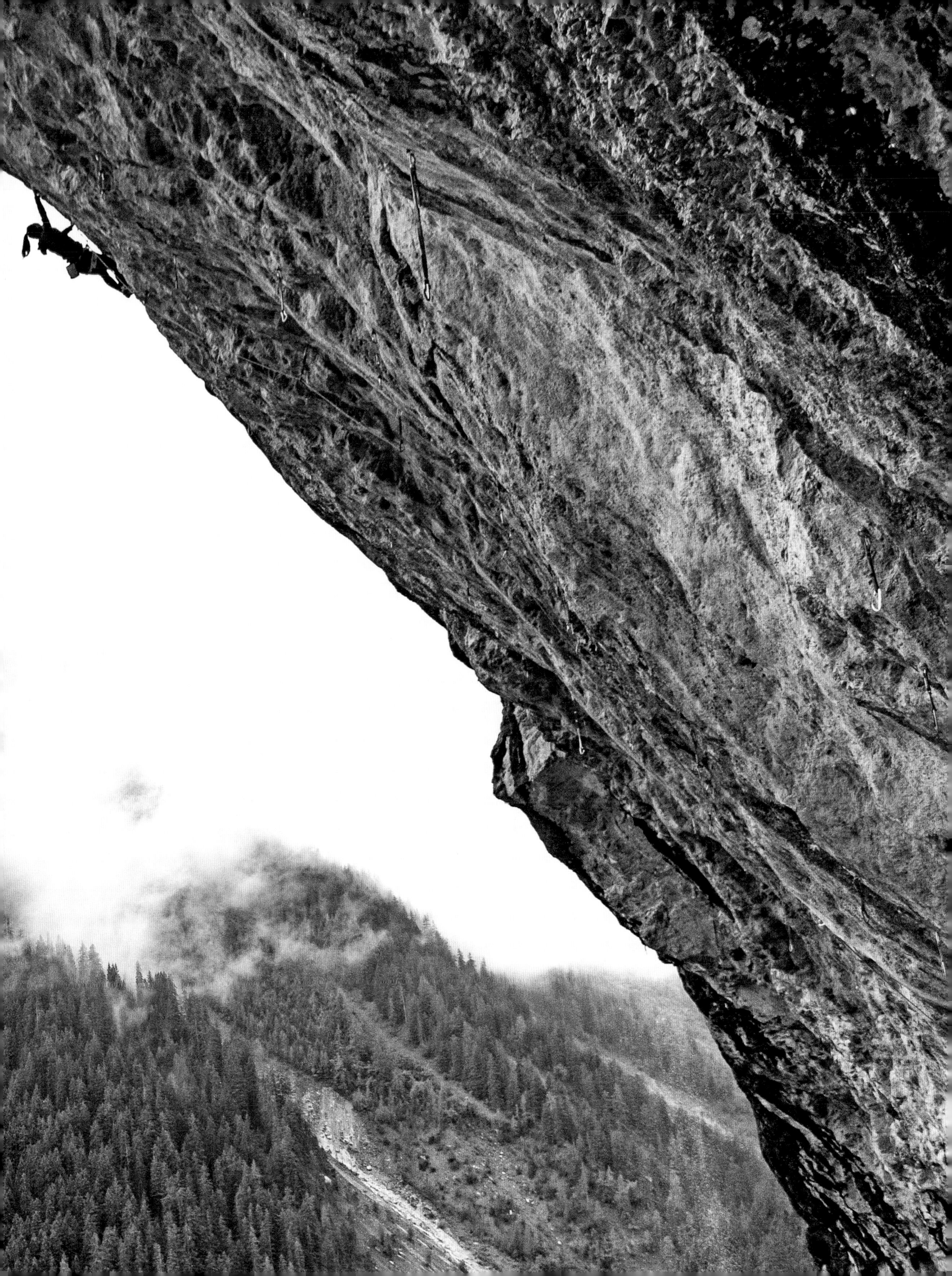

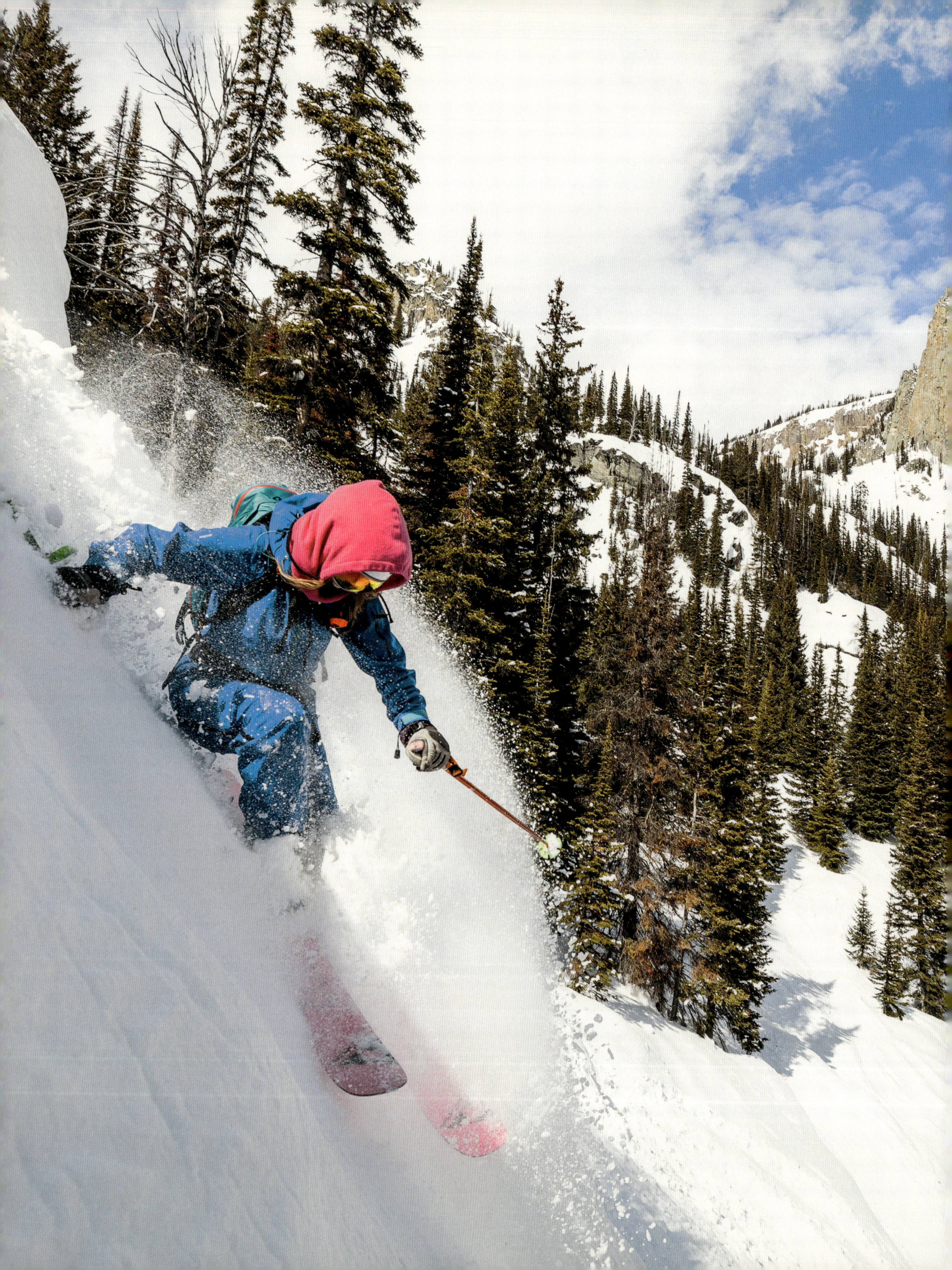

Lynsey Dyer
Big mountain skier

@lynseydyer

My name is Lynsey, a common American name with a less than common spelling. I grew up in a ski town called Sun Valley, Idaho, a mountain paradise where Hollywood stars would visit on vacation. My first passion was wildlife and conservation. In the third grade I started fundraising for whales and the rainforest. I thought I knew my purpose but I stopped taking my dream seriously when I saw that people who live on the edge of a rainforest or the ocean and need to support their families, especially in developing countries, sometimes have no better choice than to harvest the forest or the ocean to survive. I couldn't find a solution. I felt lost.

I started following the expected path laid out for most kids in the developed world. Mind your teachers, get good grades, follow the rules so that you can get into a good college, get a good job, find a husband, settle down, and keep the cycle going. For me, the only unwritten addition to that list was to ski, and to ski fast.

My dad spent time on the US ski team, also from humble beginnings. He coached our local team and drove the grooming equipment for the mountain while my mom designed ski apparel, worked in high-end retail stores, and cooked elaborate dinners for Japanese investors, all to support my brother and me on the local race team and keep us outfitted with ski passes and gear.

Though I appreciated the structure and loved my coaches, it never made much sense to me to compete with others over hundredths of a second racing around blue and red flags. Powder days got me excited and offered new ways to have fun and experience challenges and camaraderie. Attempting to keep up with my coaches on those days, I learned to point down my skis on the fall line and fly. These were some of my earliest experiences of "flow state" and "group flow." They piqued my curiosity.

Even though I struggled in school, I won the Junior Olympics in downhill and got a ski racing scholarship for college. By the time I was sixteen, my coaches and sponsors had me on the Olympic track, training and competing in speed events. It was a lonely time, though, because of bullying from my own teammates. After a long summer of training hard in the gym, I started skiing really fast. I was beating the boys. When I found out my coaches were fundraising to support me qualifying for the Olympics, I crumbled under the pressure. I wasn't all that hungry for medals and the bullying took all the fun out of skiing anyways.

By graduation I was burnt out of ski racing. After college I ended up going to art school in Europe. I had my first ever year without skiing and it helped me realize that there was more to life than my sport. It also showed me what I loved the most: powder skiing. My cousin AJ was one of the first ever female big mountain skiers and she had been encouraging me to go that way for a while, but I'd never listened. Coming back to the US, I made a choice to commit myself to the thing that made me feel most alive, to use that curiosity that caught me as a little kid.

It's been almost two decades since I made that choice. I ended up winning the Freeride tour my first season competing, then turned to film. I was in various big name ski films and commercials. I landed the biggest cliff ever by a woman, 75 feet, after being told the female body wasn't capable of it. When I didn't see women feeling welcome in the sport, I co-founded shejumps.org. I went on to make the first all-female ski film, Pretty Faces, which became a turning point in the industry.

Today I continue to ski and build up the courage to take on that first big dream, committing to conservation and wildlife. I have learned that using my voice locally does have an impact and intend to ensure that wildlife have protected overpasses and corridors throughout the north before my time on the planet is through. If I have any message, it is that our biggest challenge is not whether we can do big things; it's whether we have the audacity to consider the biggest things we might be able to create and then commit to the vision, regardless of who approves.

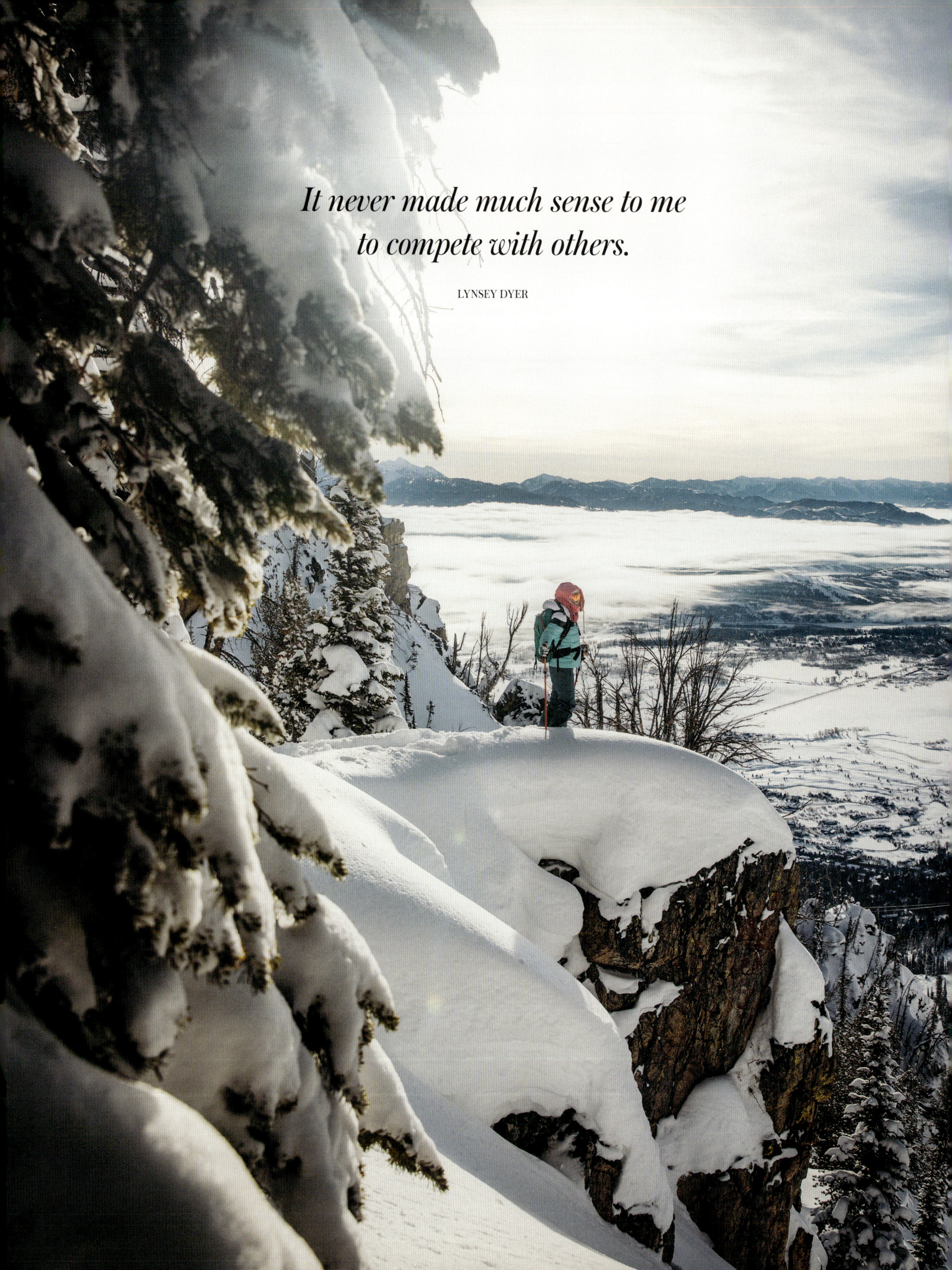

It never made much sense to me
to compete with others.

LYNSEY DYER

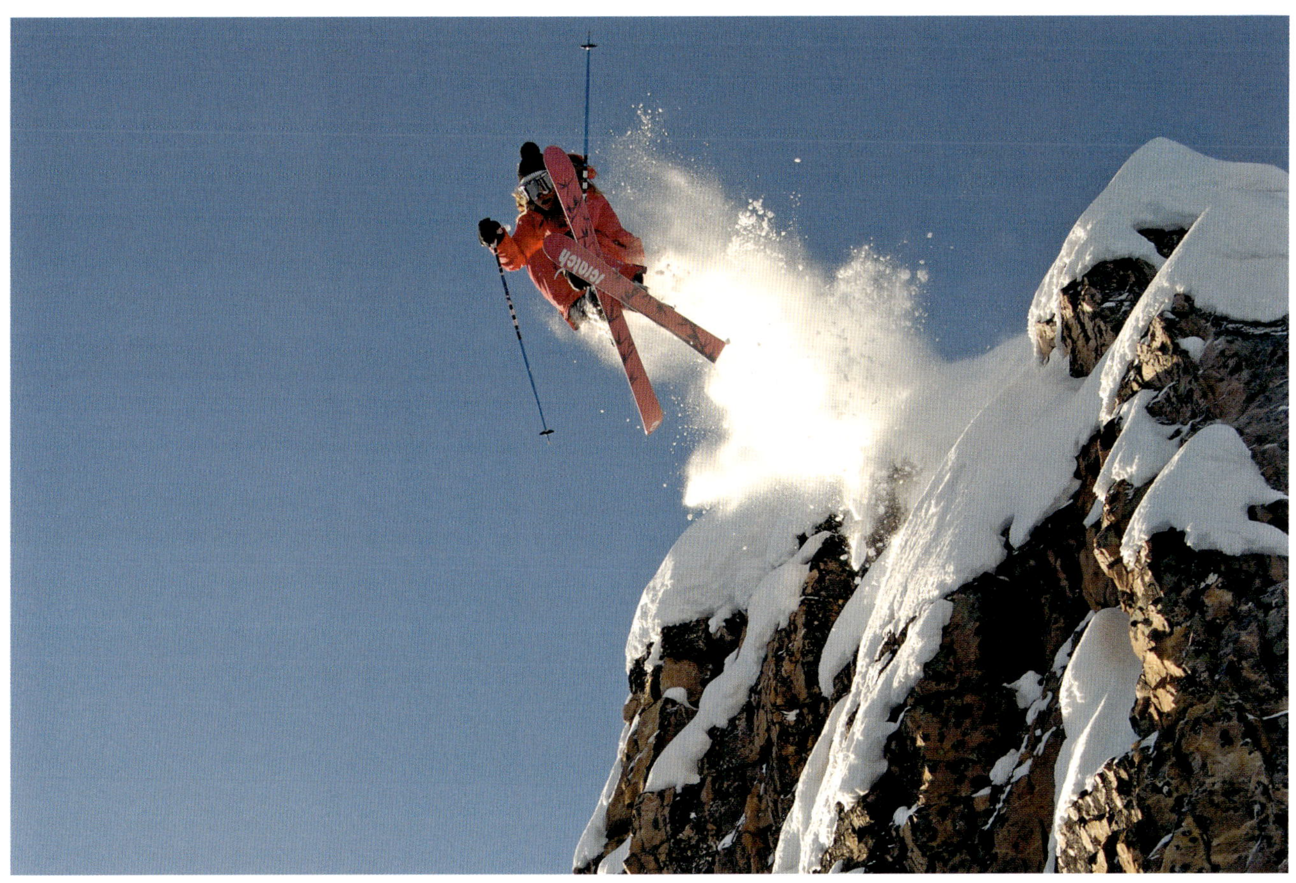

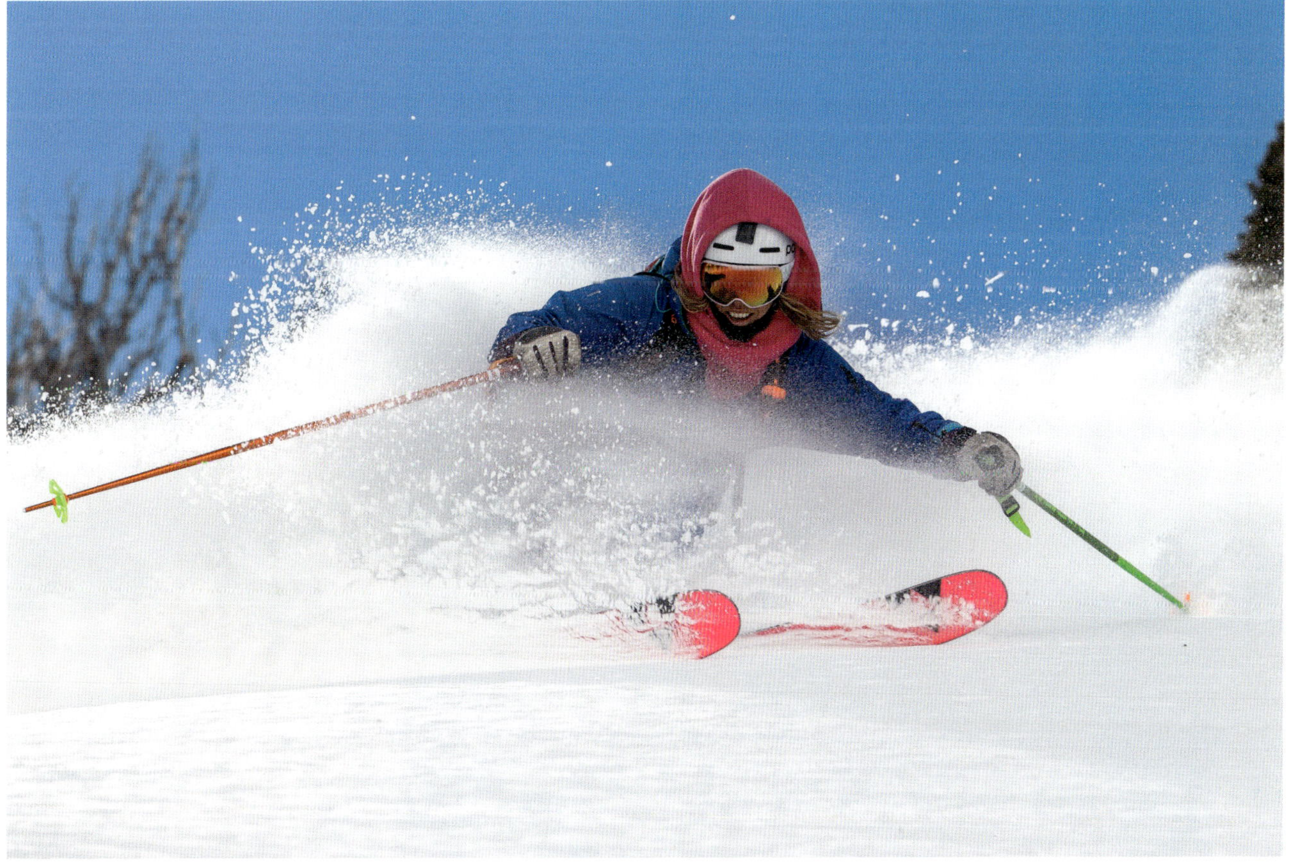

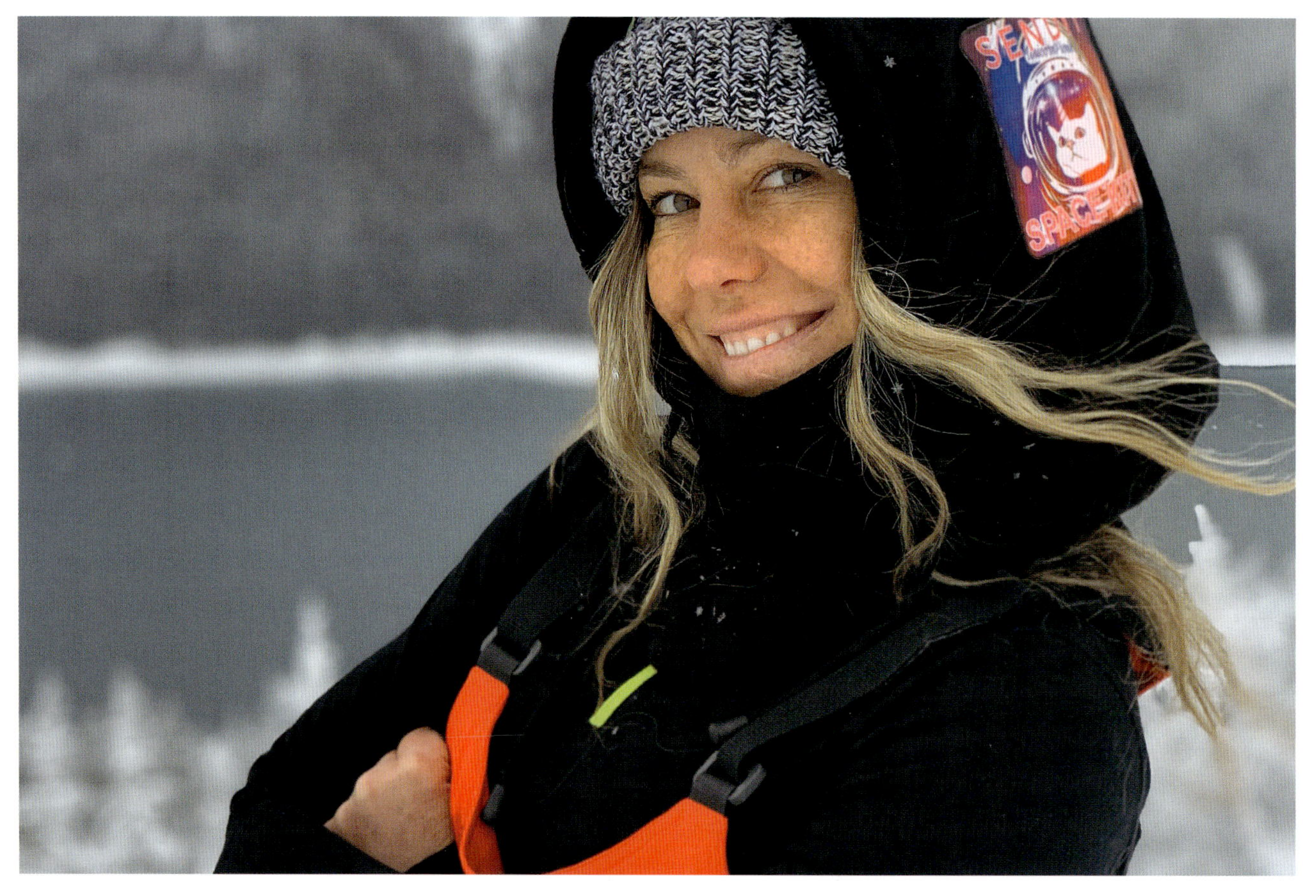

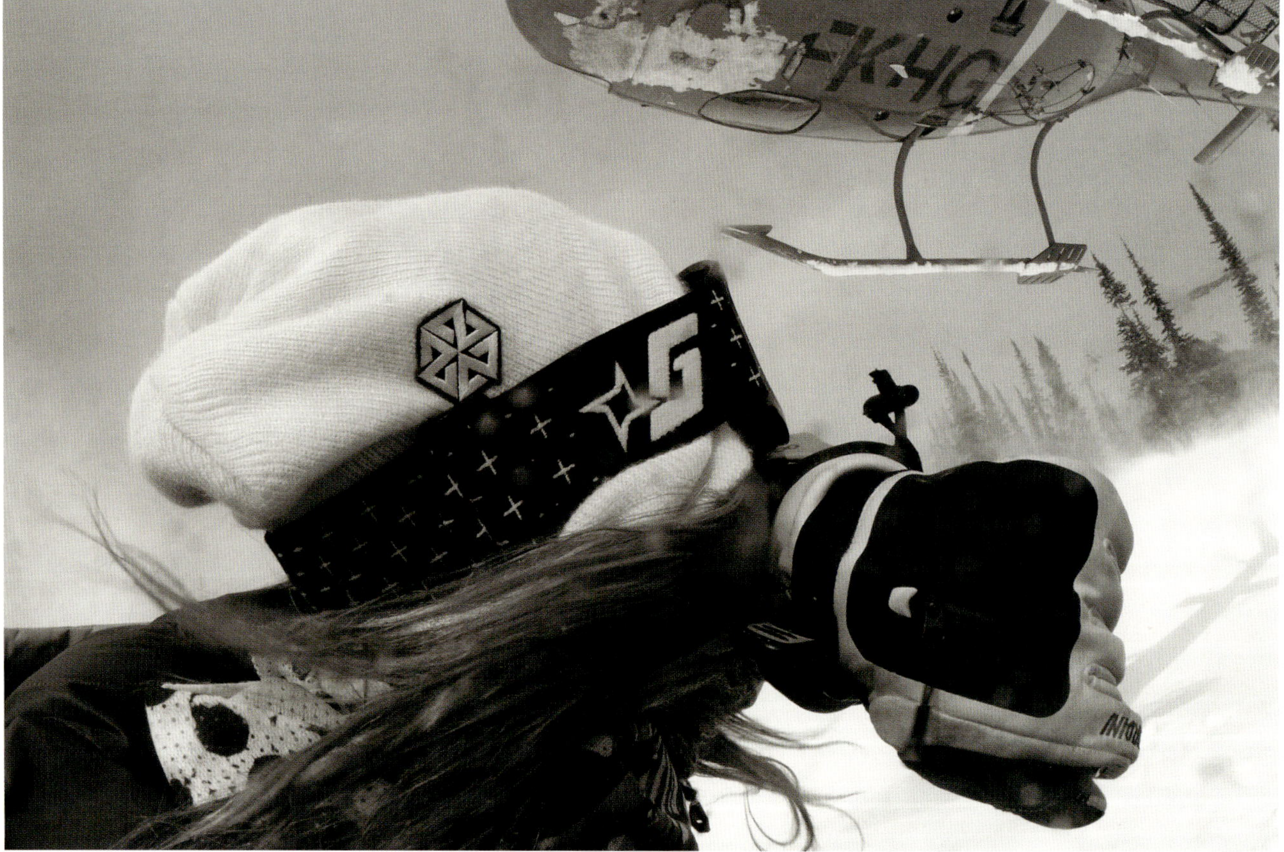

  △ Mica Heli Skiing, British Columbia, Canada   ▷ Ischgl, Austria   ▷▷ Monashee Mountains, British Columbia, Canada

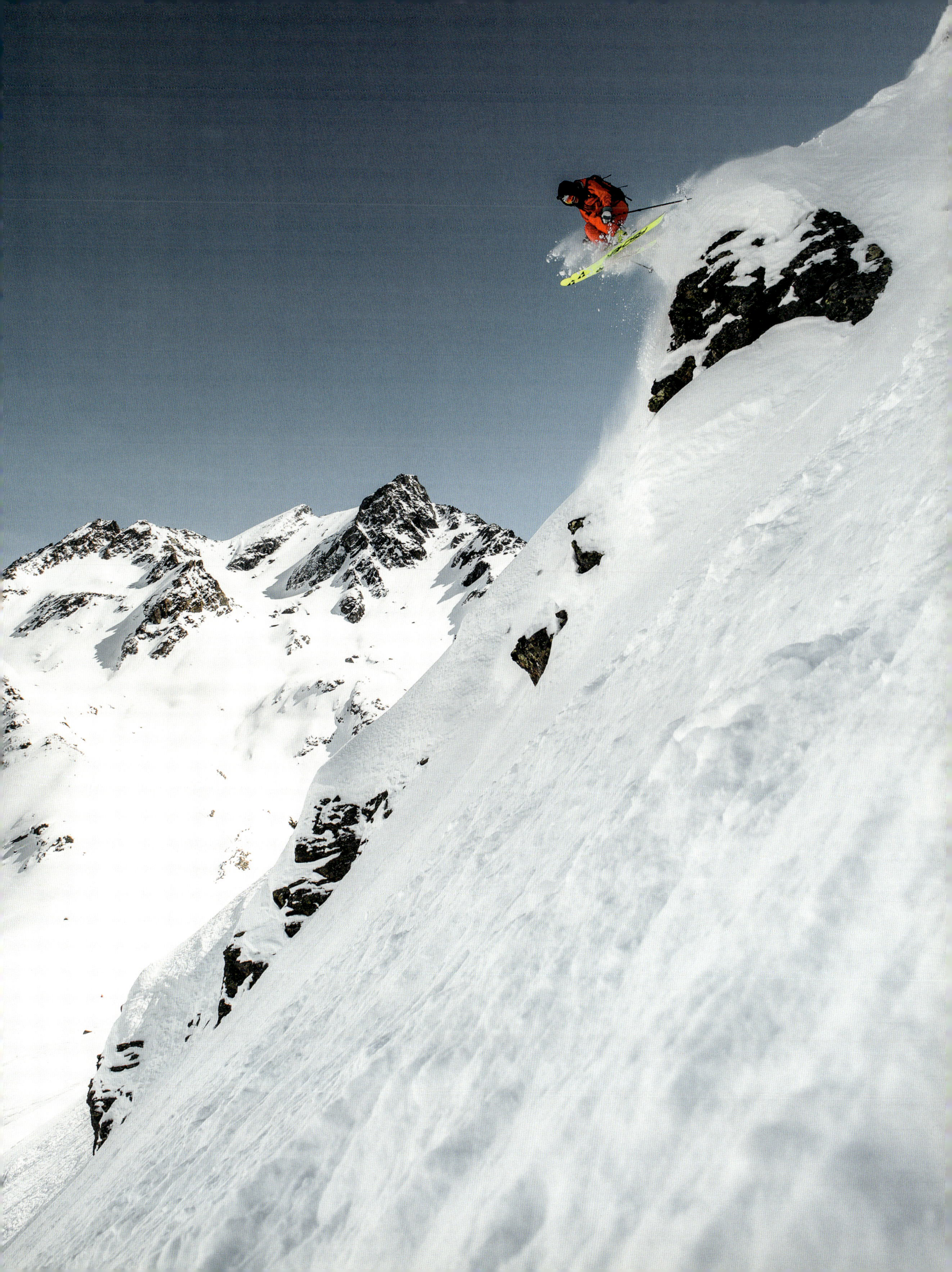

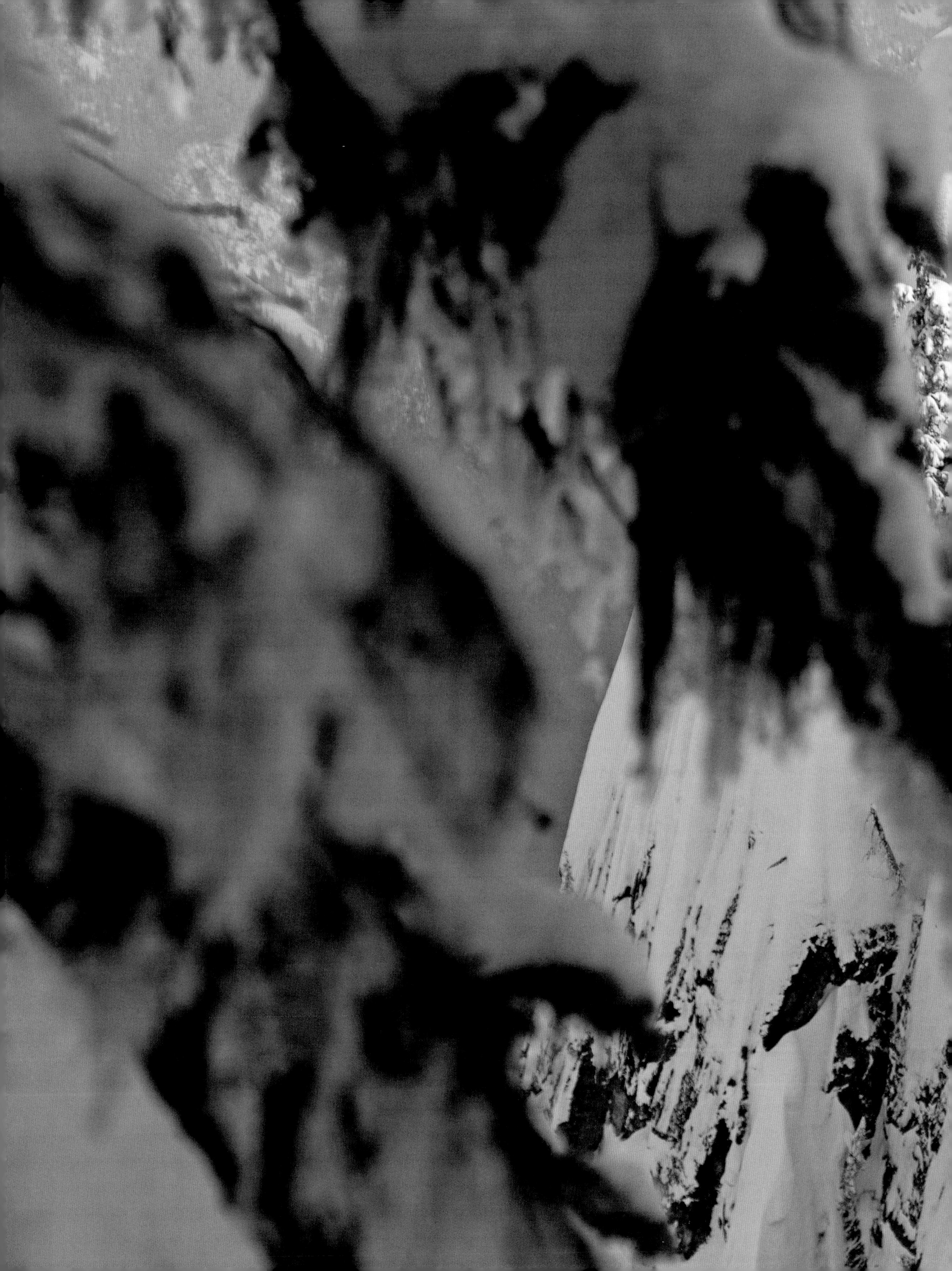

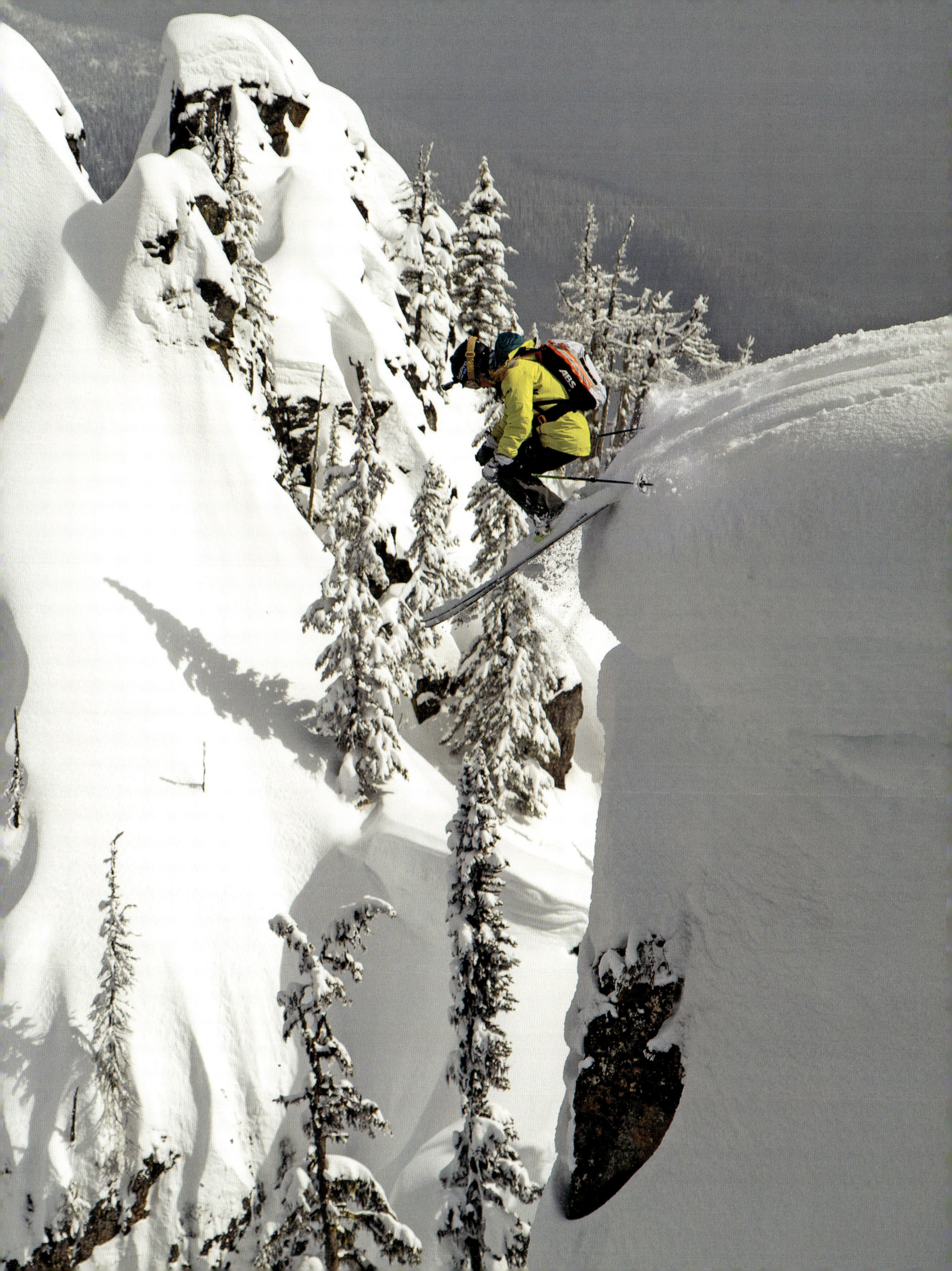

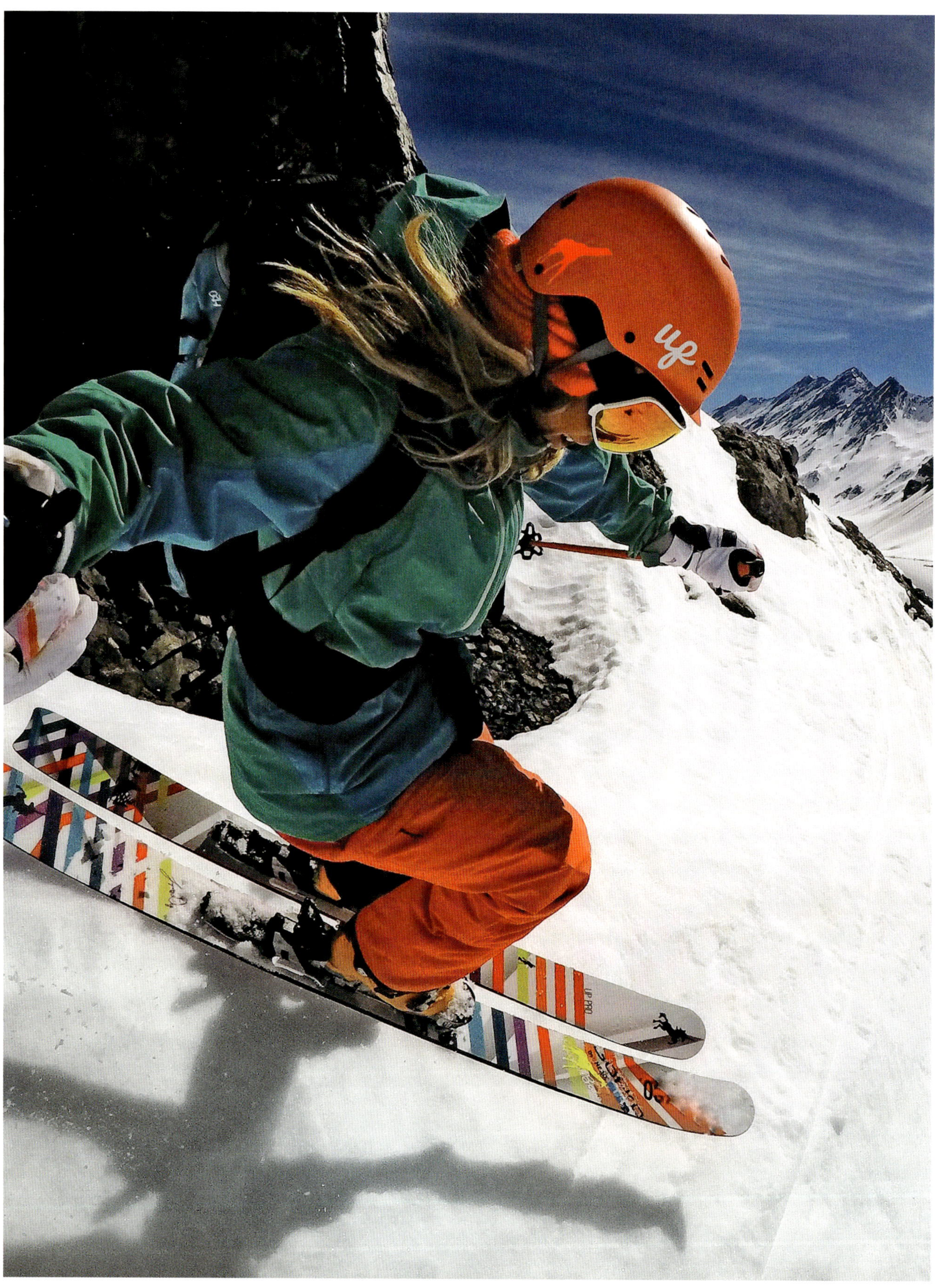

  △ Portillo, Chile   ▷ Jackson Hole, Wyoming, USA

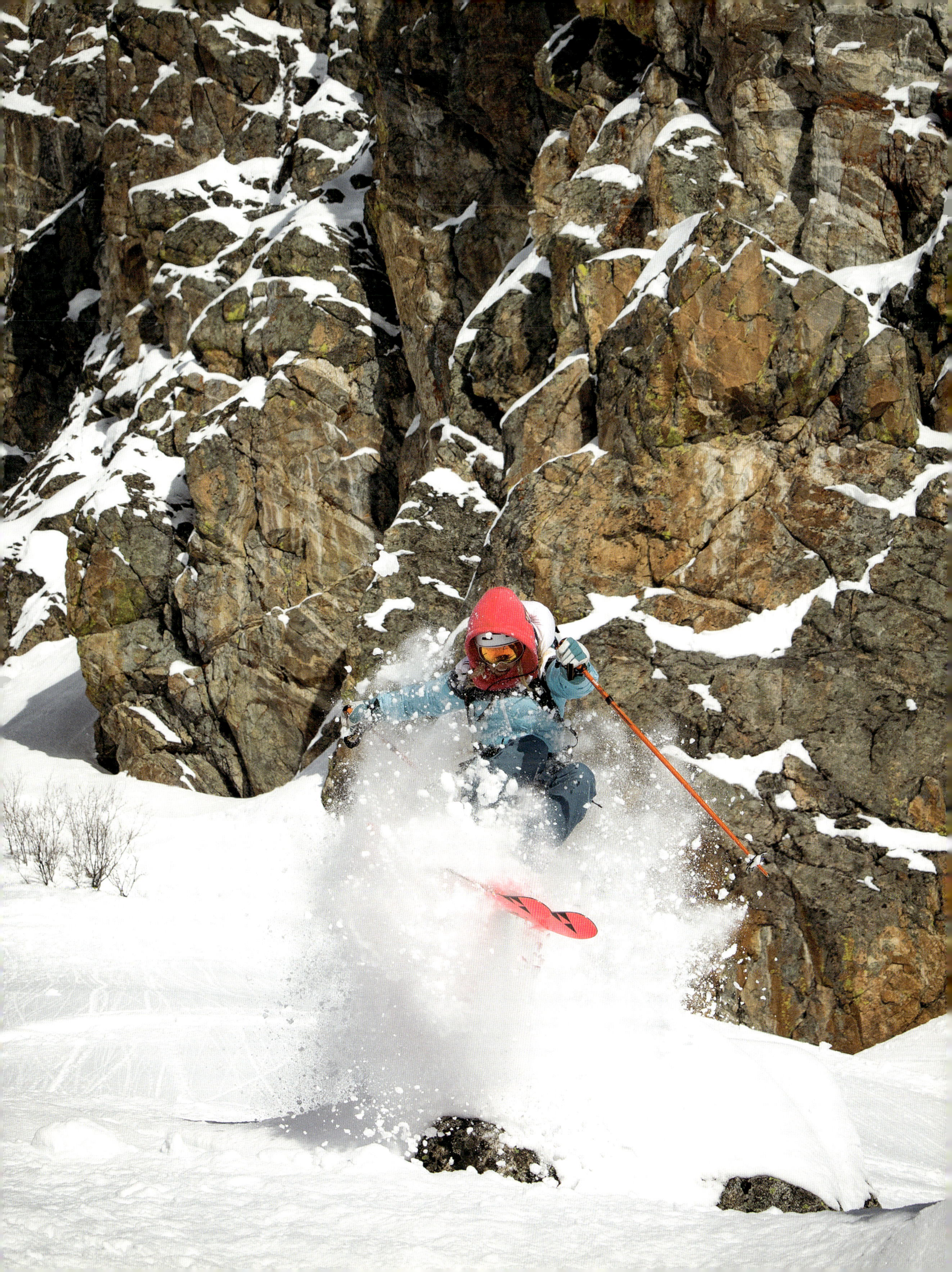

Saya Sakakibara
BMX racer

@sayasakakibara
www.sakakibarabmx.com

I am Saya Sakakibara, I am a twenty-one year-old from Sydney, Australia, and I am a professional BMX racer. I've been BMX racing since I was four years old, when I got sucked into the sport by my older brother Kai, who was already into it. We grew up racing and training with each other and ultimately toured the international circuit together.

Right now, I am training to compete and represent Australia at the Olympic Games. It has been a dream of mine since I was nine years old, when I saw BMX on TV for the first time at the 2008 Beijing Olympic Games.

I fell in love with BMX because of its challenges. Every day there is always something new to work on, whether it's trying a new jump I've never jumped before, improving my start technique, or trying to get my track speed even faster. I love that I never get bored of training or riding. Jumps, turns, and speed, all combined into a race with seven other riders, get the adrenaline pumping—and it is such a thrill!

The fast pace of BMX and the element of the unknown keep me on my toes, build up my nerves, and ultimately challenge me in new ways in every event I compete in. And that is what I love: pushing myself further than I ever thought I could and being the best I can be.

I think one of the biggest myths in extreme sports is that we don't get scared. Let me tell you, we do! (At least I do!) In BMX it's a 35–40 second race, stacked with seven other girls who are just as fast as you. And hitting a 40 foot jump at the bottom of a 25 foot high ramp is scary!

With the years of experience I've had, I've learned how to manage fear, and it's still a learning process. Because, unfortunately, fear doesn't just go away. It's always there, and we are given two options: to let the fear consume us, or to use the fear to our advantage.

For me, fear comes from not knowing what will happen, and the first thing I like to do is to accept the fear I'm experiencing. I acknowledge it is there, but then shift my focus to the things I can control—my breathing, my mental rehearsal, my processes. Then I trust that I have the ability to get over this challenge. My nerves put some good pressure on me to perform when it really counts. No one can predict the future, whether it is the outcome of a race or going to a new school, but we can find comfort in controlling what we can control and strapping in for the ride. It's okay to be scared, because everyone is. But it's what we do with that anxiety that matters and help us grow into better people.

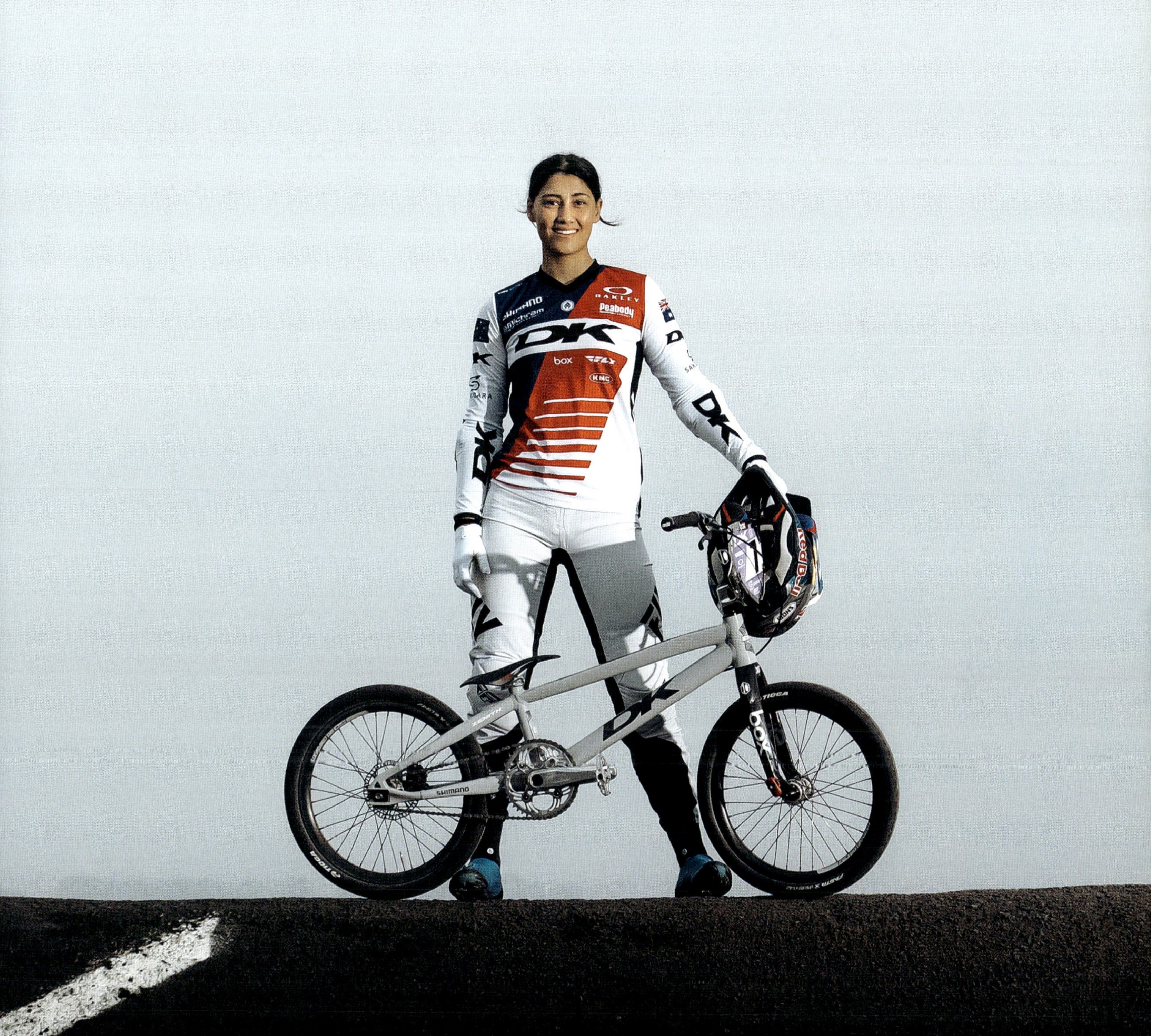

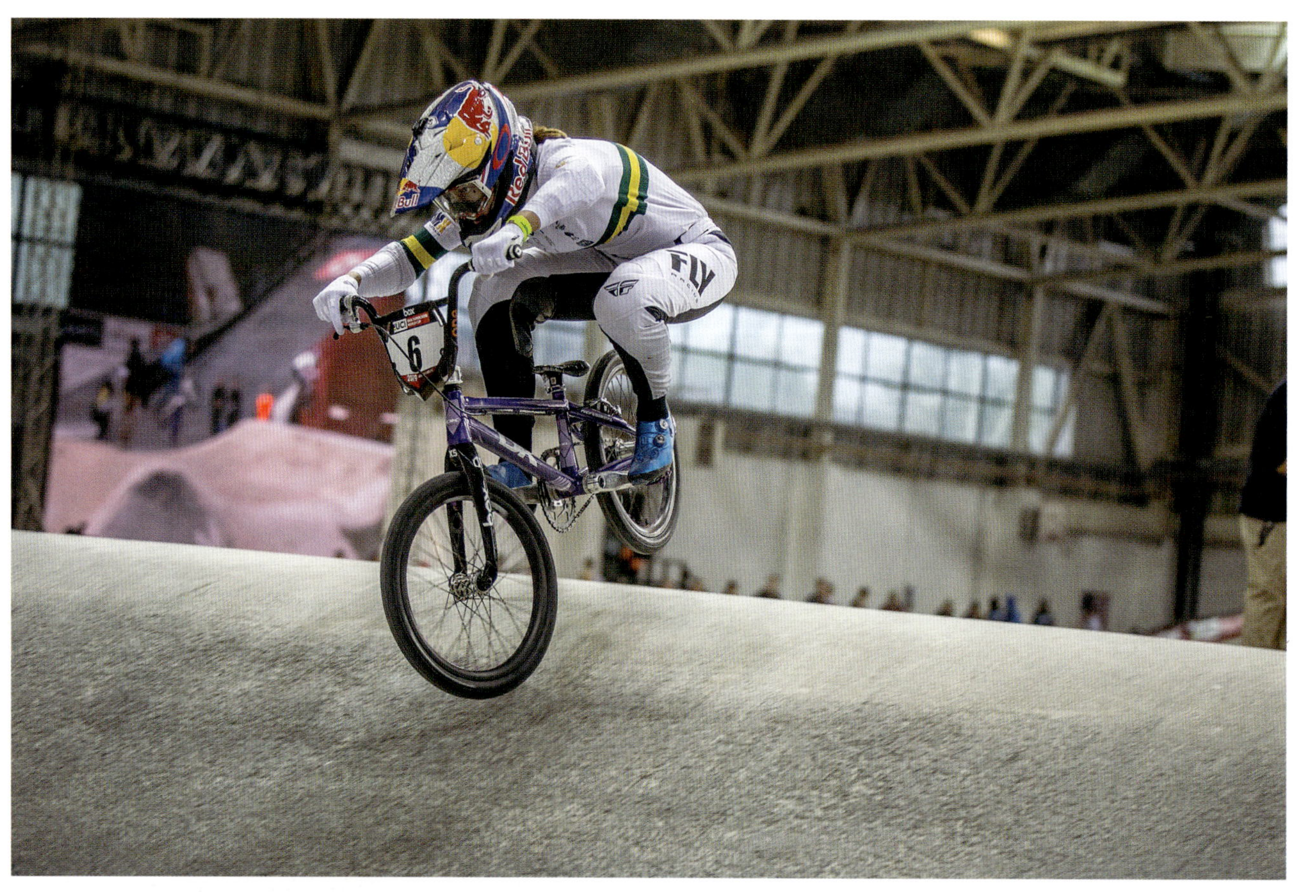

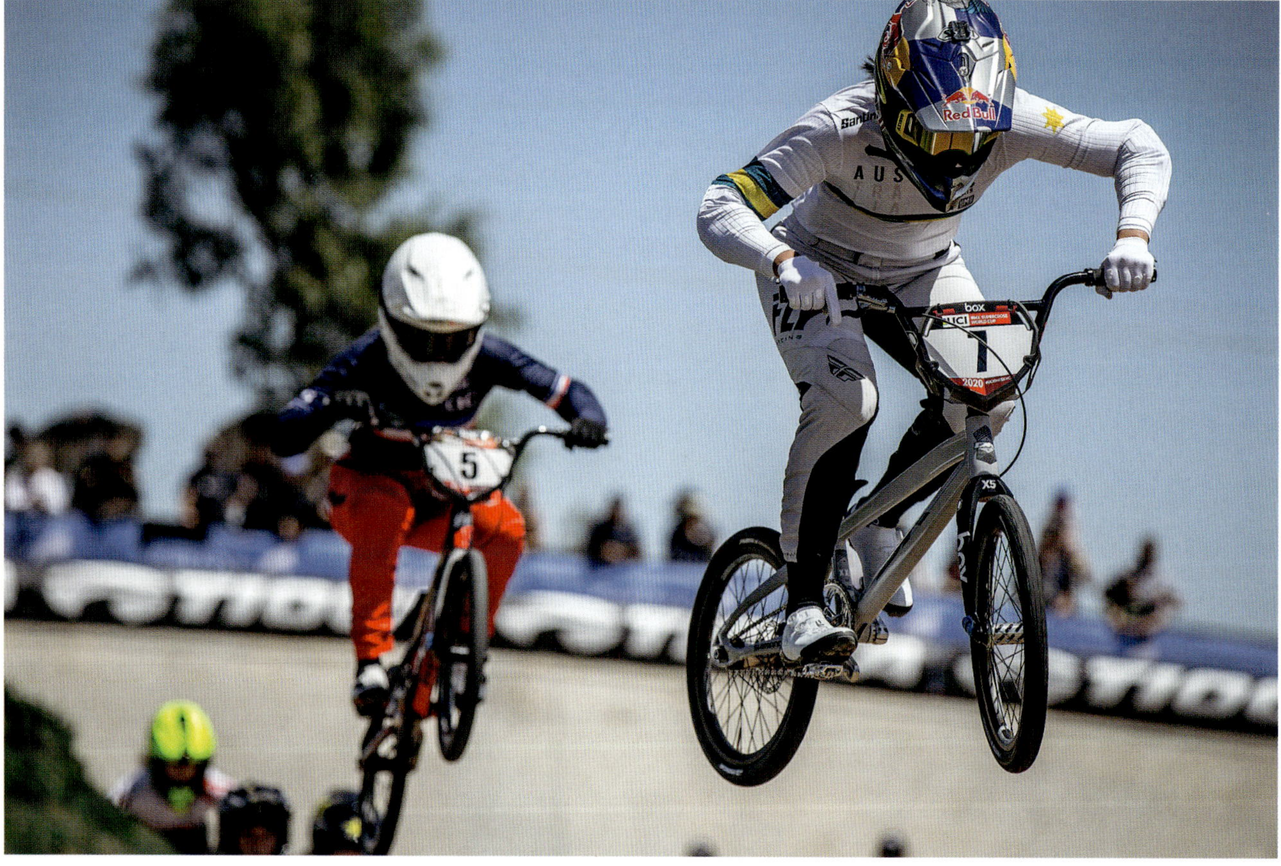

  △△ Manchester, UK   △ Shepparton, Australia   ▷ Zolder, Belgium   ▷▷ Albion Park, Australia

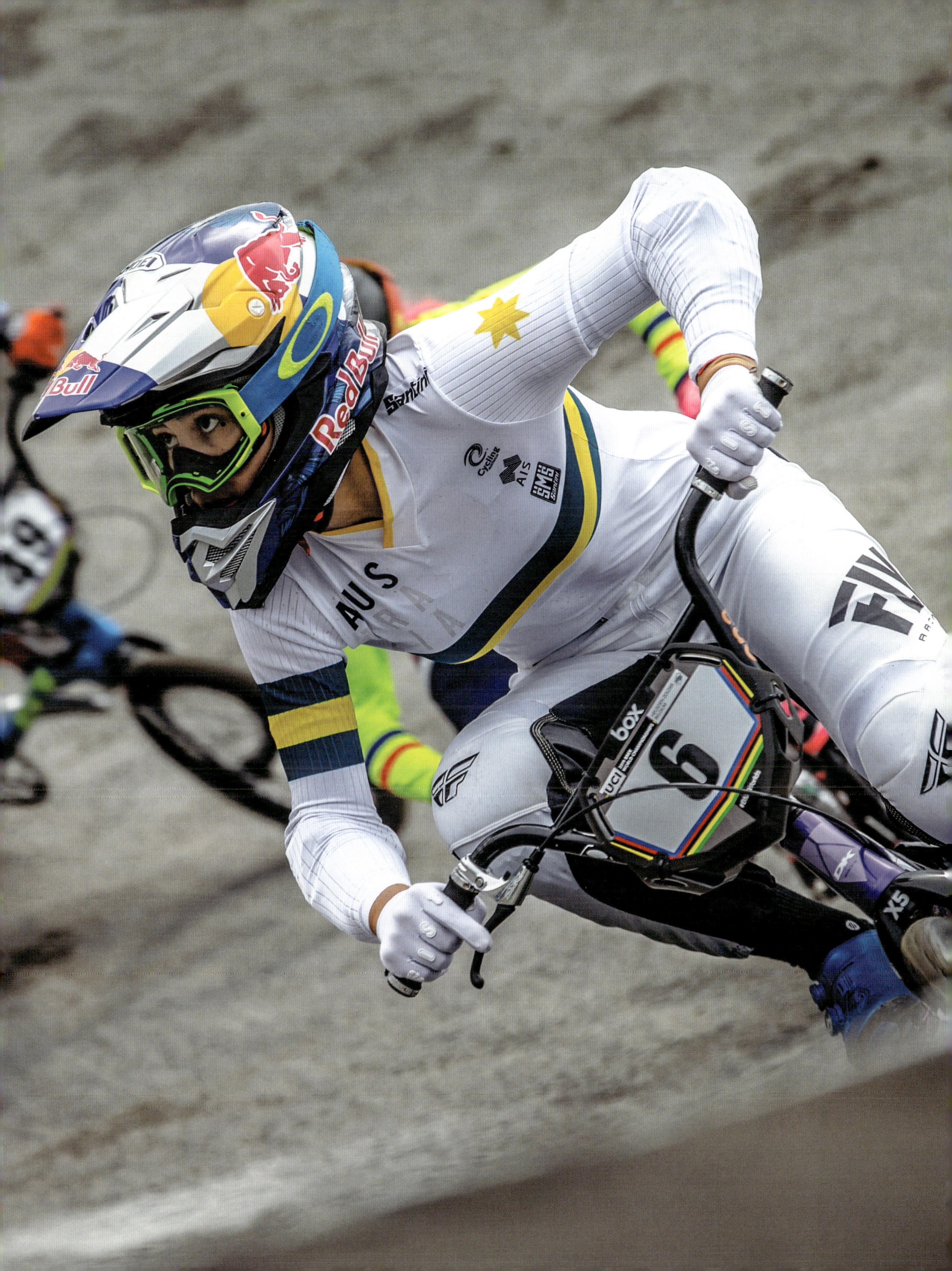

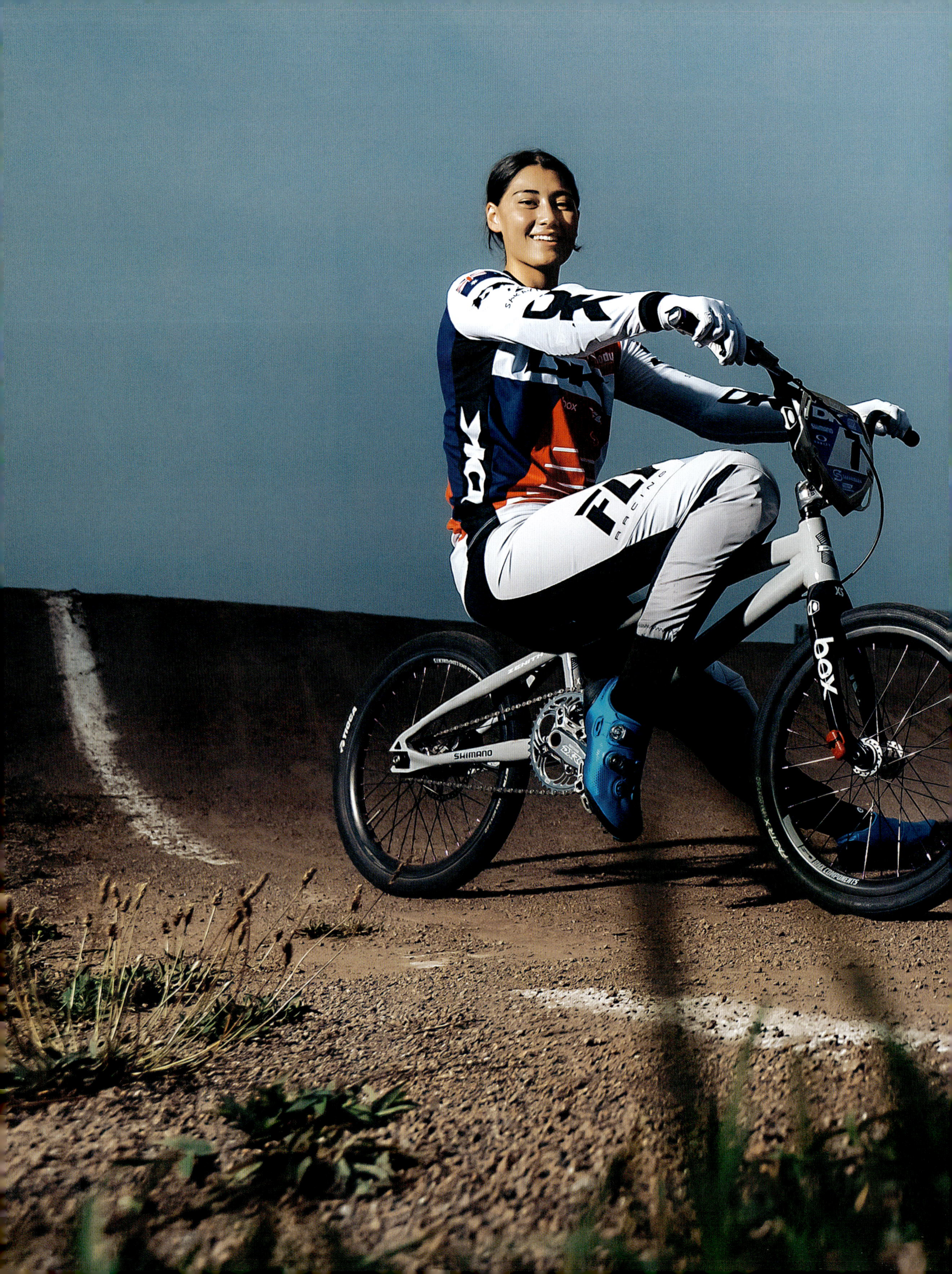

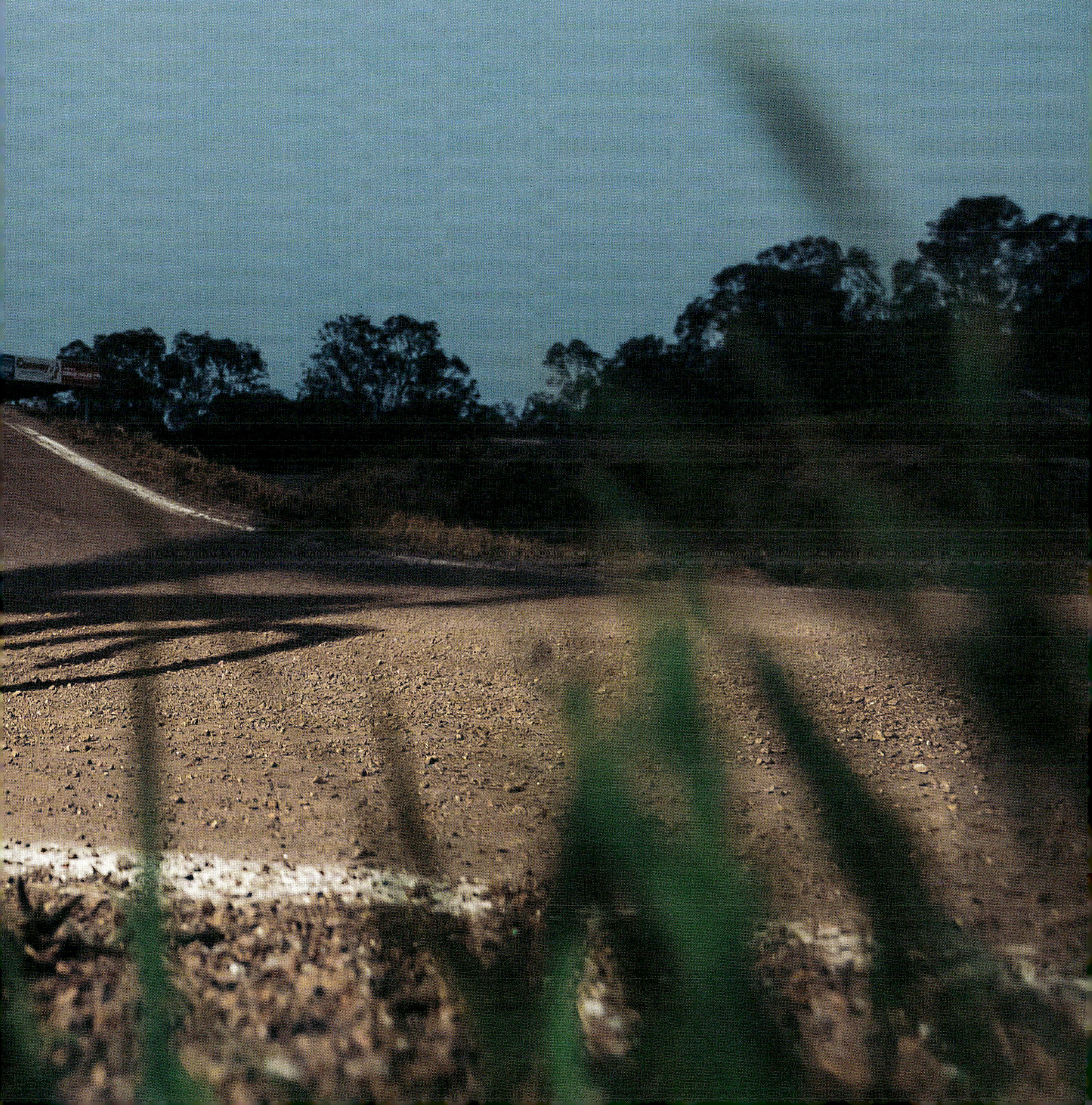
I think one of the biggest myths
in extreme sports is that we don't get scared.
Let me tell you, we do!

SAYA SAKAKIBARA

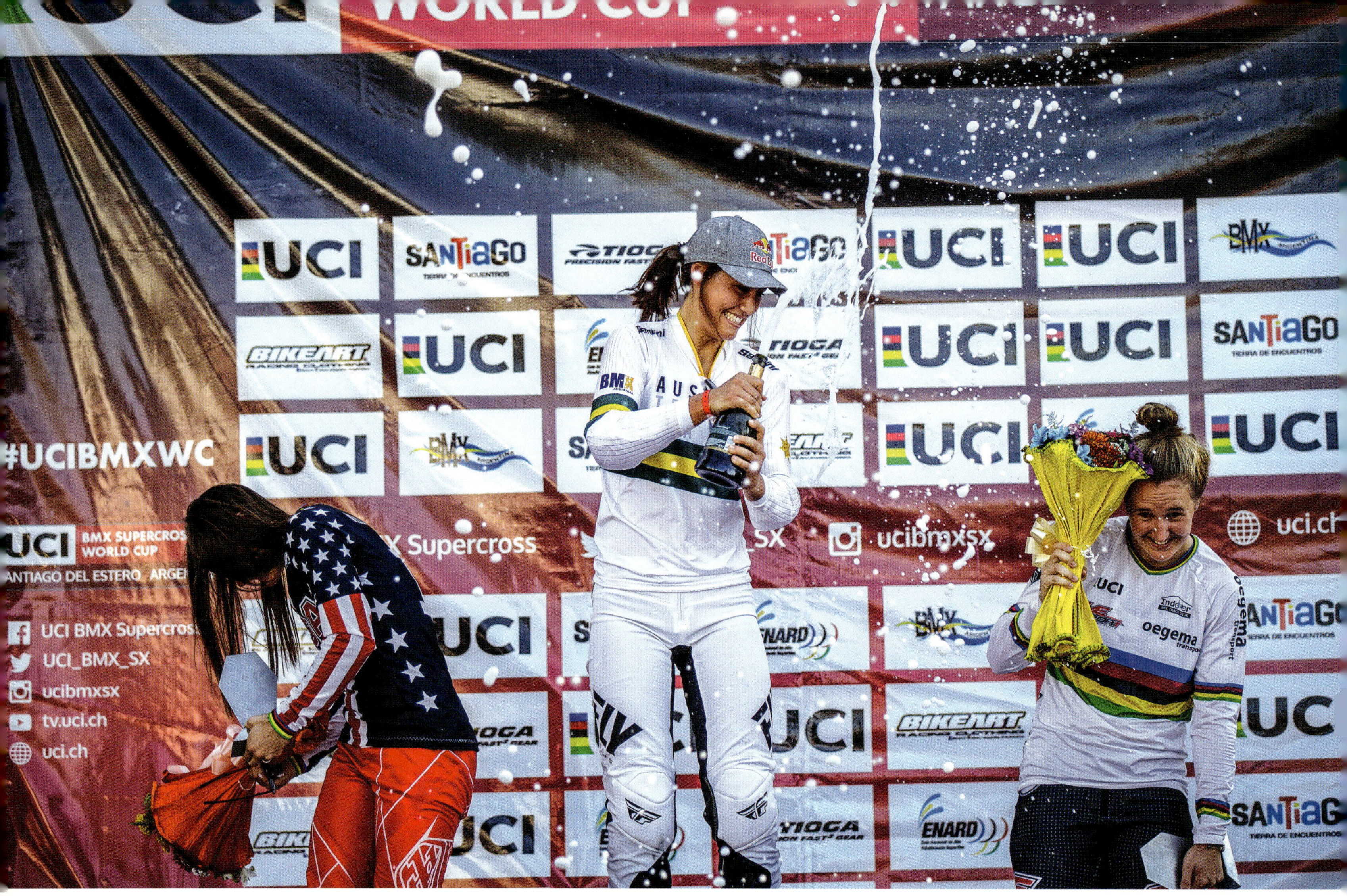
WORLD CUP
#UCIBMXWC
UCI BMX Supercross
UCI_BMX_SX
ucibmxsx
tv.uci.ch
uci.ch
ucibmxsx
UCI
SANTIAGO
TIERRA DE ENCUENTROS
BIKEART
TIOGA
ENARD
oegema
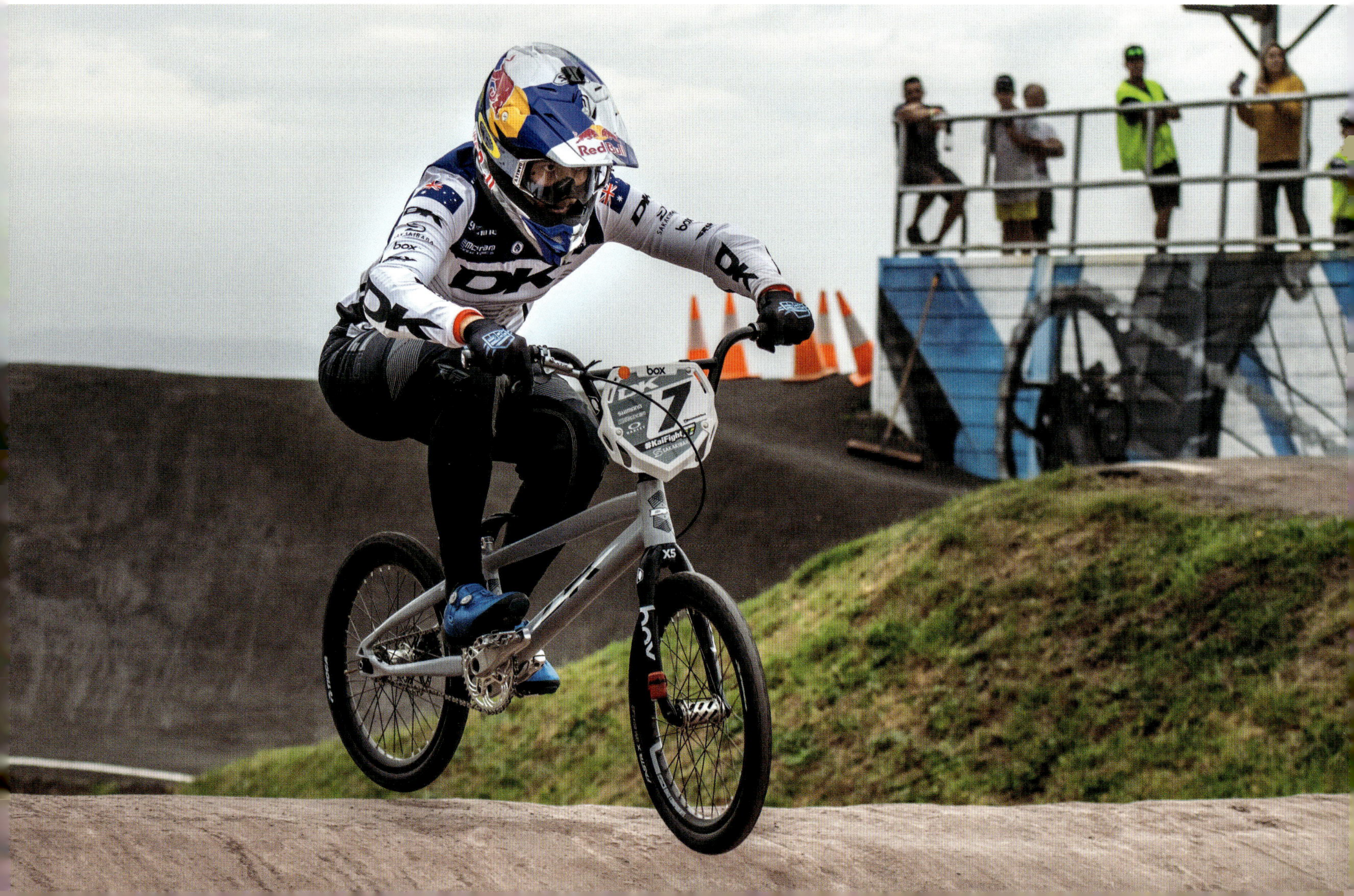
DK
Red Bull
Z

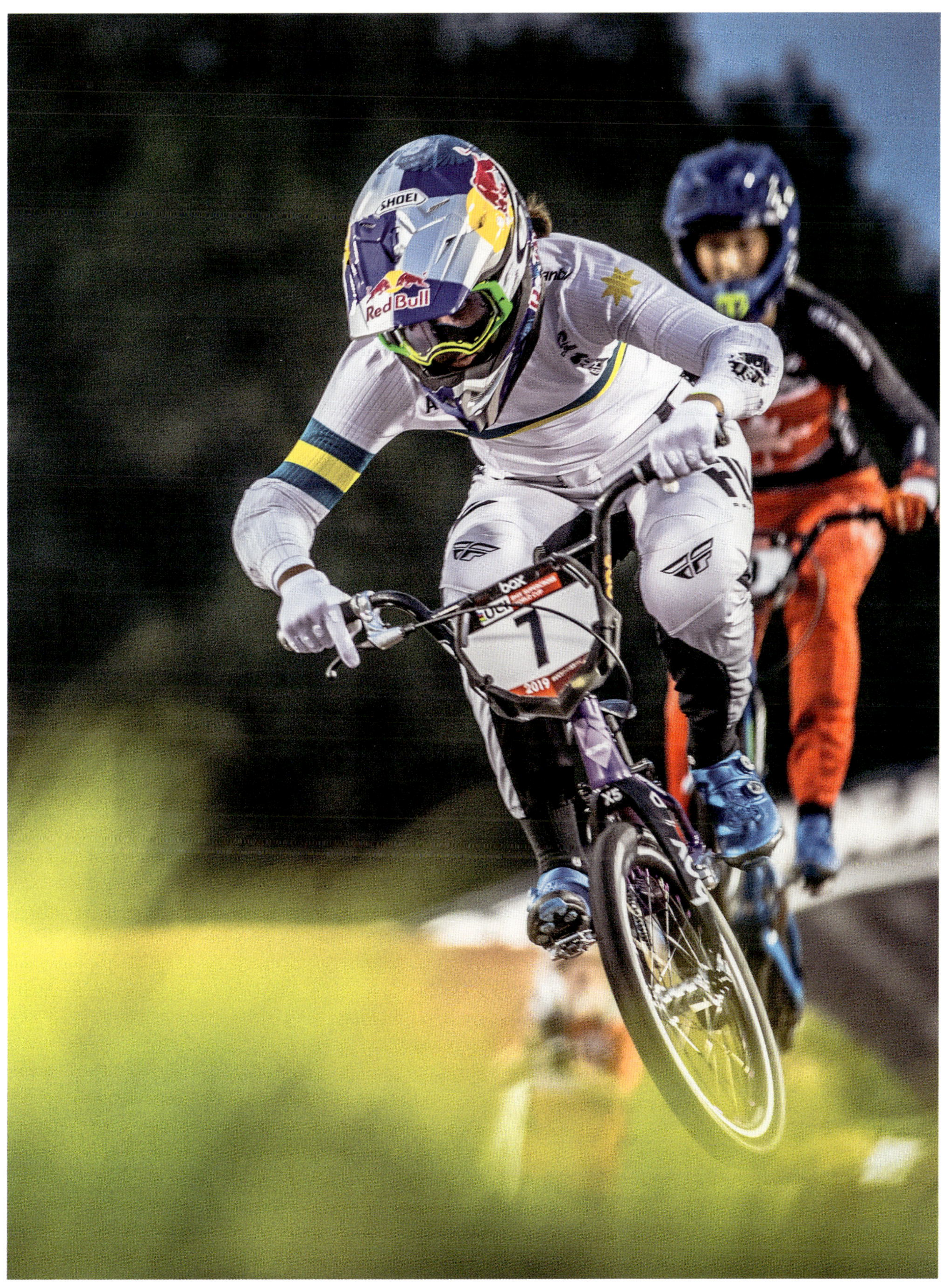

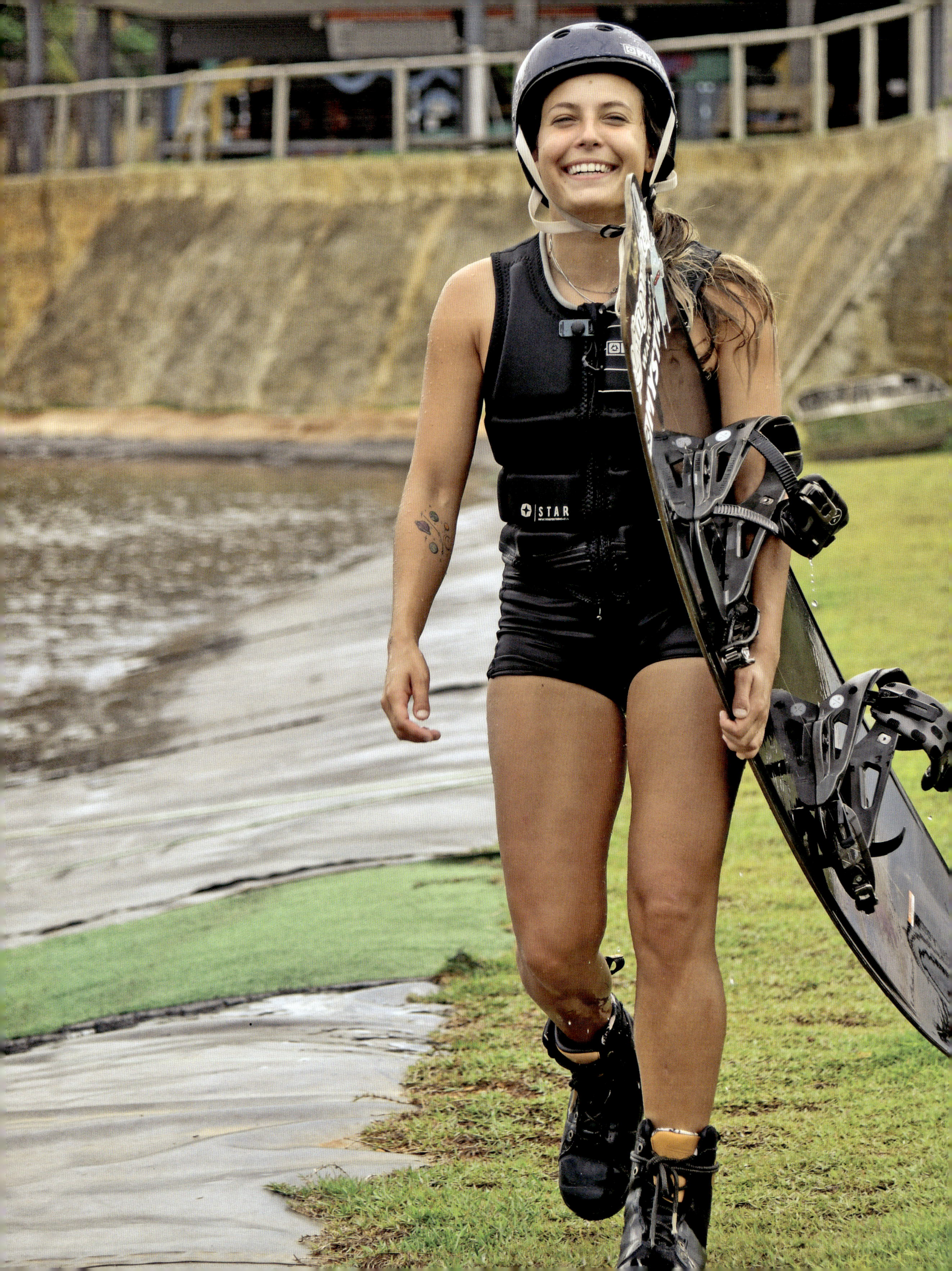

Elizaveta Pruzhanskaya
Wakeboarder

@lisabaloo

My name is Elizaveta Pruzhanskaya, but I'm mostly known as Lisa Baloo. I'm twenty-five years old and I'm from Russia. I started wakeboarding when I was eighteen and fell in love with the sport straight away. Since day one on the water I've dreamed of becoming a professional rider, winning the World Championships, getting sponsored, and living this beautiful life full of adventures.

The first years of wakeboarding were pretty hard for me since my skills were so low compared even to other Russian girls. I had to work really hard to reach the point where I was able to compete in the local wakeboarding scene. I spent the winters wakeboarding in indoor swimming pools because in Russia it is too cold to ride outside for seven months a year.

Two years after I started wakeboarding, I became the first woman in history to land the 'heart attack' trick, was named a 'national hero' by the Russian National Wake Awards, got my first partnership with a local board shop, won my first valuable competition at my home spot, Kingwinch, and was invited to the wakeboarding competition Plastic Playground in London.

I realized that I now had a chance to compete with the world's best female wakeboarders. So I packed my bags and traveled to the Philippines, where I met a lot of riders from all over the world. Their riding and lifestyle made me want to get there even harder.

In some of the competitions I took part in during the next season, I didn't even make it through the first round. But it was a priceless experience to meet and talk with different people from the international wakeboarding industry.

The next year I traveled to some other international competitions and still couldn't manage to get on the podiums. So I decided to spend the whole winter training somewhere outside Russia and ended up wakeboarding for seven months in Asia in the world's best wake parks. And I finally got my first podium at Plastic Playground in 2018. I couldn't believe it happened—I was actually crying.

The following season was my best so far. I signed up with partners and sponsors, joined my first professional photoshoots, podiumed on every international competition, and realized my first full video project, *Homeland*.

I finally started believing in myself, aiming at the podium every time I competed. Even if I didn't win, I was still confident in what I was doing and was actually having fun. Ever since, I have traveled a lot, won several competitions and awards, and got my first pro model wakeboard and pro model vest. The dream has come true.

In my career I've had people saying no to me, people who didn't believe in me. And I'd be lying if I said that I didn't care. But my dream was always so much bigger than anyone else's words. And every small success made me believe more and more that I was on the right path.

I like wakeboarding for the opportunities to be different, to live differently. It's taught me how to act when I lose, how to deal with injuries, how to be alone, how to work with emotions, how to find my comfort zone out of the comfort zone. And I am still learning something new every day. I am 100 percent happy with the life I am living now. And it wouldn't be possible without the friends, family, and partners that supported me all the way.

I consider myself a very lucky person who met really cool people that played a big role in my career. And I appreciate everyone who was always by my side, especially my partners: Kingwinch, Mystic, Hyperlite, and Hilx.

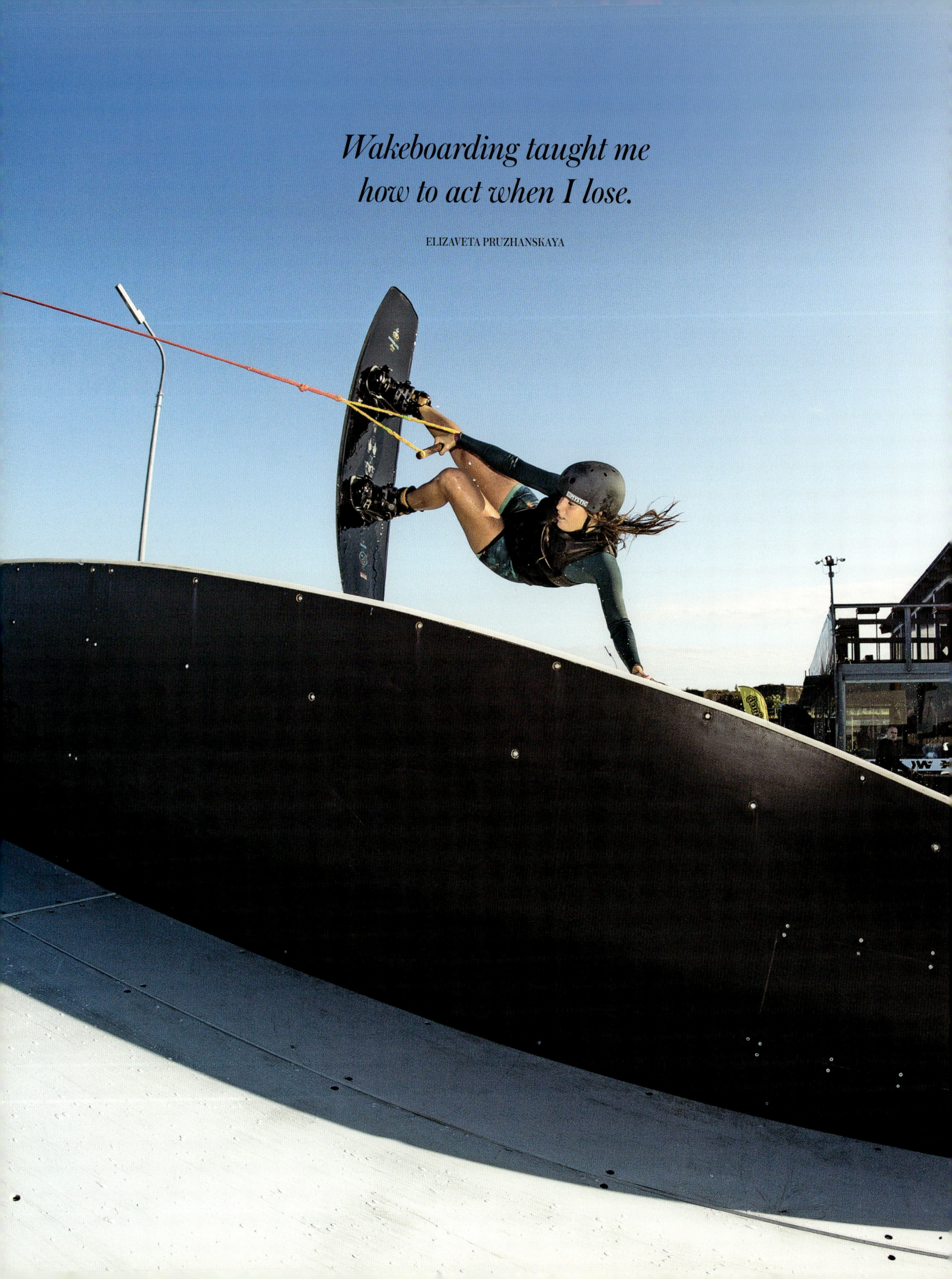

Wakeboarding taught me
how to act when I lose.

ELIZAVETA PRUZHANSKAYA

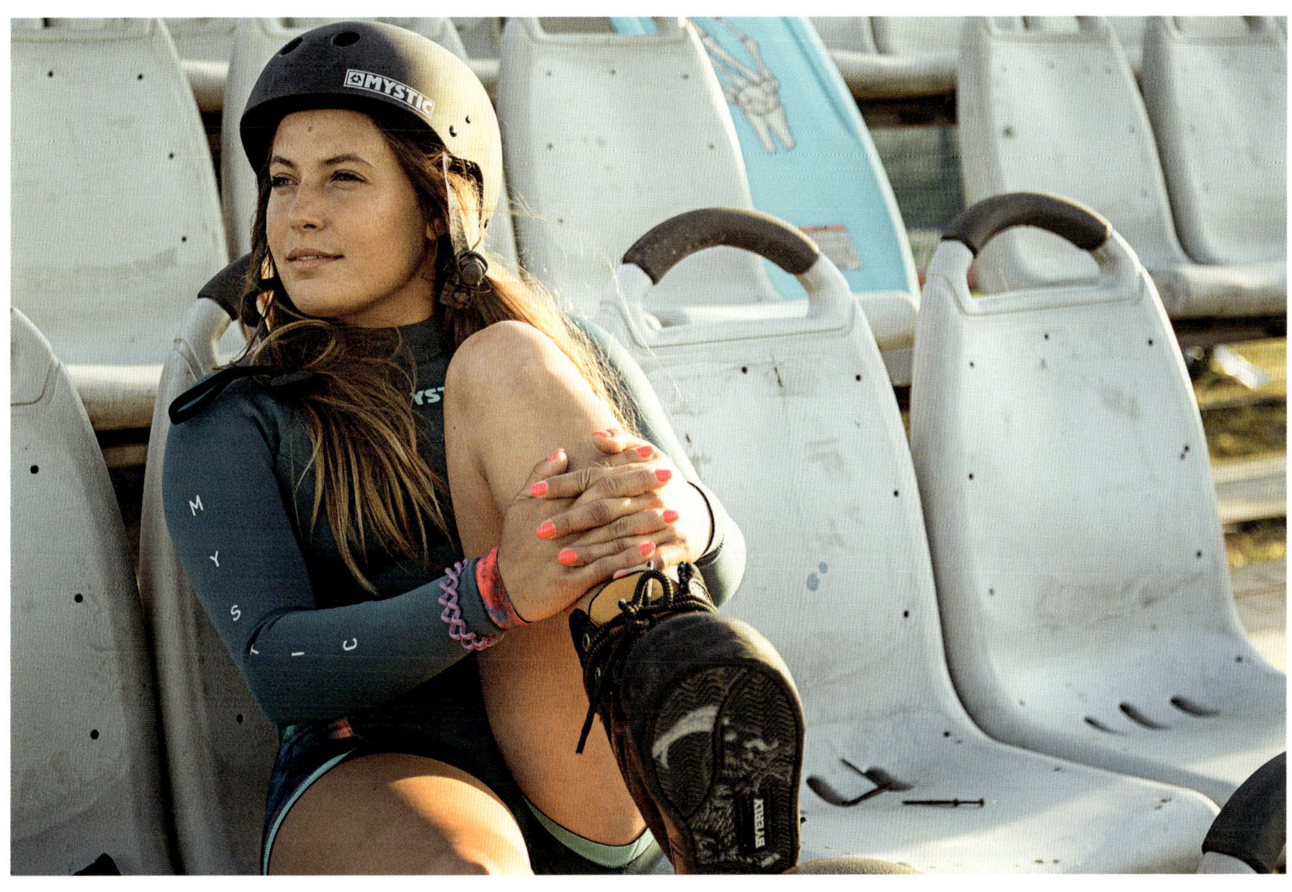

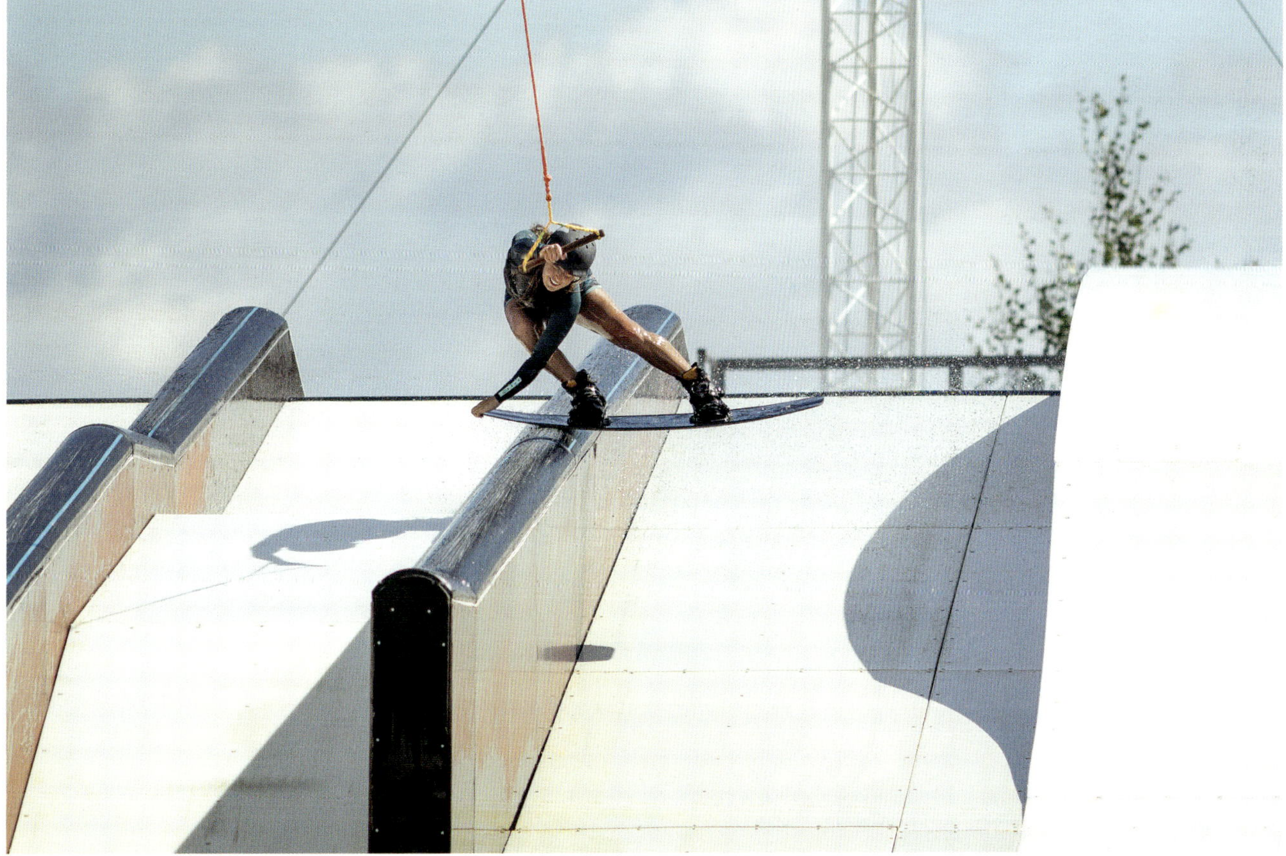

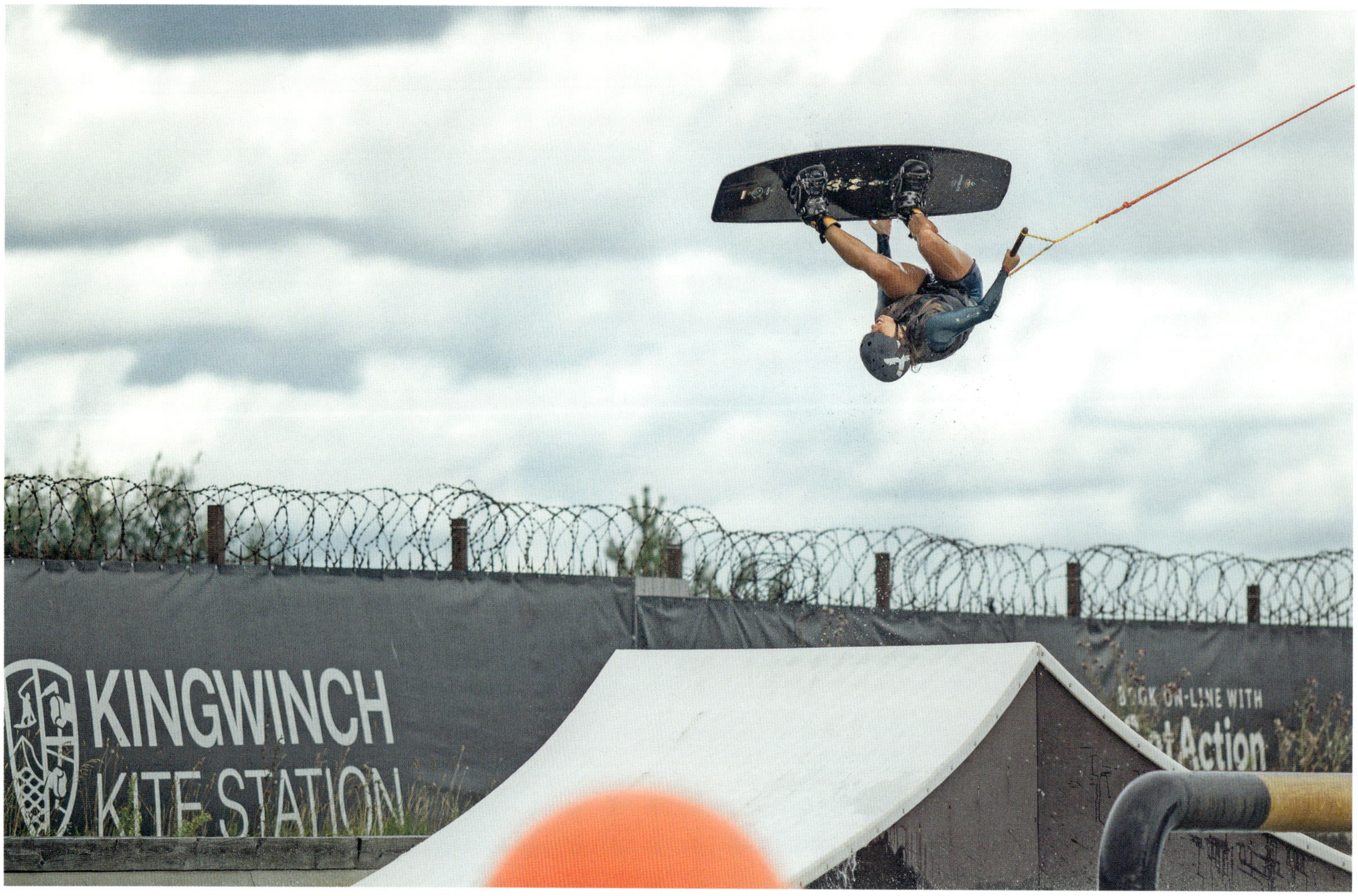

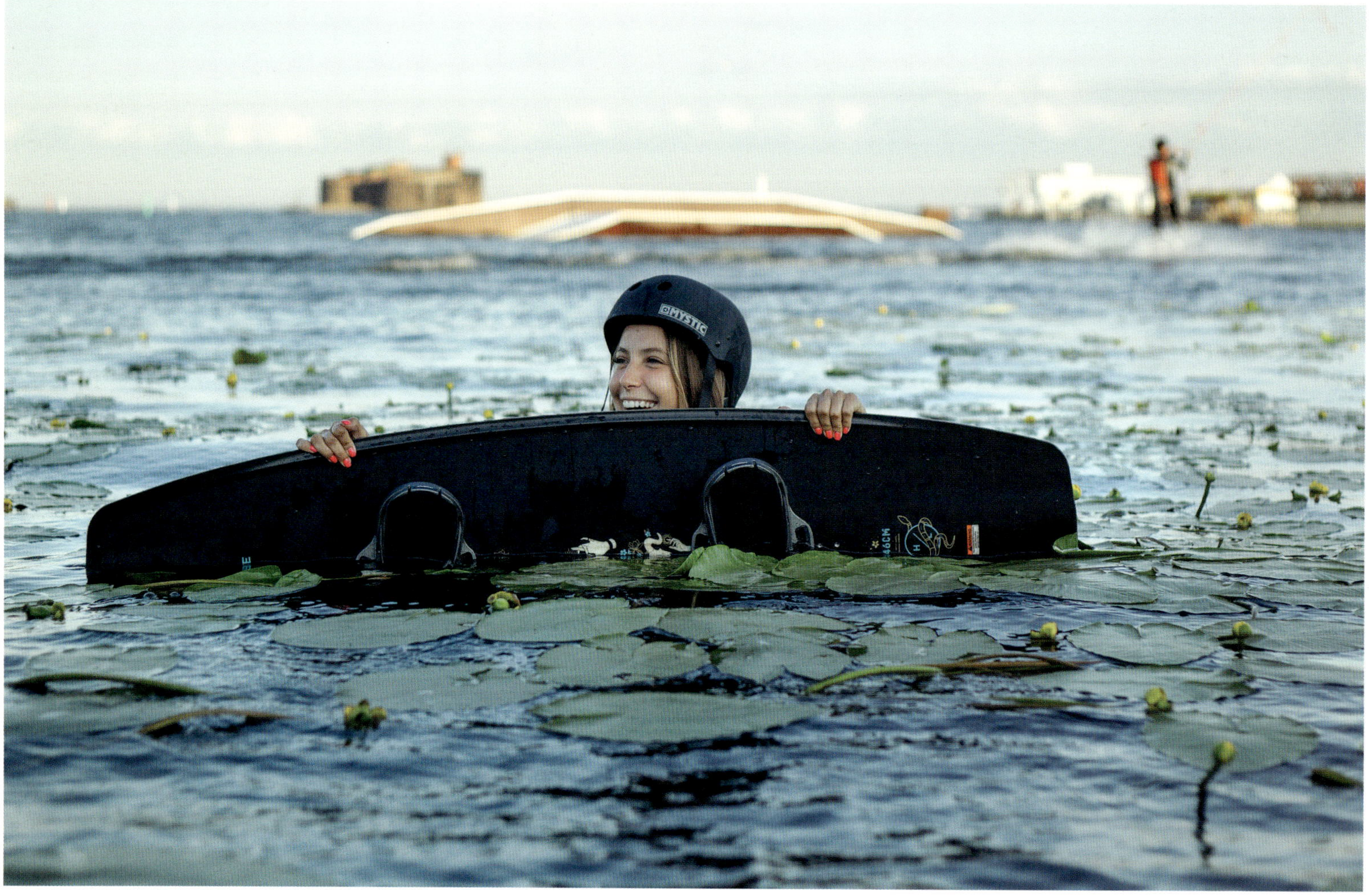

Kingwinch Wake Park   ▷ Ters Wake Park | St. Petersburg, Russia

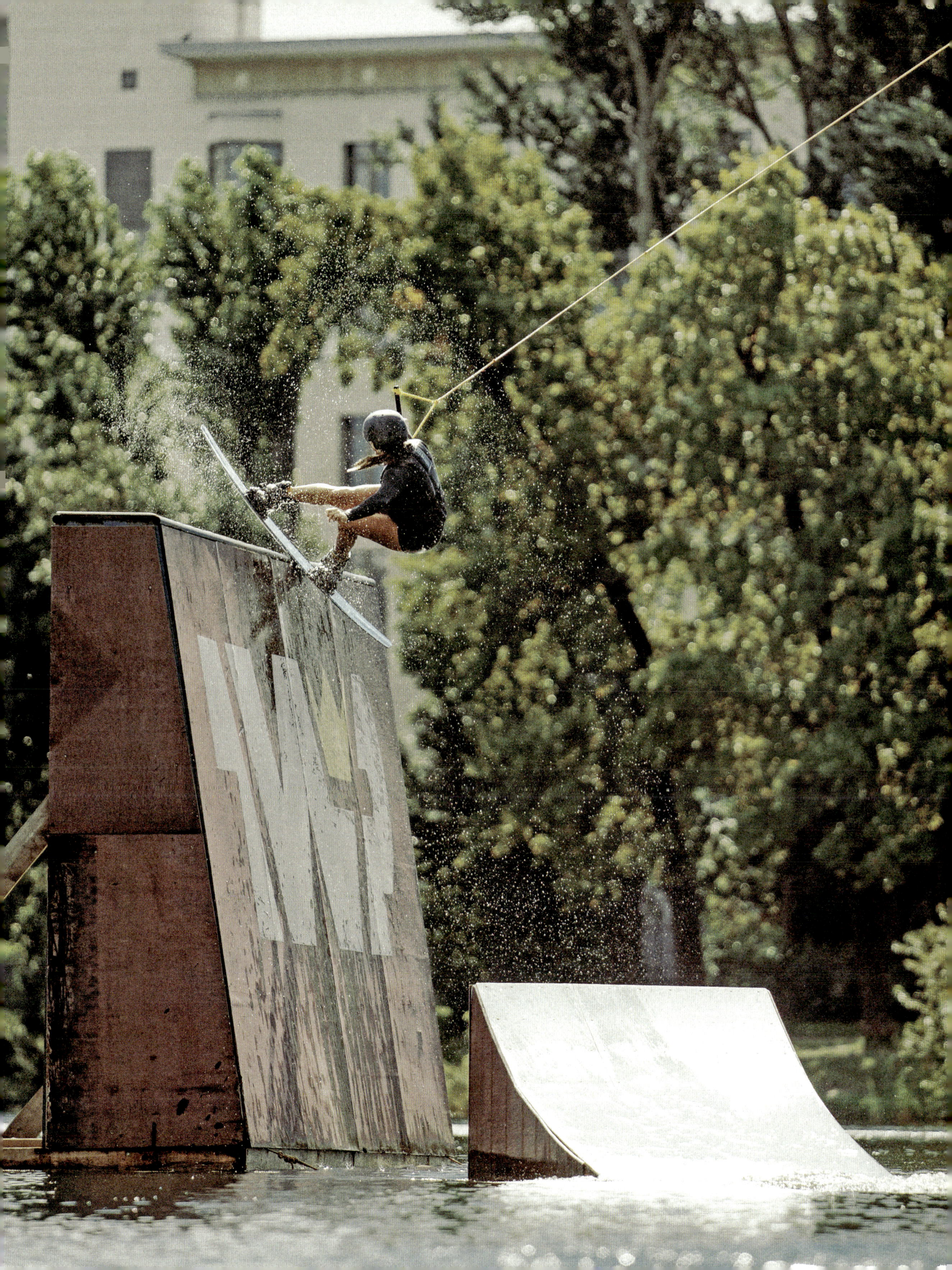

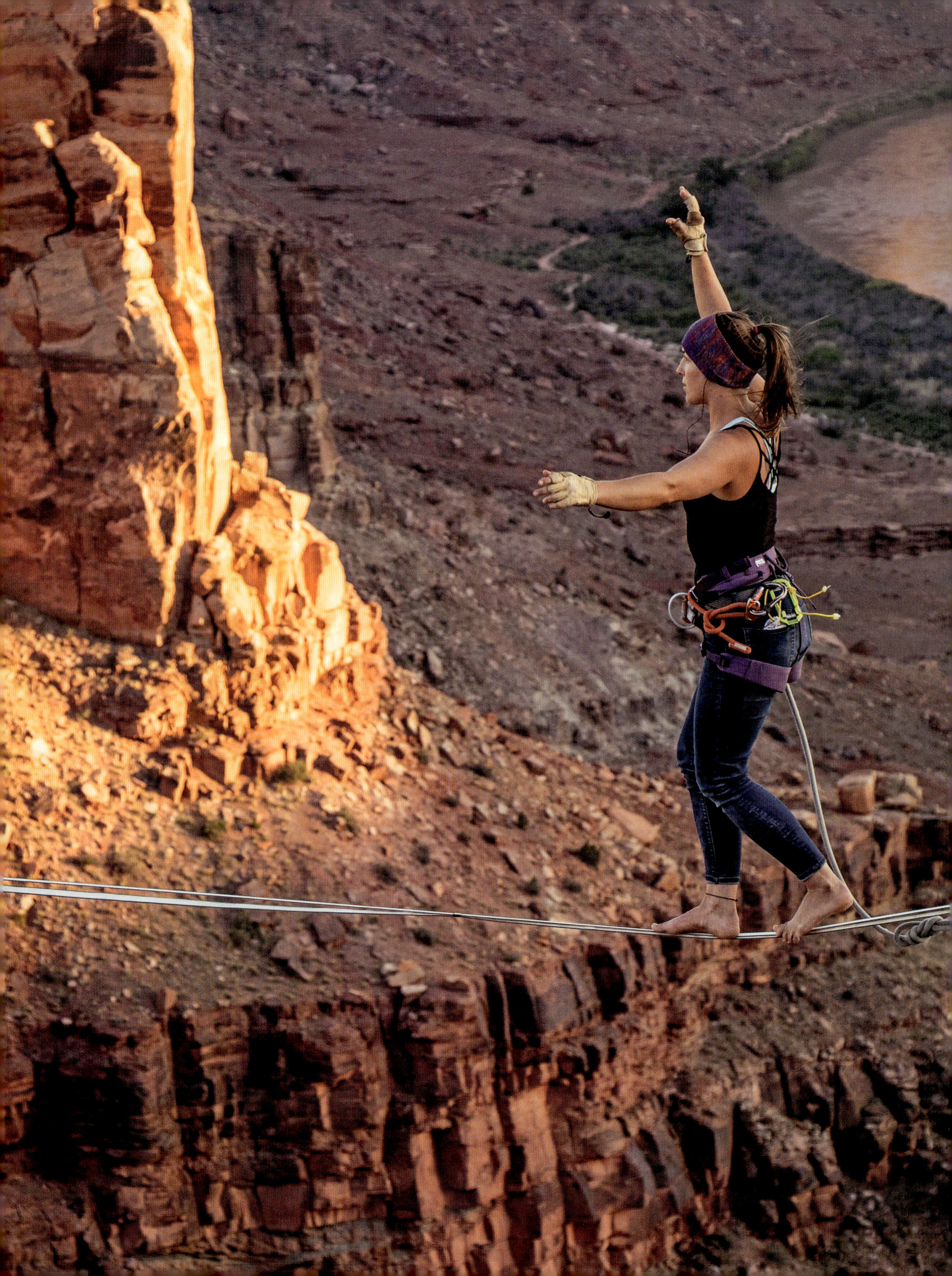

Faith Dickey
Outdoor athlete and slackliner

@thefaithdickey
www.thatslacklinegirl.com

If someone had told me as a young woman that one day, I would make a living walking and balancing across wobbly lines suspended thousands of feet in the air, I would have scoffed in disbelief. Growing up in Texas, I rarely found myself high off the ground save for the occasional tree I climbed. Yet life unfolded for me in a series of unexpected ways.

At nineteen I was working five jobs trying to save every penny for a move to New York City to study fashion at my dream college. Growing up with a single mom, my family had always struggled financially, and when it came to funding my future ambitions I was on my own. I pushed myself too hard, and one night I fell asleep at the wheel while driving home from one of my jobs. I woke up to the strange sensation of my world being turned upside down, as my car flipped over and slid to a halt, just a minute from reaching my driveway. I walked away unscathed but found myself questioning the path I was on. After the accident I started spending time at my local park to be outdoors and contemplate what I should do with myself. It was during one of these visits that I became fascinated by slacklining, when I saw a line strung up between two lofty pecan trees.

The line was only a few feet above the ground, yet I was unable to take a single step on it. It seemed impossible and it demanded a focus that was unlike anything I had ever experienced. I was immediately attracted to the peaceful feeling of pure concentration, and the way it felt to discover balance using only my body and my mind. It became my favorite hobby, and so a year later, when I decided to travel through Europe, I took a slackline with me.

After spending a few months in England, I traveled to Germany and by chance was invited to a slackline festival, where I attempted my very first highline: a slackline that is high off the ground. In order to be safe, highliners wear a harness attached to a leash that trails along the line as they walk, so if they fall, they only dangle a few feet below and can climb back up, mount the line and try again. I befriended two guys who mentored me on my first attempts. Despite knowing I was safe, the fear was like nothing else I'd ever known. I was an experienced slackliner on the ground, but as soon as I was high up everything I knew was out the window. My body became gripped with fear and I could not stand up. I tried over and over to walk, but each time, after a few steps I would lose control and fall, swinging on my leash. It felt even more impossible than the first time I tried slacklining!

I was determined to walk just one line before I gave up this newfound sport, so I threw myself at every highline I could, until finally I powered through the voice in my head telling me I wasn't good enough and, step by step, crossed an entire line. Stepping onto the rock on the other side was the most exhilarating feeling of success I'd ever had. Little did I know that was only the beginning!

A few months after setting foot on my very first highline, I had set a new Female World Record in the sport. I would for a time level the playing field in the sport of highlining, sharing the World Record with my male counterparts. Then I would go on to break my own records and set new ones for six years straight. After noticing that I was often the only woman out highlining, I formed the Women's Highline Meeting, which has taken place annually in Czechia for the last ten years. Starting with six women, the festival grew each year, and the last few have boasted sixty women from all over the world.

But most importantly, I discovered so much about myself along the way. By learning to manage and overcome my fear, I discovered that I am more than just the voice in my head and that if I truly want to reach a goal, I only have to work for it. Over time, I learned that my worth is not defined by achievements, but rather that my achievements are defined by my worth. And if faced with a challenge, the best way forward is one step at a time.

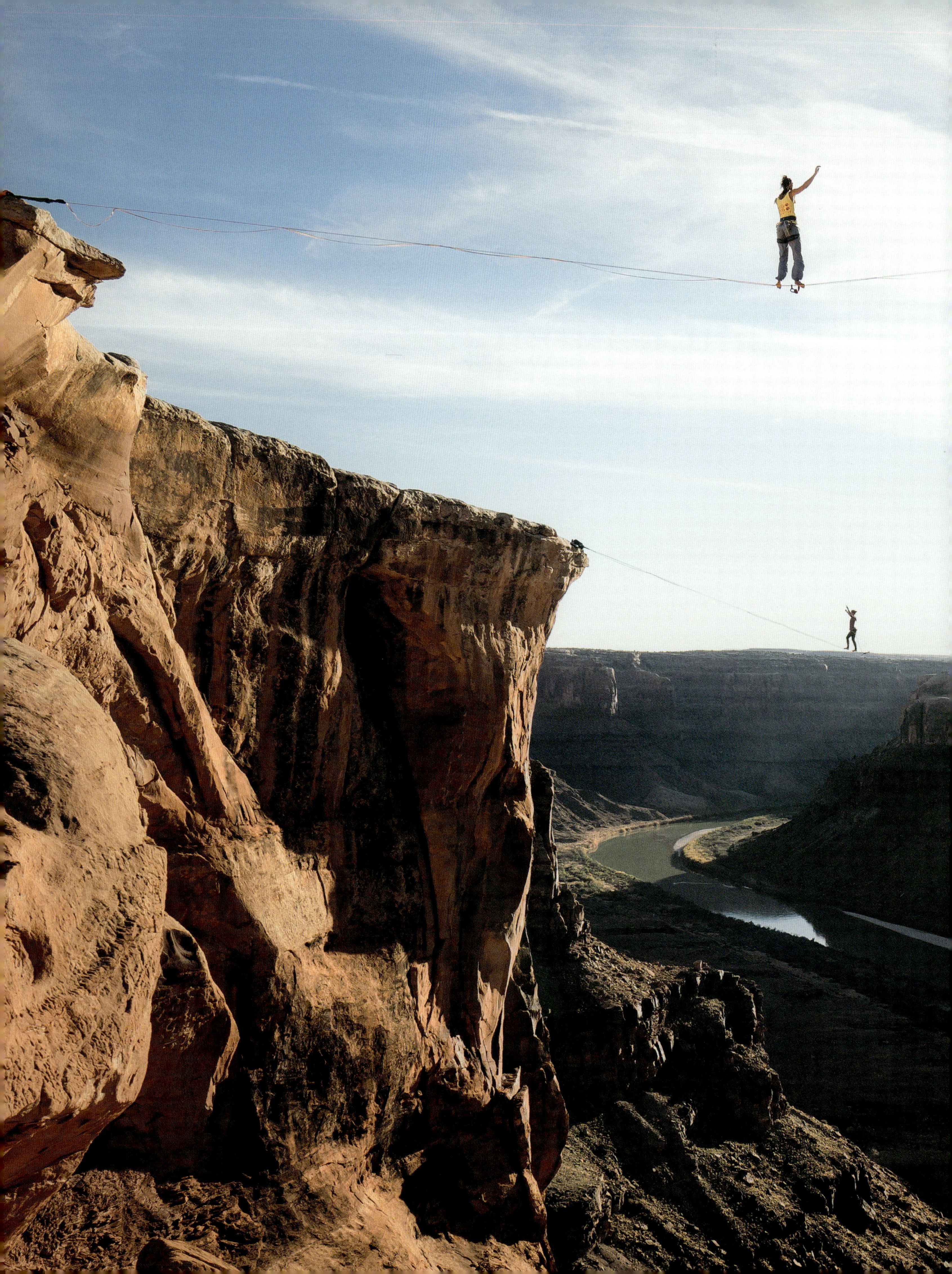

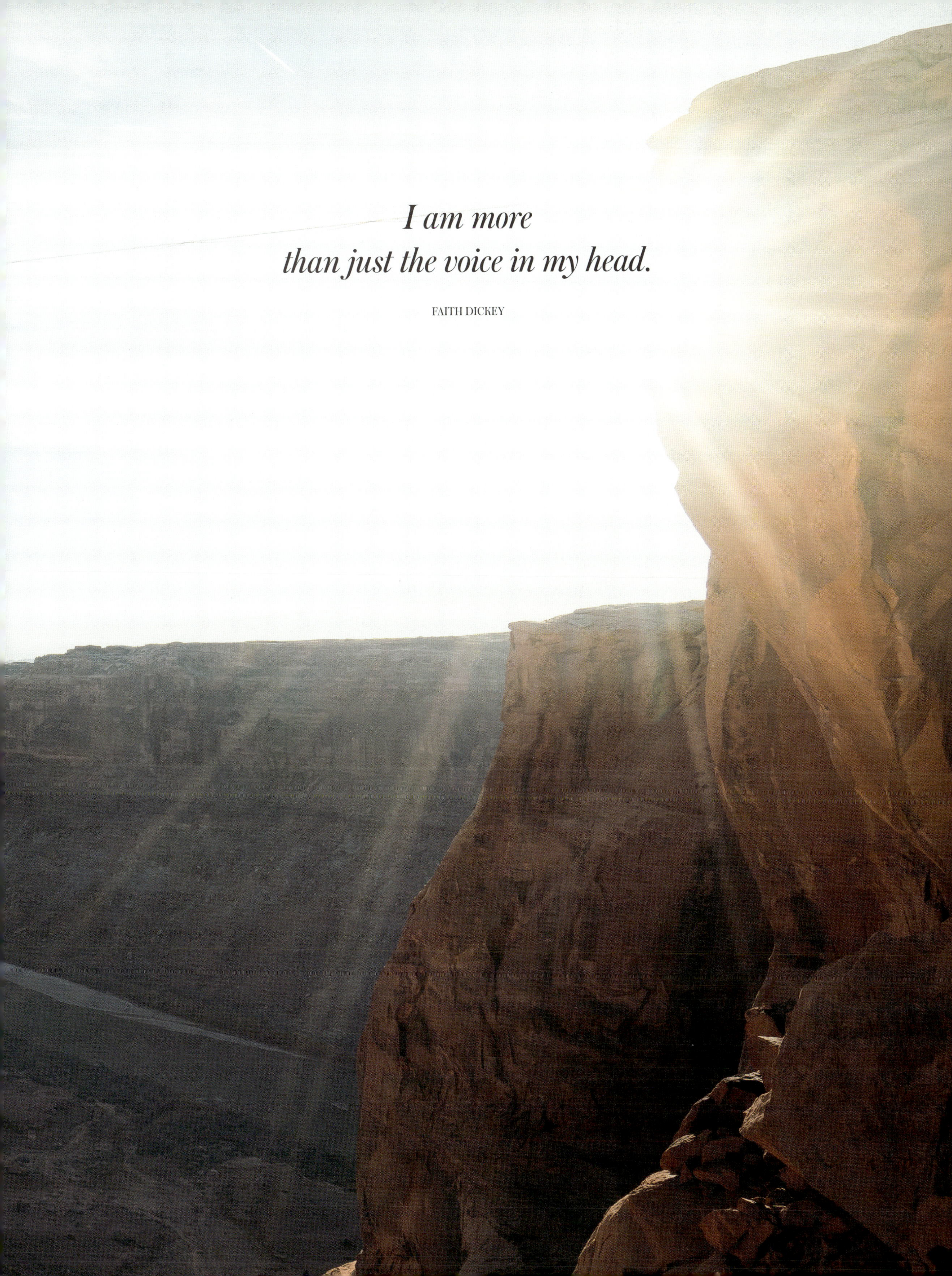
I am more
than just the voice in my head.
FAITH DICKEY

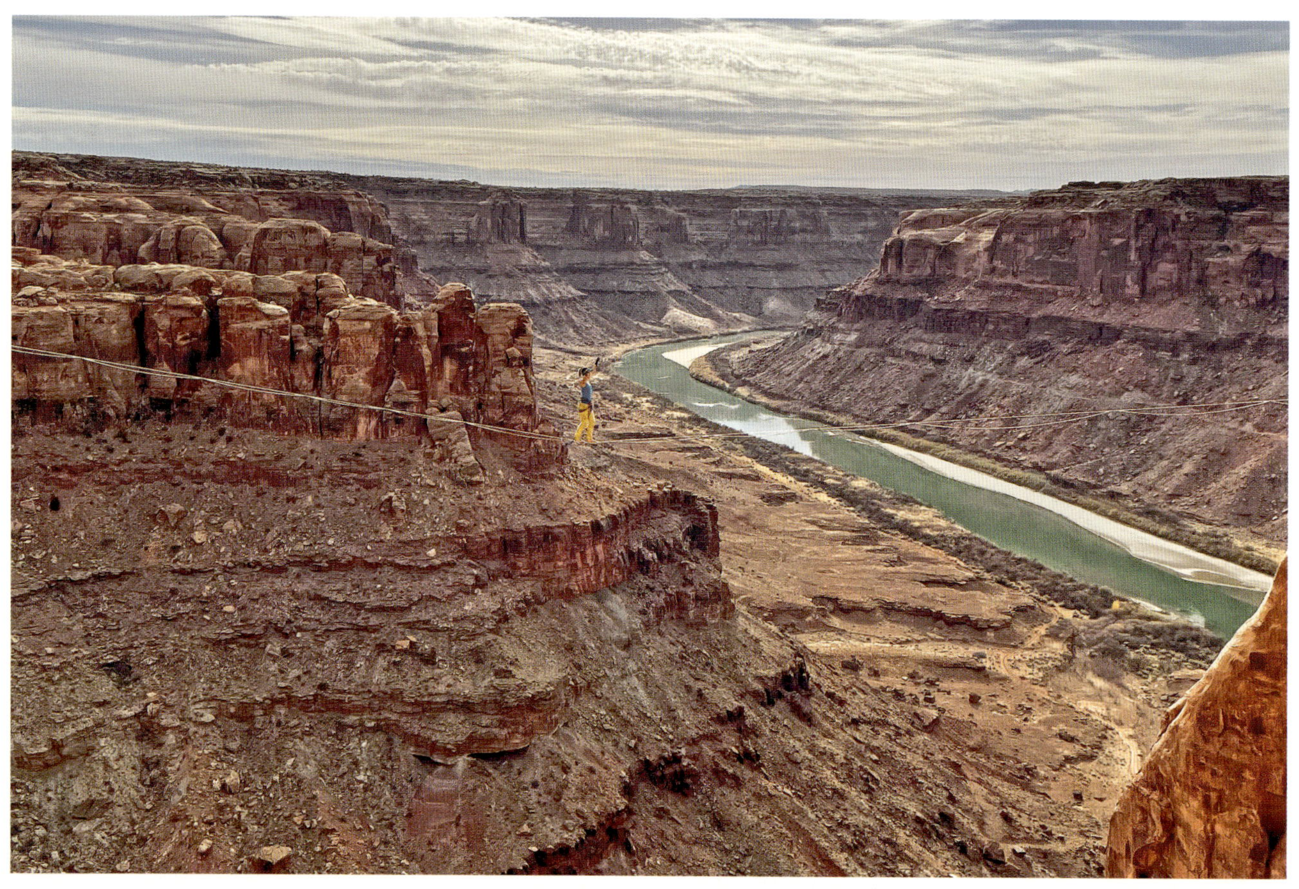

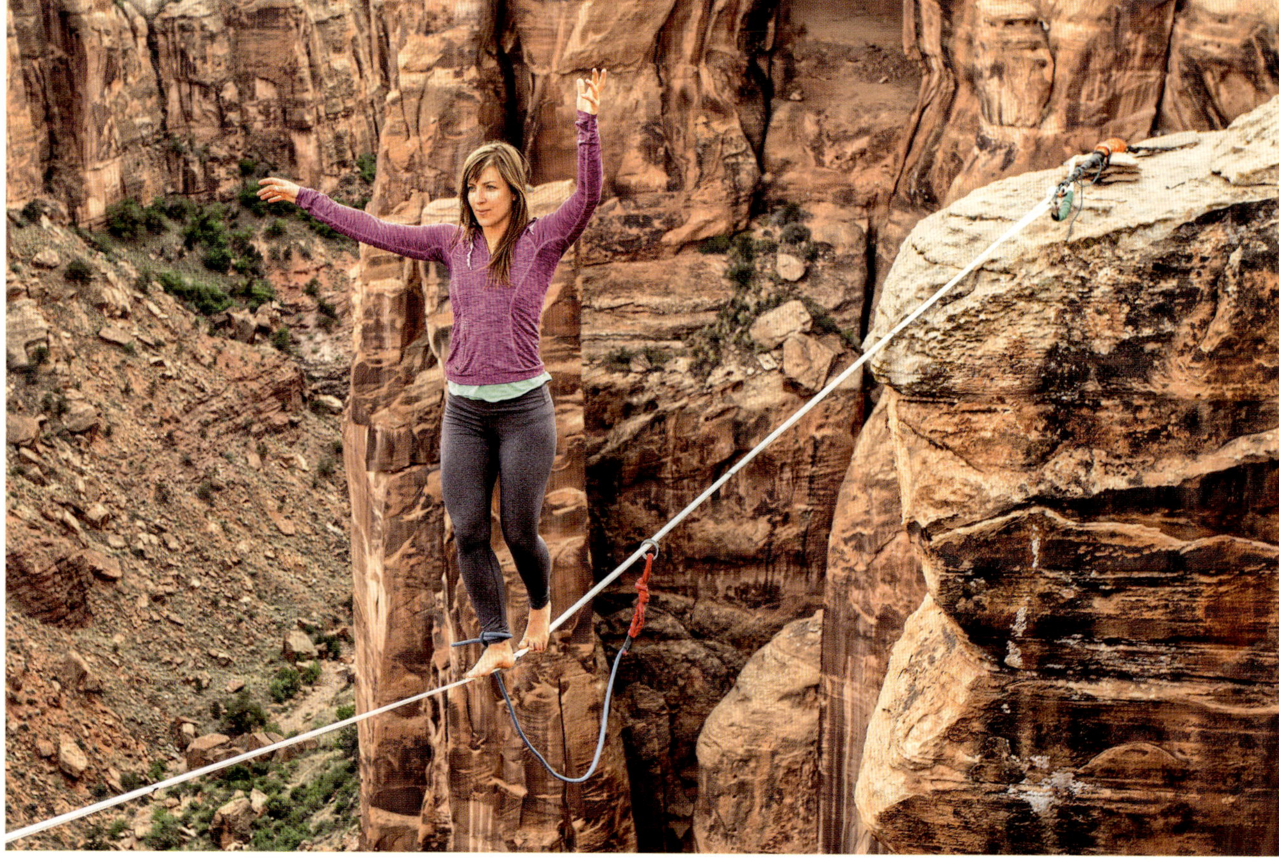

  Moab, Utah, USA

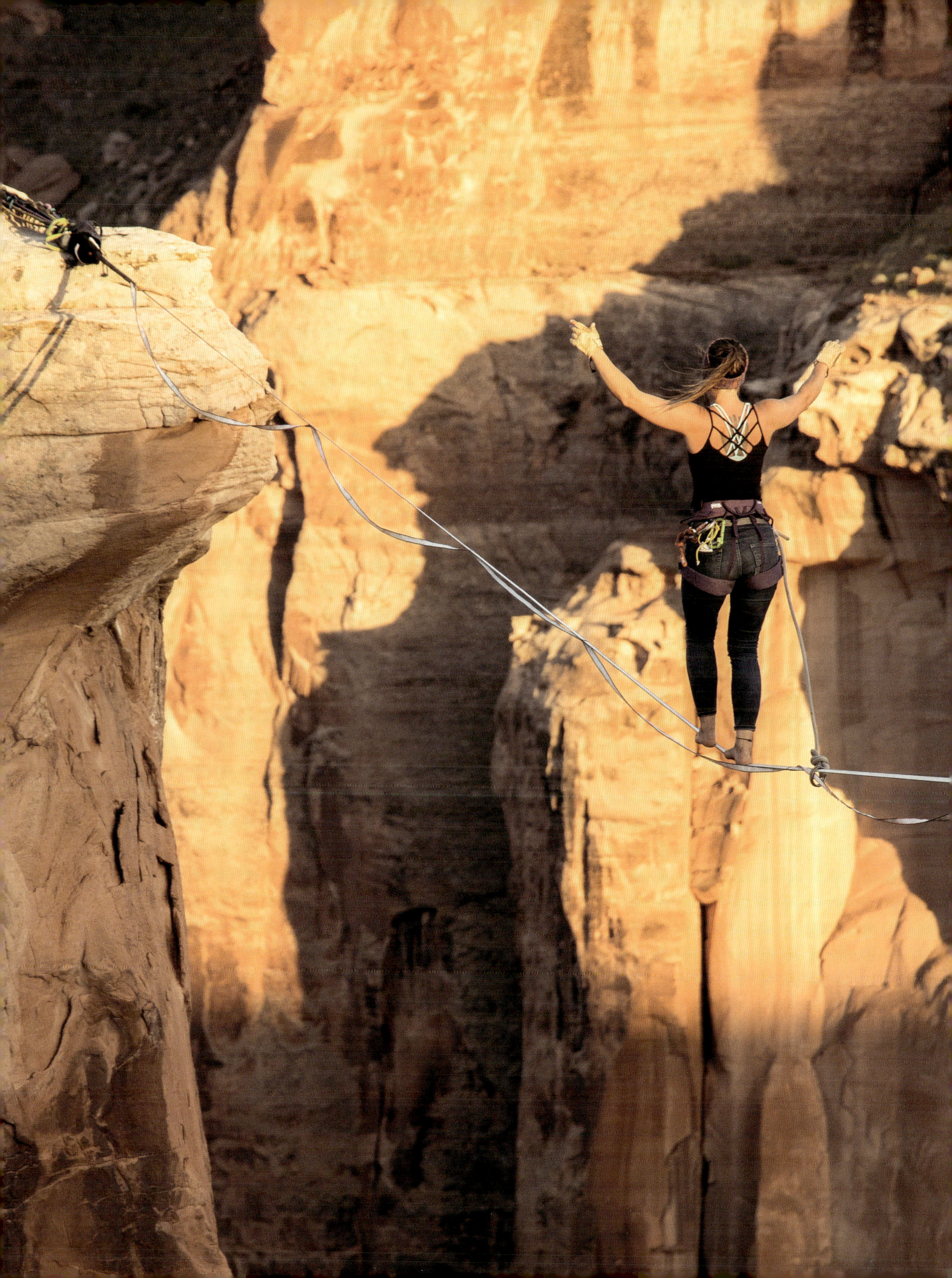

Clair Marie

BASE jumper

@thebasegirl
basegirl.com

I was born and raised in a tiny mountain town in Northern California. We were thirty minutes from the nearest gas station or grocery store and the schools were even further away. I was born with adventure in my blood. I started skiing and rock climbing when I was three years old and snowboarding as an early teen, and I spent much of my childhood outdoors, exploring my surroundings and dreaming up an epic life. I was homeschooled my entire life until I went to a community college when I was fourteen. I graduated high school when I was sixteen and set out into the world to make a name for myself and see what kind of shenanigans I could get into.

I've always had a deep desire to push myself past the social norm. I was never interested in a normal life or a normal job. The idea of the American Dream was more of a dull headache for me. When I was eight years old, I saw a BASE jumping video clip at a ski resort I was at with my mom. I remember watching that clip and thinking: That is what I am supposed to do.

I told my mom I was going to BASE jump one day and the statement was brushed off as the lofty dreams of a kid. No one really knew how deeply I felt the connection to the sport. It looked like the most freeing and amazing thing a human could do—purposely falling off a tall object, defying hundreds of thousands of years' worth of DNA pumping though my veins saying that if I jump I will die, then opening a parachute and floating peacefully to the ground.

For those who don't know, BASE stands for Building, Antenna, Span, Earth—those are the four main objects we jump from with parachutes on our backs.

I was the youngest female BASE jumper and the youngest active BASE jumper ever. I have jumped all over the world and have made it my career for almost seventeen years. Once I felt comfortable with my place in the world of BASE jumping, I expanded my career to include mountain bike racing and then becoming an active and very busy photographer and videographer. One thing I have come to realize is that I don't like to feel a ceiling above me. If I start feeling like I've reached the top, I'll shift over a bit and reinvent myself and my work. Always learning, always growing!

BASE jumping provides the ultimate freedom for me. There's no outside influence, no stress about normal life; you're just in the moment and in nature. We are so torn these days between either adhering to society's standard of how life should look or truly following our own path. Paving your own way will always be messy and emotional, difficult but also the most rewarding thing you could ever do. Having a deep respect for yourself and your passion will lead your life in a direction you never thought possible and although it will test you, it will uplift your soul in a way nothing else can. Being 100 percent true to yourself and your passion creates the space for you to grow into a person society would never allow, and that in itself is a pretty incredible thing!

   ▷ Mineral Bottom Canyon, Moab, Utah, USA

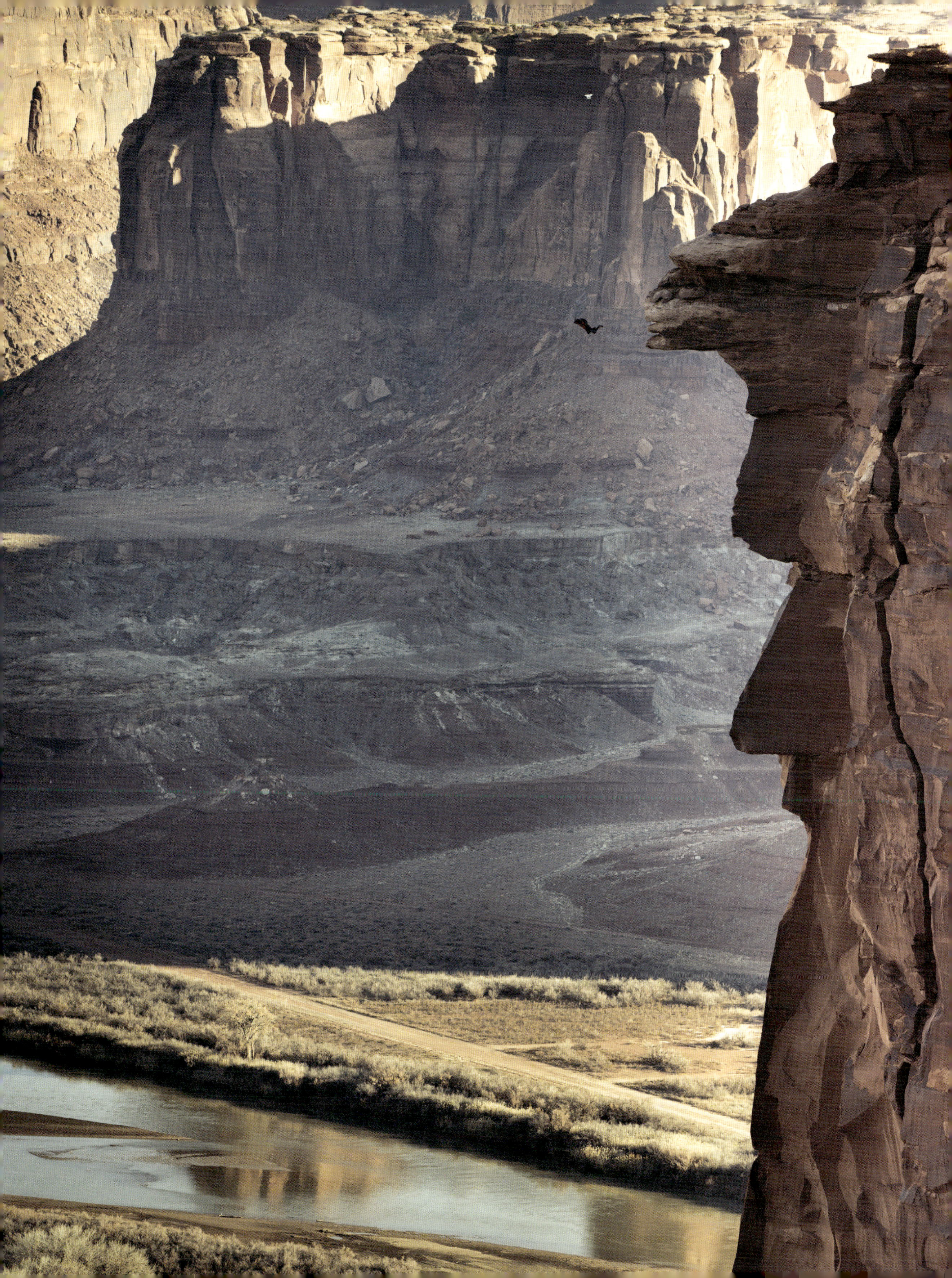

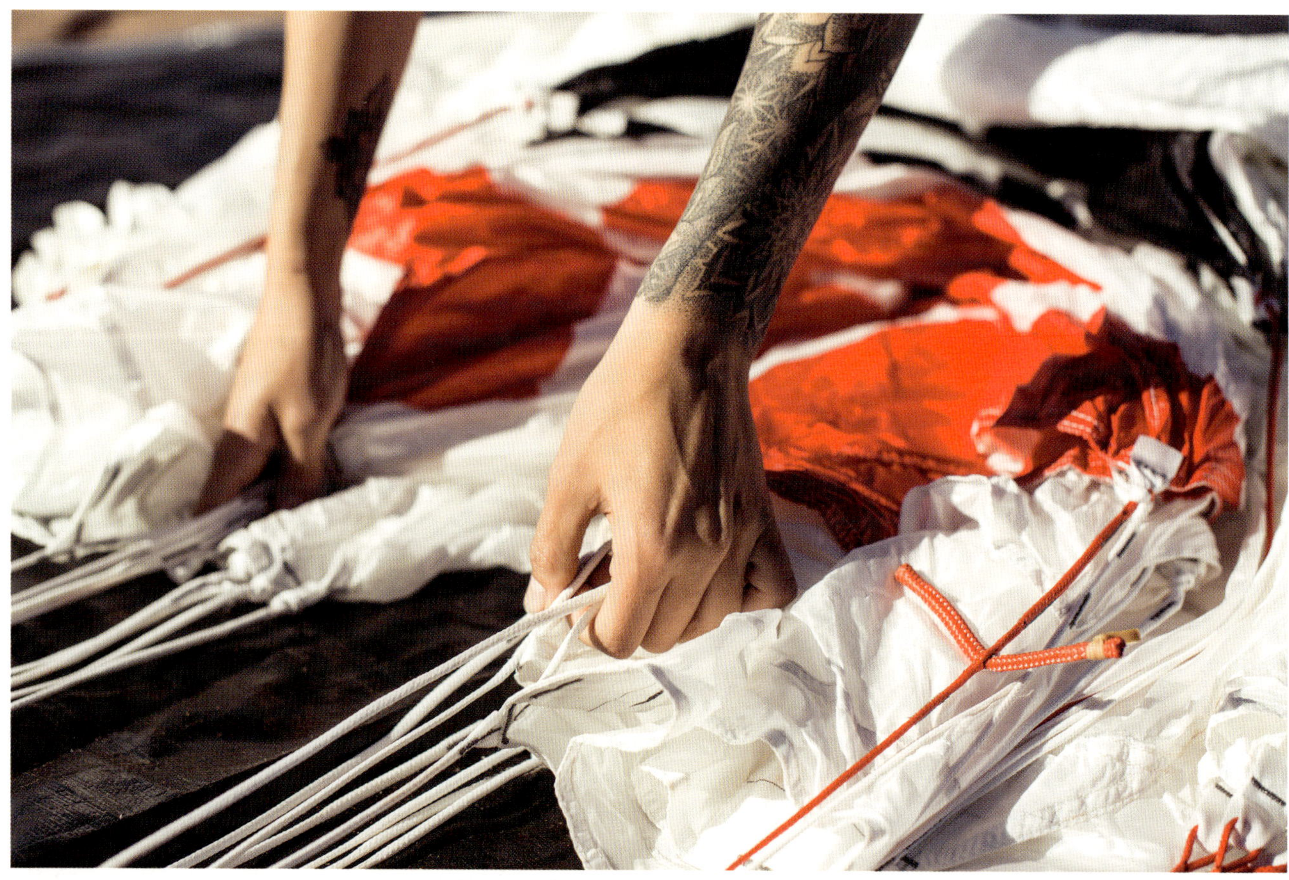

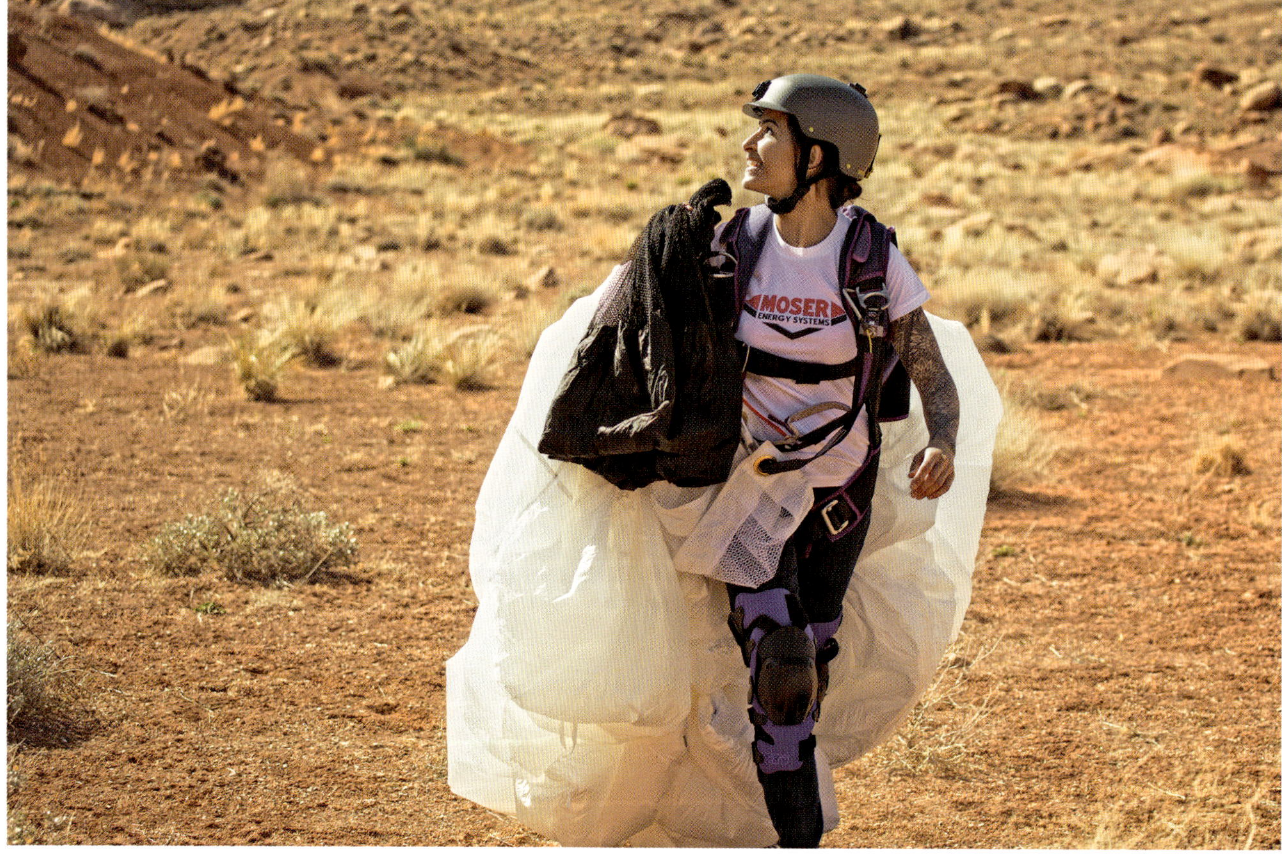

  Mineral Bottom Canyon, Moab, Utah, USA

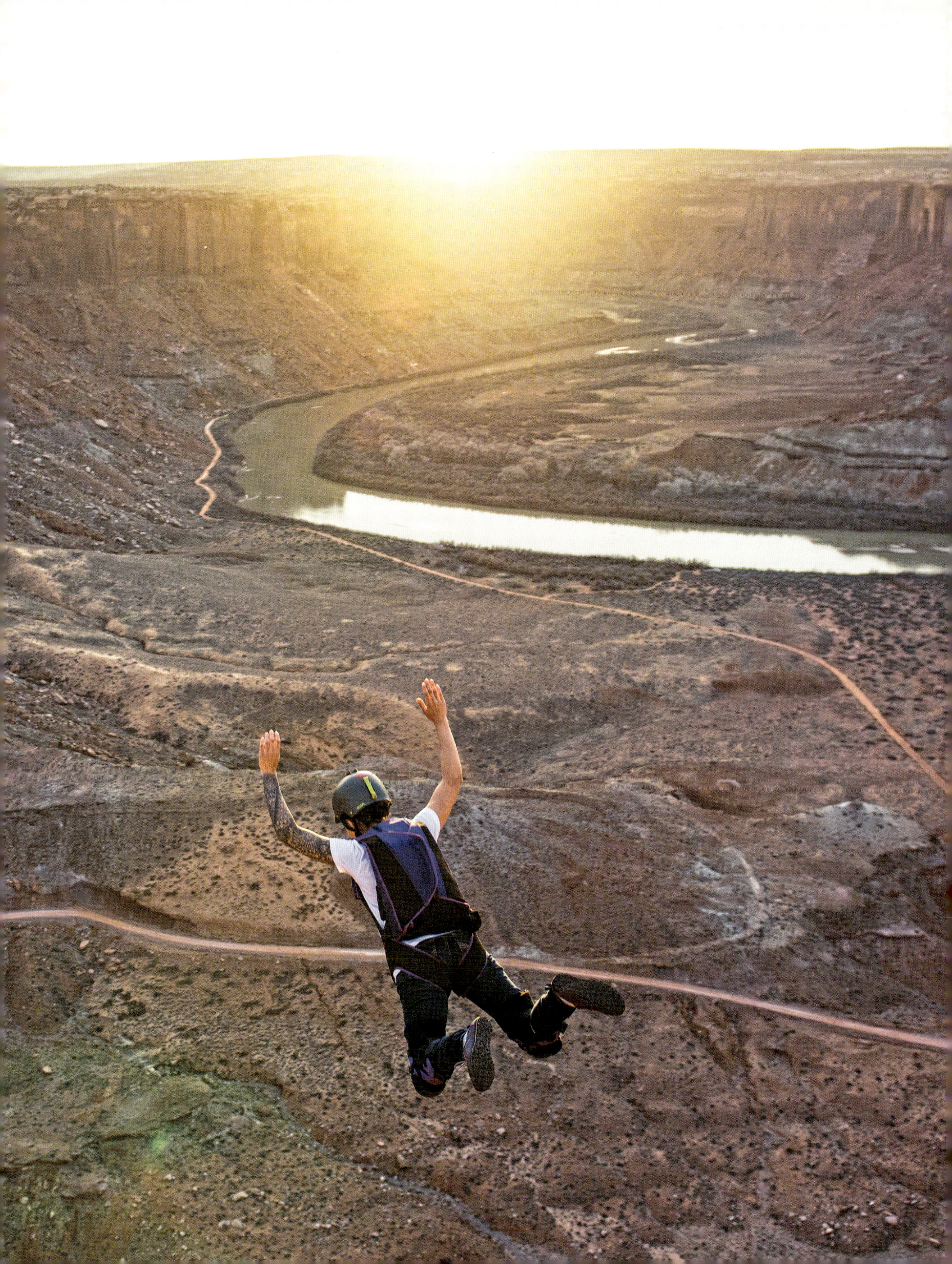

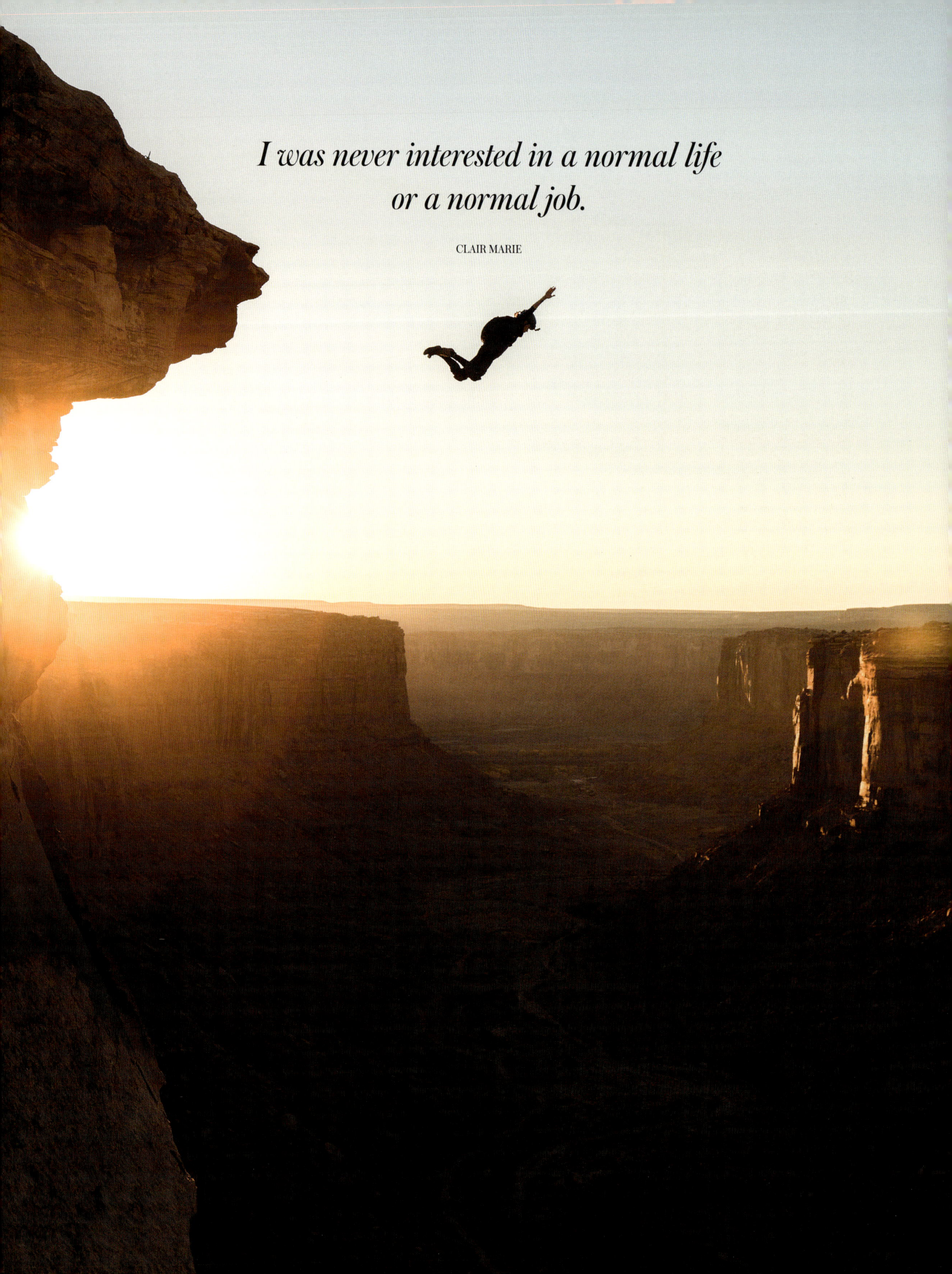

I was never interested in a normal life
or a normal job.

CLAIR MARIE

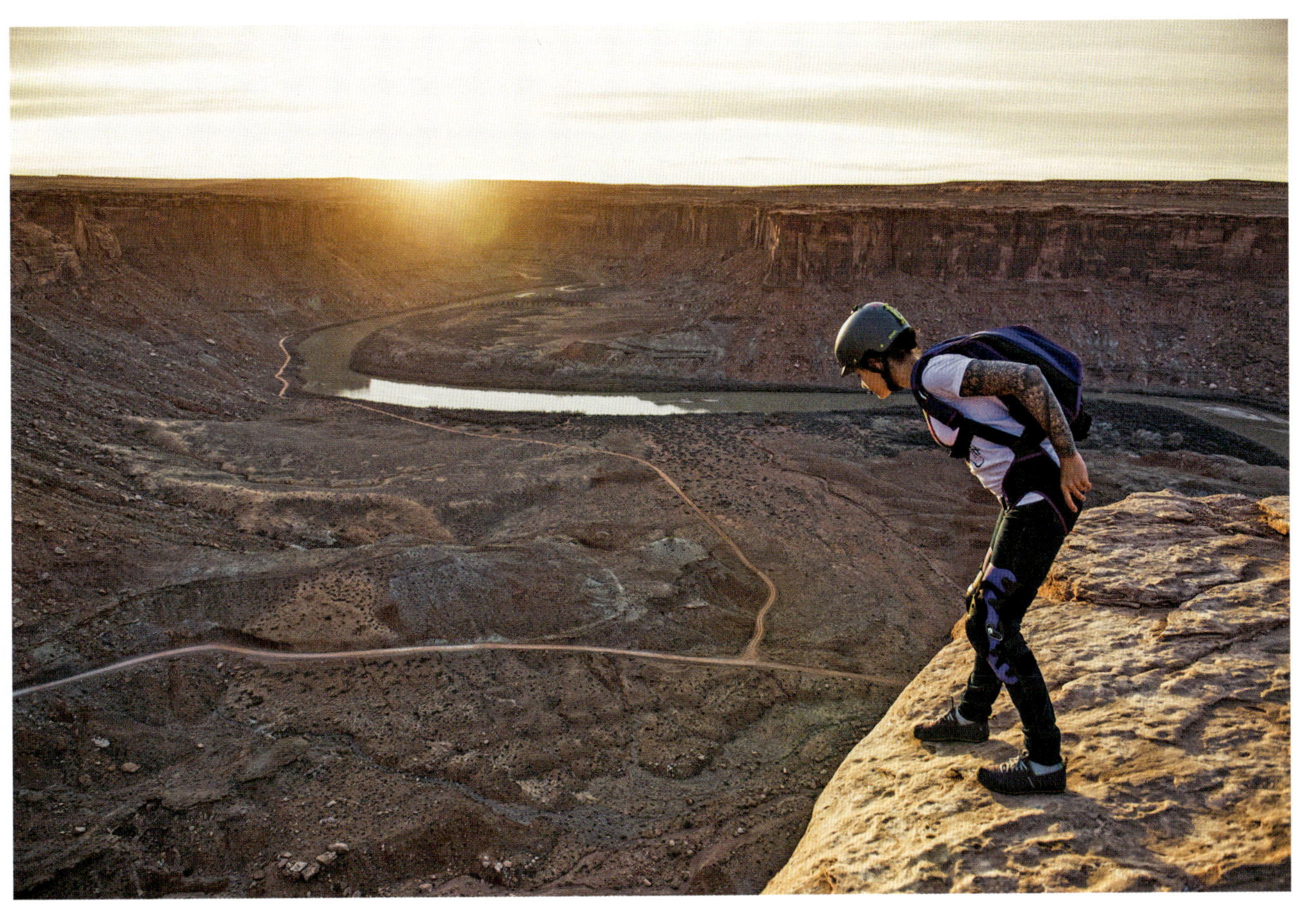

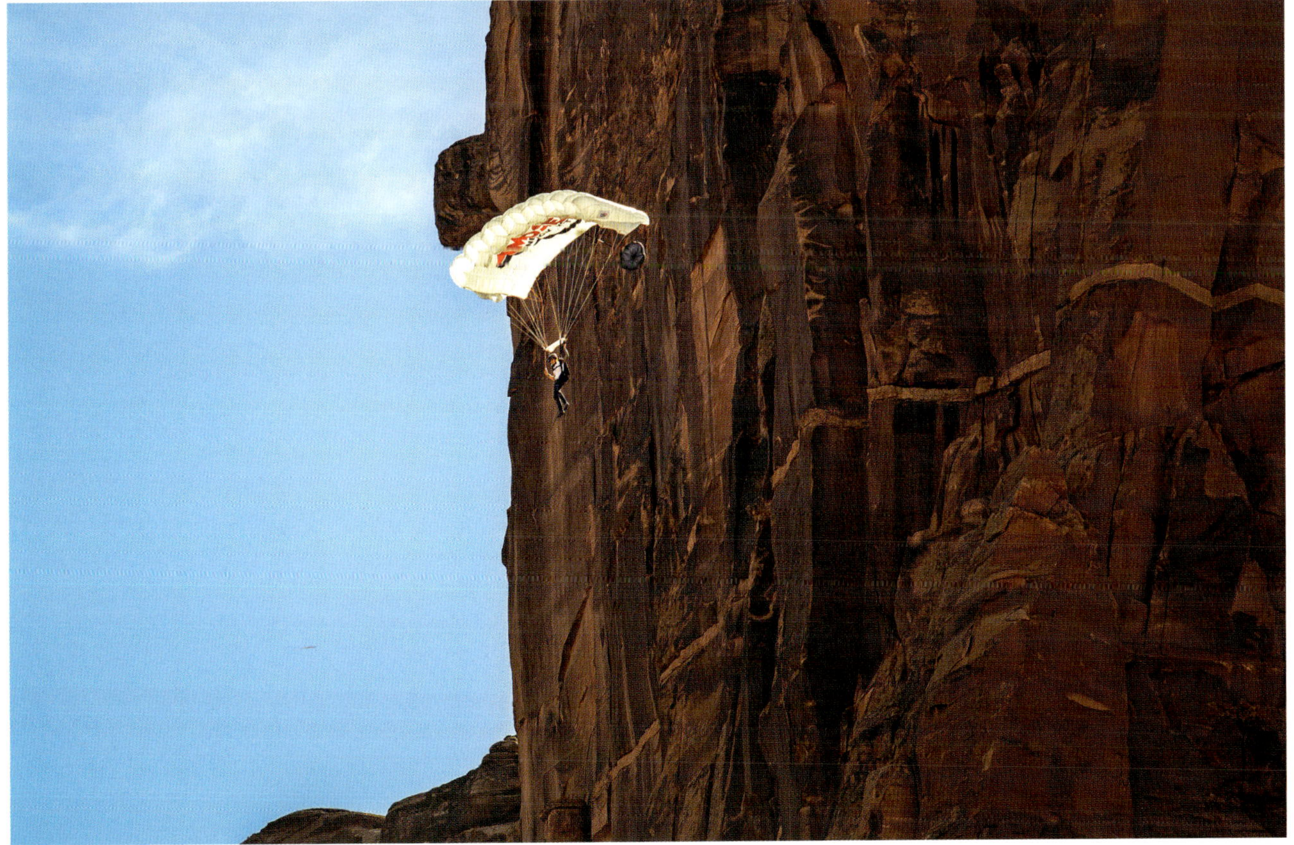

Julia Cassou
Photographer and climber

@julia.cassou
juliacassou.com

People always ask me, "When did you start photography? Where did you learn it?" The answer is simple: I can't remember. It's not something I've learned, it's about taking a breath with my soul when pressing the button and shooting.

As far back as I can remember, I've always had a camera in my hand, grabbing my father's camera as often as I could. It always felt natural to me, looking through the camera at my surroundings, finding the lines, the colors, the textures. Seeing everyday life from another perspective, transforming what is real to what I see, revealing the way I observe life— that for me is photography.

As a child I had difficulties expressing myself. My parents divorced when I was young and my mom was diagnosed as bipolar. Taking pictures was my way out, my way to protect and express myself. Later at college I discovered climbing.

In climbing you just face yourself, pushing your body and your mind to the limit. The world stops and nothing exists; you are just deeply connected to your body. I used to look at stronger climbers around me and I thought it was beautiful the way they moved, the way they released everything and revealed themselves: the purest form of freedom. Inspired by the way they moved, I started taking pictures of them.

Life is simple if you are a passionate person. Hitchhiking to a crag with my tent, camping, and climbing gear, that was all I needed to be happy: the dirtbag life was opening its arms to me and I jumped into it. For several years I was doing many things—coaching, climbing, and studying sport science—, and I forgot my photography dream. Then I traveled in India for two weeks on my own and there I reconnected with myself, and with the freedom and the purity of climbing.

Going back to France, I left my boyfriend, moved out of our house, and lived in the forest for one month. I went back to India for two months, exploring and climbing in the wild valleys of the Himalayas. I remember this particular moment: sitting in the taxi taking me back to the airport, I watched my last sunrise through the window. The city was scrolling past the window, the heaviness of the air and the humidity were constant. I took a breath, one last taste of freedom. I started asking myself what really made me happy in life. Suddenly it felt really heartbreaking to be going back home. In India I felt like I was where the universe wanted me to be, and that day, sitting in New Delhi airport, I decided to reconnect with photography. I knew what I needed to be happy: a camera, to move a lot, to be surprised by life and make every day a unique adventure. I was able to listen to the ten-year-old Julia. I put all my money into buying a van, left my apartment, quit my job, and without any real plan I hit the road.

Freedom can be really scary. The emptiness in front of you is frightening. But once you accept it and embrace it, fear becomes your best friend. I made a new start without any expectations, keeping an open mind, driving my van wherever there were climbers and taking pictures, hoping to sell them afterward. I didn't have any backup plan, and it was a very insecure feeling.

I took a risk and it was the hardest but also the best decision of my life. People always ask me, "How did you get so brave? Isn't it scary to be a girl living alone in a van?" Again, simple answer: I don't think I'm unusually brave. Anybody can do it.

Once I've decided on something, I can move mountains to achieve it. My limitless motivation for what I love is my best ally. I love testing my own physical limits, spending several hours suspended in space, jumaring hundreds of feet of rope in a day. The more adventurous a project is, the more I love it.

I think climbers can relate to this aspect of my personality. Working with a climber means that they give you their trust and allow you to step into their world. When they give a try in a project they can not be less themself, they express themself in the most beautiful way they know: while climbing. Behind my camera I'm only a spectator, trying to capture moments that describe the best of these athletes, pictures that present their performances and tell their stories. Being part of that is incredible and I feel blessed and thankful for it every day.

  ▷ Nolwen Berthier at Aiguille du Midi, Chamonix, France

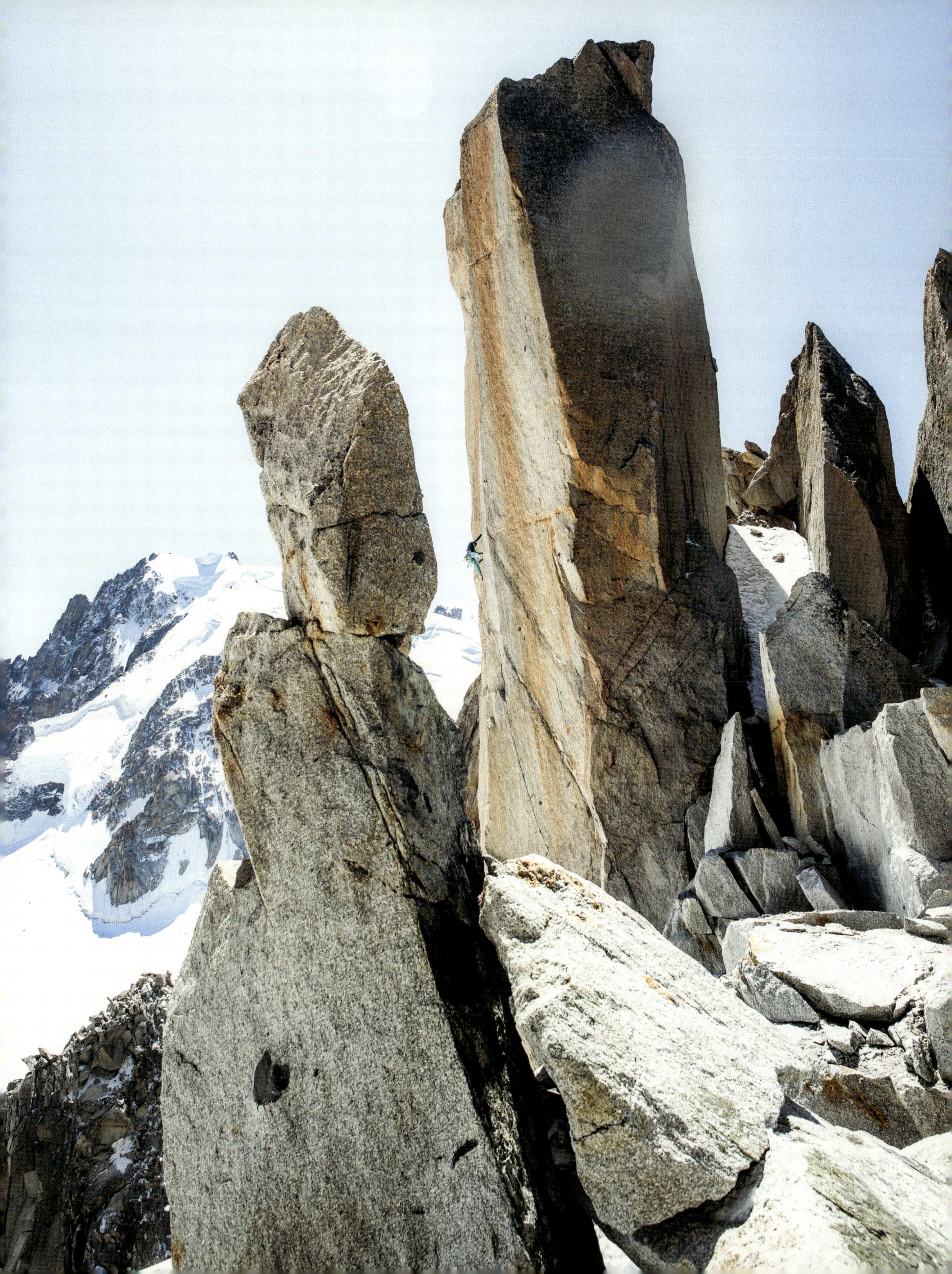

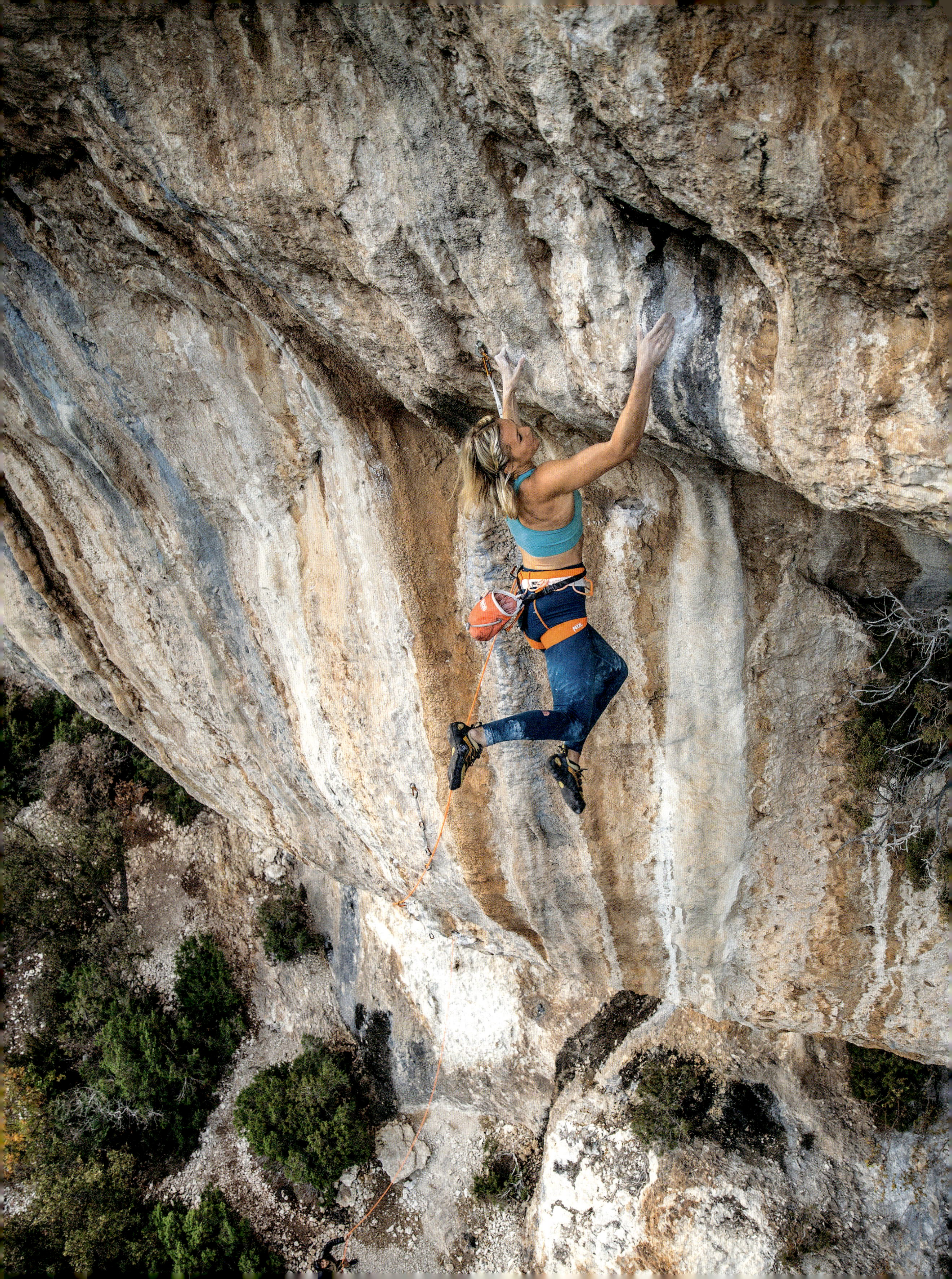

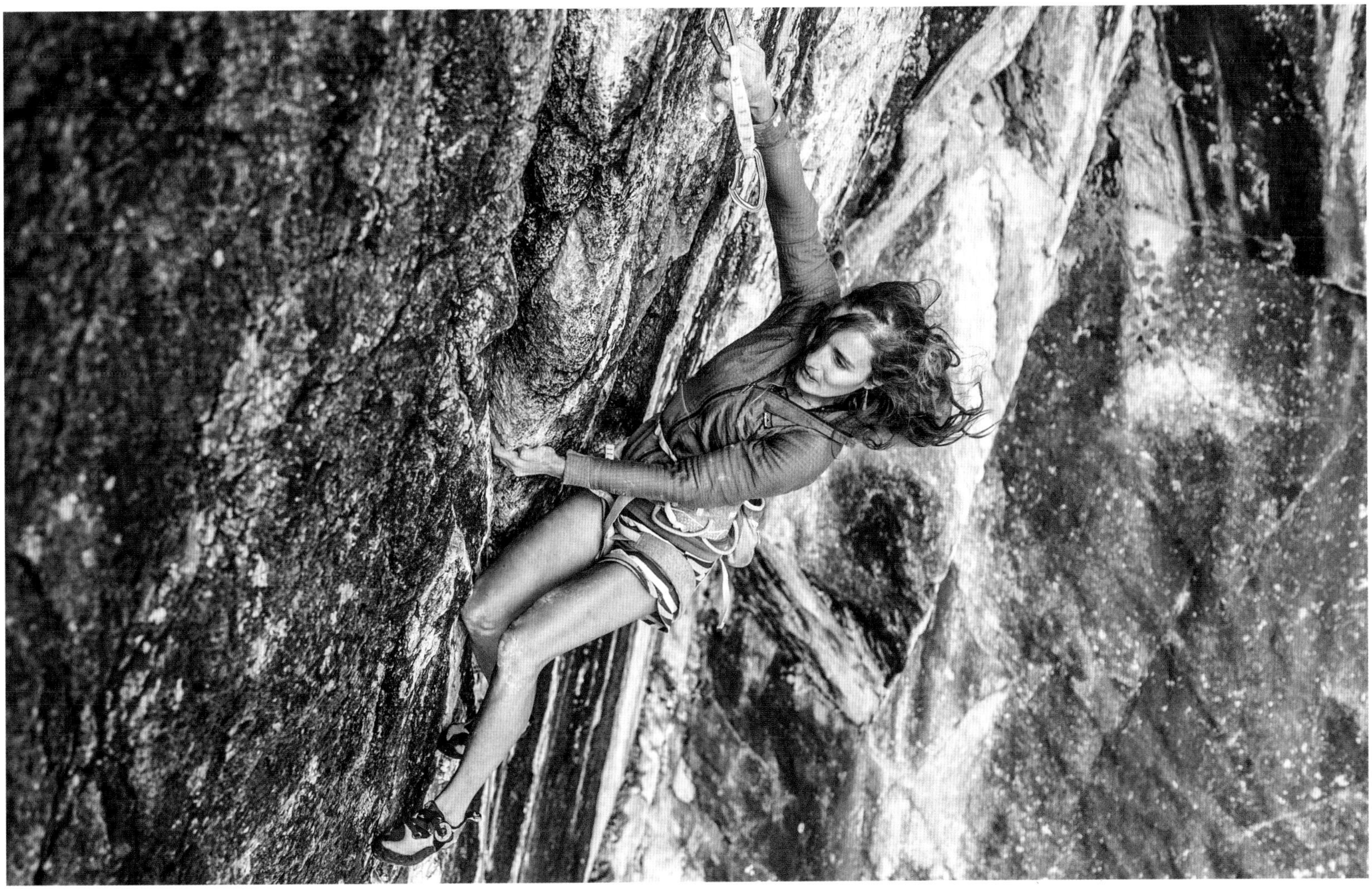

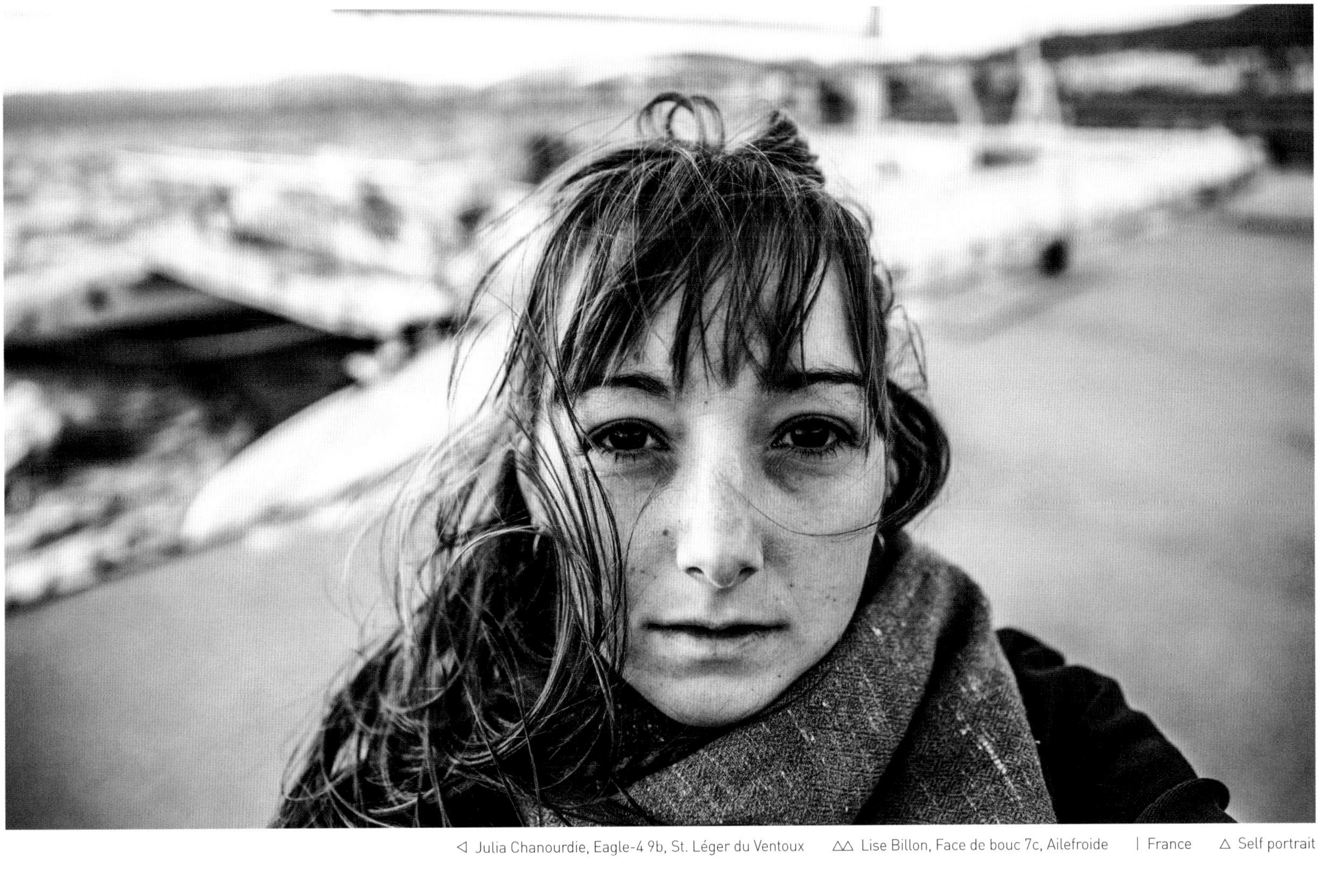

◁ Julia Chanourdie, Eagle-4 9b, St. Léger du Ventoux   △△ Lise Billon, Face de bouc 7c, Ailefroide | France   △ Self portrait

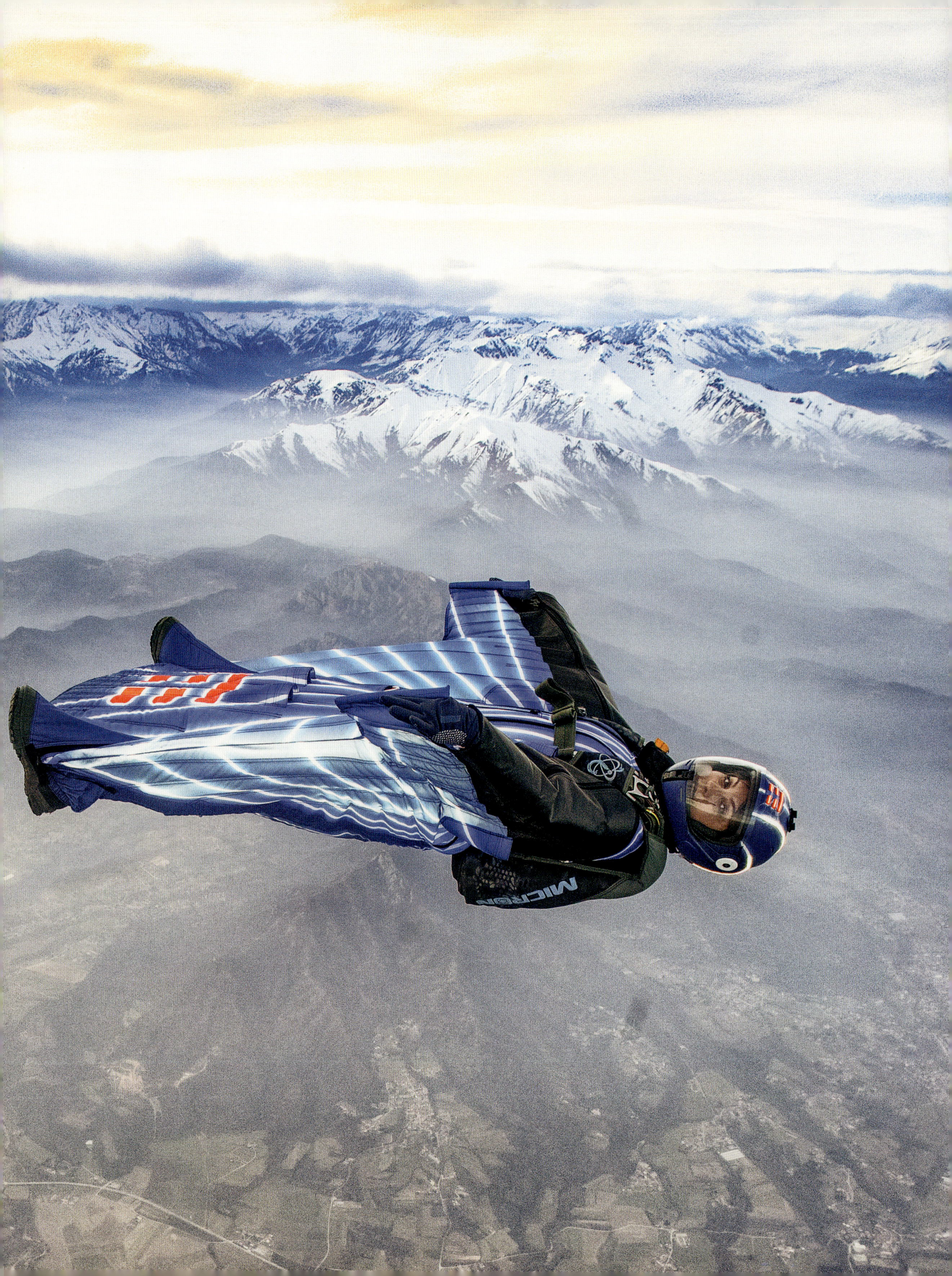

Roberta Mancino

Skydiver, BASE jumper, and wingsuit pilot

@mancinoroberta

My name is Roberta Mancino and I'm Italian. I grew up in Anzio, a small town south of Rome. Since I was very little, I've wanted to fly. I also loved the ocean and animals. I've always been very active in sports like dancing and kickboxing, and did scuba diving and freediving as a hobby. When I finished school I really wanted to do something different and get away from my small town.

Because of my dream of flying, I decided to make a skydiving career for myself. That's why I left everything I had in my country—my studies and a modeling career—to go to the USA and learn how to fly. It wasn't easy to leave my family and all of my friends and follow my dreams. I had to work in a pizzeria and sell my little Vespa to be able to

pay for my skydiving course, and with a few modeling jobs I paid for my ticket to Florida. I left with very little money and without being able to speak a word of English. It took me many years to get good at my sport and to be able to finance my training and some of my projects.

When I was in LA, I started to dream about being a stuntwoman too. In the last ten years, I've been swimming with the biggest sharks in the ocean, and I've got into BASE jumping wingsuit proximity flying.

For many people, diving with sharks and falling off things are their biggest fears, but I can say I have the best job in the world.

· MINI GUIDE ·

Extreme camps, holidays, retreats, and festivals

Wheel sports

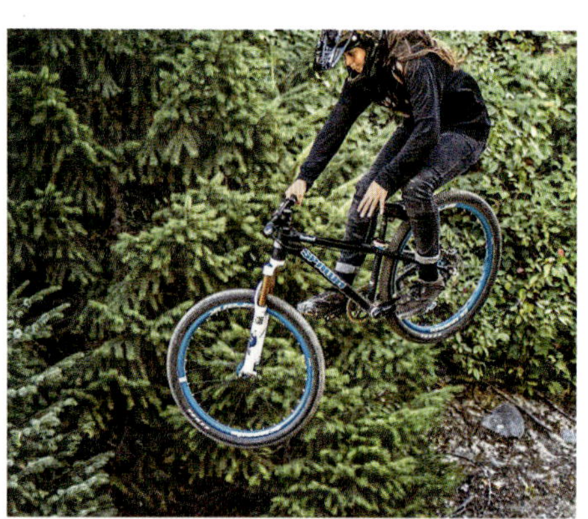

WFMBIKE
Women's Freeride
Movement programs

CANADA

www.wfmbike.com

WFM Bike (Whistler Freestyle and Mountain Bike) is a freestyle-focused jump school based out of British Columbia, Canada. We offer jump skills clinics that are progressive and tailored to your skill level. Our Women's Freeride Movement programs include air awareness training, indoor bike park sessions, coach's training, a freestyle competition, and pump track and dirt jump skills clinics. Our goal is to elevate women's freestyle biking, and we're stoked to see the progression that's already happening.

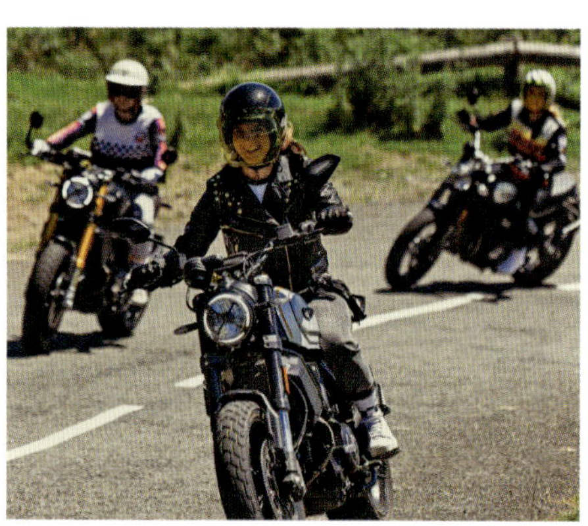

EUDOXIE
Split Chain road trip

FRANCE

eudoxie.shop
@eudoxie_unchained_lady

Eudoxie is a brand, but also a way of life. It is a source of inspiration for women in search of adventure. Every summer, it organizes a road trip called the "Split Chain," where fifteen women from different sport worlds (like skating, surfing, and snowboarding) meet for a motorcycle road trip and proudly wear the Eudoxie colours. They take to the roads of the Basque Country in France to discover breathtaking landscapes with throttle in hand. Feel and follow this unique sensation of freedom and girl power.

Winter sports

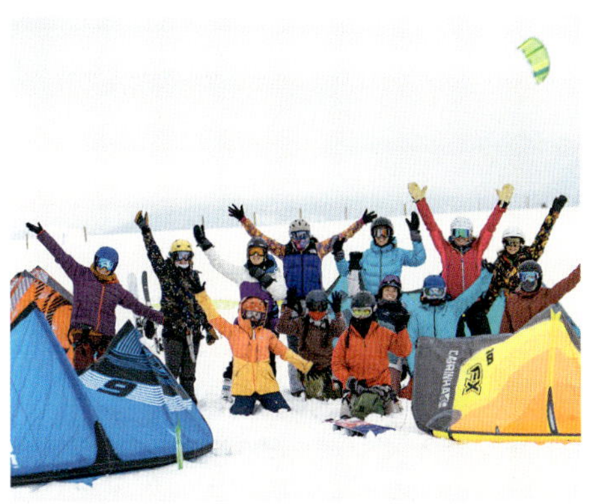

ADRENAJEN
Women's snowkite events

ALASKA, AUSTRALIA OR IDAHO

Adrenajen.com

Jennie Milton, aka Adrenajen, learned to kite by attending women's kite clinics in Australia. Inspired by other female athletes, Jen has been snowkiting and kitesurfing for seventeen years. Join Jen and learn about forecasting and location choice, set up and safety, launching, and landing. The goal is to become a safe, confident, and self-sufficient snowkiter. This event is suited to skiers or snowboarders wanting to learn to kite, or kiteboarders who love to ski or snowboard and haven't put the two sports together yet. Women learning from women and going through the fear together is a great way to learn and have fun.

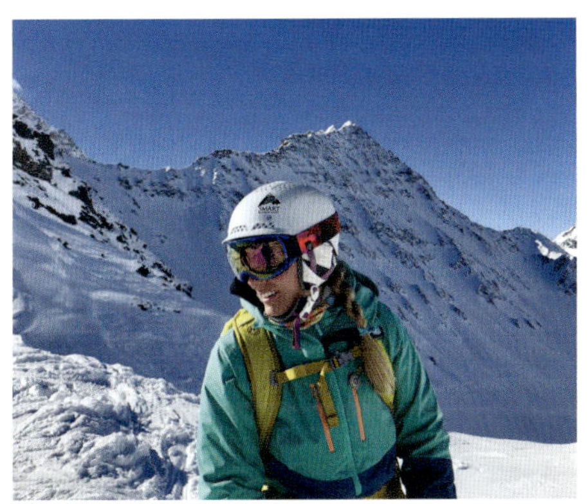

STEEP SKIING CAMPS
Women's Steep Skiing Camps with Liz Smart

WORLDWIDE

steepskiingcamps.com
@mountainguidemama

Liz Smart is the eighth woman in the USA to become a UIAGM internationally certified mountain guide. In this male-dominated profession, Liz has helped pave the way for other women to guide climbers and skiers in the high mountains. Her passion for skiing steep, big-mountain terrain brought her to the Alps, where she runs Steep Skiing Camps Worldwide. She decided to create camps specifically for women. Skiing in an all-women group is rewarding because the camaraderie between women enables them to face their fears and push their limits in ways they may not have imagined.

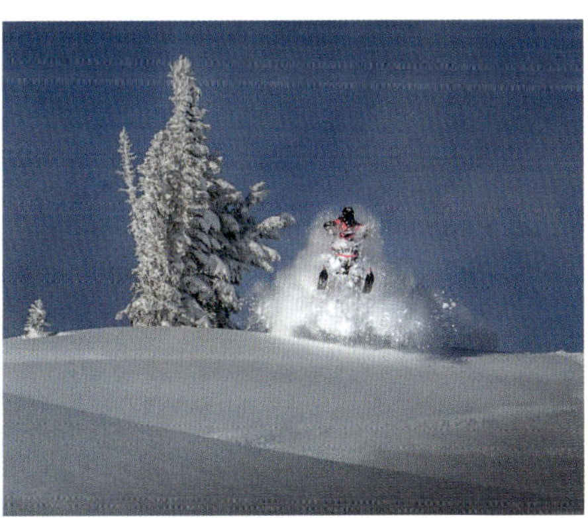

SHE SHREDS MOUNTAIN ADVENTURES
All-girls' snowmobile clinics

CANADA

sheshreds.ca
@sheshredsmountainadventures

Julie-Ann Chapman has been an "extreme girl" for over eighteen years. She is the creator of She Shreds Mountain Adventures, the first all-girls' snowmobile clinics in the world. She Shreds offers snowmobile clinics, avalanche courses, snowmobile rentals, and guided adventures for both men and women. Julie-Ann's now a mom to her son Jax and many fur babies (horses and dogs), a professional snowmobiler for Polaris, and runs her business She Shreds. You can find Julie-Ann boosting her Polaris sled off natural features and cliffs in the BC backcountry and teaching people backcountry safety and sledding skills in the winter.

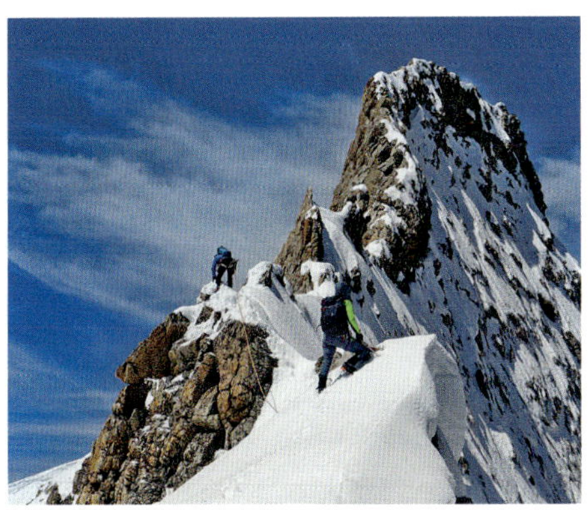

GFHM
Female mountaineering

FRANCE

gfhm.blog
@gfhmteam

Since 2010 the "High Mountain Women's Group" of the French Alpine Club has brought together eight women who receive over two years of training in mountaineering autonomy. This group shares training, mutual aid, good humor, and progress. Unlike the image that is common in the media, the team shows that female high-mountaineering can be powered by sharing and good vibes. Its development reflects the real change that is taking place, and the desire felt by more and more women to acquire autonomy in mountaineering.

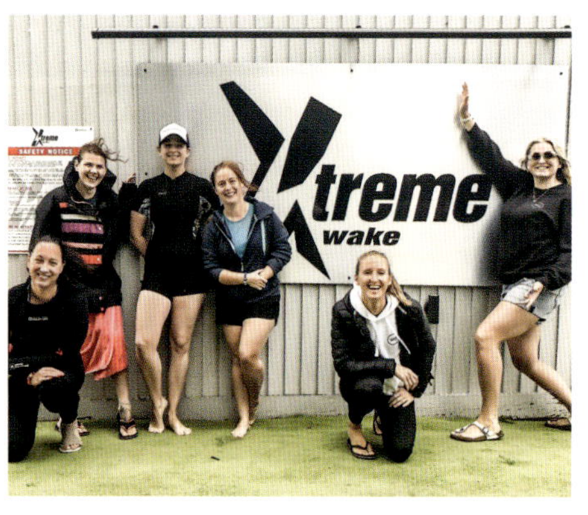

WAKE DAZE
Introducing women into
an extreme watersport
UK

wakedaze.co.uk
lexballadon.com
@_wakedaze_
@lexballadon

Wake Daze was born from Lex Balladon's love of coaching and introducing women to an extreme watersport. The main goal is to make sure that every single woman who attends learns something new, and walks away with the biggest smile and the highest level of stoke. The events have also been a great hub where women can meet other women with similar interests.

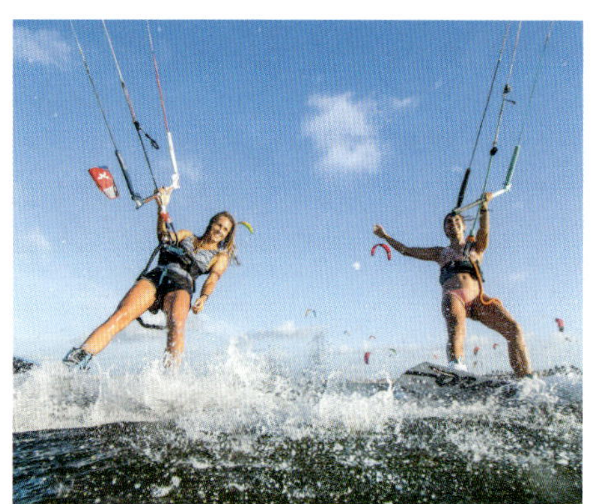

STRUT KITEBOARDING
Women's kiteboarding
and wingfoiling camp
WORLDWIDE

strutkiteboarding.com
@strutkiteboarding
@sensigraves
@colleenjcarroll

Strut Kiteboarding is a camp targeted at intermediate kiteboarders. Run and hosted by professional kiteboarders Colleen Carroll and Sensi Graves, it aims to provide an inclusive, supportive, and empowering retreat environment to help women take their skills to the next level, in locations around the world. Strut aims to de-mystify the progression around kiteboarding and give attendees the tools they need to become the best kiteboarders they can be. Join Strut kiteboarding for an empowering experience that blends kiteboarding, yoga, and laid-back vacation vibes into the kiteboarding trip you've been waiting for.

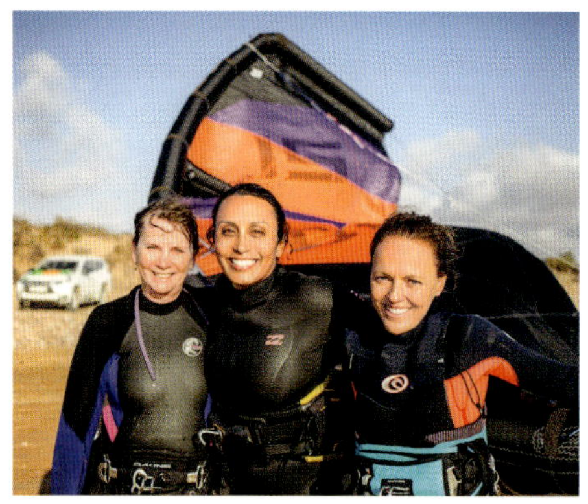

KITE SISTERS
Kitesurf retreats for ladies
WORLDWIDE

kite-sisters.com
@kitesisters

The original women-only kiteboarding and yoga camps company since 2010, Kite Sisters organizes deluxe kitesurf retreats for ladies of all ages in different destinations around the world. On all of these you can learn kitesurfing, improve, and be coached on and off the water by certified and knowledgeable coaches, while a professional and international team takes care of every single detail, delivering a unique, personalized, and high-end vacation. There's gourmet cuisine by Michelin-star chefs, yoga sessions, adventures and tours, and support and empowerment from like-minded women.

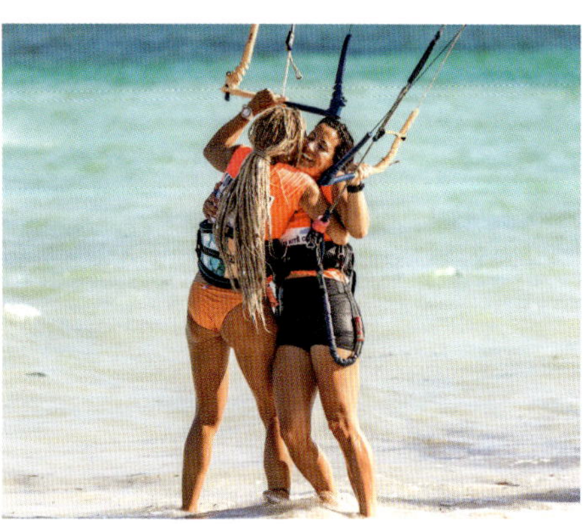

SHE FLIES
Make women the default,
not the exception
WORLDWIDE

www.she-flies.com
@sheflies_

She Flies is a social enterprise whose mission is to grow and strengthen the global wave of women in extreme sports. Its international events and campaigns make women the default, not the exception. She Flies believes in and celebrates women's uniqueness, elegant strength, and divine femininity in extreme sports. Its festivals (She Kites, She Wakes, and She Surfs) are held across Europe and its trips and virtual events reach a global community. She Flies welcomes beginners through to experienced athletes, and its strong network of professional ambassadors and close affiliates prove the power women find through community.

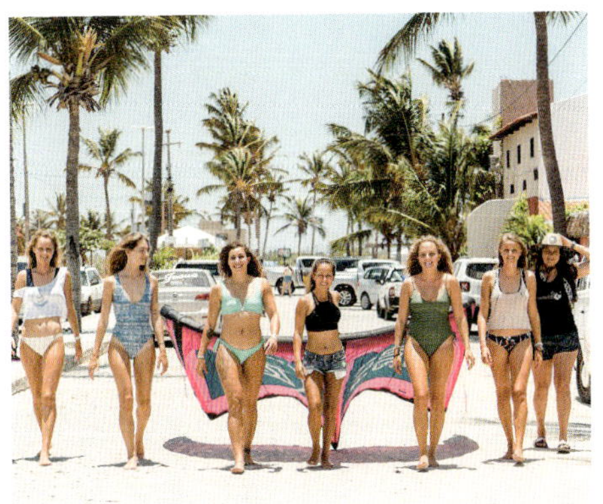

MY SALTY SISTERS
Empowerment and Kite Retreats for women
WORLDWIDE

mysaltysisters.info
@mysaltysisters

Girls support girls: with My Salty Sisters you are never alone on the water! The Empowerment and Kite Retreats show that you don't have to be a champion to be a fierce rider. Your level doesn't matter– your passion does! Join these kitesurfing retreats to unlock and nurture your female energies in a safe and open environment, live a mindful and healthy lifestyle, and kite every day with your newfound Salty Sisters. Ready for a life-changing experience?

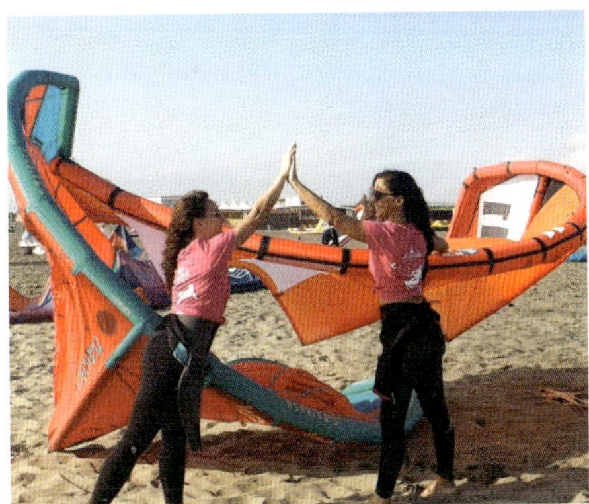

KITE GIRLS ITALIA
Community of girls
ITALIA

kitegirlsitalia.it
@kitegirlsitalia

Kite Girls Italia is a community of girls who love adrenaline and extreme sports. For them, kitesurfing isn't only a sport, but a lifestyle. They organize trips and events all around the world, following the wind, as well as collaborating with kite schools and companies to promote the sport and to share their passion.

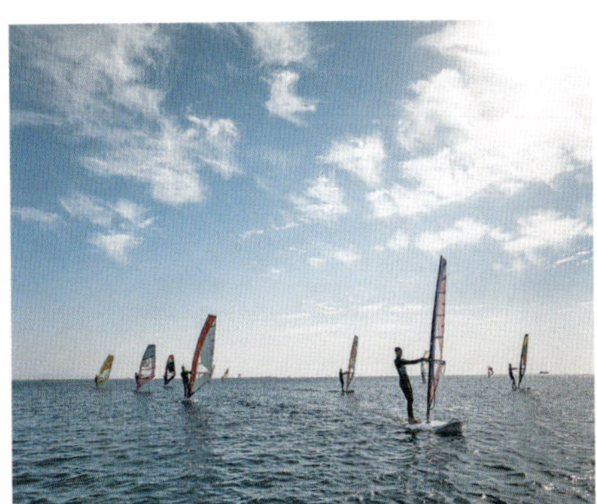

WINDSURF BEAUTIES
Windsurf camp
EGYPT

olyaraskina.ru
@windsurfbeauties

Windsurf Beauties camp is a windsurfing clinic in Dahab. Since our first camp ten years ago, it has become a tradition. Some guys do manage to sneak into our camp, and we welcome them, calling them our "Beasts." So it's Windsurf Beauties and Beasts camp nowadays! Our main destination is Dahab, Egypt, but we also travel to Greece, Mauritius, South Africa, and Morocco. We run windsurfing classes for all levels; in the evenings we do video analysis and correction. We also surf, do yoga, hike in the mountains, and have a great time together.

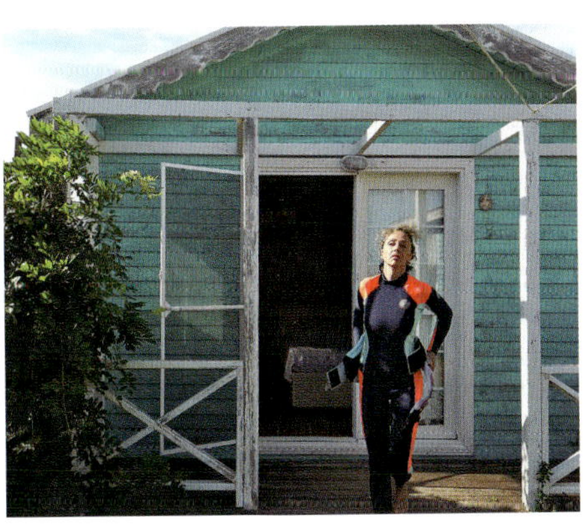

CRAZY ISLAND
All-women retreat
TURKEY

crazy-island.com
@crazyislandsurf

Crazy Island is a kite and windsurf center located at one of the windiest spots in Europe—Gokceada Island in the Aegean sea, Turkey. It is led by sisters Tina and Dolly, who'd become addicted to kite- and windsurfing. Knowing burnout well, they had the idea of an all-women surf retreat, which quickly became a working project. It's an effective program balanced between sports and relaxation—windsurfing, kitesurfing, SUP, yoga, and healthy food. During the retreat you will stay in wooden chalets with a private bathroom and terrace, surrounded by nature and the beach. Leave all of your responsibilities behind and reveal your true you!

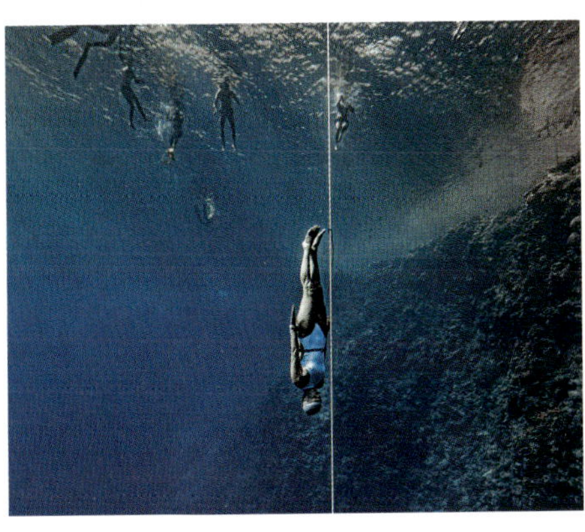

FREEDIVING WITH MOOANA
Apnea training
PORTUGAL AND SPAIN

mooana-retreat.com
@seasoulstories / @mooana_retreat
@ruth_osborn
@aidafreediving
@montedagua.homestay

Freediving is one of the oldest forms of diving. It is holding your breath under water and diving without having to surface for oxygen. This form of diving is commonly experienced as a way to find inner peace and relaxation. Conchita Rossler, with her ocean-based project Mooana, offers unique freedive certifications and apnea training camps. In collaboration with British freediving athlete and instructor Ruth Osborn, spend beautiful weekends freedive training in Ibiza. With Mooana, AIDA certification or equivalent courses in Portugal with professional certified trainers can be joined on request.

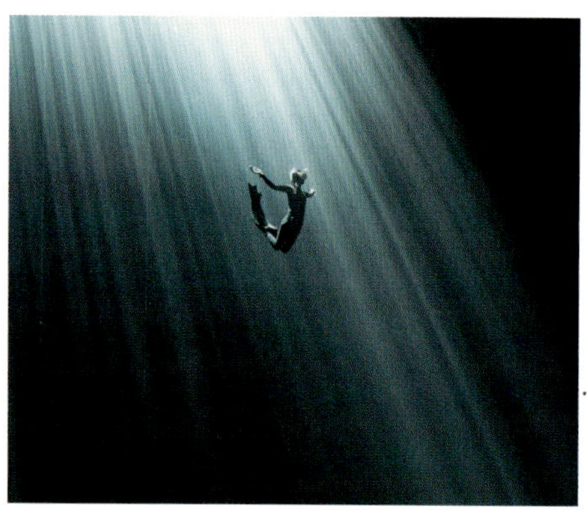

AMANCAY FREEDIVING
Female freediving instructors

MEXICO

amancayfreediving.com
@amancayfreediving

Based at the beautiful Riviera Maya in Mexico, Amancay Freediving is owned by two sisters. It is run by female freediving instructors from all over the globe with a passion for traveling, adventure, and water. We offer freediving experience for all levels. Freediving is not just a sport. While discovering the water's depths we discover ourselves by overcoming fear and limits from a new perspective. It can be challenging, but at the same time soothing; it helps us grow and be stronger!

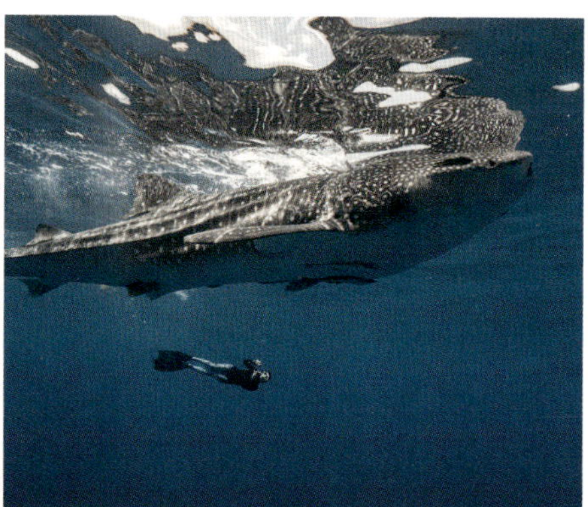

GIRLS THAT SCUBA
Freediving retreat for woman

MEXICO

girlsthatscuba.com
@girlsthatfreedive
@girlsthatscuba

Girls that Scuba is the biggest female diving network in the world, founded with the goal of creating a space for women to connect and share their passion for the ocean. With this in mind, Girls that Scuba has co-created with Amancay Freediving a unique freediving retreat for women from all over the world, introducing them to freediving for the first time in one of the most magical places on earth. You will have the chance to combine your freediving Level 1 course with scuba diving in the amazing Cenotes, and last but not least, since the retreat is held during whale shark season, you will be able to swim with the biggest fish in the world!

Mountain sports

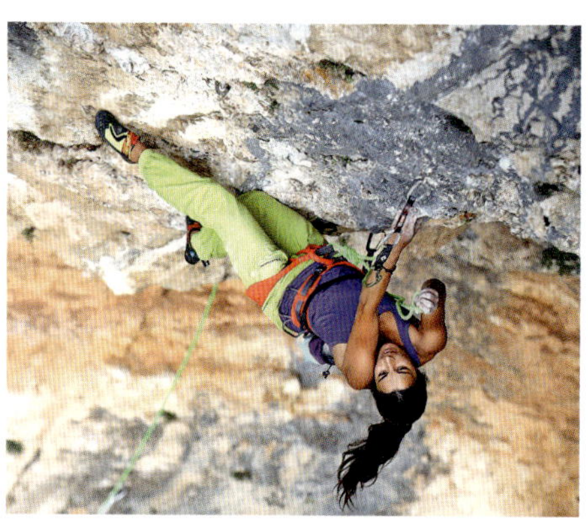

ROCKBUSTERS
**Women-only climbing coaches
by Daila Ojeda**

EUROPE

rockbusters.net
@rockbusters_climbing

Rockbusters women's rock climbing course is designed to provide a comfortable, safe, and supportive environment for female climbers to improve their technique, power, mental game, and overall climbing performance. The event is led by Daila Ojeda, one of the best female climbers. Women can and do climb as well as men, and possess different strengths. Our women-only courses focus on discovering what our bodies are capable of, and how far we can get with the use of precise footwork, increased flexibility, and good mind control.

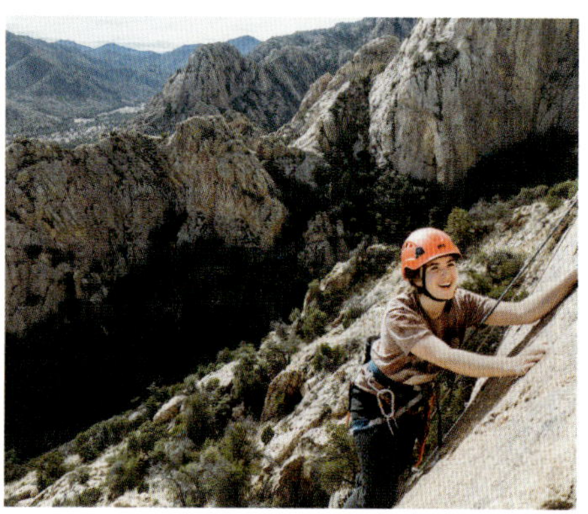

NOLS
**Women's Southwest
Rock Climbing**

USA

www.nols.edu
@NOLSedu

NOLS has been the leader in wilderness education since 1965. This rock climbing course is part of our selection of all-women's expeditions, and all levels of experience are welcome. In the living desert of Arizona's Cochise Stronghold, women build community and pursue audacious goals. The course progression covers technical skills, like risk assessment and climbing technique, and the seven skills of NOLS' core leadership curriculum. Combined, this progression builds an inclusive community and prepares participants to continue exploring the outdoors long after the course concludes.

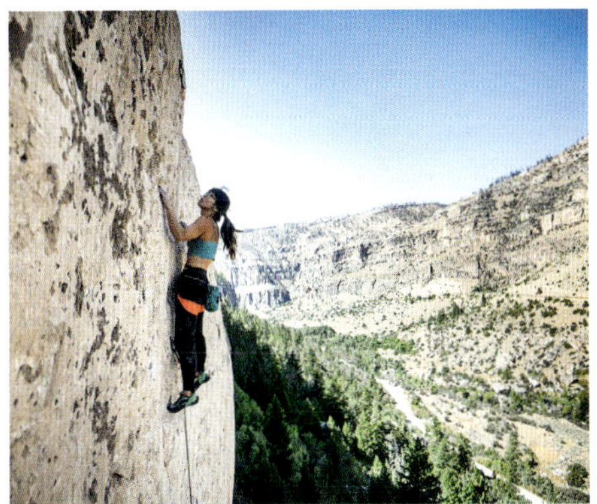

NO MAN'S LAND
FILM FESTIVAL

Film festival

VIRTUAL

nomanslandfilmfestival.org
@nomanslandfilmfestival

No Man's Land Film Festival—the premier all-women adventure film festival—meets a need and desire to highlight and connect women in pursuit of the radical. No Man's Land strives to motivate audiences to implement and inspire change through human collaboration, while cultivating a deep interest in exploring the vastness of the planet. The festival celebrates and uplifts gender-diverse identities and is committed to creating a safe and inclusive space that champions the experiences of women, nonbinary people, and trans men. No Man's Land is redefining the feminine in adventure and sport through film.

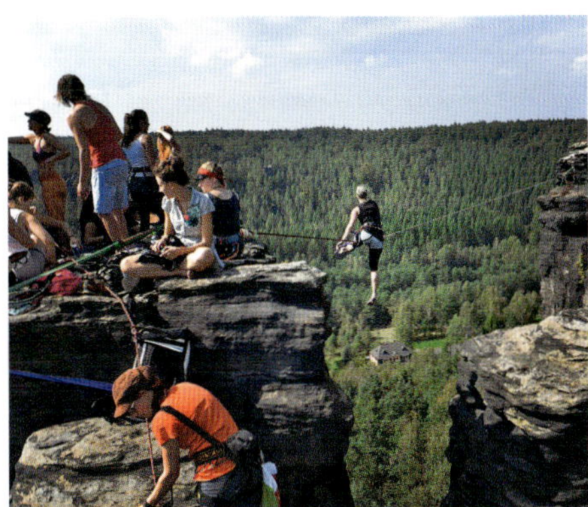

WOMEN'S HIGHLINE
MEETING

A space by women, for women

CZECHIA

womenshighlinemeeting.com
@womenshighlinemeeting

The Women's Highline Meeting occurs annually in the rural, forested valley of Ostrov, Czechia. Starting in 2009, it was formed through an organic desire to create a female-driven festival that engaged and connected women from around the world with a shared interest in the sport of slacklining and highlining. The point of the festival is to create a space by women, for women, especially within the realm of outdoor sports, which are usually male-dominated. The meeting aims to cultivate independence and sharing in a supportive environment, and to help increase the representation of women in outdoor sports.

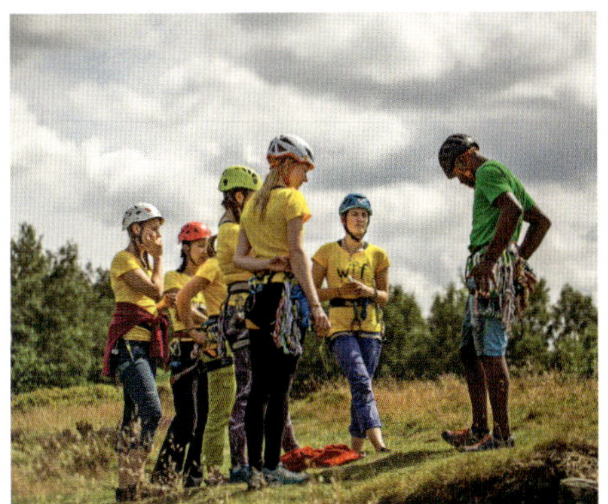

WOMEN'S TRAD FESTIVAL

Women-focused

UK

womenstradfestival.co.uk
@womenstradfestival

This annual festival held in the Peak District is women-focused, but we create a supportive, inclusive, and fun space where people of all ages, genders, and abilities can come together and learn to trad climb. The event is grounded upon three core values: sustainability, mental well-being, and accessibility. We work to empower new climbers to gain trad skills, we support women in outdoor leadership, and we are helping to create a community of psyched, strong female trad climbers. We, a four-strong team of women who run Women's Trad Festival, love to climb and adventure.

Air sports

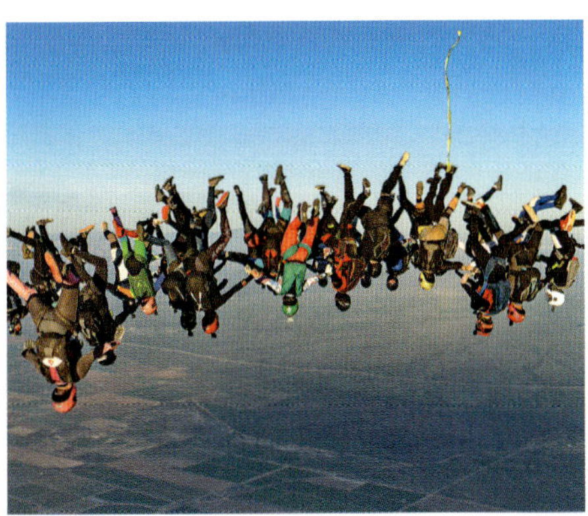

WOMEN'S SKYDIVING
NETWORK

Women in skydiving

WORLDWIDE

womensskydivingnetwork.org
@womensskydivingnetwork

The Women's Skydiving Network (WSN) is an inclusive movement for female skydivers (and future female skydivers!) to connect, inspire, and champion each other as we live bright, brave lives and grow our presence and participation in skydiving and beyond.

PHOTO CREDITS

A

ABBI HEARNE
thehearnes.com
@abbihearne
Page: 234

ADAM CLARK
adamclarkphoto.com
@acpictures
Page: 180b

ADAM KLINGETEG
adamklingeteg.com
@adamklingeteg
Page: 205

ALEX ST JEAN
alexstjean.com
@alexstjeanphoto
Page: 185b

AMY JIMMERSON
amyjimmersonphoto.com
@amyjimmerson
Pages: 202 - 209

ANDY GREEN
andygreenimages.com.au
@andygreenimages
Pages: 211 - 214

ANDRE MAGARAO
for Crazyfly Kiteboarding
andremagarao.com
@andre_magarao
Pages: 120 - 121

ANKI GRØTHE
ankigrothe.com
@ankigrothe
Pages: 137 - 142 - 143

ANTON HILDING LILLJEGREN
Page: 55

ARMANDO GOEDGEDRAG
artmandomultimedia.com
@artmando_multimedia
Pages: 106 - 107 - back cover

AUSTIN SCHMITZ
austinschmitz.com
@austinschmitzphoto
Pages: 14t - 17b

B

BÁRBARA COMPANY ESPEJO
Pages: 154 - 160b

BENJAMIN DITTO
bendittophoto.com
@benjaminbditto
Pages: 200 - 203b

BERTRAND DELAPIERRE
Pages: 74 - 77b

BILLY STEVENS
billystevensmedia.ca
@skid1
Page: 243 (SHE SHREDS)

BRITT MOORE
brittmoore86.com
@brittmoore86
Pages: 144 - 146 -147

BRYAN SODERLIND
bryansoderlind.com
@thegoldenbear
Page: 131

C

CARRO DJUPSJÖ
wakecarro.com
@wakecarro
Page: 129b

CHRIS ROGERS
chrismrogers.com
@cmrog
Page: 133

CHRISTIE OLIVER
Pages: 149b

CRAIG DUTTON
craigdutton.com
@craigdutton
Pages: 212 - 213 - 216t - 217

D

DAAN VERHOEVEN
@daanverhoevenfreediver
Pages: 2 - 40 - 41 - 42
43 - 184 - 186

DAVE MODY
@dave.mody
Pages: cover - 26 - 27

DAVID WYBENGA
Page: 247 (Women's Skydiving)

DEAN TREML
@deantreml
Pages: 91 - 92 - 94 - 95 - 96t

DREW SMITH

DREW SMITH
drewsmithmedia.com
@ _drew_smith_
Page: 16

DYLAN MILLER
@dylanmiller
Page: 130

E

EMILY TROMBLY
emilytrombly.com
@emilytrombly
Page: 247 (No Man's Land)

EVGENY PAVLOV
@ponchikz
Pages: 220 - 221 - 222

F

FAITH DICKEY
thatslacklinegirl.com
@thefaithdickey
Pages: 224 - 228t - 229

FRANCISCO RIZQUEZ
imfpluss.com
@fpluss1
Pages: 23 - 24 - 29

FUKA JAZ
@fukajaz
Pages: 117 - 123

G

GUILLEM CASANOVA
guillemcasanova.com
@guillem_casanova
Page: 177

H

HANNAH SHORE
hannahshore.com
@wild_shore
Page: 115

HILDE RØRVIK NORDSTRAND
@superhildern
Page: 136

HUGO VINCENT
@hugovincentphotography
Pages: 190 - 192

HUUB WAALDIJK
huubwaaldijk.com
@huubwaaldijk
Page: 245 (FREEDIVING
WITH MOOANA)

I

IAN CURRY-LINDAHL
@iancurrylindahl
Page: 132

ISABELLE FABRE
isabellefabre.fr
@isabelle.fabre
Page: 118

J

JACQUES HOLST
jacquesholst.com
@jacquesholst
Pages: 138 - 139 - 140 - 141

JAN NOVAK
@jan_novak_photography
Pages: 194 - 195t - 246 (Rockbusters)

JANCSI HADIK
@jancsihadik
Page: 198

JENNIE MILTON SELFIE
@adrenajen
Pages: 58 - 59t

JESSIE KUSTERS
knotsandshots.nl
@knotsandshots
Pages: 45 - 46 - 47b

JOHN CARTER
Pages: 100 - 101 - 102 - 105

JORDI SARAGOSSA
saragossa.cat
@jsaragossa
Pages: 176t - 179 - 181 - 250
back cover

JULIA CASSOU
juliacassou.com
@julia.cassou
Pages: 195b - 196 - 197 - 237
238 - 239 - back cover

K

KIE WILLIS
basefilms.ae
@kieparkour
Pages: 152 - 155 - 156 - 158b - 159
160t - 161

KIRILL UMRIKHIN
kirillumrikhin.com
@kirillumrikhin
Pages: 162 - 165 - 166 - 168 - 169
170 - 245 (Windsurf Beauties)

b - bottom

t - top

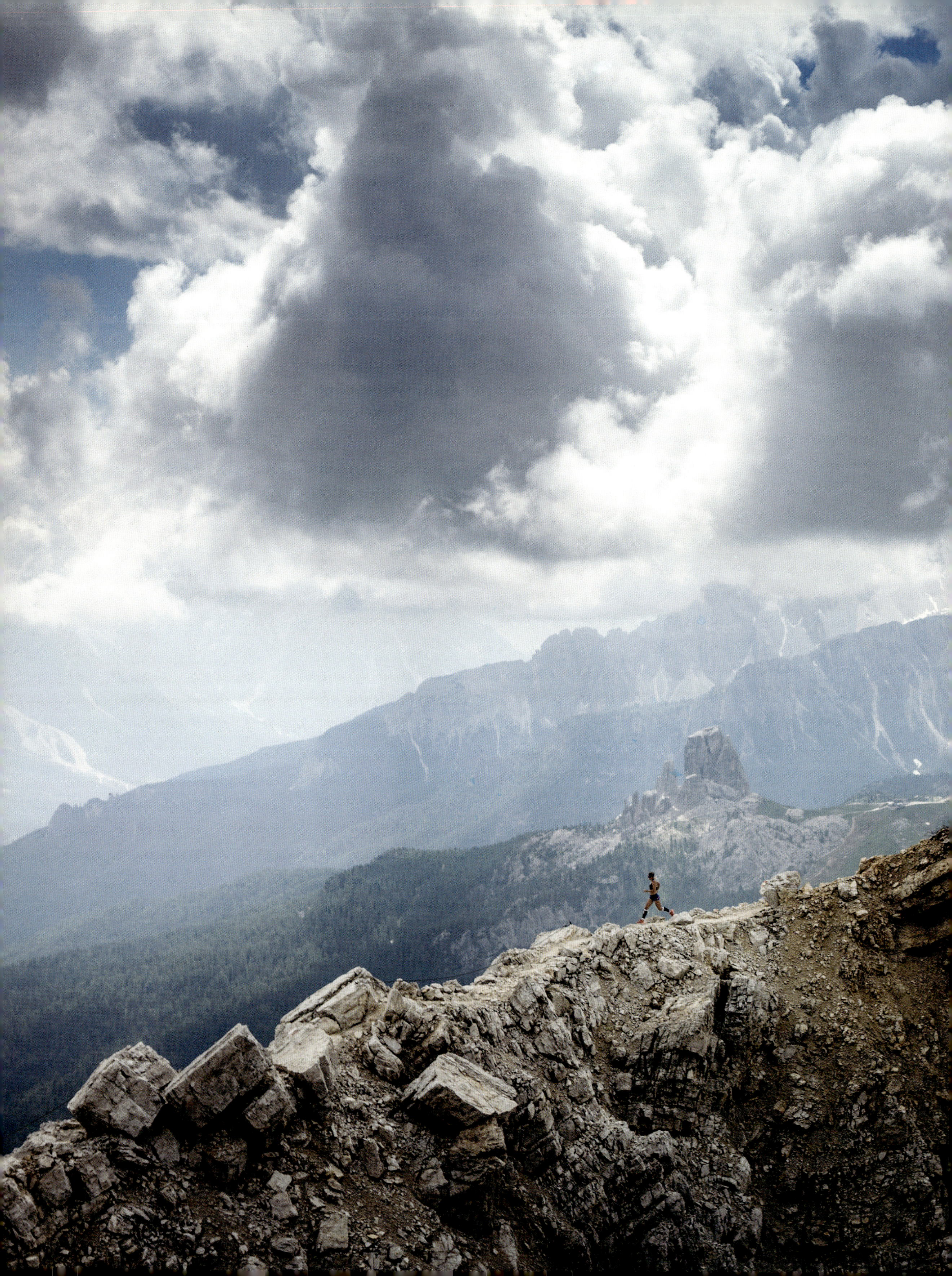

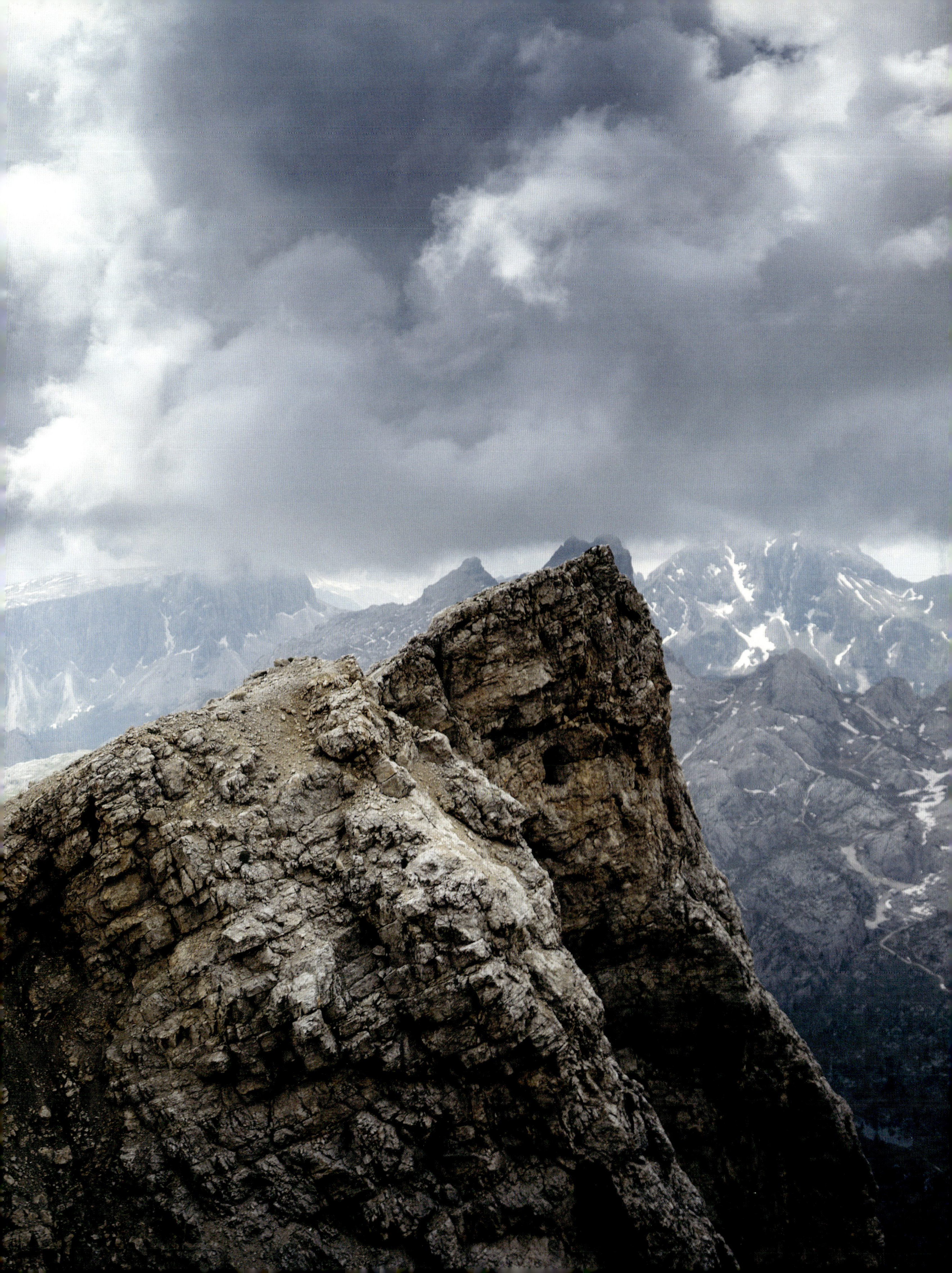

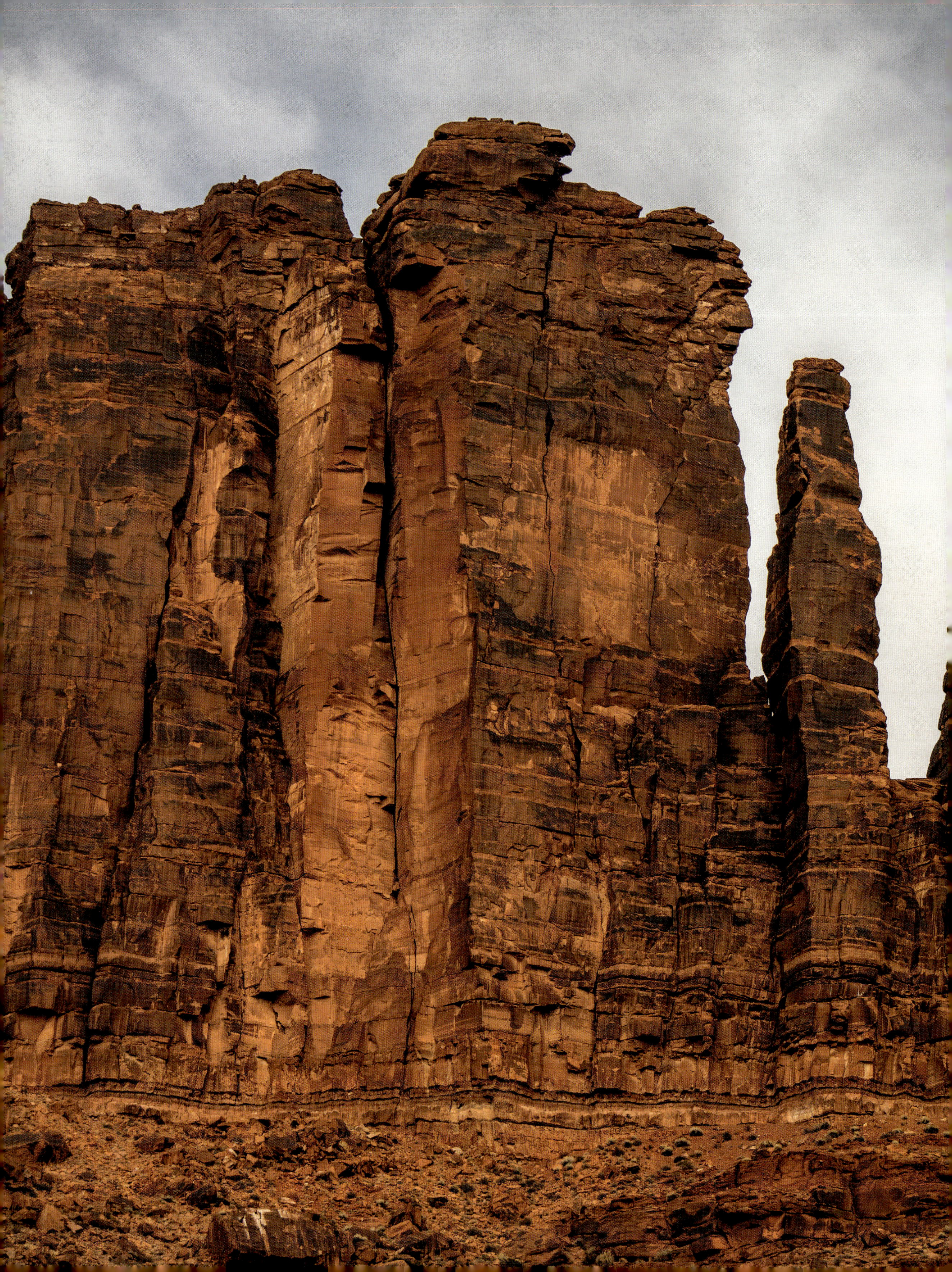

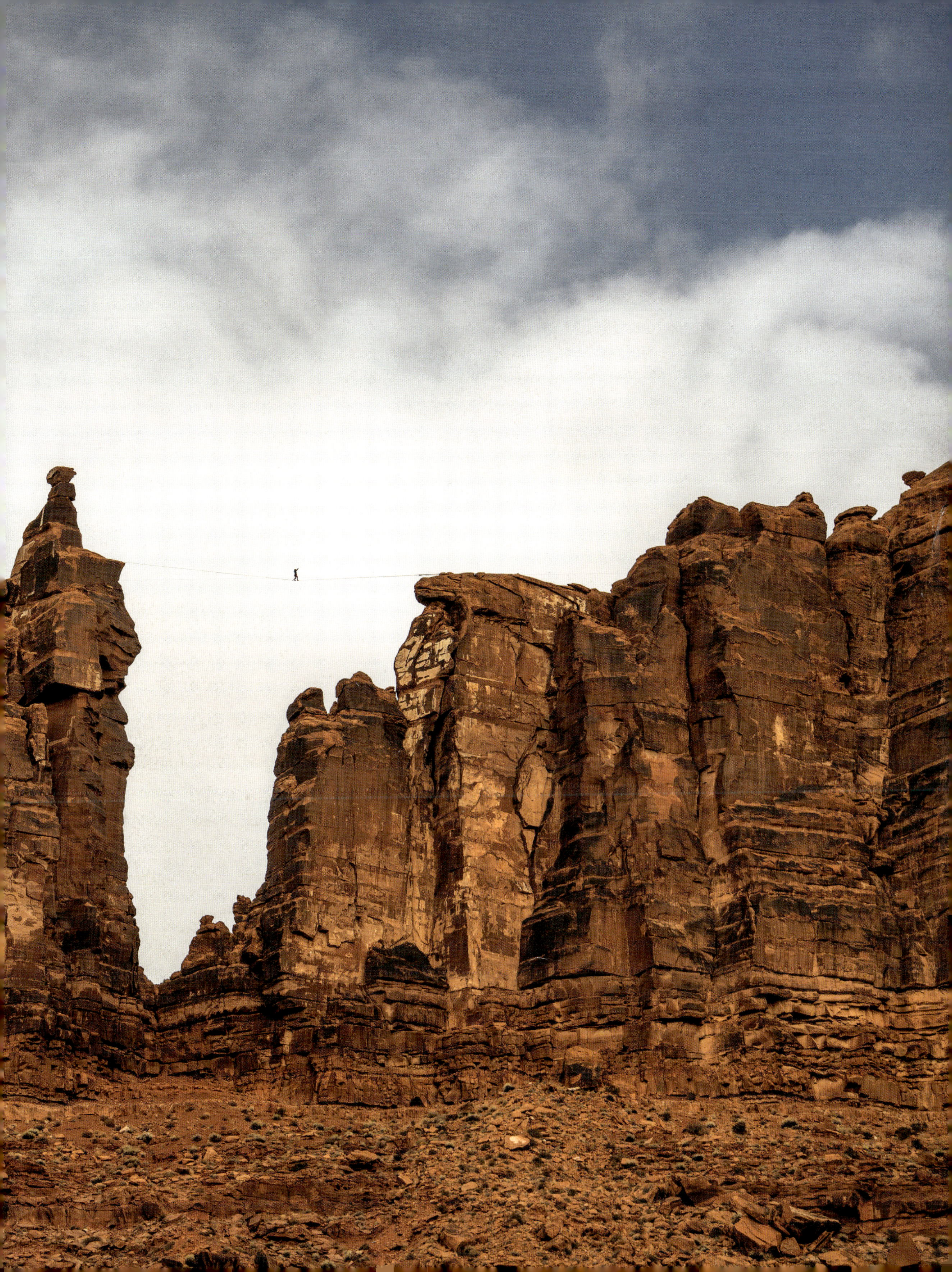

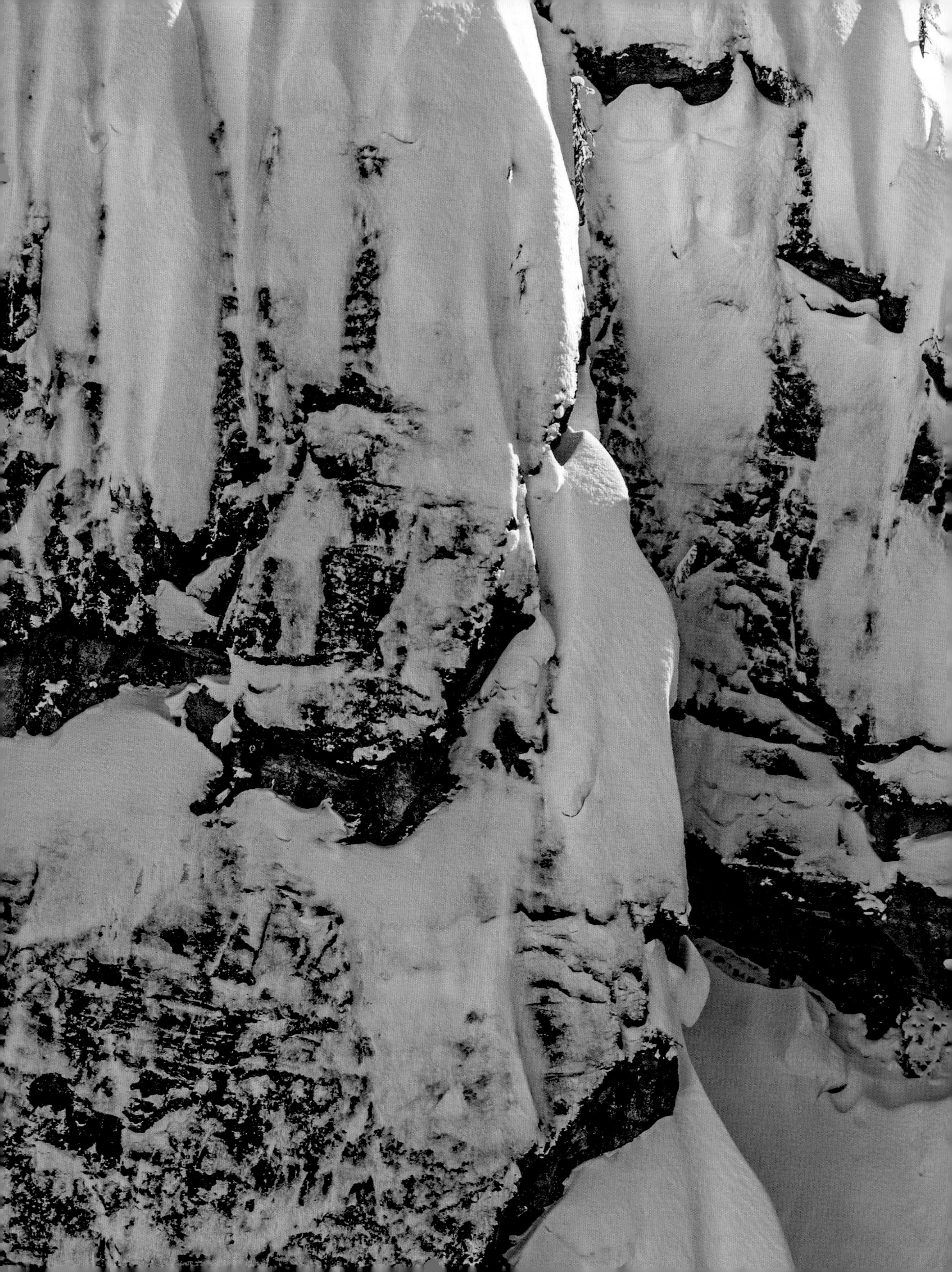

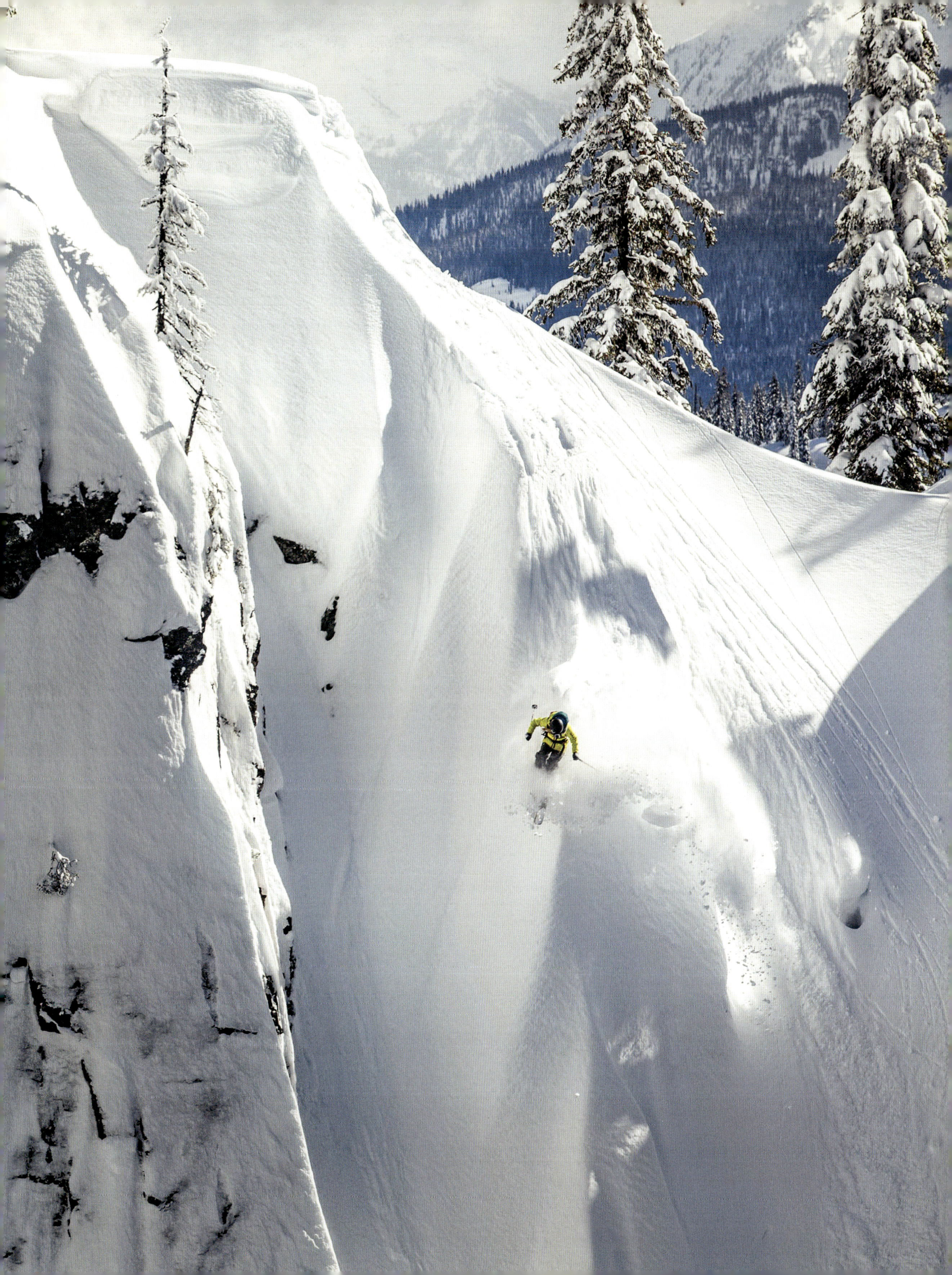

© Prestel Verlag, Munich · London · New York, 2021
A member of Penguin Random House Verlagsgruppe GmbH
Neumarkter Strasse 28 · 81673 Munich

Copyright © Carolina Amell, 2021
This edition published by agreement with Carolina Amell
www.amellcarolina.com

Text copyright © the contributing authors
Photography copyright © the contributing photographers, see photo credits pp. 248/249

Cover: Rita Arnaus, photo by Dave Mody
Back cover: Photos by Julia Cassou (top left), Romina Amato (top right),
Sebastien Baritussio (middle), Jordi Saragossa (bottom left), Armando Goedgedrag (bottom right)

Library of Congress Control Number is available; a CIP catalogue record for this book
is available from the British Library.

In respect to links in the book, the Publisher expressly notes that no illegal content
was discernible on the linked sites at the time the links were created. The Publisher
has no influence at all over the current and future design, content or authorship of
the linked sites. For this reason the Publisher expressly disassociates itself from all
content on linked sites that has been altered since the link was created and assumes
no liability for such content.

Editorial direction: Julie Kiefer
Concept and coordination: Carolina Amell
Photo research: Carolina Amell
Design and layout: Carolina Amell
Copyediting: Martha Jay
Production management: Friederike Schirge
Separations: Ludwig Media, Zell am See
Printing and binding: DZS Grafik, d.o.o., Ljubljana
Paper: Profibulk

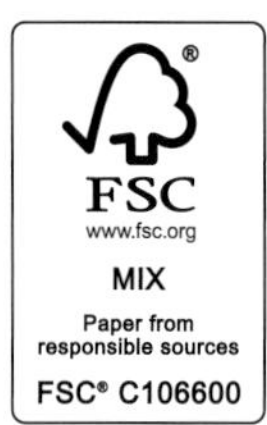

Penguin Random House Verlagsgruppe FSC® N001967

Printed in Slovenia

ISBN 978-3-7913-8785-7

www.prestel.com